# Educational Psychology for Teachers

**2**nd edition

# Educational Psychology for Teachers

Anita E. Woolfolk
Lorraine McCune-Nicolich
*Rutgers University*

Prentice-Hall, Inc., Englewood Cliffs, New Jersey 07632

**Library of Congress Cataloging in Publication Data**

Woolfolk, Anita E.
  Educational psychology for teachers.

  Bibliography: p. 593
  Includes index.
  1. Educational psychology.  I. Nicolich, Lorraine
McCune.  II. Title.
LB1051.W74     1984     370.15     83-13696
ISBN 0-13-240465-6

**Development Editor:** Jeannine Ciliotta
**Cover and Interior Design:** Lee Cohen
**Editorial Production/Supervision:** Barbara Kelly Kittle
**Photo Researcher:** Anita Duncan
**Manufacturing Buyer:** Ron Chapman
**Cover Photo:** 4 × 5

Printed in the United States of America

10  9  8  7  6  5  4  3  2  1

**Chapter Opener Photo Credits:**

1: Carmine L. Galasso
2: UNICEF photo by Satyan
3: Ken Karp
4: Diane Stanford
5: Ken Karp
6: Ken Karp
7: Leslie Deeb
8: Ken Karp

 9: Chuck Iossi
10: Elizabeth Hamlin, Stock/Boston
11: Ken Karp
12: Ken Karp
13: Frieda Leinwand, Monkmeyer Press
14: Ken Karp
15: Ken Karp

ISBN 0-13-240465-6

Prentice-Hall International, Inc., *London*
Prentice-Hall of Australia Pty. Limited, *Sydney*
Editora Prentice-Hall do Brasil, Ltda., *Rio de Janeiro*
Prentice-Hall Canada Inc., *Toronto*
Prentice-Hall of India Private Limited, *New Delhi*
Prentice-Hall of Japan, Inc., *Tokyo*
Prentice-Hall of Southeast Asia Pte. Ltd., *Singapore*
Whitehall Books Limited, *Wellington, New Zealand*

**To Elizabeth**

and her teachers

# Contents

## LEARNING THEORY AND PRACTICE

## MOTIVATION AND MANAGEMENT

## EFFECTIVE TEACHING

# MEASUREMENT AND EVALUATION

# Preface

Many people reading this book will be enrolled in an educational psychology course as part of their professional preparation in teaching, counseling, speech therapy, or psychology. Even though the title emphasizes the role of the teacher, the material in this text should be of interest to anyone who is concerned about education and learning, from the nursery school volunteer to the instructor in a community program for handicapped adults. No prior background in psychology or education is necessary to understand this material. It is as free of jargon and technical language as possible.

Since the first edition of *Educational Psychology for Teachers* appeared, exciting developments have occurred in the field. This edition has incorporated the new insights while retaining the best qualities of the previous work. The second edition continues to emphasize the educational implications of research on development, learning, and teaching. Instead of separating theories from applications, the text shows how information in educational psychology can be used to solve the everyday problems of teaching. To make the connections between knowledge and practice both clear and interesting, many examples, actual case studies, guidelines, and ideas from experienced teachers fill the upcoming pages. Professors and students who used the first edition found these features very helpful. But what about the new developments?

This revision reflects the growing importance of cognitive perspectives for educational psychology. The old chapters on cognitive views of learning have been completely redone and now include material on perception, attention, the structure of knowledge, schema theory, the organization of information in memory, information processing, comprehension, learning strategies, concept teaching, metacognitive abilities, problem solving, and expertise. In addition, there is a new chapter on individual differences placed early in the book so you will have a better understanding of students before you encounter information on educational principles and strategies for teaching these complicated persons. The first part of the chapter discusses the origins of differences including the roles of heredity and environment, the effects of various child rearing styles, and cultural differences. The second part of the chapter explores three specific dimensions of individual difference: intelligence, creativity, and cognitive style.

The three chapters of the book on motivation and management have been brought together in a section that includes discussions of cognitive, social learning, and humanistic perspectives on student motivation, methods for coping with problem behavior, systems for organizing and managing elementary and secondary classrooms, as well as research-based ideas for establishing procedures and setting rules, dealing with conflict, encouraging communication, and becoming an effective leader.

# The Plan of the Book

Part 1 begins with you, the prospective teacher, and the questions you are probably asking yourself about a career in teaching. What are the joys and problems teachers can expect? How can educational psychology increase the joys by helping to solve the problems? In Part 2, "Human Growth and Development," we turn to the students. How do they develop mentally, physically, socially, and emotionally? Where do individual differences come from and what do they mean for teachers? The next three units are the heart of the book. Part 3, "Learning Theory and Practice," looks at learning from two major perspectives: behavioral and cognitive, with an emphasis on the latter. Findings in this area have important implications for instruction at every level. Part 4, "Motivation and Management," discusses how to motivate and manage today's students. The information in these chapters is based on the most recent research in real classrooms. Part 5, "Effective Teaching," has chapters on designing instruction, using effective teaching strategies, and working with exceptional students. Finally, Part 6, "Measurement and Evaluation," gives the information needed to determine how well students have learned.

## New Appendices

In addition to the 15 chapters, there are two new appendices. Appendix A, "Research in Educational Psychology," discusses key terms, methods, and concepts in psychological research. Readers go through the processes of planning and evaluating a study. Appendix B, "Computer-Based Education," is a very current introduction to the area designed for students who have no background in computers. Readers will gain an understanding of basic terms and concepts plus an appreciation of the range of classroom applications. In addition, the appendix describes selecting and utilizing hardware and software to make the most of this revolutionary tool. Each appendix follows the appropriate chapter in the body of the text instead of being "lost" at the end of the book. Your instructor may incorporate the material into class or may tell you to disregard it. If it is not assigned as part of your class work you might still find these sections to be worthwhile reading.

## Current Theory and Research

Almost 400 new references have been added to this edition, bringing prospective teachers the most current information. Topics include metacognition, the development of friendships, social cognition, schema theory, cognitive behavior modification, the psychology of instruction, studies of expert knowledge and studies of expert classroom managers, research on teaching effectiveness, the future of mainstreaming, and controversies in testing and grading.

## Readability and Relevance

The responses of hundreds of students who read the first edition were analyzed to make this edition even more understandable and interesting.

Jargon and technical language are avoided. When a new term is introduced, it appears in **boldface** type along with a brief definition. The concepts and principles discussed are related to life inside and outside the classroom. Many examples were contributed by student teachers and master teachers around the country. Other case studies are taken from personal experience. To add further interest, this edition includes special boxed material that emphasizes the role of educational psychology beyond the classroom.

## Aids to Understanding

At the beginning of each chapter you will find an *outline* of the key topics with page numbers for quick reference, an *overview* that will orient you to what follows, and a list of *learning objectives*.

Within the chapter, *headings* and *marginal annotations* point out themes, questions, and problems as they arise, so you can easily look up information in the chapter. These also serve as a quick review of the important points of the chapter. Throughout the text you will see terms highlighted in **boldface** type. These terms are explained as soon as they are presented and a complete definition is given in the *glossary* at the end of the book. Throughout the book, graphs, figures and even the pictures have been chosen to make the text more understandable.

Each chapter ends with a *summary* of the main ideas and applications and a list of the *key terms* from the chapter to make review easier. Several *suggested readings*, including books, short articles, and major texts, are provided for further exploration of the topics presented in the chapter.

## Guidelines

An important reason for studying educational psychology is to gain skills in solving classroom problems. Often texts give pages of theory and research findings, but little assistance in translating theory into practice. This text is different. Included in each chapter are several sets of Guidelines or teaching tips. The Guidelines offer practical suggestions based on the theory and research discussed in the chapter. Each suggestion is clarified by two or three specific examples. While these Guidelines cannot cover every situation, they do provide a bridge between knowledge and practice and should help you transfer this information to new situations.

## Teachers' Forum

This highly acclaimed and popular feature from the first edition has been expanded. More teaching problems, inspired by the real life experiences of beginning and advanced teachers at every grade level, were sent to master teachers around the country. Their ideas for solutions show you how to apply information from educational psychology in everyday classroom situations. These problems and suggested solutions follow each chapter, bringing the principles of the chapter alive.

You are invited to criticize the solutions in the Teachers' Forum and suggest your own. Professors are encouraged to send case studies that they would like to see discussed in the next edition. Send letters to:

Woolfolk and Nicolich
EDUCATIONAL PSYCHOLOGY FOR TEACHERS, 2/E
College Division
Prentice-Hall
Englewood Cliffs, NJ 07632

## Supplements

Two supplements are available to make this textbok more useful. An *instructor's manual*, written by Gail King, includes expanded chapter objectives, outlines, discussion questions, student assignments, demonstrations, audio-visual aids, and class activities. It also contains a completely revised test item file prepared by Robert Pratt. The *student guide*, also written by Gail King and Robert Pratt, has chapter objectives and outlines, lists of key concepts, sample test questions, projects and case studies to enrich your understanding of education psychology and better prepare you for your class evaluations.

# ACKNOWLEDGMENTS

During the years that we worked on this textbook many people suported our efforts. Without their help we could not have completed the project.

Our writing was guided by extensive, thoughtful, and insightful reviews from the following individuals: Professor Barak Rosenshine, University of Illinois; Dr. Susan G. O'Leary, SUNY Stony Brook; Professor Penelope L. Peterson, University of Wisconsin; Professor Rickey L. George, University of Missouri; Professors Carlton James and Richard De Lisi, Rutgers The State University of NJ; Professor Betty Caldwell Griffin, Oregon State University; Professor Christopher M. Clark, Michigan State University; Professor Walter B. Kolesnik, University of Detroit; Professor Steven M. Ross, Memphis State University; Professor Ron Reeve, University of Virginia; Professor Richard S. Prawat, Michigan State University; Professor Thomas J. Shuell, SUNY Buffalo; Professor Raymond W. Kulhavy, Arizona State University; Professor Suzanne P. Waller, University of Wisconsin-Milwaukee; Professor David F. Lohman, University of Iowa; Professor Sandra Anselmo, University of Pacific; Professor Daniel O. Lynch, University of Wisconsin; Professor Mark Grabe, University of North Dakota.

Many classroom teachers contributed their experience, creativity, and expertise to the Teachers' Forum. The teachers in our forum are well aware of the demanding responsibilities of teaching. We have thoroughly enjoyed our association with these experts and are grateful for the perspective they brought to the book.

Joan M. Bloom
Providence, Rhode Island

Kristine C. Bloom
Tonawanda, New York

B. Boriand
Edinboro, Pennsylvania

R. W. Bybee and R. B. Sund
Columbus, Ohio

H. Chipley
Lookout Mt., Tennessee

R. D. Courtright
Chapel Hill, North Carolina

M. Dozortz
Buffalo, New York

J. G. Dyer
St. Louis, Missouri

D. Egan
Streetsboro, Ohio

B. Everett
Ottawa, Ohio

Patricia Frank
South Brunswick, New Jersey

Barbra Fromme
Alexandria, Virginia

James C. Fulgham
Chattanooga, Tennessee

M. C. Gallagher
Perrysburg, Ohio

Carol Gibbs
Rossville, Georgia

Wayne A. Ginty
Lockport, New York

Deborah Glace-Wnek
Monmouth Junction, New Jersey

Louis G. Harrold
Warwick, Rhode Island

Bonnie Hettman
Lima, Ohio

Dorothy E. Hopkins
Homer, New York

Larry A. Irwin
Greeley, Colorado

John E. Jungbluth
Brockport, New York

Sharon Klotz
Kiel, Wisconsin

Joan H. Lowe
Hazelwood, Missouri

B. L. Luedtke
Appleton, Wisconsin

Jim Malanowski
Columbus, Ohio

G. D. McClary
Buffalo, New York

Annamarie McNamara
Erie, Pennsylvania

Rachel D. Morton
Star, North Carolina

Darlene Reynold
Spirit Lake, Iowa

Ruth Roberts
Rochester, New York

Shirley W. Roby
Shrub Oak, New York

Charlotte Ross
Elmont, New York

Estelle Sickles
Hampstead, New York

Sandra Silverberg
Buffalo, New York

J. M. Walsh
Pawtucket, Rhode Island

Arleen Wyatt
Rossville, Georgia

The talented staff at Prentice-Hall deserves special mention. Bob Sickles, editor for the first edition, provided invaluable leadership. His wisdom, tireless efforts, and friendship will always be remembered. The development editor, Jeannine Ciliotta, skillfully guided the revisions for this second edition. Barbara Kelly Kittle regularly performed minor miracles in supervising and coordinating all aspects of the project. Shirley Chlopak, assistant to the editor, has been a participant in this project from the earliest days of the first edition. Her dedication and unfailing good humor were greatly appreciated. Mary Helen Fitzgerald worked diligently to obtain permissions for the material referenced in this text. Anita Duncan guided the collection of photographs. The text and cover designer, Lee Cohen, brought a fresh, clean look to the book. The supplements for the text were prepared under the able supervision of Gert Glassen. Gail King drew upon her years of experience with teachers to provide outstanding activities and materials for these supplements. Robert Pratt performed the impossible, creating excellent test items that are clear, fair, and at times, even entertaining.

No words are sufficient to thank the editor, Susan Katz. Her good judgment, boundless energy, creativity, and strong leadership were essential in this project, from the first discussions about revisions to the last decisions about design. She is a valued friend.

Many colleagues contributed to this project. Carol Weinstein wrote the section in Chapter 11 on the physical environment of the classroom. Steven Ross is responsible for the exciting new appendix, "Computer-Based Education." Ken Carlson, Jack Nelson, Stan Vitello, Richard De Lisi, and Rita Silverman, all of Rutgers University, provided expert advice and counsel. In addition, both the first and second editions have benefited greatly from the suggestions of Ed Emmer, University of Texas at Austin, a gifted educational psychologist and a good friend. Two extraordinary educators, Nathan Levy and Chris Cornwell, provided guidance in planning the Teachers' Forum and graciously shared examples from their own experiences.

Beverly Dretzke, Kathy Biacindo, and Shelly Carroll contributed their efforts researching special topics. Phil Griswald, Eastern Montana College, and Janet Goldstein and Maria Defino, University of Texas at Austin shared ideas about needed revisions. Natalia Bayes tirelessly typed the manuscript. Her great competence and good humor made the project more pleasant.

Finally, it is to my family, Rob and Elizabeth, that I owe inexpressible thanks for their kindness, understanding, and support during the long days and nights required to write this book. A very special thanks is due again to Jane Woolfolk who dedicated many weeks to helping me care for my family during the hectic months of work. Without her selfless efforts, a second edition could not have been written.

A. E. W.
August, 1983

Educational
Psychology
for Teachers

# 1

# Teaching and Educational Psychology

If you are like many students, you begin this course with a mixture of anticipation and wariness. Perhaps you are required to take educational psychology as part of a program in teacher education, speech therapy, nursing, or counseling. You may have chosen this class as an elective, simply because you are interested in education or psychology. No matter what your reason for enrolling, you probably have questions about teaching, schools, students, or even about yourself that you hope this course will help you answer. We have written *Educational Psychology for Teachers* with questions such as these in mind.

In this first chapter we begin not with educational psychology, but with education—more specifically, with the state of teaching today. We believe that only a person who is aware of the problems teachers face can appreciate the solutions offered by educational psychology. For this reason, we will look first at the demands, challenges, and rewards of teaching, from both the perspective of day-to-day experiences in the classroom and the broader view of education's role in our society. After introducing you briefly to the world of the teacher, we turn to a discussion of educational psychology itself. We will consider what educational psychology is and why you should study it. How can principles identified by educational psychologists benefit teachers, therapists, parents, and others interested in teaching and learning in our society? What exactly is the content of educational psychology, and where did this information come from? By the time you have finished this chapter, you will be in a much better position to answer these questions and many others, such as:

- Would teaching be a good career for me?
- What are the greatest concerns of beginning teachers?
- What are the most important issues facing educators today?
- Will I be able to get a job in teaching?
- Why should I study educational psychology?
- What roles do theory and research play in this field?
- What specific types of problems will the study of educational psychology help me to solve?

We will start with the most basic and perhaps the most difficult question of all: What is teaching?

## TEACHING: AN ART, A SCIENCE, AND A LOT OF WORK

It has been a favorite indoor sport of educators over the years to debate whether teaching is an art or a science. If it is an art, then teaching calls for inspiration, intuition, talent, and creativity — very little of which actually can be taught. If it is a science, however, teaching requires knowledge and skills that can indeed be learned. Rules describing the effects of various teacher

2

actions can be memorized and applied in the classroom. If we take the scientific argument to the extreme, teaching is merely selecting and applying the correct formula for each classroom situation.

Some educators actually do take one or the other extreme, believing that teaching is fully an art or that teaching is a science and nothing but a science. Most, however, agree that teaching has both artistic and scientific elements. Two decades ago, Charles Silberman had this to say:

> To be sure, teaching — like the practice of medicine — is very much an art, which is to say, it calls for the exercise of talent and creativity. But like medicine, it is also — or should be — a science, for it involves a repertoire of techniques, procedures, and skills that can be systematically studied and described, and therefore transmitted and improved. The great teacher, like the great doctor, is the one who adds creativity and inspiration to that basic repertoire. . . . (1966, p. 124)

Silberman's analogy to medicine is still a good one. The modern practice of medicine is based on scientific theory and research. But a doctor treating a patient also must use judgment, intuition, and creativity in solving the many medical problems for which there are no guaranteed answers. Still, the doctor cannot ignore the principles of biochemistry and, for example, give a patient a dose of medicine that is lethal at the person's body weight. Ignoring the principles that determine safe drug dosages would have results even the most creative doctor wants to avoid. The same is true in education. The teacher who does not know what scientists have discovered about learning and instruction is like the physician who does not understand the principles of biochemistry. Both could make decisions that will lead inevitably to failure.

Whether you work with youngsters or adults, in schools, hospitals, community agencies, or industry, teaching is complicated. It is essential to know a great deal about the subject matter, your students, and the processes of teaching and learning. There is also a need to possess or develop a certain flair for teaching — the artistic aspect of the role. However, much more should be included in a definition of teaching. Here we will look at several of these aspects.

## The Many Roles of a Teacher

At the most general level, a teacher is a person who helps others learn. Yet teachers do much more than explain, lecture, and drill. They also design materials, make assignments, evaluate student performance, and maintain discipline. They must keep records, arrange the classroom, create learning experiences, talk to parents, and counsel students. A teacher assumes a multitude of roles. We will discuss the major ones here. As you read, you might consider how these roles relate to your own expectations, skills, and desires.

**The Teacher as an Instructional Expert.**   Teachers must constantly make decisions about teaching materials and methods. These decisions are based on a number of factors, including the subject matter to be covered, the abilities and needs of the students, and the overall goals to be reached. What is the best way to teach subtraction to second-graders. How can I teach creative writing to a seventh-grader who has never mastered basic writing skills? What book should I use to teach reading to eleventh-graders who read

3

at a fifth-grade level but are insulted by fifth-grade readers? Should I let students cover the next assignment individually or in groups? Which would be best for this lesson: lecture, discussion, discovery learning, programmed instruction, recitation, or seatwork? Would a microcomputer be a worthwhile investment for the school, and how would I use it in my classes? Teachers make hundreds of these instructional decisions each week. In addition, they are expected to know the answers to a multitude of questions about the subject itself.

**The Teacher as Motivator.**   Nothing the teacher does results automatically or magically in student learning. The student must act. One of the most important roles teachers assume is that of motivator. For today's media-saturated students, ordinary school activities may have little appeal, as you can see in the box, "The Teacher as Entertainer" (Box 1–1). But motivation involves more than starting each lesson with something exciting. Many

---

### BOX 1–1 THE TEACHER AS ENTERTAINER

*The following are excerpts from an article entitled "Teacher Biz Needs A Little Show Biz," by Rosalie S. Lawrence,* The New York Times, *Sunday, January 6, 1980.*

As an elementary school teacher, I have come to realize that there is a big gap in my professional training. Nothing in my educational background prepared me to be a song-and-dance person.

Though I have scanned with gimlet eye the catalogues of such institutions as Columbia's Teachers College and the Bank Street College, I have yet to find a course on the "The Teacher as Entertainer" or "How to Teach in Living Color."

The truth began to dawn on my pretelevision consciousness when, each time I rolled in the movie projector to show films to my captive audience of 5- and 6-year-olds, the vocal reaction was immediate and consistent.

"Is it a cartoon?" they piped tremulously. "Are we going to see a cartoon?" Then on a more plaintive note, "We want a cartoon!"

The announcement that it was not a cartoon invariably brought forth groans and occasional boos. Obviously, any educational film that is not animated is at a great disadvantage with today's youngsters, who peered through the bars of crib and playpen at "Sesame Street" and "The Electric company." . . .

Over the years I have considered having canned laughter piped into my classroom, or at the very least, hiring a makeup and wardrobe person. . . .

The challenge is great, but the educational show must go on. In truth, a master teacher has always been a combination show person and salesman. An instructor's unfeigned love for art, literature, music and nature, if presented with joy and enthusiasm, is contagious. It can raise the curtain on higher mental realms and turn the schoolroom into a stage for genuine excitement. Live action then replaces passivity and the children's animation comes from within.

These are noble aspirations indeed, but if in today's world teachers need a little help from show biz, then I say, send in the clowns. Let's make Singing and Dancing I and II mandatory courses for all teachers. After all, as an educational trouper can tell you — that's edutainment!"

decisions have an effect on student motivation. The grading method a teacher uses, for example, can motivate students to try harder or to give up. Any classroom materials chosen with student interest and ability in mind may help motivate students to learn. The question, How can I keep my students actively involved in learning? is at the heart of effective teaching. It is something you will need to think about every day.

**The Teacher as Manager.** Most elementary school teachers spend an average of only 20 to 30 percent of the day in direct verbal interaction with students (Rosenshine, 1977). Much of the remaining 70 percent is spent in some form of management. The figure for direct teaching in secondary schools is higher, but managing the class still takes a large percentage of the teacher's time. Management includes supervising class activities, organizing lessons, completing forms, preparing tests, assigning grades, training aides, meeting with other teachers and parents, and keeping records. Given only 24 hours in the day, teachers must be skillful managers of time, projects, deadlines, and people if they hope to have any private lives beyond working hours.

As a teacher you also will have to deal with another type of management: **classroom management**, or the maintenance of a healthy learning environment relatively free of behavior problems. You have met this concept many times under the more traditional heading of discipline. Teachers need to develop a number of methods for dealing with major and minor behavior problems so the class can get on with the process of learning.

**The Teacher as Leader.** Although teachers must be concerned with the needs of each student, in reality they seldom work with individuals for an extended period of time. Teaching, almost inevitably, is leading a group of students. An effective teacher is an effective leader, using the power of the group to promote individual growth. In the role of group leader, "The teacher is expected to be a referee, detective, limiter of anxiety, target for hostile feelings and frustrations, friend and confidant, substitute parent, object of affection and crushes, and ego supporter." (Ornstein and Miller, 1980, p. 226)

**The Teacher as Counselor.** Although teachers cannot be expected to act as guidance counselors, they must be sensitive observers of human behavior. They must try to respond constructively when students' emotions are getting in the way of their learning. They must know when a particular student needs to see a mental health specialist. Often teachers are expected to administer standardized intelligence, achievement, or interest tests, and to interpret the results of these tests for the students and their parents. In every class there are students who bring their personal problems to the teacher. You should be aware of the opportunities and the dangers involved in these situations. The feelings of parents, the standards of the community, the needs of other teachers and students all must be considered.

**The Teacher as Environmental Engineer.** The term environmental engineer may seem a bit far-fetched when you think about teaching. Yet the way the physical space of a classroom is used can help or hinder learning. Changes made by a teacher may be minor (for example, posters and occasional seating in a circle for discussion), or they may involve major restructuring. School budgets usually do not allow the purchase of extra bookshelves, room dividers, or learning carrels. Thus, in their role as environmental engineers, some teachers even build or adapt furniture for their classrooms. The instructor who spends Saturday making a reading corner in a fifth-grade classroom is simply acting out one of the teacher's many roles.

**The Teacher as Model.**   No matter what you do as a teacher, you will be acting as a model for the students. Enthusiasm for a subject will more likely be taught by an enthusiastic teacher giving a less-than-perfect demonstration than by a bored instructor lecturing brilliantly on the value of the subject. At times, teachers use modeling intentionally. The demonstrations in physical education, home economics, and industrial arts offer examples of direct modeling. In many other cases, however, teachers are not so aware of their role as model. For example, teachers constantly act as models in demonstrating how to think about problems. If they force their solutions on the students, the students are likely to learn that there is one best answer—namely, that of the authority. If they involve the students in thinking through alternatives, the students are more likely to learn that they themselves are capable of dealing with problems.

Having looked at just seven of the many different roles a teacher plays, you may feel overwhelmed. Many veteran teachers agree. Having too many roles to play, too many people to please, and too few resources to succeed in all these sometimes conflicting roles appear to be major sources of stress in teaching (Pettigrew and Wolf, 1982). And trying to meet all these demands is time-consuming as well as stressful. Nine thousand readers of *Instructor* magazine responding to a survey indicated that they worked an average of 10 hours each day, including preparation time. They managed to sleep an average of 7.5 hours each night (Landsmann, 1978). Figure 1–1 gives you an

*The teacher's many roles are interdependent. One of the surest means of motivating students, for example, is to model involvement. This teacher's infectious enthusiasm clearly contributes to the motivation of her students.*

(Lynn McLaren/Photo Researcher, Inc.)

idea of what you can expect to do during the 10 or so hours a day you are likely to spend teaching or preparing. The example is taken from the experiences of a high school teacher, but the variety of demands and the many roles played translate relatively easily to any teaching position.

**Figure 1–1    A Day in the Life of a Secondary-School Teacher**

| | |
|---|---|
| *Random Thoughts on the Way to Work* | "My life happens in segments just like my eight-period day . . . lots of homework last night . . . hate grading essay papers, but really enjoyed working out today's lessons. I think they're going to work. . . . Hope I can keep Ralph quiet during fourth period. . . ." |
| *Homeroom* | "At least the flag salute quiets them down. Do I have all the attendance cards in order? Almost forgot to collect insurance forms. I figured those two would forget theirs again. 'Lost,' they say. I'll have to send a student to the office for extra forms." |
| *Period 1: U.S. History (Standard)* | "I really feel sharp today, but I think my students are half asleep. Is it just that the lesson's not going as well as it could or that they're tired? Maybe the material isn't as good as I thought." |
| *Period 2: Preparation Period* | "I have a million things to do! I'd better beef up that U.S. history lesson before sixth period. I don't want to put another class to sleep. My turn to use the phone in the lounge—my only link with the outside world. Coffee! A few minutes to talk with friends and check the mail." |
| *Period 3: Economics* | "I love this course, partly because it's elective. All the kids want to be here. We can really tackle some difficult subjects. Great lesson today! The students are really getting excited. Madeline told me before class that she wants to major in economics in college. This kind of class makes it all worthwhile." |
| *Period 4: U.S. History (Basics)* | "Basics, alias 'sweathogs.' They're rowdy but I love them. They've got character even though they don't give a damn about history. We have great lessons . . . 'Get away from the window!' . . . 'Wait until the bell rings!'" |
| *Period 5: Lunch Duty* | "How demeaning to have to sit and watch kids eat!" |
| *Period 6: U.S. History (Standard)* | "Much better lesson than in first period. Maybe you really can learn from your mistakes. Or, maybe these kids are just more awake." |
| *Period 7: Library Duty* | "It's remarkable how many students don't know the first thing about using a library. In the beginning I thought I would get some reading done during this period, but the interruptions make it impossible—a frustrating 40 minutes." |
| *Period 8: Economics* | "This lesson went so well this morning. What's different? I guess last period is a terrible time to have to talk about supply and demand. We all want to go home." |
| *End of the Day* | "I'm glad I got to speak to Jane after school. Intramurals is a great way to get to know the kids. It's easier to work with them in class now that I am learning more about them after school . . . but I'm exhausted . . . just don't want to face three new lessons tonight. Sometimes I wish I could leave my work at the office." |

*Adapted from the experiences of Howard Schober, high school social studies teacher in New Jersey.*

You can probably tell from the description in Figure 1–1 that during much of the day the teacher is the only adult in a crowd of adolescents. For many people, this isolation from other adults is one of the major disadvantages of teaching. Will it be for you? What other disadvantages can you expect to find? Will the advantages of teaching outweigh the disadvantages?

## Advantages and Disadvantages

The fact that teachers play so many roles brings with it a great deal of stress but also a number of rewards. Let us focus on the disadvantages first so we can end on a more cheerful note.

**The Disadvantages of a Career in Teaching.** Teaching can be a very lonely endeavor, even though teachers are surrounded by people all day. Most teachers give each other very little mutual support or help with problems, in part because the teacher's class is considered a solitary domain. Teachers are generally expected to solve their own problems. Even if help is available, teachers are given little time during the day to consult or plan with their colleagues.

Isolation

A great deal of the teacher's time is filled with routine paperwork. Imagine for a moment that you have given an essay test to all five of your high school classes over a one-week period at the end of the semester. The following week you have to grade about 125 papers, turn in final grades for the semester, prepare 25 lessons, take attendance, answer memos from the administration, and perhaps meet with the backpacking club as their faculty advisor. In an elementary class you might have to prepare reading and math handouts and worksheets for students whose abilities span several grade levels, correct in-class ditto sheets, workbooks, and homework assignments, keep records on 25 students in six or seven different subjects, give achievement and placement tests, keep track of PTA notices, T-shirt money (for the fundraiser), lunch money, insurance forms, school picture forms,

Routine Work

*Teaching can be a lonely occupation. Most of the time the teacher is the only adult in the room. Hours spent in preparation and organization before and after class are often solitary time.*

(Ken Karp)

library notices, bus schedules, and weekly helper assignments. The idea that a teacher's day ends at 3 or 4 o'clock is definitely a misconception.

These busy teachers face the impossible challenge of encouraging maximum achievement in all their students. Yet is often difficult to see the results. Unlike the successful portrait painter, a teacher can seldom step back and admire the finished picture.

**Lack of Concrete Results**

For such potentially frustrating work, teachers are not lavishly paid. Teachers' salaries vary greatly from one part of the country to another and from one district to another, even in the same state. Salaries tend to be highest in the Far West and in the larger cities, but the cost of living is often higher as well. In general, the average starting salary for teachers has lagged behind beginning salaries for other college graduates who have gone into

**Modest Salaries**

private industry (Ornstein and Miller, 1980). Once in the profession, teachers can expect to earn the equivalent of only about double their initial salary as a top figure. In addition, there is little opportunity for advancement unless you return to school for further preparation to become a supervisor, principal, or educational specialist. Figure 1–2 presents the average salaries for teachers in the highest-paying states and some predictions for the future. The hand of inflation can clearly be seen.

With all these problems, it is no surprise that teaching can be a very stressful profession. The survey of 9000 teachers mentioned earlier (Landsmann, 1978) indicated that many teachers had trouble leaving the day's problems at work. Seventy-five percent of the respondents said that they were sometimes ill or absent from school for reasons that were related to stress or tension. Among the sources of stress named by the teachers were

**Figure 1–2  Average Salaries in Recent Years**

| Salaries for 1981–82* | | Projections for Average Salary, 1983–1990† | |
|---|---|---|---|
| Top 10 States in Salary | Salary | Year | Average Salary |
| 1. Alaska | $33,200 | 1983–84 | $20,431 |
| 2. Massachusetts | 27,946 | 1984–85 | 21,718 |
| 3. California | 26,191 | 1985–86 | 23,086 |
| 4. District of Columbia | 25,099 | 1987–88 | 26,086 |
| 5. Nevada | 24,820 | 1988–89 | 27,729 |
| 6. Hawaii | 24,278 | 1989–90 | 29,476 |
| 7. Washington | 23,392 | | |
| 8. New York | 22,900 | | |
| 9. Michigan | 22,202 | | |
| 10. Maryland | 21,899 | | |
| U.S. average | 20,208 | | |

*From the National Education Association, **Ranking of the States, 1982.** Washington, D.C., National Education Association, 1982, p. 21.
†A. C. Ornstein, "Teacher Salaries: Past, Present, Future," **Phi Delta Kappan,** 61 (1980), p. 678.

large classes, lack of teaching materials, increasing discipline problems, and very few or no breaks (many teachers had duties during their lunch periods). Several teachers mentioned the absence of even minimal adult help, the self-imposed pressure to succeed with every student, and a generally inhospitable physical environment (rooms that were too hot, cold, drafty, dark, dirty, noisy, or just plain ugly). Other studies of teacher stress point to the strain of trying to please administrators, parents, students, and colleagues while maintaining a sane family life outside class, even though adequate resources are seldom available (Pettigrew and Wolf, 1982).

Burnout

All these factors combine to produce "teacher burnout." Around the country today there are more and more books and workshops designed to help teachers rekindle their enthusiasm and counteract the sense of being "burned out" on teaching. One school district in Washington has developed a plan that includes insurance coverage for teachers suffering long-term disabilities as a result of classroom stress or burn-out (Young, 1980).

**PEANUTS** &reg;                                                    **By Charles M. Schulz**

*Moral for teachers: There are days when even the egg shells may get to you.*

(© 1959 United Features Syndicate, Inc. Used with permission)

**The Advantages of a Career in Teaching.**    This would be a pretty grim picture if teaching did not offer some compensating advantages. An old joke quotes a university professor who said, "There are three good reasons for choosing teaching as a career: June, July, and August." This probably is the most widely held image of the advantages. However, there are other more important reasons to become a teacher.

A Valued
Profession

Even though it is not high-paying, teaching is generally a well respected profession. While teachers are seen as having less prestige than physicians, lawyers, or business executives, they are usually ranked above many other professionals, such as journalists, nurses, and the clergy (Treiman, 1977). In the eyes of the public, schools are still seen as extremely important to an individual's chances for success in life (Gallup, 1982).

Academic
Freedom

Although a teacher may at times feel lonely and isolated as the only adult in the class, this very isolation offers certain rewards. With it comes the freedom to deal with instructional and behavioral problems as they see fit. Within limits that vary greatly from school to school, a teacher is autonomous in the classroom.

Working
with People

The major reward for teachers, of course, comes from the relationships with students and the chance to make a difference in the lives of these individuals. Over 70 percent of the teachers responding to the National Education Association's poll in 1976 indicated that the desire to work with young people was one of their main reasons for entering the profession. Each year we ask our students to interview teachers about the rewards and problems of the profession. The positive factor mentioned most often is the chance to work closely with youngsters. When you return to visit teachers who were important to you and note their broad smiles or when you hear teachers tell their special success stories, you begin to understand how important these relationships can be.

**Satisfactions of Teaching**

So it seems that many of the satisfactions for teachers involve relationships with other people rather than money or status. In fact, research indicates that individuals who stay in the teaching profession (compared to those who leave) tend to value interpersonal rewards such as approval and recognition from supervisors, family, and friends. The issues of salary and participation in important decisions appear to be less important to them (Chapman and Hutcheson, 1982).

Having looked at both the advantages and disadvantages of teaching, you may be asking yourself which are more important. Of course, no one can answer this question for you. As you can see in Box 1–2, "Two Views of Teaching," different people reach different conclusions.

---

### BOX 1–2 TWO VIEWS OF TEACHING

*The following two cases were reported in the cover story of the June 16, 1980, issue of* Time *magazine. They present two different experiences of teaching exemplifying some of the advantages and disadvantages of the profession.*

"Judy," 40, says: "What got to me was that I found I was not getting results." A Bryn Mawr graduate who always wanted to be a teacher in a big city, she successfully taught English for eleven years in a Manhattan high school. Her enthusiasm began to falter three years ago when each of her five high school classes crept above the union maximum of 34 students. Says she: "No English teacher should have five classes. If you're trying to teach kids how to read and write, you simply can't do it — that's 200 students a day." In effect, Judy gave up teaching because she wanted to teach. Says she: "Many of my colleagues were not making an effort. The administration failed to recognize excellence, failed to recognize mediocrity, and failed to recognize negligence — except if you punched your timecard a few minutes late."

Carolyn Kelly, 33, whispers to a visitor: "I love this." Kelly has just led a spirited senior class debate on the best interpretation of H. G. Wells' *The Man Who Could Work Miracles.* "I feel rejuvenated when a kid expresses something in a manner that for him is totally new, totally his own."

The seniors are Kelly's star pupils. She also teaches a basic English class and acts as coordinator of teacher advisers at the Rindge and Latin School in Cambridge, Mass. If need be she can reason with students from slum backgrounds in their own street-wise slang, and she spends a good deal of time trying to make students understand that public school is still a gateway to opportunity. Says she: "My goal is not just academic; it's teaching kids what it is to be a human being."

Like most teachers she decries the loss of public support for the profession. "It is vital that we all understand how things have changed: the role of the teacher, the school, the church, the family. It does no good to isolate schools as the culprit when there are social changes that affect other institutions as well. Until we all realize that education is a reciprocal thing, we won't have understood much at all."

If you decide in favor of the advantages of teaching and continue your preparation to enter the profession, you still must face many difficult situations.

## Major Concerns of Beginning Teachers

It is impossible to talk about the concerns of teachers without taking the individual teacher's stage of development into consideration. At different points in their careers, teachers tend to be concerned about different issues. In fact, there appear to be at least three stages of psychological development for teachers: (1) a preteaching stage; (2) a beginning or early teaching stage; and (3) a mature or experienced stage (Fuller, 1969; Katz, 1972). Let us examine the stage that probably is of greatest interest to you—beginning teaching.

In the first two years of "real" teaching, most people seem quite self-oriented. Concerns usually focus on issues of adequacy. Young teachers tend to worry about lack of confidence, being accepted and liked by peers and students, making a good impression, and generally surviving from day to day and week to week (Evans, 1976). If you have had similar concerns when you imagine your first day in front of a class, you are not alone. Coates and Thoresen (1976) concluded that beginning teachers seem most anxious about the answers to five basic questions:

*Common Problems of the Early Years*

1. Will I be able to maintain discipline?
2. Will students like me?
3. Is my knowledge of the subject matter adequate?
4. How should I cope with making mistakes or running out of material?
5. How should I relate to other teachers, parents, and the administration?

Each year we ask our students, "Now that you've visited a classroom and observed things from the point of view of a prospective teacher, what do you expect to be the major problems you will encounter as a beginning teacher?" Some of the more typical answers we have collected over the years are given below:

*Problems Student Teachers Expect*

Probably the most difficult problem I will encounter as a teacher is one of discipline. I found that quite often I would lose my temper and punish with threats of detention and the like. Then on occasion, after realizing that my anger was not warranted, I would revert back and overcompensate by kidding around. This whole issue of discipline and temper versus joking around and calm is definitely something I must learn to deal with!

One problem I expect is becoming a believable authoritative figure. At the junior-high level, the students are quite restless. They can't wait to grow up. Control is important and hard to come by. Finding enough material to vary the classes is another problem. You have to get their attention, and an interesting lesson plan is very important to both teacher and students.

Frustration may be a major problem for me. In the course of observing my classes I found myself expecting a higher level of production than the students were able to give. Conversely, I have feelings of inadequacy. Granted, what I give my students will be something more than what they'd have if I hadn't been there, but will I be able to give them as much as I'd like?

Concerns don't disappear after the first few years. But most teachers do move beyond worries about adequacy to focus more on the needs of students. For this reason we believe that the experienced instructor, the one who has solved many of the initial problems of teaching, has a great deal to offer students of education. We have polled a number of successful experienced teachers for ideas about solving some of the problems of the early years.

*Experience is a good teacher, but a hard one. The beginning teacher can learn much from contacts with more experienced teachers. Lessons learned second-hand will spare the teacher many a painful first-hand experience.*

**Learning from Experienced Teachers**

These common problems and possible solutions are found at the end of each chapter in the section called "Teachers' Forum." Although the vast majority of the material in this text is based on findings of educational psychologists, the ideas suggested by these experienced teachers offer a sound supplement.

You may have noticed that teachers are quite concerned about discipline. In fact, many people, especially parents, worry about discipline (or the lack of it) in today's classrooms. Parents who move their children to private schools often cite a desire for better discipline as the main reason (Frechling, Edwards, and Richardson, 1981). In light of these concerns, we have devoted a large portion of three chapters (5, 9, and 10) in this book to managing classrooms and motivating students.

**An Emphasis on Management**

Now that we have examined the problems, joys, and concerns of teachers from the perspective of the day-to-day classroom experience, let us step back and take a look at the profession from another vantage point. Our schools are part of our society and are at times rocked, swayed, and even improved by changes in the society itself. What issues in the larger society will affect teaching in the next few years?

## SOCIAL ISSUES AFFECTING TEACHERS TODAY

In this section we discuss five issues that are likely to be a special challenge to the teachers of the 1980s.

### Criticisms Left and Right

One of the important issues facing teachers today is public dissatisfaction with the public schools. In 1974, for example, 48 percent of the people responding to the Gallup poll gave the schools a grade of A or B for quality of education. In 1979, only 34 percent of those polled were willing to give the schools such high grades, and by 1982 the figure had risen only slightly to 37 percent (Gallup, 1982). A closer examination of the 1982 survey shows that whites and residents of towns of under 50,000 were more satisfied with their schools than other groups.

**Criticisms from the Left**

Although there may be general agreement that the schools could be improved, there is no such agreement on solutions. The answers offered by educators in recent years have ranged from going "back to basics" to getting rid of schools altogether. During the 1960s and early 1970s, many solutions were suggested by such liberal and radical reformers as John Holt, Ivan Illich, Jonathan Kozol, and Neil Postman. A general theme running through their criticisms and proposed solutions is that the schools are repressive and stifle real learning and creativity. A second important theme is that the schools discriminate against minorities and the socially and economically disadvantaged while favoring the white middle class (Robinson, 1978). If you have not yet read these works, you may want to do so at some point within the next few years so that you can make your own decisions about the solutions they offer.

**Criticisms from the Right**

On the other end of the continuum are critics such as Max Rafferty and Frank Armbruster, who believe the schools are too permissive and lax in the enforcement of standards. (Robinson, 1978). Again, their works may be worth your time. More recently, there has been growing concern about national declines in achievement test scores and an increasing demand that we return to the "basics." Many Americans share this view. In 1980, 61 percent of those surveyed believed there was "not enough" emphasis on basic subjects in the schools (Gallup, 1980). Recently some researchers have suggested (though others disagree) that private schools may be more successful than public schools in educating students (Coleman et al., 1982).

## Accountability

Minimum
Competency
Tests

Some educators and politicians believe teachers and schools should be held responsible for what the student does or does not learn. In several states **minimum competency tests** are now required for graduation from high school or for promotion from one grade to the next. All students are expected to learn at least enough to pass these tests. Advocates of the accountability movement believe teachers and schools are to blame when students fail to reach a minimum level of performance.

Assumptions
About
Accountability

The position favoring accountability assumes that almost every student *can* learn the material taught in schools if given enough time and the right instruction. A second assumption is that teachers and schools play the major role in determining what students learn. Both assumptions have some truth but there are problems with accepting them completely. Students vary greatly in abilities and motivation. Many other factors besides the teacher and the school influence what the student will learn. For example, it is possible for students to be physically or psychologically absent from the classroom most of the time. No teacher can influence someone who is not there.

The call for accountability offers possibilities of both gains and losses. It may encourage teachers to examine the results of their teaching more carefully and make improvements. The progress of each student may be more carefully watched. But should teachers' jobs and salaries depend on how much their students learn?

One of the greatest problems with holding teachers responsible for student learning is the difficulty of measuring learning accurately. If standardized achievement or minimum competency tests are used to measure how well the student has learned (and thus how well the teacher has taught), will teachers be forced to teach just the material covered on the tests to protect their jobs? Will students be robbed of the chance to view themselves as partly responsible for their own learning? Perhaps teachers, students, and parents should be held jointly accountable for the student's progress.

Recently, a new and perhaps even more difficult set of demands has been placed on teachers—the responsibility for teaching students who had formerly been taught in separate, special classes.

## Mainstreaming

Public Law
94-142

The movement of as many students as possible out of special education classes and into regular classrooms is generally called **mainstreaming.** There are an estimated 8 million people in this country between the ages of 3 and 21 with learning needs or learning problems so different from their peers' that they require special instruction (Council for Exceptional Children, 1976). For years, these students, if educated at all, were kept separate from others and given labels such as "retarded" or "physically handicapped." Landmark

*One effect of budget cutting and financial problems for schools can be increased class sizes. What impact will these changes have on the teacher's methods?*

legislation passed in 1975, called Public Law 94-142, set the stage for bringing many of these young people into the mainstream of American schools.

The new legislation compelled the public schools to provide an appropriate free education for every young person. The law recognized that many students with severe problems cannot function in a regular classroom, but that other "special" students, given the needed support, can benefit greatly from spending at least some part of their school day with their more "normal" peers. At this point the future of PL 94-142 is uncertain. The principle of a free public education for certain children like the profoundly retarded is being challenged in a few states. The law may be rewritten or even repealed. Schools seldom have been given enough money to support the program (Vitello and Soskin, in press). But regular classroom teachers probably will be expected to continue working with many "special" students even if the laws are changed, because having separate classes and teachers for these children is expensive. In a time of budget cuts and inflation, it is often the regular teacher who is expected to do more. Because the demands on teachers dealing with mainstreamed students are significant, we have devoted an entire chapter (Chapter 13) to this topic.

Mainstreaming may not be every teacher's problem, but there is one question that affects everyone who wants to become a teacher: Will there be any jobs?

## The Future of the Job Market

Since 1960, the birth rate in this country has been decreasing. Twenty-eight percent fewer children were born in 1978 compared with 1959. This has led to declining school enrollments that should persist well into the 1980s (Coates, 1978). Fewer children have meant fewer jobs for teachers, although many experts are predicting a teacher shortage beginning in the mid-1980s (Bispo and Wallace, 1978; National Center for Educational Statistics, 1980). Even now there are shortages in certain fields and in some areas of the country. The supply of teachers is least adequate in mathematics, natural and physical sciences, agriculture, special education, industrial arts, distributive education, and vocational-technical subjects. It is most adequate in the social sciences, physical and health education, music, and art. Some states have teacher shortages in all subject areas; most states have too many applicants in some subjects and not enough in others (National Education Association, 1981).

Even if the market for teachers is poor in the places you want to teach, you can begin now to improve your chances for finding a job. Check with your college placement office to find out what qualities and skills local schools value in applicants. Build your credentials so that you have a good chance to fill one of the vacancies created by the resignations and retirements that occur in every school. Finally, if you are willing to relocate, you usually can find the position you want. Many rural areas as well as large cities in developing parts of the country need teachers.

## Changes in the Family

The declining birth rate is not the only change in the family affecting teachers: "Approximately 45 percent of the children born in 1976 will have lived with a single parent for some time before reaching 18 years of age" (Coates, 1978, p. 35). There has been a dramatic increase in the number of school-age children living with divorced or single parents and in the number of children born to mothers under the age of 15. These children often need extra support during times of crisis.

For reasons of necessity or by choice, the mothers of many students work outside the home. This has led to a decrease in the availability of volunteers to serve as teachers' aides, library workers, and club sponsors. In dual-career families, extra money sometimes is available for private school, decreasing the enrollments in public schools even more. But working families need preschool and after-school child care, services that could be provided in by public education.

We hope we have given you a balanced picture of the problems, concerns, rewards, and issues confronting teachers today. But this is an educational psychology book, and we have said very little so far about educational psychology. Let's turn now to the role educational psychology can play in helping teachers solve problems.

# THE ROLE OF EDUCATIONAL PSYCHOLOGY

Before you began this book, the term educational psychology may or may not have had any meaning to you other than the obvious linking of two areas of study. We begin our consideration of the role of educational psychology with a closer look at what these words mean.

## Definitions

**Education** itself has many definitions. One is "the process by which a society transmits to new members the values, beliefs, knowledge, and symbolic expressions to make communication within the society possible"

(Roemer, 1978, p. 4). In our society, schools are the institutions formally responsible for educating new members. But not all education happens in schools, nor is every lesson that people learn intentionally taught. Education may be deliberate, as in classrooms and lecture halls, or it may be unintentional, as in the transmitting of prejudices from one generation to another within the family. Whenever education takes place, deliberately or unintentionally, it is tied to **psychology,** because psychology is the study of human behavior, development, and learning. But, as is often the case, the whole meaning of the term educational psychology is more than the sum of the two parts.

Conflicting
Views About
Educational
Psychology

For as long as **educational psychology** has existed, about 80 years, there have been debates about what it really is (Grinder, 1981). Some people believe educational psychology is simply the application of *knowledge* gained from psychology to the activities of the classroom. Others believe it is the utilization of *methods* from psychology to study life in schools (Bierly, 1981). Many people argue that educational psychology is a distinct discipline, with its own theories, research methods, problems, and techniques. The movement today is toward this third view (Scandura, Frase, Gagné, Stolurow, Stolurow, and Groen, 1978). So educational psychology can be seen as a distinct discipline concerned primarily with (1) understanding the processes of teaching and learning, and (2) developing ways of improving these processes.

Educational psychologists apply knowledge from other fields and also create knowledge. They employ general scientific methods and also develop their own methods. They examine learning and teaching in the laboratory, in nursery, elementary, and secondary schools, in universities, in the military, in industry, and in many other settings as well. But no matter what the situation or subjects studied, educational psychologists are especially concerned with applying their knowledge to improve learning and instruction. Educational psychology is not something limited to the laboratory; it is intimately related to what is happening in classrooms.

In dealing with the issue of laboratory versus classroom, educational psychologists make an important distinction between learning and teaching. Most of what we know about how people learn is based on controlled research in laboratories. But knowing how people learn in a controlled environment such as the laboratory does not tell us how to teach those people in the often unpredictable environment of the classroom. Theories and methods of teaching, which are based on theories of learning, must be examined and tested outside the laboratory. Studying how people learn is only half the question. The other half is studying how to teach them. Educational psychologists do both.

The purpose of this text is to give you a large part of the most important knowledge that educational psychologists have gained over the years. Knowing what educational psychologists have learned will not automatically make you a great teacher. But not knowing this information can lead to failure in teaching or to the frustration of spending hours rediscovering what others already know. Findings from educational psychology are part of the scientific basis for becoming a teacher-artist.

We are convinced that educational psychology can play an important role in teaching. You still may be skeptical, especially about the value of research and theory. Here are some additional reasons why future teachers can benefit from the scientific approach found in a study of educational psychology.

## The Need for a Scientific Approach

Does educational psychology really have anything new to say to future teachers? After all, most teaching is just common sense, isn't it? Let's take a few minutes to examine these questions.

**No, It's Not Just Common Sense.**    In many cases, the principles set forth by educational psychologists — after much thought, research, and money spent — sound pathetically obvious. People are tempted to say, and usually do say, "Everyone knows that!" Consider these examples:

*TAKING TURNS*

What method should a teacher use in selecting students to read in a primary reading class?

*Common Sense Answer*

Teachers should call on students randomly so that everyone will have to follow the lesson carefully. If a teacher were to use the same order every time, the students would know when their turn was coming up and probably would concentrate only on the line they were going to read. They would not have to pay attention during the rest of the lesson.

*Answer Based on Research*

Research by Ogden, Brophy, and Evertson (1977) indicates that the answer to this question is not so simple. In first-grade reading classes, for example, going around the circle in order and giving each child a chance to read led to better overall achievement. The system does let students figure out when their turn is coming and practice just their own lines. This very practice, with teacher feedback, may be a more important aspect of learning to read than paying attention while others are reading, at least in the early grades. In addition, going around the circle means that teachers do not overlook certain students, perhaps those in the greatest need of practice.

*CLASSROOM MANAGEMENT*

What should a teacher do when students are repeatedly out of their seats without permission?

*Common Sense Answer*

The teacher should remind students to remain in their seats each time they are up. These repeated reminders will help them remember the rule. If the teacher does not remind them and lets students get away with breaking the rules, those students and the rest of the class might decide the teacher was not really serious about the rules.

*Answer Based on Research*

In a now classic study, Madsen, Becker, Thomas, Koser, and Plager (1968) found that the more a teacher told students to sit down when they were out of their seats, the more often the student got out of their seats without permission. When the teacher ignored students who were out of their seats and praised students who were sitting down, the rate of "out-of-seat behavior" dropped greatly. When the teacher returned to the previous system of telling students to sit down, the rate of "out-of-seat behavior" increased once again. It seems that, at least under some conditions, the more a teacher says, "Sit down!" the more the students stand up.

*SKIPPING GRADES*

Should a school encourage exceptionally bright students to skip grades or enter college early?

*Common Sense Answer*

No! Very intelligent students who are a year or two younger than their peers are likely to be social misfits. They are neither physically nor emotionally ready for dealing with older students and would be miserable in the social situations that are so important in school, especially in the later grades.

*Answer Based on Research*

Maybe! According to Martinson (1973), most careful studies indicate that gifted students who begin elementary, junior high, high school, college, or even graduate school early do as well and usually better than the nongifted students who are progressing at the normal pace. Whether acceleration is the best solution for a student depends on many specific individual characteristics, including the intelligence and maturity of the student and a consideration of the other available options. For some students, skipping grades is a very good idea.

You may have thought that educational psychologists spent their time discovering the obvious. The examples above point out the danger of this kind of thinking. When a principle is stated in simple terms, it can sound simplistic. A similar phenomenon takes place when we see a gifted dancer or athlete perform; they make it look easy because we see only the final

*The classrooms of the 1980s and 1990s will be filled with new possibilities for teaching and learning. To use these opportunities wisely, teachers will need to be aware of the results of research and the latest theories in educational psychology.*

(Ken Karp)

performance, not all the work that went into mastering the movements. With any research, it would probably be possible to make either the actual finding or its opposite sound like common sense. The issue is not what sounds sensible, but what is demonstrated when the principle is put to the test.

Research and Theory

Conducting research to test possible answers is one of two major tasks of educational psychology. The other is combining the results of various studies into theories that attempt to present a unified view of such things as teaching, learning, and development. In this book you will encounter both kinds of information: (1) the results of actual studies and experiments; and (2) descriptions of major theories about topics of importance to teachers. Here we will look briefly at each of these sources of information.

**Using Research to Solve Classroom Problems.**  Educational psychologists design and conduct many different kinds of research studies in their attempt to achieve a better understanding of both teaching and learning. A number of studies are based on classroom **observations.** Generally, the results reported in these studies are **correlations,** which are findings that show the degree of relationship between two events or measurements.

Correlations

The correlation indicates both the strength of the relationship and its direction. Correlations are expressed as numbers from 1.00 to .00 to –1.00. The closer the number is to 1.00 or –1.00, the stronger the relationship. For example, the correlation between height and weight is about .70 (a fairly strong relationship), while the correlation between height and number of languages spoken is about .00 (no relationship at all). The sign of the correlation tells the direction of the relationship. A positive correlation, such as the one between height and weight, indicates that the two factors increase or decrease together. As one gets larger, so does the other. A negative correlation means that increases in one factor are related to decreases in the other. For example, the correlation between outside temperature and the weight of clothing worn would be negative because as the temperature increases, people tend to wear clothing of decreasing weight.

It is important to note that correlations do not prove cause and effect. Height and weight are correlated. Taller people tend to weigh more than shorter people. But gaining weight does not *cause* you to grow taller. Knowing a person's weight simply allows you to make a general prediction about that person's height. Educational psychologists identify correlations so they can make predictions about important events in the classroom.

Experimentation

A second type of research allows educational psychologists to go beyond predictions and actually study cause and effect. A special kind of research called **experimentation** must be conducted to identify true **cause-and-effect relationships.** Instead of just observing an existing situation, the investigators introduce changes and note the results. First a number of comparable groups of subjects are created, usually by assigning subjects at **random** to the groups. Random means each subject had an equal chance to be in any group. In one or more of these groups, psychologists change some aspect of the situation to see if this change has the expected effect. The results in each group are then compared. A number of the studies we will examine attempt to identify cause-and-effect relationships by asking questions such as these: If teachers ignore students who are out of their seats without permission and praise students who are working hard at their desks (*cause*), will students spend more time working at their desks (*effect*)?

In many cases, both kinds of research occur together. The study by Ogden, Brophy, and Evertson (1977) described at the beginning of this section is a good example. In order to answer questions about the selection of students to recite in a primary reading class, these investigators first observed students and teachers in a number of classrooms and then measured the reading achievement of the students. They found that the teaching strategy of going around the circle asking each student to read was associated or correlated with gains in reading scores. With a simple correlation such as this, however, the researchers could not be sure that the strategy was actually causing the effect. In the second part of the study, Ogden and her colleagues asked several teachers to use the strategy of calling on each student in turn. They then compared reading achievement in these groups with achievement in groups where teachers used other strategies. This second part was, in effect, an experimental study conducted to see whether the teaching strategy would actually improve reading scores. As we have already seen, a cause-and-effect relationship did indeed seem to be involved, although the students had not been assigned randomly to the classes, so the results might have been due to other factors as well.

This has been a brief and simplified discussion of research methods. For a more complete description, see the appendix at the end of this chapter.

**Theories for Teaching.** The major goal of educational psychology is understanding the teaching-learning process, and research is a primary tool. If enough studies are completed in a certain area and findings repeatedly point to the same conclusions, we eventually arrive at a **principle.** This is the term for an established relationship between two or more factors, between a certain teaching strategy, for example, and student achievement. Principles that stand the test of time and repeated investigation become **laws** of human functioning.

Another tool for building a better understanding of the teaching-learning process is **theory.** Given a number of established principles, educational psychologists have attempted to explain not just the relationship between two or more variables, but much larger systems of relationships. Theories have been developed to explain how motivation works, how differences in intelligence occur, and even how people learn.

Note that theories attempt to explain. In dealing with such broad areas, it would be impossible to have all the answers. In this book, you will see numerous examples of educational psychologists taking different theoretical positions and disagreeing on the overall explanations of such issues as learning and motivation. If any one theory offered all the answers, disagreements would not exist.

So why, you may ask, is it necessary to deal with theories? Why not just stick to principles? The answer is that both are useful. Principles of classroom management, for example, will give you help with specific problems. A good theory of classroom management, on the other hand, will give you tools for creating solutions to a great many discipline problems. A major goal of this book is to provide you with the best and the most useful theories for your teaching. Although you may like some of the theories better than others, our suggestion is that you look at each as a possible source of solutions to the problems teachers face.

Now that we have explored the role of theory and research, let us turn to a consideration of the topics studied by educational psychologists.

*Priniciples and Laws*

*Theories*

# MAJOR AREAS OF STUDY: THE CONTENTS OF THIS BOOK

To present the major theories and principles of educational psychology in a single textbook, some system of organization is needed. We have chosen an organization that we think works quite well because it takes things as they come.

## An Orderly Progression

The Teacher

In Part One, we begin with an exploration of teaching from the teacher's point of view and then with an examination of educational psychology.

In Part Two we will look at the students—or, more specifically, at human development. As you will see, students of different ages bring a wide range of abilities and ways of thinking to the classroom. Besides having their own

The Students

characteristic styles of thinking, students of different ages also face distinct challenges in social and emotional development. As a teacher, you will want to take into account the mental, physical, emotional, and social abilities and limitations of your students. To do this, you must know something about them and about the ways individuals differ in their development.

Having introduced the students themselves, we will move to one of the most important topics in both educational psychology and the classroom:

Learning

human learning. In Part Three, we will describe the major approaches to the study of human learning, the behavioral and cognitive theories. We will also show how these theories can be applied in a number of very practical ways, including strategies for classroom management and instruction in various subject areas.

At that point we will have covered the dual foundations of teaching: the students and the processes of learning. Having dealt with the essentials, we can concentrate in Parts Four and Five on actual practice. Part Four examines theories of motivation and their applications in the classroom and then takes a

Management and Teaching

careful look at how to organize and manage classrooms. One chapter in this part explores interpersonal relationships among students and teachers. The focus is on creating conditions that keep students involved and learning. In Part Five we discuss instruction: how to set goals, select methods, create settings, group students, and teach effectively. The last chapter of this section concentrates on designing instruction for special students, for the handicapped, the gifted, and the bilingual child.

Evaluation

In Part Six, we evaluate the effectiveness of what has been taught. Here we will look at standardized tests, teacher-made tests, grading systems, mastery learning, and various alternatives to the traditional systems of evaluation.

## Putting the Book to Work

In Figure 1–3 you will find a list of sample questions drawn from different parts of this book. The questions do not begin to cover the many topics that will be included in each part. However, they will give you a sense of the kind of information we will present.

As you continue through this book, you will encounter not only questions, but also a number of possible solutions. We hope we have communicated our belief that educational psychology has a great deal to offer teachers and all those interested in education in our society.

**Figure 1–3**   **Would You Like to Know?**
**Questions Educational Psychology**
**Can Help You Answer**

| Questions | Source for Information |
|---|---|
| • What is it like to be a teacher?<br>• Why study educational psychology?<br>• What use can a teacher make of research and theory? | Part One: Education and Psychology |
| • How might my students' thinking processes differ from my own?<br>• What is the emotional and social world of my students like?<br>• How can I help my students develop a positive self-image?<br>• What is intelligence and where does it come from?<br>• Are there inborn psychological differences between males and females? | Part Two: Human Growth and Development |
| • What causes some students to develop fears about school?<br>• Should I use punishment in my classes?<br>• Why do students remember some things and forget others?<br>• How should I teach difficult concepts to slower students?<br>• Will students use what I teach them? | Part Three: Learning Theory and Practice |
| • Can sine curves ever be as interesting to students as sex education?<br>• How can I deal with a really defiant student?<br>• What should I do when angry parents accuse me of treating their child unfairly? | Part Four: Motivation and Management |
| • Where do I start in planning my first class?<br>• Is lecture better than discussion or individualized instruction?<br>• What makes an effective teacher?<br>• What should I do if I'm assigned a student who is deaf? | Part Five: Effective Instruction |
| • How can the results from standardized tests help me teach?<br>• Are grades really necessary?<br>• How should I test my students? | Part Six: Evaluation |

## SUMMARY

1. Teaching is both an art and a science. Effective teaching requires an understanding of the findings of research on learning and instruction. Teaching also calls for the creativity, talent, and judgment of an artist.

2. The disadvantages of teaching include isolation from other adults, the need to do a great deal of routine paperwork, the difficulty in actually seeing the results of the work done, and the often very modest salaries.

3. Balancing the disadvantages are the rewards of teaching: the chance to perform a valuable service, autonomy in the classroom, recognition from parents and peers, and the chance to make a difference in the lives of students.

4. The concerns of teachers change as they progress through three stages: the preteaching years, the early teaching years, and the experienced teaching years. During the beginning years, concerns tend to be focused on survival. The experienced teacher can move on to concerns about professional growth and effectiveness with a wide range of students.

5. Many societal changes are having repercussions in today's classroom. While everyone today seems to agree that the schools could be improved, no one plan for change is acceptable to all. There is a movement to hold schools and teachers accountable for student learning. New federal laws call for an appropriate education for all students, regardless of ability or handicapping condition. Declining birth rates have presented teachers with a tight job market. More and more students live in homes with just one parent and many children undergo the crisis of divorce.

6. The goals of educational psychology are to understand and to improve the teaching-learning process. Educational psychologists develop their own knowledge and methods, and also use the knowledge and methods of related disciplines such as psychology. A very important aspect of educational psychology is its concern with application, as well as its scientific approach.

7. Both observational studies and experimental research can provide valuable information for teachers. Correlations will allow you to predict events that are likely to occur in the classroom; experimental studies leading to the establishment of cause-and-effect relationships should help you implement useful changes.

8. The principles of educational psychology offer teachers a number of answers to specific problems. The theories offer perspectives for analyzing almost any situation that may arise.

**KEY TERMS**

classroom management

minimum competency testing

mainstreaming

education

psychology

educational psychology

observation

correlation

experimentation

cause-and-effect relationship

random (sample)

principle

law

theory

# Teachers' Forum

## Past Influences

What factors were most influential in making you the kind of teacher you are today?

**A Variety of Influences**

My early teaching experience in nursery school and kindergarten taught me to appreciate children as "people who are learning to live," not only recipients of subject matter. Observation of and discussions with admired and respected teachers taught me to experiment, since there are many ways to approach the teaching-learning process. Participation in an outstanding Masters Program helped me to analyze my performance, round out professional deficits, and utilize the research data to support my professional decisions and expertise. Active membership in professional associations (National Education Association, Phi Delta Kappa, Association of Teacher Educators) has fostered a strong advocacy for children and teachers and further encouraged me to "be the best that I can be."

Joan H. Lowe, Fifth-Grade Teacher
*Russell Elementary School, Hazelwood, Missouri*

## Working with Student Teachers

Imagine you've just been assigned a new student teacher who is very shy. In fact, you can't quite understand why this person has chosen to go into teaching. He's been very open with you, telling you about his great love of learning and about the wonderful experiences he himself had in school when the teacher really cared. He's also told you about his fear of failing with the students. What kinds of advice would you give him to help him build up the kind of confidence he will need to teach?

**Guidelines for a New Teacher**

To a new teacher from a not so old one: (1) You are only *you*, be yourself, naturally. (2) Do get close to your students as a *teacher.* (3) Do smile, joke, play games with your students. (4) Establish your tolerance level and expectations and (5) Be consistent in what you say and do! (6) Let the children know who you are, a person with likes, dislikes, interests, and desires. (7) Plan, plan, plan!!! Have objectives in mind with each lesson so you can evaluate (see 10 and 11). (8) Overplan so you never run short or can switch midstream. (9) Kids like variety, it is their spice of life. Use it in your teaching. (10) Evaluate yourself after each lesson for positive and negative points. . . . (11) Like yourself and what you are doing, and most of all . . . (12) Like the children and what they do.

John E. Jungbluth, Fifth- and Sixth-Grade Teacher
*Brockport Middle School, Brockport, New York*

**Fears Are Normal**

I would reassure him that all teachers begin with a desire to succeed and a dread of failure, then identify his strongest subject area to use as a starting point for increasing his confidence. I'd prepare him for the realities of the classroom and pupil-teacher interaction so he will not seek popularity or gratitude from the kids, but instead look for satisfaction from his own sense of accomplishment. . . . I'd include post-class conferences to identify instances where his shyness hindered effective instruction, and suggest alternate behaviors and responses to improve his classroom management skills.

Richard D. Courtright, Gifted and Talented Elementary Teacher
*Ephesus Road Elementary School, Chapel Hill, North Carolina*

## Family and School

Families have changed in many ways over the past few decades. Parents seem busier than ever. Life has become very full and complicated. What aspects of the family most affect a child's attitude, performance, and ability in school? As a liaison between the home and the school, how can a teacher deal with these family effects if they are negative?

**The
Importance
of Sensitivity**

The most important change in the family has to be the increasing number of single-parent families where the parent is unmarried, separated, divorced, or widowed. The teacher must be sensitive to changes in student performance or behavior and be familiar with the family situation. The teacher should *know* that it is the day his folks appear in court, or that he is moving from one parent's home to the other's, or that a birthday or significant life event of a deceased parent is near. . . . In addition, the teacher must accept the challenge of being a role model for the student, especially when both teacher and absent parent are the same gender.

Family economics—two working parents, latchkey children, parent's loss of a job—can bring stress that affects behavior and academic achievement. Job-related mobility, too, affects students whose families move frequently. A teacher must see that a new student who may have never been at *any* school more than one year is quickly integrated into the group and not allowed to flounder on the sidelines.

Richard D. Courtright, Gifted and Talented Elementary Teacher
*Ephesus Road Elementary School, Chapel Hill, North Carolina*

## Were You Prepared?

No teacher is completely ready to meet the demands of every situation. In the beginning years, teachers often feel inadequate about some aspect of their new role and wish they had been better prepared with additional information, skills, or practical experiences. In what areas, if any, did you feel a lack of preparation, and how did you deal with the situation?

**Collecting
Information
Early**

It always seemed to take me ten weeks to find out which pupils moved faster and which ones needed the added time to go over material for mastery. In addition, I seemed to find out about special musical talents, family composition, physical interests, and family travel experiences almost by accident during the school year.

Now, before the rush of the semester begins, I make a summary chart for each pupil which not only lists past test scores and report card grades, but also notes any special information. Collecting data on each incoming student allows me to plan instructional strategies and to match students with appropriate materials. The time is well spent.

Dorothy Eve Hopkins, Sixth-Grade Teacher
*Homer Intermediate School, Homer, New York*

## Accountability?

Imagine that the school board in the district where you teach is drawing up plans to make teachers accountable for student learning. Present plans call for the use of standardized achievement test scores and student evaluations to determine the results each teacher is achieving. The results will then be used in making decisions about which teachers to rehire each year. Assume that you have no real say about whether or not they implement the program. You do, however, have a say about the method they use. Do you think a combination of achievement test scores and student evaluations makes sense? If so, why? If not, what would you suggest instead?

**An Argument in Favor of Student Evaluation**

While the use of student achievement scores in teacher evaluation is both understandable and necessary, my major commitment is to student evaluation. Students see the teacher "in action" every day and have the best insight into the teacher's overall performance, including his/her affective impact. Student evaluations are by no means infallible. Some people feel that student evaluations are nothing more than popularity contests. I feel that most students are capable of making accurate, honest judgments of teachers. Student evaluations and achievement test scores both have their limitations, but I see them as our two most desirable options.

Jim Malanowski, Secondary Social Studies Teacher
*West High School, Columbus, Ohio*

**An Argument in Favor of Committee Reports**

Although I disapprove of any program where teachers' jobs depend upon accountability, I think the best way to find out the effectiveness of a teacher is to see for oneself. Perhaps a committee could make short visits to classrooms periodically throughout the year.... Student evaluations are not always reliable.... Usually they reflect the attitudes of the students toward the teacher, not necessarily the knowledge they've gained. I feel there is an overemphasis on standardized tests as far as measuring skills gained by students during a specific time period. There are many factors that go into a test score besides knowledge.... Often the goals and objectives of the teacher and students are not identical to what the achievement test is measuring.

Marilyn Dozoretz, Sixth-Grade and Prekindergarten Teacher
*Build Academy Public School, Buffalo, New York*

# Appendix

# Research in Educational Psychology

The concepts, principles, laws, and theories of educational psychology come from somewhere. One step toward a better understanding of educational psychology is knowing how information in the field is created and how to judge the information you encounter. This appendix will explore the value and limitations of research, the major road to knowledge in educational psychology. Then we will examine a specific problem to determine how research might answer questions posed by teachers. Finally, we will describe how to judge a research study by evaluating a real experiment.

When you complete this appendix, you should be able to:

- Describe four methods for making measurements.
- Distinguish between correlational and experimental methods.
- Judge research to determine if it is valid.
- Propose a study to answer a question from your teaching.

## ASKING AND ANSWERING QUESTIONS

A Sample Problem

To get a better understanding of a few of the basic methods for asking and answering questions in educational psychology, we can examine a question that might interest you: Do students' expectations about the competence of a new teacher influence the way the students behave toward the teacher? To be more specific, do students pay more attention to a teacher they expect to be good? Suppose, for our purposes here, that an educational psychologist decided to look for an answer to this question. What methods might be used to gather information?

### Forming a Research Question

Specific Question

The first step might be to frame a clear and specific question. In this case, we might begin with something like this: Do students' beliefs about a teacher's competence affect the amount of attention they pay to the teacher? Notice how specific the wording is. We will have problems if the question is too vague — for example, Do students' beliefs about a teacher affect the way they behave in class? There is too much territory to cover in answering the question. We need to be *specific* about what kinds of beliefs — beliefs about the teacher's competence, not age, intelligence, or marital status. And we need to be *specific* about what kind of behavior — attention to the teacher, not enthusiasm for the subject or anxiety about a new year.

## Choosing Variables and Selecting Measurement Techniques

At this point we are ready to identify the variables to be studied. A **variable** is any characteristic of a person or environment that can be said to change under different conditions or differ from one person to the next. In our hypothetical study, we have decided to examine two variables—student beliefs about the teacher's competence and student attention to the teacher.

Measurement The next thing we must do is decide how we will define what we mean by "beliefs" and "attention." This question leads to the issue of measurement, because our definitions will be useful only if they give us something we can measure.

To study any variable systematically, there must be a way to measure changes or compare different levels of the variable. To simplify matters, let us concentrate at this point on just one of the variables—student attention. We will need to find a way to measure the degree of attention shown by the students. The method chosen will depend in part on the design of the study and on the limitations imposed by the situation. Here we will look at four basic approaches to measurement: (1) self-report, (2) direct observation, (3) test, and (4) teacher or peer ratings.

Using the **self-report** method, we could ask the students questions about how attentive they thought they were being. Answers could be given in writing or face to face, in an interview with the students.

If we decided instead to use **direct observation,** we could send researchers into the classroom to watch the students and assess their attention. These investigators might simply rate the students (on a scale of one to five, perhaps, from very attentive to very inattentive), or they could use a stopwatch to count the number of seconds each student watched the teacher. Observers could also work from a videotape recording of the class, replaying the tape several times so that each student could be observed and his or her level of attention rechecked. These are only a few of the systems that could be designed using observers to measure attention.

A **test** would be a little more difficult to construct in this case. Many variables are measured with tests, especially those involving learning or achievement. But since attention is a process rather than a product, it is hard to design a test to measure it. One approach, however, would be to use a "vigilance task." We could see if the students were paying attention by having the teacher give an unpredictable signal, such as "stand up," during the lesson. The measure of attention in this case would be the number of people who stood up immediately (Woolfolk and Woolfolk, 1974).

Finally, we might decide to use **teacher ratings** or **peer ratings.** We could measure attention by asking the teacher or the students to rate the attention of every student in the class.

Clearly, each of these approaches has advantages and disadvantages. Using self-reports or ratings of teachers or peers means relying on the judgments of the participants themselves. Using observers or tests can be disruptive to the class, at least initially. Videotaping is difficult and expensive. Let us assume, however, that we have chosen direct observation from videotapes. We will train the observers to time student attention with a stopwatch to determine how many seconds each student looks at the teacher during a 10-minute lesson. Note that our system of measurement has given us our definition of attention: the number of seconds each student looks at the teacher during a 10-minute lesson. This seems to offer a reasonably good definition. If the measurement system did not offer a good definition, we would need to find another way of measuring.

To define and measure our first variable — students' beliefs about the teacher's competence — we could also choose from a number of methods. Let us assume, at least for the time being, that we have selected a rating system. Students' answers to the question "How competent do you think this teacher is?" should give us a good idea of student opinion.

One other definition may be in order here, although in this particular study it seems rather obvious. Since we wll be studying student beliefs and student attentiveness, the "subjects" in our investigation will be students. As you probably know, **subjects** is the term for the people (or animals) whose behavior is being measured. We would want to specify the grade, sex, and type of student to be studied. For our hypothetical study, we will select male and female sixth-graders in a predominantly middle-class school.

## Stating a Hypothesis and Choosing an Approach

Hypothesis

At this point we have our research question, the variables to be studied, the definition of these variables, the system for measuring them, and the subjects to be studied. We are now ready to add two new details: a **hypothesis** or guess about the relationship between the two variables, and a decision about what kind of approach we will use in our study. To some extent, the hypothesis will dictate the approach.

At the most general level, there are two approaches to answering research questions. The first is to describe the events and relationships in a particular situation as they take place in real life. The second approach is to step in and change one aspect of a situation and note the effects of the change. These two approaches are generally called descriptive and experimental.

**A Descriptive Approach.** One hypothesis we might establish in our study of student beliefs and attention is that students pay more attention to a teacher they believe to be competent. To test this hypothesis, we could go into a number of sixth-grade classrooms and ask students to rate their teachers on competence. Ideally, we would conduct the study in a middle school where sixth-graders usually have more than one teacher each day. We could then observe the students and measure their level of attention to each teacher. At this point we could get some idea about whether believing that a teacher is competent and paying attention to that teacher go together.

Correlation

Let's assume, for the sake of the argument, that the two variables do go together. What we have now is a **correlation.** If two variables tend to occur together, they are correlated. We have just assumed such a correlation between beliefs and attention. Other variables that are correlated are height and weight, income and education, and colder temperatures and falling leaves. A taller person, for example, is likely to weigh more than a shorter person. A richer person is likely to have completed more years of education than a poorer person. And, for the sake of the argument, we are now assuming that a student who believes a teacher to be competent is more likely to pay attention to that teacher,

But what does this correlation give us? If educational psychologists know that two variables are correlated, they can then make predictions about one of the variables based on knowledge of the other variable. For example, because the IQ scores of parents and children are correlated, educators can predict a child's IQ based on that of the mother or father. The prediction may not be correct every time, because the correlation between parents' IQs and children's IQs is not perfect. But the prediction is likely to be correct or nearly correct much more often than a prediction based on no information at all. Several studies have found a correlation between a teacher's enthusiasm and student learning (Rosenshine and Furst, 1973). If we have information about a teacher's enthusiasm, we can make a prediction about the achievement level of the students in his or her class.

**Correlation and Cause**

But this last example brings us to a very important point about correlation and prediction, mentioned briefly in Chapter 1. Knowing that two variables tend to occur together does not tell us that one variable is actually *causing* the other. Although enthusiastic teachers may tend to have students who achieve more than the students of unenthusiastic teachers, we cannot say that teacher enthusiasm leads to or causes student achievement. We know only that teacher enthusiasm and student achievement tend to occur together. Perhaps teaching students who are achieving more makes a teacher more enthusiastic. Perhaps a third factor—the interesting materials a teacher has chosen to work with, for example—causes both teacher enthusiasm and student achievement. Knowing that two variables are correlated does not tell you that one variable is causing the other. You should not argue from correlation to cause, but you can make predictions.

Although being able to predict levels of one variable from information about levels of another is useful, teachers are often interested in finding out what factors actually will *cause* a desired change in behavior. For this, they would need a different kind of research—research based on experimental manipulation.

**An Experimental Approach.** Returning to our original question about student beliefs and attention, suppose we made a different hypothesis. Rather than just hypothesizing that student attention and beliefs about teacher competence go together, we could hypothesize that one of the factors actually causing students to pay attention is the belief that a teacher is competent. In this case, the hypothesis states a causal relationship. To test this hypothesis, we must change one of the variables to see if this change actually causes changes in the other variable. In our study, this assumed cause—known as the **independent variable**—is the belief that the teacher is competent. The purpose of our experiment will be to see if changes in this variable really cause changes in the other variable—the **dependent variable** of student attention to the teacher.

**Independent and Dependent Variables**

**Random Selection**

Assume that we create three comparable groups of students by randomly assigning the students to the groups. Since the selection and assignment of students to groups is totally **random**—by chance, based on no particular plan—the three groups should be very similar.

**Control Group**

We then tell one group of students that the teacher they are about to meet is a "very good" teacher; we tell the second group that the teacher they will have is "not a very good" teacher; and we tell the third group nothing about the teacher they are going to have. This final group serves as the **control**

**group.** It will give us information about what happens when there is no experimental manipulation. At some point in the experiment we would ask the students what they believed about the teacher to make sure they had accepted the description they were given.

Next, the teacher, actually the same person in all three cases, teaches the same lesson to each group. Of course the teacher should not be told about the experimental manipulation. We videotape the students in each group as they listen to the teacher. Later, raters viewing the tapes measure the number of seconds each student in the three groups has looked at the teacher. (You may have noticed that although the definition and measurement of the attention variable remains the same as it was in the descriptive study, the definition and measurement of the belief variable has changed. As you can see, such a change is necessary to turn the study into an experiment.)

What kind of results can we expect? If we find that students who believed the teacher was competent paid attention most of the time, students who believed the teacher was not very good paid very little attention, and students who were given no information paid a moderate amount of attention, have we proved our hypothesis? No! It is assumed in educational psychology and in psychology that hypotheses are never really proved by one study because each study tests the hypothesis in only one specific situation. Hypotheses are "supported" but never proved by the positive results of a single study. So have we supported the hypothesis that student beliefs affect student attention? The answer to this question depends on how well we designed and carried out the study.

Since this is just a hypothetical study, we can assume, once again for the sake of the argument, that we did everything just right. If you read the following list of requirements for a "true experiment," set forth by Van Mondrans, Black, Keysor, Olsen, Shelley, and Williams, you will see that we were indeed on the right track:

**True Experiment**

> The "true experiment" is usually defined as one in which the investigator can (a) manipulate at least one independent variable; (b) randomly select and assign subjects to experimental treatments; and (c) compare the treatment group(s) with one or more control groups on at least one dependent variable. (1977, p. 51)

However, with a real experiment, we would need to know more about exactly how every step of the investigation was conducted. And we would also want to know whether other researchers could come up with the same results if they did the same experiment.

# IS THE RESEARCH VALID?

**Analyzing
Research**

Being able to evaluate research studies has a dual payoff. The kind of thinking needed is in and of itself valuable. It is the same kind of thinking needed to evaluate any complex idea, plan, argument, or project. In all these cases, you need to search for errors, oversights, inconsistencies, or alternative explanations. The analytical ability necessary to evaluate research is useful in any occupation, from law to business to motorcycle maintenance. The second payoff is more specifically valuable for teachers. As an educator, you will have to evaluate research done in your school district or reported in professional journals to determine if the findings are relevant to your own situation.

To be valid, the results of an experiment must pass several tests. Changes in the dependent variable must be due solely to the manipulation of the independent variable. This means, for one thing, that the experimental and control groups must be exactly the same in every way except one — the differences in the independent variable. In the following pages, we will look at eight questions that can be asked in an evaluaion of a research experiment.

*1. Were the groups to be studied reasonably equal before the experiment began?* If the subjects vary greatly from group to group, any changes found at the end of the experiment may be the results of the original differences in the groups and not of changes in the independent variable. Random assignment of subjects to groups usually takes care of this problem. If instead of randomly selecting the subjects in our own study we had used three different sixth-grade classes, our results would be questionable. Maybe one class already had more generally attentive students or maybe as a group these students had learned to be more generally attentive. If they had been given the teacher labeled "very good" in the experiment, their high degree of attention would have been relatively meaningless. With random selection from a number of sixth-grade classes, however, each group is likely to have gotten an equal share of the generally attentive and generally inattentive students.

*2. Were all the variables except the independent variable controlled so that the only real difference in the treatment of each group was the change in the independent variable?* We have just seen that the subjects in each group must be equivalent. This principle is equally true of everything else in the experiment. If different procedures were used with each group, it would be difficult to determine which of the differences caused the results. In our study, for example, if we had used different teachers or different lessons in each group, we would have run into this problem in evaluating the results. The students' attention to the teacher could have been based on many things other than the initial statement given by the experimenter about the teacher's competence (the independent variable).

*3. Were the measurement procedures applied consistently to each group?* Unreliable results may at times be caused by an inconsistent measurement system. In our study, if we had used a different videotape rater for each group, we could not have trusted our results. Perhaps one rater would give credit for student attention when students had their faces pointed toward the teacher even if their bodies were turned away. Perhaps another rater would give credit only if the students' entire bodies were directed toward the teacher. Ideally, one rater should make all the measurements. If more are used, there must be some test of the raters' ability to agree on the results. One way to check this would be to see if they agreed when measuring the same students' behaviors.

*4. Are the results of the study due to the experimental procedures rather than to the novelty of the situation?* It is always possible that subjects will respond in some special way to any change, at least temporarily. This possibility was pointed out dramatically by studies conducted at the Western Electric Plant in Hawthorne, Illinois. Investigators were trying to determine which changes in the plant environment would lead to greater worker productivity. As it

Hawthorne
Effect

turned out, everything they tried, every change in the working conditions, seemed to lead to greater productivity, at least for a while (Roethlisberger and Dickson, 1939). In other words, the workers were reacting not to the changes themselves, but to the fact that something new was happening. Because the experiment took place in Hawthorne, Illinois, such results are now said to be examples of the **Hawthorne effect.** Our control group helped us avoid this problem. Although the independent variable of a "good" or "bad" teacher label was not applied to the control group, these students were given the special attention of being in an experiment. If their attention ratings had been particularly high, we might have suspected the Hawthorne effect for all three groups.

*5. Has the investigator who designed the study biased the results in any way?* There are a number of obvious and subtle ways in which an investigator can influence the participants in an experiment. The investigator may have no intention of doing so, but still may communicate to the subjects what he or she expects them to do in a given situation (Rosenthal, 1976). In our study, for example, if the investigator had told the teacher involved what the purpose of the experiment was, the teacher might have expected less attention from one of the groups and unintentionally done something to increase or decrease the attention actually given. If the investigator had told the videotape raters the purpose of the experiment, the same thing might have happened. Without meaning to, they might have looked harder for attention in one of the groups. To eliminate these problems, both teacher and raters would have to be unaware of the independent variable being studied.

*6. Is it reasonably certain that the results did not occur simply by chance?* To answer this question, researchers use statistics. The general agreement is that differences among the groups can be considered "significant" if these differences could have occurred by chance only 5 times out of 100. In reading a research report, you might see the results stated in the following manner: "The difference between the groups was significant ($p < .05$)." Unless you are planning to do your own scientific research, the most important part of this is probably the word "significant." The mathematical statement means that the probability ($p$) of such a difference occurring by chance factors alone in less than ($<$) five in one hundred (.05).

*7. Will the findings in this particular study be likely to fit other, similar situations?* This is really a question of generalization. How similar does a new situation have to be to get the same reuslts? Consider our own experiment. Would we get similar results under these conditions:

With much older or younger students?
With students who are more or less intelligent?
With students who already know the teacher?
With different teachers or different lessons?
With the removal of the videotape cameras?
With a lesson that lasts more than 10 minutes?

We cannot answer these questions until the study has been repeated with many different subjects in many different situations. This brings us to the question of **replication.**

*8. Has the study been replicated?* A study has been replicated if it has been repeated and the same results are found. Replication may involve exactly the same study conditions or changes in conditions that will give us a better idea of the extent to which the findings can be applied to other situations. If results have been replicated in well-designed studies, the findings form the basis for principles and laws.

Since our own study was only hypothetical, we cannot get a replication of it. But we can look at a similar study done by Feldman and Prohaska (1979). Analyzing this study should be useful to you in two ways. First, it will provide a model for considering other research articles you will find in textbooks and in professional journals. Second, the results of the study itself will probably be of interest because they suggest ways in which student expectations may cause teachers to be more or less effective.

## A SAMPLE STUDY: THE EFFECT OF STUDENT EXPECTATIONS

Feldman and Prohaska's 1979 study concerns student expectations about a teacher's competence and the effect of these expectations on the students' and the teacher's behavior. (Remember that we were looking only at student behavior in our hypothetical study.) You may want to read the study in the *Journal of Educational Psychology* (vol. 71, no. 4, 1979). At the beginning of the article you will find specific information: the names of the authors, the university where they work, the name of the article, the name of the journal, and the basic facts about the study. The basic facts describing the design and results of the study are usually included in a brief summary, called an found not at the end but at the beginning of such an article.

*Can students' expectations about a teacher influence their behavior in class? Certainly students are not shy about sharing their impressions and opinions with friends.*

(Ken Karp)

## Essential Data

Subjects

The subjects in Feldman and Prohaska's first experiment were undergraduate female volunteers from an introductory psychology class. They were randomly assigned to a positive-expectation group or a negative-expectation group.

Procedures

Each subject arrived separately at the experimental center and was told she would have to wait a few minutes before she could see the teacher. While she waited, she met another student who had supposedly just been working with the teacher and was now completing a questionnaire evaluating the teacher. Actually, this student, a male, was a **confederate** of the experimenter — an assistant pretending to be one of the subjects. The confederate played one of two roles, depending on whether he was meeting a subject from the positive-expectation group or the negative-expectation group. (The subjects, of course, did not know what group they were in.) When the confederate met a subject from the positive group, he told her the teacher had been really good, effective, and friendly. He then gave her a completed questionnaire (which also said good things about the teacher) and asked her to turn it in for him, since he had to leave. When the confederate met a subject from the negative group, he said very uncomplimentary things about the teacher and gave the subject a questionnaire with very negative comments on it.

The subject then went into a room and met the teacher, who was the same person for both groups. The teacher did not know the subject had been given any expectation at all. While she taught two mini-lessons, she and the subject were secretly videotaped. After the two lessons, the subject took a short quiz on the material and filled out a questionnaire just like the one she had seen the confederate completing. The same procedure was repeated for each subject.

Measurement System

Finally, the videotapes of all the subjects were shown to trained coders who were unaware of the actual experimental conditions. These coders measured three things: (1) percentage of time each subject looked at the teacher, (2) each subject's forward body lean toward the teacher, and (3) each subject's general body orientation toward the teacher. Taken together, these student behaviors could be called "paying attention." When the coders rated the same subject's videotape, their ratings of the three behaviors were highly correlated. Thus we can assume that the coders agreed about how to use the measurement technique.

Results

Results showed that the subjects who expected the teacher to be "bad" rated the lesson as significantly more difficult, less interesting, and less effective than the subjects who expected the teacher to be "good." They also found the teacher to be less competent, less intelligent, less likable, and less enthusiastic than the other subjects did. Furthermore, the subjects who expected the teacher to be "bad" learned significantly less from one of the two mini-lessons, as measured by the short quiz. They also leaned forward less often and looked at the teacher less than the subjects who expected the teacher to be good.

How would you evaluate this study? The full report (Feldman and Prohaska, 1979) gives many more details, but based on our summary alone, what can you tell about the validity of the findings?

### Judging Validity

**Criticisms?**

If you look at the Guidelines for Evaluating a Research Study, it appears that conditions 1, 3, 5, and 6 have been met. (Do you agree?) We cannot yet be certain about condition 2—equal treatment of the subjects—because in this first experiment we have no detailed information about the way the teacher behaved toward the subjects. We only know that the teacher was instructed to give the same lesson, in the same way, to each subject. But what if the differences in the subjects' behavior toward the teacher—the differences that were found in the study—caused the teacher to give the lesson in different ways to different students? Perhaps after the first minute or so, subjects were reacting to real differences in the way the teacher delivered the lesson.

Feldman and Prohaska looked at this very real possibility in their second experiment. They found that students' nonverbal behavior (leaning forward or looking at the teacher) actually could affect how well the teacher taught the lesson. Although this may, to some extent, lessen the validity of their first experiment, it is a worthy finding in and of itself.

You may have noticed that we have not yet discussed conditions 4, 7, and 8. Feldman and Prohaska did not include a control gorup. The fact that the two experimental groups reacted in significantly different ways, however, shows that they were not simply reacting to the novelty of the situation. If both groups had been particularly eager or bored, we might have had good reason to expect the Hawthorne effect.

# *Guidelines*

## *Evaluating a Research Study*

**1. Ideally, you should be able to answer "yes" to each of these eight conditions:**

**EXAMPLES**
- Equality of the experimental groups before the experiment.
- Equal treatment of the groups except for the independent variable.
- Use of a consistent measurement process.
- Control for the Hawthorne effect.
- Nonbiased participation by experimenters and raters.
- Results that are statistically significant.
- Ability to generalize to other similar situations.
- Replication.

**2. You will also want to consider these two questions:**

**EXAMPLES**
- Are there alternative explanations for the results that were achieved?
- Are the differences among the groups large enough to have educational as well as statistical significance?

**Significance**

The answers to conditions 7 and 8 will have to await further research. The evaluation of student expectations is a relatively new topic. Until now, research has placed more emphasis on the study of the effects of teacher expectations about students. In some ways, it is exciting to be in on a new type of experimentation. At the same time, it is frustrating not to have as much information as we would like to have about replication and the ability to generalize. We can say, however, that two respected educational psychologists have reported findings that seem to support our initial hypothesis. In some cases, at least, student expectations about a teacher's competence do have an effect not only on the students' behavior, but also on the teacher's behavior.

The answers to the last two questions given in the Guidelines are equally difficult to answer. It is almost always possible to offer alternative explanations for the findings of any study. In a well-controlled study, an attempt is made to eliminate as many of these alternative explanations as possible. The question of educational versus statistical significance is also one on which reasonable people might easily differ. How large a difference between the test scores of the two groups is large enough to warrant a change in educational practice? This question must be answered in part by the individual teacher. Do the potential gains offered by the findings seem worthwhile enough to make whatever change is called for?

## SUMMARY

1. Besides helping you answer your questions about teaching, research can offer data to support your viewpoint when others disagree and methods for carrying out your own studies.

2. There are two general approaches to research in educational psychology: (1) descriptive studies, in which correlational relationships are examined; and (2) experimental studies, where cause-and-effect relationships are found. An experimental study involves the carefully controlled manipulation of an independent variable (the presumed cause).

3. In evaluating research, just as in evaluating any complex idea, you must make judgments about how valid the results are. If a research study meets all or most of the Guidelines we listed, you must still decide if the results will truly generalize to your situation and whether the change involved is worth making.

## KEY TERMS

| | |
|---|---|
| variable | correlation |
| self-report | independent variable |
| direct observation | dependent variable |
| test | control group |
| teacher rating | Hawthorne effect |
| peer rating | replication |
| subjects | abstract |
| hypothesis | confederate |

**40**

# SUGGESTIONS FOR FURTHER READING AND STUDY

BORG, W. R. and GALL, M. D. *Educational research: An introduction* (4th ed.). New York: Longman, 1983. This latest version of a comprehensive text describes the entire research process from identifying the problem to writing the finished report.

FARLEY, F. H. and GORDON, N. J. *Psychology and education: The state of the union.* Berkeley, Calif.: McCutchan, 1981. This book has chapters written by authorities in different areas of educational psychology. Topics include individual differences, development, learning and instruction, and the future of the discipline.

GALLUP, G. H. Gallup Poll of the public's attitudes towards the public schools. *Phi Delta Kappan.* Each year the September issue of this journal reports results of the annual Gallup Poll on the public schools.

HOUSE E. R. and LAPAN, S. D. *Survival in the classroom: Negotiating with kids, colleagues, and bosses.* Boston: Allyn and Bacon, 1978. This book, written for both new and experienced teachers offers chapters on discipline, teacher credibility, communication with parents, dealing with bosses, getting a job, getting tenure, students' rights, and negotiating for resources.

RYAN, K., NEWMAN, K., MAGER, G., APPLEGATE, J., LASHLEY, T., FLORA, R., and JOHNSON, J. (Eds). *Biting the apple: Accounts of first-year teachers.* New York, Longman, 1980. This book is filled with real stories about the first year of teaching. The experiences are interesting, funny, inspiring, but, at times, depressing.

SCANDURA, J. M., FRASE, L. T., GAGNE, R., STOLUROW, L., and GROEN, G. Current status and future directions of educational psychology as a discipline. *Educational Psychologists,* 1978, *13,* 43–56. In this article, the profession of educational psychology looks at itself, its goals, and its future. The article gives a good view of the current state of the discipline.

SOWELL, EVELYN and CASEY, RITA, *Analyzing educational research.* Belmont, California: Wadsworth, 1982. A book for people who need to read and understand educational research. Included are examples of complete reports and hands-on exercises in applying results.

TREFFINGER, D. J., DAVIS, J. K., and RIPPLE, R. E. *Handbook on teaching and educational psychology.* New York: Academic Press, 1977. Part One of this book is four chapters written by four different groups about the nature and organization of educational psychology. In these chapters you will find the history, contents, methods, and future directions of the field.

## *Journals in the Field*

Some information about educational psychology can be found in professional education journals. These journals may include specific descriptions of research but are more likely to have general articles describing current topics in education. Examples of such journals are:

*Contemporary Education Review*
*Childhood Education*
*Educational Researcher*
*Educational Leadership*
*Harvard Educational Review*
*Journal of Education*

*Journal of Teacher Education*
*Phi Delta Kappan*
*The Review of Education*
*School Review*
*Teaching Exceptional Children*
*Theory into Practice*

Other journals specialize in reports of research studies or reviews of several studies on one topic. Some examples are:

*Adolescence*
*American Educational Research Journal*
*Child Development*
*Contemporary Educational Psychology*
*Cognitive Psychology*
*Educational and Psychological Measurement*
*Exceptional Children*
*Elementary School Journal*
*Human Development*
*Journal of Applied Behavior Analysis*
*Journal of Applied Developmental Psychology*

*Journal of Educational Psychology*
*Journal of Educational Research*
*Journal of Experimental Child Psychology*
*Journal of Experimental Education*
*Journal of Learning Disabilities*
*Journal of School Psychology*
*Monographs of the Society for Research in Child Development*
*Psychology in the Schools*
*Sex Roles*

# 2

# Cognitive Development and Language

How does the mind of the average 8-year-old work? What about the mind of the average 14-year-old? Can you really explain geometry to second-graders? Can you explain existentialism to seventh-graders? The material in this chapter will help you answer these questions and many others about how young people think and how their thinking changes over time. These changes in thinking and understanding are called cognitive development.

In this chapter we will begin with a discussion of the general principles of human development. Then we will turn to what is perhaps the most influential of all modern theories of cognitive development, that presented by Jean Piaget. Piaget's ideas have important implications about what to teach students and when to teach it. But Piaget's theory is not the only explanation of how cognitive development takes place.

After considering his ideas, we will look at what has been called the American question: Can cognitive development be speeded up? Should teachers try to help students move from one stage of cognitive development to the next as quickly as possible? Or is it better to let students proceed at their own pace? We turn next to the theorists who emphasize developmental changes in how children process information. Last, we will explore the topic of language and the role of the school in developing this important ability.

By the time you have completed this chapter, you should have a basic understanding of cognitive development. More specifically, you should be able to do the following:

- State three general principles of human development and give examples of each.
- Describe Piaget's four stages of cognitive development and tell how you might teach a concept to a person at each stage of development.
- Argue for and against methods for accelerating cognitive development.
- Present alternative views about cognitive and metacognitive development.
- Discuss how childrens' attention and memory abilities change over time.
- Describe the role language plays in cognitive development.

First, however, we will look at the concept of development itself.

## DEVELOPMENT: TOWARD A GENERAL DEFINITION

**A General Definition of Development**

The term **development** in its most general psychological sense refers to certain changes that occur in human beings (or animals) between conception and death. The term is not applied to all changes, but rather to those that appear in orderly ways and remain for a reasonably long period of time. A temporary change due to a brief illness, for example, is not considered to be a part of development. There is also a value judgment made by psychologists in determining which changes qualify as development. The changes, at least those that occur early in life, are generally assumed to be for the better and to result in behavior that is more adaptive, more organized, more effective, more complex, and of a higher level (Mussen, Conger, and Kagan, 1979).

Human development can be broken into a number of different aspects. **Physical development,** as you might guess, deals with changes in the body. **Personal development** is the term generally used for changes in an individual's personality. **Social development** refers to changes in the way an individual relates to others. And, as we have seen, **cognitive development** refers to changes in the way a person thinks.

**Maturation v.
Experience**

Many of the changes involved in human development are simply a matter of growth and maturation. **Maturation** refers to changes that occur naturally and spontaneously and are, to a large extent, genetically programmed. Such changes emerge over time relatively unaffected by the environment, except in cases of malnutrition or severe illness. Much of a person's physical development would fall into this category. Other changes are brought about through learning as individuals interact with their environment. Such changes make up a large part of a person's social development. But what about the development of thinking and personality? Most psychologists agree that both maturation and interaction with the environment are important in these two areas of development, although theorists vary greatly in the amount of emphasis they place on each.

There is also a difference of opinion about the way development takes place. Does it follow certain predictable stages? Are later changes dependent on a number of very specific earlier changes? Or is development relatively flexible, with changes coming in different orders for different people? Again, we can find theorists who favor each of these views.

Although there is great disagreement about what is involved in development and about the way it takes place, there are a few general principles almost all theorists would support.

1. *People develop at different rates.* In your own classroom, you will have a whole range of examples of different development rates. Some students will be larger, better coordinated, or more mature in their thinking and social relationships. Others will be much slower in these areas. Except in rare cases of very rapid or very slow development, such differences are normal and to be expected in any large group of students.

2. *Development is relatively orderly.* People tend to develop certain abilities before others. In infancy they crawl before they walk, babble before they talk, and see the world through their own eyes before they can begin to imagine how others see it. In school, they will master addition before algebra, *Bambi* before Shakespeare, and so on. Theorists may disagree on exactly what comes before what, but they all seem to find a relatively logical sense of progression.

3. *Development takes place gradually.* Very rarely will changes appear overnight. A student who cannot manipulate a pencil or answer a hypothetical question may well develop this ability, but the change is likely to take time. Even Piaget, who believes that children do move from one specific stage to another, sees these changes as taking place slowly over time.

With these three principles, we will close this brief introduction to development in general and turn to that aspect of human development with perhaps the greatest relevance for teachers: the development of thinking.

*The progression of development is relatively orderly. For example, students can work with concrete materials in doing arithmetic problems before they can perform some of the same operations mentally or with symbols like numbers.*

## A COMPREHENSIVE THEORY ABOUT THINKING: THE WORK OF PIAGET

During the past half-century, Jean Piaget devised a model describing how humans go about making sense of their world by gathering and organizing information (Piaget, 1954, 1963, 1970). His theory emphasizes a number of distinct stages through which a person must go to develop the thinking processes of an adult.

Although Piaget's ideas about how thinking develops have been very influential, his methods have been criticized for not being defined and specified clearly enough to allow replication (Larsen, 1977). He has also been criticized for basing his conclusions on detailed observation of just a few children. As you can see in Box 2–1, this criticism is based on a misconception about how Piaget gathered his data.

Piaget's Clinical Method

Piaget used the clinical method, approaching the study of children through extended, unstructured interviews, asking and probing, following up on the responses of each child. He also asked children to perform particular tasks and talked to them about their solutions to the problems presented. For

## BOX 2–1 JEAN PIAGET (1896–1980)

*Excerpts from an obituary by David Elkind,* American Psychologist 36 *(1981), pp. 911–913.*

I heard of Jean Piaget's death on my car radio as I was driving home from work on September 16. It was an unusual way to hear of a mentor's death, sandwiched in between other local and national news items. I had known that he was ill, so the news was not unexpected, but it was hearing it on the radio, announced so matter of factly, that left me a little numb. . . .

In Geneva I had the opportunity to view Piaget's research enterprise at first hand. Piaget was located in the Institute of Educational Science, which was committed both to teacher training and to research. Prospective teachers took courses in intellectual development taught by Piaget and others. (At the institute, a student had to hand in a bluebook to the Professor each time he or she attended class, and the Professor had to sign it. Every time Piaget lectured he was simultaneously signing from 200–300 bluebooks!) These students also had to learn to administer the Piagetian semiclinical interview.

As a consequence of this arrangement Piaget had a large pool of research assistants and, since they were teachers in training for the Canton of Geneva, open access to the Genevan schools. Accordingly, and contrary to the erroneous assumption sometimes made on the basis of Piaget's infancy books (for which he did study only his own three children), most of his research was carried out with large samples (hundreds of children) examined by teachers in training who had undergone rigorous preparation for their role in data collection. Piaget thus had, in effect, an institute precisely geared to the conduct of his research without the necessity of soliciting research grants. . . .

Driving back I told Piaget a story that I thought would amuse him. I reported a remark made by my youngest son, Ricky, when we were driving to the toy store. He said that it was better to go to the toy store in the station wagon than in the sedan because (since it was longer) we would "get there faster." I thought it was a nice anecdotal support for Piaget's finding that for young children speed was essentially "overtaking." But Piaget was amused in an unexpected way. "Oh," he remarked, "you Americans, you always have two cars." . . .

Piaget himself was always most open to responsible critiques of his work. To me, one of the most moving moments I ever experienced listening to Piaget give a public address occurred at one of the Jean Piaget Society meetings in Philadelphia. Piaget suggested at that meeting (he was then 80 years old) that perhaps some children could attain conservation by strategies other than those he had previously outlined. For a man of his years to change a fundamental tenet of his theory was, I think, a remarkable testament to his extraordinary scientific commitment.

Another dimension of Piaget's integrity was his reluctance to produce disciples. He said, "To the extent that there are Piagetians, to that extent I have failed. . . ."

obvious reasons, such methods are hard to reproduce in a scientifically controlled fashion.

In recent years, however, more formal research has supported many of Piaget's basic ideas; others are still under investigation. Piaget's theory thus continues to have a great impact on the study of cognitive development. His ideas should give you, as a teacher, a number of suggestions about how to design instruction that is appropriate for your students.

## Readiness and Thinking

According to Piaget (1954), certain ways of thinking that are quite simple for an adult are not so simple for a child. There are specific limitations on the kinds of material that can be taught at a given time in a young person's life. Sometimes all you need to do to teach a new concept is give a student a few basic facts as background. At other times, however, all the background facts in the world will be useless. The student simply will not be ready to learn the concept. With some students, you can discuss the general causes of civil wars and then ask why they think our own Civil War took place in 1861. But what if the students respond with "When is 1861?" Obviously their concepts of time are different from your own. They may think, for example, that they will someday catch up to a sibling in age, or they may confuse the past and the future (Sinclair, 1973). In order to experience some of these differences in thinking at first hand, try asking children of various ages the questions listed in Figure 2–1.

Ability to learn a particular fact or idea is limited by the mental tools the student brings to the problem. For example, if you ask a young child who has not learned how to multiply how much is ten 12s, the child may well give you the answer after carefully adding $12 + 12 + 12 + 12 + 12 + 12 + 12 + 12 + 12 + 12 + 12 = 120$. The child used current knowledge to solve the problem. An older child might multiply 12 by 10 or simply add a 0 to 12, depending on his or her understanding of how best to solve the problem.

In Piaget's view, a person's mental tools are the internal processes each of us uses to perceive and structure reality. The reality of a child is not necessarily the same as the reality of an adult because these internal processes are subject to change. One of the reasons the processes do change is the fact that a child is constantly trying to make sense of the world.

**Different Ways of Thinking**

**Changing Mental Tools**

**Figure 2–1**   **Questions to Ask Children**

What does it mean to be alive?
Can you name some things that are alive?
Is the moon alive?
Where do dreams come from?
Where do they go?
Which is farther, to go from the bottom of
    the hill all the way to the top or go
    from the top of the hill all the way to
    the bottom?
Can a person live in Chicago and in Illinois
    at the same time?
Will you be just as old as your big brother
    some day?
When is yesterday?
Where does the sun go at night?

## Making Sense of the World

Piaget assumes an internal set of organizational principles (mental tools) with which a person must attempt to build an understanding of the world. He also assumes that each person's internal organization changes radically but slowly during the period from birth to maturity. This development is more than the adding of new facts and ideas to an existing fund of information. Instead, it involves major changes in thinking itself. We will look first at the processes through which the changes are made and then at the factors that cause these changes to take place.

**Processes of Change: Organization and Adaptation.**   The basis of Piaget's theoretical position on learning and thinking can be traced to his early research in biology. This research dealt with developmental changes in mollusks (shellfish such as clams) that are moved by environmental factors from still to turbulent areas of large lakes. Mollusks that make this transition show a pattern of development very different from that of their relatives who reside in calmer waters. In order to keep from being washed off the rocks, the mollusks in the turbulent waters must make extraordinarily vigorous movements of the foot. This activity, in turn, leads to changes in the growth of the shell, which becomes wider and shorter than that of the mollusks who have not been moved to a turbulent location.

*Early Research in Biology*

As a result of this research, Piaget concluded that all species inherit two basic tendencies, both of which are evident in the description of the fast-footed mollusk. The first of these tendencies is **adaptation**: the mollusk changed its behavior in response to the turbulent water. The second is **organization**: the structure of the mollusk's shell was altered by the constant fast footwork. In other words, environmental influences lead to adaptive changes in behavior, which in turn change the organization and structure of the organism in predictable ways.

*Adaptation and Organization*

*Jean Piaget observes two boys taking the task of learning very seriously. According to Piaget, learning is not merely an accumulation of information, but an adaptation and reorganization of the thinking process itself, with certain types of learning appropriate to certain stages of growth.*

(Wayne Behling/The Ipsilanti Press)

Piaget's theory of cognitive development is analogous in many ways to the occurrence of changes in the mollusk. According to Piaget, as young people develop in accord with their genetic potential, they change their behavior to adapt to their environment. These adaptive changes then lead to a stable and predictable pattern of changes in cognitive organization and structure. Let's look more closely at organization and adaptation as they apply not to mollusks, but to humans.

**Organizational Changes.** According to Piaget, people are born with a tendency to organize their intellectual processes, or **cognitive structures** as he called them. These cognitive structures are our physical and psychological systems for understanding and interacting with the world. Simple structures are continually combined and coordinated to become more sophisticated and thus more effective. Very young infants, for example, either look at an object or grasp it when it comes in contact with their hands. They cannot do both together. As they develop, however, the infants organize these two separate behavioral structures into a coordinated higher-level structure of looking, reaching for, and grasping the object (Ginsburg and Opper, 1979).

Schemes

Piaget has given a special name to these mental structures that people are continually reorganizing into better systems for interacting with the world. In his theory, these changing internal structures are called **schemes.** Schemes are the basic building blocks of thinking. They are organized systems of actions or thoughts that allow us mentally to represent or "think about" the objects and events in our world. These systems give us ways to organize data from the outside world into patterns so we can make sense of what we encounter and respond appropriately. Schemes may be very small and specific—the sucking through a straw scheme or the recognizing a rose scheme, for example. Or they may be larger and more general—the drinking scheme or the categorizing plants scheme. As behavior is organized to become more sophisticated and more suited to the environment, a person's thinking processes also become more organized and new schemes develop.

In addition to the tendency to organize their cognitive structures, people, like the fast-footed mollusks, also inherit the tendency to adapt to their environment.

**Adaptive Changes.** Piaget believed that from the moment of birth, a person begins to look for ways to adapt more satisfactorily to the environment. Two basic processes are involved in adaptation: assimilation and accommodation.

**Assimilation** takes place when people use their existing schemes to make sense of events in their world. Assimilation involves trying to understand something new by fitting it into what we already know. At times we may have to distort the new information to make it fit. For example, the first time most children see a zebra, they call it a horse. They try to match the new data from the outside world with an existing scheme for identifying animals. A baby trying to suck on a new rattle is attempting to assimilate the novel event by applying an existing scheme.

**Accommodation** takes place when the person must change existing schemes to respond to a new situation. If data cannot be made to fit any existing schemes, then more appropriate structures must be developed. We adjust our thinking to fit the new information instead of adjusting the information to fit our thinking. Children demonstrate accommodation when they add the scheme for recognizing zebras to their other systems for identifying animals. The baby sucking the rattle soon develops new behaviors for dealing with the situation. With a little trial and error, the baby is likely to learn such appropriate rattle behavior as shaking or even throwing (less appropriate to parents but fine as far as the infant is concerned).

People adapt to their increasingly complex environments by using existing schemes whenever they work (assimilation) or by modifying and adding to their schemes whenever something new is needed (accommodation). In fact, both processes are required most of the time. Even using an established pattern such as sucking to act on an unfamiliar baby bottle may require some accommodation, since the new nipple may be slightly larger or smaller or have holes of a different size than the last bottle encountered.

Whenever new instances are assimilated into an existing scheme, the scheme is enlarged and changed somewhat, so assimilation involves some accommodation. There are also times when neither assimilation nor accommodation are used. If the events people encounter are too unfamiliar, they may be ignored. Experience is filtered to fit the kind of thinking a person is doing at a given time. But thinking changes over time, as we all know. We look next at the four factors that play major roles in the development of thinking.

**Assimilation and Accommodation Work Together** *(margin note)*

## Four Factors Influencing Development

In Piaget's theory, developmental changes in the thinking processes are brought about by the interaction of four different factors. Perhaps the most basic of these is *maturation,* the emergence of biological changes that are genetically programmed in each human being at conception. Of all the factors this is the least changeable, but it does provide a biological basis for the other changes to come.

**Maturation** *(margin note)*

The second factor contributing to changes in the thinking process is *activity.* A person who is acting on the environment, exploring, testing, observing, or just actively thinking about a problem is engaging in experiences that may alter his or her thinking processes. With physical maturation comes increasing ability to act on the environment and learn from it. When the coordination of a young child is reasonably developed, for example, the child may discover principles about balance by experimenting with a seesaw.

**Activity** *(margin note)*

The third factor affecting the development of thinking is *social transmission,* or learning from others. Without social transmission, people would need to reinvent all the knowledge already offered by their culture. The amount people can learn from social transmission will vary according to their stage of cognitive development. A child at a certain level of development, for example, may be ready to understand a verbal explanation of the principle of balance. A younger child, as we have seen, may actually have to manipulate something like a seesaw again and again before beginning to understand.

**Social Transmission** *(margin note)*

Maturation, activity, and social transmission influence cognitive development. The actual changes in thinking take place through the process of **equilibration**—the act of searching for a balance or for equilibrium. Briefly, the process is something like this. If an event that does not fit any of a person's schemes is noticed, the result is a state of disequilibrium—that is, a lack of balance. Piaget assumes that people generally prefer a state of balance or equilibrium. Thus they continually test the adequacy of their thinking processes.

**Equilibration** *(margin note)*

If they apply a particular scheme to act upon an event and it works, then equilibrium exists. If the scheme does not produce a satisfying result, then disequilibrium exists and the person becomes uncomfortable. This is what helps thinking change and move ahead. We continually assimilate new information using existing schemes and accommodate our thinking when necessary in order to maintain a fit between our schemes for understanding the world and the data the world provides. Thus equilibration, this search for fit or balance, leads to changes in cognitive organization and the development of more effective systems for thinking.

There are at least three basic ways of achieving the satisfactory fit between an event and an internal scheme. First, a person may encounter a familiar event and assimilate it directly into an existing scheme. A simplified example of this is when a very young student forms the plural of a word by adding s and the plural works. Second, a person may encounter an unfamiliar event that does not fit any existing schemes exactly but can be accommodated with only a small change into a scheme that does exist. An example of this is a young student forming the plural of the word party. The "add s" scheme is simply enlarged a little to include "drop the y and add ies." Third, a person may encounter a totally unfamiliar event and find it necessary to form a whole new scheme to accommodate the event. An example of this is found in the primary student who must give the plural for the word "louse."

By now, we have made the point a number of times that young people's thinking is not like that of adults. We have suggested that learners at ages 5 and 10 are even more different than a simple observation of their size would indicate. Piaget's theory considers development over time as a progression of stages. He believed that all young people pass through the same four stages in their cognitive development. Furthermore, they pass through these same stages in exactly the same order.

## Four Stages of Cognitive Development

Piaget's four stages of cognitive development are sensorimotor, preoperational, concrete operational, and formal operational. When these stages are presented, they are generally associated with specific ages, as in Figure 2–2.

Before you read any further, however, please understand that these are only general guidelines. Knowing a student's age is never a guarantee that you know his or her stage of cognitive development. Even being 16 or 17 does not guarantee that a person has reached the final stage of formal operations (Ashton, 1978). It also may be possible for a person to be at more than one stage at a time. Piaget was interested in the kinds of thinking abilities people are able to use. Often people can use one level of thinking to solve one kind of problem, and other levels of thinking to solve different problems. So the stages describe ways of thinking, not labels that can be applied directly to students.

As we examine the four stages, keep in mind that there is a definite continuity in thinking. The stages in many ways are cumulative. As adaptation proceeds, each kind of thinking from the previous stage is incorporated and integrated into the stage that follows. We all continue to use

the actions of infancy (such as sucking), although as we grow older we acquire other ways of dealing with the environment we may wish to use instead. You, for example, may have developed very sophisticated abstract

**Figure 2–2   Piaget's Stages of Cognitive Development**

| Stage | Approximate Age | Characteristics |
|---|---|---|
| Sensorimotor | 0–2 years | Begins to make use of imitation, memory, and thought. Begins to recognize that objects do not cease to exist when they are hidden. Moves from reflex actions to goal-directed activity. |
| Preoperational | 2–7 years | Gradual language development and ability to think in symbolic form. Able to think operations through logically in one direction. Has difficulties seeing another person's point of view. |
| Concrete operational | 7–11 years | Able to solve concrete (hands-on) problems in logical fashion. Understands laws of conservation and is able to classify and seriate. Understands reversibility. |
| Formal operational | 11–15 years | Able to solve abstract problems in logical fashion. Thinking becomes more scientific. Develops concerns about social issues, identity. |

*From **Piaget's theory of cognitive development: An introduction for students of psychology and education**, 2d ed., by Barry J. Wadsworth. Copyright © 1979 by Longman Inc. Reprinted with permission of Longman.*

thinking abilities in your major area of study. But when someone asks how many months until you finish school, you may return to a more primitive and concrete method of solving the problem, perhaps counting on your fingers.

We will begin with a brief discussion of the sensorimotor stage. Because of the cumulative nature of the stages, an understanding of the earlier stages should give you a better sense of how your students developed the thinking they bring to your class.

**Infancy: The Sensorimotor Stage.**   The earliest period is called the **sensorimotor stage** because the development at this stage is based upon information that is obtained from the senses (sensori) and from the actions or body movements (motor) of the infant. The greatest conquest of infancy is the realization that objects in the environment are really out there whether the baby is perceiving them or not. This basic understanding, called **object permanence**, arises from many activities with and observations of objects and people appearing, disappearing, and reappearing. Infants who search for objects that have fallen or rolled out of sight indicate that they understand the objects continue to exist even when they are not perceived.

Recognizing Object Permanence

A second major accomplishment of the sensorimotor period is the beginning of logical **goal-directed actions.** Think of the familiar dumping bottle toy that babies enjoy. It is usually made of plastic with a cover and several colorful items inside that can be dumped out and replaced. If you give a bottle like this to a 6-month-old baby, the baby is likely to have a frustrating time trying to get to the toys inside. Shaking the bottle is not enough unless it is first inverted. Inverting it does no good unless the cover is removed. Even if the cover is removed, the items may jam in the opening. At this age, the baby is not likely to have a sufficiently organized, systematic approach or scheme to get the items out.

But suppose you give the dumping bottle to an older child, one who has mastered the basics of the sensorimotor stage. This child, at age 2, will probably be able to deal with the bottle in a much more orderly fashion. Through trial and error the child will slowly build a "bottle dumping" scheme: (1) get the cover off; (2) turn the bottle upside down; (3) shake if the items jam; and (4) watch the items fall on the floor. Once this sequence is learned, the child will be able to deal with the dumping bottle efficiently on future occasions. Separate lower-level schemes have been organized into a higher-level scheme.

If you keep watching, you may notice that the child is soon able to reverse this action. The items can be picked up one by one, put in the bottle which has been turned right side up, and finally the cover can be replaced. According to Case (1978a), this accomplishment of reversible actions is a basic characteristic of the sensorimotor stage. As we will soon see, however, the accomplishment of reversible thinking, being able to imagine the reverse of a sequence of actions, takes much longer.

**Early Childhood to the Early Elementary Years: The Preoperational Stage.** Sensorimotor intelligence is not very effective for planning ahead or keeping track of information. For this children need what Piaget called **operations,** or actions that are carried out mentally rather than physically. The child at the second stage is only beginning to master these operations. Thus the stage is called **preoperational.**

According to Piaget, the first step from action to thinking is the internalization of action. By the end of the sensorimotor stage the child can use many action schemes. However, as long as these schemes remain tied to action, they are of no use in recalling the past or predicting the future. The first type of thinking separate from action involves making these schemes symbolic.

A symbol is something that stands for or represents something else. So if you form a mental picture of someone dumping a bottle, or consider it through the use of language as we have done here in writing about it, your thoughts represent the action and are symbolic. Another way to represent reality is by miming the action, but not really carrying it out. The child's earliest use of symbols is generally of this second type. Children who are not yet able to talk will often use action symbols—pretending to drink from an empty cup, touching a comb to their hair, showing that they know what each object is for. This behavior also shows that their schemes are becoming more general and less tied to specific actions. The eating scheme, for example, may be used in play as well as for getting food.

As the child advances through the preoperational stage, this ability to think about objects in symbolic form remains somewhat limited to thinking in one direction only. A Piagetian road-building task provides a good example of

(Burt Glinn/Magnum Photos, Inc.)

*The girl on the right has built a road "just like" the experimenter's, demonstrating the one-way logic characteristic of the preoperational stage of learning. If the child has not yet moved beyond this stage, he or she will probably have difficulty demonstrating reversible thinking and will not be able to build a road "going the other way."*

**One-Way Logic**

this kind of **one-way logic.** Two sets of small objects and two strips of paper (roads) are needed. The child is given one road and set of objects, the experimenter the other. The experimenter then lines up the objects along the road and asks the child to make a road "just like mine." If the child has achieved the one-way logic of the preoperational stage, he or she will probably be able to do this.

To see if the child has moved beyond the preoperational stage, the experimenter may then ask the child to carry out a task calling for reversible thinking. Again the experimenter builds a road but this time asks the child to "build one just like mine, but going the other way." As you can see in Figure 2–3, the preoperational child may start out just fine. Soon, however, the child is likely to start placing things in the same order as the experimenter has, rather than in reverse order. The child may then go back and forth in confusion between the two orders. Reversible thinking calls for the ability to keep the entire system in mind. The preoperational child is not likely to be able to do this.

**Difficulty with Conservation**

Reversible thinking is involved in other tasks that are difficult for the preoperational child. A child at this stage also has difficulty thinking through

**Figure 2–3   Reversing the Objects at the Preoperational Stage**

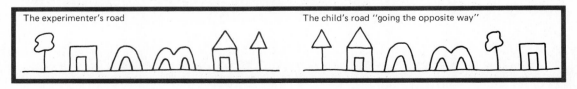

The experimenter's road          The child's road "going the opposite way"

problems that involve the **conservation** of matter. Conservation is the understanding that the amount or number of something remains the same even if the arrangement or appearance is changed, as long as nothing is added and nothing is taken away. You know that if you tear a piece of paper you have been writing on into several pieces, you will still have the same amount of paper. To prove this, you know that you can reverse the process by taping the pieces back together. The preoperational child, however, is not able to imagine such a reversal.

A Piagetian Task  A classic example of this is found in the preoperational child's response to the following Piagetian task. A child is shown two identical glasses, both short and fat in shape (see Figure 2–4). Both have exactly the same amount of colored water in them. The experimenter asks the child if each glass has the same amount of water, and the child answers "yes." The experimenter then pours the water from one of the glasses into a tall, thin glass, lines this glass up with the other short, fat glass, and asks the child once again if each glass has the same amount of water. Now the child is likely to insist that there is more water in the tall, thin glass because the water level is higher. The preoperational child cannot understand that increased diameter compensates for shorter height. The child has difficulty focusing on more than one aspect of the situation at a time. Piaget called this ability **decentration.** The child who says the tall glass has more water is "centering" attention on the dimension of height. Children at the preoperational stage have trouble freeing themselves from their own perception of how the world appears. What looks like more must be more, even if logic says otherwise.

Egocentric Thinking  In addition to being unable to use reversible thinking, unable to decenter thinking, and being fooled by appearances, Piaget felt that preoperational children are very **egocentric,** tending to see the world and the experiences of others from their own viewpoint. "Egocentric" as Piaget intended it does not mean selfish; it simply means children often assume that other people share their feelings, reactions, and perspectives. For example, children at this stage may believe you see the same view as they do, even though you are facing toward another direction in the room. A child might ask you about an animal she had seen through the window and be very disappointed when you could not answer, even though you had been sitting with your back to the window the entire time. During this period children are also likely to believe everyone feels the same way they do about things. These children center on their own perceptions and on the way the situation appears to them (Muss, 1982).

However, recent research has shown that young children are not totally egocentric in every situation. They are able to take into account the perspectives of others to a certain degree. Children as young as 4 change the way they talk to 2-year-olds by speaking in simpler sentences, and even before age 2 children show toys to adults by turning the front of the toy to face

**Figure 2–4    Conservation at the Preoperational Stage**

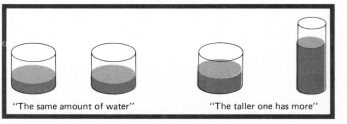

"The same amount of water"          "The taller one has more"

the other person. So young children seem quite able to take the needs and different perspectives of others into account, at least in certain situations (Gelman, 1979).

Dealing with preoperational children, at home or in school, offers both problems and rewards. Since you may well have students who use these ways of thinking, at least to solve certain problems, we include a set of Guidelines here.

# Guidelines

## Teaching the Preoperational Student

1. **Use concrete props and visual aids whenever possible to illustrate your lessons and help children understand what you are talking about.**

EXAMPLES
- Physical demonstrations.
- Drawings and illustrations.

2. **Make instructions relatively short, using actions as well as words, again so that the students will not get confused.**

EXAMPLES
- After giving instructions, ask a student to demonstrate them as a model for the rest of the class.
- Explain a game by acting out the part of a participant.

3. **Do not expect the students to find it easy to see the world from someone else's perspective since they are likely to be very egocentric at this point.**

EXAMPLES
- Avoid social studies lessons about worlds too far removed from the child's experience.
- Avoid long lectures on sharing.

4. **Give children a great deal of physical practice with the facts and skills that will serve as building blocks for later development.**

EXAMPLES
- Use of cut-out letters to build words.
- Avoid overuse of workbooks and other strictly paper and pencil tasks.

5. **Encourage the manipulation of physical objects that can change in shape while retaining a constant mass, giving the students a chance to move toward the understanding of conservation and two-way logic needed in the next stage.**

EXAMPLES
- Chances to play with clay, water, or sand.
- Conversations about the changes the students are experiencing in manipulating objects.

6. **Give many opportunities to experience the world in order to build a foundation for concept learning and language.**

EXAMPLES
- Take many field trips.
- Give them words to describe what they are seeing, doing, touching, tasting, and smelling.

**Later Elementary to the Middle School Years: The Concrete Operational Stage.** If you teach any grade from kindergarten through twelfth, a knowledge of the thinking processes at the concrete operational stage will be helpful. In the early grades the students are moving toward this logical system of thought. In the middle grades it is in full flower, ready to be applied and extended by classroom work. In the high school years it is available to the student whose thinking may not have moved on to the higher stage of formal operations.

Piaget coined the term **concrete operations** to describe this stage of "hands-on" thinking. The basic characteristics of the stage are that the student recognizes (1) the logical stability of the physical world; (2) the fact that elements can be changed or transformed and still conserve many of their original characteristics; and (3) that these changes can be reversed.

**Conquering
Conservation**

Conservation of quantity is probably the most basic of all concrete operations. We already have shown the difficulty the preoperational child has with conservation. Remember the tall, thin glass that had more water? If the child in this experiment had been able to use concrete operations, he or she would have realized that the amount of water in the two glasses remained the same.

**Basic Aspects
of Reasoning**

A student's ability to solve conservation problems depends on understanding three basic aspects of reasoning: identity, compensation, and reversibility. With **identity,** the student knows that if nothing is added or taken away, the material remains the same. With **compensation,** the student knows that an apparent change in one direction can be compensated for by a change in another direction. (That is, if the liquid goes higher in the glass, the glass must be narrower.) With **reversibility,** the student can mentally cancel out the change that has been made. Note especially that the student at this stage, with an understanding of reversibility, has mastered two-way thinking.

Another important operation mastered at this stage is **classification.** Classification depends on a student's ability to focus on a single characteristic of objects and group the objects according to that single characteristic. Given 12 objects of assorted color and shape, the concrete operational student can invariably pick out the ones that are round. More advanced classification at this stage involves recognizing that one class fits into another. While daisies and daffodils may each be in a class by themselves, both fit into the class of flowers, and flowers are members of the plant family. A hammer can be both a hammer and a tool. With reversibility, the concrete operational student also can see that there is more than one way to classify a group of objects. Big and small disks of two different shapes and two different colors can be classified and then reclassified in three different ways: by color, size, and shape.

**Classifying**

**Seriation** is the process of making an orderly arrangement from large to small or vice versa. This understanding permits a student to construct a logical series where $A < B < C$ and so on. The preoperational student is likely to get stuck on an idea such as this: "$A$ is smaller than $C$, and $B$ is smaller than $C$, so both $A$ and $B$ are small." The fact that $B$ might be larger than $A$ is likely to get lost in the shuffle. The preoperational child has difficulty with the idea that $B$ can be larger than one object but smaller than another.

**Order
in Relationships**

With the ability to think through operations such as those involved in conservation, classification, and seriation, the student at the concrete operational stage has finally developed a complete and very logical system of thinking. This system of thinking, however, is still limited to physical reality, to thoughts about real things that can be internalized and considered mentally. The operations at this stage do not extend to the consideration of hypotheses about abstract ideas and possibilities. Using operations to think about thinking evolves later at the formal operation stage. Given these limitations, we have again included a set of Guidelines to help you in dealing with students at this stage.

# Guidelines

## Teaching the Concrete Operational Student

**1. Continue to use concrete props and visual aids, especially when dealing with sophisticated material.**

EXAMPLES
- Time-lines for history lessons.
- Three-dimensional models in science.

**2. Continue to give students a chance to manipulate objects and test them out.**

EXAMPLES
- Simple scientific experiments in which the students can participate.
- Craftwork to illustrate some of the daily occupations of people of an earlier period (Wadsworth, 1978).

**3. Make sure that lectures and readings are brief and well organized.**

EXAMPLES
- Materials that present a progression of ideas from step to step.
- Short stories or books with short, logical chapters, moving to longer reading assignments only when the students are ready.

**4. Ask students to deal with no more than three or four variables at a time (Hallam, 1969).**

EXAMPLES
- Readings with a limited number of characters.
- Experiments with a limited number of steps.

**5. Use familiar examples to help explain more complex ideas so students will have a beginning point for assimilating new information.**

EXAMPLES
- Comparison of the students' own lives with those of the characters in a story.
- Story problems in mathematics.

**6. Give opportunities to classify and group objects and ideas on increasingly complex levels.**

EXAMPLES
- Give students separate sentences on slips of paper to be grouped into paragraphs.
- Use outlines, hierarchies, and analogies to show the relationship of unknown new material to already acquired knowledge.

**7. Present problems which require logical, analytical thinking to solve.**

EXAMPLES
- Materials such as Mind Twisters, Brain Teasers, and riddles.
- Discussions focused on open-ended questions which stimulate thinking, e.g. "Are the mind and the brain the same thing?"

Students at the concrete operational stage are centered on reality. Their logic is based on concrete situations that can be organized, classified, or manipulated. Predictions can easily be generated at this stage, given the right kind of question. What would happen if you rolled out a round ball of pie dough? It would get big and flat and be better suited for holding a pie filling. This seems to be correct enough. But the question is a limited one, which could be verified by actually rolling the dough out and noting the results.

Solving Real World Problems

The concrete operational student can also deal with questions that call for the repetition of facts learned by rote memory. Ask such a student, "What would happen if the president were impeached?" and you are likely to learn that the vice-president would become president. For a more complete answer, taking into account the effects this event would have on the world and on individuals, concrete operations are not enough. Several different conditions (the reason for the action, the state of the economy, the stock market, foreign reactions, the power and popularity of the vice-president, the strength of the president's party in Congress) need to be considered and coordinated. This kind of coordination is part of what Piaget has called formal operations.

**Junior High and High School Years: The Formal Operational Stage.** As you will soon see, some students remain at the concrete operational stage throughout their school years, even throughout life. However, new physical and social experiences, usually those that take place in school, eventually present most students with problems they want to solve but cannot with concrete operations. It is fine to be able to pick out the red objects, to order items from large to small, but what happens when a number of variables interact, as in a laboratory experiment? Then a mental system for controlling sets of variables and working through a set of possibilities is needed. These are the abilities Piaget calls **formal operations.**

The Need for Formal Operations

At the level of formal operations, all the earlier characteristics of operations continue in force. Formal thinking is reversible, internal, and organized in a system, the parts of which depend on each other. The focus of thinking, however, shifts so that the real situation that is experienced is seen as only one of many different possible situations. In order for this to happen, the students need to be able systematically to generate a good number of the different possibilities.

Scientific Reasoning

Formal operations include what we normally think of as scientific reasoning. Hypotheses can be made and mental experiments set up to test them, with variables isolated or controlled. Although the formal operational student is able to use this type of thinking, the student will not necessarily be aware of the process or be able to describe it to you. It is the logician who describes systems for reasoning. The student simply makes use of the new mental tools.

Making Systematic Combinations

The following experiment can help to identify students who are capable of applying formal operations. The purpose is to test whether a person can systematically determine the number of different possibilities that exist within a reasonably limited framework. Ask a student: "How many different meals can be made if a shopper has bought the following for this week: (1) three meats—hamburger, chicken, and steak; (2) three vegetables—broccoli, spinach, and green beans; and (3) three starches—rice, noodles, and potatoes." (Only balanced meals, please!) A student capable of formal operations would begin by laying out the possibilities systematically:

Hamburger, broccoli, rice
Hamburger, broccoli, noodles
Hamburger, broccoli, potatoes
Hamburger, spinach, rice
Hamburger, spinach, noodles
And so on

A student at the concrete operational stage would be much less systematic; he or she might start with favorite foods and continue in the order of preference. It would not be unusual for the student to mention only three meals, using each food only once. The underlying system of combinations is not yet available.

**Failure
to Master
Formal
Operations**

Although most psychologists agree there is a level of thinking that is more sophisticated than concrete operations, the question of how universal formal thinking is, even among adults, is still under investigation. According to Neimark (1975), the three early stages of Piaget's theory are forced on most people by the regularities of the physical environment. Formal operations, however, are not so closely tied to the physical environment, and it would seem that not everyone reaches this stage. Neimark has speculated that this last stage may be "a refinement of an advanced culture rather than a necessary condition for survival" (Neimark, 1975, p. 556). Dale (1970) found that fewer than 75 percent of the 15-year-olds tested were able to solve a problem involving chemical combinations similar to those found in high school lab experiments. Kohlberg and Gilligan (1971) found that only 30 to 50 percent of the older adolescents they studied could successfully carry out

*Formal operations are particularly crucial in science courses. Many students in this chemistry class will be ready to use formal operations, but some students probably will be lost if this type of thinking is required to understand the material.*

(Ken Karp)

formal operation tasks. Based upon these findings, we can speculate that anywhere from one-half to two-thirds of the students in most American high schools may be unable to use formal operations consistently in solving problems.

Piaget himself (1974) suggested that even most adults may be able to use formal operational thought in only a few areas, areas where they have the greatest experience or interest. De Lisi and Staudt (1980) found support for this idea. In their experiment, college students with three different majors (physics, political science, and English) were asked to solve several types of problems. Almost all the students were able to use formal operations when the problems were similar to the type encountered in their major. When confronted with problems unlike those in their major, only about half of the students applied formal thinking in finding solutions.

Many of the tasks presented to high school and even junior high students require a good deal of formal thinking. Science and mathematics are especially likely to require formal operations. Students who have not learned to go beyond the information that lies before them, to form and test hypotheses, are likely to fall by the wayside in these courses.

If the problems presented to students are clearly beyond their comprehension, they may try to achieve "success" by developing certain shortcuts, by memorizing formulas or lists of steps. These systems may be helpful, but real understanding will take place only if students are able to go beyond this superficial use of memorization. This understanding requires formal operational thinking. If you are teaching junior high or high school students, be alert to the possibility that many of your students have not yet mastered formal thinking. The Guidelines presented on the next page take this possibility into consideration. Since many secondary students will be still working toward the attainment of formal operations, we have emphasized the transitional stage.

# IMPLICATIONS OF PIAGET'S THEORY

Piaget's major purpose was to reach a better understanding of the way thought develops, not to offer suggestions to teachers. In fact, most of the suggestions given in the Guidelines and in the pages that follow have been offered by others.

There are at least two basic questions for teachers in any theory of cognitive development. First, how can you as a teacher determine the current cognitive abilities of the students you are teaching? This is essentially a question of readiness. Second, and perhaps even more important, once you know the abilities of your students, what teaching strategies should you use?

## Determining Cognitive Abilities

As a teacher, how will you know whether students in your class are having trouble because they lack the necessary thinking abilities or because they simply have not learned the basic facts? Case (1978b) suggests one strategy. First you must determine the cognitive level required to master the tasks students are expected to learn. What mental operations are needed to succeed in the lessons you have planned? If you are teaching a social studies unit on

What Do
the Lessons
Call for?

# *Guidelines*

## Teaching Students Who Are Beginning to Use Formal Operations

**1. Continue to use many of the teaching strategies and materials appropriate for students at the concrete operational stage.**

EXAMPLES
- Visual aids such as charts and illustrations, as well as simple but somewhat more sophisticated graphs and diagrams.
- Well organized materials that offer step by step explanations.

**2. Give students an opportunity to explore many hypothetical questions.**

EXAMPLES
- Questions about social issues.
- Consideration of hypothetical "other worlds."

**3. Encourage students to explain how they solve problems.**

EXAMPLES
- Ask students to work in pairs with one student acting as the problem solver, thinking aloud while tackling a problem, and the other student acting as the listener, checking to see that all the steps are mentioned and that everything seems logical (Bauman, 1978).
- Make sure that at least some of the tests you give ask for more than rote memory or one final answer; essay questions, for example, might ask students to justify two different positions on an issue.

**4. Whenever possible, teach broad concepts, not just facts, using materials and ideas relevant to the students.**

EXAMPLES
- While discussing the Civil War, consider what other issues have divided the country since then.
- Use lyrics from popular music to teach poetic devices, to reflect on social problems, and so on.

children in other lands, for example, you are expecting students to go beyond their own immediate experience. The material assumes at least a concrete operational level of development. For the egocentric student in the earliest grades, this leap outside immediate physical experience may be impossible (Renner, Stafford, Lawson, McKinnon, Frist, and Kellogg, 1976). You might practice your ability to recognize the characteristics of the different stages by completing the exercise in Figure 2–5 on the next page.

Once you have analyzed your lessons to see what kinds of thinking abilities they require, you are ready to determine if your students have the abilities needed. To do this, Case suggests you observe your students carefully as they try to solve the problems you have presented. What kind of logic do they use? Do they focus on only one aspect of the situation? Are they fooled by appearances? Do they suggest solutions systematically or by guessing and forgetting what they have already tried? Ask your students how

What Can the Students Do?

**Figure 2–5    Different Thinking at Different Stages**

Match the following examples with the appropriate stage and characteristic below:

1. Mary wants more cookies. Her mother breaks in half the ones she has already and Mary is satisfied.
2. Jill is able to understand that some people say one thing but act in ways that are not congruent with their statements.
3. When given a set of cards picturing the steps in baking a cake, Sally can put them in the proper order.
4. Johnny wants you to pick up his spoon and put it on his table so he can drop it again.
5. *Mother:* "How do you think Molly feels when you take her doll away? *Child:* "She feels like I want to play with it."
6. Karen can predict the movement of a body, taking into account several influences simultaneously.

STAGES

a. Sensorimotor
b. Preoperational

c. Concrete operational
d. Formal operational

CHARACTERISTICS

A. Goal-directed activity: cause-and-effect relationship.
B. Hasn't achieved conservation.
C. Egocentrism.
D. Combinatorial logic.
E. Can hold more than one premise in mind at the same time.
F. Seriation of actions.

ANSWERS

1. (b, B).   2. (d, E).   3. (c, F).   4. (a, A).   5. (b, C).   6. (d, D).

they tried to solve the problem. Listen for their strategies. Try to understand the kind of thinking that is behind repeated mistakes or problems. The students are the best sources of information about their own thinking abilities.

## Choosing Teaching Strategies

Perhaps the most important implication of Piaget's theory for teaching is what Hunt (1961) has called "the problem of the match." Teachers must not underestimate or overestimate the current thinking abilities of their students. The Problem Students must be neither bored by work that is too simple nor left behind by of the Match teaching they cannot understand. According to Hunt, disequilibrium must be kept "just right" to encourage growth. Of course, many materials and lessons can be understood at several levels. Classics such as *Alice in Wonderland*, myths, and fairy tales can be enjoyed at concrete or more symbolic levels.

At every level of cognitive development, you will also want to see that students are actively engaged in the learning process. They must be able to incorporate the information you present into their own schemes. To do this, they must act on the information in some way. Schooling must give the students a chance to experience the world (Farnham-Diggory, 1972).

This active experience, even at the earliest school levels, should not be limited to the physical manipulation of objects. It should also include mental manipulation of ideas that arise out of class projects or experiments. Often this mental manipulation can even be turned into games.

**Applying Principles in New Situations**

Another important part of healthy cognitive development is being able to apply and test the principles learned in one situation to new situations. Teachers should continually ask students to apply recently learned principles in different situations. If the principle applies, the student will gain practice in using it. If the principle does not fit, disequilibrium and perhaps new thinking abilities may develop.

**Social Interaction**

Students at every stage also need to interact with teachers and peers to test their thinking, to be challenged, to receive feedback, and to watch how others work out problems. Disequilibrium is often set in motion quite naturally when the teacher or another student suggests a new way of thinking about something.

The mistakes students make can also be very useful if treated with care and sensitivity. They can give you clues about a student's thinking strategies. They can also serve to point out to students the limitations of their current strategies.

As a general rule, students should do, manipulate, observe, experience, then talk and write (to the teacher and each other) about what they have experienced. Concrete experiences provide the raw materials for thinking. Communicating with others makes students use, test, and sometimes change their thinking abilities (Ashton, 1978).

When the issue of changing or improving cognitive abilities is discussed, a question often arises. If we can improve teaching by matching methods and materials to the cognitive abilities of students, perhaps we can accelerate cognitive development. Piaget called this "the American question," which gives you a hint about his position on the matter.

*The students in this class are learning about the states by creating a puzzle. The pieces are large enough for little hands to manipulate. This project should help the children understand how they can be in one state and in the United States at the same time.*

(Kenneth P. Davis)

# SPEEDING UP COGNITIVE DEVELOPMENT: PRO AND CON

The position of Piaget and most psychologists who attempt to apply his theory to education is that development should not be speeded up. This traditional view can be summarized in the words of Wadsworth:

**The Piagetian Position**

The function of the teacher is not to accelerate the development of the child or speed up the rate of movement from stage to stage. The function of the teacher is to insure that development within each stage is thoroughly integrated and complete. (Wadsworth, 1978, p. 117)

According to Piaget, cognitive development is based on the self-directed actions and thoughts of the student, not on the teacher's actions. Adult explanations often do not mesh with the student's thinking. Until students have created an appropriate scheme, they cannot assimilate what the teacher is saying. If you do try to teach a student something the student is not ready to learn, he or she may learn to give the "correct" verbal answer. But this will not really affect the way the student thinks about this problem or others. Therefore, acceleration is useless. The second argument is that acceleration is inefficient. This argument can be summed up in one question: Why spend a long time teaching something at one stage when students will learn it by themselves much more rapidly and thoroughly at another stage?

Some of the strongest arguments in favor of speeding up cognitive development are based on the results of cross-cultural studies comparing children growing up in different cultures. These results suggest that certain cognitive abilities are indeed influenced by the environment and education. Children of pottery-making families in one area of Mexico, for example, learn conservation of substance earlier than their peers in families who do not make pottery (Ashton, 1978). Ashton also reports research indicating that children in different cultures appear to master the various forms of conservation in different orders. Furthermore, children in non-Western cultures appear to acquire conservation operations later than children in Western cultures. These results may be due to the way the ability to conserve is measured in the studies. But it seems likely that some factors in the environment, not just the naturally evolving internal structures of the child, are involved.

**What Can Be Accelerated?**

Research supporting the idea of acceleration also offers a number of specific suggestions for teachers. You are more likely to be successful in teaching some things than in teaching others (Ashton, 1978). Goodnow (1969), for example, has concluded from several studies of children in different cultures that schooling is not much help in teaching conservation of mass and weight, but it can be very useful in teaching tasks that call for the use of words or visual images. Schools also seem to be helpful in teaching formal thinking (Philip and Kelly, 1974). Schools may, in fact, be critical in helping students move to the stage of formal operations (Ashton, 1978).

We believe that the first of these two options for acceleration—namely, a stress on the present stage combined with opportunities to advance—has the most to offer. If acceleration is indeed impossible, then this system, with its stress on the present stage, can't do much harm. On the other hand, if acceleration is possible, students will be given ample opportunities to move to the next stage. Given this preference, we have included a few ideas for this

66

kind of mild acceleration in the Guidelines and suggestions we gave earlier, along with more traditional ideas for trying to match the students' present stages.

# ANOTHER PERSPECTIVE: INFORMATION PROCESSING

Piaget's theory of cognitive development is perhaps the most influential, but there are a number of other ways of viewing cognitive growth. In this section we will examine some very recent research done by a group that stresses the importance of information processing.

**Information processing** is the study of how humans perceive, comprehend, and remember the information they gain from the world around them. Recently the principles of information processing have been applied to explain cognitive development. According to Klahr (1978), cognitive development can be described as the ongoing improvement of a person's system for processing information. Over time, a person develops a faster, more complex, sophisticated, and powerful "computer" to solve the problems the world presents.

*Your Own "Personal Computer"*

The information processing theorists have been less interested in creating a comprehensive description of cognitive development, like the one offered by Piaget, and more interested in studying specific cognitive processes like perception, attention, memory, and hypothesis testing (Hetherington and Parke, 1979). In Chapters 6 and 7, we will examine these processes in depth because they are central to an understanding of how cognitive theorists view human learning. Right now we will consider briefly how two important cognitive abilities, attention and memory, develop in children.

## Attention

John Flavell (1977) has described four aspects of attention that appear to develop as children mature:

*Controling Attention*

1. As they grow older, children are more able to control their attention. They not only have longer attention spans, they also become better at focusing on what is important and ignoring irrelevant details. In addition, they can simultaneously pay attention to more than one dimension of a stimulus. How would you relate these improved abilities to better performance on a conservation task?

*Fitting Attention to the Task*

2. As they develop, children become better at fitting their attentional skills to the task. Older children can focus on both height and width when determining if the tall, thin glass has more liquid than the short, fat glass, but would focus only on height if the glasses were the same size and shape.

*Planning*

3. Children improve in their ability to plan how they will direct their attention. They look for clues to tell them what is important and are ready to pay attention. For example, older children may be able to tell from the teacher's gestures and voice tone that the next part of the lesson is important and prepare themselves to really "pay attention."

*Monitoring*

4. Finally, children improve their abilities to monitor their attention, decide if they are using the right strategy, and change approaches when needed to follow a complicated series of events.

# Memory and Metacognitive Abilities

Developmental
Improvement
in Memory

The information processing theorists have been particularly interested in the development of memory. Research indicates that young children have very limited short-term memory. In one study by Case (1978b), for example, children of 7 and 8 could remember the number of items in only three small sets at a time. Case (1980) suggests that the total amount of space available for processing information is the same at each age, but young children must use quite a bit of this space remembering how to execute basic operations, like reaching, or finding the right label for an object, or counting. As children become more proficient, they can use the operations more efficiently. Learning a new operation takes up quite a bit of the child's working memory. Once the operation is mastered, however, there is more working memory available for short-term storage of new information. In addition, as children grow older they develop more effective strategies for remembering information and monitoring how well they are remembering.

According to Case (1978a), young children often use reasonable but incorrect strategies for solving problems because of their limited memories. They try to oversimplify the task by ignoring important information or skipping steps to reach a correct solution. They may, for example, consider only the height of the water in a glass, not the diameter of the glass, when comparing quantities, because this approach demands less of their memory. It may well be that students could handle more mature ways of thinking if they did not have to remember large amounts of information while using these more sophisticated processes.

Teaching
Strategies

Case (1980) suggests the following procedures for instruction based on the information processing theory of cognitive development. First, observe the children who are failing at a particular task and determine how they are trying to oversimplify the task. Second, find some way to emphasize for the children what they are ignoring and why their oversimplified approach won't work. Then demonstrate a better strategy. Finally, have the students practice using the new approach. Throughout this process, try to minimize the amount of information the students have to remember by reducing the number of items involved, using familiar terms, emphasizing what is really important, keeping the steps small, and giving lots of practice so each step will become as automatic as possible.

You may have noticed that one characteristic of cognitive development seems to be a growing ability to monitor and direct your own thinking, to keep track of how well you are paying attention or to select an effective strategy for solving a problem. The general term to describe this activity of monitoring your own cognitive processes is metacognition.

**Metacognition** literally means knowledge about knowledge. Recently researchers have begun to study how people develop knowledge about their own thinking and the thinking of others. For example, as children grow older they become more able to determine if they have understood instructions (Markman, 1977) or if they have studied enough to remember a set of items (Flavell, Friedrichs, and Hoyt, 1970). Older children automatically use more efficient techniques than younger children for memorizing information (Flavell & Wellman, 1977; Pressley, 1982). Researchers still have much to learn about how metacognitive abilities develop, but many are enthusiastic about the possible implications for education:

(Ken Karp)

*One important metacognitive ability is knowing when you don't understand and changing strategies to find a more effective approach. Improvements in this ability are part of cognitive development.*

Importance of Metacognitive Knowledge

. . . I am absolutely convinced that there is, overall, far too little rather than enough or too much cognitive monitoring in this world. This is true for adults as well as for children, but it is especially true for children. For example, I find it hard to believe that children who do more cognitive monitoring would not learn better in and out of school than children who do less. I also think that increasing the quantity and quality of children's metacognitive knowledge and monitoring skills through systematic training may be feasible as well as desirable. (Flavell, 1979, p. 910)

We will return to this issue in Chapters 6 and 7 when we discuss what teachers can do to help students use more effective cognitive learning strategies. Now we will turn to a topic that has been mentioned repeatedly in this chapter—language.

# THE DEVELOPMENT OF LANGUAGE

The language adults use is just as complicated as their thinking. In fact, if you try diagramming some of the sentences you hear in lecture classes, you may think it is even more so. As you may have come to expect, there is much disagreement about how people develop this complex process of communication.

## How Does Language Develop?

The Role of Reward

One of the most widely held views of language development assumes that children learn language just as they learn anything else, by repeating those behaviors that lead to some kind of positive result. The child makes a sound, the parent smiles and replies. The child says "MMM" in the presence of milk, the parent says, "Yes, milk, milk," and gives the child a drink. The child learns to say milk because it leads to a happy parent and a drink of milk.

**69**

Children add new words by imitating the sounds they hear and improve their use of language when they are corrected by the adults around them.

Such a theory is in many ways convincing, but an important question remains. What originally induced the infant to make any sounds at all? Was the baby trying to make the sounds that an adult made? Research has shown that many of a child's earliest utterances are original. They are things the child has apparently never heard before. And they are unlikely to be rewarded because they are "incorrect." Examples are found in phrases such as "paper find" and "car mosquito." The meaning of such utterances may be clear from the situation and intonation, but it is unlikely that the child has heard the phrases before or been rewarded for saying them (R. Brown, 1973). In addition, researchers studying interactions between young children and their parents discovered that parents rarely correct pronunciation and grammar during the early stages of language development. They are much more likely to respond to the content of the child's remarks (Brown and Hanlon, 1970). In fact, if parents spent all their time correcting the child's language and never "heard" what the child was trying to say, the child might give up trying to master a system as complicated as language.

Motherese

Parents make language learning easier for their children in other ways as well. There is a tendency for most people to speak in "motherese," when they interact with children (Gelman and Shatz, 1977). This style of speaking involves short sentences that are grammatically simple and correct (quite a contrast to the usual adult conversations filled with false starts, rambling sentences, digressions, incorrect grammar, and mispronounced words). Sentences addressed to children are generally in the present tense, with few or no abstract words. Questions and commands predominate. The adult often exaggerates intonation and speaks in a higher pitch, a bit like a bad actor. The same thing may be repeated in slightly different ways such as:

> "Who is that? Is that Eric? Look in the mirror? Is that Eric? Hi, Eric. That's you. That's Eric in the mirror. See Eric."

Adults caring for children seem continually to adapt their language to stay just ahead of the child. Before children begin talking, adults may direct long, complicated sentences to them. But as soon as the child utters identifiable words, the language of adults becomes simple. Then as the child progresses adults tend to change their language to stay just a bit more advanced than the child's current level of development, thus encouraging new understanding (Moskowitz, 1978).

Does Motherese
Help?

Does motherese help children learn language? The conditions for learning seem right. Adults simplify the complexities of language to make the puzzle easier to solve. Questions and repetitions may encourage interaction, practice, and ultimately, learning. Exaggerated voice tone and high pitch may help children focus their attention and give them clues to the meaning of the words and sentences. However, the role of simplifying language in helping children learn is not clear. Several studies have shown that children whose parents are very careful to speak "motherese" do not learn to talk any faster than children whose parents are much less careful to simplify their language (Newport, Gleitman, and Gleitman, 1977).

Figuring-Out
Language

It is likely that many factors play a role in language development. Humans may be born with a special capacity for language (Chomsky, 1965). But children develop language as they develop other cognitive abilities, by actively trying to make sense of what they hear, looking for patterns and making up rules to put together the jigsaw puzzle of language (Moskowitz, 1978). Reward and correction play a role in helping children learn "correct" language, but the child's thinking and creativity in putting together the parts of this complicated system are very important. In the process they make some very logical "mistakes," as you will see.

## Stages in the Process

Children communicate before they speak through crying, smiling, and body movements. But by the end of the first year, more or less, most children have spoken their first word. They have entered what psychologists imaginatively call the one-word stage. For the next three or four months they add slowly to their vocabulary until they have around 10 words. After this point, words are added rapidly. By about 20 months the vocabulary includes approximately 50 words (Nelson, 1973). The early vocabularies of most children are filled with object names and some adjectives, verbs, and proper names (Nelson, 1981).

**One-Word Stage**

Even at this early stage, language is more complex than it appears on the surface. One word can be used to communicate a variety of complex ideas. For example, the first author's daughter's first word was "ite" (translated: light). Said loudly while reaching toward the light switch on the wall, "ITE!" meant, "I want to flip the switch on and off (and on and off and on and off)." When someone else flipped the switch while she was playing on the floor, Elizabeth might remark, "ite," meaning, "I know what you just did. You turned on the light." When single words are used in this way they are called **holophrases** because they express complex ideas or whole phrases.

A second characteristic of this period is overgeneralization. Children may use one word to cover a range of concepts. For example, on a trip to the zoo, the 13-month-old son of a friend pointed excitedly at every animal including peacocks and elephants, saying: "doug, doug" (translated: dog, dog). This was the only word he had that came close to being adequate. He wisely rejected his other possibilities, "bye-bye," "more," "mama," and "dada." He used the language tools available to him to make sense of his world and to communicate.

At about 18 months many children enter the two-word stage. They begin to string words together in two-word sentences like "Daddy book," "play car," "allgone milk," and "more light." This speech is **telegraphic** (R. Brown, 1973). The nonessential details are left out and the words that carry the most meaning are included, as in the telegram, "Arriving 8:35 P.M., track 12." Even though sentences are short, **semantics** or meaning can be complex. Children can express possession ("Daddy book"), recurrence ("more light"), action-object ("play car"), and even disappearence or nonexistence ("allgone milk").

**Two-Word Stage**

For about one year, children continue to focus on the essential words even as they lengthen their sentences. At a certain point that varies from child to child, new features are added. Children begin to elaborate their simple language by adding plurals, endings on verbs such as *-ed* and *-ing,* and small words like "and," "but," or "in." In the process of figuring out the rules governing these aspects of language, children make some very interesting mistakes.

*Children create interesting rules as they try to figure out our complicated language.*

Applying Rules

For a brief time children may use irregular forms of particular words properly, as if they simply are saying what they have heard. Then, as they begin to learn rules, they **overregularize** words by applying the rule to everything. Children who had said, "Our car is broken," begin to insist, "Our car is *broked*." Parents often wonder why their child seems to be "regressing." Actually, these "mistakes" show how logical and rational children can be as they try to assimilate new words into existing schemes. Because most languages have so many irregular words, accommodation is necessary in mastering language.

By about age 5 or 6, most children have mastered the basics of their native language. A few types of constructions, like passive voice, are still difficult at this age, but a remarkable amount has been accomplished. "Ten linguists working full time for 10 years to analyze the structure of the English language could not program a computer with the ability acquired by an average child in the first 10 or even five years of life" (Moskowitz, 1978, p. 92).

Thus far we have described general stages in language learning. In the next section we will consider differences in the languages themselves.

## Dialects: Variations within English

A **dialect** is a variation of a language spoken by a particular group. The rules for a language define how words should be pronounced, how meaning should be expressed, and the way the basic parts of speech should be put together to form sentences. Dialects appear to differ in their rules in these areas, but it is important to remember that these differences are not errors. Each dialect variation within a language is just as logical, complex, and rule-governed as the standard dialect.

When the Double Negative Is Correct

An example of this is the use of the double negative. In standard English the redundancy of the double negative is not allowed. But in many nonstandard dialects, just as in many other languages (for instance, Russian, French, Spanish, and Hungarian), the double negative is required by the grammatical rules. To say "I don't want anything" in Spanish, you must literally say "I don't want nothing," or *No quiero nada.*

Another area in which nonstandard dialects differ from standard English is in pronunciation, which can lead to problems in spelling. In black English, for instance, there is less attention paid to pronouncing the ends of words than there is in standard English. A lack of attention to final consonants, such as *s*, can lead to failure to indicate possession, third person singular verbs, and plurals in the standard way. So "John's book" might be "John book," and words such as "thinks," "wasps," and "lists" may be difficult to pronounce. When endings are not pronounced there are more homonyms (words that sound alike but have different meanings) in the student's language than the unknowing teacher would expect. Even without the confusions caused by dialect differences, there are many homonyms in English. Usually special attention is given to words such as these as they come up in the spelling lesson. If the teacher is aware of the special homonyms in student dialects, direct teaching of these spelling differences is also possible.

Now we turn to a very important issue. While the various dialects may be equally logical, complex, and rule-governed, are they equally useful in school learning? Do students who speak a dialect such as black English understand standard English well enough to progress in school? Cherry-Peisach (1965) conducted an experiment presenting samples of "teacher speech" and "peer speech" to lower- and middle-class black and white students in first, third, and fifth grades. These students listened to audiotapes and read printed materials that contained missing words. Cherry-Peisach reported that middle-class students were better than lower-class students at guessing the missing words, regardless of the student's race or grade level. She concluded that lower-class students probably understand more language than they can produce, but they may still have definite problems understanding the language of the classroom.

What is the teacher's role in this situation? What can and should be done about the child who speaks a nonstandard dialect or about any student whose language is "incorrect" because it follows a different set of rules?

## Teaching and Language

If the theorists who emphasize the role of thinking and logical rule-learning in language development are correct, children are likely to continue generating "incorrect" language until they have reached a stage at which it is possible to remember all the correct patterns or schemes. In this case, certain things may be difficult, if not impossible, to teach young students.

Other experiments point strongly to the possibility that students at different ages (or stages) have specifically limited abilities to benefit from corrective feedback. McNeill (1966) presents an example. A child said to his mother, "Nobody don't like me." The mother responded, "No, say 'Nobody likes me.' " The boy tried to correct and said "Nobody don't like me." The mother tried again, with the same results. After seven more identical statements and attempted corrections, the boy suddenly got the point and said "Oh! Nobody don't *likes* me." Even though he was trying, the boy had difficulty discriminating between the two versions. He had a rule to follow and could not violate it. Children who come to school speaking a different dialect have similar problems.

What does all this mean for teachers? How can they cope with such language diversity in the classroom? First, they can ensure comprehension by repeating instructions using different words or asking students to paraphrase or give examples showing their meaning. Throughout the school year, they can develop the language abilities and knowledge of their students in a variety of ways. Courtney Cazden (1968) suggests these possibilities: (1) Enrich the students' language environment by focusing on the idea expressed, extending the idea beyond the students' meaning. This maintains interest while introduc-

(Ken Karp)

*One of the best ways for children to learn language is in conversations with adults. Here the teacher is giving her full attention to such a conversation.*

ing different grammatical constructions that the student can observe and perhaps adopt. For example, if a student says, "I writed my name on my picture," the teacher could respond, "You wrote your name above the rocket. Where is your astronaut going?" (2) Word meanings are most easily learned through planned conversations with an adult where the adult includes the new words in the conversation. Reading is also a potent form of language stimulation. Often the social situation involved in reading to students leads to conversations about the pictures or the ideas in the books.

It seems generally agreed that the first key to language development in school is to encourage students to use their language by talking, listening, reading, and writing. Around the age of 5 students begin to develop **metalinguistic** awareness. This means their understanding about language and how it works becomes explicit. They have knowledge about language itself. They are ready to study and extend the rules that have been implicit or out of awareness. This process continues throughout life as we all become more able to manipulate and comprehend language in sophisticated ways. (We will examine other issues related to language and teaching in Chapter 13 when we consider bilingual and multicultural education.)

Meta Language

## SUMMARY

1. Theorists differ greatly in their approach to the study of development, especially in the emphasis they place on the individual or the environment and in the decision they make about the overall structure of development. All developmental theorists, however, tend to agree on three principles: (1) People develop at different rates; (2) development is relatively orderly; and (3) development takes place gradually.

2. Piaget's theory is based on the assumption that people actively create their own knowledge by acting on objects, people, and ideas, and by noting the effects of these actions. The process is one of adaptation (through assimilation and accommodation) and organizational changes (the development of schemes).

3. Maturation, activity, and social transmission all play major roles, as does the need for equilibrium. Thinking grows when the equilibrium of a person's world view is threatened, and accommodation is used to restore this equilibrium.

4. As young people develop, Piaget believes they pass through four stages: sensorimotor, preoperational, concrete operational, and the formal operational.

5. Some theorists believe teachers should restrict their teaching to the current level of a student's cognitive development; others believe cognitive development should be encouraged or even stressed (accelerated).

6. Explanations of cognitive development based on information processing are concerned with specific cognitive skills like attention, memory, and the ability to monitor thinking processes. Growing and developing capabilities to focus attention, use strategies to remember information, and keep track of progress lead to more sophisticated thinking and reasoning abilities.

7. According to some research, the development of language seems to be very closely related to cognitive development. Children use different approaches to solve the puzzle of language. But children everywhere generally move from holophrasic to telegraphic speech and finally complete most of their basic problem solving about language at around age 5 or 6.

## KEY TERMS

| | | |
|---|---|---|
| development | object permanence | seriation |
| physical development | goal-directed activity | formal operations |
| personal development | operations | information processing |
| social development | preoperational | metacognition |
| cognitive development | one-way logic | holophrases |
| maturation | conservation | overgeneralization |
| adaptation | decentration | telegraphic |
| organization | egocentric | semantics |
| schemes | concrete operations | overregularization |
| assimilation | identity | dialect |
| accommodation | compensation | metalinguistic |
| equilibration | reversibility | |
| sensorimotor | classification | |

## SUGGESTIONS FOR FURTHER READING AND STUDY

BYBEE, R. W. and SUND, R. B. *Piaget for educators* (2nd ed.). Columbus, Ohio: Charles E. Merrill, 1982. After describing Piaget's theory and discussing the characteristics of the four stages of cognitive development, the authors give many examples of how to extend this information to teaching situations.

FLAVELL, J. H. Metacognition and cognitive monitoring: A new area of cognitive developmental inquiry. *American Psychologist*, 1979, 34, 906–911. One of the most active researchers and theorists exploring metacognitive processes describes his view on the meaning of findings in this area.

INHELDER, B. and PIAGET, J. *The growth of logical thinking from childhood to adolescence.* New York: Basic Books, 1973. Here you will find a full description of Piaget's theory in his own words.

PIAGET, J. *The science of education and the psychology of the child.* New York: Orion Press, 1970. This volume presents Piaget's ideas about education and the problems that occur when teaching does not fit the child's thinking abilities.

MOSOKOWITZ, B. A. The acquisition of language. *Scientific American*, 1978, 239, 92–108. A very readable overview of how language develops.

# Teachers' Forum

## Workbooks Overused?

Math workbooks and texts for all grades use pictures, numbers, graphs, and so on to present math concepts. While symbolic representation may be appropriate for some students at certain ages, it is not sufficient for all students in all grades. Also, the overuse of workbooks may make the students emphasize "getting the right answer" rather than understanding the process. What suggestions would you make to a beginning teacher who might rely heavily on the workbook in lesson plans?

**Matching Teaching to the Student**

A major goal of mathematics instruction should be to guide the learner from the concrete, to the semi-concrete, to the abstract stage of reasoning. It is imperative that the teacher determine at which stage each individual learner is presently functioning and build from there. As a general rule, math workbooks concentrate mainly on the semi-concrete stage. They tend to disregard students requiring more concrete explanations while limiting students capable of more abstract work. In addition, math workbooks by their very nature tend to stress product—the correct answer—as opposed to process, the how or the why. Once these limitations are understood it is still possible to use workbooks in the math curriculum, but only as a supplement, never as the core. Depending upon need, workbooks could be augmented by the use of manipulative materials or high-level word problems. Regardless of the stage at which the learner is operating, however, explanations of how answers were arrived at should always be required.

Jacqueline M. Walsh, Sixth-Grade Teacher
*Agnes E. Little Elementary School, Pawtucket, Rhode Island*

**The Value of Concrete Materials**

As a primary grade teacher for many years, I have found that it is of the utmost importance for young children to use concrete materials in order to understand math concepts. If I teach place value, then every child has sticks and rubber bands to create tens, ones, hundreds, and so on. There are so many commercial aids—flannel board materials, counting beads, toy clocks, play money, Cuisinaire rods. . . . But you really don't have to buy anything—use the children themselves and relate math to incidents with which they are familiar.

Charlotte Ross, Second-Grade Teacher
*Conert Avenue School, Elmont, New York*

## Fingers in Math

Imagine that a few of the students in your class have great difficulty with abstract thinking about numbers. To figure out any problem, they must use props such as counting on their fingers or drawing pictures of the objects involved in the problem. The other students think this is funny, and you are afraid the students involved may refuse to do any number work at all. What steps would you take to help the students who are having problems with numbers or to stop the other students from making fun of them?

**A Gradual
Transition**

Perhaps, a brief study of the history of mathematics and the counting procedures used by humans could serve as a reminder that we once had only fingers, toes, feet, objects and pictures in the beginning.

To help the students having problems, all that might be necessary would be granting permission to use any concrete method available while at the same time attempting to determine their learning styles or their learning disability and applying techniques that gradually wean them away from the constant use of concrete techniques to the more abstract.

Jacqueline G. Dyer, Second- to Eighth-Grade Teacher
*Classical Junior Academy, St. Louis, Missouri*

**Building
Self-Worth**

Very early in the school year, I begin building an attitude of self-worth. We discuss our likes and dislikes, our strengths and weaknesses. I try to help them understand that each individual will be seen doing something that he is very good at and struggling with something that will be difficult for him. Once this is established, we begin to notice areas in which we can help each other. Thus, if a child is having difficulty with abstract concepts, I would assign a more capable child as his "helper," asking him to share some of his learning "secrets." At the same time, I would provide numerous activities on the concrete level which the child can do independently.

Joan M. Bloom, First-Grade Teacher
*Henry Barnard Lab School for Rhode Island College, Providence, Rhode Island*

## The Problem of the Match

It is not unusual for a class in the upper elementary grades through high school to contain students with abilities ranging from the early concrete operational stage through formal operations. This is especially true in smaller school districts, where enrollments are too small to allow ability grouping. In courses that build on previous skills, such as math and reading, you usually have to group within the class. But in other areas—for example, social studies—how can you teach the same information to the entire class in such a way as to prevent either frustration or boredom?

**Diversify
Assignments**

Present the topic orally to the entire class with lively concrete illustrations and with some class discussion. Then in the follow-up time, diversify assignments. Extension and application of concepts will challenge those who have already gotten the message. A second explanation and provision for practice of drillable items will reinforce your presentation for those who need a second exposure. Even in testing, accommodation can be made. The first page of the test contains the basic information everyone must master. The second page has two versions. Each version tests the objectives of the study group.

Dorothy Eve Hopkins, Sixth-Grade Teacher
*Homer Intermediate School, Homer, New York*

# 3

# Personal and Social Development

As we all know from experience, schooling involves more than cognitive development. In this chapter, we examine the development of self-concept, emotions, attitudes, values, and social relationships. We begin with the work of Erik Erikson, whose comprehensive theory of personal and social development offers a helpful framework for study. Next we explore several recent ideas about the development of social knowledge. How do we come to understand the feelings and intentions of others? What factors determine our views about morality? Do moral actions follow from moral beliefs? What can teachers do to foster such personal qualities as honesty, cooperation, altruism, and self-esteem? In the final section, we consider the question of affective education—education for emotional growth—in the public schools.

By the time you have completed this chapter, you should have a number of new ways of looking at the students you will be teaching. More specifically, you should be able to do the following:

- List several implications for teaching in Erikson's theory.
- Describe the child's changing view of friendship.
- Describe the problems of early- and late-maturing students.
- Tell how teachers can foster positive self-concepts in their students.
- Describe Kohlberg's six stages of moral reasoning and give an example of each.
- Take a stand on affective and moral education.

# A COMPREHENSIVE THEORY: THE WORK OF ERIKSON

Erik Erikson (1963) offers a basic framework for understanding the needs of young people in relation to the society in which they grow and develop, learn, and later make their contributions. While Erikson's approach is not the only explanation of personal and social development, we have chosen it to organize our discussion for several reasons. First, Erikson emphasizes the continuing development of the individual's view of self, as well as the person's relationships with others. Teachers must be concerned with both. Because he describes development throughout life, Erikson provides a framework for understanding past and future influences on students. Finally, his theory has implications for teachers at every grade level.

Erikson's Stages    Like Piaget, Erikson sees a person's development as a passage through a series of stages, each with its special accomplishments. However, Erikson uses the term "stage" to imply differences in forms of motivation and interests, not differences in structure. In this section, we will look briefly at all the stages in Erikson's theory, stages that begin with infancy and end with old age. Of course, a teacher's role is more often related to young people between the ages of 5 and 18. But, in fact the stages are interdependent, so

*Erik Erikson formulated a comprehensive theory of emotional development involving a series of eight critical stages, each leading to a positive or a negative outcome. The successful resolution of each crisis contributes to strengths of personality and to the ability to meet future crises.*

accomplishments at later stages depend on the results of the earlier years. In many cases, the accomplishments of earlier periods have to be reestablished in the various new settings of the school.

## Tasks for All Ages

**Role of Society**

Erikson developed his theory while studying how young people learn to live in their social environment. He was particularly interested in the relationship between the culture in which a child is reared and the kind of adult the child becomes. Erikson began with the hypothesis that all humans have the same basic needs and that each society must provide in some way for the needs of the developing person. He then studied childrearing practices in several societies and found recurring themes in emotional and social changes across the life span.

The resulting theory, essentially a **psychosocial theory,** is based in part on Freud's description of personality development. However, Erikson has gone beyond the sexual aspects of Freud's work and included the growing competence expected of individuals as they move toward adulthood and assume increasing responsibility for themselves and others. In the later years, a new type of competence is required: the ability to face declining influence and physical weakness.

**The Role of Developmental Crises**

Erikson suggests that at each stage the individual faces a crucial **developmental crisis.** In order to proceed satisfactorily through future stages, the person must resolve the crisis of the present stage. The way in which he or she resolves the crisis will have a lasting effect on that person's self-image and view of society. An unhealthy resolution of problems in the early stages has a negative effect throughout life. None of these developmental crises is ever permanently resolved, but if individuals are successful in resolving the crisis when it is first encountered, they will have a reasonably solid foundation for future dealings with that particular crisis and with others.

**Figure 3–1    Erikson's Stages of Personal and Social Development**

| Stage | Approximate Age | Important People Involved | Approximate Stage in Piaget's Theory |
|---|---|---|---|
| Trust v. mistrust | 0–1 years | Maternal figure | Sensorimotor |
| Autonomy v. doubt | 1–2 years | Parental figures | Sensorimotor |
| Initiative v. guilt | 2–6 years | Family | Preoperational |
| Industry v. inferiority | 6–12 years | Family, neighbor-hood, and school | Concrete operational |
| Identity v. role diffusion | Adolescence | Family, school, and peers | Formal operational |
| Intimacy v. isolation | Young adulthood | Friends and acquain-tances | Formal operational |
| Generativity v. self-absorption | Young and middle adulthood | Family, friends, and work world | Formal operational |
| Integrity v. despair | Later adulthood | Family, friends, and humanity | Formal operational |

*Adaptation of Erikson chart from **Childhood and Society**, 2d Ed. by Erik H. Erikson, is used with the permission of W. W. Norton & Company, Inc. Copyright © 1963, 1950 by W. W. Norton & Company, Inc. Erik H. Erikson's Literary Estate and Hogarth Press are also gratefully acknowledged.*

Figure 3–1 presents all eight stages, each carrying the label of the developmental crisis of the stage. The figure also gives approximate ages, the important people involved at each stage, and some idea of how Erikson's stages relate to Piaget's. As we discuss Erikson's tasks we will relate these personal and social milestones to Piaget's stages of cognitive development. We do this because the mental tools available to people at different stages will determine, in part, the sense they can make of their personal and social experiences.

### Infancy: Trust v. Mistrust

*The Need to Trust*    Erikson identifies **trust v. mistrust** as the basic alternative of infancy. The transition from the womb to the outside world marks the beginning of the infant's need to trust. In the first months of life babies begin to find out whether they can depend on the world around them. According to Erikson, the infant will develop a sense of trust if needs for food and care are met with comforting regularity. Closeness and responsiveness on the part of the parents in these early months contribute greatly to this sense of trust.

Infants encountering this need to trust are in the early part of the sensorimotor stage. They are just beginning to learn that they are separate from the world around them and that other objects and people exist even when they cannot see them. This realization of separateness is part of what makes trust so important: infants must trust the aspects of their world that are beyond their control.

Recent research on infant attachment supports Erikson's theory. Mary Ainsworth (1979) has studied the differences between babies who are "securely attached" to their mothers and those who are "anxiously attached." Babies in the first group have mothers who are more responsive to their needs. Ainsworth suggests that these babies come to see their mothers as accessible or available when needed. They can use their mothers as a secure base for exploring the world, knowing they can "trust" their mothers to respond when necessary. These babies are more cooperative and less aggressive with their mothers. As they grow older, they become more competent and sympathetic with peers and explore their environment with greater enthusiasm and persistence than the anxiously attached babies.

## Early Childhood: Autonomy v. Doubt

Erikson's second stage, **autonomy v. doubt** marks the beginning of self-control and self-confidence. Young children exercise this autonomy or self-control by beginning to do more and more on their own. During this period, parents must tread a fine line; they must be protective but not overprotective.

The way the parents handle this has a strong influence on the child's achievement of autonomy. The alternative to autonomy—doubt—means that children doubt their abilities to manage the world on their own terms. Erikson believes that children who experience too much doubt will lack confidence in their own powers throughout life. This confidence is especially important in the early years when children must assume many responsibilities for self-care (feeding, toileting, and dressing, to name just a few).

This stage, like the first, ties in with Piaget's sensorimotor stage. Children in the later part of the sensorimotor period have developed the physical and mental abilities needed to achieve some control of their own lives. A sense of autonomy is in many ways based on the ability to carry out the goal-directed activities of Piaget's stage.

Before we leave this section on the early stages, a word about the people involved is in order. In Figure 3–1, we listed the "maternal figure" as the most important person in the first stage, and "parental figures" in the second. Erikson himself assumed that the mother would naturally be the single most important figure in the earliest stage. However, more recent research shows that fathers can play an equal role at this time. Lamb (1978), for example, has concluded that infants become attached to their mothers and fathers at about the same time. Although most infants turn to their mothers when they are distressed, they do *not* show predicted preferences for their mothers during the first year. In fact, in the second year, male infants generally develop preferences for their fathers. Finally, it appears that mothers and fathers play and interact with their infants in qualitatively different ways. Fathers, for example, are more likely to play in physical or novel ways, while mothers tend to play more traditional games such as peek-a-boo and do the routine caregiving tasks. Lamb concludes that both the mother and father make "independent and important contributions to the sociopersonality development of the child" (Lamb, 1978, p. 104).

Since there are such predictable differences in the ways mothers and fathers interact with their babies, Lamb (1979) believes that this is a main factor influencing the development of gender identity. We all may learn very

early what it means to be a male or a female through the actions of our parents in the first years of our lives. Our parents may teach us how to be male and female in other ways as well. Birns (1976) reports a number of studies that indicate both parents play more roughly and vigorously with sons than with daughters. Parents tend to touch male infants more at first and then shift to keeping male toddlers at a greater distance. They also seem to spend more time interacting socially with sons, trying to get the babies to laugh or smile.

After the first two stages, the child enters a slowly broadening world where feelings of trust and autonomy will be very important. At this point, the child has a new task to master.

## Preschool or Kindergarten: Initiative

According to Erikson, the child must now face the alternative of **initiative v. guilt**. For Erikson, initiative is the "willingness to undertake, plan, and attack a task for the sake of being active" (Erikson, 1963, p. 255). This period, from approximately 2 to 6, is an exciting time when children begin to test their powers at "grown-up" tasks. The 4-year-old perched on a chair stirring cookie batter or solemnly passing tools to a parent who is fixing a broken bicycle is involved in important work. The youngster is beginning to channel the energy and enthusiasm of childhood into more adultlike activities. But with this change comes a growing understanding that some activities *should*

*not* be done. At times the child may feel guilty, torn between what he or she wants to do and what should be done. The challenge of this period is to retain a zest for initiating activities while learning not to act on every impulse.

Children at this stage require confirmation from adults that their initiative is accepted and that their contributions, no matter how small, are truly valued. In short, the childen are eager for responsibility. Successful growth during this period rests upon the children's ability to feel that they are accepted for themselves. Again, adults tread a fine line, this time in providing supervision without interference. If children are not allowed to do things on their own, a sense of guilt may develop because they come to believe that what they want to do is always "wrong." They may learn that they cannot trust their own judgment.

**Learning about Adult Roles.**    Although children at this period are relatively egocentric, they can imagine themselves playing various roles. They may even begin to imitate the roles of important people around them—for example, by playing house and school. These children are often hero-worshippers and take great interest in the ideals society offers. Preschool books showing doctors, firefighters, artists, and teachers are intriguing for most children as they begin to learn what the future might hold for them. Initiative points the children toward reality, leading to pretend games based on adult roles. Television is also a source for many pretend games, supplementing what the children have learned from their families and communities. Children learn early which roles are ordinarily male and female and reflect this in their play. But there are many other ways for children to learn about sex roles and initiative.

As children move into early childhood, the different treatment of the sexes we saw during infancy seems to continue. A number of researchers have

(Laimute E. Druskis)

*Preschool children are eager to learn about the world of adults. They often imitate the activities of important people in their lives as they try out various roles.*

Sex Roles  found that boys are given more freedom to roam the neighborhood than girls and are allowed to do potentially dangerous acts such as playing with sharp scissors or crossing the street alone at an earlier age than girls. Independence and initiative seem to be encouraged in boys to a greater extent than in girls. Lois Hoffman (1977) suggests that girls are not so much trained in dependency as they are deprived of the independence training offered to boys.

**The Effects of Day Care.**    In the first few years of the stage of initiative v. guilt, most children remain in the family. With recent increases in two-career families and single parents, however, more and more children are spending part of their daily lives in group settings outside the family. This means that broader influences have an effect on the child's resolution of the conflict at this stage.

Research on Day Care    What are the effects of this broader scope? In the past few years, researchers have examined the results of day care experiences on both the intellectual and emotional development of children. Belsky and Steinberg (1978), for example, have found that day care generally has neither a positive nor a negative effect on intellectual development. For children from disadvantaged environments, however, high-quality day care seems to prevent some of the decline in IQ scores that is often seen as these children proceed through school. Evidence also suggests that day care is not disruptive to the child's emotional bonds with parents, even if it begins before the child's first birthday. But children who attend day care centers do tend to interact more

**85**

with their peers in both positive and negative ways. Some results indicate that children in day care centers may be more aggressive toward other children and adults. The effect of this aggression in later years has not yet been determined.

Clearly, not every situation involving a working mother is the same. Recent studies have looked at the factors that lead to successful adjustment for children with working mothers. It appears that problems can be avoided if mothers are sensitive to the special needs of their children and compensate for time away by having more direct interaction with their children when they are at home (L. Hoffman, 1979). This is often difficult for families with many children and few financial resources. It also requires great energy.

Because you may be teaching children of this age, in preschool or kindergarten, we have included a set of Guidelines directed toward the encouragement of initiative and the avoidance of guilt.

# Guidelines

## Encouraging Initiative in the Preschool Child

**1. Encourage initiative in many aspects of classroom work.**

**EXAMPLES**
- Student-run projects.
- Choices that students may make for themselves.

**2. Make use of the sense of initiative in work with basic skills.**

**EXAMPLES**
- Have a free choice time in which a child may select an educational game or activity.
- As much as possible, avoid interrupting a child who is very involved and concentrated on what he is doing.

**3. Make sure that each child has a chance to experience success.**

**EXAMPLES**
- Individualized tasks and assignments on student's level of difficulty.
- Non-competitive games that invite enthusiastic participation, e.g. New Games.

**4. Encourage make-believe with a wide variety of roles.**

**EXAMPLES**
- Pretend games focusing on roles children are already familiar with.
- Switching roles to give all children a chance to lead.

**5. Avoid scolding or devaluating a child because he tries something on his own.**

**EXAMPLES**
- Be flexible. Incorporate children's ideas, suggestions, and comments into class activities and discussions.
- If a child initiates an inappropriate or dangerous activity, restructure his efforts within acceptable limits rather than completely squelching his ideas.

## Elementary and Middle School Years: Industry

In the early school years, students are developing what Erikson calls a sense of industry. They are beginning to see the relationship between steady attention and perseverance and the pleasure of a job completed. This is also the period when students are beginning to conquer the physical environment with concrete operations. While play satisifed them before, they now desire productive work on their own and are physically and mentally ready for it. The alternative at this stage is **industry v. inferiority**.

Research on Industriousness

A recent study by George and Caroline Vaillant (1981) supports Erikson's notion of the importance of industry. These researchers followed 450 men for 35 years. Their conclusion was that the men who had been the most industrious and willing to work as children were the most well-adjusted and well-paid as adults and had the most satisfying personal relationships. The willingness and ability to work hard as a child was more important for success in later life than other early factors such as social position, family experiences, or intelligence.

In many traditional societies, this period brings the child into direct involvement with the adult world of work. For American children, however, this period brings something else: a need to conquer the world of the school. The activities provided—academics, sports, clubs, performing arts—are the arenas to demonstrate accomplishment for most children between the ages of 6 and 16.

**Moving Outside the Family: The Role of Friends.**   During their early school years, children move rather freely in and out of three overlapping worlds: the home, the school, and the neighborhood. Parents remain important, even though the children spend increasing amounts of time with other children in the neighborhood and the school.

*For young children, friends are people who share their toys with you when you play together. Friendship is based on immediate experience.*

(UNICEF photo by Tom Marotta)

**Development of Friendships**

In recent years, psychologists have studied the development of friendships and found that the meaning of friendship changes as children mature (Damon, 1977; Selman, 1976; Youniss, 1980). Damon describes three levels of friendship. At the first level, friends are people you play with often, usually sharing food or toys and acting "nice" toward each other. But friendships can begin and end quickly, based on acts of kindness or "meanness." There is little sense of friends having stable characteristics, so moment to moment actions define the friendship. Teachers working with young children should be aware that these rapidly changing allegiances are a normal part of development.

Friendships at the next level are defined by willingness to help each other when help is needed. Children begin to base their choices for friends on personal qualities in the other such as kindness or trustworthiness. The descriptions of friendship in Box 3–1 reflect many of these concerns.

---

### BOX 3–1 WHAT IS A FRIEND?

*Children's views of friendship change as they mature. The themes in these developing views seem to be from short-lived and frequently changing friendships based on sharing possessions and being "nice" to each other to long-term, durable relationships based on enduring personality characteristics and mutual trust. This progression is evident below in the descriptions of friends given by children at different ages. The statement by Elizabeth Woolfolk is taken from the homework assignment of the first author's daughter. All the students in her second-grade class wrote an essay on friendship. The statements by Tony, Julie, Deborah, Elizabeth, Douvan, and Joseph Aselson are taken from Zick Rubin's book,* Children's Friendships *(1980, p. 31).*

We're friends now because we know each other's names. *Tony, age 3½*

A friend is nice to you and helpful, playful and caring. Friends give you cards when you are sick and call you. My friends play outside with me. We play camping. Friends lend you things and help you with your homework. I have four best friends. My friends' ages are seven, eight, twelve and fourteen. My friends and I go to movies. We go to the mall and shop. I go over to my friends' house for dinner and they come to mine. We have sleep-overs. We watch TV too. Also my friends and I color and draw. We listen to records and play board games. My friends and I have lots of fun. *Elizabeth Woolfolk, age 7.*

Friends don't snatch or act snobby, and they don't argue or disagree. If you're nice to them, they'll be nice to you. *Julie, age 8.*

A friend is someone that you can share secrets with at 3 in the morning with Clearasil on your face. *Deborah, age 13.*

The friendship we have in mind is characterized by mutual trust; it permits a fairly free expression of emotion; it allows the shedding of privacies (although not inappropriately); it can absorb, within limits, conflict between the pair; it involves the discussion of personally crucial themes, it provides occasions to enrich and enlarge the self through the encounter of differences. *Elizabeth Douvan and Joseph Adelson, adults*

At the highest level, friends are seen as people who share common interests and values, faithfully keep your most private revelations a secret, and provide psychological support when necessary. Friendship is a long-term proposition and usually cannot be destroyed by one incident. This changing conception of friendship may reflect changes in cognitive abilities as children move from basing judgments on the immediate situation to being able to take several factors into account at the same time and finally to using abstract concepts (such as trust and shared values) to judge people.

Teachers sometimes forget the importance of these developing friendships. Life can be very difficult for a student whose peer relationships are unsatisfying, whatever the basis for friendship in his or her age group. A teacher should be aware of how each student gets along with the group. Are there outcasts? Do some students play the bully role? Careful adult intervention can often correct such problems.

**Student Popularity**

As a teacher, you may wonder what makes some students more popular than others. Hartup (1970) has found that several characteristics taken together seem to be associated with being popular. These include being outgoing, kind, nonaggressive, sensitive to the interests and needs of others, unruffled by simple problems, and having an easygoing enthusiasm. Asher, Ogden, and Gottman (1977) add these characteristics to the list. Popular students in elementary and high schools tend to be friendly, academically successful, more attractive, more physically mature or taller, the youngest member of their family, and very skilled at sports or other activities that are respected by the peer group. But remember that these results are based on average tendencies; they do not hold for all individuals. They simply give a picture of a few characteristics that tend to be valued among children. You will encounter many popular children who do not fit these patterns at all.

**Making, and Keeping Friends**

**The Role of Teachers.** Even if every student cannot be one of the most popular, most can and do have friends. Making and keeping friends requires many skills:

> "These skills include the abilities to gain entry into group activities, to be approving and supporting of one's peers, to manage conflict appropriately, and to exercise sensitivity and tact. They are subtle skills, by no means easy to learn, and the fact that most children ultimately succeed in acquiring them is itself one of the most remarkable aspects of social development." (Rubin, 1980, p. 47)

But not all students acquire these skills readily. In the early school years, part of the teacher's role is to balance students' need to learn the curriculum with their need to establish healthy peer relationships. We have included both sets of needs in the Guidelines given for teaching students at this stage.

So far, we have examined the emotional development and needs of children and young students going through the first four stages of Erikson's theory and the first three of Piaget's. The child has now developed (or failed to develop) a sense of trust, autonomy, initiative, and industry. We turn next to the needs of the young person moving into the secondary school years and toward the challenges of adulthood.

# Guidelines

*Encouraging Industry and Healthy Peer Relationships in Elementary School Students*

**1. Make sure that students have opportunities to set and work toward realistic goals.**

EXAMPLES
- Many relatively short projects that offer true gains.
- Student involvement in choice of projects.

**2. Know something about the friendship structure of your classroom and try to find ways to encourage isolates to get involved.**

EXAMPLES
- Give isolates responsibilities that they can handle.
- Help students learn game skills needed to take part in peer activities.

**3. Give students a chance to think about fairness and justice.**

EXAMPLES
- Use the Golden Rule as a basis for discussions of conflict. ("How would you feel if someone did that to you?")
- Discussion of class rules.
- Clear statement of class rules and their rationale.

**4. Let students have a chance to show their independence and responsibility.**

EXAMPLES
- Tolerance of some mistakes.
- Student participation in classroom duties and "housekeeping."

**5. Provide encouragement to students who seem discouraged.**

EXAMPLES
- Use individual contracts and charts that show student's progress.
- Recognize students for their accomplishments.

## Adolescence: The Search for Identity

During the period of adolescence, the central issue is the development of an identity that will provide a firm basis for adulthood. The individual has been developing a sense of self since infancy, but at adolescence there is for the first time a conscious effort to answer the question, Who am I? The alternative at this point is **identity v. role diffusion.** Erikson notes that the accomplishments of the early stages have prepared the way for this task. Each of the earlier accomplishments now serves as a foundation for the search for identity. Having established a sense of basic trust, the young person is now searching for people and ideas to have faith in. The autonomy achieved in childhood leads to an insistence on the chance to decide freely about future careers and lifestyles. During the period of initiative, the young person is likely to have had a chance to play at various roles in preparation for achieving one or more of them. The development of industry leaves the young person with a sense of competence and a belief in his or her ability to make meaningful contributions to the world.

*During adolescence, students face the questions, "Who am I?" "What do I want to become?" In a world filled with possibilities, answering these questions is not easy.*

(Ken Karp)

**Physical Development in Adolescence.**    Physically, adolescents begin to look like adults. But the physical changes occurring just before and during adolescence can have significant effects on the individual's identity. Figure 3–2 provides a graphic representation of the physical maturation of males and females as they move through puberty to adulthood. The most striking part of the graph is, of course, the earlier growth spurt found among the female students. On the average, females mature about two years ahead of males (Rogers, 1981).

Throughout elementary school, many of the girls are likely to be as large or larger than the boys in their classes. This gives the girls some advantage in physical activities, an advantage that is often countered by the feeling that boys should be better at sports. The really significant effects of different growth rates, for both males and females, seem to come at the beginning of puberty.

Fein (1978) describes a number of differences between individuals who mature early and those who are late maturers. First, there seems to be an academic advantage in early maturation. Students who are physically mature tend to score higher on the average on most tests of mental ability than less mature students of the same age. Second, early maturation seems to have certain special advantages for boys. Early-maturing boys are more likely to enjoy high social status, to be leaders, and to be popular. Later-maturing boys tend to be less popular, more talkative, and more attention-seeking. For girls, early physical maturity seems to be less important in determining social status. But maturing way ahead of classmates can be a definite disadvantage. Being larger than everyone else in the class is not a valued characteristic for girls in our culture.

Sex Differences in Physical Development

Early and Late Maturers

**91**

## Figure 3–2  Growth During the School Years

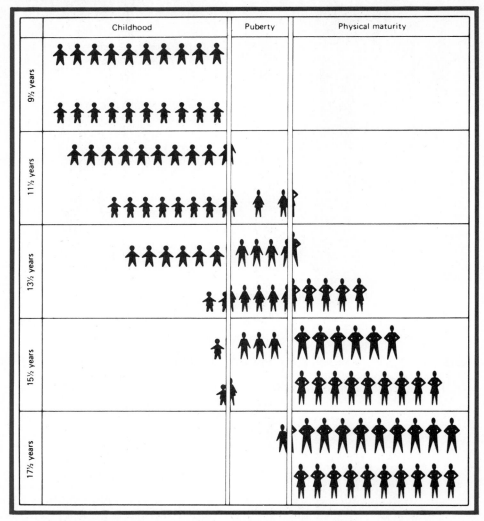

From D. Rogers, *Adolescents and Youth,* 4/e. Englewood Cliffs, NJ: Prentice-Hall, 1981, p. 70. Used with permission of Prentice-Hall, Inc.

From the students' point of view, probably the most important aspect of development during these years is the emergence of sexual maturity. In our culture, the sexually mature adolescent is physically and hormonally equipped for sexual relationships but probably will go through an extended period of continued education or other training before society considers him or her ready for marriage. In previous decades, males were more likely than females to have sexual intercourse before marriage. Today about 60 percent of all unmarried teenagers (boys and girls) have sexual intercourse by age 19 (Rosen and Hall, 1983). The emotional impact of these early experiences may have repercussions in the school, both for the students involved and for others who hear about them.

# Guidelines

## Dealing With Physical Differences in the Classroom

**1. Make allowances in the class for larger and smaller students.**

EXAMPLES
- Smaller students in the front.
- Avoidance of games that will draw attention to major differences.

**2. Help students obtain factual information about differences in physical development.**

EXAMPLES
- Science projects on growth rates.
- General school programs on sexual development.

**3. Expect some adolescents to be somewhat clumsy and occasionally inattentive.**

EXAMPLES
- Avoidance of requests that will highlight clumsiness.
- Avoidance of reprimands for occasional lapses.

**4. Accept the fact that concerns about appearance and the opposite sex will occupy much of the time and energy of adolescents.**

EXAMPLES
- Deal with some of these issues in curriculum-related materials.
- Offer models of people involved in other equally important concerns.

---

Teachers are likely to have students who vary greatly in size, maturity, and sexual sophistication in almost every class. As we have seen, being very different from other students appears to be a plus only for boys who mature earlier than their peers. For everyone else, being very different can cause problems in emotional and social development. We have offered a set of Guidelines for dealing with these problems.

Adolescent development does not end with the attainment of physical and sexual maturity. The junior and senior high school years are a time to begin assembling the pieces of one's own being into a sense of identity or a more mature self-concept.

**Self-Concept: Origins and Influences.**   **Self-concept,** like many other psychological terms, is part of our everyday conversation. We talk about people who have a "low self-concept" or individuals whose self-concept is not "strong." Used this way, self-concept sounds like a chemical in the blood or a type of muscle. In psychology, the term generally refers to "the composite of ideas, feelings, and attitudes people have about themselves" (Hilgard, Atkinson and Atkinson, 1979, p. 605), or more broadly to "a person's perception of him or herself" (Shavelson and Bolus, 1982).

A Scheme about Self

We could consider the self-concept to be our attempt to explain ourselves to ourselves, to build a scheme (in Piaget's terms) that organizes our impressions, feelings, and attitudes about ourselves. But this model or scheme is not permanent, unified, or unchanging. It is "a complex system of ideas, feelings, and desires, not necessarily well articulated or coherent" (Bromley, 1978, p. 164). Our pereception of ourself varies from situation to situation and goes through many changes as we grow older. We will take a brief look backward at the self-concept as it develops before adolescence, and then consider the role of the school in relation to the self-concept.

**Changes
in Self-concept**

Young children see themselves in terms of their physical appearance, name, actions, and abilities, but do not yet have a sense of their enduring characteristics or "personality." They evaluate themselves as they evaluate friends at Damon's level one described above—in terms of concrete actions, immediate events, and appearances. As they mature, children move from concrete and fragmented views of themselves to more abstract, organized, and objective views that include psychological characteristics. As with friendship, changing conceptions of the self can be linked to cognitive development. Again, the progression is from ideas based on appearances, immediate experiences, and actions to ideas based on abstractions and enduring qualities that are conserved despite alterations in appearances. Below are examples of three British children's descriptions of themselves showing this trend (Bromley, 1978).

**Examples**

*A BOY AGED 7*

I am 7 and I have hazel brown hair and my hobby is stamp collecting. I am good at football and I am quite good at sums and my favourite game is football and I love school and I like reading books and my favourite car is an Austin.

*A BOY AGED 9*

I have dark brown hair, brown eyes and a fair face. I am a quick worker but am often lazy. I am good but often cheeky and naughty. My character is sometimes funny and sometimes serious. My behavior is sometimes silly and stupid and often good it is often funny my daddy thinks.

*A GIRL AGED 14*

I am a very temperamental person, sometimes, well most of the time, I am happy. Then now and again I just go moody for no reason at all. I enjoy being different from everybody else, and like to think of myself as being fairly modern. When I am nervous I talk a lot, and this gives some important new acquaintances a bad impression when I am trying to make a good one. I worry a lot about getting married and having a family, because I am frightened that I will make a mess of it.

**Many Aspects
of Self-concept**

The developing self-concepts evident in these examples are influenced by many factors. Parents play a major role in the early years, but friends and teachers become very important as the child grows older. Shavelson and his colleagues have devised a model of the way a student's self-concept may be organized (Shavelson and Bolus, 1982; Shavelson, Hubner and Stanton, 1976). In this model, a student's general self-concept can be divided into two parts, an academic and a nonacademic self-concept (see Figure 3–3). On the academic side, self-concept is based on how well the student performs in different academic areas. On the nonacademic side, self-concept is based on relationships with peers and other important people, on emotional states, and on physical qualities.

**Figure 3–3   One View of the Organization of Self-Concept in the School Years**

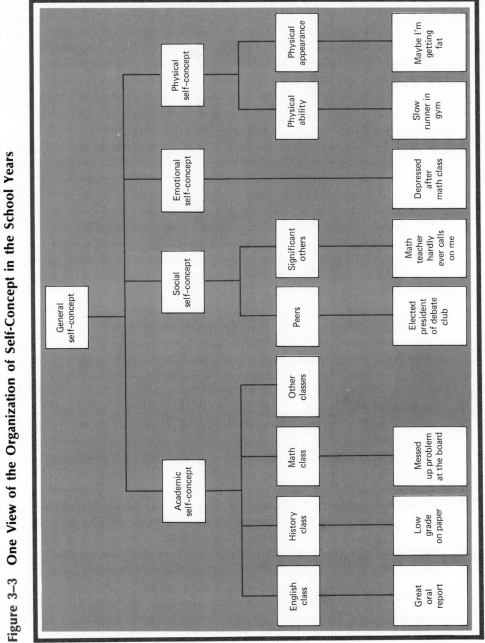

*Adapted from F. J. Shavelson, J. J. Hubner, and G. C. Stanton. Self-concept: Validation of construct interpretation. **Review of Educational Research**, 1976, **46**, 413. Copyright 1976, **AERA**, Washington, D.C.*

Shavelson also offers an explanation of how such a self-concept is developed. Students evaluate their own specific behaviors in particular situations. They are continually asking, in effect, "How am I doing?" To answer this question, they compare their performance with the performances of others and with their own standards. They also look to the verbal and nonverbal reactions of people who are important to them for answers to this question. Another factor, as you will see in the chapter on motivation, is the individual's explanation for success or failure in each situation. Successes will not build a positive self-concept if the person takes no credit for the outcome. Over time, a concept of self evolves in the different areas and a general self-concept emerges. Thus we have different concepts of ourselves in different situations. Some views may be more positive than others, depending on how well we do in each area and on our beliefs about our own contributions to the outcomes (Griffin, Chassin and Young, 1981). When the perceptions that develop are generally positive, the term high self-esteem is often used to describe the person's self-evaluation.

For teachers, there are at least two important questions to ask about self-concept. One is the question of how self-concept affects a student's behavior in school. The other is the question of how life in school affects a student's self-concept.

**Self-concept and Schooling**

In answer to the first question, it appears that students with higher self-esteem (positive self-concepts) are somewhat more likely to be successful in school (Purkey, 1970), although the strength of the relationship varies greatly depending on the characteristics of the subjects studied and the methods used (Hansford and Hattie, 1982). In addition, a more positive self-concept is related to more favorable attitudes toward school (Metcalfe, 1981) and more positive behavior in the classroom (Reynolds, 1980). Of course, as we discussed in Chapter 1, knowing that two variables are related (correlated) does not tell us that one is causing the other. It may be that high achievement leads to positive self-concept, or vice versa. In fact, it probably works both ways (Shavelson and Bolus, 1982; West, Fish and Stevens, 1980).

In answer to the second question of how school affects self-concept, Bloom (1973) said: "Successful experiences in school are no guarantee of a generally positive self-concept, but they increase the probabilities that such will be the case" (p. 142). Given this responsibility, what can teachers do? In their book *Teacher Behavior and Pupil Self-Concept*, Kash and Borich (1978) offer several suggestions. We have listed a number of them in Figure 3–4.

**Identity: Becoming an Individual.** When children reach adolescence, they begin to make conscious decisions about who they are and what they believe. Identity refers to this organization of the individual's drives, abilities, beliefs, and history into a structure of self. It is quite similar to self-concept, but involves more deliberate choices and decisions, particularly about vocation, sexual orientation, and a "philosophy of life" (Marcia, 1982).

**Marcia's Identity Alternatives**

James Marcia identified four different alternatives for the adolescent during the period of identity v. role diffusion. The first is **identity achievement**, meaning that the individual has considered the possibilities, made personal choices, and is pursuing those choices. **Foreclosures** are people who are committed to particular goals, but these goals were selected by parents, not the people themselves. **Identity diffusion** occurs when individuals reach no conclusions and have no firm direction, even though they may have gone through periods of trying to make decisions. Finally, adolescents experienc-

**Figure 3–4    Suggestions for Encouraging the Development of Positive Self-Concept**

1. Value and accept all pupils, for their attempts as well as their accomplishments.
2. Create a climate that is physically and psychologically safe for students.
3. Become aware of your own personal biases (everyone has some biases).
4. Make sure that your procedures for teaching and grouping students are really necessary, not just a convenient way of handling problem students or avoiding contact with some students.
5. Make standards of evaluation clear.
6. Model appropriate methods of self-criticism and self-reward.
7. Avoid destructive competition and encourage students to compete with their own prior levels of achievement.
8. Accept a student even when you must reject a particular behavior.
9. Remember that positive self-concept grows from success in operating in the world *and* from being valued by important people in the environment. It takes both kinds of experiences to build a positive self-concept.

*Adapted from M. M. Kash and G. Borich.* **Teacher behavior and pupil self-concept.** *Reading, Mass.: Addison-Wesley, 1978, pp. 217, 260.*

ing a **moratorium** are in the midst of struggling with choices. This is the true meaning of an identity crisis. Research on these four alternatives indicates that people who work hard to resolve identity crises are firmer in their sense of who they are and less influenced by outside forces. Figure 3–5 gives examples of each alternative.

Views of Self and Others

**Identity and Sex Roles.**   One very important aspect of identity is sex role. Like self-concept, an individual's view of what it means to be male or female develops over many years. Younger children tend to have more stereotyped notions of sex roles than older children, but all ages seem to have more rigid and traditional ideas about male occupations than about what females do. In addition, children seem to have less stereotyped concepts of themselves than of others. They tend to see themselves as **androgynous** (having both

**Figure 3–5    Marcia's Identity Statuses**

During many interviews over the past 15 years, James Marcia has asked adolescents questions about how they see themselves. One topic concerns commitment to vocational choices, such as: *"How willing would you be to give up your plans to become a _____ if something better came along?"* Based on responses similar to those below, he has identified four types or identity statuses.

*Identity Diffusion.* "I'm always willing to go with something better. I'd change in a minute if there was a better possibility."

*Foreclosure.* "No, my family and I have been pointing toward _____ ever since I can remember. I can't imagine doing anything else. I wouldn't feel comfortable with another choice."

*Moratorium.* "Well maybe I'd be willing to change, but I think _____ or something like it is the best for me. I'm not completely certain, but other options just don't seem quite right."

*Identity Achieved.* "Well, if you say it would be better, I guess I'd have to consider it, but it's hard to imagine anything really better for me. I thought about this decision for a long time and I think it's the right one for me."

masculine and feminine qualities), even though they may categorize other people as masculine or feminine. It appears that we must be able to see ourselves as androgynous before we can recognize this in others (Guttentag and Longfellow, 1978).

**The School and Sex Roles**

You already have seen how parents often teach children to adopt traditional sex roles. Schools also may foster stereotyped views of sex roles in a number of ways. Most of the textbooks produced for the early grades before 1970 portrayed both males and females in sexually stereotyped roles. Materials for the later grades often omitted women altogether from illustrations and text. In a study of 2760 stories in 134 books by 16 publishers, a group called Women on Words and Images (1975) found the total number of stories dealing with males or male animals to be four times greater than the number of stories dealing with females or female animals. They also found that females tended to be shown in the home, behaving passively and expressing fear or incompetence. Males usually were more dominant and adventurous and often rescued the females. Textbook publishers have recognized these problems to some extent in recent years. However, it still makes sense to check your teaching materials for such stereotypes.

# Guidelines

## Encouraging Identity Formation in Secondary School Students

**1. Give students many models for career choices and other adult roles.**

EXAMPLES
- Models from literature and history.
- Guest speakers.

**2. Encourage students to develop interest in many activities.**

EXAMPLES
- Extra-curricular clubs and activities.
- Worthwhile hobbies.

**3. Help students find assistance in working out personal problems.**

EXAMPLES
- School counseling services.
- Outside services.

**4. Give students a chance to examine some of the choices they must make.**

EXAMPLES
- Lessons centering on career choices.
- Units on changing family life.

**5. Check to see if the textbooks and other materials you are using are presenting an honest view of the options open to both females and males.**

EXAMPLES
- Are both males and females portrayed in traditional and nontraditional roles at work, at leisure, and at home?
- What effects are the materials likely to have on the self-images and aspirations of the female students? of the male students?

The teacher's own attitude toward sex differences also may be influential. When teachers want boxes carried to the basement, they may ask for male volunteers. If refreshments are needed or flowers must be arranged, they may again fall into the stereotype and ask for female volunteers. Such requests, repeated again and again, can help strengthen students' beliefs that these are valid expectations (Levitan and Chananie, 1972; Jackson and Lahaderne, 1971).

**The Role of Teachers.** The teacher is often the most appropriate and available adult to help adolescents in their search for themselves as well as in their search for knowledge. Teachers can offer students ideas and people to have faith in. Teachers can support the students' need for free choice of careers. They can give encouragement to aspirations while giving objective feedback on students' accomplishments in the subject area. When students are asked to list reasons for choosing a particular major, they often mention the importance of an effective, demanding, and warm teacher. The Guidelines here offer a number of suggestions for helping students in their search for identity.

6. **Make adjustments in your teaching to compensate for any inadequacies you find in the materials.**

EXAMPLES
- Discuss your findings with the students and ask them to help you find similar biases in other materials.
- Locate additional materials to fill gaps noticed in the regular materials.

7. **Watch for any unintended biases in your own classroom practices.**

EXAMPLES
- Do you group students by sex for certain activities?
- Do you tend to call on one sex or the other for certain answers, boys for math and girls for poetry, for example?

8. **Look for ways in which your school may be limiting the options open to male or female students.**

EXAMPLES
- What advice is given by guidance counselors to students in course selection and career decisions?
- Is there a good sports program for both girls and boys?

9. **Be tolerant of teen-age fads as long as they do not offend others or interfere with learning.**

EXAMPLES
- No strict dress or hair codes.
- Discussion of the purposes of fads of earlier eras.

10. **Give students realistic feedback about themselves.**

EXAMPLES
- Point out how their behavior produces certain consequences.
- In addition to grading, comment on the strengths and weaknesses in their work.

*Not only should blatant and subtle sexual stereotypes be avoided, but positive examples showing full and friendly equality of the sexes should be presented whenever possible.*

*(Reprinted with permission of Macmillan Publishing Co., Inc. from Who Can? by Florence Perry Heide and Sylvia Worth Van Clief. (Series r, The New Macmillan Reading Program—Carl B. Smith and Ronald Wardhaugh, Senior Authors.) Copyright © 1975 Macmillan Publishing Co., Inc.)*

**The Role of Formal Operations**

The process of identity formation may only begin in the school years. Formal operations may be needed to complete the process (Leadbeater and Dionne, 1981; Marcia, 1980). Erikson himself sees a role for formal operations in the identity formation of the young person, since the person must choose "from among all the possible and imaginable relations" that are available (Erikson, 1968, p. 245). And as we have seen, the stage of formal operations is not always achieved in school. Like formal operations, identity formation may be an extended process.

The educational experience of the junior and senior high school years can provide a foundation not only for the formation of identity, but also for the later achievement of intimacy, generativity, and integrity. Let us turn briefly to these last three stages before we leave our discussion of Erikson.

## Beyond the School Years: Intimacy, Generativity, and Integrity

**Intimacy**

The terms intimacy, generativity, and integrity refer to the *quality* of human relations rather than to the roles people perform. The first of these stages is **intimacy v. isolation.** Intimacy in this sense refers to a person's willingness to relate to another person on a deep level, to have a relationship based on more than mutual need and reciprocity. It means giving one's self without asking what will be received in return. Sexual relations are not a necessary part of intimacy. People can be sexually intimate without having the personal commitment called for in true intimacy. However, within a truly intimate relationship, mutual sexual satisfaction can act to increase the closeness of the people involved. Since intimacy calls for the giving of one's self, there is always the fear of being overwhelmed. A person who has not achieved a sufficient sense of identity cannot partake fully of intimacy.

**Generativity**

The alternative at the next stage is **generativity v. self-absorption.** Generativity extends the act of caring beyond a single other person to the needs of the future generations. While generativity sometimes refers to having children, it is probably the broader meaning of the term that should be emphasized. Erikson sees this broader perspective as similar to the Hindu principle of the maintenance of the world. There is a time in the life cycle when death appears realistically certain, rather than a far-off eventuality. A person does best at that time to put aside thoughts of death "and balance its certainty with the only happiness that is lasting: to increase, by whatever is yours to give, the good will and higher order in your sector of the world" (Erikson, 1974, p. 124).

This second view of generativity offers certain implications for the schools. Many students are concerned about the future of the environment and the American dream of equality for all citizens. These issues suggest the importance of looking ahead and leaving behind a world others can enjoy. Encouraging students to appreciate the consequences of today's decisions for the generations to come will help to prepare them for the challenges of generativity v. self-absorption.

Integrity

The last of Erikson's stages is **integrity v. despair.** The number of aged is increasing in our society. As this happens, there is an increasing societal focus on the needs of the elderly and on what it means to be old. Several of the student teachers in our classes have designed social studies units on this theme for junior and senior high school students. Response to these units has been excellent. Such projects can help adolescents prepare for the last task they will face.

Erikson's work provides the most complete and integrated theory of personal and social development throughout life, but there are other more specific areas of study of great importance to teachers. We will look at some of these next.

# UNDERSTANDING AND LIVING WITH OTHERS

Here we will consider several recent directions in research and theorizing on personal and social development. This work does not necessarily contradict the ideas of Erikson, but instead focuses on more specific aspects of the developing individual. We will discuss how people come to understand the feelings and intentions of others. Then we will explore an area that has interested psychologists and philosophers for years: How do people develop a sense of right and wrong? Finally, we will ask how moral thinking relates to behavior and how individuals learn to be helpful and cooperative.

## Social Cognition: Understanding Social Relations

Stages
in
Understanding
Others

Psychologists interested in **social cognition** study questions about "how children conceptualize other people and how they come to understand the thoughts, emotions, intentions, and viewpoints of others" (Shantz, 1975, p. 1). Martin Hoffman (1979) describes four stages in the child's concept of other people. For about the first year, children do not distinguish between themselves and others in their world. Toward the end of the first year, children develop "person permanence" or the awareness that other people are separate physical beings. But children at this stage still believe others have thoughts and feelings identical to their own. During the next two years children move toward an understanding that, in a particular situation, other people have feelings and ideas that are separate from their own. But children are 8 to 12 years old before they fully understand that other people have personal identities, separate life histories, and futures. Around this time in your life you may remember being intrigued with the idea that all the people passing you in cars on a busy street led separate lives filled with unique experiences and that they were the "heroes" in their own "movies."

How do young people develop **empathy,** or the ability to feel an emotion as it is experienced by others? M. L. Hoffman (1978, 1979) suggests that this ability is related to the progression in understanding the separate identities of others described above. Both adults and children respond emotionally to signs of distress in others. But young children do not combine these emotional reactions with an accurate view of the separate life experiences of other people. Very young children may respond to seeing another child hurt as if they had been hurt themselves. As they become aware that other people are separate, the children recognize when others are distressed, but assume that the reactions of others are the same as their own, like the 18-month-old boy who brought his own mother to comfort a crying friend, even though the friend's mother was available to help (M. Hoffman, 1979). As children develop, they become more able to imagine how other people feel in a given situation. By late childhood they are able to respond emotionally not only to the immediate distress of another person, but also to a more abstract notion of the life situation of others. At this point the older child can accurately imagine how others feel, even if the child has not had similar experiences.

Teachers can encourage the development of empathy by allowing students to work and talk together and discuss emotional reactions to various experiences. With children in the later elementary and secondary grades,

*One way to encourage the development of empathy is to allow students to work out minor disputes by themselves. The two students here may emerge from this confrontation with a better appreciation of each other's feelings.*

(The University of Texas at Austin News and Information Service. Photo by J. Godwin)

they also can resist the temptation to settle disputes by quoting rules or acting as a judge, choosing instead to help the combatants see each other's view of the incident.

Understanding
Intention
As childen mature they become more sophisticated in their descriptions of how others feel. Instead of categorizing the emotions of others in broad generalities like "happy," and "sad," or "mad," older children recognize specific feelings such as jealousy, disgust, and nervousness. They also begin to consider the intentions of the other person and how these intentions relate to emotions (N. Gordon, 1981). Understanding intentions also plays a major role in the child's view of right and wrong, as you will see in the next section.

## Moral Development

In a world of rising crime rates and the diminishing influence of traditional sources of moral guidance, the issue of how people develop a sense of right and wrong is more than an interesting question for psychologists. It is a topic of great importance to parents, teachers, and all those who influence the development of children.

Morality and
Discipline Styles
Parents play a major role in moral development. Children are more likely to adopt moral standards if parents discipline them by pointing out the harmful consequences of the child's misbehavior for other people and if the parents show a great deal of affection when they are not disciplining their children. Discipline based on threats and punishment is more likely to lead to a view of morality based on fear of getting caught and being punished (M. Hoffman, 1979). So a parent who threatens a child with, "If I ever catch you again hitting your little brother, I'll whip you so hard you won't sit down for a week!" is teaching the child to be kind only to avoid punishment. In addition, the child may learn that it's OK to hit someone smaller, as long as you don't get "caught," and it's expected for larger people (like parents) to hit smaller people (like their children) when they are angry.

Kohlberg's
Stages
**Stages of Moral Development.**   One of the best-known psychologists in the field of moral development is Lawrence Kohlberg (1963, 1975). Kohlberg has proposed a detailed sequence of stages of moral reasoning and has led the field in studying their evolution. He has divided moral development into three levels: (1) preconventional, where judgment is based solely on a person's own needs and perceptions; (2) conventional, where the expectations of society and law are taken into account; and (3) postconventional, where judgments are based on principles that go beyond specific laws. Each of these three levels is then divided into stages, as in Figure 3–6.

Moral Dilemmas
In numerous studies, Kohlberg has evaluated the moral reasoning of different subjects, both children and adults, by presenting them with hypothetical stories or **moral dilemmas.** These stories describe situations in which a person must make a difficult decision. Actually these are dilemmas that are impossible to solve, situations in which the "rightness" or "wrongness" of any action is questionable. The subjects are then asked what the person in the story should do and why.

One of the most commonly used moral judgment stories can be summarized as follows: A man's wife is dying. There is one drug that could save her, but it is very expensive, and the druggist who invented it will not sell it at a price low enough for the man to buy it. Finally the man gets desperate and considers stealing the drug for his wife. What should he do and why?

## Figure 3–6 Kohlberg's Levels and Stages of Moral Reasoning

**Level 1.** *Preconventional.* Judgment based on personal needs and perceptions and on the physical power of the rule makers.
   **Stage 1.**   Obedience only because of fear of punishment; deference to power
   **Stage 2.**   Meeting own needs and making "fair trades"; the morality of reciprocity.

**Level 2.** *Conventional.* Judgment based on social expectations and the belief that one must be loyal to one's family, group, or nation and maintain the social order.
   **Stage 3.**   Good behavior is the behavior that pleases or helps others; the good-boy/nice-girl orientation.
   **Stage 4.**   Judgment based on respect for authority and a feeling that one must do one's duty, maintain the social order for its own sake, and promote "law and order."

**Level 3.** *Postconventional.* Judgment based on principles that go beyond specific laws or the authority of the people who make the laws.
   **Stage 5.**   Rules based on social consensus; feeling that rules can be changed if there is a good reason; valuing of general individual rights agreed upon by the whole society.
   **Stage 6.**   Decisions based upon self-chosen ethical principles. The principles are abstract and universal, such as justice and equality.

*Adapted from Stages of moral development, © 1958 by Lawrence Kohlberg. **Phi Delta Kappa,** 1975, **61,** 10.*

*Kohlberg's first stage of preconventional moral reasoning holds that stealing is wrong because you might get caught and be punished. This shoplifter is certain that he can pull off the perfect crime. Is his behavior "moral" by any conceivable stretch of the imagination?*

(Sepp Seitz/Woodfin Camp & Associates)

Presented with this story, subjects at different levels are likely to give answers such as these:

*Level 1:* "It's wrong to steal the drug because you might get caught."
*Level 2:* "It's wrong to steal the drug because the law says it is wrong to steal."
*Level 3:* "It's okay to steal the drug because human life must be preserved, but the man may have to face the consequences and go to jail."

**Preconventional Level**

At level 1, the subject seems to be most swayed by the personal results of the action. In deciding whether to tell a parent about an older brother's bad behavior, a young child at level 1 might think: "Well, it may be right to tell because if I don't my mother might find out and spank me. But it may be right to keep quiet, because my brother might find out and beat me up." The "right" thing to do is the action with the most acceptable personal consequence.

**Conventional Level**

At level 2, the subject is able to look beyond the immediate personal results and consider the views of others. A child at this level will generally consider laws, religious or civil, to be of great importance. The fact that laws can change usually is not recognized. It is possible, of course, that the child at this level will agree that the man should steal the drug. The reasoning will generally be that it is all right to do so because the man loves his wife. The child may also begin to take intention into account. Stealing the drug to save his wife may be considered right because of the man's good intentions.

**Postconventional Level**

At level 3, the subject is able to consider the underlying values involved in the decision. It should be no surprise that this type of judgment generally occurs at the time when the young person is capable of formal operations. The ability to look at the current state of affairs as only one of many possible situations applies to laws as well as to physical events.

**The Stage Theory: An Evaluation.** Movement through these stages is based on several changes in children as they mature. Children at level 1 base their judgment on personal consequences because they are unable to put themselves in the role of the other or recognize how other people might feel in the situation. In addition, children are likely to see rules as concrete and absolute. As they develop the ability to be empathetic and to use formal operational thinking, children are able to see the perspectives of others and imagine other bases for rules. Kohlberg believes that we move from one stage to another to resolve the cognitive conflict experienced when we are exposed to higher stages of moral reasoning in particular situations. So equilibration and social interaction play important roles in moral development.

**Criticisms of Kohlberg**

Kohlberg's stage theory has been criticized on several points. First, the stages do not seem to be separate and sequenced. People often give reasons for moral choices that reflect several different stages simultaneously. Second, the ordering of the stages reflects two biases. More women than men are identified as being at stage 3 versus stage 4, partly because women tend to value pleasing others and being merciful. These qualities are seen as representing lower levels of moral reasoning (Gilligan, 1977). Stage 6 reasoning is biased in favor of Western libertarian values that emphasize individualism. In cultures that are more family- and group-centered, the highest moral level might involve putting the opinions of the group ahead of decisions based on individual conscience. In recent years, Kohberg has questioned the inclusion of stage 6. Very few people, other than trained philosophers, reason naturally at this level. The controversy over these issues continues today (Reimer, Paolitto and Hersh, 1983).

**Implications for Teachers.**    You may well be wondering what implications this discussion of moral development has for the teacher. These ideas may help you deal with student opinions when moral questions come up in class. Certain issues arise in most classrooms — cheating, bullying, and the destruction of school property, among others. Knowing that students are likely to have different views about right and wrong may help you in these situations.

Role of Teachers

Some educators believe schools should help students develop higher levels of moral reasoning. Classroom discussion of moral dilemmas is one method for achieving this goal. The best dilemmas are those that have or might arise in the class. What should be done about stealing, fights, and the abuse of privileges? The following is an example of how one teacher used the events of the week for discussion:

> [The teacher] decided that at the end of each week the children would discuss a slice of moral life from their classroom. During the week, they were invited to complete a sentence written on a chart at the front of the room: "This was the week when _____." On Friday, the class eagerly discussed the chart's various entries: e.g. "there were fights on the morning bus," "someone had money taken," "Mrs. _____ kept the projector too long and we couldn't see the movie because you had to send it back." . . . talking about in-school problems led children to raise dilemmas from their lives outside school. . . . (Reimer, Paolitto and Hersh, 1983, pp. 122–123)

During the discussion of moral dilemmas, students are likely to encounter challenges from other students that will create disequilibrium and cause them to examine their own moral reasoning. Students can be helped to see many sides of an issue and possibly to move to a higher stage of moral reasoning. Teachers may attempt to encourage this movement by presenting conflicting arguments based on reasoning one stage above that being used by the students (following Kohlberg's scheme). This technique is called "plus-one matching" (Lockwood, 1978). Generally, however, the teacher's role is to lead the discussion. The students are the ones who should talk, give reasons, and respond to other students. The discussion group should be small. If necessary, ask students to respond to each other's ideas. To keep the discussion organized, list student opinions and reasons (Lickona, 1977).

Research on
Moral Education

In summarizing the research on moral dilemmas in the classroom, Lockwood (1978) draws two conclusions. First, he finds that the direct discussion approach (with or without plus-one matching) generally produces significant development in moral reasoning, at least in some students. The success of the approach varies greatly from student to student. Second, he finds that changes seem most likely at Kohlberg's second and third stages. Students already at stage 4 or above are less likely to change.

It is important to distinguish between moral reasoning (what the person says should be done and why) and moral action (what the person would actually do). The reasons given for a particular action may not be related to actual behavior and decision making (Wonderly and Kupfermid, 1980). For example, in one study 15 percent of students at the postconventional level of reasoning cheated on a task. Fifty-five percent of students at the conventional

Reasoning v.
Behaving

level and 70 percent of the students at the preconventional level also cheated (Kohlberg, 1975). The fact that some students at the postconventional (principled) level cheated suggests there is more to moral action than simply reasoning about what is right. In the next section we will consider what factors influence **prosocial behavior,** those actions that are benefical to others and to social relationships.

## Prosocial Behaviors

What does influence people to behave in positive ways? We cannot look at every type of behavior, but we will explore two issues of great interest to teachers: honesty, and dealing with aggressive impulses.

Who Cheats?

**Honesty.**     Results of research on cheating in school have led to several fairly consistent conclusions. Whether or not people will cheat depends more on the situation than on the personality of the individual, although individuals seem to have a general tendency to act honestly or dishonestly in similar situations (R. Burton, 1963). A student who cheats in math class is probably more likely to cheat in other classes, but may never consider lying to a friend or taking candy from the local grocery store. However, most students will cheat if the pressure to perform well is great and the chances of being caught are slim.

As children grow older, there is a stronger relationship between beliefs about the value of honesty and behavior in real situations (Staub, 1979). There are few sex differences in actual behavior. When asked why students cheat, the 1100 high school subjects in a study by Schab (1980) listed three reasons: (1) too lazy to study; (2) fear of failure; (3) parental insistence on grades. The students in this study were very pessimistic about the incidence of cheating. Both boys and girls in the survey believed that over 97 percent of their peers had cheated at one time or another. This estimate may be high and depends on how cheating is defined.

The Role of Models

**Aggression.**     **Aggression** is not to be confused with assertiveness, which is the clear asserting of a legitimate right. Helen Bee (1981) gives this example of the difference between the two types of behavior: "A child who says, 'That's my toy!' is showing assertiveness. If he bashes his playmate over the head to reclaim it, he has shown aggression" (p. 350). Learning by watching others plays an important role in the expression of aggression. Albert Bandura and his colleagues have demonstrated repeatedly that children will be generally more aggressive after watching others act aggressively (Bandura, Ross and Ross, 1963). (The details of these studies are reported in Chapter 5.)

One very real source of aggressive models is found in almost every home in America — television. Over 90 percent of the households in this country have more than one television set. The average child watches three to four hours per day (Moody, 1980). The effects of this intensive exposure have been hotly debated, as you can see in Box 3–2.

What Can Teacher's Do?

The most obvious thing teachers can do to discourage aggression is to present a nonaggressive model. There are a number of other factors to keep in mind with young children. If the school environment provides too few favorite toys, students are more likely to grab from each other, leading to

## BOX 3–2 TV VIOLENCE

Anyone who has watched television knows that violence is a part of many programs. The average dramatic show has about 8 acts of physical violence per hour, while children's cartoons may have anywhere from 20 to 30 incidents per hour (Gerber and Gross, 1974). In most programs the heroes are just as likely as the villains to use force for solving problems, and these solutions bring rewards. In cartoons, violence seems to have no real, permanent consequences. Wile E. Coyote in the Roadrunner cartoons returns no matter how many times he is squashed by boulders, flattened by trucks, incinerated, or hurled from cliffs (Bee, 1981).

But does all this violence have any effect on the children who watch TV for hours each day? Many psychologists, parents, and teachers say "yes." Some research has shown that children who watch more television are more violent in their play (Liebert and Schwartzberg, 1977) and have more positive attitudes about violence as a way to deal with problem situations (Dominick and Greenberg, 1972). Teachers and parents believe they see the effects of TV violence in children's behavior. For example, the following statement appeared in an article on television in *The New York Times* "Spring Education Supplement":

"I can spot the heavy TV viewers right away," said Alison Stopford, a kindergarten teacher for 20 years, first in Britain and now in the Central School in Mamaroneck, N.Y. "They are usually the children whose play is copied from TV superheroes—the ones you see standing on top of the tables with towels or aprons tied around their necks as capes like Batman has. They do a lot of aimless punching and shouting. The heavy viewers are often the ones who can't sit still and listen to a story without squirming and interrupting incessantly. But if I put on a film, they will sit motionless and stare at it." (Moody, 1980, p. 17)

Still, the observations of teachers or reports of correlations between television viewing and violent play do not prove that watching TV *causes* children to be more violent. In one study that actually controlled the TV viewing of a large group of boys, ages 9 to 15, the researchers found that children who watched more violent programs were no more violent in their actions than those who watched programs without violence (Feshbach and Singer, 1971). But these were short-term effects. Perhaps there are subtle, long-range effects of viewing violence on TV. It is a complex issue, but it is possible that television violence has adverse effects on certain individuals under specific conditions. For example, children whose parents applaud the violent solutions to problems seen on television may encourage their children to "learn" from the TV.

verbal and physical fights. If there is too little play space, students are more likely to trip over one another or shove, leading again to conflict. (Bandura, 1973; Shantz and Voydanoff, 1973). Certain activities and toys, such as stories about cowboys and Indians, toy guns, and soldiers, seem to encourage children to play more aggressively (Roedell, Slaby and Robinson, 1976). Figure 3–7 presents some other ideas about helping younger students cope with aggressive impulses.

**Figure 3–7    Suggestions for Encouraging Presocial Behaviors**

1. Discuss the way certain actions might affect other people's feelings.
2. Emphasize the similarities among people.
3. Suggest specific ways in which students can be cooperative and helpful.
4. Set up situations where students are likely to cooperate and help each other; group projects and group incentives are among the many possibilities.
5. Provide examples of sharing, helping, and cooperating.
6. Provide enough space and materials so that students can work without competing for resources.
7. Do not allow an aggressor to benefit from aggressive acts.
8. Model a reasoned and cooperative approach to social conflict.
9. Discuss and demonstrate nonaggressive problem solving methods at times when aggression is *not* taking place.
10. Step between the aggressor and the victim. Comfort the victim while ignoring the aggressor. (This applies only with small children.)

Adapted from W. C. Roedell, R. G. Slaby, and H. B. Robinson, *Social development in young children: A report for teachers.* National Institute of Education, U.S. Department of Health, Education, and Welfare, Washington, D.C., 1976, pp. 7–18.

# EDUCATION FOR EMOTIONAL GROWTH

Changing Views about Affective Education

Educational goals have fluctuated greatly over the years. At times, the emphasis has been solely on cognitive outcomes. At other times, there has been an equal concern with social and affective, or emotional, outcomes (Shavelson, Hubner and Stanton, 1976). Early in the century there was a strong emphasis on cognitive achievement which Callahan (1962) has called the "cult of efficiency." Emphasis shifted in the 1930s to a concern with social and affective learning (Aiken, 1942). Then came Sputnik and a flurry of interest in teaching the basics, especially mathematics and science (Bruner, 1960). The 1960s brought criticism of teaching the intellect while ignoring the feelings of the "whole person." As a result, personal and social development were once again included in the curriculum. In the late 1970s, reports of declining achievement-test scores and high school graduates who could not read, write, or calculate brought the cry "back to basics" (Armbruster, 1977). In 1975, four out of five Americans polled in the annual Gallup Poll of attitudes toward public schools believed that schools should teach something about morals and moral behavior. Although what constituted moral behavior varied from conservative concern with respect for authority to liberal concern with human rights, the majority of the American public agreed that moral education belonged in the classroom. Critics of affective education raised several issues, including: (1) schools should stick to cognitive goals and leave affective education to the family; (2) the most significant values schools can teach are those already present in the traditional curriculum, such as those placed on knowledge and academic achievement. How do today's teachers feel?

## What Do Teachers Think?

A recent study by Richard Prawat and his colleagues asked this question (Prawat, Anderson, Diamond, McKeague and Whitmer, 1981). The researchers interviewed 40 elementary school teachers from 24 schools to determine what teachers really believe about encouraging personal and social development in schools and how their thinking influences their behavior. By asking the teachers a series of indirect and probing questions, then analyzing the 3600 pages of interview transcripts, Prawat reached these conclusions: (1) Over twice as many teachers emphasized affective as opposed to cognitive goals. The affective goals included interpersonal skills, independence, self-discipline, responsibility, self-worth, self-understanding, enthusiasm for learning, and "manners." (2) Most teachers judged how good their day had been based on affective accomplishments such as getting everyone to cooperate and participate enthusiastically in the activities of the day. (3) When teachers described their ideal student, they stressed personal qualities (eager, self-motivated, sets high standards, and well behaved but not too "good" or conforming) as much as academic abilities. (4) The teachers' views about the importance of personal and social development were related to their behavior. For example, teachers who emphasized independence had fewer class rules about when and how to move around the room. Teachers who were most concerned about self-worth had fewer quietness rules.

**Elementary Teachers Emphasize Affective Goals** *(margin note)*

## What Do Teachers Do?

A second goal of Prawat's study was to identify the strategies most often used to encourage personal development. The most frequent approach involved group discussions of ideas, feelings, or problems. Next, teachers relied on rewards and praise to encourage interpersonal skills, cooperation, independence, and so on. Many teachers tried to foster feelings of self-worth in small ways, such as meeting students at the door when they came to class. Some commercially prepared materials were used to teach lessons on affective goals directly, and these goals were also incorporated into academic lessons.

**Emotions and Thinking** *(margin note)*

The teachers in Prawat's study worked with elementary school children and may have been more focused on emotional and social development than subject specialists in high schools. But these elementary teachers believe that both social-emotional and cognitive development should receive attention in schools. In practice, it is very difficult to separate emotions from thinking.

> In psychological works the distinction often made between cognitive and social-emotional processes is a simplistic convenience not in accord with actual psychological functioning. . . . This point was noted by Piaget (1967) as he discussed the inseparability of cognition and affectivity. He suggested that affectivity provides the energetic component to cognitive processes. The message behind this material is clear: the prudent educator is interested not only in cognitive processes but also in affectivity. (N. Gordon, 1981, pp. 136–137)

Where do you stand? Should moral behavior be taught in classrooms, or by people outside the school such as parents? Is affective education a frill or an inseparable part of all learning? If you decide to include specific lessons on personal and social development in your teaching, there are many factors to keep in mind. We have listed several in the Guidelines given here.

# *Guidelines*

## *Judging an Affective Education Program*

**1. Moral education programs should help students examine the kinds of dilemmas they are currently facing or will face in the near future.**

**EXAMPLES**
- In elementary school, discussions of rivalries with siblings, teasing, stealing, prejudice, treatment of new students in the class, behavior toward handicapped classmates.
- In high school, discussions of cheating, letting friends drive when they are intoxicated, conforming to be more popular, protecting a friend who has broken a rule.

**2. Programs should help students see the perspectives of others.**

**EXAMPLES**
- Ask students to describe their understanding of the views of another, then have the other person confirm or correct the perception.
- Have students exchange roles and try to "become" the other person in a discussion.

**3. Help students make connections between expressed values and actions.**

**EXAMPLES**
- Follow discussion of "What should be done'?" with "How would you act? What would be your first step? What problems might arise?"
- Help students see inconsistencies between their values and their own actions.

**4. Safeguard the privacy of all participants.**

**EXAMPLES**
- Remind students that they can "pass" and not answer questions in a discussion.
- Intervene if peer pressure is forcing a student to say more that he or she wants to.
- Don't reinforce a pattern of telling "secrets."

**5. Make sure students listen to each other.**

**EXAMPLES**
- Keep groups small.
- Be a good listener yourself and recognize students who pay careful attention to each other.

**6. As much as possible, your class (and ideally, the school) should reflect concern for moral issues and values.**

**EXAMPLES**
- Make clear distinctions between rules based on administrative convenience (keeping the room orderly) and rules based on moral issues (respecting the privacy of others).
- Enforce standards uniformly. Be careful about showing favoritism.

*Adapted from J. W. Eiseman, What criteria should public school moral education programs meet? The Review of Education, 1981, pp. 226–227.*

## SUMMARY

1. The work of Erik Erikson offers a comprehensive theory of emotional development from infancy to old age. Erikson believes that people go through eight stages, each of which involves a central developmental crisis that must be resolved. Adequate resolution of the crisis leads to increased personal and social competence and a stronger foundation for solving future crises.

2. According to Erikson, in infancy a person needs to develop both a sense of trust and a sense of autonomy. In early childhood and in the preschool or kindergarten years, the focus is on the development of a sense of initiative. The elementary years are devoted to the need to achieve a sense of industry. In the secondary school years, the student begins to focus on a sense of identity.

3. Three important aspects of establishing an identity involve the individual's physical characteristics, self-concept, and sex role.

4. Research seems to indicate that maturing more quickly than others in the same grade is a social plus for boys, but a social disadvantage for girls. Some of the physical changes that take place in adolescence cause problems for both girls and boys.

5. Our concept of ourselves changes as we mature, becoming increasingly complex and abstract, but it is not a unified or stable notion. Instead, our self-concept has many dimensions, based upon different roles and situations.

6. Although differences in the behavior of males and females have been identified, it is not yet clear whether these differences are a result of biology, socialization, or perhaps a combination of both. Research has documented several ways in which males and females are treated differently beginning in infancy.

7. Teachers can play a major role in the resolution of the identity crisis. Establishing a firm identity, which may or may not be completed within the school years, plays an important role in the three final stages in Erikson's theory, where the focus is on intimacy, generativity, and integrity.

8. Children pass through several stages in their conception of other people, moving from a belief that everyone has thoughts and feelings identical to their own to an appreciation of the separate identities of others.

9. Lawrence Kohlberg's theory of moral development includes three levels: (1) a preconventional level where judgments are based on self-interest; (2) a conventional level where judgments are based on social expectations; and (3) a postconventional level where judgments are based on more abstract ethical principles.

10. Over the years the focus in education has shifted back and forth from an emphasis on cognitive goals to an attempt to include more affective goals. Today's teachers, at least at the elementary school level, believe affective goals should be a part of schooling.

## KEY TERMS

psychosocial theory

developmental crisis

trust v. mistrust

autonomy v. doubt

initiative v. guilt

industry v. inferiority

identity v. role diffusion

self-concept

identity achievement

foreclosure

identity diffusion

moratorium

androgynous

intimacy v. isolation

generativity v. self-absorption

integrity v. despair

social cognition

empathy

moral dilemmas

prosocial behavior

aggression

# SUGGESTIONS FOR FURTHER READING AND STUDY

PRAWAT, R. S. Teacher perceptions of student affect. *American Educational Research Journal,* 1980, *17,* 61–73. This study reports results of interviews with 84 elementary school teachers who describe their perceptions of significant classroom situations that involve students' feelings and affective behaviors.

ERIKSON, E. *Childhood and society* (2nd ed.). New York: W. W. Norton, 1963. In this book, which is not at all dry or "theoretical," you will find a complete description of Erikson's ideas about personal and social development.

ERIKSON, E. *Identity, youth, and crisis.* New York: W. W. Norton, 1968. If you are teaching any of the secondary grades, you may find this book on the adolescent's search for a personal identity especially rewarding.

KASH, M. M. and BORICH, G. *Teacher behavior and pupil self-concept.* Reading, Mass.: Addison-Wesley, 1978. This volume offers a very thorough look at the practical research that has been done on how teachers can influence the self-concepts of their students. Each chapter ends with a list of recommendations for teachers.

LICKONA, T. How to encourage moral development. *Learning,* March, 1977. Lickona's brief article includes descriptions of many practical methods teachers can use to encourage moral development.

REIMER J., PAOLITTO, D. P., and HERSH, R. H. *Promoting moral development: From Piaget to Kohlberg* (2nd. ed.). New York: Longman, 1983. This book has a full explanation of both Piaget's and Kohlberg's theories plus several chapters on how to apply the theories in teaching.

RUBIN, Z. *Children's friendships.* Cambridge, Mass.: Harvard University Press, 1980. This book is a combination of current theoretical perspectives on the development of friendships and lively examples, often in the words of the children themselves.

SHAVELSON, R. J. and BOLUS, R. Self-concept: The interplay of theory and method. *Journal of Educational Psychology,* 1982, *74,* 3–17. Read this article for a complete explanation of the many factors that may influence self-concept.

# Teachers' Forum

## Withdrawn Students

Because they do not cause any problems, withdrawn children are often ignored in the classroom. When you have students in your class who are social isolates, how do you help them make friends and become members of the classroom group?

**Encouraging Involvement**

The first step is to "emphasize the positive" and help them develop feelings of self-worth by showing recognition and appreciation for their obvious strengths with both concrete and abstract praise. Arrange seating in clusters so children can work together with partners who share and supplement skills and abilities. Establish committees or informal groups to accomplish preestablished goals (bulletin boards, science projects, bookbinding, and so on). Be sure outside play is organized so all children can be included in an activity. Request the help of principal, custodian, parents—anyone available—to have positive, rewarding contacts with these children so they will feel more comfortable about taking the risks involved in establishing contacts with significant others and participating in living.

Joan H. Low, Fifth-Grade Teacher
*Russell Elementary School, Hazelwood, Missouri*

## Group Rivalry

Imagine you are facing this situation in your class. Recently a definite rivalry has been developing between two groups of students in the class. Each group is like a club. Members dress alike, talk alike, and even seem to use the same gestures. The two groups ridicule each other, play tricks on each other, and occasionally there are fights. The fights take place out of class, but many of the tricks take place in class and are becoming increasingly disruptive and even cruel. What approach would you take? Would you emphasize classroom order, defusing the rivalry, or both?

**Dealing with the Group Leaders**

I must first ask myself: "How involved do I want to get? Will I be getting in over my head if I attempt to solve the broader problem?" With these questions answered, it seems that I could successfully defuse the rivalry through classroom action. First, I would privately appeal to the leaders in both groups. By acknowledging their influence and asking for their help, I would hope to gain their support. This is really nothing more than ego seduction. With them on my side, I could then focus on team building through group goals and possibly even discuss their rivalry in class without the risk of a showdown.

Jim Malanowski, Secondary Social Studies Teacher
*West High School, Columbus, Ohio*

# Queen Kong

Imagine that one of the students in your class is very large. In fact, she's obese. The other students are merciless in their teasing, calling her Queen Kong among many other clever but heartless names. The girl is miserable but doesn't seem to know how to make friends or cope with the teasing. She is, however, a very good student and seems very eager to please you, the teacher. What steps, if any, would you take to help this student? What, if anything, would you say to the rest of the class?

**A Step-by-Step Approach**

I would first try to help this girl gain some self-confidence by asking her to help me correct some papers or do a bulletin board display in my classroom during her free time. I would then ask her to help another student in the class who is not doing very well (peer tutoring), perhaps a girl who I know would be nice to her and who may strike up a friendship with her on the basis of mutual need. I would then plan a few small group activities in the class in which it would be advantageous to have someone who is a good student in the group. I would only say something to the class if on a given day the girl was not in class. I might point out that everyone has strong and weak points and that we should make an effort to overlook the weak points of a person, whether they be physical or personality, and admire them for their strong points.

Kristine C. Bloom, Secondary French Teacher
*Tonawanda High School, Tonawanda, New York*

**A Parallel with Ethnic Discrimination**

I would try to keep contact with the girl without neglecting the rest of the class. I would also reinforce her strong points and try to point out any ways in which she could share them with others in the class. In most classes, it would be embarrassing to confront her problem directly in class. I had a home room where a skinny, homely retarded boy was laughed at and mocked by a group led by a large, handsome football player. In English class, we studied a story about an Indian boy who was discriminated against and I asked each student to put himself in the place of the Indian. "How would it feel," I asked, "to be laughed at for something you had no control over and could not change?" Then I asked several students for their reactions, including the football player. Never again has he mocked or laughed at the retarded boy in home room.

Bonnie Everett, Secondary French and English Teacher
*Ottawa-Glandorf High School, Ottawa, Ohio*

**A Focus on Tolerance and Individual Guidance**

There are two basic problems that need attention [the class's attitude and the girl's inability to cope]. Class discussion and/or human relation experiments on tolerance of individual differences might be helpful. Included in this could be self-inventories and positive reactions to other individuals. Queen Kong herself needs individual guidance in coping skills. During class it might improve self-image and peer relationships if the teacher would put this student in a leadership role and provide verbal reinforcement when appropriate. A conference with the school nurse and parents might help set the scene for proper diet and weight loss over a period of time.

Darline Reynolds, Junior High School Teacher
*Spirit Lake Junior High School, Spirit Lake, Iowa*

# 4

# Individual Differences

**OVERVIEW**     Every child is unique. This is a statement both educators and psychologists would affirm. But so far we have talked little about individuals. We have discussed principles of development that apply to everyone — stages, processes, conflicts, and tasks. Because we are human, our development *is* similar in many ways. But not in every way. Even within the same family there are marked contrasts among members in appearance, interests, abilities, and temperament. Some people learn very quickly in school. Others are not interested in learning. Where do such wide-ranging differences originate, and what do they mean for teachers? These are the questions we will consider now.

In this chapter we examine the roles of heredity and environment in creating differences among individuals. After a brief discussion of how characteristics are transmitted genetically from parents to children, we consider the concept of heritability. Next we turn to the effects of environment and the influences of social class, culture, and the family on the child, as well as the effect of the child on the family. The second half of the chapter focuses on three types of differences among individuals: intellectual ability, creativity, and cognitive style. Many other categories of variation exist, but these were selected because they are particularly significant in classrooms.

In discussing the many ways individuals vary, we hope to communicate two important messages. First, the number of abilities, styles, behaviors, and characteristics that fall within the normal range of human functioning is great. Too often adults, particularly teachers, are quick to label a child as "abnormal" in some way. Each individual's combination of heredity and environment creates a unique pattern of characteristics. Most of the differences among individuals, though great at times, are normal. Second, not all differences among students in school performance are due to differences in intelligence or effort. Many other factors, such as cultural differences and cognitive style, play significant roles in shaping classroom behavior and achievement.

When you complete this chapter, you should be able to do the following:

- Discuss the concept of heritability in human development.
- Describe the roles of social class and culture in creating individual similarities and differences.
- Give examples of the likely effects of several childrearing practices.
- Develop a personal concept of the meaning of IQ in teaching.
- List five specific teaching behaviors that might encourage creativity.
- Describe the educational implications of student differences in cognitive style.

Now to our first question. Why are there so many differences among individuals?

## THE ORIGIN OF DIFFERENCES

If you look across the room in any class, you will see a host of individual differences. Even children of approximately the same age vary greatly in appearance, abilities, temperament, interests, and attitudes — to name only a few possibilities. Where do these differences come from? For hundreds of years there has been debate over the importance of nature versus nurture (or heredity versus environment) in creating human variation. Until fairly recently, it was difficult even to consider this question scientifically because little was known about behavior genetics, the study of genetic factors involved in characteristics such as intelligence, musical ability, or moods. Even with modern methods for studying the question, we are far from definite answers. The more we learn, the more complex the phenomena appear.

## Methods for Studying Differences

To determine the influences of heredity and environment on plants or animals, scientists can use techniques like selective breeding, special diet, and controlled environments. But people are not likely to cooperate in such "experiments." To study the roles of heredity and environment in humans, scientists have relied on methods like comparing the similarities between identical twins (who developed from the same original egg and sperm and thus have identical genes) and fraternal twins (who developed from two different eggs fertilized by separate sperm). Other psychologists have studied identical twins who were separated and reared in different families, twins in the same family who were given different experiences, and children in adoptive or foster homes (Buss and Poley, 1976; Willerman, 1979).

Each of these approaches has problems. Identical twins are not only genetically the same, they also tend to be treated very similarly by the family and others. You may have known families that seemed to consider their two children to be one unit. ("Here comes Nancy with the twins." "The twins hate to visit the dentist.") Because they were born at the same time, fraternal twins have more similar experiences than regular siblings born several years apart. It is difficult to separate the effects of being treated similarly or having the same experiences from the effects of heredity. Sometimes adoption agencies try to "match" the adoptive parents to the biological parents, confusing the picture when adopted children are studied. The result is that our information about human behavior genetics is far from perfect.

## Hereditary Factors

At conception, 23 **chromosomes** from your mother and 23 from your father came together to give you the 46 chromosomes you have in almost every cell of your body. These chromosomes carry the information that determines many of your characteristics — your sex, height, blood type, whether you will become bald, and perhaps other qualities such as abilities and temperament. Each chromosome has about 20,000 **genes**. The gene is the basic unit of heredity and carries biochemical information from one generation to the next.

Certain characteristics — eye color for example — can be determined by a single pair of genes, one from the mother and one from the father. The gene for certain eye colors such as brown is *dominant* meaning that this gene determines eye color no matter what the other gene is in the pair. The gene for other eye colors such as blue is *recessive*, meaning it will not determine eye color unless the other gene in the pair is for blue eyes as well. As you can see in Figure 4–1, even this simple relationship between two genes can have complicated results.

Behavior Genetics

Twin Studies

Dominant and Recessive Genes

**119**

Figure 4–1    **Dominant and Recessive Genes and Eye Color**

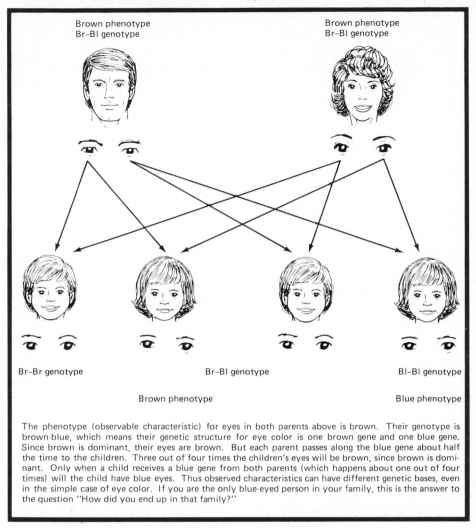

The phenotype (observable characteristic) for eyes in both parents above is brown. Their genotype is brown-blue, which means their genetic structure for eye color is one brown gene and one blue gene. Since brown is dominant, their eyes are brown. But each parent passes along the blue gene about half the time to the children. Three out of four times the children's eyes will be brown, since brown is dominant. Only when a child receives a blue gene from both parents (which happens about one out of four times) will the child have blue eyes. Thus observed characteristics can have different genetic bases, even in the simple case of eye color. If you are the only blue-eyed person in your family, this is the answer to the question "How did you end up in that family?"

Phenotype v.
Genotype

This discussion of dominant and recessive genes brings up an important distinction in genetics, the difference between phenotype and genotype. **Phenotype** is the actual characteristic or behavior we observe in an individual—eye color or artistic ability, for example. But the **genotype** is the individual's underlying genetic makeup. You cannot be sure of a person's genetic structure by studying outward appearances. Two brown-eyed people may have the same or different genetic codes for eye color, as you can see in Figure 4–1.

Most human characteristics are more complicated than eye color. Even characteristics that seem straightforward, such as height, are influenced by more than one pair of genes. When many genes influence a particular characteristic, the phenomenon is called **polygenetic inheritance.** The influences on intelligence, talents, dispositions, and temperament are polygenetic. Each gene adds a note to produce the final symphony (Morris, 1982).

Your experience tells you there is great variation in the phenotypic or observable expression of many human characteristics, from foot size to singing voice. How much of this outward variation is due to genotypic or genetic differences among individuals? The answer to this question for certain characteristics can be expressed as a **heritability ratio.** This term means the proportion of the variation occurring in a particular characteristic that is due to genetic differences. With animals or plants, heritability ratios can be determined by controlling environmental conditions and observing differences over several generations. Heritability can vary from 0.00 (none of the variance is due to heredity) to 1.00 (all of the variance is due to heredity).

With people, heritability ratios must be estimated based on the methods described earlier. Scientists have also learned about the role of heredity and environment from the experiences of children born without particular senses (sight or hearing, for example). But agreement on heritability is seldom perfect. For example, depending on who did the calculating, you may see the heritability of intelligence as .80, .70, .50, or even .40 (Gleitman, 1981).

As you encounter heritability figures such as those above, you should keep several cautions in mind (Buss and Poley, 1976). First, the figures themselves refer to the relative contribution of heredity for the population as a whole, and *not* for particular individuals. Both heredity and environment are 100 percent necessary to produce a given characteristic in a particular individual. Small changes in any number of factors could have caused large changes in the outcome. Second, even behavior that is 100 percent heritable may be modifiable by changes in environment. For example, the genetic disorder commonly called PKU disease (discussed in Chapter 13) causes severe mental retardation. This retardation is completely genetic in origin, but the effects can be minimized or even eliminated if the disorder is detected early enough. So "inheritable" does not mean "unchangeable." Third, heritability is a relative concept. The ratio determined applies only for the particular population and conditions being studied. This means that comparisons across different races or very different environmental conditions are not appropriate.

## The Role of the Environment

Many environmental factors influence individuals, some beginning before birth. Different experiences are available to people, depending on income, status, cultural group, sex, and education. In addition, every family creates a different environment for its members.

**Socioeconomic Differences.** **Socioeconomic status,** or **SES,** is the term used by sociologists for variations in wealth, power, and prestige. Most researchers identify three levels of SES—upper, middle, and lower. These levels may be defined somewhat differently from one study to the next, so a person who is labeled lower class in one study might be called middle class in another. No single variable, not even income, is an effective measure of SES.

*(Paul Conklin/Monkmeyer Press Photo Service)*

*This stark classroom in Appalachia is an example of the limited educational resources often available to the rural poor in our country. There is no computer-assisted instruction in this school.*

Backman (1972) describes an index of SES that reflects father's education and occupation, mother's education, family income, the value of the home, and the specific facilities and economic goods in the home, such as a television, radio, and typewriter. But it is rare to find SES so carefully defined in research; keep this in mind when you read about SES differences in studies.

As you will see when we discuss types of individual differences, there are many relationships between SES and variations among individuals. For example, it is well documented that higher SES students of all ethnic groups show higher average levels of achievement on test scores (Backman, 1972), receive better grades, and stay in school longer than low SES students. The correlation between socioeconomic status and achievement in grade 6 is about .50 (Loehlin, Lindzey, and Spuhler, 1979).

Effects of SES    What effects of low status might explain the poorer school achievement of many low SES students, besides the obvious economic problems of limited income? Being labeled lower class makes life more difficult. People of higher status generally command a greater portion of the group's resources. Children of poverty see that they cannot easily attain the advantages of their middle-class peers. Others may respond to them in terms of class rather than individual worth. Self-esteem may be affected adversely. Adjustment to school may be more difficult for these children, since schools tend to value and expect the behaviors more often taught in middle-class homes.

**Cultural Differences.**    There are many definitions of **culture.** Most include a view of culture as the rules, expectations, attitudes, beliefs, and values that guide behavior in a particular group of people. Culture involves a total life style. In the United States, we have not one but many cultures. Students growing up in a small rural town in the Deep South are part of a different cultural group, in many ways, from students in a large urban center or students in a West Coast suburb. All these individuals share many common experiences and values, especially through television and the mass media, but other aspects of their lives are different, shaped by different ethnic, regional, or language backgrounds.

In what ways might the existence of different cultural groups promote variation among individuals? Within a particular culture, the effect is to encourage similarity among members. But the effect for the population as a whole is to create diversity among people. Each group teaches its members certain "lessons" about living. Cultures differ in (1) rules for how to conduct interpersonal relationships, (2) orientations toward time, (3) view of the ideal personality, (4) ideas about the appropriate relationship between humanity and the rest of the natural world, and (5) the most cherished value (Maehr, 1974). Thus, depending on your cultural background, your views on these subjects may be quite different from the views of many other individuals who also call themselves Americans.

In the five areas listed above, the behaviors and values learned in the child's home and neighborhood may not fit the expectations of the school and its teachers. In general, schools expect and reward the behaviors, attitudes, and abilities fostered by white, middle-class America — the culture of most teachers. Figures 4–2 presents a few examples of potential conflict. But the generalities do not hold for every group or for every individual within a group. What these comparisons should do is give you some idea of the role of culture in creating variations among individuals. As you will see in Chapter 13, there is increasing interest in valuing and preserving these differences instead of trying to create one national culture — the old idea of the "melting pot."

To this point we have been discussing the effects of growing up in particular SES or cultural groups. But there is a problem with these generalizations. In every group there are great differences among individuals. Think about your own neighbors for a moment. Even though they may share your culture and SES background, they probably differ from you in many important ways. Being a member of a particular group cannot magically create certain characteristics in people. Something more direct must happen in the day-to-day life of the individual. In searching for specific factors that influence individual differences, psychologists have often focused on a factor that can have powerful effects — the family.

**Figure 4–2  Some Potential Areas of Cultural Conflict**

| Areas in Which the Culture "Teaches Lessons" | School's Expectation (Majority Culture Belief) | Student's Expectation (Minority Culture Belief) |
|---|---|---|
| Interpersonal relationship | Students will compete and value individual accomplishment. | Students will help each other; the group, not the individual, is the source of accomplishment (many Native American and Mexican-American groups). |
| Orientation toward time | Plan for the future, work, and save now for a better future for yourself. | Focus on the present, trust the cultural group to provide for the future (certain native American tribes); or Value the past, tradition, and ancestors (certain Oriental cultures). |
| Valued personality type | Busy. | Methodical, relaxed, meditative (some Oriental and Mexican-American cultures). |
| Relationship of humanity to nature | Control nature, use technology to "improve" nature. | One with nature, respect and live with nature (native Americans). |
| Most cherished values | Individual freedom. | Loyalty to the group and tradition (certain Oriental cultures). |

*Adapted from M. L. Maehr.* **Sociocultural origins of achievement.** *Monterey, Calif.: Brooks/Cole, 1974.*

Development of Competence

**Childrearing Practices.**  Since 1965, Burton White and his colleagues at Harvard University have been studying the effects of early experiences on the development of "competence" in young children (White, Kaban, Attanucci, and Shapiro, 1978). White defines competence to include both social and cognitive skills such as getting and maintaining the attention of adults in reasonable and acceptable ways, recognizing when a job is too difficult and securing the right help, expressing both affection and annoyance to adults and peers, leading, following, and competing with peers, showing pride in accomplishments, playing make-believe games about adult roles, developing good language abilities, noticing details and discrepancies, planning and anticipating consequences, dealing with abstractions and making interesting associations, carrying out complicated activities, seeing another person's point of view, and paying attention to a task while keeping track of what is happening around you. These abilities characterize competent children as young as 3.

Childrearing practices that encourage these qualities, according to White, include structuring the environment so the child can explore freely and safely without restrictions, being sensitive to the child's needs and interests at a given moment and responding appropriately, recognizing achievement, encouraging curiosity and competitiveness, and talking to the child about topics of immediate interest. These and many other practices were followed by parents of the most competent children (White, 1975; White, Kaban, Attanucci, and Shapiro, 1978).

SES Differences
in Childrearing

Several researchers have observed mothers as they try to help their children perform a task to see if there are differences among SES groups. Studies have shown that higher SES mothers talk more, give more verbal guidance, help their children see reasons, make plans, and anticipate consequences, direct their children's attention to the relevant details in a problem, and generally encourage the child to solve the problem rather than imposing a solution (Willerman, 1979). These interaction styles may account for some of the differences among children from various SES groups.

One of the most extensive studies of childrearing practices has been directed by Diana Baumrind, who for two decades has studied parental discipline styles. Her research has identified three types of parents. Figure 4–3 shows these three categories and the associated characteristics of the children.

Each family is different from others in many ways. Even within a particular family, the experiences of one child will not be like those of siblings. Research has found quite a few differences among children, based on their position in the family. For example, first-born children tend to be more oriented toward adults, self-controlled, conforming, anxious, fearful of failure, studious, and passive than later-born children (Hetherington and Parke, 1979). Before you decide that first-borns are "cursed" by their position in the family, you should know that first-borns also tend to be high achievers. They are more likely to earn high scores on intelligence tests, make good grades in college, be National Merit Scholars, or be cited in *Who's Who* (Hilgard, Atkinson and Atkinson, 1979).

Birth-Order
Differences

The picture is less clear for later-born children. Their experiences may vary greatly, depending on the number of older and younger children and the family situation. There are tendencies for middle children to be more extroverted and less achievement-oriented than first-borns, while the often indulged "baby" of the family has many of the advantages of first-borns with few of the problems. These last children are high achievers, popular with friends, and more optimistic, secure, and confident than first-borns (Hetherington and Parke, 1979). Of course, all these characteristics are true for large-group comparisons only; many individuals do not fit these descriptions.

## Figure 4–3    Parental Discipline Styles

| Type | Parents' Behavior and Characteristics | Child's Behavior and Characteristics |
|---|---|---|
| Authoritative | Demanding; controlling; communicative; loving; use corporal punishment at times, but generally reward good behavior instead of punishing bad; firm but willing to listen to their children; give explanations for rules; consistent; follow through with threats and promises; not afraid of conflict. | Assertive; self-reliant; self-controlled; content, friendly, cooperative; high self-esteem; high achievers; appropriately disagree with adults. |
| Authoritarian | Controlling; detached; won't listen to child; give orders; use punishment often; enforce rules "because they are the rules"; cold. | Unhappy; withdrawn; distrustful; hostile; low achievers. |
| Permissive | Warm but not demanding or controlling; few rules or punishments; lack confidence in their childrearing skills; inconsistent. | Little self-control or self-reliance; unhappy; boys tend to be low achievers. |

*Adapted from D. Baumrind, The development of instrumental competence through socialization. In A. Pick (Ed.),* **Minnesota Symposium on Child Psychology,** *Vol. 7. Minneapolis: University of Minnesota Press, 1973.*

**Children of Divorce.**    Lately there has been a great deal of interest in studying the effects on children of two particular aspects of family life — divorce and the single-parent home. It is now estimated that 40 percent of current marriages of young adults will end in divorce. As we said in Chapter 1, almost 50 percent of the children born in 1970 will spend some time living in a single-parent family (Hetherington, 1979). Divorce is a stressful event for all participants, even under the best circumstances. The actual separation of the parents may have been preceded by years of conflict in the home, or may come as a shock to all, including friends and children. During the divorce itself, conflict may increase as property and custody rights are being decided. Children may have to cope with angry, tired, anxious parents.

Stresses of Divorce

After the divorce is settled, more changes may disrupt the children's lives. The parent who has custody, still usually the mother, may have to move to a less expensive house, find new sources of income, go to work for the first time, or work longer hours. For the child, this can mean important friendships left behind in the old neighborhood or school, just when support is needed the most. It may mean having only one parent who has less time

*Many young children today live in families touched by divorce. Students who suddenly become moody, easily frustrated, or withdrawn may be experiencing trouble at home.*

than ever to be with the children. Money shortages lead to fewer toys, trips, and less recreation in general. To add to all these adjustments, the childen may be asked to accept their parent's lover or even a new stepparent (Guerney, 1981). Not every situation is the same, of course. In some divorces there are few conflicts, ample resources, and the continuing support of friends and extended family.

Effects of Divorce

Just as no two divorces are the same, the effects of divorce on children vary from one situation to the next. The first two years after the divorce seem to be the hardest for both boys and girls. Long-term adjustment appears to be most difficult for boys. They tend to show a higher rate of behavior and interpersonal problems at home and in school than girls in general or boys from intact families (Hetherington, 1979). But living with one fairly content, if married, parent may be better than living in a conflict-filled situation with two unhappy parents. The Guidelines on the next page offer suggestions for helping students through this difficult time.

**Child Abuse.**    All teachers must be alert to another situation that develops in many families—child abuse. Accurate information about the number of abused children in this country is hard to find; estimates range from 1.4 to 1.9 million children per year. If they receive help, about half of the parents can change, but without assistance probably only about 5 percent improve (Starr, 1979). As a teacher, you must alert your principal, school psychologist, or social worker if you suspect abuse. Many children die each year because no one would "get involved."

# *Guidelines*

## *Helping Children of Divorce*

**1. Notice any sudden changes in behavior that might indicate problems at home.**

**EXAMPLES**
- Repeated headaches or stomach pains, rapid weight gain or loss, fatigue or excess "energy."
- Moodiness, temper tantrums, difficulty in paying attention or concentrating.

**2. Talk with students about their attitude or behavior changes. This may give you an opportunity to find out about unusual stresses, including divorce.**

**EXAMPLES**
- Be a good listener. The students may have no other adult willing to hear their concerns.
- Let the students know you are available for talks.

**3. Don't take aggressive outbursts personally. The student may be very angry at his or her parents, but direct the anger instead at teachers or classmates.**

**EXAMPLES**
- If you must discipline the student, make sure you do so calmly.
- Don't hold a grudge or force an elaborate public apology.

**4. Watch your language to make sure you avoid stereotypes about "happy" (two-parent) homes.**

**EXAMPLES**
- You might simply say "Your families ..." instead of "Your mothers and fathers ..." when addressing the class.
- Statements such as "We need volunteers for room mother," "Your father can fix it for you," or "Get your father to throw you some long passes for practice" may be hard for some students to take.

**5. Help students to maintain their self-esteem.**

**EXAMPLES**
- Recognize a job well done.
- Make sure the student understands assignments and can handle the workload. This generally is not the time to pile on very new and difficult work.

**6. Find out what resources are available at your school.**

**EXAMPLES**
- Talk to the school psychologist, guidance counselor, principal, or social worker about students who seem to need outside help to cope with the situation.
- Consider establishing a "rap group," led by a trained adult, for students going through divorce. Often each child thinks his or her situation and problems are unique.

**7. If necessary, let the parents know about the student's signs of stress. They may be unaware of the effects the divorce is having on their child. Be ready to suggest sources of help.**

The causes of child abuse are complex. The child may be disappointing to the parents (the wrong sex, unattractive, unhealthy, or slow to develop). Parents with unrealistic expectations about how children should behave and people who were disciplined harshly themselves are at greater risk of lashing out against their own children (Berger, 1980). Too often parents attribute adult motivations to the child's behavior, assuming the child is intentionally being difficult, when in fact the child simply does not understand what is expected. But the child's behavior may play a role too, even though he or she does not mean to be difficult. Often parents who abuse one of their children say that the child drove them to the beatings by annoying, persistent, loud crying or other inappropriate behaviors that did not respond to the usual discipline techniques. There is evidence that certain abused children may be especially difficult because even when they are placed in foster homes, these children are abused by foster parents who have not treated children improperly before (Bell, 1979).

We have discussed the effects of many hereditary and environmental factors on children. Now let's try to put these influences together in a more integrated view of the origin of individual differences.

## Current Views: A Complicated Interaction

Human beings are complicated. They are influenced by their environment, but also create and shape that environment. The effects of various experiences depend on so many factors, such as the timing of the event, how long it lasts, what happens next, and the meaning of the event to the individual and the family. The same behaviors on the part of parents seems to have different effects on different children, often in the same family (Bell, 1979).

The temperament of each child (which is biologically determined to a great extent) may influence how parents treat the child and how easily influenced the child actually is. For example, parents of more passive young children may become very protective, particularly if the children are boys and vulnerable in the rough world of other preschool boys. Thus a biologically determined characteristic (passive temperament) helps create a particular environment (protective parenting) that can have lasting effects (Kagan, 1979).

Children can have effects on teachers as well as on parents. For example, students who are nonverbally positive, smile, nod at the teacher, and pay attention are more likely to be seen by the teacher as interested and intelligent. The teacher may feel and act more positively toward them and see

them as more "teachable" (Woolfolk and Brooks, 1983). These students help to create warm, supportive environments for themselves in school. Timing is a key factor as well. A current burning interest will cause one student to make the most of a particular experience when others remain unaffected. A book about the stars for the first author's daughter, purchased immediately after a trip to the Hayden Planetarium, was read with excitement. A similar book received earlier was never opened.

The research on the effects of children on adults has several implications. First, it shows one way heredity and environment interact to produce individual differences. Second, it removes from parents and teachers some of the pressure to create perfect children by always implementing the "right" childrearing strategy. Parents and teachers are not sculptors working with a lump of clay, solely responsible for the product. Instead, parent and child are two powerful human beings, negotiating their relationship day-to-day. Their goals are seldom the same. Parents and teachers must be sensitive to the differences among children and their needs. But these adults also much have the courage to face conflict and set limits. Diane Baumrind's years of research on childrearing demonstrate that adult guidance and control are necessary. "Friction and conflict characterize optimal child-rearing situations" (Bell, 1979, p. 825). Great affection is necessary too. Teachers like parents, must have the energy and courage to face a room filled with different and developing individuals.

In the second half of this chapter we examine three important categories of student differences: intelligence, creativity, and cognitive style.

# INDIVIDUAL DIFFERENCES IN INTELLIGENCE

Because the concept of **intelligence** is so important in education and so often misunderstood, we will spend quite a few pages discussing it. We begin with a basic question. What is intelligence?

## What Does Intelligence Mean?

The idea that people vary along a dimension similar to what we call intelligence has been with us for a long time. Plato discussed these variations over 2000 years ago. Most early theories about the basic nature of intelligence involved one or all of the following three themes: (1) the capacity to learn; (2) the total of all the knowledge a person has acquired, and (3) the ability to adapt successfully to new situations and to the environment in general (Robinson and Robinson, 1976).

By 1921, consensus about the meaning of intelligence seemed almost impossible. In that year, 12 psychologists gave 12 different views about the nature of intelligence in a symposium on the subject, reported in the *Journal of Educational Psychology* (Sattler, 1982). Today opinion is still divided. A few psychologists believe that intelligence is nothing more than a label used to describe the skills measured by intelligence tests. In other words, intelligence is what intelligence tests measure. Other psychologists believe intelligence is much more than simply what it takes to do well on IQ tests. They link intelligence to successful coping in the world. David Wechsler, the person responsible for three of the most frequently used individual intelligence tests, defines intelligence as "the aggregate or global capacity of the individual to act purposefully, to think rationally, and to deal effectively with his environment" (Wechsler, 1958, p. 7). This brings us to a central question about intelligence: Is it a general quality or a collection of many specific abilities?

*Disagreement About Intelligence*

**Intelligence: One Ability or Many?** Wechsler's use of the phrase "aggregate or global capacity" reflects an important and unresolved issue concerning the nature of intelligence. Some theorists believe intelligence is a basic ability that affects performance on all cognitively oriented tasks. An "intelligent" person will do well in computing mathematical problems, in analyzing poetry, in taking history essay examinations, and in solving riddles. Evidence

*One Basic Ability?*

for this position comes from correlational evaluations of intelligence tests. In study after study, high positive correlations are found among all the different tests that are supposedly measuring separate intellectual abilities (McNemar, 1964). But the correlations are not perfect. What could explain these results?

Several approaches have been taken to explain the persistent but less than perfect relationships among the various mental tasks. Charles Spearman (1927) suggested there was one factor, which he called g or general intelligence, that was common to all tests of mental abilities. Different types of tests assess g to a greater or lesser extent. In addition, each type of test requires some very specific abilities or skills that are different from g. Spearman assumed that individuals vary in both general intelligence and specific abilities and that together these factors determine performance on mental tasks.

**Several Abilities?**

Critics of Spearman's position insisted that there were several "primary mental abilities," not just one. Thurstone (1938) listed verbal comprehension, reasoning, spatial relations, numerical ability, word fluency, and perceptual speed as the major mental abilities underlying intellectual tasks. But tests of these "separate" factors showed that ability in one area was correlated with ability in the others. Even though people tended to perform better on some tests than on others, in general those who made high scores on the reasoning test did pretty well on the test of spatial relations, while low scores on the verbal test tended to go along with low scores in numerical ability, word fluency, and so on.

J. P. Guilford (1967) is perhaps the most prominent modern proponent of multiple cognitive abilities. His research indicates three **"faces of intellect"**: mental operations, types of content, and different products. Mental operations are divided into five different categories: cognition, memory, divergent thinking, convergent thinking, and evaluation. The types of content on which people operate are divided into four different categories: figural, semantic, symbolic, and behavioral. The different products that may result are divided into six categories: units, classes, relations, systems, transformation, and implications. (Are you still there?)

**Guilford's Faces of Intellect**

Carrying out a cognitive task is essentially using a mental operation on some specific content to achieve a product. For example, listing the next number in the sequence 3, 6, 12, . . . requires a convergent operation (there is only one right answer) about symbolic content (numbers) to achieve a relationship product (each number is double the one before). Think for a minute about how many combinations of operations, contents, and products there are. As you may have calculated, there are 120, or $5 \times 4 \times 6$. Figure 4–4 offers a pictorial representation of these 120 mental abilities. Guilford contends that each of us varies in our competence in each of the 120 abilities. Tests have been developed for many of the 120 areas, but some of the abilities still exist only in theory.

Guilford's model of intelligence has several advantages as well as one major drawback. The model is based on research findings from genetics, neurology, the biological sciences, and experimental psychology (Pyle, 1979). It broadens our view of the nature of intellect by adding factors related to social judgment, (for example, the evaluation of the behavior of others to determine implications) and creativity (divergent thinking) (Gleitman, 1981). We will discuss the latter contribution later in this chapter. Certainly human mental abilities must be complex, but Guilford's model may be too complex to serve as a guide for predicting behavior in real situations and planning

**Figure 4–4    Guilford's Model of the Three Faces of Intelligence**

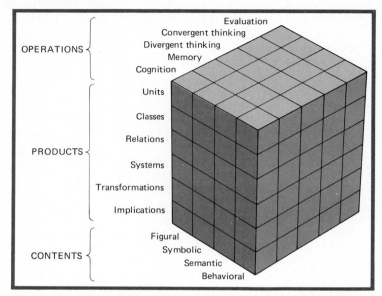

From **The Naure of Human Intelligence** by J. P. Guilford. Copyright © 1967 by McGraw-Hill Book Company. Used with permission of McGraw-Hill Book Co.

instruction. In addition, the problem of explaining the persistent correlations among all these "separate" mental abilities remains.

*Current Views*

Most current theories assume there is something like general intelligence or a common factor involved in all cognitively oriented tasks, even though more than one factor is needed to explain intelligence (Horn and Donaldson, 1980). Detterman described the problem of making sense of this complicated system:

> All mental abilities are more or less related to all others. Since we are dealing with a complex system, the human mind, this is just what should be expected. The dilemma is that we will have to attempt to understand a complex, integrated system by studying its parts behaving, at times, as if they were independent. You have to start some place when you are eating a plate of spaghetti. (Dettermen, 1979, p. 250)

*Components of Intelligence*

In the past few years, psychologists have looked to research on cognitive development and information processing for guidance in "eating the spaghetti." They have analyzed the items from many different types of mental tests to determine what abilities are needed to do well on the tests. At times they have studied the strategies used by individuals who consistently score high on a particular type of test. Based on this work, a new way of looking at intelligence is emerging. One approach (Sternberg, 1980) suggests there are five types of components, each serving a different function. The functions are acquisition of new information, retention (memory), transfer of information to new problems, performance or execution of a strategy, and metacognition or the executive function (making decisions about what strategy to use and monitoring progress).

Some components are very general and may be necessary in almost every cognitive task. For example, metacognition is always operating to select strategies and keep track of progress. This may help to explain the pesistent correlations among all types of mental tests. People who are effective in selecting good problem-solving strategies, monitoring progress, and moving to a new approach when the first one fails are more likely to be successful on all types of tests. Individuals who lack metacognitive abilities will have trouble with a wide range of tasks, from verbal comprehension to spatial relations. You may remember from Chapter 2 that metacognitive abilities become better developed as children grow older. These abilities also seem to be better in individuals who perform well on mental tests. (We will discuss the components of information processing and how they might be improved in Chapters 6 and 7 on cognitive views of learning.)

Although the components view of intelligence is controversial, it does suggest a way to relate mental abilities and learning. Other psychologists have different explanations for the processes involved in intelligent actions, and research in the next decade should provide exciting clues to this important question. By understanding exactly what more intelligent people *do* when they solve problems, we should be able to help all students behave in more "intelligent" ways.

Even though psychologists do not agree about what intelligence is, they do agree that it is related to the type of learning that goes on in schools. In fact, scores on intelligence tests predict school achievement quite well. There is a very good explanation for this relationship between intelligence and school performance. It has to do with how IQ is measured.

### How Is Intelligence Measured?

A brief history of intelligence testing should give you some insight into the reasons intelligence is measured as it is today.

**Binet's Dilemma.**    In 1904, Alfred Binet was confronted with the following problem by the minister of public instruction in Paris: How can students who will need special teaching and extra help be identified early in their school careers, before they fail in regular classes? At the time, many of these students, who are now called mentally retarded, were likely to spend several years in regular classes, falling farther and farther behind, when they might have been in classes designed to meet their needs. Other students, particularly those from low SES homes, were forced to leave school because of the often biased opinions of teachers that these students were unable to learn.

After trying many different types of test items, Binet finally identified 58, several for each age level from 3 to 13. In identifying the items to be included on the final test, Binet and his collaborator Theodore Simon searched for items that did not measure achievement in school subjects, but still discriminated between students who were doing well in school and students of the same age who were doing poorly. Trial and error led to the final 58 types of tests. Binet and Simon selected the items by comparing the performance of students in regular schools with the performance of students the same age in institutions for the retarded.

Binet and Simon also devised an ingenious system for clustering the tests by age group. If an item was successfully completed by 60 to 90 percent of all 6-year-old children, that item was placed at the 6-year level. A child who succeeded on all the 6-year items was considered to have a **mental age** of 6, whether the child was actually 5, 6, or 7 years old. A child who succeeded on some of the items for 5-year-olds, some for 6-year-olds, and some for 7-year-olds, might also earn a mental age of 6 overall.

The concept of **intelligence quotient** or **IQ** was added after the test was brought to the United States and revised at Stanford University to give us the Stanford-Binet. This score was computed by comparing the mental age score to the person's actual chronological age. The formula was

$$\text{Intelligence quotient} = \frac{\text{mental age}}{\text{chronological age}} \times 100$$

The early Stanford-Binet has been revised several times. The practice of computing a mental age has been replaced by the concept of **deviation IQ**. A person's performance on the test is compared to a sample of people of the same age who have taken the test. The IQ score is determined by how much better or worse than average the person did.

**The Wechsler Scales.** A second series of intelligence tests has been developed by David Wechsler. Like the Stanford-Binet, the Wechsler Scales must be given individually by a trained professional and take 1 to 2 hours to complete. Wechsler devised three scales: the Wechsler Adult Intelligence

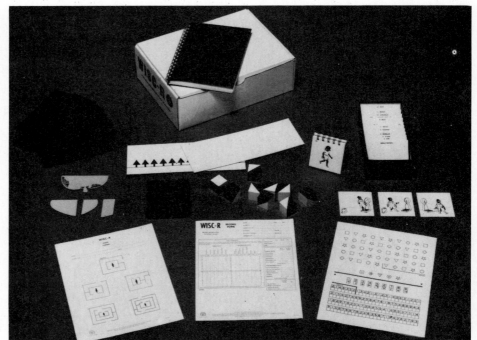

*It takes a trained professional from one to two hours to use these materials in giving the WISC-R test to children. The test is used with children between the ages of 6 and 16 and yields verbal, performance, and overall IQ scores.*

(The Psychological Corporation)

Scale (WAIS-R, the revised version), the Wechsler Intelligence Scale for Children (WISC-R, the revised version), and the Wechsler Preschool and Primary Scale of Intelligence (WPPSI).

**Individual and Group Tests**

Some of you may have experienced an individual intelligence test. More likely, you were given a group intelligence test with many other students. An individually administered test is much more likely to yield an accurate picture of a person's abilities. When students take tests in a group they may do poorly because they do not understand the instructions, because their pencil breaks, because they are distracted by other students, or because they do not "shine" on paper and pencil tests. Most of the questions on an individual test are asked orally and do not require reading or writing. On an individual test, a student may pay closer attention, be less distracted, and be more motivated to do well, because an adult is working directly with the student. As a teacher, you should be very wary of IQ scores based upon group tests.

Since scores on an individual test such as the WISC-R are more accurate reflections of a student's true abilities, we can turn to this test for samples of what the test makers consider to be intelligent behavior. The WISC-R includes both verbal and performance items. On the verbal test, students may be asked to do the following things:

**Verbal Items**

1. Define words.
2. Answer questions requiring commonsense knowledge and social judgment, such as "Why should you tell the truth?"
3. Solve mathematical problems without using a pencil and paper.
4. Tell how things are alike—for example, a house and a barn.
5. Remember a series of digits, forward and backward.
6. Answer questions on general information, such as "Where is France?" or "When is Thanksgiving?"

On the performance test, students are asked to carry out tasks such as these:

**Performance Items**

1. Identify the missing element in a picture.
2. Assemble cut up pictures similar to jigsaw puzzles.
3. Arrange pictures in a logical order to tell a story.
4. Replicate a design from a picture using three-dimensional blocks.
5. Copy symbols quickly, using pencil and paper.

Like the WISC-R, the WAIS-R and WPPSI are designed to measure both verbal and nonverbal, or performance, intelligence, but the separation is not perfect. Verbal skills are needed to understand directions for the performance items and to complete the tests successfully. Still, a much higher score on the performance scale may indicate that a student has problems with oral language but has mastered many of the concepts appropriate for his or her age. This is especially likely to happen when the student's first language was not English.

In addition to requiring verbal skills, many of the tests on both the performance and verbal scales are timed. Working quickly results in a higher score. Students lose points if they do not work well under time pressure or if poor motor coordination slows them down on the object manipulations. In a later section we will discuss other reasons why some students, especially non-native speakers and minority students, may have difficulties with the questions on intelligence tests. For now, let us turn to how test scores are interpreted.

**What Does an IQ Score Mean?** In Chapter 14 we will spend quite a bit of time discussing the meaning of scores on standardized tests. For now, we can take a brief look at the IQ score. Individual intelligence tests are designed so that they have certain statistical characteristics. They are similar to the college entrance tests you probably took in high school in that both types of tests have a standard average score. For IQ tests, the average score is 100. Fifty percent of the people from the general population who take the tests will score above 100, and 50 percent will score below. About 68 percent of the general population will obtain IQ scores between 85 and 115. Only about 16 percent of the population will receive scores below 85, and only 16 percent will score above 115. These figures are true for white, native-born Americans whose first language was standard English. As you will see later, the numbers are inappropriate guides for evaluating scores of other groups of students.

People often wonder what IQ scores mean in terms of future achievement. We have already said that intelligence test scores predict achievement in schools quite well, at least for large groups. But do people who score high on IQ tests achieve more in life? Here the answer is less clear. It appears that IQ scores and school achievement are not highly correlated with income and success in later life when number of years of education is held constant.

If you complete college, your chances of doing well in your career cannot be predicted accurately from your scores on IQ tests, compared with others who have the same education (McClelland, 1973). Within a particular type of job, success does not seem to be related to measured intelligence (Jencks et al., 1972). Other factors like motivation, social skills, and luck may make the difference. However, the average IQ scores of members of different occupations vary quite a bit. The highest average scores are found among top civil servants, professors, and research scientists, while other occupations such as unskilled laborers have the lowest average scores. But within every group there are individuals with higher and lower scores (Sattler, 1982).

This brings us to a very important question about intelligence: How much can intelligence be influenced by education and other aspects of the environment?

## Intelligence: Nature or Nurture?

A topic of great controversy is whether intelligence should be seen as something innately limited or as an achievement. In other words, is intelligence a potential that cannot be exceeded or simply the current level of functioning a person has attained, based upon experience and education?

Because it is much more difficult to study heritability in people than in plants and animals, it is almost impossible to separate intelligence "in the genes" from intelligence "due to experience." Mental abilities, to the extent that they are determined by heredity, are polygenetic or influenced by many sets of genes. There is no simple relationship like that found with eye color (which isn't very simple either).

**Figure 4–5  Kinship and Intelligence: Average Correlations between the IQ Test Scores of Various Related and Unrelated People**

|  | Correlation |
|---|---|
| Genetically identical | |
| Same individual tested twice | .87 |
| Identical twins reared together | .86 |
| Genetically related | |
| Fraternal twins reared together | .62 |
| Ordinary brothers and sisters reared together | .34 |
| One parent and child, living together | .35 |
| Genetically unrelated | |
| Unrelated children, reared together | .25 |
| Adoptive parents–adoptive child | .15 |

*Adapted from R. Plomin, and J. C. DeFries, Genetics and intelligence: Recent data. **Intelligence,** 1980, **4,** pp. 15–24.*

Kinship and IQ

Efforts to understand the roles of heredity and environment have often focused on studies of kinship and IQ similarity. In a recent summary of this work, Plomin and DeFries (1980) looked at research conducted from 1976 through 1979 by computing the average correlation, or relationship, for IQ scores among different kinship groups. A correlation of 1.0 is a perfect relationship and a correlation of around 0.0 is considered no relationship at all. If intelligence were determined completely by genes, it would be possible to calculate exactly the correlation between the IQ scores of two related people. Identical twins (who have identical genes) would have IQs that correlated perfectly at 1.0. Unrelated children (who have completely different genes) would have IQs that correlated around 0.0. Some of the results of the Plomin and DeFries (1980) study are shown in Figure 4–5.

Heredity and Environment

As you can see, the closer the kinship relationship, the higher the correlation. Identical twins are more similar in their abilities than fraternal (nonidentical) twins, brothers and sisters, or parents and children. This supports the idea that heredity is a strong factor in determining intelligence. But the role of environment is indicated as well. Unrelated children reared together are more similar in abilities than genetic determination would lead us to expect. Since unrelated children have no genes in common, a correlation approaching 0.0 would be expected if IQ were determined entirely by heredity. Instead, the correlation appears to be around 0.25. So the similar environment in which the unrelated children were reared apparently has had an effect on the development of their intelligence (Vernon, 1979). Of course, the fact that adoption agencies often try to "match" the adopting parents with the biological parents may mean that adopted children are similar in heredity to adopted brothers and sisters.

A recent study by Sandra Scarr and David Yee (1980) examined the role of heredity and environment for a large group of adopted adolescents, the oldest sample studied thus far using this particular method. These children had been adopted as infants. The researchers compared the children's IQ, aptitude, and school achievement test scores with estimates of their adoptive parents' and natural mothers' IQs and with several environmental character-istics of the adoptive home (parents' education, income, father's occupation). The same comparisons were made for a large sample of adolescents reared by their natural parents.

Scarr and Yee found that environmental variations among the adoptive families were a substantial source of differences among the adolescents in school achievement test scores, but contributed practically nothing to differences among individuals in IQ scores. In addition, the natural mother's educational level "correlated more highly with the adopted adolescents' test scores than the adoptive parents' educational levels, even though the children had lived with these parents for the past 18 years" (p. 7). The parents and children in this study were all working- and upper-class whites. Environmental differences within this group were not associated with individual differences in IQ scores. This doesn't mean that very deprived or extremely enriched environmental conditions would have no effect on intelligence or that the same results would be found for other ethnic groups. But it does show a powerful influence of heredity on intelligence test scores.

Are intellectual abilities due more to heredity or to environment? The most accurate statement that can be made is that intellectual abilities, like many human characteristics, are strongly influenced by both. As a teacher, it is especially important for you to realize that cognitive abilities, like any other abilities, are always improvable. Intelligence is a *current state of affairs*, affected by past experiences and open to future changes (probably within limits, but limits that are not yet fully understood).

There is one other problem with IQ testing that has caused a great deal of controversy. Students from cultural backgrounds other than white middle- and upper-class milieus seem to have different patterns of performance.

## Cultural Differences and IQ Testing

Students from lower socioeconomic classes tend to score lower on mental abilities tests than middle- and upper-class students do, regardless of ethnicity. But black students, on the average, score below Puerto Ricans, who score below whites. The average difference between blacks and whites on
Ethnic and SES
Differences most measures of intelligence is around 15 points (Loehlin, Lindsey and Spuhler, 1979). Few psychologists dispute the existence of these differences in performance, but there is great disagreement about the cause of the differences and what they really mean.

Because there is evidence that intellectual abilities are determined, in part, by heredity, some psychologists have suggested that these differences among groups on average test scores indicate genetic differences. Other psychologists point out that an estimate of the heritability of any characteristic within a particular group does not tell us anything about differences between groups unless environmental conditions have been identical for both groups. Given the very different economic, social, and educational conditions that histori-cally have affected many racial and ethnic groups, the influence of genetic differences (if any) probably is small compared to the influence of culture and experience (Vernon, 1979).

A third explanation for the differences among various groups in measured intelligence is that the tests themselves are biased against minorities. We will examine this last suggestion more thoroughly in Chapter 14 when we discuss factors that influence standardized test results.

No matter what the explanation for differences in IQ scores, there is extensive overlap in the distribution of scores for blacks and whites. Many black students will have IQ scores above the mean for white students and many white students will have IQ scores below the mean for black students. Since you will teach individual students and not the whole population, you should avoid making predictions about the abilities of any one student based on social class, race, or ethnicity. The range of abilities is much greater within each racial or ethnic group than between groups. Since the goal of education is to help students move forward from wherever they are, it really does not matter if heredity or environment or both have caused students to be where they are when they enter your class. The crucial question is how you help the students learn. The Guidelines given here should be of help not only in dealing with this particular issue, but also in the general interpretation of IQ scores.

# Guidelines

## Interpreting IQ Scores

**1. Check to see if the score is based on an individual or a group test.**

EXAMPLES
- Individual tests include the Wechsler Scales (WPPSI, WISC-R, WAIS-R), the Stanford-Binet, the McCarthy Scales of Children's Abilities, the Woodcock-Johnson Psycho-Educational Battery, and the Kaufman Assessment Battery for Children.
- Group tests include the Lorge-Thorndike Intelligence Tests, the Analysis of Learning Potential, the Kuhlman-Anderson Intelligence Tests, the Otis-Lennon Mental Abilities Test, and the School and College Ability Tests (SCAT).

**2. Remember that IQ scores are estimates.**

EXAMPLES
- Ignore small differences in scores among students.

**3. Be wary of IQ scores, especially group test scores for minority students and students whose native language is not English.**

EXAMPLES
- If a student's ability with English is very limited, question the results of the test.
- Even scores on "culture-free" IQ tests are lower for disadvantaged students.

**4. Remember that IQ scores reflect a student's past experiences and previous learning.**

EXAMPLES
- Consider these scores predictors of school abilities, not measures of innate intellectual abilities.
- If students are doing well in your class, do not change your opinion or expectations because a score seems low.

## Improving Intelligence

In light of the differences in test scores among ethnic groups, several educators and psychologists have attempted to design educational programs that would eliminate these discrepancies. Have they been successful? The answer appears to depend on how you define success.

*An Experiment That Raised IQ*

Craig Ramey and Ron Haskins (1981a, 1981b) designed an intensive educational day care program for infants from very poor homes. The average IQ of the children's mothers was around 82. Given the home conditions and the mothers' IQ, these children were considered "at risk" to develop below-normal intelligence. The project began when the infants were 4 months old or younger. All children in the study received improved nutrition, health care, and social services. Half the children, chosen at random, also attended the special educational program every day. At ages 2, 3, 4, and 5 years, the average IQ score of the children in the educational program was significantly higher than the average score of the children who were reared at home.

Other studies have shown dramatic improvements of 30 to 40 IQ points for children from deprived situations such as orphanages (Hunt, 1981). The problem has been that these differences seem to fade as the children progress through school. By junior or senior high, often earlier, the children who participated in the early educational programs have the same average IQ scores as peers who had no special teaching (Jensen, 1981). However, there are differences, for participants of some programs at least, on factors such as school motivation and achievement (Schweinhart and Weikart, 1980), grade retention, and placement in remedial education programs (Ramey and Haskins, 1981b).

*IQ Can Be Changed*

Two conclusions make sense. Intelligence, as measured by IQ tests, can be changed and often is in the normal course of development. Without participating in any special program, one out of seven middle-class children in a 15-year study changed as much as 40 points or more in IQ between ages 2½ and 17 (McCall, 1981). Even if the heritability of intelligence is .80, as some suggest, IQ changes of up to 45 points could follow from alterations in environmental conditions (Jensen, 1981). But if special teaching methods and enrichment do not continue throughout school, the IQ gains of high-risk children probably will not hold up. Other types of gains, perhaps more related to success in life, do seem to last.

There is another question about group differences in intelligence that has been debated recently—are there sex differences in mental abilities?

## Sex and Mental Abilities

From infancy through the preschool years, most studies find no differences between boys and girls in mental and motor development. When any differences are noted, they usually favor girls but are quite small (Willerman, 1979). During the school years and beyond, psychologists find no differences in general intelligence on the standard measures, but these tests have been designed and standardized to minimize sex differences. Usually items that favor one sex are eliminated or balanced by adding an equal number of items that favor the other sex. But even though the overall IQ scores of males and females are not significantly different on the average, scores on several

*Early Sex Differences*

140

subtests show sex differences. For example, on the WAIS, Matarazzo (1972) found that men performed significantly better on the arithmetic test, while women were superior on a test requiring them to copy symbols quickly and accurately. Results such as these bring the question of sex differences in specific abilities.

Before the school years there appear to be few differences between boys and girls in specific abilities, although girls may have the edge in verbal skills. But then the picture changes. Maccoby and Jacklin (1974) report the following

well-documented differences in school-aged childen: (1) girls excel in verbal ability; (2) boys show better performance on visual and spatial tasks; (3) boys are superior in mathematical ability.

Not all psychologists agree with these conclusions. The contention of male superiority in mathematical ability has been a frequent target for debate. One factor complicating the issue is the fact that girls take fewer courses in

mathematics than boys. As soon as mathematics courses become optional in school, many girls tend to avoid them. Thus the girls do not develop their abilities in this area (and in the process, limit their college and career choices, since college entrance and many jobs require some proficiency in mathematics). Fenema and Sherman (1977) found that the performance of males and females in mathematics was comparable when the actual number of previous math courses taken by each student was considered. Other researchers have reported that boys are superior in mathematics, even when participation in previous math courses is taken into account (Benbow and Stanley, 1980; Kolata, 1980). As you can see in Box 4–1, there are strong opinions, and evidence, on both sides of this issue.

It is possible that there are biologically based sex differences in specific mental abilities. But a wide range of abilities occurs in both groups. Even if boys did have an edge in mathematics as a group, this wouldn't mean that all boys would be superior to all girls. In every class there will be many girls with excellent potential for mathematics and many boys who have great difficulty. We don't know what the situation would be like if all students, boys and girls, received appropriate instruction and encouragement in math. For example, Patricia Casserly of the Educational Testing Service has studied 20 high schools where no sex differences are found in mathematics performance. Even though the schools are not alike in all ways, they share several common features. The teachers have strong backgrounds in mathematics, engineering, or science, not just in general education. They are enthusiastic about mathematics. The brightest students, male and female, are grouped together for instruction in math, and there is heavy emphasis on reasoning in the classes (Kolata, 1980).

Recently a few psychologists have turned their attention to studying a phenomenon called **brain lateralization.** In the human being, the brain is organized so that the two hemispheres or halves of the brain are involved in somewhat different abilities. You may have read about the "split brain"

research. It appears that, for most people, the right hemisphere of the brain controls nonverbal, spatial abilities and the left side of the brain tends to be involved with verbal skills, language, and verbal reasoning. It has been suggested lately that men's brains tend to be more "lateralized" or specialized, while women may tend to use both sides of the brain for verbal and spatial reasoning (Fairweather, 1980). The next decade should yield more information on this topic.

## BOX 4–1 SEX AND MATHEMATICS

*Are there genetic differences in mathematical ability? Recent data from the Study of Mathematically Precocious Youth has set off a debate across the country. Below are summaries from articles that take very different positions on the issue:*

YES, there probably are sex differences in mathematical ability. This is the position of Camilla Benbow and Julian Stanley, investigators in the Study of Mathematically Precocious Youth at Johns Hopkins University (1980). In this program about 10,000 seventh- and eighth-graders who are strong math students have taken the SAT college entrance test, designed for eleventh- and twelfth-graders. Students who perform very well on the mathematics portion of the SAT may go on to participate in a special mathematics program. Benbow and Stanley claim that this testing provides good information about inherent mathematical ability because the boys and girls taking the test have had the same number of mathematics courses. They believe the results of the SATs shows that boys have more math ability. A few of their findings are listed below:

| Test | Grade | Mean SAT Math Score | | Highest Score | | Percentage Above 600 | |
|------|-------|------|-------|------|-------|------|-------|
|      |       | Boys | Girls | Boys | Girls | Boys | Girls |
| 1973 | 7     | 495  | 440   | 800  | 620   | 8.1  | 1.1   |
|      | 8 +   | 551  | 511   | 800  | 650   | 22.7 | 8.2   |
| 1979 | 7 + 8 | 436  | 404   | 790  | 760   | 3.2  | 0.9   |

In some schools there are no differences in mathematics achievement between males and females. Teachers in these schools have a strong background in science and mathematics, and reasoning is emphasized in the classes.

(Ken Karp)

Based on these figures and knowing that the students had the same course background in mathematics, you might wonder if Benbow and Stanley are right. Several psychologists disagree, however.

*NO,* the case for genetic differences is not strong. Alice Schafer and Mary Gray, both professors of mathematics, have this reply:

> There are at least two problems with this hypothesis. First, environmental and cultural factors have not been ruled out. Anyone who thinks that seventh graders are free from environmental influences can hardly be living in the real world. While the formal training of all students may be essentially the same, the issues of who helps with mathematics homework, of what sort of toys and games children are exposed to, of what the expectations of parents and teachers are, and a multitude of other factors cannot be lightly set aside. Second, it is not clear that SAT mathematics scores are a good measure of inherent mathematical ability. . . . Certainly there is no evidence that SAT scores are good predictors of creative ability in mathematics. Not a single student identified as mathematically precocious — boy or girl — has gone on to do graduate work in mathematics, although a number are in or have completed graduate work in other fields (Schafer and Gray, 1980)

Shelia Tobias (1982) adds some other information. She cites evidence suggesting that boys are more likely than girls to study for the math portion of the SAT. She also notes that the number of boys who outperform the top-scoring girl has been falling in recent years. In 1972, 19 percent of the boys who took the test scored above the top girl. By 1978, only .1 percent of the boys scored higher than the best girl, and in 1979 only one boy had a higher score than the top-scoring girl. Tobias believes "Until and unless girls are encouraged to experience the world as boys do, it is unreasonable to assume, as Benbow and Stanley have done, that the boys and girls they tested had identical exposure to mathematics" (p. 16).

## Age and Mental Abilities

As the number of older people in our society increases, interest has grown in studying the changing pattern of mental abilities across the life span. There are many myths about the effects of aging on intellectual performance. As a result of early research, most psychologists assumed that intelligence increased throughout childhood, peaked in adolescence or early adulthood, and declined from then on (Papalia and Olds, 1981). This conclusion has been criticized because it is based on comparisons of the test performances of younger and older people. Since these groups may have had very different experiences, the lower IQ scores found for the older group may not represent decline with age. For example, the older group probably had less education, on the average, and poorer health care in childhood. Critics suggest that the same people must be tested from childhood through old age to see if a decline in intelligence actually occurs for most people. Studies of this type, called **longitudinal,** often have found no decrease in IQ. But the issue is more complicated than the question of decline versus no decline. It is likely that different types of abilities are affected in different ways by aging.

One concept that may be helpful in understanding the changes in intelligence that come with age is the distinction between fluid and crystallized intelligence (Cattell, 1963). The first factor, **fluid intelligence,** involves many basic processes such as solving problems, reasoning, forming concepts, drawing inferences, and dealing with abstractions. The main characteristic of fluid intelligence is that it is not dependent on formal education. This type of ability is probably dependent on the physiological structure of the body, particularly of the brain and nervous system, and the experiences we have that directly affect these systems, such as early nutrition and disease (Horn and Donaldson, 1980). Fluid ability is sometimes considered the basic ability to solve new or unpracticed problems without formal training. As the body and nervous system grow and develop throughout childhood and adolescence, fluid abilities develop as well. But injury and deterioration in later life adversely affect these abilities (Havighurst, 1981).

**Crystallized intelligence** is made up of those abilities that are highly valued and directly taught by the culture. Reading, vocabulary, general information, making change, balancing your checkbook, taking tests, and behaving appropriately in a religious service are crystallized abilities in our culture (Horn and Donaldson, 1980). The distinction between fluid and crystallized intelligence is sometimes seen as the difference between inherited capacity to learn and learning based on experience, but this is not accurate. Heredity and learning play a role in both types of abilities. Havighurst (1981) describes crystallized abilities as "the collective intelligence of a society that is passed on from one generation to the next by means of schooling, the parental word, personal example, or instruction, or is learned through experience" (pp. 186–187). Fluid abilities develop without this attention to learning.

As people grow older, they decline in their fluid intelligence as well as in the ability to remember and retrieve new information very quickly. Crystallized abilities do not decrease and may improve if the individual stays intellectually active. Even though the neurological deterioration that comes with age may hurt fluid abilities, we can continue to add to our store of knowledge and increase our technical proficiency throughout life (Horn and Donaldson, 1980).

We turn now to another characteristic that concerns teachers—one that has proved as hard to define and as complex as intelligence.

*Fluid and Crystallized Intelligence* (margin note)

*Changes with Age* (margin note)

# THE QUESTION OF CREATIVITY

To some psychologists, **creativity** is a personal quality or trait. We often talk about *creative* people. But what is it that makes a person creative? According to Davis, "the single most important characteristic of the highly creative individual is creative *attitudes*. The concept of creative attitudes is broadly defined to include purposes, values, and a number of personality traits that together predispose an individual to think in an independent, flexible, and imaginative way" (Davis, 1976, p. 219). Other psychologists suggest that creativity is not a personality trait but a skill or process that produces a "creative" product, such as a painting, invention, computer program, or solution to a personal problem.

At the heart of the concept of creativity we find the notion of *newness.* Creativity results not in imitation, but in a new, original, independent, and

*Trait or Process?* (margin note)

*Flexibility and imagination are part of the creative process. Sometimes these qualities are stimulated by working with others.*

(Ken Karp)

imaginative way of thinking about or doing something. Although we frequently associate the arts with the word "creative," any subject can be approached in a creative manner.

## Assessing Creativity

All the usual research problems are present when psychologists attempt to study creativity. "How shall we define creativity?" becomes "How shall we measure creativity?" Several answers have been proposed. One answer has been to equate creativity with **divergent thinking,** the ability to come up with many different, often unconventional ideas or answers (Mansfield, Busse, and Krepelka, 1978). **Convergent thinking** is the more common ability to come up with one correct but conventional answer. This solution for measuring creativity is not perfect, but certain divergent thinking tests, given under certain conditions, do seem to predict actual creative behavior fairly well (Barron and Harrington, 1981).

Creativity Tests     E. P. Torrance has developed two types of creativity tests, verbal and graphic (Torrance, 1972; Torrance and Hall, 1980). In the verbal test, a person might be instructed to think up as many uses as possible for a tin can or asked how a toy might be changed to make it more fun to play with. On the figural test, the person might be given 30 pairs of parallel vertical lines and asked to create 30 different drawings, each drawing including one pair of lines (Hudgins, 1977).

Responses to all these tasks are scored for originality, fluency, and flexibility, three aspects of divergent thinking. Originality is usually determined statistically. To be original, a response must be given by fewer than 5 or 10 people out of every 100 who take the test. Fluency is simply the number of different responses. Flexibility is generally measured by counting the number of different categories of responses. For instance, if a person gives 100 uses for a tin can, but each one was as some type of container, the fluency score might be high but the flexibility score would be quite low.

Originality, Fluency, and Flexibility

In general, it appears that at least average intelligence is required to be creative, but above this point, IQ and creativity are not related. Very intelligent people can be quite creative, very conventional, or anywhere in between. People of average intelligence can also be more or less creative. In fact, it is likely that creativity is a bit like intelligence. We all have intelligence and creativity, but some people seem to have more of either or both qualities.

Intelligence and Creativity

## Creativity in the Classroom

Should teachers promote creative thinking? If so, how can this be done? Teachers are not always the best judges of creativity. In fact, Torrance (1972) reports data from a 12-year follow-up study indicating no relationship between teachers' judgments of their students' creative abilities and the actual creativity evident in products made by those students as adults. Even though creative students may be difficult to identify, we believe creativity is worth fostering. Certainly the many economic, social, and environmental problems now facing our society will require creative solutions.

Teacher Judgment

**What Can Be Done to Encourage Creativity?**   Perhaps the most important step teachers can take to encourage creativity is to make sure students know their creativity will be appreciated. All too often teachers stifle creative ideas without realizing the effects of their actions. Teachers are in an excellent position to encourage or discourage creativity through their acceptance or rejection of the unusual and imaginative. Rejection may be fatal to creativity.

In addition to encouraging creativity through everyday interactions with students, teachers can try brainstorming.

**The Brainstorming Strategy.**   The basic tenet of **brainstorming** is to separate the generation of ideas from the evaluation of ideas (Osborn, 1963). You probably are quite familiar with the usual sequence of events when a group is trying to solve a problem:

LEADER:        We have to decide on a senior project.
PARTICIPANT 1: How about cleaning up the river by the park?
PARTICIPANT 2: No, that won't work. Someone's bound to get hurt.
PARTICIPANT 1: Not necessarily. Five years ago the senior class did it and everything went fine.
PARTICIPANT 2: Yes, but . . .

In discussions such as the one above, the attempt to have creative ideas and solve a problem often turns into a debate about the merits of one idea. Many participants become bored and "tune out." The principle of brainstorming is to generate as many ideas as possible, no matter how impractical they seem at first. Evaluation, discussion, or criticism of the ideas is left until

Deferring Evaluation

all possible suggestions have been made. In this way, one idea may inspire others. Perhaps more important, people do not withhold what could be creative solutions, fearing that they will be criticized. After all the ideas are in, they can be evaluated and possibly modified or combined to produce a creative answer to the original problem.

Individuals as well as groups may benefit from brainstorming. In writing this book, for example, it has sometimes been helpful simply to list all the different topics that could be covered in a chapter, then leave the list and return to it later to evaluate the ideas. Individual brainstorming can be especially helpful when you or your students do not know where to begin on a large project. If you agree that creativity should be encouraged in the schools, you will find the Guidelines here helpful. We turn our attention now to individual differences you may find less familiar than intelligence and creativity.

# *Guidelines*

## *Encouraging Creativity*

### 1. Accept and encourage divergent thinking.

**EXAMPLES**
- During class discussion, ask: "Can anyone suggest a different way of looking at this question?"
- Reinforce attempts at unusual solutions to problems, even if the final product is not perfect.

### 2. Tolerate dissent.

**EXAMPLES**
- Ask students to support dissenting opinions.
- Make sure nonconforming students have an equal chance to be granted classroom privileges.

### 3. Encourage students to trust their own judgment.

**EXAMPLES**
- When students ask questions you think they can answer, rephrase or clarify the questions and direct them back to the students.
- Give ungraded assignments from time to time.

### 4. Emphasize that everyone is capable of creativity in some form.

**EXAMPLES**
- Avoid describing the feats of great artists or inventors as if they were superhuman accomplishments.
- Recognize creative efforts in each student's work.

### 5. Be a stimulus for creative thinking.

**EXAMPLES**
- Use a class brainstorming session whenever possible.
- Model creative problem solving by suggesting unusual solutions for class problems.

*The boy on the left is obviously enjoying "the circus," while the boy on the right has actually joined it. Playfulness and imagination of this type seem to be closely tied to the development of creativity in adults.*

# VARIATIONS IN COGNITIVE STYLES

The notion of **cognitive styles** is fairly new. It grew out of research on how people perceive and organize information from the world around them. Results from these studies suggest that individuals differ in how they approach the experimental tasks, but these variations do not reflect levels of intelligence or patterns of special abilities (Tyler, 1974). Instead, they have to do with "preferred ways that different individuals have for processing and organizing information and for responding to environmental stimuli" (Shuell, 1981a, p. 46). For example, certain individuals tend to respond very quickly in most situations. Others are more reflective and slower to respond, even though both types of people are equally knowledgable about the task at hand.

Styles of Thinking

Cognitive styles are often described as falling on the borderline between mental abilities and personality traits (Shuell, 1981). They are styles of "thinking" and thus are probably influenced by and influence cognitive abilities (Brodzinsky, 1982). But these preferred ways of dealing with the world also affect social relationships and personal qualities.

## Field Dependence and Independence

Characteristics of Field-dependent and Independent Individuals

In the early 1940s Herman Witkin became intrigued by the observation that certain airline pilots would fly into a bank of clouds and fly out upside down, without realizing that they had changed position. His interest led to a great deal of research on how people separate one factor—for example, true upright position—from the total visual field (Willerman, 1979). Based on this research, Witkin identified the cognitive styles of *field-dependence* and *field-independence*. People who are field-dependent tend to perceive a pattern as a whole. They have difficulty focusing on one aspect of a situation or analyzing a pattern into different parts. Field-independent people are more likely to perceive separate parts of a total pattern and to be able to analyze a pattern into its components (Wittrock, 1978). In addition, field-dependent individuals tend to be more oriented toward people and social relationships, while field-independent individuals are more likely to be task-oriented (Sigel and Brodzinsky, 1977).

There appear to be developmental trends in field dependence. As children grow older, they generally become more field-independent, at least until the middle teenage years. Then development levels off until later adult life, when there is a tendency to become more field-dependent. Even with these changes, over the years people remain fairly stable in comparison with others their age. So a person who tends to be field-dependent as a child may become more independent with age but still be less independent than peers who have also changed with age. Some studies show that boys tend to be more field-independent than girls, but this probably is related to the way girls are socialized in our culture or to the testing situation itself. Parents who encourage self-reliance and curiosity, who are confident, and do not stress conformity or obedience tend to foster field-independence in their children (Sigel and Brodzinsky, 1977). These conditions are more likely to occur for boys than for girls in our society. In Eskimo society, in contrast, girls are given considerable independence, and no sex differences are found in this cognitive style (Willerman, 1979).

This discussion may seem to imply that it is "better" to be more field-independent. But each style has advantages and disadvantages. For example, field-dependent individuals are superior in remembering social information such as conversations or interpersonal interactions, perhaps because they are more attuned to social relationships. Field-independent people are better at analyzing complex, unstructured material and organizing it to solve problems (Shuell, 1981a, 1981b).

While you will not necessarily be able to determine all the variations in your student's cognitive styles, you should be aware that the students approach problems in different ways. Some may need help in learning to pick out important features and ignore irrelevant details not because they are less intelligent, but because they tend to perceive patterns as wholes and have trouble analyzing. They may seem lost in less structured situations and need clear, step-by-step instructions. Many students find it particularly difficult to organize information from several sources. Other students may be great at organizing, but seem less sensitive to the feelings of others and not as effective in social situations. Figure 4–6 presents some of the other learning characteristics of field-dependent and field-independent individuals.

*The task of organizing information from many different sources can be difficult for students who have a field-dependent cognitive style. They have trouble breaking information down into units and recombining the parts into new patterns.*

(Ken Karp)

**Figure 4–6**  **Learning Characteristics of Field-Dependent and Field-Independent Students**

| Field-Dependent | Field-Independent |
|---|---|
| • Are better at learning material with social content<br>• Have better memory for social information<br>• Require externally defined structure, goals, and reinforcement<br>• Are more affected by criticism<br>• Have greater difficulty learning unstructured material<br>• May need to be taught how to use mnemonics<br>• Tend to accept the organization given and be unable to reorganize<br>• May need more explicit instruction on how to solve problems | • May need help in focusing attention on material with social content<br>• May have to be taught how to use context in understanding social information<br>• Tend to have self-defined goals and reinforcement<br>• Are less affected by criticism<br>• Can impose their own structure on unstructured situations<br>• Can analyze a situation and reorganize it<br>• Are more likely to be able to solve problems without explicit instructions and guidance |

*Adapted from H. A. Witkin, C. A. Moore, D. R. Goodenough, and R. W. Cox, Field dependent and field independent cognitive styles and their educational implications.* **Review of Educational Research,** *1977,* **47,** *17–27. © 1977,* **AERA,** *Washington, D.C.*

## Impulsive and Reflective Styles

You may be the type of individual who responds very quicky; you finish multiple-choice tests long before your friends. Or you may still be checking your answers when the instructor is collecting the papers. If you fit the first description, you could be a true impulsive individual. But not everyone who works fast is impulsive. Some people are simply very bright and quick to understand. These individuals are called *fast-accurate* in the jargon of psychology. The true impulsive individual is one who responds very quickly but also makes quite a few errors in the process. If you are not the first, but the last to finish the test, you may be a truly reflective individual, or you may have studied the wrong material for the test. The reflective person is one who is slow and careful to respond, but tends to answer correctly. Those who are slow and make many errors are called *slow-inaccurate.*

The most common method for measuring impulsive-reflective style is the Matching Familiar Figures test. An item from one version of this test is shown in Figure 4–7. The goal is to find the teddy bear from the bottom group that is exactly the same as the one on top. Impulsive children tend to select the first match that looks right without scanning all the examples and comparing each with the top bear. You can see how the tendency to go with the first reasonable choice could cause a low score on this test. The same thing often happens in college classes when some students hurry through a multiple-choice test, selecting the first good answer they find and never even reading the better (correct) answer listed after their selection.

As with field-dependence, the cognitive style of impulsive-reflective is not highly related to intelligence within the normal range. However, as children grow older they generally become more reflective, and for school-age children being more reflective does seem to improve performance on many school

*Assessing Impulsivity*

**Figure 4–7  Measuring Reflective-Impulsive Styles**

J. Kagan, B. L. Rosman, D. Day, J. Albert, and W. Phillips. Information processing in the child: Significance of analytic and reflective attitudes. **Psychological Monographs,** 1964, **78,** 1 (Whole 578). (Copyright © 1964 by the American Psychological Association and reproduced with permission.)

tasks, such as reading (Messer, 1976). In addition, more reflective children are less likely to fail one of the early grades (Messer, 1970). It is not clear what influences the development of this cognitive style, although genetic factors may play a role (Sigel and Brodzinsky, 1977).

Students can learn to be more reflective if they are taught specific strategies. One that has proved successful in many situations is **self-instruction.** Students learn to give themselves reminders to go slowly and carefully. They "talk themselves through" the tasks, saying things such as "Okay, what is it I have to do? . . . copy the picture with the different lines. I

**Becoming More Reflective**

have to go slowly and carefully. Okay, draw the line down, down, good; then to the right, that's it; now...." (Meichenbaum, 1977, p. 32). Another possibility is learning scanning strategies. For example, students might be encouraged to cross off each alternative as they consider it so no possibilities will be ignored. They might work in pairs and talk about why each possibility is right or wrong. In math classes, impulsive children need to be given specific strategies for checking their work.

We have also encountered several bright students who seem too reflective. They turn 30 minutes of homework into an all-night project. These children may be afraid of failure, or they may be bored with the assignment. They need help in learning to work steadily through a project.

The message for teachers in the work on cognitive styles is that not all differences in class performance are due to differences in ability or effort. We all probably have preferred ways of processing new information, as well as blind spots in our approaches to new tasks. Flexibility and a willingness to experiment with different methods for different students are the keys.

## SUMMARY

1. Many human characteristics are influenced by the thousands of genes we receive from our parents. Most characteristics are polygenetic, influenced by many genes.

2. It is impossible to tell the exact genetic makeup of an individual from outward appearances. Scientists can calculate the heritability of various characteristics, but even traits or behaviors that are highly heritable can often be influenced by experience.

3. People grow up in very different environments. Experiences and resources may be limited by the socioeconomic status of the family. Being a member of a particular cultural group may mean being taught different values, behaviors, attitudes, and expectations.

4. The important consideration seems to be the specific influences in the life of the individual, particularly those related to family structure and relationships. In addition, different children encourage different reactions from parents and later from friends, teachers, and other people. Day-to-day life is a constant interchange between the child and the environment, with each influencing the other.

5. Even though we all talk about intelligence, there is little agreement about what it is. Some psychologists believe intelligence is a collection of separate abilities; others believe it is a general mental ability to learn new information and cope with the world.

6. As IQ is measured today, with individually administered tests such as the Stanford-Binet or the Wechsler Scales, it is closely related to ability to learn and succeed in school.

7. IQ scores must be interpreted with caution, particularly for minority students. Different groups tend to have different patterns of performance on measures of certain general and specific abilities.

8. Though both heredity and environment play a part, intelligence is always open to change over time; it is not fixed.

9. Creativity involves the production of something new. Divergent and convergent thinking patterns may play a role in creativity.

10. There are characteristic differences among people in the ways they prefer to organize and process information. These differences, called cognitive styles, are not related to intelligence or effort, but they do affect performance in school.

11. One cognitive style is field-dependent or field-independent; another is reflective or impulsive.

**KEY TERMS**

chromosomes

genes

phenotype

genotype

polygentic inheritance

heritability ratio

socioeconomic status (SES)

culture

intelligence

faces of intellect

mental age

intelligence quotient (IQ)

deviation IQ

brain lateralization

longitudinal study

fluid and crystallized intelligence

creativity

divergent and convergent thinking

brainstorming

cognitive styles

self-instruction

## SUGGESTIONS FOR FURTHER READING AND STUDY

ALLERS, R. D. *Divorce, children, and the schools.* Princeton, NJ: Princeton Book Company, 1982. This book discusses the child's experience of divorce as well a suggestions for teachers and other school personnel.

BELL, R. Q. Parent, child, and reciprocal influences. *American Psychologist,* 1979, *34,* 821–826. A brief summary of the more recent views on how children help to create the environments that influence them.

SHEULL, T. J. Dimensions of individual differences. In F. H. FARLEY and N. J. GORDON (Eds.), *Psychology and education: The state of the union.* Berkeley, CA: McCutchan, 1981. An overview of several important ways that individuals differ, with examples of recent research in each area.

TOBIAS, S. Sexist equations. *Psychology Today,* 1982, *16,* 14–17. A brief discussion of the possible explanations and remedies for sex differences in math achievement.

VERNON, P. E. *Intelligence: Heredity and environment.* San Francisco: Freeman, 1979. Here you will find a very thorough evaluation of the roles of heredity and environment in the development of intelligence. Vernon synthesizes an extensive number of older and more recent studies, presenting a view that is both balanced and opinionated.

WHITE, B. *The first three years of life.* Englewood Cliffs, NJ: Prentice-Hall, 1979. This book is written to be a guide for parents and preschool teachers about how to help children develop competence.

# Teachers' Forum

## Coping with Differentness

Suppose you have in your class a student who is very different from you. He is from a different culture, has different values, and even his temperament is different from your own. As a result, there is a strain between the two of you, and you tend to avoid interacting with him. The students, following your example, also shy away from him. How would you go about establishing a relationship with this student to reverse this trend toward estrangement and isolation?

**Valuing Differences**

I've been known to play up student strengths and competencies: "John, as an auto mechanics student, can you say if it is possible to crash a car that way?" "Can a math student figure out if that canoe could get down the Ohio in one day?" "We're mostly from the North in this class. Fred, how is the South different?" Once a student knows you value his accomplishments and differences as a teaching tool, he begins to value them himself.

Bonnie Hettman, High School Teacher
*Lima Central Catholic High School, Lima, Ohio*

**Educating Yourself**

This is the time to do some personal growing. Understand your resistance to this personality type and have a chat with the school psychologist for a beginning. Visit some adults from his culture with whom you can relate. Get a flavor for his childhood experience. Read some articles about his background. As a professional, it is your job to make the connections that will enable the student to learn. Bring examples from his cultural experience to your teaching and modify some of your expectations to match his temperament. Accommodation should pay off for both teacher and students.

Dorothy Eve Hopkins, Sixth-Grade Teacher
*Homer Intermediate School, Homer, New York*

## In the Meantime . . .

You have a transfer student who is very slow in understanding new material and whose general achievement level is way below grade level. You have referred him for testing but it will be two months before the overloaded testing department will be able to see him. In the interim, how can you determine what he needs right now so the two months (which is almost 1/4 of the school year) will not be wasted?

**Teacher Diagnosis**

In the area of reading, an individual reading inventory (IRI), professionally prepared or teacher-made, which requires the child to read and respond to graded passages, will provide a realistic picture of reading ability by distinguishing among independent, instructional, and frustrational levels. Graded word lists are also helpful in determining the learner's vocabulary level. In the area of mathematics, a simple teacher-made diagnostic test consisting of a variety of examples representing the basic function areas is an invaluable tool for uncovering strengths and weaknesses. It goes without saying that once diagnosis has been accomplished, instruction in all subject areas must be geared to the ability level of the learner in question. Peer-tutoring sessions as well as enlisting the help of willing parents are approaches that could aid greatly in reinforcing initial instruction.

Jacqueline M. Walsh, Sixth-Grade Teacher
*Agnes E. Little Elementary School, Pawtucket, Rhode Island*

**Language Arts**  Since I am a language arts teacher, this is how I would test the child in reading, spelling, and language so he could immediately begin instruction. I would use an informal reading inventory that usually accompanies the basal reading series to determine his instructional reading level. To insure success, I would begin with easier materials and work up. You could use the Writing and Spelling List Placement Test to determine where to start the child in spelling. Since there is no test available like this for language, I would ask the child to write a few paragraphs so I could diagnose strengths and weaknesses in this area.

Sharon Klotz, Sixth-Grade Language Arts Teacher
*Kiel Middle School, Kiel, Wisconsin*

## Original Thinking

Imagine that you have just finished grading the essay questions on your unit examination. Many of the answers were straight from the book and terribly uncreative, showing no original thinking and no ability to go beyond the information given. You are particularly concerned about two of your brighter students who seem to work very hard at giving you back your own words on the test. How would you handle this problem? What would you say to the class when you returned the papers? What, if anything, would you do about the two students who are so eager to quote you? How might you encourage more creativity in your students?

**Ask the Right Question**  The problem here lies with the essay questions rather than the students. When you pass back the exam, let the students know you are looking for original thinking. Make a joke of "Where's your imagination?" In the next test, make sure you are using questions that permit room for creativity. Remember that pupils have years of training to spit back answers rather than to think.

Dorothy Egan, Seventh- and Eighth-Grade Teacher
*Streetsboro Middle School, Streetsboro, Ohio*

# 5

# Behavioral Views of Learning

If you were asked to give ten to twenty different examples of learning, what would your response be? If you are like most people, you might begin by listing school subjects or certain activities, things you had purposely set about mastering at some point in your life. You might also list different emotional reactions or insights you have had. But unless you've already had a few courses in psychology, it is likely that the examples you would choose would cover only a few of the aspects included in the psychological definition of learning. We will spend the next three chapters looking at learning and its many classroom applications.

We begin this chapter with a very general definition. It is a definition that takes into account the opposing views of different theoretical groups. We will then highlight one of these groups, the behavioral theorists, throughout the rest of the chapter. (The other major group, the cognitivists, will be highlighted in Chapters 6 and 7). Our discussion in this chapter will focus on four different behavioral learning processes. Finally, we will look at two of the teaching aids behavioral theorists offer classroom teachers, programmed instruction and the Keller Plan.

By the time you have completed this chapter, you should have a much better idea of what is involved in learning. More specifically, you should be able to do the following:

- Offer a reasonably precise definition of learning.
- Give both positive and negative examples of learning through the principle of contiguity.
- Compare classical and operant conditioning, giving examples of each.
- Give examples of four different kinds of consequences that may follow any behavior and the result each is likely to have on future behavior.
- Describe situations in which a teacher may wish to use modeling.
- Give three specific examples of the ways in which you might use behavioral principles to solve problems that could arise in your own classroom.

Before you can begin to use behavioral principles, you must know a great deal more about learning itself. We will begin with a definition.

## LEARNING: TOWARD A GENERAL DEFINITION

One way to understand the psychological meaning of learning, is to note what it is *not*. First, learning is not something found only in the classroom. It takes place constantly, every day of our lives. Second, it is not something that is "correct." If a students misspells a word on a test, one cannot say that the student did not learn to spell the word, only that the student learned the wrong spelling. Third, learning does not have to be deliberate or conscious. A

**What Learning Is Not**

*Encouraged by her teacher, Paula is not just learning to print her name, but developing self-concept and personal pride as well. Attitudes and emotions are as much a part of classroom learning as are knowledge and skills.*

(Ann Meyer/Photo Researchers, Inc.)

tennis player may have learned a bad method of tossing the ball before serving, but the player could be completely unaware of the pattern until the instructor points it out. Finally, learning does not always involve knowledge or skills such as spelling and tennis. Attitudes and emotions can also be learned (W. Hill, 1981).

Learning always involves a change in the person who is learning. The change may be for the better or for the worse, deliberate or unintentional. To qualify as learning, this change must be brought about by experience, by the interaction of a person with his or her environment. Changes due simply to maturation, such as walking, do not indicate that any learning has taken place. Temporary changes due to illness, fatigue, or hunger are also excluded from a general definition of learning. A person who has gone without food for two days does not learn to be hungry, and a person who is ill does not learn to run more slowly.

With these two factors—change and experience—we can develop a definition. Learning is a change in a person that comes about as a result of experience. But, you might well ask, "a change in what aspect of the person?" It is the answer to this question that has traditionally separated the behavioral definition of learning from the cognitive definition. We will examine these two different views and see if we can come up with a broader definition.

**Change and Experience**

## Behavioral and Cognitive Views

Most of the psychologists discussed in this chapter — that is, those holding the **behavioral** view — would state that learning is a change in behavior, in the way a person acts in a particular situation. Theorists such as J. B. Watson, E. L. Thorndike, and B. F. Skinner are considered behavioral psychologists because they have focused almost solely on observable behavior and behavioral changes. In fact, many of the early behaviorists refused even to discuss the concepts of thinking or emotion, since thoughts and emotions could not be observed directly.

In contrast, **cognitive** psychologists such as Jean Piaget, Robert Glaser, John Anderson, and David Ausubel would say that learning itself is an internal process that cannot be observed directly. It is a change in a person's ability to respond in a particular situation. According to the cognitive view, the change in behavior that strict behaviorists call learning is only a reflection of the internal change. Again in contrast to the behaviorists, cognitive psychologists studying learning are interested in such unobservable variables as knowledge, meaning, intention, feeling, creativity, expectations, and thought.

Behavioral and cognitive views differ in many other important ways, and the differences are apparent in the methods each group has used to study learning. A great deal of the early work on behavioral learning principles was done with animals in controlled laboratory settings. These studies were an attempt to identify a few general laws of learning that would apply to all higher organisms (including humans) regardless of age, intelligence, or individual differences. The laws they were seeking could be used to predict and control changes in the behavior of any organism (Estes, 1975). Cognitive psychologists, on the other hand, have been more interested in explaining how learning takes place in humans of different ages and abilities. They have attempted to find out how different people solve problems, learn concepts, perceive and remember information, and accomplish many other complex mental tasks.

The important thing for teachers is that both cognitive and behavioral psychologists offer helpful information. Teachers must, after all, be concerned with observable student behavior — that is, the actual work done on assignments or behavior in class — and with less observable qualities, such as abstract thinking and attitudes.

So far, we have highlighted the differences between behavioral and cognitive views. In recent years, these two approaches have moved closer together and now share many ideas. A group of behavioral psychologists, often called the **neobehaviorists,** has expanded the view of learning to include such internal, unobservable events as expectations, intentions, beliefs, and thoughts. A prime example of this expanded behavioral view is found in Albert Bandura's **social learning theory,** which equates learning with much more than observable behavior. Social learning theorists emphasize that people may "know" more than their behavior indicates. Learning is seen as the **acquisition** and behavior as the observable **performance.** In describing social learning theory, Bandura (1971) said:

> Man is a thinking organism possessing capabilities that provide him with some power of self-direction. To the extent that traditional behavioral theories could be faulted, it was for providing an incomplete rather than an inaccurate account of

*Early Behavioral Views*

*Cognitive Views*

*Differences in Methods*

*Neobehavioral Views*

human behavior. The social learning theory places special emphasis on the important roles played by vicarious, symbolic, and self-regulatory processes. (p. 2)

We will look at some of Bandura's findings in the section of this chapter on observational learning and return to social learning theory when we discuss cognitive views of learning in the next two chapters.

A General
Definition

Taking into account the traditional behavioral and cognitive views and the more recent work of the social learning theorists, we can suggest this general definition of learning: **Learning** is an internal change in a person, the formation of new associations, or the potential for new responses. Learning is a relatively permanent change in a person's capabilities. Because we cannot actually observe these changes, we must infer that new associations and responses have been acquired when we observe changes in performance in a particular situation. This definition acknowledges the fact that learning is a process taking place within a person (the cognitive view), but also emphasizes the importance of changes in observable behavior as indications that learning has taken place (the behavioral view). Although this definition probably would not be acceptable to psychologists who hold extreme behavioral or cognitive views of learning, we believe it is a reasonable beginning.

Four Processes

Because this chapter focuses on behavioral views of learning, we will be more concerned, for the time being, with the changes in observable behavior. These changes can take place through four different learning processes: contiguity, classical conditioning, operant conditioning, and vicarious conditioning or observational learning. We will devote an entire section to each of the processes later in the chapter. First, however, let's step into an actual classroom and see some of these processes at work. Don't worry about identifying the various processes at this point; it should all become very clear as you read the rest of the chapter.

## Learning Is Not Always What It Seems to Be

Elizabeth was beginning her first day of solo teaching. After weeks of working with her cooperating teacher in an eighth-grade social studies class, she was ready to take over. As she moved from behind the desk to the front of the room, she saw another adult approach the classroom door. It was Mr. Ross, her supervisor from college. Elizabeth's neck and facial muscles suddenly became very tense.

"I've stopped by to observe your teaching," Mr. Ross said. "This will be my first of four visits. I tried to reach you last night to tell you I had changed my schedule and was coming today. No one answered."

Elizabeth was beginning to feel weak and nauseated. Her worst fear was confirmed. He was going to observe her on her first solo day. She tried to hide her reaction, but without much success. Her hand trembled as she gathered the notes for the lesson. Elizabeth had planned a slightly unorthodox introduction, and she now found herself wishing she had chosen something a bit less risky. After a few seconds of reflection, she decided to stick to the original plan.

"Let's start today with a kind of game. I will say some words. I want you to tell me the first words that you can think of when you hear my words. Don't bother to raise your hands. Just say the words out loud and I will write them on the board. Don't all speak at once, though. Wait until someone else has finished to say your word. Okay, here is the first word: slavery."

"Civil War." "Lincoln." "Freedom." "Emancipation Proclamation." The answers came very quickly, and Elizabeth was relieved to see that the students understood the game.

"All right, very good," she said. "Now try another one: South."

"Carolina." "Pacific." "No, the Confederacy, you dummy." "Gone with the Wind." "Clark Gable." With this last answer, a ripple of laughter moved across the room.

"Clark Gable!" Elizabeth sighed dreamily, looking "starstruck" for a moment.

By now the students were laughing, and Elizabeth joined them. "Okay, settle down," she said. "Here is another word: North."

"Bluebellies." (The students continued to laugh.) "Yellowbellies." "Belly-dancers." (More laughter and a few appropriate gestures.)

"Just a minute," Elizabeth pleaded. "These ideas are getting a little off base!"

"Off base? Baseball," shouted the boy who had first mentioned Clark Gable.

"Popcorn." "Hotdogs." "Drive-in movies." "Gone with the Wind." "Clark Gable." The responses now came too fast for Elizabeth to stop them.

For some reason, the Clark Gable line got an even bigger laugh the second time around, and Elizabeth realized she had lost the class. At this point, her cooperating teacher would have sent "Clark Gable" and a few others in the fan club to the principal's office. But Elizabeth feared her college supervisor would see that approach as a failure to handle the situation constructively. She looked to the back of the room and saw Mr. Ross writing in a notebook and shaking his head.

It appears, on the surface at least, that very little learning of any sort could have taken place in Elizabeth's classroom. If you consider the psychological definition of learning, however, you can see evidence for a good deal of learning. Four events can be singled out for our purposes here, each related to a different learning process. First, the students were able to associate the words "Carolina" and "Pacific" with the word "South." Second, Elizabeth's hands trembled and she became nauseated when her college supervisor entered the room. Third, one student continued to disrupt the class with inappropriate answers to questions. And fourth, after Elizabeth laughed at a student comment, the class joined in her laughter. In the next four sections we will examine these four different kinds of learning, with special attention to the third type.

## CONTIGUITY: LEARNING THROUGH SIMPLE ASSOCIATIONS

Simply phrased, the principle of **contiguity** states that whenever two sensations occur together over and over again, they will become associated. Later, when only one of these sensations (a **stimulus**) occurs, the other will be remembered too (a **response**). Some early twentieth-century psychologists claimed that this principle explains most learning. Edwin Guthrie, for example, believed that "If you do something in a given situation, the next time you are in that situation you will tend to do the same thing again" (W. Hill, 1971, pp. 42–43).

**Figure 5–1    Contiguity as a Part of Rote Memory**

| Stimulus | Response |
|---|---|
| 1 + 1 = _____ | 2 |
| *i* before e except after _____ | c |
| The capital of Texas is _____ | Austin |
| The capital of Brazil is _____ | Brasília |
| Strontium burns with a _____ | red flame |

Many of us learned quite a few basic facts in school through the repetitive pairing of a stimulus and a (hopefully) correct response. A number of examples of this kind of learning are given in Figure 5–1.

**Drill and Practice**

The items in Figure 5–1 represent deliberate attempts to learn through the use of contiguity. The student repeats "The capital of Texas is Austin" over and over until seeing the stimulus "The capital of Texas is _____" on a test brings to mind the response "Austin." Spelling drills in the earlier grades and the memorizing of vocabulary words in foreign language classes are other examples of the positive use of contiguity. Some results of contiguous learning were also evident in Elizabeth's class. When she said "South," students associated the word with "Carolina" and "Pacific." They had heard these words together many times.

**Stereotypes**

As we mentioned earlier, not all learning is deliberate and, of course, not all learning leads to positive results. Children may develop stereotypes about the way people are or should be through contiguous learning. The media consistently present the image of a mother of young children as a young, attractive, full-time homemaker. In our thinking, we may tend to associate the idea of "mother" with this picture. Yet a large number of women in this country with children under 5 are employed full time. And many of them are in their thirties or forties.

Even though, as we will see shortly, there is more to learning than contiguity, this principle can be used to help students learn. We have included a short set of Guidelines for applying contiguity in the classroom.

# *Guidelines*

## *Using Contiguity*

**1. Whenever possible, encourage students to practice pairing the desired responses with the appropriate stimuli.**

**EXAMPLES**
- Math and language drills.
- Repeated practice in carrying out some new behavior such as putting away supplies when finished with them.

**2. Discourage the repetition of inappropriate responses or behavior.**

**EXAMPLES**
- Correct a student's poor throwing motion before it becomes a habit.
- Check the first few answers on a written drill assignment to make sure students have the right idea.

The process of contiguity plays a major role in another, more complex learning process. It has been called by various names: classical conditioning, respondent conditioning, and signal learning, among others. Here we will use the first name.

# CLASSICAL CONDITIONING: PAIRING AUTOMATIC RESPONSES WITH NEW STIMULI

Through the process of **classical conditioning,** humans and animals can learn to respond automatically to a stimulus that once had no effect or a very different effect on them. The learned response might be an emotional reaction, such as fear or pleasure, or a physiological response, such as muscle tension. These normally involuntary responses can be conditioned, or learned, so that they will occur automatically in particular situations. Looking at an early experiment involving classical conditioning should help make this kind of learning process clearer.

## Pavlov's Dilemma and Discovery

In a Russian laboratory in the 1920s, a scientist was plagued by a series of setbacks. He was trying to answer questions about the digestive system of dogs, including how long it took a dog to secrete digestive juices after it had been fed. But this time period kept changing. At first, the dogs salivated in the expected manner while they were being fed. Then the dogs began to

*Pavlov's apparatus for classical conditioning of a dog's salivation. The experimenter sits behind a two-way mirror and controls the presentation of the conditioned stimulus (tone) and the unconditioned stimulus (food). A tube runs from the dog's salivary glands to a vial, where the drops of saliva are collected as a way of measuring the strength of the dog's response.*

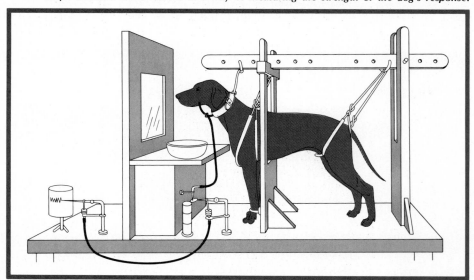

(C. G. Morris, **Psychology: An Introduction,** 4/e. Prentice-Hall, 1982, p. 136. Used with permission of Prentice-Hall, Inc.)

Before
Conditioning

Conditioning

salivate as soon as they saw the food. Finally, they salivated as soon as they saw the scientist enter the room. Because Ivan Pavlov decided to make a detour from his original experiments and examine these unexpected interferences in his work, we now have a better understanding of an important form of learning—classical conditioning.

In one of his first experiments directed toward the study of learning, Pavlov began by sounding a tuning fork and recording the dog's response. As expected, there was no salivation. Then he fed the dog. The response was salivation. The food in this case was an **unconditioned stimulus (US)** because it brought forth an automatic response of salivation. The salivation was an **unconditioned response (UR),** again because it occurred automatically. No prior learning or "conditioning" was needed to establish the· natural connection between food and salivation. The sound of the tuning fork, on the other hand, was at this point a neutral stimulus (NS) because it brought forth no response.

Using these three elements—the food, the salivation, and the tuning fork—Pavlov demonstrated that a dog could be conditioned to salivate after hearing the tuning fork. He did this by contiguous pairing of the sound with food. At the beginning of the experiment, he sounded the fork and then quickly fed the dog. After repeating this several times, the dog began to salivate after hearing the sound but before receiving the food. Now the tone was a **conditioned stimulus (CS)** that could bring forth salivation by itself. The response of salivating after the tone, now a **conditioned response (CR),** was similar to the original response to the food. Figure 5–2 shows a schematic diagram of what happened in Pavlov's laboratory.

You may be wondering what salivating dogs have to do with classroom learning. There are a number of reasons why research conducted with animals can be of value. Using animals makes it possible to isolate the effect of a few variables on some basic learning process. Also, animals don't worry about how well they are doing or try to outguess the researchers, the way people often do.

Pavlov's findings and those of others who have studied classical conditioning have at least two implications for teachers. First, it is possible that many of our emotional reactions to various situations are learned in part through

**Figure 5–2**  **Classical Conditioning in Pavlov's Laboratory**

| Before Conditioning | Conditioning | After Conditioning |
|---|---|---|
| Unconditioned stimulus (food) ↓ Unconditioned response (salivation) | 1. Present tone 2. Wait a second 3. Present food 4. Repeat 5. And repeat | Unconditioned stimulus (food) ↓ Unconditioned response (salivation) |
| *BUT* Neutral stimulus (tone) ↓ No noticeable response (no salivation) | | *AND* Conditioned stimulus (tone) ↓ Conditioned response (salivation) |

"PERHAPS, DR. PAVLOV, HE COULD BE TAUGHT TO SEAL ENVELOPES."

(Sidney Harris)

classical conditioning. Second, procedures based on classical conditioning can be used to help people learn more adaptive emotional responses. For example, people can learn to be less fearful and anxious in situations that have become threatening to them, such as speaking in public or taking tests. Emotions and attitudes as well as facts and ideas are learned in classrooms, and sometimes this emotional learning can interfere with academic learning. Let us consider a few examples.

## Examples of Classical Conditioning: Desirable and Undesirable

Fear and Anxiety

There is no absolute proof that we learn to be fearful and anxious in school through classical conditioning (Brewer, 1974), but consider these possibilities. A young child who is initially fearless on the playground could be involved in a painful accident on a swing. Later, the child may refuse to get on the swing again and seem fearful of other playground equipment and even of recess itself. A previously neutral stimulus, the swing, now automatically brings the response of fear. Other examples include learning to fear or hate school after several embarrassing or frightening experiences. A student may also learn to be very anxious or even physically sick during tests because tests have been associated with failure and possible painful punishment or ridicule at home. Finally, a student may learn the very common fear of speaking before a group.

Of course, positive emotional responses can be learned as well. If students frequently experience success in school, they will probably respond to new learning tasks with confidence rather than anxiety. Students who have been relatively successful in algebra will be more likely to face a new subject such as geometry with a relaxed attitude. In contrast, students who have found algebra a source of failure or even humiliation may face the first day of geometry with sweaty palms.

To develop the concept of classical conditioning a bit more, let us return for a moment to Elizabeth's classroom and consider three new terms.

## Generalization, Discrimination, and Extinction

Do you remember Elizabeth's response to the arrival of her supervisor? It is very possible that she had previously had bad experiences speaking publicly, especially when her performance was being evaluated. It is also possible that she had had unpleasant experiences in her college supervisor's class. Her trembling hands and nausea could be conditioned responses brought forth by people or situations associated with unpleasant, frightening, or embarrassing events in the past. These emotional responses may have spread to other similar situations, such as the new one she was facing.

But how does this spreading of responses to new situations occur? How could an embarrassing past event, possibly with a totally different cast of characters, lead Elizabeth to fear the presence of her advisor in her classroom? How can a child come to fear all swings and even slides and seesaws, when the child's bad experience was with only one particular swing?

Pavlov demonstrated one answer to this question with his dogs: the process of **generalization**. After the dogs learned to salivate to one particular tone, they would also salivate after hearing other tones. The response of salivating generalized to stimuli that were *similar* to the original CS. Elizabeth may have been ridiculed by one college professor and now her conditioned response of anxiety has generalized to similar stimuli—that is, other college professors.

Does this mean that Elizabeth will fear *all* speaking experiences? No. Elizabeth was not anxious about speaking to her class when her supervisor was not present. What she was doing is called **discrimination**—that is, responding differently to similar but not identical situations. Pavlov's dogs were also capable of discriminating when they learned that the food always followed one of the tones and not the others. Thus, it is possible that only adults (or only college professors, or only this particular professor) are capable of bringing forth Elizabeth's fear reaction.

Discrimination occurs because of another process called **extinction**. If a conditioned stimulus is presented repeatedly but not followed by the unconditioned stimulus (the tone but no food), the conditioned response (salivating after the tone) will finally go away. So if Elizabeth had initially been afraid of lecturing to her class but had never experienced anything unpleasant in doing so, her fear of speaking before the class would finally be extinguished. In other words, she would be able to discriminate between her class and other similar anxiety-arousing events.

We have just seen the effect classical conditioning may have on a teacher. Now let's look more closely at the positive effects it may have on students.

## Classroom Applications

The examples we have given so far have described a number of different ways in which emotional responses can be conditioned in humans. Generally, the conditioning involved was haphazard, with no Pavlovian scientist pulling strings. However, classical conditioning can also be used quite directly for positive changes in the classroom. In every class, most teachers meet several students who are overly concerned about their performance, who are fearful and withdrawn, who would rather not attempt a new activity than risk the chance of failure. These students may have learned to fear certain kinds of new situations because they had very unpleasant experiences in similar situations in the past. Techniques based on classical conditioning can be used to help students learn other responses to frightening situations.

**Prevention.** One general procedure suggested by classical conditioning is prevention. To prevent the development of negative emotional reactions to school situations, teachers can attempt to associate positive stimuli with experiences in school. This could mean preparing students in the early grades for potentially frightening experiences by telling them what is about to happen and encouraging the children to talk about their concerns. It could also mean making the classroom a pleasant and comfortable physical environment. (In Chapter 11 we will describe comfortable classrooms, appropriate for learning.) Finally, at every grade level students sometimes need to be protected from embarrassment, especially in a public situation, through well-timed interventions by the teacher.

**Cures.** Once a student has developed a fearful or anxious reaction to some aspect of school, other procedures are suggested by the classical conditioning model. One of the least complicated approaches is to use the principle of extinction. Encourage students to put themselves in the problem situation and then make sure unpleasant events do not follow. If, for example, a student is mildly fearful of the guinea pig in your classroom, you could encourage the student to touch the animal if you are certain no negative results will follow. After several uneventful contacts with the animal, the student's fear of it should be extinguished.

**Gradual Extinction.** Many fears that students have will not be so easily extinguished because the students will not put themselves in the problem situation. If a student absolutely refuses to take part in gym class, he or she will never learn that the embarrassment or pain of the past will not occur again. And even if the student is willing to take part, it is possible that the anxiety the student feels will actually interfere with performance, and failure or other unpleasant experiences will continue. The learned response of anxiety may be perpetuated. This is a definite possibility in cases of severe test anxiety. Extreme anxiety while taking a test leads to poor performance, which in turn leads to more anxiety. In these situations, simple extinction will not change the student's behavior, because unpleasant experiences will continue to be associated with the situation.

One approach for coping with these more difficult situations is gradual extinction. If a student is too fearful to participate in gym class, he or she can gradually work out the problem by taking small steps toward the goal.

# Guidelines

## Using Classical Conditioning

**1. Try to associate positive, pleasant events with learning tasks.**

**EXAMPLES**
- Use more group competition and less competition among individuals.
- When evaluating student performance, make positive as well as negative comments.

**2. Encourage students to put themselves into feared situations voluntarily if you are fairly certain that there will be no negative results.**

**EXAMPLES**
- Class presentations with no pressure to be perfect.
- Involving shy students in group work.

**3. If a student's fears are too strong for immediate participation, devise small steps toward that goal.**

**EXAMPLES**
- Oral presentations beginning with very small groups.
- Daily, then weekly, then major tests.

**4. Help students discriminate the conditions which may make a behavior appropriate or inappropriate.**

**EXAMPLES**
- Talking without raising your hand is acceptable in small group conversations but not in large class discussions.
- Throwing a temper tantrum may be expected from a young child, but not an adolescent.

Clarizio (1971) suggests that such a student first read exciting stories about sports figures, then watch others play at recess, then keep score, and then slowly get more and more involved in the activities in gym. A student who is anxious about tests can also be asked to take small steps, perhaps a number of short quizzes of varying difficulty, given in a noncompetitive situation. The Guidelines give other ideas for using classical conditioning in the classroom.

## OPERANT CONDITIONING: TRYING NEW RESPONSES

So far, we have concentrated on the relatively automatic learning of emotional responses such as fear, anxiety, and relaxation. Clearly, not all human learning is of this type. Emotional responses form only a small part of the things we learn: moreover, learners are often quite actively involved in the learning process. People constantly take deliberate action; they "operate" on their environment. These operations or actions have results, positive and negative. Operant conditioning is the behavioral learning process that involves these deliberate actions.

## The Work of Thorndike and Skinner

Thorndike's
Early Work

Thorndike and Skinner both played major roles in developing the knowledge we now have of operant conditioning. Edward Thorndike's (1913) early work was with cats he placed in problem boxes. To escape from the box and reach food outside, the cats had to pull out a bolt or perform some other task. They had to act on their environment. During the frenzied movements that followed the closing of the box, the cats eventually made the correct movement to escape, usually by accident. After repeating the process several times, the cats learned to make the correct response almost immediately. Thorndike decided, on the basis of these experiments, that one important law of learning was the **law of effect:** any act that produces a satisfying effect in a given situation will tend to be repeated in that situation. Because pulling out a bolt produced satisfaction (access to food), that movement was repeated when the cats found themselves in the box again.

Skinner's Early
Work

Thorndike thus established the basis for operant conditioning, but the person generally thought to be responsible for developing the concept is B. F. Skinner (1953). Skinner began with the belief that the principles of classical conditioning accounted for only a small portion of the behaviors that are learned. Many behaviors are not simple responses to stimuli, but deliberate

*B. F. Skinner observes a rat searching for food in a "Skinner box." This device enabled Skinner to develop his notion of operant conditioning: since behavior is affected by its consequences, control of these consequences provides some control over behavior.*

actions. According to Skinner, these deliberate actions, or **operants** are affected and changed by the consequences that follow them. Thus **operant conditioning** or **operant learning,** involves control of the consequences of behavior.

To study the effects of consequences on behavior under carefully controlled conditions, Skinner designed a special cagelike apparatus. The subjects of Skinner's studies were usually rats or pigeons placed in the cages, which soon came to be called **Skinner boxes.** A typical Skinner box is a small enclosure containing only a food tray and a lever or bar (for rats) or a disk (for pigeons). The lever or disk is connected to a food hopper. Modifications of this basic box include lights close to the lever or disk and electrified floors used to shock the animals.

You can probably imagine how such a box might be used to study the effects of positive consequences (food) or unpleasant consequences (shocks). A hungry pigeon is placed in the box and proceeds to explore it. Since pigeons tend to peck, the animal will eventually get around to pecking the disk. At that point, a small food pellet will drop into the food tray. The hungry animal eats the pellet, moves around the box, and soon pecks the disk again. There is more food, and before long the pigeon is pecking and eating continuously. The next time the pigeon is placed in the box, it will go directly to the disk and begin pecking.

Using this approach, Skinner has been able to study many questions about the effects of consequences on behavior. For example, how is the rate of pecking affected if the pigeons do not get food every time they peck? How long will the pigeon continue to peck if no food follows at all? How does the negative effect of a shock compare with the positive effect of food?

## The ABCs of Operant Conditioning

"Behavior," like "response" and "action," is simply a word for what a person does in a particular situation. Speaking, moving, gesturing, drawing, crying, hitting, and maintaining eye contact are all behaviors. None of these behaviors occur alone; all are in some way associated with other events in the environment. Conceptually, we may think of a behavior as being sandwiched between two sets of environmental influences: those that precede it (its **antecedents**) and those that follow it (its **consequences**) (Mahoney and Thoresen, 1974). This relationship can be shown very simply as antecedent → behavior → consequence, or A → B → C.

**Antecedents and Consequences of Behavior**

If behavior is influenced by its antecedents and its consequences, then it can be changed by a change in the antecedents, the consequences, or both. Let us first consider the alteration of consequences. Much more research has been conducted on the effects of consequences. According to the behavioral view, the consequences determine to a great extent whether the person will repeat the action in the future.

## Controlling the Consequences

The consequences brought about by a particular behavior can be pleasant or unpleasant for the person involved. Variations in the timing of the consequences may also have an effect on the person. Here we will look at several types of consequences and at the effects of different timing schedules.

**Reinforcement.** "Reinforcement" is a common word in everyday conversation. When most people use the term, they mean something like "reward." But "reinforcement" and "reinforcer" have particular meanings in psychology. A **reinforcer** is one type of consequence. The effect of the consequence determines whether the consequence is a reinforcer. Any consequence is a reinforcer if it increases the frequency of the behavior it follows. Using the ABC notion of behavior, we can say that behaviors followed by reinforcers are likely to be repeated in the future. **Reinforcement** is the process of using a reinforcer to increase the frequency of a behavior. When you see the term reinforcement, you should immediately think about a behavior increasing. Put another way, whenever you see a behavior persisting or increasing over time, you can assume something is reinforcing that behavior.

It is important to remember that the event reinforcing the behavior may not seem pleasant or desirable to you. Reinforcers are defined by their effect of increasing behavior. Students who are sent to the principal's office repeatedly for the same offense may be indicating that the trip is in some way reinforcing for them, even if it hardly seems reinforcing to you. Whether the consequences of any action are reinforcing probably depends on the individual's perception of the event and the meaning it holds for her or him. The chance to give an oral report to the entire class may be a very enjoyable event for one student and a task to be avoided at all costs for another. Another way of defining reinforcer is to say that a reinforcer is an event a person will work to attain.

There are two types of reinforcement. The first, called **positive reinforcement,** occurs when a stimulus is *presented* following a particular behavior. Examples include money and praise presented to students when they bring home As on their report cards, or cheers and laughter presented by other students following the class clown's silly answers during reading group. Notice that positive reinforcement can occur even when the behavior being reinforced (shouting out silly answers) is not "positive" from the teacher's

*Reinforcement can be deceptive. Though intended as punishment, this trip to the principal's office may actually be reinforcement in disguise for the student seeking attention or diversion. If the unwanted behavior persists or even increases after the visit, what is the teacher's next resort?*

(Cary Wolinsky/Stock, Boston)

point of view. The expert on old movies in Elizabeth's class continued to shout "Clark Gable," so the consequences—teacher attention and laughter from other students—were reinforcing for him. Positive reinforcement of inappropriate behaviors occurs unintentionally in many classrooms. Without realizing it, many teachers help maintain problem behaviors by inadvertently reinforcing these behaviors.

**Removing a
Stimulus**

The second kind of reinforcement, called **negative reinforcement,** involves the *removal* or termination of an aversive (unpleasant) stimulus. A stimulus is **aversive** if you will do something in order to escape it. If a particular action causes the removal or disappearance of something that is aversive, the action is likely to be repeated when the person again is faced with a similar situation. Consider the students who are repeatedly sent to the principal's office. Their rule-breaking probably is being reinforced in some way because they continue to do it. The misbehavior may be getting them out of "bad" situations such as a test or a class that causes anxiety. If so, the misbehavior is being maintained through negative reinforcement.

The terms "positive" and "negative" reinforcement often are confusing. It may help if you remember that reinforcement always refers to a process that increases behavior. Positive and negative tell you how the increase came about. Positive reinforcement means something was *presented* following a behavior, and the behavior increased. Negative reinforcement means something was *removed* following a behavior, and the behavior increased. Think of the terms "positive" and "negative" as similar to the terms "positive" and "negative" describing numbers. Positive reinforcement (like positive numbers) involves the *addition* or appearance of a stimulus. Negative reinforcement (like negative numbers) involves the *subtraction* or removal of a stimulus. In both cases, the behavior is likely to occur again in similar situations. The concept of negative reinforcement might be clearer to you if you read the example in Box 5–1.

---

## BOX 5–1 AN EVERYDAY EXAMPLE OF NEGATIVE REINFORCEMENT

*The following example of negative reinforcement is taken from a new book by John and Janice Baldwin (1981) called* Behavioral Principles in Everyday Life.

*AVOIDING THE TOLL TROLL*

There are . . . ways to cope with the problems of urban transportation and fuel conservation. A method utilizing negative reinforcement was tried in San Francisco. The Oakland Bay Bridge is a toll bridge that funnels many commuters into San Francisco each day. Because the people entering San Francisco would cause less urban congestion and use less fuel if they rode in car pools (rather than one person per car), people who rode together were rewarded. Cars with three or more people were allowed to cross the bridge without paying a toll and without having to slow down for toll booths. Thus, the use of car pools was negatively reinforced by the avoidance of two aversive events: (1) paying the regular toll, and (2) being delayed by the toll lines. Due to negative reinforcement, the percentage of people using car pools rose significantly, which in turn helped relieve the urban traffic.

Figure 5–3 **Reinforcement and Punishment**

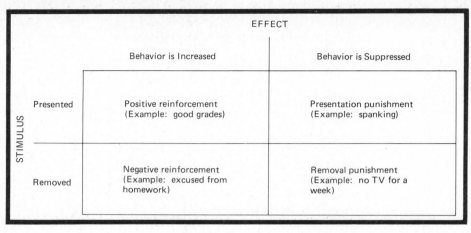

|  | | EFFECT | |
|---|---|---|---|
|  | | Behavior is Increased | Behavior is Suppressed |
| STIMULUS | Presented | Positive reinforcement (Example: good grades) | Presentation punishment (Example: spanking) |
|  | Removed | Negative reinforcement (Example: excused from homework) | Removal punishment (Example: no TV for a week) |

**A Decrease in Behavior**

**Punishment.** Negative reinforcement is often confused with punishment. The process of reinforcement (positive or negative) involves an increase in behavior. **Punishment,** on the other hand, involves a decrease in or suppression of behavior. A behavior followed by a **punisher** is less likey to be repeated in similar situations in the future. Again, the effect defines a consequence as a punisher. In the hope of increasing good writing, a teacher may try to use reinforcement ("You did such good work on those written reports that I'm going to let you present them to the entire class!") only to find the students behave as if they have been punished. They stop working hard on written reports.

**Presenting a Stimulus**

**Removing a Stimulus**

Like reinforcement, punishment may take one of two forms. The first type has been called punishment I or positive punishment, but we find these names misleading. We have chosen the name **presentation punishment.** It occurs when the appearance of a stimulus following the behavior suppresses or decreases the behavior. When teachers use demerits, extra work, running laps, and so on, they are attempting to use this kind of punishment. The other type of punishment, **removal punishment,** involves the disappearance or removal of a stimulus. When teachers or parents take away privileges after a young person has behaved inappropriately, they are applying this second kind of punishment. With both types, the effect is to decrease the behavior that led to the punishment. Figure 5–3 summarizes the four different processes we have just discussed: the two different kinds of reinforcement and the two different kinds of punishment.

### Reinforcement Schedules

**Continuous and Intermittent Schedules**

When people are learning a new behavior, they will learn it faster if they are reinforced for every correct response. This is a **continuous reinforcement** schedule. Once the response has been mastered, however, it is generally better to reinforce on an **intermittent schedule,** often but not every time. There are several reasons for using intermittent schedules to maintain established skills. One is simply that reinforcing every correct response would be time-consuming and practically impossible for the classroom

**Figure 5–4** **Effects of Different Reinforcement Schedules**

| Schedule | Definition | Example | Pattern of Responses |
|---|---|---|---|
| Fixed-interval | Predictable reinforcement based on set time interval. | Reinforcing the first response given after each 5-minute interval. | Increasing responses toward end of interval; pause after reinforcement. |
| Variable-interval | Unpredictable reinforcement based on varying time interval. | Reinforcing the first response given after 5 minutes, then after 7 minutes, then 3, then 9. | Slow, steady rate of responding; very little pause after reinforcement. |
| Fixed-ratio | Predictable reinforcement based on set number of responses. | Reinforcing every tenth response. | High rate of responding; pause after reinforcement. |
| Variable-ratio | Unpredictable reinforcement based on varying number of responses. | Reinforcing the tenth response, then the seventh response, then the ninth, then the twelfth. | Very high rate of responding; little pause after reinforcement. |

teacher. Another is that intermittent reinforcement helps the student learn to demonstrate new behaviors even when there is no reinforcement.

Types of Intermittent Schedules

There are four basic types of intermittent reinforcement schedules. Two are based on the amount of time that passes between reinforcers, and these are called interval schedules. The other two are based on the number of responses given between reinforcers, and these are called ratio schedules. Figure 5–4 offers a summary of the four different schedules. Not much research has been done in the classroom to test the effects of different reinforcement schedules on students. However, we can make some good guesses based on studies in other areas (Ferster and Skinner, 1957).

Effects on "Taking Breaks"

**Response Patterns.**    First, let's look at the effect different schedules have on the timing of responses. When reinforcement is based on a **fixed-interval** standard (every 5 minutes, for example), the reward is predictable. Reinforcement will always be given for the first response that occurs after a certain time period. Because the reinforcement is so predictable, there tends to be a pause right after the reinforcement is given. Assume, for example, that you know your teacher will stop by the library every 15 minutes to praise those who are working. No one in the library has a watch. Still, after about 12 minutes you all begin to focus on your reading so the teacher will not catch you talking. Just after the teacher completes one of the visits and praises you for working, however, you can relax and take a break, knowing that your chance for reinforcement (or punishment) will not come around again for several minutes.

Under a **variable-interval** reinforcement schedule, however, the pattern of responding is quite different. If the teacher described above stopped by on a highly unpredictable basis, sometimes returning just 45 seconds after the last visit, there would probably be fewer breaks or pauses after each visit. A teacher who wants some serious studying to take place would be happier with a variable-interval schedule.

This same principle holds for **fixed-ratio** and **variable-ratio** schedules. If you know a teacher is only interested in completed papers (a fixed-ratio schedule), you would be likely to pause after each paper and take a few days off before beginning the large job involved in writing a new paper. If you are like many other students, you might even take a week or two off and end up tackling it all the last night. However, if the teacher asked for partial results at unpredictable stages and graded you on progress (a variable-ratio schedule), you would be more likely to do a little work each day. Again, a teacher who wants students to spend two weeks on a project, not just one or two days, might be happier with a variable-ratio schedule.

**Speed of Performance.** Different reinforcement schedules can also have an effect on the speed at which a person performs. If reinforcement is based on the number of responses a person gives—a ratio rather than an interval schedule—the person has more control over the timing of the reinforcement. The faster the person accumulates the correct number of responses, the faster the reinforcement will come. A teacher who says, "As soon as you complete

*How might the teacher in this chemistry laboratory use information about the effects of various reinforcement schedules to encourage continuous work in the group projects? What can be done to keep the student productively involved, even when the teacher is working with another group?*

(Sybil Shelton/Monkmeyer)

these 10 problems correctly, you may go to the student lounge," can thus expect higher rates of performance than a teacher who says: "Work on these 10 problems for the next 20 minutes. Then I will check your papers and those with 10 correct may go to the lounge."

**Persistence.**    The third aspect of performance affected by different schedules is persistence. If reinforcement is withdrawn completely, the person is likely to slow down and finally stop giving a particular response. In other words, the behavior will probaby be extinguished. The rate of extinction will depend in large part on the schedule of reinforcement before the reinforcement stopped.

If the reinforcement has followed every response (continuous reinforcement), the person will quickly stop responding when the reinforcement stops. Fixed schedules (interval or ratio) also lead to relatively quick extinction. If people have been reinforced every five minutes or after five responses, they will soon stop responding when reinforcement does not follow the expected pattern. Both continuous and fixed patterns of reinforcement are quite predictable: We come to expect reinforcement at certain points and generally are quick to give up when the reinforcement does not meet our expectations. To encourage persistence of responding, variable schedules are most appropriate. As you can see in Box 5–2, Skinner saw many everyday examples of learning principles and schedules of reinforcement in action.

An understanding of the types of consequences along with some knowledge of the effects of various schedules of reinforcement should give you a much better sense of control over the consequences of behavior. However, if you remember the ABC model of learning we presented earlier, you know that antecedents can also have a marked effect on behavior.

---

### BOX 5–2 THOUGHTS OF A BEHAVIORIST

*For over 25 years, B. F. Skinner has maintained the practice of keeping notebooks to record his thoughts and ideas whenever they occur, day or night. Below is an excerpt from one of these notebooks that has been published* (Notebooks: B. F. Skinner, *Robert Epstein, editor). Prentice-Hall, 1980.*

At a concert or in listening to recorded music I have often found myself impatiently waiting for a piece of music to end, even though I am enjoying it. In part I may be inclined to escape from an uncomfortable seat or to get to bed, since the tendency is strong when the seat is noticeably uncomfortable or the hour late, but it is also a matter of the relative importance of the end of a piece of music. The music builds up to a termination which is maximally reinforcing. (I have noticed that the end of one sonata induces me to start playing another even when, midway, I am bored.)

There are many activities in which the major reinforcement comes at the end of a long chain of responses. In sex, the activity is repetitive, and in scientific research, it is often diverse, but in both the great moment comes at the end. The end competes with the beginning and middle.

I now see that I have been discussing large fixed ratios.

## Controlling the Antecedents

What Would
Happen If?

Antecedents provide information about which behaviors are appropriate in a given situation—that is, which behaviors will lead to positive consequences and which to negative. Quite often a kind of antecedent cue is involved. The antecedent cue of a principal standing in the hall provides information to students about the probable consequences of running or attempting to break into a locker. We often respond to such antecedent cues without fully realizing that they are influencing our behavior. But cues can be used deliberately in teaching.

Cueing

By definition, **cueing** is the act of providing an antecedent stimulus just before a particular behavior is to take place. Cueing is particularly useful in setting the stage for behaviors that must occur at a specific time but are easily forgotten. In working with young people, teachers (and parents, for that matter) often find themselves correcting behaviors after the fact. For example, they may remind children to do better next time or ask students, "When are you going to start remembering to. . . . ?" Such reminders often lead to irritation. The mistake is already made and the young person is left with only two choices, to promise to try harder or to say, "Why don't you leave me alone." Neither response is very satisfying.

Establishing a nonjudgmental cue can help avoid these negative confrontations. When a student performs the appropriate behavior after the presentation of the cue, the teacher can reinforce the student's accomplishment instead of punishing the student's failure. In some situations, without cueing teachers might never have a chance to reinforce appropriate behaviors, since students might not remember to perform them (Knapczyk and Livingston, 1974).

Once a response has been appropriately cued, the cueing may gradually be faded out. Cueing may also become less direct. Krumboltz and Krumboltz (1972) give these examples of direct and indirect cueing:

Examples

A journalism teacher tells her class, "Since this is a news article, remember to write the story just as objectively as possible even if you feel it's a one-sided issue." This cue tells students which behaviors are appropriate and avoids after-the-fact reminders and the lowered grades that would occur if the stories were too subjective. After students have written several objective stories, the teacher might move to a less direct cue, possibly saying, "Remember, this is a *news* story."

A student council advisor asks, "Is there any way we can get more facts before we reach a decision?" With these words the advisor avoids the need to berate the students for basing their decision on a limited set of facts. A less direct cue in this situation might be "Are you satisfied with the information we have?"

Such a method might also have worked in Elizabeth's classroom. To begin her game, Elizabeth might have said something like this: "When you play this game, it is sometimes hard to resist the temptation to make silly remarks. You can all help by not laughing if someone makes a remark that is just a joke." After the first few serious remarks, she could have then said: "You are doing a good job of sticking to the subject. We can play the game for a few more minutes before I begin the lesson since you are giving such good words."

The uses of operant conditioning in the classroom are numerous. To help you summarize the many points made here, we have included a set of Guidelines on this subject.

# *Guidelines*

## Using Operant Conditioning

**1. Make sure that positive behavior in class is reinforced.**

EXAMPLES
- Meaningful rewards for academic efforts such as free time at the end of class, extra recess time.
- Avoidance of meaningless rewards, possibly through class discussion of different rewards.

**2. Give plenty of reinforcement when establishing new behaviors.**

EXAMPLES
- Give extra praise for good work or attempts when students are beginning some new project.
- When dealing with problem behavior, recognize and reinforce every positive action.

**3. After new behaviors are established, give reinforcement on an unpredictable schedule to encourage persistence.**

EXAMPLES
- Surprise rewards for good participation in class.
- Unpredictable grading of homework.

**4. Use cueing to help establish new behaviors.**

EXAMPLES
- Humorous signs listing classroom rules such as: You are going to remember to put away your materials today, aren't you?
- Review of step-by-step process when assigning some major written project.

# LEARNING BY OBSERVING OTHERS

Modeling

When Elizabeth laughed at "Clark Gable's" comments in class, she provided a model for her students. Through her behavior, Elizabeth communicated that laughing was appropriate in this situation. Soon the students were laughing along with her, and she did not try to stop them until it was too late. This is one type of learning through observation. The process is called vicarious conditioning because another person is performing the actions and experiencing the consequences. The observer is learning vicariously—that is, through the experience of someone else. Today the more common name for this type of learning is **observational learning** or **modeling**.

## Operant versus Observational Learning

Bandura's Early Work

Bandura is responsible for much of what we know today about observational learning. In the early 1960s he was already at work showing ways in which cognitive processes are important in learning. In a classic study, he demonstrated that children were more aggressive after watching an aggres-

179

sive model, a film of an aggressive model, or a cartoon depicting violence than they were after viewing a nonaggressive model or no model at all (Bandura, 1963). The repeated demonstration that people and even less sophisticated animals can learn merely by observing another person or animal learn has offered a challenge to the behaviorist idea that cognitive factors are unnecessary in an explanation of learning. Observation can be a very efficient learning process. The first time children hold hairbrushes, cups, tennis rackets, or steering wheels, they usually brush, drink, swing, or steer as well as they can, given their present muscle development and coordination. Through modeling we learn not only how to perform a behavior, but also what will happen to us in specific situations if we do perform it. For example, you may slow down on a certain street because you have seen many people being stopped by police on that street.

Despite the striking differences, learning through observation does follow many of the patterns of other forms of conditioning. Observers who witness models being reinforced on an intermittent schedule, for example, show greater persistence than observers who watch a model being reinforced continuously (S. Berger, 1971). Like the other forms of learning, modeling has a number of different uses in the classroom.

### Classroom Applications of Observational Learning

A dramatic example of the impact of modeling is found in a study by O'Connor (1969). He began by identifying a group of preschool children who were very isolated from their peers and seemed unable to play normally. Half

**Figure 5–5**  **The Results of Vicarious Reinforcement**

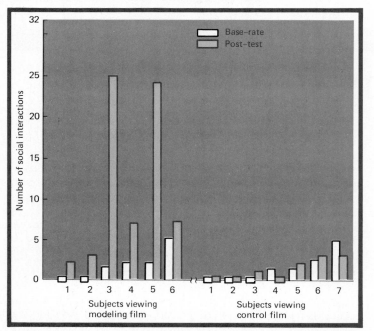

*From R. D. O'Connor. Modification of social withdrawal through symbolic modeling. **Journal of Applied Behavior Analysis**, 1969, **2**, 20.*

of this group was shown a film in which a child gradually moved from playing alone to playing with peers. Positive consequences followed the increased social interaction of the child in the film. The other half of the group was shown a film with no human characters. The children who saw the first film increased their own interactions with their peers dramatically, as shown in Figure 5–5.

Although such dramatic results are not always possible, the process of modeling deserves considerable attention. Studies have indicated that modeling can be used to achieve three different effects. First, it can teach new behaviors. Second, it can help encourage or elicit old behaviors. Finally, it may strengthen or weaken certain inhibitions for the purpose of helping students overcome problems like shyness or fear.

**Teaching New Behaviors.** A wide range of new behaviors, such as speaking a foreign language, developing skills in sports, and tasting wine properly, are acquired through observing others. The appropriate if often embarrassing use of colorful language by children is another example. Through modeling, people may even develop strong emotional reactions to situations they themselves have never experienced, such as flying. A child who watches a friend fall from a swing and break an arm may become fearful of swings. Throughout the school years, but particularily during adolescence, students often learn how to dress, talk, and behave by observing the interactions of their "popular" peers (Baldwin and Baldwin, 1981).

*The Teacher as a Model*

Given all this, consider the role of the classroom teacher. Teachers serve as models for the acquisition of a tremendous range of new behaviors, from pronouncing vocabulary words to being enthusiastic about learning. According to Bandura (1977), learning new behavior through observation of someone else may well be more efficient than learning the behavior through direct reinforcement. For teachers, this fact presents endless opportunities, as well as some obvious need for care.

*This teacher's role as model pervades everything he does. Not only is he showing his students how to do something, but he is conveying enthusiasm, interest, and commitment to learning.*

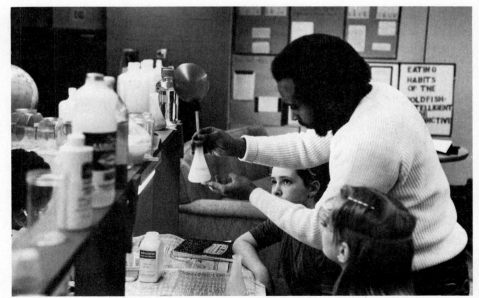

(Ken Karp)

**Encouraging Old Behaviors.**   The preschool students viewing O'Conner's film were probably already able to interact with their peers. They simply didn't do it very often. The effect of viewing the film was to draw forth behaviors already in the students' repertoire. All of us have had the experience of looking for cues from other people when we find ourselves in unfamiliar situations. Observing the behavior of others tells us which of our old behaviors to use: the proper fork for eating the salad, when to leave a gathering, what kind of language is appropriate, and so on.

This phenomenon was demonstrated in a classroom by Broden, Bruce, Mitchell, Carter, and Hall (1970). Two disruptive boys were seated near each other. When the teacher paid more attention to one of the boys as his involvement in his work improved, the other boy's behavior improved also. Both boys were already able to pay attention. They just did not do so very often until the teacher made use of observational learning.

**Strengthening or Weakening Inhibitions.**   If a class witnesses one student breaking a class rule and getting away with it, they may learn that undesirable consequences do not follow rule-breaking. Members of the class may be less inhibited in the future about breaking this rule. If the rule-breaker is a well-liked, high-status class leader, the effect of the modeling may be even more pronounced. One psychologist has called this phenomenon the **ripple effect** (Kounin, 1970). You saw an example in Elizabeth's class. When she laughed and did not stop the first few students from giggling, she encouraged more laughter.

Using the Ripple
Effect

The ripple effect can also work for the teacher's benefit. When the teacher deals effectively with a rule-breaker, especially a class leader, the idea of breaking this rule may be suppressed in the other students viewing the transaction. This does not mean that teachers must reprimand each student who breaks a rule. As we will see in a later chapter on classroom management, praising appropriate behavior while ignoring inappropriate behavior is sometimes much more effective. But once a teacher has called for a particular action, following through is an important part of capitalizing on the ripple effect.

The ripple effect could have been used to great advantage in Elizabeth's class. Remember the problems she had with the game? If all else had failed, she could have dealt with the situation by calling the game to a halt early and saying: "Linda, Carol, David, and Steven, you gave some thoughtful answers. You may hand out these papers (or leave for lunch early, or lead the small discussion groups today, or skip your homework assignment tonight)." While this strategy might not have salvaged the game for the day, it could have had a positive effect on the other students. They could have learned through observation how to conduct themselves. The next time Elizabeth introduces a game, students might be ready to participate more appropriately since they had seen how appropriate participation produced desirable consequences.

Quite a bit of research has been conducted on observational learning. A few of the more important conclusions are these: (1) High-status models and models similar to the observer are more likely to be imitated. (2) Complex skills require more observations to be imitated accurately. (3) Both hostile behavior and moral standards are readily imitated by observers. (4) When the behaviors of the model are rewarded, they are more likely to be imitated (Bower and Hilgard, 1981). We have included a set of Guidelines here.

# *Guidelines*

## *Using Observational Learning*

**1. Model those behaviors you want your students to learn.**

EXAMPLES
- Show enthusiasm for the subject you teach.
- Be willing to demonstrate both physical and mental tasks you expect the student to perform.

**2. Use peers as models.**

EXAMPLES
- In group work, pair students who do well with those who are having difficulties.
- Ask students to explain lessons to the class or to a small group.

**3. Make sure that students see that positive behaviors lead to reinforcement for others.**

EXAMPLES
- Point out the connection between positive behavior and positive consequences in stories.
- When a student is misbehaving, try to find another student near by who can be reinforced for behaving more appropriately.

**4. Enlist the help of popular students in modeling behaviors you want for the entire class.**

EXAMPLES
- Ask a well-liked student to be friendly to a class isolate.
- Let high status students lead some activity or project if you need to gain class cooperation.

---

Many teaching strategies are based on behavioral principles of learning. Chapter 9 is devoted to a closer look at several of these strategies. In that chapter we will examine specific applications and how to implement them. Before closing this chapter, however, we consider two very well developed applications of behavioral principles that have evolved their own technology.

# BEHAVIORAL TECHNOLOGY

The application of behavioral principles of learning to classroom teaching has taken many forms. Two of the more well developed are programmed instruction and the Personalized System of Instruction (PSI), generally known as the Keller Plan.

## Programmed Instruction

Definition of Programmed Instruction

As with many other concepts in educational psychology, no one definition of **programmed instruction** would satisfy everyone. The safest definition is that it is a set of instructional materials students can use to teach themselves about a particular topic. Furthermore, it is a set of materials that has been developed in keeping with several key principles, many of them behavioral in origin. According to O'Day, Kulhavy, Anderson, and Malczynski (1971), these principles include:

1. Specification of the goal to be mastered by the learner.
2. Careful pilot testing of the material.
3. Self-pacing to allow learners to move through the material at their own rate.
4. The need for definite responses from the learner.
5. Immediate feedback so the learner will know if a response is correct.
6. A division into small steps.

If you consider only the first three principles (goals, tested materials, and self-pacing), you might wonder how programmed instruction is any different from a carefully written, clear, and logical textbook. The last three principles (constant responding, immediate feedback, and small steps) are the ones that actually set programmed instruction apart from other written materials.

**Step-by-Step Frames**

The small steps used in programmed instruction are generally called **frames.** Most contain some text or information and at least one question requiring a student response. Students read the material, answer the question(s) immediately, check to see if the response is correct, and then move on to the next frame. The step from one frame to the next is so small that students can expect to be correct most of the time. But, of course, they are not always correct. There are two different kinds of programmed instruction, each with a different way of handling wrong answers.

**Skinnerian Programming**

**Linear Programs.** The linear approach is often called Skinnerian programming, because Skinner was its founder and prime advocate. One of its most distinctive features is that students must create an answer, not just select one from a multiple-choice format. They cover the correct response until they are ready to check their own answer. In **linear programs** students move through a fixed sequence of frames designed to lead them from one concept to the next with as few errors as possible. If students do make a wrong response, they learn of their error immediately, see the correct answer, and move on to the next frame. Figure 5–6 offers an example of a linear program for teaching high school physics.

**Error-Free Learning**

Linear programmers believe students should make errors on no more than 5 to 10 percent of the frames. To keep errors at this low level, the developers of the programs pilot-test the frames, identifying those that give students the most trouble. These error-causing frames are then improved or broken down into smaller steps to make success more likely (O'Day, Kulhavy, Anderson and Malczynski, 1971). In addition, many of the frames contain some kind of prompt or clue to help students create the correct answer. For example, students may be given four-letter lines to fill in when the correct answer has exactly four letters. Other clues include giving the first half of a two-word answer or providing a picture.

The linear programmers' emphasis on error-free learning goes back to Skinner's belief that wrong answers strengthen unwanted responses (Skinner, 1954). Advocates of **branching programs** are less concerned about eliminating wrong answers and, in fact, use wrong answers as part of the teaching approach.

**Figure 5–6** **A Linear Program for Physics**

| Sentence to Be Completed | Word to Be Supplied |
|---|---|
| 1. The important parts of a flashlight are the battery and the bulb. When we "turn on" a flashlight, we close a switch which connects the battery with the _____. | bulb |
| 2. When we turn on a flashlight, an electric current flows through the fine wire in the _____ and causes it to grow hot. | bulb |
| 3. When the hot wire glows brightly, we say that it gives off or sends out heat and _____. | light |
| 4. The fine wire in the bulb is called a filament. The bulb "lights up" when the filament is heated by the passage of a(n) _____ current. | electric |
| 5. When a weak battery produces little current, the fine wire, or _____, does not get very hot. | filament |

From B. F. Skinner, Teaching Machines. *Science*, 1958, **128**, p. 973.

Multiple-Choice
Programs

**Branching Programs.** This second approach to programmed instruction is often called multiple-choice programming because students are given several choices for each response. After each choice, students are told to go to a particular frame for more information. If they choose the correct answer, they will be directed to a frame that says, in effect, "You're right. Congratulations! Here's another problem." If they choose the wrong answer, they are sent to a frame telling them they are wrong, giving a remedial explanation, and then sending them back to try again. Crowder (1960) is the person usually credited with establishing this approach to programmed instruction.

Advantages of
Branching
Programs

The advantage of branching programs is that the developer can first test a frame to find the most common student errors and misconceptions. Then remediation frames can be designed to correct these common errors. Unfortunately, developers often skip this stage and simply try to imagine the most likely wrong answers. This method, though faster, is not as accurate. Much of the power of branching programs is lost when the frames are not tested first (O'Day, Kulhavy, Anderson and Malczynski, 1971).

A second potential advantage of branching programs is that very bright or well-prepared students can move through the material quickly, skipping the remediation, while slower students receive all the help they need. The disadvantage of branching programs is that they do not lend themselves very well to materials such as handouts or books. Turning back and forth to find the next frame can get very confusing. Once you lose your place in a branching program book, it is very difficult to find it again.

**The Usefulness of Programmed Instruction.** Research comparing the effectiveness of linear and branching programs has failed to demonstrate that one type is better than the other (Silberman, Melaragno, Coulson and Estevan, 1961; O'Day, Kulhavy, Anderson and Malczynski, 1971). Similarly, research has not demonstrated that programmed instruction is any better or any worse than other forms of teaching, although Langer's review of 112 studies indicated that programmed instruction has led to significantly more student learning in about 40 percent of the studies examined (Langer, 1972). As we will continue to discover throughout this text, no one method is best all the time for every subject and student.

Our experience with programmed instruction is that the process of designing a program for students can be very enlightening in and of itself. Trying to break material down into small steps helps teachers realize how much they often take for granted in their teaching. We all frequently take large steps in our explanations, leaving many students behind. In addition, seeing the students' wrong answers can help you improve your teaching by pinpointing key misunderstandings.

For the students, there are other benefits. Feedback based on these key misunderstandings is more likely to clear up problems than a general rehash of the material. It is also likely that some students will prefer self-pacing and the chance to correct their own errors offered by programmed materials. Using this method, students are not put on the spot publicly for their mistakes.

There are a number of cases in which programmed instruction may prove valuable. Having these materials available to reteach concepts can be very helpful if only a few students need extra help. Low-achieving students and very anxious students often benefit from programmed instruction, probably because it is clear, well organized, and allows the students to repeat parts they do not understand the first time through (Cronbach and Snow, 1977; Tobias, 1981, 1982). Finally, you might consider asking students to write programs themselves. This activity not only helps the students learn the material, but it also provides you with programs that might be appropriate for slower students.

*When to Use Programmed Instruction*

As a teacher, you probably would write linear rather than branching programs for your students. A really sophisticated branching program is difficult to create and even more difficult to put on paper. For this reason, branching programs are often presented by computers. This is just one of the many uses of the computer in the classroom. Computers are becoming so important in education that we have included a special section on their role following Chapter 11, "Designing Instruction: Objectives, Formats, and Settings." The advent of the computer has added new possibilities for designing instruction in the 1980s, but more on this later. For now, let's end this chapter with a look at a system that does not require any special equipment, the Keller Plan.

## The Keller Plan

In the mid-1960s, Fred Keller developed an approach to individualizing instruction that does not rely on any special materials or machines. The system makes use of several behavioral principles (specific goals, small steps, and immediate feedback) as well as lectures, demonstrations, and tutoring (Keller, 1966). It has been used mostly for college teaching and has been very carefully researched.

*Steps in PSI*

The **Keller Plan,** also called the **Personalized System of Instruction (PSI),** has a number of basic components (Robin, 1976). First, course readings are broken down into small units, each with specific goals and study guides. Students move at their own pace through the units and then come to class for testing. Proctors, usually students who have successfully completed the course, administer an oral or written test for the unit in class and give immediate feedback. If students have mastered the unit (generally with a score of 80 percent or better), they can go on to the next. If not, they must repeat the unit and take another test. Grades depend on the number of units successfully completed and perhaps to a small extent on a midterm and a final examination. Lectures and demonstrations are used more to motivate students than to present information.

**Research on PSI**

Evaluations of PSI have been very positive. In a review of 39 studies comparing the Keller approach with other teaching methods, Robin (1976) found significantly higher student achievement in 30 of the 39 studies. Using sophisticated statistical procedures to analyze the results of 75 studies with college students, Kulik, Kulik, and Cohen (1979) found that students in Keller Plan courses scored an average of 8 percentage points higher on final exams and 14 percentage points higher on tests given several months after the course had ended, when compared with students in conventional classes. Final grades of the Keller Plan students were higher, in keeping with their higher achievement on the tests. The percentage of students who completed the courses and the average time required for the course were almost the same for the Keller Plan and the conventional courses. Students found the former more enjoyable, demanding, and higher in overall quality than regular classes.

A number of studies have examined the Keller Plan to determine which components are the most important for student learning. The most important elements appear to be (1) specfic goals; (2) frequent testing; (3) proctoring; (4) having to master one unit before moving on to the next; and (5) a relatively high level for mastery. Self-pacing and lectures do not seem necessary, and tests can be either oral or written. As you might expect, the experience of proctoring turns out to be useful in helping proctors learn as well as in helping the students (K. Johnson and Ruskin, 1977). Even if you do not use the entire Keller Plan, you might consider incorporating some of the effective features into your teaching, especially if you work with high school students.

## SUMMARY

1. In defining learning, theorists disagree about the role of thinking, although most would agree that learning is demonstrated when a person responds to a situation in a new way and that new response continues to occur in similar situations.

2. Behavioral theorists place special emphasis on environmental stimuli and observable responses.

3. In contiguity learning, if two events occur together repeatedly, they will become associated. Later when only one event is present, the other will also be remembered.

4. In classical conditioning, a previously neutral stimulus is repeatedly paired with a stimulus that is already capable of bringing forth an emotional or physiological response. After several pairings in which the conditioned stimulus precedes the unconditioned stimulus and signals its appearance, the conditioned stimulus alone will bring forth a response similar to the original emotional or physiological response.

5. Operant conditioning is concerned with the deliberate responses of people to their environment. These responses are sandwiched between antecedent stimuli and consequent events.

6. In order to change behavior (and promote learning) a teacher can change the antecedents or the consequences of a student's behavior.

7. The consequences following an action may be positive or negative for the person involved. If the person continues to behave in the same manner, the consequences of the behavior are apparently reinforcing for that person. If the person discontinues certain actions, the consequences of the behavior apparently represent a form of punishment for that person.

8. The scheduling of reinforcement can have a major influence on the distribution, speed, and persistence of responses. Pauses after reinforcement are found with fixed schedules. The highest rates of responding are found with ratio schedules. The greatest persistence occurs with variable schedules.

9. Antecedent cues can be used to tell students which behaviors will be followed by positive consequences and which will be followed by negative consequences.

10. Vicarious conditioning, or learning through observation, can be useful in a number of ways: in teaching new behaviors, in encouraging old behaviors, and in strengthening or weakening inhibitions.

11. Programmed instruction offers a systematic application of the principles of behavioral learning in which students teach themselves using specially prepared materials.

12. Another method making use of behavioral principles is the Keller Plan, or the Personalized System of Instruction (PSI).

## KEY TERMS

behavioral (psychology)

cognitive (psychology)

Neobehaviorists

social learning theory

learning

contiguity learning

stimulus and response

classical conditioning

unconditioned stimulus (US)

unconditioned response (UR)

neutral stimulus

conditioned stimulus (CS)

conditioned response (CR)

generalization

discrimination

extinction

law of effect (Thorndike)

operants

operant conditioning (learning)

Skinner box

antecedent

consequence

reinforcer/reinforcement

positive reinforcement

negative reinforcement

aversive stimulus

punisher/punishment

presentation punishment

removal punishment

continuous reinforcement

intermittent reinforcement

fixed-interval schedule

variable-interval schedule

fixed-ratio schedule

variable-ratio schedule

cueing

observational learning (modeling)

ripple effect

programmed instruction

frame

linear program

branching program

Keller Plan/Personalized System
    of Instruction (PSI)

# SUGGESTIONS FOR FURTHER READING AND STUDY

BALDWIN, J. D. and BALDWIN, J. I. *Behavioral principles in everyday life*. Englewood Cliffs, NJ: Prentice-Hall, 1981. The focus here is on using behavioral principles in a variety of real life situations, not just the classroom.

BANDURA, A. *Social learning theory*. Englewood Cliffs, N.J.: Prentice-Hall, 1977. Bandura's book offers an excellent statement of the present findings of the social learning theorists. The book is not light reading but it is very thorough and informative.

BOWER, G. H. and HILGARD, E. R. *Theories of learning* (5th Ed.). Englewood Cliffs, NJ: Prentice-Hall, 1981. This is a classic reference on the range of learning theories, from behavioral to cognitive.

HILL, W. F. *Principles of learning: A handbook of application*. Sherman Oaks, CA: Alfred Publishers, 1981. While this book emphasizes applications of behavioral views, it goes on to discuss language, memory, thinking, and moral development.

MACMILLIAM, D., FORNESS, S. R., and TRUMBALL, B. M. The role of punishment in the classroom. *Exceptional Children*, 1973, *40*, 85–96. Here you will find a description of how and when to use punishment. The article includes cautions, procedures, and guidelines for the appropriate use of this type of consequence.

MCKEACHIE, W. J. The rise and fall of the laws of learning. *Review of Educational Research*, 1974, *3*, 7–11. This is a classic criticism of behavioral principles of learning. McKeachie gives a brief history of the development of this area, then describes the problems he sees in applying behavior principles to classroom learning.

RACHLIN, H. *Behaviorism in everyday life*. Englewood Cliffs, New Jersey: Prentice-Hall, 1980. A concise and very readable discussion of how ordinary experiences can be understood in terms of bbehavioral principles.

SKINNER, B. F. *About behaviorism*. New York: Knopf, 1974. This book will take you beyond operand conditioning in the classroom to the application of behavioral principles in society itself.

SKINNER, B. F. *The technology of teaching*. Englewood Cliffs, New Jersey: Prentice-Hall, 1968. Skinner himself had many ideas about applying behavioral principles to learning in schools. His book is a very clear and cogent argument for the value of these principles in teaching.

# Teachers' Forum

## Being Comfortable with Being Positive

One of the principles of operant conditioning is this: To increase a child's desirable behavior, positively reinforce that behavior when it occurs. Teachers are told, "Catch the child being good." However, in the course of a busy school day it often is difficult, especially for beginning teachers, not only to act on this advice, but also to feel natural and comfortable doing so. How did you get yourself in the habit of noticing desirable behaviors? Did you feel awkward at first compared to how you feel now?

**The Importance of Practice**

After ten years of teaching, I still make every effort to "catch *each* child being good." Yes, I did feel awkward the first few months of my first year. However, now it's part of my philosophy of teaching as well as in daily living: to reward, compliment, and praise. I got myself in the habit of noticing students' desirable behavior by rewarding appropriate actions, good work habits, and acceptable social skills. When I make a request, I reward those who comply immediately. When I wish to change a student's undesirable behavior, I seat that student by another who exhibits the desired behavior — so it can be rewarded and reinforced.

Patricia Frank, Fourth- and Fifth-Grade Teacher
*Cambridge School, South Brunswick, New Jersey*

**Being Genuine**

I certainly did feel awkward about a lot of things when I first began teaching. It is no easy task for a beginning teacher to focus on curriculum, individual differences, learning problems, and at the same time look for positive behaviors when usually the most negative stand out. I think it is important to try to be a positive person in general. I don't believe you can "catch a child being good" very often unless you have developed the habit in your out-of-school life as well. If you try to do it just because "the book says so," it will be false reinforcement at best and probably inconsistent. The other side of the coin is to ignore negative behavior unless it is harmful to others.

Joan Bloom, First-Grade Teacher
*Henry Barnard Lab School for Rhode Island College, Providence, Rhode Island*

**A Variety of Rewards**

During class and study time, I walk around the room and tell students quietly at their desks how well they are doing. At the end of each week I have an Award Day. I hand out awards to the child having the best spelling sentences, the neatest penmanship, the most improved student, the student having all work completed on time and to the best of his ability, and so on. At the end of each month, one student is chosen as Student of the Month. His picture is taken and posted in the hallway with the other sixth-grade students chosen. His name is announced over the public address, and he receives an award signed by the principal and his teachers.

Sharon Klotz, Sixth-Grade Language Arts Teacher
*Kiel Middle School, Kiel, Wisconsin*

## A "Poor-Me" Student

Imagine that you have in your class a capable, attractive student who is continually running herself down. She makes statements such as "I'm not smart enough to do this," "Nobody wants to work with me," "I always do badly," "I don't have any friends," and so on. How can you use behavior modification to help this student stop her self-depreciation and develop a more positive attitude toward herself and school?

**Genuine Recognition**

Nothing beats a positive, encouraging attitude, reinforced with honest and frequent praise distributed in some way to each child. But when the "poor-me" child surfaces, perhaps it's time to develop a special ongoing unit on self-esteem. How about instituting a weekly awarding of "superlatives," complete with fancy badges and ceremonial presentation. Select the attributes you want to salute, like "Friendliest," "Quietest," "Best Listener," "Neatest," and "Best Helper." Precede the unit with class discussions of people's differences and uniqueness, the good qualities we all possess, and the importance of knowing that everybody has at least one thing he does well. Even "poor-me" might find out she's valued for some special reasons.

Harriet Chipley, Elementary Art Teacher
*Lookout Mountain Elementary School, Lookout Mountain, Tennessee*

## Sick of Oral Assignments?

Imagine that one of your students asks to go see the school nurse at least twice a week. According to the nurse, most but not all of the complaints have been groundless. Once he did actually have severe stomach cramps. Another time it turned out that he was actually coming down with the flu. Nine out of 10 times, however, there has been nothing wrong at all. Recently you have noticed that he tends to get sick during oral assignments. What steps would you take in this situation?

**Looking for Sources of Reinforcement**

The nurse may be providing some type of positive reinforcement to this student which may not be all bad. I think that after a discussion with this student, I would give him two passes to the nurse each week. Any passes not used could be traded for privileges such as being an observer during assignments, or no homework, or other rewards that the student might choose.

Darline Reynold, Junior High School Teacher
*Spirit Lake Junior High School, Spirit Lake, Iowa*

**Determining the Seriousness of the Problem**

In this case, my job is to discover how serious his problem is. First, I would try the following: (1) Establish the pattern of his behavior by observation; (2) suggest he stay with the class, but if he feels worse in 10 minutes, he may go to the nurse; (3) suggest he give his speech first, then go to the nurse; (4) rather than a solo speech assignment, include him in a panel presentation; (5) suggest he write and then simply read his assignment. If these attempts do not seem to solve the problem, I would then do the following: (1) Alert his advisor that a discussion of this problem is urgent; (2) have a class discussion on how all students view speech assignments; (3) assure the student privately that this is a normal fear and try to work with him on a possible solution.

Shirley Wilson Roby, Sixth-Grade Reading Teacher
*Lakeland Middle School, Shrub Oak, New York*

# 6

# Cognitive
# Views
# of Learning

OVERVIEW     In this chapter we turn from behavioral views of learning to a different perspective, the cognitive orientation. Essentially, this means a shift from "viewing the learners and their behaviors as products of incoming environmental stimuli" to seeing the learners as "sources of plans, intentions, goals, ideas, memories, and emotions actively used to attend to, select, and construct meaning from stimuli and knowledge from experience" (Wittrock, 1982, pp. 1–2). But although the cognitive focus is on internal activities such as thinking and feeling, external factors such as teaching strategies and materials can play a major role in helping students learn.

We will begin with a discussion of a general cognitive model of learning and memory. Then we will consider how people take in information from the constantly changing world around them. Next we will explore how ideas, facts, concepts, rules, and other forms of knowledge are organized and represented so they can be stored and used. We will spend quite a bit of time examining learning, remembering, and forgetting, including ways to improve memory skills. All these facets of human learning and memory have important implications for teaching, and we will examine several of these. Finally we will seek answers to this question: Why do some people learn and remember better than others?

By the time you complete this chapter, you should have a number of new ideas about the ways learning takes place and how to improve your own learning. More specifically, you should be able to do the following:

- Describe a model of human learning from the cognitive perspective.
- Give examples of the role of perception in learning.
- Discuss how the representation of knowledge influences learning.
- Describe the role of schemata in learning and remembering.
- Develop a plan for teaching the basic terms from your subject in a meaningful way.
- Use memory strategies or study skills derived from cognitive theory to prepare for the test you may have to take on this chapter.

But before you can appreciate any applications, you need a better understanding of the cognitive perspective on learning.

## LEARNING: THE COGNITIVE VIEW

Learning Is
More than
Practice and
Reward

As we mentioned at the beginning of Chapter 5, a number of psychologists have long believed that behavioral principles provide only part of the answer to questions about how we learn. For example, the behavioral notion that we remember best those events that are practiced and rewarded is contradicted often in everyday life. You probably have at least one friend whose telephone number you have to look up each time you call. Although you dial the number frequently (practice) and enjoy the conversations (reward), you have not learned the telephone number. Yet you may remember a particular joke, movie scene, conversation, or your SAT scores, even though these events happened only once and were not practiced (M. Hunt, 1982).

## Elements of Cognitive Perspectives

Cognitive theorists believe that learning is the result of our attempts to make sense of the world. To do this, we use all the mental tools at our disposal. The way we think about situations, as well as our beliefs, expectations, and feelings, influence how and what we learn. Two students may experience the same class but learn two entirely different lessons. What each student learns depends on what each already knows and how the new information is processed.

**Beliefs Influence**
**Learning**

As an example of how beliefs and thoughts can influence learning, Wittrock (1978) describes an early study by Kaufman, Baron and Knapp (1966). These researchers told subjects they would be reinforced on a particular schedule as they worked on a task. Actually, a different reinforcement schedule was used. But the subjects' behavior was affected more by the schedule they thought they were under than by the actual schedule being applied. Thus an internal event, a belief in this case, was more influential than an external event, the actual reinforcement schedule. Cognitive theorists cite findings such as these to demonstrate that there is more to learning than responding to antecedents and consequences. Our interpretation of an event or its meaning for us also influences learning.

**Role of**
**Reinforcement**

Both behavioral and cognitive theorists believe reinforcement is important in learning, but for different reasons. The strict behaviorist states that reinforcement strengthens responses; cognitive theorists see reinforcement as a source of feedback. This feedback provides information about what is likely to happen if the behaviors are repeated. In the cognitive view, reinforcement for the learner is the reduction of uncertainty that leads to a sense of mastery and understanding. In other words, reinforcement comes from constructing an effective way of understanding the world and accomplishing goals.

**Active Learner**

The cognitive view of learning sees people as active. They initiate experiences that lead to learning, seek out information to solve problems, rearrange and reorganize what they already know to achieve new learning. Instead of being passively influenced by environmental events, people actively choose, decide, practice, pay attention, ignore, and make many other responses as they pursue goals. One of the most important influences in this process is what the individual brings to the learning situation. Cognitive psychologists are becoming more and more interested in the role of knowledge in learning. What we already know determines to a great extent what we will learn, remember, and forget (Peeck, van der Bosch and Kreupeling, 1982; Resnick, 1981).

Bransford (1979) offers a brief description of the major concerns of cognitive theorists. Essentially these concerns are about "how people learn, understand, and remember information, and why some people do these things better than others" (p. 3). There is not one cognitive theory of learning. In fact, cognitive psychologists have tended to investigate particular aspects of learning, such as how adults remember verbal information or how children comprehend stories. They have not sought general laws of learning that apply to all organisms (animals as well as people) in all situations. They have

*Rather than the environment shaping the student, a cognitive learning theory emphasizes the mind acting upon and interacting with the environment. What sorts of "wheels" might be turning in this boy's mind as he listens to his teacher's explanation?*

been most interested in the types of learning only humans can accomplish: reasoning, problem solving, language, and so on. Thus we cannot present one unified theory and say it is *the* cognitive theory of learning.

**Two Cognitive Approaches**

But although there are many cognitive perspectives on learning, there are only two major categories of theories. The first is the information processing approach, which relies heavily on the computer as a model for human learning and memory. The second view, often called constructivist, emphasizes the role of the individual in building an understanding of the world (Neisser, 1976). We will draw from both approaches, since both have implications for teaching.

## A Model of Learning

Learning can be described as the accumulation, organization, and use of knowledge. Something is learned when it becomes a relatively permanent part of our store of knowledge, available for solving problems and accumulating more knowledge. In this view, learning is closely tied to memory. Everything learned is stored in memory. If something exists in your memory, you learned it.

**Taking in Information**

The first step in learning is **perception** or recognizing events in the world. We must take in sights, sounds, smells, and give meaning to them. A pattern of light on the retina must be recognized as an apple or a word or another person. In this endeavor, practice makes perfect. Words that once required careful attention to figure out are later recognized automatically. Attention also plays a major role: we do not perceive what we ignore. For example, if you read this entire paragraph while listening to the words of a new song by your favorite performer, you probably will perceive more about the song than about the paragraph. Many other factors influence perception, including expectations, beliefs, and several general principles for organizing information from the senses, as you will see later.

| | |
|---|---|
| Representing Information | If we could only perceive the world, we would be in big trouble. In fact, life would be virtually impossible for us. We must hold on to the perception in some way and store information as knowledge for future use. One major question for cognitive psychologists is how we represent knowledge in memory. Do we hold pictures or images in our minds? Do we remember words and sentences? What do we have to do to new information to store it? Without memory and learning, each encounter with a particular event would be new. Even following the path of a moving object would be impossible because we could not remember from one moment to the next that the object had been somewhere else. |
| Storing and Retrieving Information | Of course, many cognitive psychologists are concerned with memory itself. How do humans remember, and why do they forget? How do you retrieve the required knowledge when you need it? Many models of memory have been suggested. Most assume that there are several memory systems with different characteristics, some that hold a great deal of information for a very short period of time, others that hold less but allow the individual to work with the information, and a long-term memory that may store certain types of knowledge permanently. We will discuss these systems later. Now let's take a closer look at the cognitive approach to learning, beginning with how we perceive the world. |

## PERCEPTION AND ATTENTION

| | |
|---|---|
| Perception | **Perception** refers to the meaning we attach to the information received through our senses. This meaning is constructed partly from objective reality and partly from the way we organize the information. Smith (1975) summarizes these points as follows: |

> It is important to grasp that the eyes merely look and the brain sees. And what the brain sees may be determined as much by cognitive structure as by the information from the world outside. We perceive what the brain decides is in front of our eyes. (F. Smith, 1975, pp. 26–27).

To illustrate this phenomenen, Smith presents the following exercise. Look at the marks below:

$$|3$$

If asked what the letter is, you would say "B." If asked what the number is, you would say "13." The actual marks remain the same; the perception, their meaning, changes based on your expectation to recognize a number or a letter. To a young child without the appropriate cognitive structures to perceive either a number or a letter, the marks probably would be meaningless.

How do we organize sensory information to perceive? Psychologists have several ideas, beginning with the Gestalt principles of organization, named for the school of psychology that first identified them.

## Early Views of Perception

Gestalt
Psychology

Some of our present-day understanding of perception is based on studies conducted in Germany by psychologists called **Gestalt** theorists. The word "Gestalt," which means pattern or configuration, refers to the belief that people tend to organize their perceptions into patterns or relationships in order to make sense of the world. The basic principle of Gestalt psychology, called **Prägnanz,** states that we recognize patterns by reorganizing stimuli so that they become simpler, more complete, and more regular than they actually are. Consider, for example, the following marks:

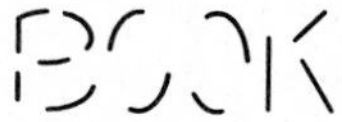

$$BOOK$$

These marks are likely to be perceived as the word "book" because such a perception is simpler, more complete, and regular than the original series of unrelated marks of varing sizes and shapes. Notice too how you use what you already know, the word "book" in this case, to construct a familiar pattern from these marks. There are many other principles for organizing stimuli, as depicted in Figure 6–1.

**Figure 6–1**   **Gestalt Principles of Organization**

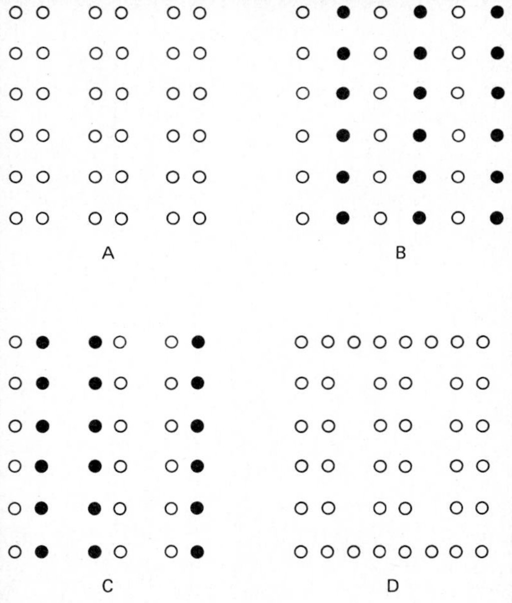

Three Gestalt principles: (a) Proximity: The six columns of dots are organized into pairs instead of six separate columns. (B) Similarity: We see six columns instead of five rows because the similar figures run up and down, not across. (C) When the effect of proximity and similarity oppose each other, the figure seems unstable. (D) Closure: We see two rectangles instead of pairs of columns.

Adapted from S. Farnham-Diggory. **Cognitive processes in education: A psychological preparation for teaching and curriculum development.** New York: Harper and Row, 1972. Used with permission of publisher.

**Figure 6–2   A Matter of Perception**

*BEELDRECHT, Amsterdam/V.A.G.A., New York. Collection Haags Gemeentemuseum—The Hague.*

**Figure-ground** is another key concept of Gestalt psychology. Viewing any scene—a painting, a photograph, or a film—a person will tend to focus attention on a basic figure and to note more detail. The rest of the stimulus becomes less important and is forced into the more vague, undifferentiated background (Travers, 1982). An example can be found in Figure 6–2. What do you see on your first glance? If you recognize devils, first you are seeing black figures against a white background. If you see angels, then you have made white the figure and black the ground. Which perception is correct? Neither? Both? It all depends on your perception. Another example is found in the common experience of learning a new word, only to find it suddenly popping up on almost every page you read. The new word becomes the figure, whereas before it was part of the ground because it was meaningless to you.

Implications
for Teachers

As a teacher you might notice that a particular behavior of one student has become "figure" to you, while the same behavior in other students is "ground." It may seem that one student is constantly turning in papers late, or losing a pencil, or giving excellent answers when, in fact, a number of students are behaving in the same way. If this happens, it may be a good idea to check your perceptions by making an objective assessment of the behavior of all the students. Why are you noticing the good or bad behavior of one student? Are you letting your attitudes and expectations concerning one student color your perceptions?

## Current Ideas about Perception

Bottom-Up
Processing

The Gestalt principles are valid explanations of certain aspects of perception, but they are not the whole story. For example, you would not have seen the marks earlier as the word "book" if you were not familar with English. There are two current explanations for how we recognize patterns and give meaning to sensory events. The first is called **feature analysis.** This suggests that we search a new stimulus for basic elements or features in order to recognize it. Anderson (1980) gives this example: A capital letter A consists of two relatively straight lines at a 45-degree angle ( $\wedge$ ) and a horizontal line (—), combined in a particular way. Whenever we see these features, or anything close enough, we recognize an A. Thus $A$ , $A$ , $A$ , $A$ , $A$ , $A$ might all be perceived as As. This is called **bottom-up processing** because the stimulus must be analyzed into specific features or building blocks and "assembled" into a meaningful pattern. This is a slow process at first, as you know if you have tried to help a young child learn to recognize bs and ds or ps and qs. After a while the process becomes automatic, and little attention is needed to tell the difference between these pairs of very similar letters.

Top-Down
Processing

If all perception relied on bottom-up feature analysis, learning might be very slow. In fact, if reading were based entirely on bottom-up processing, we would have to analyze and combine about 15,000 features to read just one page, since each letter has about 5 features (Anderson, 1980). Luckily humans are capable of another type of perception based on context, often called **top-down processing.** We do not need to analyze every feature in a particular stimulus to make sense of it. Much of the information is redundant anyway. To recognize patterns rapidly, we use the context of the situation, what we know about words or pictures or the way the world generally operates. If you catch only a fleeting glimpse of a medium-sized, four-legged animal being led down a city street, you are likely to perceive a dog, based on the context and what you know about the situation. Of course you may be wrong, but not very often.

Expectations

The patterns people perceive are based on their prior knowledge, what they expect to see, the concepts they understand, and many other factors as well. An example is found in a recent experience of the first author. A young neighbor had never seen the author in her college office, although she had visited often in her home. When the neighbor decided to take some courses at the college and encountered the author in her college office, she had a hard time placing her face. She finally remarked, "Mrs. Woolfolk, what are you doing here?" Her expectations had interfered with her ability to use pattern recognition to identify a familiar face.

In everyday life we use both bottom-up and top-down processing. For example, if you heard the sentence:

For dinner I had fried tr . . .

but missed the last word, you would use feature analysis to identify a set of possible words (those beginning with "tr," thus eliminating "chicken" and "shrimp"). You must also be aware of the context, since items like "trash" and "tractor" usually are not on the menu for dinner. Combining what you know about features of words with what you know about the context, you would fill in the word "trout" (Anderson, 1980).

### The Role of Attention

Our senses are bombarded with sights and sounds every second. If every variation in color, movement, sound, smell, temperature, and so on had to be perceived, life would be impossible. By paying attention to certain stimuli and ignoring others, we select from all these possibilities what will be processed. But attention is limited. Unless you are very accomplished at two demanding tasks, you probably cannot do both at once. When you were learning to drive, knit, or type, you had to concentrate. However, if you are accomplished at these tasks, you may be able to do one of them and, at the same time, talk, listen to music, or compose a letter. This is because many processes that require attention and concentration at first, become automatic with practice.

Practice

Thus the first-grade reader who must sound out each word and pay attention to almost every letter becomes a fast, fluent reader in time.

So people make sense of the vast amount of sensory stimuli around them by paying attention to certain aspects of the situation and by using Gestalt principles, feature detection, and the context of the situation (including what they know about similar situations) to recognize patterns. This describes perception. But perception occurs in the present. In order to understand and learn, something must be "stored." In the next section we examine how patterns, ideas, concepts, and other types of information are represented mentally so they can be remembered.

## THE STRUCTURE OF KNOWLEDGE: NETWORKS AND SCHEMATA

You know you have acquired a great deal of information over the years. How is that knowledge represented in your memory? As pictures, images, diagrams, words, sentences, or outlines? Some psychologists would say so.

Pavio's Dual
Code Theory

They believe information is stored as visual images and verbal units (Pavio, 1971). This explanation is called the **dual code theory of memory.** Psychologists who hold this view suggest that certain concepts are easier to remember than others because they can be coded both visually and verbally. Concepts such as truth, which have no clear image, are harder to remember than concepts such as your Aunt Mildred, who has both a visual image and a verbal description.

But there are problems with the dual-code theory. It is true that we have images and verbal memories. We remember the words to a song. You are able to visualize places you have visited, people you have met, particular shapes such as a cube, or whole scenes from favorite movies. You can even mentally transform these visualizations — imagining, for example, how your best friend would look in glasses or what happens when you cut a cube diagonally. But your memory for a person is more than just an image, since you are able to recognize friends or relatives even when their appearance is greatly altered.

Meaning Helps
Memory

Research has shown that we remember the *meaning* of a picture or of verbal information, not just a copy of the information. For example, if we can

**Figure 6–3** **An Apparently Meaningless Picture. Subjects Show Better Memory for this Picture When They Can Recognize the Dog.**

*From S. Wiseman and U. Neisser. **Perceptual organization as a determinant of visual recognition memory.** **American Journal of Psychology,** 1974, **87,** 675–81. Reprinted with permission of APA.*

interpret a picture or give it meaning, it is much easier to remember. You will have an easier time remembering the picture in Figure 6–3 if you recognize the dog near the center. Without this interpretation, the picture is a random series of dots. So we do not simply take a "snapshot" of the picture; meaning aids remembering.

The same is true of verbal information. If remembering and using what you read in your college courses required that you hold the words themselves in memory, you would have a hard time. Instead, we remember the meaning, but not the exact words of what we read (Anderson, 1980). If meaning is such a significant factor in remembering, how is meaning stored? Let us see.

## Propositional Networks

Network
of Meaning

A **propositional network** is an interconnected set of concepts and relationships. A proposition is the smallest unit of information that can be judged true or false. The statement "Ida borrowed the antique tablecloth" has two propositions:

**1.** Ida borrowed the tablecloth.
**2.** The tablecloth is an antique.

**Figure 6–4  A Propositional Network**

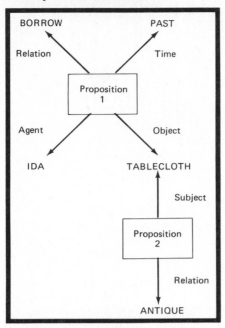

*Adapted from Anderson (1980) and Gentner (1975).*

The sentence can be represented by the network in Figure 6–4. The diagram shows the simple relationship in which Ida does the borrowing (or is the *agent*) and the *object* of the borrowing is the tablecloth. Since the verb is in the past tense, the time of the action is in the past. The same propositional network would apply to these sentences: "The antique tablecloth was borrowed by Ida" or "Ida borrowed the tablecloth, which was an antique." The meaning is the same, and this is what is stored in memory. Even though they may have slightly different methods of diagramming the networks, many cognitive psychologists believe certain types of knowledge are organized and represented in memory in propositional networks like the one in Figure 6–4.

You may be saying that you do not have anything like Figure 6–4 in your memory. Of course this is only a diagram of how you might store the meaning of a sentence. You wouldn't have little boxes and lines in your head somewhere. Cognitive psychologists create metaphors to communicate what the various cognitive processes might be like. They say that people behave *as if* knowledge were stored as shown in Figure 6–4. This view of memory fits the results of experiments on human learning.

**Translating Propositions into Words and Images**

When you recall information, you probably recall it as words and images. You translate the meaning represented by the propositional networks into familiar verbal and pictorial codes. So you aren't aware of the existence of anything like networks; they are not part of your conscious memory (Anderson, 1980).

When you hear a sentence like "Ida borrowed the antique tablecloth," you probably know even more about it than the propositions in Figure 6–4. This is because you have schemata about borrowing, tablecloths, antiques, and maybe about Ida herself.

### Schemata

Schemata
as Guides

You encountered the word "schemata" when we discussed Piaget's theory of cognitive development. (In that chapter we used the term preferred by most developmental psychologists, schemes, but the meaning is very similar.) **Schemata** are data structures or procedures for organizing the parts of a specific experience into a meaningful system (Greeno, 1980). A **schema** (the singular form) is a pattern or guide for understanding an event. The schema tells you what specific information to look for in a particular situation, what to expect. The schema is like a stereotype, specifying the "standard" relationships and sequence of events involved with an object or situation (Rumelhart and Ortony, 1977).

In order to make sense of most events in life, we need to understand concepts and make inferences. Reading "Ida borrowed the antique tablecloth," most of us know without being told that the lender does not have the tablecloth now because it is in Ida's possession and that Ida has an obligation to return the cloth to the lender (Gentner, 1975). None of this information is explicitly stated in the original sentence, but instead is part of our schema for understanding the meaning of "borrow." Other schema allow us to be fairly certain that the cloth is not plastic (if it is a real antique) and that Ida is having some kind of party. Our schema about Ida may allow us to predict how promptly the cloth will be returned and in what condition.

Understanding
Stories

Another example of the application of schema is in understanding stories. For example, a newspaper story about a robbery will not tell you that robbery

*This demonstration should help the students understand the rotation of the earth as it orbits the sun. But to understand why the rotation of the earth causes day and night, the students must have a schema about light and shadows. They must know that a source of light cannot "turn corners" to illuminate the back of an object.*

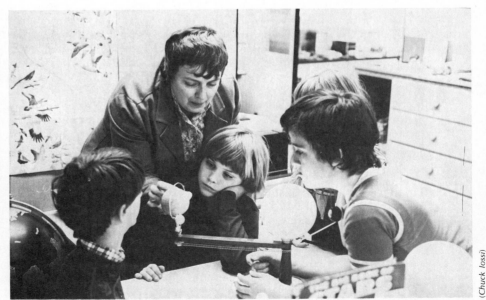

(Chuck Iossi)

is against the law, because the journalist can assume the readers know this already. It is part of their schema for "robbery."

Many cognitive psychologists believe schemata are the "key units of the comprehension process" (Rumelhart and Ortony, 1977, p. 111). To comprehend a story, we select a schema that seems appropriate for making sense of it. Then we use this framework to decide which details are important, what information to seek, and as you will see later in this chapter, what to remember. It is as though the schema is a theory about what should occur in the story. The schema guides us in "interrogating" the text, filling in the specific information we expect to find so the story makes sense (Resnick, 1981). Without the appropriate schemata, trying to understand a story or textbook is a very slow and difficult process, something like finding your way through a new town without a map.

Stereotypes

Representing and storing knowledge of the world in schemata has advantages and disadvantages. Having a well-developed schema about Ida lets us recognize her (even as her appearance changes), remember many of her characteristics, and make predictions about her behavior. But it also allows us to be wrong. We may have incorporated incorrect or biased information into our Ida schema. For example, if Ida is a member of an ethnic group and we believe that group is dishonest, we probably would assume that Ida will keep the tablecloth. Racial and ethnic stereotypes can also function as schemata for understanding (or misunderstanding) and responding to individuals.

We have been discussing how events are perceived and how knowledge is represented in memory. Now it is time to look more closely at the memory systems themselves.

# MEMORY AND LEARNING

Why do we remember some things and forget others? To begin answering this question, we consider one model of memory that is accepted by many cognitive psychologists. This model assumes that people have at least three types of memory systems. These include a sensory register for taking in perceptions, a short-term or working memory, and a long-term memory (Atkinson and Shiffrin, 1968, 1971).

## The Receptors and the Sensory Register

Receptors

Stimuli from the environment (sight, sounds, smells, and so on) constantly bombard our receptors. Receptors are the components of the sensory system for seeing, hearing, tasting, smelling, and feeling. The patterns of neural activity produced when stimuli reach the receptors are registered by the **sensory register** for only about one-quarter of a second. But in this brief time, we have a chance to select information for further processing (Wrightsman, Sigelman and Sanford, 1979). This phenomenon was demonstrated by Sperling (1963). Subjects in his experiment saw three rows of four letters projected for a few seconds or less on a screen. Recalling all 12 letters, even immediately, was impossible for the subjects. But when the experimenter signaled the subjects to recall just the first, second, or third row right after the letters were removed, the success rate was very high. The experimenter did not tell them in advance which row to watch, so the subjects must have held all the numbers in memory very briefly. For a fraction of a second they held a "picture" of the display and could "read" any one row of numbers. But by the time they recalled one row, they had lost the traces of the others.

Lindsay and Norman (1977) suggest several activities you can use to experience this brief holding of sensory information in your own sensory register. Two are given below.

> Tap your fingers against your arm. Feel the immediate sensations. Then stop tapping and note how the sensations fade away so that at first you still retain the actual feeling of the tapping, but later only the recollection that your arm was tapped.

> Wave a pencil (or your finger) back and forth in front of your eyes while you stare straight ahead. See the shadowy image that trails behind the object.

In each of these cases, the sensory input remains very briefly after the stimulus has left. You can feel a trace of the tap and see a trace of the pencil after the actual stimulus has moved. Thus, for a fraction of a second, the data from a sensory experience remain intact. It may be appealing to think of it as a photograph or an echo, but the data is probably some kind of neural activity that continues after the sensory signal stops.

**Perceiving Patterns**

Because the sensory register holds everything briefly, we have a chance to make sense of it, to organize it, through perception (Lindsay and Norman, 1977). This is necessary since there is much more information available in the sensory register than can possibly enter the next system: the short-term memory. Instead of perceiving everything, we pay attention to certain features of the total content in the sensory register and look for patterns, as we discussed in the earlier section on perception.

## Short-Term Memory

Once transformed into patterns of images or sounds, the information in the sensory register can enter the **short-term memory.** The stay here, like that in the sensory register, is short, probably about 20 seconds. Information can be held for a longer period of time only if you do something with it. To prevent forgetting most people **rehearse** or repeat the information mentally until it is no longer needed. As long as you focus on and repeat the information in the short-term memory, it is available. In fact, information can be maintained in short-term memory indefinitely through rehearsal. Most children discover rehearsal on their own at around age 10, as we noted in Chapter 2. This involves metamemory, or "knowing about" memory.

**Importance of Short-Term Memory**

It may seem to you that a memory system with a 20-second time limit is not very useful—but without this system you would forget what you read in the first part of a sentence before you finished the last few words. This would make understanding sentences very difficult. Yet it would be a disadvantage to remember permanently every sentence you ever read. Finding a particular bit of information in all that sea of knowledge would be impossible. So it is helpful to have a system that allows temporary storage.

**Capacity**

Short-term memory is limited not only in the length of time unrehearsed information can be retained, but also in the number of items that can be held at one time. In experimental situations, it appears that only about five to seven separate items can be held in short-term memory at one time (G. A. Miller, 1956). This limitation can be seen in many daily experiences. It is quite common to rehearse a phone number after looking it up, as you walk across the room to make the call. But if you have two friends to call in succession, would it occur to you to try to keep both numbers in mind? Probably not. Experience tells us that two phone numbers (14 digits) probably cannot be simultaneously stored. In any event, the first conversation would wipe out the second number.

The seven-unit limitation seems to hold in experimental learning tasks. But, as Anderson (1980) points out, while you dial that seven-digit phone number, you have other things in your memory at the same time — how to dial a telephone, who you are calling, and why. This is because the short-term memory is the working memory. Information must be brought into short-term memory and held while it is being used. We are aware of the contents of short-term or working memory because it is the information we are thinking about at the moment.

Of course, most of us know a great deal — for example, many more than two telephone numbers. But these have been learned over a long period of time and are not as accessible as a number you have just looked up and are about to dial. They are part of long-term memory and require a bit of effort to retrieve. To move from short-term to long-term memory, other transformations of the information are required.

## Long-Term Memory

The transformation of information so that it can become part of **long-term memory** is one of the most critical aspects of learning. Certainly teachers are interested in helping students remember for longer than 20 seconds. So the encoding processes that transform information at this point are of special importance to teachers.

Craik and Lockhart (1972) suggest that there is one major difference between information assumed to be in short-term memory and the information recalled over longer periods of time. The difference is how thoroughly and deeply the information has been processed. In fact, Craik and Lockhart first proposed their **levels of processing theory** as an alternative to the three stages model. They suggested that the sensory register really involves representations that are relatively unanalyzed, while limited analysis and processing leads to representations such as those assumed to be in short-term memory. Thoroughly processed and organized information is the type considered to be in long-term memory. Thus what determines how long information is remembered is not the type of memory system, but how completely the information is analyzed and connected with other information.

More recently Craik (1979) has suggested that the stages model and the levels of processing views are not entirely incompatible. There may be different structural components or stages of memory similar to the sensory register, short-term, and long-term distinctions, as well as different strategies or levels of processing that "move" information from one stage to the next (Reed, 1982).

Several factors or strategies seem to be important in learning new information so it is easy to retrieve when needed. The first is **elaboration.** Elaboration involves adding meaning by connecting one bit of new informa-

(Ken Karp)

*One way to elaborate new information and make it easier to remember is to connect the verbal information with a visual image. These students can see the results of mixing the chemicals because the gas produced fills the balloon. They have an image to associate with the formula.*

tion with other associations or with existing knowledge. The connecting occurs when the new information is incorporated into propositional networks and schemata. We often do this automatically. A paragraph we are reading about a historical figure reminds us of something we already know about that time period. A scene from a film is associated with a similar experience in our own lives.

**Using Elaboration to Remember**

When information becomes an organized part of a network or schema, there are several routes to follow to retrieve the original information. For example, if you were asked to memorize the sentence, "Ida borrowed the antique tablecloth," and elaborated this sentence by picturing your aunt setting the table, or added to the sentence, "and she sold it to buy booze," or remembered a particular old lace tablecloth at your home, or completed the story to include a big dinner party, you would have a much better chance of remembering the sentence.

Even if you later remembered only something about your own aunt, you might be able mentally to move from the proposition about your aunt to the proposition about Aunt Ida and finally remember the original sentence. If you could remember only the idea of dishonestly selling something to buy booze, you might infer that the article did not belong to the seller and that it was stolen or borrowed, thus finding the right association to lead you to Ida's borrowed tablecloth. So elaborating on new information gives extra paths for following the propositional networks back to the original idea as well as additional information for making inferences about that idea. Both factors improve learning and remembering (Anderson, 1980).

**A Study of Elaboration**

One study shows the power of elaboration in learning (Hyde and Jenkins, 1973). Subjects saw words presented very rapidly, but only half the subjects were told to learn the words. This half was called the intentional learning group, while the other subjects were called the incidental learning group. In both groups, subjects were told either to check each word for two letters or to rate the pleasantness of the word. The experimenters assumed that rating the pleasantness of each word would require more elaboration than simply scanning for two letters, since subjects would have to make associations and have reasons to make the pleasantness ratings.

All subjects were tested to see how many of the words they could remember. The subjects who had rated the pleasantness of the words recalled significantly more. Subjects applying this strategy recalled about 68 percent of the words, whether they had been told to memorize the words or not. Students trying to learn the words but applying the letter-checking procedure learned only about 43 percent of the words, nearly the same number as the group checking for letters but not trying to memorize the words. So intention to learn made no difference, perhaps because the subjects were applying ineffective strategies, such as repeating the words over and over (Anderson, 1980). The effects of a good learning strategy seem very powerful, stronger even than "trying hard" to learn. Of course, if intention to learn causes you to process the information more deeply, positive results should follow.

**Organization
and Memory**

A second factor that improves learning is *organization*, which is related to elaboration. Material that is well organized is easier to learn and remember than bits and pieces of information. For example, Figure 6–5 shows how the concepts of positive and negative reinforcement can be placed in a hierarchical organization. Here you see that there are two types of consequences and each of these can be further broken down into two types with examples of each. This is one way of organizing the concepts to see interrelationships. Understanding this organizational system can help you learn and remember more specific examples of behavioral techniques. Placing concepts in an organizational framework such as a hierarchical structure is one way to elaborate on the information.

**Context and
Memory**

A third factor that influences learning and remembering is *context*. Evidently certain aspects of the physical and emotional context of material are

**Figure 6–5    A Coding System for the Concept "Consequence"**

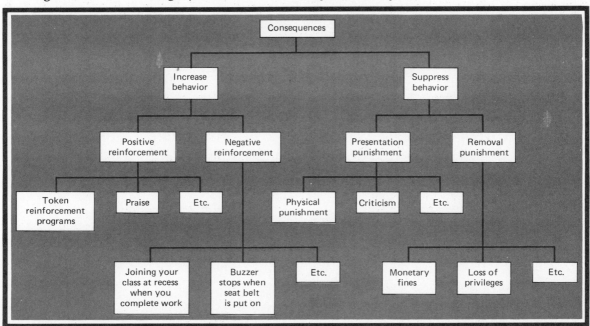

learned along with the information and become part of the propositional networks. Later, if you try to remember the information it will be easier if the context is similar. This has been demonstrated in the laboratory by having students learn material in one type of room, then take a test in a similar or a different room. Performance was better in the similar room (Smith, Glenberg, and Bjork, 1978). So studying for a test under "testlike" conditions might improve your score.

Once information has entered long-term memory, it apparently becomes permanently available. This means that anything you have remembered for more than a few minutes without active rehearsal has become a part of your long-term memory. Of course, the problem is to find it when it is needed. It also appears that the capacity of long-term memory is unlimited for all practical purposes. Theoretically, we should be able to remember as much as we want. How can we make the most effective use of this practically unlimited capacity to learn and remember? The major challenge is the integration of the new material you want to learn into the structure of what already exists in long-term memory.

Figure 6–6 is a graphic representation of the various memory systems. Of course, people do not have separate "boxes" in their heads. Like many aspects of psychology, this is a metaphor, not an anatomical drawing. And it is not the only view of memory. As we mentioned earlier, some psychologists prefer to emphasize different levels of processing, not different memory systems.

## Figure 6–6  A Model of Memory

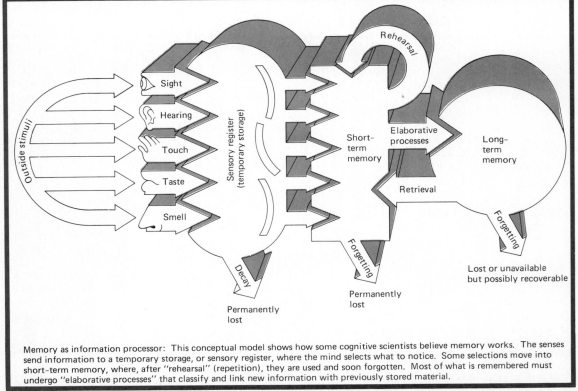

Memory as information processor: This conceptual model shows how some cognitive scientists believe memory works. The senses send information to a temporary storage, or sensory register, where the mind selects what to notice. Some selections move into short-term memory, where, after "rehearsal" (repetition), they are used and soon forgotten. Most of what is remembered must undergo "elaborative processes" that classify and link new information with previously stored material.

*Adapted from Hunt (1982, p. 32).*

## Figure 6–7  Short- and Long-Term Memory

| Type of Memory | Capacity | Persistence | Access | Input |
|---|---|---|---|---|
| Short term | Limited | Very brief | Immediate | Very fast |
| Long term | Practically unlimited | Practically unlimited | Depends on organization | Relatively slow |

*Adapted from F. Smith,* **Comprehension and learning: A conceptual framework for teachers.** *© 1975 Holt, Rinehart, and Winston. Reprinted by permission of publisher and CBS College Publishing.*

## A Comparison of the Two Memory Systems

Suppose you were asked to recite all the telephone numbers you know. It is an alarming task and possibly a ridiculous one, but take it seriously for a moment. You might begin with your own number, then move to family members, close friends, work numbers, doctors, and so on. You would go from the most familiar numbers to less familiar categories. By using these categories, you would give yourself cues for retrieving numbers available in long-term memory.

Remembering a phone number that you know but use infrequently is a much more difficult task than repeating a new number you have just looked up. The difference between these tasks demonstrates some of the basic differences between short- and long-term memory. Access from long-term memory depends on organization; some strategy or cue is needed to bring about recall. Items in short-term memory are immediately available. Information in short-term memory is limited in quantity, but enters the system very quickly. Long-term memory includes an enormous amount of information, which enters the system relatively slowly. Figure 6–7 offers a brief comparison of the two memory systems.

Where Is Memory?

A note of caution should be added about memory. People often tend to think of memory as a place. But if there is a specific location for information stored in the brain, it has not been found and probably will not be. Since memory includes both process and storage, it is probably distributed throughout the brain in the form of neurons, neural activity, and large molecules such as DNA and RNA that have the potential for storing large quantities of information.

## Why Do People Forget?

With such an amazing capacity to store information, why do we forget so much? As we said earlier, it appears that nothing is really forgotten once it enters long-term memory, and everything that people remember without active rehearsal for more than a few minutes is stored in long-term memory.

Interference and Decay

**Forgetting and Short-Term Memory.**  Information is lost from short-term memory through **interference** and the passage of time (Lindsay and Norman, 1977). As new information enters short-term memory, the trace of the older information becomes weaker. Remembering new things interferes with remembering old things. At a certain point, the limited capacity of short-term memory is simply filled and old information is lost, as shown in Figure 6–6.

Otherwise the new information could not be taken in. Information is also lost from short-term memory by **time decay**. The longer information is held in the short-term memory, the weaker it becomes until it simply disappears. Forgetting is very useful. Without it, people would quickly overload their short-term memories and learning would cease.

**Forgetting and Long-Term Memory.** Information lost from short-term memory is actually forgotten. But it appears that information stored in long-term memory can always be retrieved, given the appropriate conditions. Electrical stimulation to certain parts of the brain can cause people to remember the most distant childhood experiences (Penfield, 1969). Even without this physical stimulation, retrieval is still almost always possible if the right cues can be found to guide a person to the desired information.

Reconstruction
and Memory

Lindsay and Norman (1977) suggest that successful retrieval is really a problem-solving process that makes use of logic, cues, and other knowledge to reconstruct the information, sometimes incorrectly, by using our current knowledge to fill in the missing parts. Information that is thoroughly elaborated or well organized is easier to retrieve, as we mentioned earlier. This is true in part because you have more cues for making correct inferences and reconstructing accurately. Isolated bits of information may prove difficult to find. You probably have had the experience of looking for a book, saying to yourself, "I know it's blue with white letters." When the book is later found, it turns out to be different, perhaps green with white letters. Maybe the color of the object was encoded incorrectly in or never reached your long-term memory.

Tip-of-
the-Tongue
Phenomenon

You did, however, retrieve part of the information. This may be an example of what Brown and McNeill (1966) called a tip-of-the-tongue state, the ability to "almost" remember by retrieving parts of the lost information. You may have experienced this phenomenon on tests. These partially correct reconstructions of information demonstrate that memory is more than a simple retrieval. If the memory of the book were stored simply as a visual image, remembering would be all or none. Once you have found the image, you would have all the correct information. Instead, we often retrieve parts and reconstruct the rest.

Bartlett's Work

The role of reconstruction in memory was demonstrated in famous studies conducted in England by Bartlett (1932). He read a complex, unfamiliar story about a tribe of North American Indians to students at Cambridge University. He then asked the students to retell the story after waiting different lengths of time. These recalled stories were generally shorter and were translated into the concepts and language of the Cambridge students. For example, the story told of a seal hunt, but many students remembered a "fishing trip," an activity closer to their experience. Instead of remembering the exact words of the story, the students remembered the meaning, but the meaning they remembered often was altered somewhat to fit their cultural expectations and stereotypes—in other words, their schemata. Bartlett even called these cognitive structures that influence memory *schemata*.

Not all reconstructed memories are distorted. In fact, reconstruction strategies often lead to remarkable successes. Consider this question, which Lindsay and Norman proposed to a group of subjects: "What were you doing on Monday afternoon in the third week of September two years ago?"

(Lindsay and Norman, 1977, p. 372). One subject solved this seemingly impossible retrieval problem by following the steps listed below:

1. Come on. How should I know?
2. OK. Let's see: Two years ago . . .
3. I would be in high school in Pittsburgh . . .
4. That would be my senior year.
5. Third week in September — that's just after summer — that would be the fall term . . .
6. Let me see. I think I had chemistry lab on Mondays.
7. I don't know. I was probably in the chemistry lab . . .
8. Wait a minute — that would be the second week of school. I remember he started off with the atomic table — a big, fancy chart. I thought he was crazy, trying to make us memorize that thing.
9. You know, I think I can remember sitting . . .

A number of other theories have been suggested to explain why people forget and what is needed to remember. We will look at some of them next.

Suppression **Other Explanations of Forgetting.** Freud suggested that we sometimes intentionally forget or suppress certain experiences we do not really want to remember. But this cannot explain why some painful experiences are remembered vividly while others that are pleasant or neutral are forgotten.

Context Aids Remembering Another explanation of forgetting is that the memory trace simply fades away when the information is not used frequently. For example, you might have had no problem remembering the names of all the people you worked with last summer while you were seeing them every day, but according to this theory you have probably forgotten them by now. The difficulty with this theory is that we sometimes remember information we have not used in years. Given the proper cues, for instance, you might remember or reconstruct the names of the other students in your ninth-grade English class. If you were in the same context, remembering could be even easier. For example, the first author's memory was recently jogged by a visit to her elementary school. Leaving the school and following the old bicycle route home, she remembered the name of her fifth-grade boyfriend, whose house was on that route, plus the name of his brother and his dog.

Interference The idea that interference causes forgetting in long-term as well as short-term memory seems to be supported by evidence from research. Newer memories may interfere with or obscure older memories by becoming confused with them. When new verbal associations make it difficult for a person to remember older information, the interference is called *retroactive* interference. If memories of older associations make it difficult to remember new information, the interference is called *proactive* interference (Crouse, 1971). Research on the learning of higher-level information such as rules and propositions indicates that interference is likely to occur only if the new information directly contradicts the old (Anderson and Myrow, 1971).

The interference explanation of forgetting does not contradict the notion that we never really forget anything stored in long-term memory. The interference is not necessarily occurring in the long-term memory itself, but probably occurs when the information is retrieved and brought back into short-term memory. So the problem is still retrieving and reconstructing accurately (Gagné, 1974).

# IMPLICATIONS OF THE COGNITIVE PERSPECTIVE

There are a number of ways to use cognitive models of learning in the classroom. First we will look at general teaching strategies, particularly those involved in designing lessons. Then we will focus on helping students remember new information.

## Teaching Strategies

Teachers can help students to pay attention to lessons; to identify what is important, difficult, or unfamiliar; to retrieve previously learned information; and to comprehend new material by connecting it with information already in long-term memory.

Using Novelty **Focusing Attention.**   Many factors influence student attention. Eye-catching or startling phenomena can draw attention at the beginning of a lesson. A teacher might begin a science lesson on pressure by blowing up a balloon until it pops. Bright colors, unusual placement of words, underlining, highlighting written or spoken words, changes in loudness, lighting, pace, or unexpected events can all be used to gain attention. Teachers may also appeal to the interests of the students. A teacher might introduce a lesson with an intriguing question such as this: "Would you like to know what causes thunder?" Finally, a teacher might consider incorporating nonverbal stimuli such as gestures, movements, demonstrations, and pictures (Gagné and Briggs, 1979). These nonverbal events often gain attention simply because they are different. There is some evidence, however, that students learn more when the teacher is more animated in delivering a lecture (Kaufman, 1976). Figure 6–8 offers additional ideas for getting the students' attention.

**Figure 6–8    Suggestions for Focusing Attention**

1. Tell students the purpose of the lesson. Indicate how learning the material will be useful or important to them.
2. Ask students why they think learning the material will be important.
3. Arouse curiosity with questions such as "What would happen if . . . ?"
4. Create shock by staging an unexpected event such as a loud argument just before a lesson on communication.
5. Alter the physical environment by changing the arrangement of the room or moving to a different setting.
6. Shift sensory channels by giving a lesson that requires students to touch, smell, or taste.
7. Use movements, gestures, and voice inflection by walking around the room, pointing, speaking softly and then more emphatically.
8. Avoid distracting behaviors such as tapping a pencil or touching your hair.

*Adapted from E. Emmer and G. Millett, **Improving teaching through experimentation: A laboratory approach,** © 1970, pp. 65–68. Englewood Cliffs, N.J. Adapted by permission of Prentice-Hall.*

*This teacher is helping students focus on the most important parts of the presentation by highlighting key features on the board.*

(Norman Hurst/Stock, Boston)

A Caution

One caution about the use of stimulus change to capture students' attention has been suggested by Skinner (1968). Surprising events, pictures, or movements in a lesson capitalize on our instinctive responses to novelty. Skinner believes that such techniques may make the students less interested in the aspects of the lesson that are more familiar and ordinary. So you may want to be careful with novelty. In order to learn, students must pay attention, even to material that is not very exciting.

Studying the Right Material

**Identifying What Is Important, Difficult, and Unfamiliar.** Students often pay attention and study hard, but they focus on the wrong material. They may spend time learning unessential details and miss major points. They may concentrate on material they already know and avoid tackling the unfamiliar or difficult task (Dansereau, 1978). Some students are better than others at judging when they truly understand an idea. Knowing when you know is a metacognitive task that many students, particularly the younger and less able, find difficult.

Learning can be enhanced if teachers help students perceive the important features of new information. One strategy for doing this is to make the purpose of the lesson very clear. If students know what they will be expected to do with the information, they should be more able to focus on the important features (Gagné and Briggs, 1979). (We will deal more thoroughly with how to communicate purposes in Chapter 11.)

Highlighting Important Features

In written or graphic materials, important features can be highlighted using italics, bold print, underlining, or symbols such as stars. The chapter outlines, topic headings, and margin notes in this book are examples of this strategy. All are meant to help you recognize important features and thus detect patterns and relationships in the material. In oral presentations, teachers can highlight differences and similarities among the ideas being presented and give different examples of the concepts being taught. When a new idea could easily be confused with previous information, the teacher should point out the critical differences. Difficult or tricky parts of a lesson should be given extra attention.

**Helping Students Retrieve Previously Learned Information.** Cognitive theorists believe learning is a matter of integrating new information with existing cognitive structures. Before integration can be made, students must be able to retrieve the information they already know (Peeck, van der Bosch and Kreupeling, 1982). The prior learning may be in many different forms — concepts, definitions, and rules. When it is needed to master new information, the prior learning must be available.

An Example

Gagné and Briggs offer an example of how a teacher might encourage retrieval:

> ... when children are being taught about rainfall in relation to mountains, the question may be asked, "Do you remember what the air is like in a cloud which has traveled over land in the summer?" (The air is warm.) The further question may then be asked, "What is the temperature of the land on a high mountain likely to be?" (Cold.) This line of questioning recalls previously learned rules, and obviously leads to a strand of learning which will culminate with the acquisition of a new rule concerning the effects of cooling on a warm, moisture-laden cloud. (Gagné and Briggs, 1979, p. 157)

Other strategies for helping students bring the necessary prior learning into their working memories include capsule reviews, demonstrations, and discussions of key vocabulary.

**Helping Students Comprehend and Combine Information.** Volumes have been written on comprehension of written material. Out of all this work have come several techniques that seem to aid comprehension. These include forming mental images of the verbal material as you read, restating the material in your own words, reorganizing the information as you read, or answering questions about the material as you go along (Dansereau, 1978). A well-developed method for improving comprehension is the PQ4R system described in Chapter 7.

Meaningful
Learning

Perhaps the best single method of helping students comprehend lessons and combine old information with new is to make each lesson as **meaningful** as possible. Meaningful lessons are presented in vocabulary that makes sense to the students. New terms are clarified through the use of more familiar words and ideas. Meaningful lessons are also well organized, with clear connections between the different elements of the lesson. Finally, meaningful lessons make natural use of old information to help students understand new information by giving examples or analogies.

An Example

The importance of meaningful lessons is emphasized in an example presented by Smith (1975). Consider the three lines below:

1. KYBVODUWGPJMSQTXNOGMCTRSO
2. READY JUMP WHEAT POOR BUT SEEK
3. KNIGHTS RODE HORSES INTO WAR

Begin by covering all but the first line. Look at it for a second, close the book, and write down all the letters you remember. Then repeat this procedure with the second and third lines. Each line has the same number of letters, but the chances are great that you remembered all the letters in the third line, a good number of letters in the second line, and very few in the first line.

The first line makes no sense. There is no way to organize it in a brief glance. The second line is more meaningful. You do not have to see each letter because you bring prior knowledge of spelling rules and vocabulary to the task. The third line is the most meaningful. Just a glance and you can probably remember all of it because you bring to this task prior knowledge not only of spelling and vocabulary, but also of rules about syntax and probably some historical information about knights (they didn't ride in tanks). This sentence is meaningful because you have existing schemata for assimilating it. It is fairly easy to associate the words and meaning with other information already in long-term memory.

The challenge for teachers is to make learning less like memorizing the first line and more like memorizing the third line. Although this may seem obvious, think about the times when you yourself have read a sentence in a text or heard an explanation from a professor that might just as well have been KYBVODUGPJMSQTXNOGMCTRSO.

## Strategies for Helping Students Remember

Lindsay and Norman (1977) present three general rules for improving memory. First, memorization calls for effort; it seldom comes easily. Second, the material being memorized should be related to other things. Paraphrasing and visualizing may help. Third, memorization requires organization. Material can be divided into smaller pieces and then put back together in meaningful patterns. Students should also look for structure in the material itself and use mnemonic aids where possible.

 **Mnemonics**

This last suggestion, the use of mnemonics, has become quite popular lately, although it has been around a long time. **Mnemonics** is the art of memory, a very respectable art in ancient Greece. Before paper, pens, books, recording equipment, and other external memory aids were developed, quite a bit of material simply had to be memorized. Orators, musicians, and poets had few alternatives but to memorize their presentations. Even when written notes for speeches were possible, the style of speaking valued in ancient times required fluency. A great orator was supposed to seem spontaneous, even in delivering a carefully prepared speech (Bellezza, 1981).

The purpose of mnemonics is to connect the new material to be learned with information that is already well known. The many different mnemonic

**PEANUTS ®**                                                    **By Charles M. Schulz**

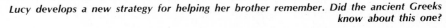

*Lucy develops a new strategy for helping her brother remember. Did the ancient Greeks know about this one?*

strategies are most helpful when the material to be memorized has very little inherent meaning, such as lists of vocabulary words or a sequence of errands. Psychologists and educators have become quite interested in mnemonics lately because these procedures seem to lead to impressive improvements in learning. Carlson, Kincaid, Lance, and Hodgson (1976) found that college students who spontaneously applied mnemonic methods to learn course material had an average grade point of 2.80, while students who did not had an average 2.37. In a recent extensive review of research on the keyword mnemonic method, Pressley, Levin, and Delaney (1982) concluded that it greatly improves performance in learning foreign language vocabulary definitions for students from preschool through college, and in a wide variety of languages from Spanish to Malay.

Among the several useful mnemonic systems are peg systems such as loci, peg words, and first letters; chaining systems such as linking, stories, and rhymes; and other systems based on word meanings, such as the keyword method. As you will see, many of these strategies use imagery.

**Peg-Type Mnemonics.**    Peg-type methods require that you memorize a standard list of places or words. Then, whenever you want to learn a list of items, you associate this information with the "pegs" already in memory. One peg-type approach, the *loci method*, derives its name from the plural form of the Latin word *locus*, meaning "place." This method gave us the expression "In the first place" (Hunter, 1956).

To use the loci method, you must first imagine a very familiar place, such as your own house or apartment. Now pick out particular locations, such as the table by the front door, the sofa, the chair near the fireplace, and the dining-room table. Memorize this list of places, in order. They will be your pegs for all future loci memory tasks. Whenever you have a list to remember, simply place each item from the list in one of these locations in the house. Visualize each item sitting in its spot. When you want to remember the items, all you have to do is take an imaginary walk through the house and see what is on the table by the front door, the sofa, the chair, and the dining-room table. The same locations serve as pegs every time you have a list to remember.

The *peg word method* has often been used by entertainers to dazzle the public with feats of memory. In the most formal variation of the method, you begin by learning a set of peg words. Lindsay and Norman (1977) suggest 10 simple words that incorporate rhyming to make the list easier to learn:

| | |
|---|---|
| One is bun. | Six is sticks. |
| Two is shoe. | Seven is heaven. |
| Three is tree. | Eight is gate. |
| Four is door. | Nine is line. |
| Five is hive. | Ten is hen. |

When you know the peg words, new lists of items to be learned can be associated with these words through an image. For example, if you have to stop at the cleaners, the bank, the Post Office, and the supermarket on your way home from school, you might imagine your clothes that need cleaning with huge *buns* in the pockets. Next you could see money stuffed into a pair of *shoes*. Then you could envision letters hanging like leaves on a *tree*. Finally, you might imagine smashing down a *door* with a shopping cart.

**Acronyms**     The pegs we have discussed thus far are used over and over to learn new material, generally material that will be needed for only a short period of time. Another type of peg approach involves learning a set of pegs to remember information for long periods of time. One example is found in *acronyms*—phrases or sentences in which the first letter of each word represents an item on a list. You may be familiar with a sentence known by all young music students, Every Good Boy Does Fine. The first letter of each word stands for the name of a line of the G clef: e, g, b, d, f. Another is "Men Very Easily Make Jugs Serve Useful Nocturnal Purposes." (No sexism intended.) Here the first letter of each word corresponds to the first letter of the planets in order from the sun: Mercury, Venus, Earth, Mars, Jupiter, Saturn, Uranus, Neptune, and Pluto (Higbee, 1977). In both cases, the first letter of each word in the sentence provides the peg. In addition, the words must make sense to complete the sentence, so this approach has some characteristics of the chain-type method. One item is linked to the next in order.

**Linking Systems**     **Chain-Type Methods.**     Chain-type mnemonics connect the first item to be memorized with the second, the second with the third, the third with the fourth, and so on. For example, with *linking systems* each item on a list is linked to the next through some visual association. If you have to stop at the cleaners, the bank, the Post Office, and the supermarket, you might begin by imagining the cleaner cleaning the money that is going to be sent to the bank. Then you might imagine the money stuffed in letters. Finally, you might imagine these letters in a shopping cart. In each case, one visual cue leads you to the next.

Other chain-type approaches include incorporating all the items to be memorized into a story and making use of rhymes such as "Thirty days hath September." Both approaches can be effective, as you probably know from experience with the latter.

**Keyword Method**     **The Keyword Method.**     The mnemonic system that has been most extensively applied in teaching is the *keyword method*. Although the idea has a long history, research by Atkinson and his colleagues in the mid-1970s sparked serious interest, especially in foreign language teaching (R. C. Atkinson, 1975; Atkinson and Raugh, 1975). As we mentioned earlier, this research has demonstrated impressive results.

The approach has two stages. First, you must identify an English word, preferably a concrete noun, that sounds like the foreign word or a part of it. Next, you associate the meaning of the foreign word with the selected English word through an image or sentence. For example, the Spanish word *carta* (meaning "letter") sounds like the English word "cart." Cart becomes the keyword, and you imagine a cart filled with letters on its way to the Post Office or make up a sentence, such as "The cart full of letters tipped over" (Pressley, Levin and Delaney, 1982). Figure 6–9 offers another example of this method in teaching Spanish vocabulary.

Joel Levin and his colleagues have applied variations of the keyword method to teach elementary-school students foreign languages, states and capitals, and other material. For example, to associate Annapolis and Maryland, the key words would be "apple" and "marry." An image that connects these words might involve two apples getting married. Other possible applications of the method include learning names of presidents,

**219**

**Figure 6–9    Using Keywords to Learn Spanish.**

**Purpose:** The memorization of the Spanish word **pato**, which means duck.

**Method:** The student would select an English word that sounds like an important part of the Spanish word. The first syllable of the Spanish word sounds like the English word pot, so that word might easily be chosen. Then the student would imagine a duck with a pot on its head.

**Visual Image:**

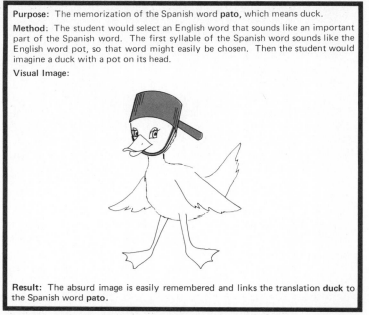

**Result:** The absurd image is easily remembered and links the translation **duck** to the Spanish word **pato**.

Adapted from Images are a Key to Learning. Wisconsin Research and Development Center News, Spring, 1979, pp. 1–2.

explorers, inventors, or principal products of a state (Levin, 1981; Levin, Berry Miller and Bartell, 1982; Levin and Pressley, in press).

Imagery    In general, techniques that use imagery are more appropriate for students in late elementary and secondary grades. Young students have some difficulty forming their own images. This is less true of memory aids that rely on auditory cues, rhymes such as "*i* before *e* except after *c*," and "Thirty days hath September." In general, research suggests that younger and less able students may need help in finding appropriate images or keywords. More teacher structure in supplying these links is often necessary with younger students (Pressley, Levin and Delaney, 1982).

Chunking    **Chunking.**    A final mnemonic device is *chunking*. Individual bits of information are put together in some meaningful way so that short-term memory can retain more. The number of bits of information is the problem for short-term memory, not the size of each bit. Thus, if the six digits 3, 5, 4, 8, 7, and 0 have to be remembered, it is easier to put them together into three chunks of two digits each (35, 48, 70) or two chunks of three digits each (354, 870). With these changes, there would only be three or two bits of information to hold at one time.

## Rote Memorization

Some things need to be learned by rote, but probably not many. We all learned the alphabet and the names of the numerals from 1 to 10 by rote.

After 10, the whole procedure became a lot easier because prior knowledge of the first 10 numbers helped us crack the system. The learning became meaningful because of this related prior knowledge.

Memorizing
Lists

How might a student go about memorizing the abbreviations of the chemical elements by rote in a single weekend? One possibility might be to break the list of elements into a number of separate lists and practice each one intermittently throughout the weekend. A student might also ask a friend to hear recitations of the short lists and later ask the friend to pick elements at random and give a test.

This system makes use of a number of strategies that have been documented by psychologists to be appropriate for learning meaningless material: (1) part learning; (2) a means of combatting the serial-position effect; and (3) distributed practice.

Breaking the list into segments is an example of **part learning.** Since only a few items can make it into long-term memory at a time, it is sensible to concentrate on a limited number of items. From a reinforcement point of view, the intermediate success of learning each partial list can encourage the student to continue. If the entire list is practiced as a unit, reinforcement is delayed until the end of a very long task. The student may give up in frustration before success is achieved.

When a list of similar items is memorized, the best retention occurs with the items at the beginning and the end of the list. The middle is often forgotten. This is called the **serial-position effect.** By breaking a long list into several short lists, the student can turn this psychological fact into an advantage. The beginning and end of each short list will now be easier to remember, leaving fewer middle items to cause problems. Words should be practiced in different orders to avoid having the same words in the middle each time. Even though this method has advantages, it will not save time over learning the one long list. The total time for learning one long list and several short lists is about the same when the items are the same.

Types
of Practice

A final strategy for making the memorization of a long list easier is the use of **distributed practice.** A student who studied the abbreviations of the chemical elements intermittently throughout the weekend will probably do much better than a student who tried to memorize the entire list Sunday night. Studying for an extended period, rather than for briefer periods with rest time in between, is called **massed practice.** There are several reasons why distributed practice is more effective. Too long a study session leads to fatigue, and motivation lags. In addition, forgetting begins promptly at the end of the learning session. If several sessions are used, what is forgotten from one session can be relearned in the next. The relearning will be faster than starting from scratch because forgetting is only partial and some items will be familiar.

If your subject requires certain amounts of rote memorization, you might want to teach the strategies mentioned above to your students. The approaches may seem obvious, but students who have not learned them through experience can benefit from such instruction. Students vary greatly in their knowledge about how to memorize. Metamemory skills are important in school, but many students will not develop them without your help.

As you can see, the cognitive model of learning and memory has many implications for teaching. We have summarized a few of these implications in the form of Guidelines.

# *Guidelines*

## *Applying the Ideas of the Information Processing Theorists*

**1. Make sure you have the students' attention.**

EXAMPLES
- Use, but do not overuse, novelty in presenting materials.
- Move around the room, use gestures, and avoid speaking in a monotone.

**2. Help students focus on the most important information.**

EXAMPLES
- Highlight important points with pauses, writing on the board, or review.
- Ask students to summarize the important points in a presentation.

**3. Help students combine new information with old information.**

EXAMPLES
- Show relationship of new information to previous knowledge or familiar experiences through the use of outlines, diagrams, analogies, examples, or demonstrations.
- Give assignments that specifically call for the use of new information along with information already learned.

**4. Help students remember.**

EXAMPLES
- Help students develop images or verbal cues for remembering important ideas.
- Teach strategies for memorization.

**5. Provide for repetition of information.**

EXAMPLES
- Give frequent, short tests.
- Begin a class by asking questions about yesterday's lesson.

**6. Present new material in a clear, organized manner.**

EXAMPLES
- "Tell students what you're going to say, say it, then tell them what you've said."
- Make the purpose of the lesson very clear.

## LEARNING ABOUT LEARNING: METACOGNITIVE ABILITIES

Thus far we have discussed general principles of cognitive perspectives on learning that seem to apply to most people. But experience tells us that individuals differ in how well or how quickly they learn. As we said at the beginning of this chapter, one question that intrigues many cognitive psychologists is why some people learn and remember better than others. Researchers have looked for answers by studying differences between younger and older learners as well as differences between more and less able learners. Results of both types of comparisons point to the importance of metacognitive abilities.

You have encountered the phrase "metacognitive abilities" several times in this text. **Metacognition** is knowledge of your own cognitive processes and products (Flavell, 1976). As children develop, they become more sophisticated in their understanding of how to control and monitor their own learning, how to remember (metamemory), and how to use language (metalanguage).

The metacognitive ability to monitor your own performance and employ different strategies in order to learn and remember develops and improves with age. Identifying the main idea, checking to determine if you understand, changing strategies when one is not working, predicting outcomes, planning, deciding how to apportion time and effort, rehearsing information, forming associations and images, using mnemonics and organizing new material to make it easier to remember are all skills that are more difficult for younger and less able students. In general, metacognitive abilities such as these begin to develop around ages 5 to 7 and improve throughout school, but there is great variability even among students of the same age. Most children go through a transitional period when they can apply a particular strategy if reminded, but will not do it on their own (Brown, Campione and Day, 1981).

Since very competent students appear to have more well-developed metacognitive abilities, many psychologists have suggested that these learning strategies be taught directly to children. For example, younger and less able students have difficulty knowing when they understand something (Flavell, Friedrichs and Hoyt, 1970). To overcome this difficulty, Ann Brown and her colleagues taught mildly retarded students a few simple techniques for learning a long list of items and checking their memory before a test (Brown, Campione and Barclay, 1979). One of the techniques is to cover the next item on the list and try to recall it before you look at it. Another checking technique is to recall sections of the list. If students cannot name the next item on the list or recite sections from memory, they are not ready to take a test on the entire list. The older children in this study (mental age of about 8) improved significantly when they were taught these simple methods for checking their own progress, and they were still applying the strategies a year later. The younger students (mental age of about 6) benefited very little from the training.

In addition to having trouble knowing when they know, younger and less able children are not as skilled at knowing what they know (A. Brown, 1980). For example, earlier we discussed the tip-of-the-tongue phenomenon. Older children and adults are fairly accurate in predicting when they know something but cannot retrieve it at the moment. Younger children do not seem to have this ability. In addition, older individuals can tell you what they do not know as well as what they cannot know. Asked for Charles Dickens' telephone number, you would probably reply that you cannot know his number because telephones did not exist during Dickens' lifetime (Norman, 1973). You use reasoning as well as retrieval to determine what you know.

Younger children also have difficulty deciding what they need to know to perform well on a test (A. Brown, 1980). For example, it is not until around the fifth grade that most students understand it is easier to remember the gist of a story than to remember the exact words (Kreutzer, Leonard and Flavell, 1975). Younger students often are quite inflexible in the way they study a passage, not matching studying to the actual goal of the lesson. Even when they understand the goal of the lesson and can predict the best strategies for

(Ken Karp)

*Younger children often have trouble recognizing when a particular approach is not working and a new one should be tried. They may become very frustrated and need the teacher's help to "change gears."*

reaching the goal, younger children do not always follow their own advice and use the best strategy (A. Brown, 1980).

**Problems Requiring Metacognitive Abilities**

Because younger and less able children have not fully developed their metacognitive abilities, they have difficulty with the following (A. Brown, 1980):

1. Recognizing when a problem has gotten harder and a new approach is needed.
2. Inferring that an assumption is true, based on the information available.
3. Predicting the outcome of using a particular learning strategy in a given situation.
4. Planning ahead and apportioning time for studying.
5. Monitoring attempts to learn and changing approaches when necessary.

Simply teaching students strategies for dealing with these problems is not enough; students also must be taught how to monitor their use of the strategy. In other words, you need to give the students a way to check and test to see if they are applying the new strategy (Brown, Campione and Day, 1981). Ideas about how to accomplish both goals will be found in the next chapter, where we will explore two major types of instructional strategies based on cognitive views.

## SUMMARY

1. Cognitive psychologists study how people understand, represent, and remember information. They are interested in individual differences in specific learning situations.
2. In order to make sense of the vast amount of stimulation that reaches our senses, we must ignore some stimuli and recognize patterns in others, a process known as perception.

3. Early investigation of this process was conducted by the Gestalt theorists. Their contributions include the Gestalt principles for organizing stimuli (proximity, similarity, closure, and figure-ground, among others).

4. Perception is also influenced by feature analysis or bottom-up processing, and context or top-down processing.

5. Information must be represented in memory to be of any value in the future.

6. Most cognitive psychologists agree that information may be stored in several ways: as images, as words, or in propositional networks.

7. The networks indicate relationships among concepts. More general patterns for understanding events are called schemata, which are stereotypes of what to expect in particular situations.

8. People transform information in order to remember it. A limited amount of information can be held briefly in short-term memory, and can be maintained for a long time if it is rehearsed. To be retained without rehearsal, the information must be processed more deeply by being elaborated, organized, and integrated into the individual's store of knowledge.

9. Information is lost from short-term memory through interference and the passage of time.

10. Once in long-term memory, information is never really forgotten, but it may be hard to find. Given the right cues, we can usually reconstruct the original material by making associations and using logic and schemata describing what "should be" to fill in the gaps.

11. Teaching implications of the cognitive perspective include helping students to pay attention to the lesson; to identify the important, unfamiliar, and difficult aspects of new material; to retrieve prior knowledge so it is available to elaborate and organize the new information; and to connect the new information with what they already know. Students also can learn special memory strategies such as mnemonics.

12. As children grow older, they develop metacognitive skills. They monitor their understanding, fit study strategies to the purposes of assignments, and actively process the information they are attempting to learn.

**KEY TERMS**

perception

Gestalt theory

Prägnanz

figure-ground

feature analysis

bottom-up and top-down processing

dual code theory of memory

propositional network

schema, schemata

sensory register

short-term memory

rehearsal

long-term memory

levels of processing theory

elaboration

interference

time decay

meaningful

mnemonics

part-learning

serial-position effect

distributed and massed practice

metacognition

Suggestions for further reading and study are found on page 266.

# Teachers' Forum

## The Lower Third of the Class

Imagine you have just graded the final test for the first large unit of the year. You find that about two-thirds of the students seem to have mastered the material in the unit. The other third, however, seems to be totally lost. Somehow or other they have failed to memorize the basic vocabulary and facts they must know before they can do the more complicated work in the next unit. These students often have difficulty remembering material from one day or week to the next. How could you help these students retain and retrieve the information?

***Strategies for Learning***

I use mnemonic devices and spelling tricks to help students do rote memory work. Also, acting out situations can help students personalize and thus retain information—for example: Laurie is the sun, Steve is the earth, Susie is the moon. Steve is the person who most needs to understand what the earth does. Laurie stands in the center, Steve rotates around her, and Susie revolves around Steve. After repeating a few times on subsequent days, Steve learned this (he was a freshman in college at the time).

Bonnie Hettman, High School Teacher
*Lima Central Catholic High School, Lima, Ohio*

***Differentiated Assignments***

Grouping the class seems to be a logical solution to handling sharp differences in styles of learning. But in class, review would become tedious and a problem for the two-thirds who have already mastered the material. Differentiate homework assignments by planning exercises that review and use the vocabulary and facts. Gear these exercises so they use the previous lesson's facts also. By preprinting two sets of homework assignments—extension for the top two-thirds and basic fact-vocabulary exercises for the bottom one-third of the class—instructional time won't be lost, and learning needs will be matched.

Dorothy Eve Hopkins, Sixth-Grade Teacher
*Homer Intermediate School, Homer, New York*

***Prior Knowledge and Meaningful Learning***

First I would continue with the students who achieved mastery of the material. The third who were not proficient obviously have needs that must be determined. These are some of the questions I would want answered: Do the students' learning styles coincide with the instructional methods used? Are the students developmentally ready to master the material? Do the students have the background information or skills necessary to assimilate what I am expecting them to learn? Is the material relevant to them? Is memorization the most efficient means of learning the facts? Were the test instrument and results valid? Answers to these questions would determine how to proceed.

Annamarie McNamara, First-Grade Teacher
*Robison School, Erie, Pennsylvania*

## A Problem Text

Imagine that one of the books you are using this year is much too complicated for the students. Many of the students have complained that it is too hard to read. The real problem, however, seems to lie not in the reading level, but in the fact that the text jumps so quickly from one idea to another without giving examples, and without offering any logical organizational framework. Although you would like to change books, you have been told you will have to wait three years. Your request for funds for supplementary materials has also been turned down.

**Help Students Create Organization**

Since you are stuck with the text, the logical option is to outline the course material and to share the outline with your students. Helping them to see the connections and the development of logical thought is the only hope you have. The text then can be used as a ready reference since it seems to have plenty of information. In addition, lead the pupils to use other sources. The teacher's ability to present an overview as well as to relate the presently taught material to the overview will be critical to pupils' mastery.

Dorothy Eve Hopkins, Sixth-Grade Teacher
*Homer Intermediate School, Homer, New York*

**Create a Learning Center**

I would use the textbook strictly as reference material. I would create a learning center that would present one topic at a time. The learning center would present these topics in what I considered a logical sequence. The children would be given many types of activities to fulfill at the center, and would use information provided by me, the textbook, and other appropriate materials. This would also be a perfect time to incorporate a lesson on the use of an index so that students would learn how to find specific facts. . . .

Marilyn Dozoretz, Elementary and Prekindergarten Teacher
*Build Academy Public School, Buffalo, New York*

**Organize Student Groups**

If every teacher could write his own textbooks, education would approach Utopia. First, I would organize rotating student groups for an "overhaul" job. One committee would restructure the entire book. What a lesson in organization! Another would cite examples where necessary. Great experience in creative writing! Still another group would rephrase difficult passages, perhaps on tape. What better way to teach précis, word choice, and speaking skills? Finally, I'd compile all our work and send it to local tightfists and unaware editors with the following notation: "When a textbook committee hands you a lemon, make lemonade!"

Rachel D. Morton, Middle-School Language-Arts Teacher
*Star Middle School, Star, North Carolina*

**Supplement the Text**

I would continue to use the book and supplement it with teacher-made materials. Such materials would consist of outlines of chapters (to remedy lack of organizational framework) and numerous examples that I feel are most necessary. Since the reading level is not inappropriate, I feel retaining the text is a more satisfactory solution than discarding it altogether. (One should not throw out the baby with the bath water.) Some of the reorganization may be accomplished by the students—part of the learning process also.

Louise G. Harrold, Fourth-Grade Teacher
*Greenwood School, Warwick, Rhode Island*

# 7

# Instruction from the Cognitive Perspective

**OVERVIEW**    In the previous chapter we discussed how people perceive, understand, and remember information. We also examined the metacognitive skills that make individuals effective learners. The focus of this chapter is on instruction. We will be concerned with the implications of cognitive theories for the day-to-day tasks of teaching.

Schools are interested in many different types of knowledge. Students are expected to learn verbal information, concepts, principles, attitudes, and skills. In addition, we hope they will leave our classrooms ready to solve new problems and continue learning throughout life. Here we will explore what is known about designing instruction for these different types of learning goals. First we will consider how to teach concepts and verbal information, with special attention to the ideas of Jerome Bruner and David Ausubel. While it may seem that teaching facts, concepts, and principles is the goal of schools, most educators agree that more is required. Students must be able to apply this information in solving problems and must transfer what they learn to new experiences inside and outside the classroom. Thus we will spend several pages examining what is known about problem solving in both routine and unfamiliar situations. Then we will look at research on concept learning and problem solving in specific subjects such as mathematics, science, and reading. In the last section of this chapter, we will discuss how to encourage the transfer of learning from one situation to another.

By the time you finish this chapter, you should be able to do the following:

- Select an important concept in your subject and design a way to teach it to a particular grade level.
- Develop a lesson based on Bruner's discovery approach.
- Develop a lesson using Ausubel's expository approach.
- Describe the steps in solving complex problems.
- Discuss the implications of cognitive theories for instruction in science, mathematics, and reading.
- List three ways a teacher might encourage positive transfer of learning.

## LEARNING OUTCOMES: GAGNÉ

Humans are remarkably versatile. We learn a wide variety of skills and have a great deal of knowledge about the world. Robert Gagné has categorized the possible outcomes of learning under five headings: attitudes, motor skills, verbal information, intellectual skills, and cognitive strategies (1974; 1977).

Attitudes      **Attitudes** are probably learned through positive and negative experiences and modeling. For example, if you are a member of the golf team and receive a great deal of recognition for your performance on the team, you are likely to have a positive attitude toward golf. If a respected friend, teacher, coach, parent, or sibling has a positive view of golf, this could encourage you to develop a favorable attitude as well.

**Motor Skills**

Another type of learning involves the acquisition of **motor skill,** the ability to coordinate movements. Much of the learning of young children falls into this category. Children learn to walk, tie their shoes, "pump" on the swing, throw and catch a ball, run, skip, and print. Older students must master skilled movements for sports. In addition, many subjects require motor skills as part of the learning experience. Students may have to use a scale or centrifuge in chemistry lab, dissect a frog in a biology class, type in a business or journalism class, work with a potter's wheel in art, or thread a sewing machine in home economics. Motor skills have two components. The first is the rule that describes what to do or how to make the movements. The second is the actual muscle movement that becomes more accurate and smoother with practice and feedback.

**Verbal Information**

**Verbal information** could be described as "knowing what." Included in this category is the content of most lessons, facts, names, descriptions, dates, characteristics.

**Intellectual Skills**

**Intellectual skills** have been characterized as the "knowing how." Intellectual skills make it possible for people to use symbols and communicate. Through symbols we can interact with the environment indirectly, using mental manipulations and calculations to solve problems.

Not all intellectual skills are the same. Gagné suggests that there is a heirarchy of different intellectual skills and each skill is a prerequisite for mastering the skill above. The first intellectual skill of interest to teachers is *discrimination,* or making distinctions among symbols. This is a prerequisite for the next skill, forming *concepts.* In learning concepts, students must be able to make discriminations among separate elements, then classify and sort the elements into groups. The next step in the heirarchy is relating different concepts through *rules.* For example, the rule about calculating area states a relationship among the concepts of length, width, and area. Finally, rules can be combined into more complex, *higher-order rules.* To design an experiment comparing teaching methods, for instance, we must combine rules about selecting subjects, designing treatments, and evaluating results.

**Cognitive Strategies**

The final category described by Gagné is **cognitive strategies.** These are the skills involved in processing information by directing attention, selecting patterns from the sensory register, deciding which information in short-term memory will be rehearsed, elaborating and organizing information, and selecting a retrieval strategy. When students use the key word method to learn a list of French verbs, they are applying a cognitive strategy. Actually, when such a strategy is applied deliberately, it would be called metacognitive in the current terminology. We discussed these skills in the previous chapter when we considered the abilities of older and more able students. In this chapter we will examine a related topic, problem solving. Again, the research in this area is extensive and the implications for teaching are great, so we will devote an entire section to the topic. Figure 7–1 is a summary of the five possible learning outcomes described by Gagné. Now let's turn to the question of how to teach one important category of outcomes, concepts and rules.

**Figure 7–1**    **Gagné's Types of Learning Outcomes**

| Types of Learning Outcomes | Examples |
| --- | --- |
| Intellectual skills | Demonstrating the use of symbols by: |
| Discriminations | Distinguishing between *p* and *q* or a circle and oval |
| Concepts | Categorizing paintings by artist, style, period, subject matter |
| Rules | Demonstrating that water freezes at 32°F or 0°C |
| Higher-order rules | Predicting the amount of growth of a plant based upon water, fertilizer, and sun available |
| Verbal information | Stating the most famous works of a particular author, dates of publication, and so on |
| Attitudes | Choosing to join the backpacking club, listening to the Rolling Stones, or electing to take German |
| Motor skills | Mastering a front walkover, or throwing a straight pot on a wheel |
| Cognitive strategies | Using the loci method to remember a series of points to make in a speech or using analogies to solve a problem |

Adapted from R. M. Gagné. **Essentials of learning for instruction.** Hinsdale, Ill.: Dryden Press, 1974, p. 68.

# TEACHING AND LEARNING ABOUT CONCEPTS

The word "concept" has appeared repeatedly throughout this text. It is common in everyday conversation as well. In fact, most of what we know about the world involves concepts and relationships among concepts (Bourne, Dominowski and Loftus, 1979). Let's take a moment now to look more closely at the concept of *concept.*

## What Is a Concept?

Concepts
as Categories

**Concepts** are categories used to group similar events, ideas, or objects. When we talk about a particular concept such as *student* or *war*, we refer to a category of objects or events that are similar to one another. The concept *student*, for example, refers to all instances that fit into the category of people who study a subject. The people may be old or young, in school or not, study baseball or Bach, but they can all be categorized as students. Concepts are abstraction, creations of the mind to organize experience. We never see the pure concept *student.* We only see individual examples.

By forming concepts, we are able to organize the vast amount of information we encounter into meaningful units. For instance, there are about 7.5 million discriminable differences in colors. By categorizing these colors into a dozen or so groups, we manage to deal with this diversity fairly well (Bruner, 1973). Without the ability to form concepts, life would be a confusing series of unrelated experiences. Every new object encountered would require a new name, a new set of rules for recognition, and a new response. The load on memory would be tremendous. There would be no way of grouping like things together, no shorthand for talking and thinking about similar objects and events. Communication would be virtually impossible.

Defining
Attributes

Traditionally psychologists have assumed that members of a category share a set of **defining attributes** or distinctive features. For example, books contain pages of printed, drawn, or photographed material, are bound along one edge, and are of sufficient length to distinguish them from magazines or professional journals. We might have included shape as a distinctive feature, since most books have four sides. But the children of both authors have enjoyed several books shaped like Raggedy-Ann, Winnie-the-Pooh, and other forms that were not rectangular or square. Shape is not really a defining attribute of the concept book, even though most books share one shape. Shape in the case of this concept is an irrelevant attribute. You probably recognize the relationship between the distinctive features notion of concepts and the feature detection process in perception. Both theories suggest that we recognize specific examples of a concept by noting the critical or key features that define membership in that particular category.

Criticisms of the
Traditional View

Recently these long-popular views about the nature of concepts and category systems have been challenged. Critics have raised questions about how concepts are formed in the real world. While some concepts such as equilateral triangle have clear-cut defining attributes, most concepts do not. For example, take the concept of lobby. What are the defining attributes of a lobby? While we might have difficulty listing these attributes, we know a lobby when we see one. What about the concept of bird? A first thought might be that birds are animals that fly. But is an ostrich a bird? What about a penguin? These animals do not fly, but they are birds.

Prototypes

According to critics of the traditional view of concept learning, we have a **prototype** of a lobby and a bird, an image that captures the essence of these concepts. The prototype is the best representative of a category. Consider the concept of bird. The best representative of this category probably is a robin (Rosch, 1973). Potential members of the category may be very similar to the prototype (sparrow), or similar in some ways but different in others (chicken, ostrich). Thus whether something fits into a category is a matter of degree. Some events, objects, or ideas are simply better examples of the concept than others (Rosch, 1975). It is likely that children first learn concepts in the real world from best examples or prototypes (Tennyson, 1981). You can see that the idea of prototypes is related to schema theories of perception and memory.

Combining the
Two Views

The distinctive features and the prototype view of concept learning may not be totally incompatible. Concepts may be defined by a set of features that most members share. If a particular animal has enough of these features, we decide it is a bird, even though the list of features you check for "birdness" might vary from someone else's list. A biologist probably has a very sophisticated set of features for identifying examples of the category bird. But the prototype of the category can be seen as the example that has all (or most) of the defining features (Bourne, Dominowski and Loftus, 1979). We may learn concepts initially based on prototypes, but refine our schema for determining what is and what is not a member of the category based on a more sophisticated understanding of the defining attributes of the concept (Tennyson, 1981). Often this more highly developed understanding is a goal of instruction in school subjects such as science.

Most of the current approaches to teaching concepts rely heavily on an analysis of distinctive or defining attributes and less on identifying prototypes. We will present these traditional teaching strategies because they have been tested more thoroughly in classrooms. But approaches that combine both distinctive features and prototypes in teaching concepts are being developed and appear to be promising (Tennyson, 1981).

## Strategies for Teaching

No matter what strategy you select for teaching concepts, you probably will need these four components in the lesson: (1) the name of the concept, (2) a definition of the concept, (3) distinctive attributes of the concept, and (4) examples and nonexamples of the concept (Eggen, Kauchak and Harder, 1979).

Concept Name

The verbal label that identifies the concept, its name, is not the same as the concept itself. The label is important for communicating, but it is somewhat arbitrary. Simply learning a label does not mean the person understands the concept, although the label is necessary.

Concept Definition

A definition makes the nature of the concept clearer. A good definition has two elements: A reference to the more general category that includes the new concept, and a statement of the defining attributes of the concept (Klausmeier, 1976). For example, an equilateral triangle is defined as a plane, simple, closed figure (general category), with three equal sides and three equal angles (defining attributes). Reviewing the research on the role of definitions in concept learning, Tennyson and Park (1980) conclude that giving a definition improves performance on later tests of the concept, that a definition plus examples and nonexamples is better than the examples and nonexamples alone, and that providing a definition allows the teacher to use fewer examples to reach the same degree of understanding.

Relevant and Irrelevant Attributes

The identification of relevant and irrelevant attributes or features is another aspect of teaching concepts. The attributes of size, shape of ears, tusks, and trunk are relevant for categorizing animals as African or Asian elephants. On the other hand, gentleness is not a relevant characteristic for classifying elephants. The ability to fly is not a relevant attribute for classifying animals as birds, even though many birds fly.

Examples and Nonexamples

Examples are essential in teaching concepts. More examples are needed in teaching complicated concepts and in working with younger or less able students. Both examples and nonexamples (or **positive instances** and **negative instances**) are necessary to make the boundaries of the category clear.

The examples should be chosen to show the wide range of possibilities included in the category. They should vary greatly on attributes that are irrelevant to the concept and might be a source of confusion to the student. In teaching the concept of bird, examples should include ostriches and penguins, birds that vary on an irrelevant attribute for the category, the ability to fly. Since size is an irrelevant attribute, birds of many sizes should be included as examples. This will prevent *undergeneralization,* or excluding some animals from their rightful place in the category of bird. Nonexamples should be very close to the concept but miss by one or just a few critical

(*Leslie Deeb*)

attributes. For example, the figure △ is not an example of an equilateral triangle because it is not closed, even though it meets all the other criteria for the category. Including this type of example will prevent *overgeneralization* to figures that are not equilateral triangles.

**Rule-Eg and Eg-Rule**

These four components (concept name, definition, distinctive attributes, and examples) will be part of most teaching about concepts at every grade level. But the way these parts are assembled to create a lesson can vary. In general, concepts may be taught *deductively*, moving from a general rule to specific examples, or *inductively*, moving from many specific examples to an understanding of the rule. The deductive method is sometimes called the **rule-eg method.** We will see an example of this approach when we examine David Ausubel's expository teaching strategy. The inductive method, sometimes called the **eg-rule method,** is exemplified by Jerome Bruner's discovery learning, which we explore next.

## LEARNING THROUGH DISCOVERY: BRUNER

**Structure**

Jerome Bruner believes teachers should provide problem situations that stimulate students to discover for themselves the structure of the subject matter. **Structure** is made up of the fundamental ideas, relationships, or patterns of the subject—that is, the essential information. Particular facts and details are not part of the basic structure. If students really understand the basic structure, they should be able to figure out many of these details on their own. Thus Bruner believes that classroom learning should take place inductively, moving from specific examples presented by the teacher to generalizations about the structure of the subject that are discovered by the students.

The basic structure of subject matter is made up of concepts, but these concepts must be related to one another. For example, you might learn the meaning of the following terms: plane, simple, closed, figure, quadrilateral, triangle, isoscles, scalene, equilateral, right. Knowing these terms, you would **Relating Concepts** be on your way to understanding one aspect of geometry. But how do these terms relate to one another? If you can place the terms into a **coding system** such as the one in Figure 7–2, you will have a better understanding of the

**Figure 7–2    A Coding System for Triangles**

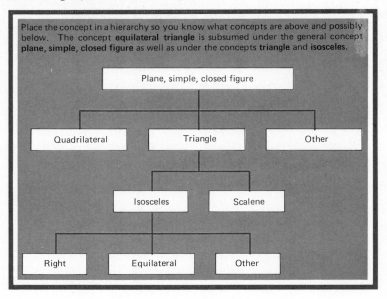

basic structure of this part of geometry. At the top of the coding system is the most general concept, in this case "plane, simple, closed figure." More specific concepts are arranged under the general concept.

## Classroom Applications

Intuitive
Thinking

Bruner suggests that teachers nurture **intuitive thinking.** Students should be encouraged to make intuitive guesses based on incomplete evidence, then check out these guesses more systematically (Bruner, 1960). For instance, after learning about ocean currents and the shipping industry, students might be shown old maps of three harbors and asked to guess which one became a major port. The guesses could then be checked by more systematic research. This research might be pursued with a bit more interest than usual, since the students would be finding out if their guesses were right or wrong. Unfortunately, educational practices often discourage intuitive thinking by punishing wrong guesses and rewarding safe but uncreative right answers.

Discovery
Learning

In discovery learning, a teacher organizes the class so the students learn through their own active involvement. A distinction usually is made between **discovery learning,** where the students are on their own to a very great extent, and **guided discovery,** in which the teacher provides some direction. For most situations, guided discovery is better. Students are presented with intriguing questions, baffling situations, or interesting problems. Instead of explaining how to solve the problem, the teacher provides the appropriate material and encourages students to make observations, form hypotheses, and test solutions. This process requires both intuitive and analytical thinking. The teacher guides discovery by asking leading questions: What would happen if you combined these two ideas? How would you test your guess? The teacher also provides feedback about the direction the problem-

**Figure 7–3    A Discovery Exercise for the Elementary Grades**

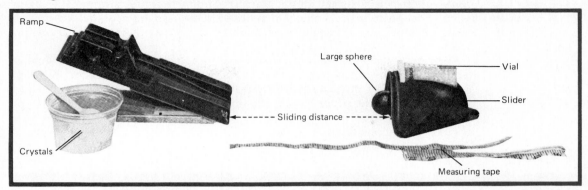

From *Energy Sources,* pamphlet prepared by the Science Curriculum Improvement Study. Copyright © 1971 by the Regents of the University of California. Published by Rand McNally & Co., Chicago, Ill.

solving activities are taking. This feedback must be given at the right time so students can revise their approach or continue toward a correct solution.

**An Example of Guided Discovery**

Let us consider one example of a guided discovery lesson for fourth- or fifth-graders studying energy sources in science class. The activity is taken from the Science Curriculum Improvement Study (SCIS) program (Karplus and Lawson, 1974). The materials used for the discovery activity are presented in Figure 7–3. The purpose of the lesson is to determine if the weight of the slider affects the distance that it slides. To answer this question, students place the slider at the base of a ramp so the two touch. Then they roll a metal ball down the ramp. Of course, when the ball hits the slider, it pushes the slider along the surface.

Students have to repeat this procedure twice, each time measuring exactly how far the ball pushes the empty slider. Next, a plastic vial is placed on the

*These students are discovering the relationships among the variables of weight, size, and distance traveled. Results of experiments with specific balls should point to general principles.*

(Chuck Iossi)

slider to add weight. The procedure is repeated to see how far the slider will move when it is weighed down slightly. Again this measurement is taken twice. The procedure is repeated with more weight (crystals added to the vial). Throughout the experiment, students record their observations in notebooks.

The next step is to compute an average for each set of two observations at each weight. The averages are plotted on a graph. Finally, the teacher can ask: What is the effect of increased weight on the distance traveled? How could the distance that the slider traveled be improved for each weight? The concept of friction can then be introduced.

Here are some Guidelines for applying Bruner's suggestions in other classroom situations.

# Guidelines

## Applying Bruner's Ideas in the Classroom

**1. Present many examples of the concept you are teaching.**

EXAMPLES
- In teaching about shapes, draw the shapes, show pictures of the shapes found in everyday objects, pass around examples, and let the students make the shapes with their own bodies.
- Ask students, "What are the different ways something can stand for something else, like a red light standing for stop?" (Bruner, 1966, p. 98).

**2. Emphasize the basic structure of new material.**

EXAMPLES
- Do not give too much detailed information.
- Clarify the structure with outlines, hierarchies, or demonstrations.

**3. Help students build coding systems.**

EXAMPLES
- Ask questions such as these: What else could you call this apple? (fruit). What do we do with fruit? (eat). What do we call things we eat? (food).
- Make up games that require students to create sets of like objects.

**4. Apply new learning to many different situations and kinds of problems.**

EXAMPLES
- Calculate the area of each tile on the classroom floor, then of all the tiles in the room, and then of the room in general.
- Have students use new words in many different contexts.

**5. Pose a problem to students and let them try to find the answer.**

EXAMPLES
- Ask questions such as this: "How could the human hand be improved?"
- Help students find ways to keep track of the hypotheses and data they generate, possibly by charting it yourself initially.

**6. Encourage students to make intuitive guesses.**

EXAMPLES
- Instead of giving a definition for a word, say: "Let's guess what it might mean by looking at the words around it."
- Give students a map of ancient Greece and ask where they think the major cities were.

# RECEPTION LEARNING: AUSUBEL

Expository
Teaching

David Ausubel's (1963, 1977) views of learning offer an interesting contrast to those of Bruner. His view is that learning should occur through reception, not discovery. Teachers should present materials to students in a carefully organized, sequenced, and somewhat finished form. Students will thus receive the most usable material. Ausubel calls this method **expository teaching.** It is best suited for meaningful verbal learning, or the learning of verbal information, ideas, and relationships among verbal concepts. The method is not useful in teaching physical skills or the multiplication tables.

Subsumers

Ausubel, like Bruner, believes people learn by organizing new information into coding systems. Ausubel calls the general concept at the top of the coding system the **subsumer** because all other concepts are subsumed under it, as in Figure 7–2. But unlike Bruner, Ausubel believes learning should progress deductively—that is, from an understanding of the general concepts to an understanding of specifics. Bruner, you may remember, believes learning should take place inductively, with the person using specifics to discover generalizations.

Ausubel suggests that people in most disciplines acquire knowledge through reception learning rather than through discovery. Concepts, principles, and ideas are presented to them, not discovered by them. The more organized and focused the presentation, the more thoroughly the person will learn. While this might sound like rote learning, it is not. The purpose of teaching is to help students understand the meaning of information so they can combine the new material sensibly with what they already know. Simply memorizing the content of a text or lecture is not meaningful learning; connections must be made with existing knowledge. Our discussion in the previous chapter indicated that rote memorization is a very ineffective learning strategy. Even so, it is often used by students because many teachers want rote recall. Sometimes teachers prefer the sound of their own words to an equally correct answer in the students' own words (Ausubel, 1977).

## Characteristics of Expository Teaching

Four
Characteristics

Ausubel's expository approach to teaching has four major characteristics. First, it calls for a great deal of interaction between teacher and students. Although the teacher may do the initial presentation, students' ideas and responses are solicited throughout each lesson. Second, it makes great use of examples. Although the stress is on *verbal* learning, examples may include drawings, diagrams, or pictures. Third, it is deductive. The most general and inclusive concepts are presented first, and the more specific concepts are derived from them. Finally, it is sequential. Certain steps must be followed in the presentation of the material. These steps are the initial presentation of an advance organizer, followed by subordinate content.

**Advance Organizers.** Meaningful learning generally occurs when there is a potential fit between the student's schemata and the material to be learned. To make this fit more likely, a lesson following Ausubel's strategy always begins with an **advance organizer,** an introductory statement of high-level concepts broad enough to encompass the information that will follow. Advance organizers can take three different forms: the definition of a concept, a generalization, or an analogy comparing new material with some well-known example (Eggen, Kauchak and Harder, 1979).

Types of
Organizers

The definition and generalization types of organizers are appropriate when the material to be learned is unfamiliar and the student has few "anchoring ideas" for making sense of the new information. These organizers give the key abstract ideas and relationships so the students have a conceptual framework or foundation for interpreting the new material. The analogy organizer is appropriate when the information to be learned has some familiar aspects (Rickards, 1980).

Purposes of
Organizers

The purpose of advance organizers is to give students the information they will need to make sense of the lesson or to help them remember and apply knowledge they already have but may not realize is relevant to the lesson. The organizer thus acts as a kind of conceptual bridge between new material and old (Faw and Waller, 1976). Textbooks often contain such advance organizers — the chapter overviews in this book are examples. These organizers serve three purposes. They direct your attention to what is important in the upcoming material. They highlight relationships among ideas that will be presented. And finally, they remind you of things you already know that will be relevant when you encounter the new material.

**Subordinate Content.** Once you have presented an advance organizer, the next step is to organize the subordinate content in terms of basic similarities and differences. Then you will need to provide examples and nonexamples of the various subconcepts. Finally, you must help students see the relationships between the examples you have been discussing and the general ideas given in the advance organizer.

## Classroom Applications

The characteristics and components of expository learning should become clearer after you have read the following extended example.

An Example of
an Expository
Lesson

**An Expository Lesson.** Assume you have decided to teach a ninth-grade geography class a lesson on one of the elements of the physical environment, the various landforms. Eggan, Kauchak, and Harder (1979) describe how you might use Ausubel's strategy in such a lesson. First, you arrange the students' desks so the students can see the board, one another, and you. Since this is an interactive lesson, you want the arrangement of the desks to encourage give-and-take between students and teacher. You will also be writing on the board, so you want students to be able to see it.

Next, you write the advance organizer on the board: *Landforms are land surfaces that have characteristic shapes and compositions.* On a table that all the students can see, you place three unlabeled objects: one with a high, relatively flat surface, one with a low, rough surface, and one with a high, peaked surface, as shown in Figure 7–4.

You are now ready to present the subordinate content. The first step is to note the basic similarities and differences in the three objects you have presented. For example, you might ask students to tell you what differences they find in the objects. After a series of appropriate responses, you could ask them to tell you the similarities. After this series of answers, you might take a moment to underscore the goals of the lesson. The students are going to learn

**Figure 7–4   Models of Three Types of Landforms.**

Adapted from P. D. Eggen, D. P. Kauchak, and R. J. Harder. **Strategies for teachers: Information processing in the classroom,** Englewood Cliffs, NJ: Prentice-hall, 1979, p. 260.

about the basic landforms and their characteristic shapes. By the end of the lesson, they should be able to identify each of the three types.

The next step is to add subordinate examples. These could be provided by you or by the students. After one student identifies the third object as a mountain, you might ask for specific examples of mountains, followed by questions about the characteristics of the mountains the students name. You could follow a similar procedure with the other two types of landforms: first an identification of the type (plateau, hill), and then a discussion of specific examples and the characteristics of these examples.

The final step is to help the students put it all together. Contrasts and comparisons are now drawn among all the landforms identified. What characteristics do all three share? How do specific examples differ? How can all of them be used to expand upon the original advance organizer?

**Similarities and Differences**

As you can see, this lesson in geography makes use of all four characteristics of expository teaching: interaction, examples, deduction, and sequence. The emphasis on both similarities and differences reflects another one of Ausubel's basic ideas about learning: To learn new material, students need to see *similarities* between what they already know and what they are trying to learn. Once students have learned the new material, they need to be able to see the *differences* between the new information and the old. Otherwise, the new may become mixed up with the old.

**When Is Ausubel's Approach Most Effective?**   Although expository teaching offers a number of ideas for teachers, its appropriateness may vary from situation to situation. Just as few teachers depend solely on discovery learning, few depend solely on expository teaching.

**Teaching Relationships**

The expository approach is appropriate for teaching relationships among concepts, but not for teaching the concepts themselves. If students do not yet know the concepts, certain problems arise. Imagine, for example, that the students in the geography class described above had no idea what a plateau, a hill, or a mountain was. They would have had a hard time offering specific examples. The discussion of differences and similarities would have had little meaning for them.

**Age Levels**

Expository teaching also requires that students be able to manipulate ideas mentally, even if the ideas are based on physical realities such as mountains or hills. So expository teaching is generally more appropriate for students at or above junior-high level, although advance organizers appear to have moderately positive effects on learning for students at all grade levels (Luiten, Ames and Acklerson, 1980).

(Sybil Shelton/Monkmeyer Press Photo Service)

*The teacher here uses the rule-example method of teaching concepts, a deductive or expository method. Having first presented general definitions of "land uses" and "water uses," he then elicits examples of each from his students.*

**Effectiveness**     Given the most appropriate situation—namely, a lesson on relationships among concepts for older students—how effective is the expository approach? As with discovery learning, this is a difficult question to answer. Barnes and Clawson (1975), Faw and Waller (1976), and Luiten, Ames, and Acklerson (1980) have reviewed many studies of the use of advance organizers and conclude that this approach does help. General, abstract organizers do seem to aid learning, especially when the material is particularly novel or difficult (Faw and Waller, 1976) or involves higher-level, more complex learning (Shuell, 1981b). This approach seems to aid students of all ability levels, but those who benefit most are the students with the greatest prior knowledge in the area (Shuell, 1981b).

A related question involves the effect of expository teaching as contrasted with discovery learning. The discovery method seems to be more appropriate for young students who can benefit from concrete experiences. However, research comparing discovery and expository approaches with young children has not indicated clear superiority for the discovery method (Cantor, Dunlap and Rettie, 1982). Expository teaching seems to be more efficient, as well as more useful, for teaching abstract relationships. It also offers a good means of helping students retain important information.

If you decide to use expository teaching, the Guidelines given here may be helpful. However, cognitive theorists offer much more than just discovery and expository methods of learning. In the next section we will consider a very important topic for teachers, how to solve problems.

# *Guidelines*

## *Applying Ausubel's Ideas in the Classroom*

**1. Use advance organizers.**

EXAMPLES
- Give a list of definitions of the most important terms you will be using in a lesson.
- Briefly describe the major concept you will be discussing.

**2. Use a number of examples.**

EXAMPLES
- In a mathematics class, ask students to give examples of the right triangles they can find in the room around them.
- In a science class, pass around pictures showing numerous examples of animals or plants that are being discussed.

**3. Focus on both similarities and differences.**

EXAMPLES
- In a history class, ask students to list ways in which the North and South were alike and different before the Civil War.
- In a biology class, ask students to tell you what would have to be different to make spiders fit into the category of insects.

**4. Present material in an organized fashion.**

EXAMPLES
- Use simple diagrams whenever possible
- Start a lesson with an overview, give partial summaries of important points throughout, and end with a general summary.

**5. Discourage rote learning of material that could be learned more meaningfully.**

EXAMPLES
- When students give an answer from the book, ask them to give it in their own words or to give an example.
- Include activities that give students a chance to explain ideas to each other.

# PROBLEM SOLVING

Definition    "Educational programs have the important ultimate purpose of teaching students to solve problems—mathematical and physical problems, health problems, social problems, and problems of personal adjustment (Gagné, 1977, p. 177). **Problem solving** is usually defined as formulating new answers, going beyond the simple application of previously learned rules to create a solution. Problem solving is what happens when routine or automatic responses do not fit the current situation.

Before we examine different approaches to problem solving, consider the problems in Box 7–1, which have been used by researchers studying this topic.

## Steps in Problem Solving

In general, there are four stages in problem solving. The first is understanding or representing the problem. The second is selecting or planning the solution, followed by executing the plan and then evaluating the results (Wessells, 1982).

**What Is the Problem?**

**Understanding the Problem.** The first step in problem solving is to decide exactly what the problem is. This often means finding the relevant information in the problem and ignoring irrelevant details. For example, consider problem 1 in Box 7–1. How many times would you have to remove a sock from the drawer before you are certain to have a match? In this case, the information about the 4 to 5 ratio of black socks to brown socks is irrelevant. As long as you have only two different colors of socks in the drawer, you will have to remove only three socks before two of them are bound to match.

**Representing the Problem**

In addition to identifying the relevant information in a problem, you must develop an accurate or helpful representation of the situation involved. For example, if you assumed that the two men playing the five checker games in the second problem were playing each other, then it would be impossible for the men to win the same number of games with no ties. But the problem did not say the men were playing against each other, merely that they each played five games.

244

Consider the fourth question in Box 7–1. This problem can be solved by using an object in an unconventional way. If you tie the hammer or the pliers to the end of one rope and start it swinging like a pendulum, you will be able to catch it while you are standing across the room holding the other rope. You can use the weight of the tool to make the rope come to you instead of trying to stretch to reach the rope. People often fail to solve this problem because they seldom consider unconventional uses for materials that have a specific function. This difficulty is called **functional fixedness** (Duncker, 1945). Trying to reach out with the pliers and grasp the other end of the rope is an example of fixing your attention on the usual function of the pliers. Often, problem solving requires seeing things in new ways.

A related block to effective problem solving is rigidity or set, sometimes called **response set.** In the matchstick question, you probably figured out how to solve the first example quite quickly. You simply move one match from the right side over to the left to make $\backslash/\,| = \backslash/\,|$. Questions two and three can also be solved without too much difficulty by changing the $\backslash/$ to an $\times$, or vice versa. But the fourth example (taken from Raudsepp and Haugh, 1977) probably has you stumped. We had the same reaction. To solve this problem, you must change sets. What has worked before will not work this time. Consider making a major change of set by switching from Roman to Arabic numbers and creating a mathematical symbol with your one match move. The answer lies in using both an Arabic number and a square root, changing $\backslash/\,|| = |$ to $\backslash/\overline{\mathstrut}\, = |$, which is simply the symbolic way of saying that the square root of 1 equals 1.

While functional fixedness and response set interfere with finding a helpful way to represent a problem, other factors can lead to a representation that quickly suggests a solution. The Gestalt psychologists believed that insight is a key to problem solving. **Insight** is the sudden reorganization or reconceptualization of a problem that leads to an immediate recognition of the solution.

The first author had an experience with insight while trying to solve the following problem: How can 10 trees be planted in 5 rows so that there are 4 trees in each row (Sternberg and Davidson, 1982)? Clearly many or all of the trees had to appear in more than one row. She tried several patterns, erasing and moving dots to simulate trees. Then she reached a point where the dots looked something like pattern A in Figure 7–5. This configuration suddenly

**Figure 7–5   An Insightful Solution**

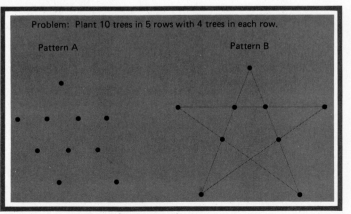

*Adapted in part from Sternberg and Davidson, 1982.*

suggested a star, which turns out to be the solution, as you can see in pattern B.

Need for Flexibility

Functional fixedness, response set, and insight point to the importance of flexibility in understanding problems. If you get started with an inaccurate or inefficient representation of the true problem, it will be difficult, or at least very time-consuming, to reach a solution (Wessels, 1982). For example, in the tree problem, trying to work with parallel rows is a dead end. Until you abandon this strategy, little progress is likely. Sometimes it is helpful to "play" with the problem, to seek a better way of understanding it. Ask yourself: What do I know? What do I need to know to answer this question?

Strategies for Problem Solving

**Selecting the Approach.** After deciding what the problem is, you must plan a strategy. You could conclude that the current situation is the same as a previous problem and try what has worked before. Success is likely with this approach only if the two situations are in fact quite similar. Another strategy that sometimes works but is not very efficient is the **generate-test method.** This involves trying possible solutions in a relatively haphazard manner. For example, if you wanted to name the capital of Ohio, you might start recalling names of cities in that state and evaluating each name as a possible capital (Wessells, 1982). If the potential number of solutions is small this might make sense, but most problems should be approached in a more organized fashion.

A promising method would be to try **analogical thinking,** or reasoning by analogy (Copi, 1961). This limits your search for solutions to situations that bear some resemblance to the one you currently face. You do not have to test every possibility that pops into your mind.

Using Analogical Thinking

To solve the X-ray problem presented earlier, you might imagine an analogous situation, such as how to bring a heavy load across a ravine when the whole load must get across at the same time and the material you have for building the bridge is not strong enough to support the entire load. One way to transport a heavy load across a weak bridge so that the whole load arrives at the same time and the bridge does not break would be to build several small bridges, divide the load, and time the crossing so that each small load arrived simultaneously. The solution to the X-ray problem is analogous. Direct several rays of weaker intensity through the body at various spots, converging on the tumor. The X ray will be intense enough to destroy tissue only at the point where all the rays converge.

*One strategy that helps students improve their problem solving capabilities is to work in pairs, discussing reasons for each step taken.*

(Ken Karp)

In addition to thinking analogically, verbalizing, trying to put into words what you are doing and why, helps solve problems. For example, Gagné and Smith (1962) found that when ninth- and tenth-grade subjects were instructed to state a reason for each step they were taking, they were much more successful in solving the problem than students who did not state reasons. Finally, active involvement improves problem solving. Research on teaching problem-solving skills indicates that presenting solutions to students is the least effective way to help them learn to solve problems in the future (Gagné, 1977).

**Evaluating the Results.**  After you identify a solution and implement it, you should evaluate the results. This involves checking for evidence that both confirms and disconfirms your choice. Often people stop before they have identified the *best* solution if they find an answer that works in some cases. For example, the first author recently tested a high school student with the following problem:

$$8X + 4Y = 28$$
$$4X - 2Y = 10$$

The student quickly wrote: $X = 2$, $Y = 3$. This solution works for the first equation, but not for the second. The student found evidence to confirm the solution, but did not keep checking to see if the solution fit all aspects of the problem.

## Effective Problem Solving: General Principles

Most psychologists agree that effective problem solving is based on an ample store of knowledge about the problem area. Students must have the appropriate vocabulary and concepts. For example, finding a solution to the X-ray problem would be difficult without a basic knowledge of the meaning of the words, "tumor," "X ray," "tissue," and "healthy." In the matchstick problem, you must understand Roman and Arabic numbers as well as the concept of square root. In addition, you must know that the square root of 1 equals 1. A good supply of knowledge, facts, concepts, and procedures seems to be important for solving problems in various fields. A chemist in one study described the first step in finding a solution to be "so thorough a study of the problem and of the data that your mind is quite completely saturated with the subject" (Platt and Baker, 1931). This rich store of knowledge must be organized in ways that make it easy to retrieve when needed, perhaps in interconnected propositional networks or schemata.

In addition to having a rich store of well-organized prior knowledge, expert problem solvers are persistent. Motivation plays an important role as well: "Successful problem-solvers are often those who simply are willing to put in the necessary effort" (Sternberg and Davidson, 1982, p. 44).

An early study by Bloom and Broder (1950) summarizes many of the factors associated with successful problem solving. These researchers found that successful problem solvers generally had six things in common. First, they made sure that they understood exactly what the nature of the problem was. Unsuccessful problem solvers often tried to solve a problem that was different from the one actually presented to them. Second, the successful problem solvers tried to understand the ideas in the problem by making associations with other, more familiar ideas. Third, they tended to plan their approach to solving the problem more carefully and systematically. Fourth, they refused to give up when conventional answers proved inadequate. Fifth, they tended to follow a line of reasoning without getting sidetracked. Sixth, they believed they had a good chance of solving the problem. Finally, to be an expert problem solver in a given field requires mastery of specific procedures and operations in that field (Greeno, 1982). Before we consider the development of expertise in a particular field, we can summarize the general principles for effective problem solving in the form of Guidelines.

# Guidelines

## Problem Solving

**1. Make sure students have the necessary prior knowledge to understand the problem.**

EXAMPLES
- Consider the use of task analysis (described in Chapter 11).
- Supply necessary information before presenting the problem.

**2. Ask students if they are sure they understand the problem.**

EXAMPLES
- Can they separate relevant from irrelevant information?
- Are they aware of any assumptions they are making?
- Encourage them to try to visualize the problem.

**3. Encourage attempts to see problems from different angles.**

EXAMPLES
- Suggest different possibilities and then ask students to offer additional possibilities.
- Develop exercises involving unconventional uses for common objects.

**4. Encourage the use of analogies.**

EXAMPLES
- Ask students to describe similar situations.
- Suggest analogies in everyday lessons.

**5. Help students develop systematic ways of considering alternatives.**

EXAMPLES
- Model appropriate problem-solving techniques.
- Ask "What would hapen if . . . ?"

**6. Ask students to explain the steps they take in solving problems.**

EXAMPLES
- Ask students to draw a line down the middle of an answer sheet and write the answers on one side and the reasons for the answers on the other.
- Have students teach their problem-solving methods to other students.

**7. Let students do the thinking; do not simply provide solutions.**

EXAMPLES
- Offer individual problems as well as group problems so that each student has a chance to provide solutions.
- Give partial credit if students have good reasons for the "wrong" solutions they choose.

## Becoming an Expert in One Field

One of the most exciting recent accomplishments of cognitive psychology is a more complete understanding of human competence. Psychologists have moved from studying simple laboratory tasks such as memorizing nonsense syllables to investigating complex learning such as mathematics and reading. One aspect of this interest is the study of experts. Researchers have tried to understand how experts in particular fields comprehend, remember, and solve problems.

Types of Knowledge

In understanding the differences between experts and beginners in any field, it is helpful to make the distinction between two types of knowledge. **Declarative knowledge** is the content or information of the field—the facts, concepts, and principles. When we think of experts, we usually think of people who have more of this type of knowledge. But experts also differ in their **procedural knowledge,** or cognitive strategies for solving problems. The processes experts apply in solving problems are often quite different from those of beginners.

Chess Experts

The modern study of expertise began with investigations of chess masters (Simon and Chase, 1973). Results indicated that masters can quickly recognize about 50,000 different arrangements of chess pieces. They can look at one of these patterns for a few seconds and remember where every piece on the board was placed. It is as though they have a "vocabulary" of 50,000 patterns. For the masters, patterns of pieces are like words. You probably know a very large number of words. If shown any one of these words for just a few seconds, you could remember every letter in the word in the right order (assuming you could spell the word). The task would be similar to the "Knights rode horses" memory problem we presented in the previous chapter.

But a series of nonsense words is hard to remember. An analogous situation holds for chess masters. When chess pieces are placed on a board randomly, masters are no better than the average individual at remembering the positions of the pieces. So the configurations of chess pieces are like words and the master's memory is for patterns that make sense or could occur in a game. Thus "high-level competence in this case does not appear to reside in conscious analytical thinking processes. The chess master is a superior recognizer rather than a deep thinker" (Glaser, 1981, p. 931).

Recognizing Patterns

A similar phenomenon may occur in other fields such as physics. There may be a kind of intuition or immediate recognition of how to solve problems that is based on recognizing patterns and knowing the "right moves" for those patterns. Experts in physics, for example, appear to organize their knowledge differently from beginners. Beginners attempt to solve problems in physics by organizing their knowledge around the objects and details directly indicated in the problem; experts organize their knowledge around central principles of physics. With this type of organization, experts can find the patterns needed to solve a particular problem very quickly without putting a heavy strain on working memory. There is less "bottom-up processing" or analyzing of details in the problem. Experts literally don't have to think as hard or consider as many details (Glaser, 1981).

"Unlearning" Wrong Information

But physics is different from chess in at least one way. Most beginners approach physics with a great deal of misinformation and apprehension. Many of our intuitive ideas about the physical world are wrong and do not fit modern theories of physics, as you can see in Box 7–2 on Forces. So learning physics means unlearning old, incorrect schemata as well as building new correct ones (McWilliams, 1982). Most people have no comparable inaccurate notions about chess.

The study of experts points to the importance of how knowledge is organized. Because knowledge is organized around general principles, experts can quickly recognize familiar patterns in new problems. These patterns suggest possible procedures for solving the problems.

---

## BOX 7–2 FORCES IN PHYSICS

When students are faced with learning about the motion of bodies in physics, they not only must learn new information, they also must "unlearn" certain common sense ideas. For example, when asked to draw the forces acting on a ball that has been thrown straight up into the air, many people include the force from the throw "pushing" the ball up and the force of gravity "pulling" the ball back to the ground. But the first idea, that a force is acting on the ball to push it up, is not correct. This idea is in contradiction to Newton's laws of motion, principles that must be understood in physics courses.

A study by Audrey Champagne, Leopold Klopfer, and John Anderson (1980) provides another example of the interference of common sense ideas in learning physics. The subjects were college students in an introductory physics class for nonmajors. Before the course, students saw a demonstraton of objects in free fall in various situations. The students were asked questions about the motion of the objects and then had to justify their answers.

Analyses of the answers indicated that one student in five believed that the objects reached maximum speed immediately and then dropped at a constant rate. Four out of five believed that, all other things being equal, heavier objects fall faster than lighter objects. These beliefs were held in spite of the fact that 70 percent of the class had taken high school physics.

The formal rules of Newtonian mechanics, based on a frictionless world, do not fit well our everyday intuitive beliefs about motion. These common sense ideas are more like the basic notions of Aristotle. In addition, common sense belief systems often are quite flexible. Contradictions are easily rationalized. For example, the authors state:

> Most students thought that objects fall at a constant speed. They argued, as Aristotle did, that the speed depends only on the weight (mass) of the object, which also remains constant. However, some students had learned the specific fact that objects accelerate in free fall. One might think this piece of knowledge is sufficient contradiction of the Aristotelian belief to engender a major disruption of the system. Instead we found that students rationalized the acceleration by hypothesizing that the force of gravity increases closer to the ground. They supported the hypothesis by noting that there is little or no gravity in outer space (p. 1078).

Because the common sense ideas make sense and because students can explain away contradictions, learning a new system is difficult. The researchers suggest that students examine both Aristotelian and Newtonian systems so that they can compare the two and see the advantages of Newton's laws. If it seems like a waste of time to teach a system and then tell students they should reject it, remember that they may never really accept Newton's laws until they confront their own common sense ideas and reject them.

# LEARNING STRATEGIES AND PROBLEM SOLVING IN SCHOOL

As research on problem solving, like work in most of cognitive psychology, focuses more on complex problems, the findings have important implications for how people solve problems in school subjects. Here we will look at mathematics, science, and reading.

## Mathematics and Science

Role of Schemata

Let us consider the problem-solving steps we described earlier as they apply to story problems in arithmetic. The first step is to understand or represent the problem. This means translating the verbal presentation of the problem into an arithmetic expression. Research in this area suggests that students need a number of basic story problem schemata for recognizing what is being asked. These schemata might be as simple as a "putting things together" or "losing some things" schema (Lindvall, Tamburino and Robinson, 1982) or more complicated, such as an "area measuring" or a "velocity" schema (Gagné, 1982). If these schemata are well developed, students will be less confused by tricky words such as "more" in a problem that really requires subtraction or "fewer" in an addition problem (Resnick, 1981).

When we discussed expert problem solvers, we said they have a large store of patterns to apply in solving specific problems. They see a new problem as an instance of a particular pattern and thus know the right moves for solving the problem without analyzing all the details of the new situation. This style of seeing the whole pattern contradicts one recommended method for teaching story problems that involves sentence-by-sentence direct translation of words into equations (Resnick, 1981).

Representing the Problem

Research suggests that effective problem solvers create some type of qualitative representation of a mathematical problem before they select the actual number operations (Lindvall, Tamburino and Robinson, 1982; Heller and Greeno, 1979; Simon and Simon, 1978). In understanding a story problem, it may be helpful to represent the problem with a diagram. As an example, Figure 7–6 shows diagrams for representing eight types of simple addition and subtraction story problems. When these procedures were taught to primary grade students, their performance on story problems improved significantly (Lindvall, Tamburino and Robinson, 1982).

The researchers stress that these diagramming methods should *not* be taught as just another computation procedure. Students should be encouraged to create their own way of diagramming. A lesson based on the "losing some things" schema is found in Figure 7–7. A problem stated in the manner of the problem in Figure 7–7 often gives students trouble because the unknown is in the middle of the story. Stated algebraically, the problem would be $8 - X = 3$. But the computation needed is $8 - 3 = ?$ The "losing some things" schema and diagram handle this problem easily.

Accurate Computations

After representing the problem, the next step is to carry out the computations. Errors can occur at this point because students have developed systematic "bugs" in their procedures (Brown and Vanlehn, 1982). To become expert problem solvers in mathematics, basic computation operations must be learned correctly and thoroughly. In fact, Gagné (1982) suggests that many operations should be "automatized," or learned and practiced so completely that little attention is needed to complete them accurately. Then attention and working memory can be directed to the more difficult or unfamiliar aspects of

**Figure 7–6    Representing Addition and Subtraction Story Problems**

| Problem Type | Story Example | Diagram Taught |
|---|---|---|
| **1.** Combine (putting sets together) | Ann had 3 apples. Jill had 4 apples. How many apples did they have altogether? | |
| **2.** Separate (taking set apart) | Together Bob and Tony had 8 toy cars. 3 of these were Bob's. How many did Tony have? | |
| **3.** Change increase (getting more things) | Sue had 5 pencils. She got 4 more pencils. How many did she have then? | |
| **4.** Change decrease (losing some things) | May had 7 cookies. She then ate 3 of them. How many did she have left? | |
| **5.** Compare—more (how many more) | Rick had 6 kites. Dan had 8 kites. How many more kites did Dan have than Rick? | |
| **6.** Compare—less (how many less) | Len had 5 books. Rita had 9 books. How many less books did Len have than Rita? | |
| **7.** Equalize—take away (making same size—take away) | Jim had 4 cookies. Al had 7 cookies. How many cookies would Al have to eat to have as many as Jim? | |
| **8.** Equalize—add on (making same size—add on) | Sally had 8 rings. Jan had 5 rings. How many more would Jan have to get to have as many as Sally? | |

*Adapted from Lindvall, Tamburino and Robinson, 1982.*

the problem. To provide the amount of practice necessary to make mathematical operations automatic, Gagné suggests scheduled reviews spaced throughout the day (distributed practice), competitions, games, and computer-assisted instruction.

The last step in solving mathematical problems is to validate the answer. This might mean applying a checking routine such as adding to check the result of a subtraction problem or adding the column from bottom to top instead of top to bottom. Another possibility is estimating the answer. For example, if the computation was $11 \times 21$, the answer should be around 200, since $10 \times 20$ is 200. A student who finds an answer of 2311 or 23 or 562 should quickly realize these cannot be correct. Estimating an answer is particularly important when students rely on calculators. They must be able to judge the answer, since they cannot go back and spot an error in the figures.

**Figure 7–7    A Lesson Based on the "Losing Some Things" Schema**

| Lesson 15: Losing Some Things |
| --- |

*Lesson objective:* Given a written story problem of the losing some things type, the pupil will be able to draw the appropriate story diagram and write and solve the correct number sentence.

*Story example:* "Bob had 8 pencils. He lost some of his pencils. He then had 3 left. How many pencils did Bob lose?"

**1.** Show with blocks.

**2.** Draw story diagram (dots):
—Start set.
—The "take away" loop.
—Number remaining.

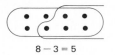

8 − 3 = 5

**3.** Draw story diagram (numerals):

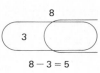

8 − 3 = 5

—Place number in start set above loop.
—Draw "take away" loop.
—Place number in "remaining set" space.

**4.** Write number sentence. Solve.

**5.** Check answer.

*Adapted from Lindvall, Tamburino and Robinson, 1982.*

*Being able to estimate answers is particularly important when students do computations on calculators. One possibility is working in pairs. One student estimates, the other calculates, and then they change roles.*

(Ken Karp)

In science, many of the issues found in mathematical problem solving also apply. Students must have a good store of well-organized prior knowledge on which to base new learning. They need appropriate patterns or schemata for making sense of new information. But in science there are special difficulties that might be caused by the students' existing schemata. Students often bring mistaken models of the physical world to their science classes. You saw one example in the box on forces in physics in the previous section. It seems logical that there is a force acting to "push" an object up after the object has been hurled into the air. This is the way very early scientists viewed the world. But it is a model that contradicts Newtonian laws of motion. It also makes learning and working with Newton's laws difficult.

Another example is provided by Roger Osbourne (1981). He studied the models students have about how electric current flows in a circuit to light a bulb. Some students think the current flows from the battery to the light bulb in one direction and in only half of the circuit. At the bulb, the current is "burned" like fuel to produce the light. Other students think the light is caused when current (coming in two directions from the two different poles of the battery) collides in the bulb and makes it glow. Of course, there are students who have an accurate model of how the current flows. But even when teachers try to correct the erroneous models and go on to demonstrate that the students' views are wrong, students often "stick to their guns," claiming that this particular circuit is an exception, but all other circuits would act in keeping with their model (Wittrock, 1982).

These two examples show that science teachers must understand their students' representations or models of the concepts and principles involved in the lessons. Students often memorize a formula or procedure, then apply it in the wrong situation because they have an inadequate model of the problem. This also causes difficulties when the students encounter unfamiliar problems they should be able to solve, but cannot because they do not have an accurate view of the principles involved.

## Learning to Read

Constructing
Meaning

Several researchers suggest that comprehending what you read is a constructive process in which you create meaning by (1) relating your experience and knowledge to the information on the page, and (2) relating one part of the text to other parts to make it all fit together. Students can accomplish the first connection by imagining themselves in the story, forming an opinion, creating images about the story, or thinking of examples from their own lives. The second type of connection can be made by answering questions about the story, noticing the organization (headings, topic sentences, summaries), paraphrasing the main points of the story, graphing or diagramming the relationships in the story, illustrating the story, and so on. All these possibilities make the reader elaborate on the information in the story, organize it, and thus process it more deeply.

For teachers, this means knowing the students and their capabilities. Can the students form an image, an example, an analogy? Can they summarize or paraphrase? Do they recognize and use headings? If the answers are "No," students may need to be taught these skills as part of their instruction in how to read.

**PQ4R**      Over the years there have been many suggestions about how to understand and remember what you read. One of the most enduring systems is the SQ3R (survey, question, read, recite, review) approach developed by F. P. Robinson (1961). This and similar systems have proved effective with many types of students (Sargent, Huus and Andersen, 1970). A more recent variation is called PQ4R (Thomas and Robinson, 1972). In this system the extra *R* is for *reflection*. The phases are preview, question, read, reflect, recite, review. If you were applying the PQ4R method to study this text, you would do the following:

**Preview.**      Introduce yourself to the chapter you are about to read by surveying the major topics and sections. Read the overview, the objectives, the section headings and subheadings, the summary, and perhaps the initial sentences of the major sections. If you have the Study Guide for this book, you might look over the chapter objectives and outlines. Formulate your general purposes for reading each section, such as identifying the main idea or the biases of the author.

**Question.**      Create questions about each major section related to your purposes. One way is to turn the headings and subheadings into questions. For example, in this chapter you might ask: "How can I help students learn to read?" "What are some effective learning strategies for mathematics?" If you are beginning to use this method of reading, it often is helpful to write down brief questions as they come to mind.

**Read.**      At last! The questions you have formulated can be answered through reading. You should pay attention to the main ideas, supporting details, and other data in keeping with your purposes. You may have to adjust your reading speed to suit the difficulty of the material and your purpose for reading.

**Reflect.**      While you are reading, try to think of examples or create images of the material. Make connections between what you are reading and what you already know.

**Recite.**      After reading each section, sit back and think about your initial purposes and questions. Can you answer the questions without looking at the book? In doing this, your mind has a second chance to connect what you have read with what you already know. If your mind is blank after reading the section, it may have been too difficult to read comfortably or you may have been daydreaming. Reciting helps you monitor your understanding and tells you when to reread before moving on to the next section. Reciting should take place after each headed section, but might be required more often in reading difficult material.

**Review.**      Effective review helps limit forgetting and incorporates new material more permanently into your memory. As study progresses, review should be cumulative, including the sections and chapters you read previously. Rereading is one form of review, but trying to answer key questions without referring to the book is the best way to review. Wrong answers can direct you to areas that need more study, particularly before an exam.

Anderson (1980) suggests several reasons why PQ4R works. First, following the steps makes students more aware of the organization of the chapter. (How often have you skipped reading headings entirely and thus missed major clues to the organizational structure of the information?) Next, these steps require the student to study the chapter in sections instead of trying to learn all the information at once. This makes use of distributed practice. Creating and answering questions about the material forces the student to process the information more deeply and with greater elaboration. Reciting and reviewing with questions in mind encourages more connections to be made between the new information and what the student already knows.

The PQ4R method is most appropriate for older children. In fact, very little is known about teaching study skills to students before about grade 9. The effective application of study skills probably requires metacognitive development beyond the range of most very young children.

Thus far we have discussed learning and problem solving in particular subjects. The next sections examine more general learning strategies.

## Study Aids

Do you underline or highlight key phrases in your text? Are our words turning yellow at this very moment? What about outlining or taking notes? The research on these study techniques shows mixed results. Some investigations have shown that rereading is better than taking notes or underlining, and others have found no differences. A third group finds note-taking effective.

When particular study techniques do work, they seem to involve active thinking or processing, not simply copying words and phrases from the text. For example, outlining, paraphrasing, and creating images appear to improve comprehension and memory (Anderson, 1980; Bretzig and Kulhavy, 1979). Answering questions while reading seems to be one of the best methods. All these approaches require processing and elaboration. Two other important factors seem to be spending time concentrating on the material, either to make notes or to reread, and having the material available for reference when studying. The more you focus on and process the text, the more you learn.

## Teacher Guidelines

What can we conclude from all this information about "expert performance" and learning strategies? First, teachers must take responsibility for helping students learn study skills. Only a few individuals in your class will
be "expert students." Armbruster and Anderson (1981) make these suggestions for teachers: (1) Teach students the importance of knowing what they are studying for, so they can match study with the task or test. (2) Teach students how to use the elements of the texts (headings, objectives) to improve studying. (3) Teach students how to make the best of what they already know, their own interests, motivations, strengths and weaknesses. (4) Teach specific study strategies and how to monitor these strategies. For example, most students must be taught how to outline and how to recognize a good outline.

Second, even if you don't enter teaching, you can benefit from these guidelines on how to become an "expert learner."

# Guidelines

## Becoming Expert Learners

**1. Make sure you have the necessary declarative knowledge (facts, concepts, ideas) to understand new information.**

EXAMPLES
- Keep definitions of key vocabulary available as you study.
- Review required facts and concepts before attempting new material.

**2. Find out what type of test the teacher will give (essay, short answer) and study the material with that in mind.**

EXAMPLES
- If there will be a test with detailed questions, study by practicing writing answers to likely questions.
- If a multiple-choice test is expected, use mnemonics to associate key terms and their definitions.

**3. Make sure you are familiar with the organization of the materials to be learned.**

EXAMPLES
- Preview the headings, introductions, topic sentences, and summaries of the text.
- Be alert for words and phrases that signal relationships, such as "on the other hand," "because," "first, second," "however," "since."

**4. Know yourself and use your cognitive skills deliberately to learn.**

EXAMPLES
- Relate the new material through examples and analogies to something you like and understand well, such as sports, hobbies, or films.
- If one study technique is not working, try another—the goal is to stay involved, not to use a particular strategy.

**5. Study the right information in the right way.**

EXAMPLES
- Ask the teacher for a study outline for the test.
- Spend your time on the important, difficult, and unfamiliar material that will be required for the test or assignment.
- Keep a list of the parts of the text that give you trouble and spend more time on those pages.
- Process the important information thoroughly by using mnemonics, forming images, creating examples, answering questions, making notes in your own words, and elaborating on the text. Do not just try to memorize the author's words—create your own.

**6. Monitor your own comprehension.**

EXAMPLES
- Use questioning to check your understanding.
- When reading speed slows down, decide if the information in the passage is important. If it is, note the problem so you can reread or get help to understand. If it is not important, ignore it.

*Adapted from Armbruster and Anderson (1981).*

*Most students have to be taught the study skills of outlining and taking notes. Some individuals, like this boy, need extra help and practice, perhaps before school or during a free period.*

(Ken Karp)

## TEACHING FOR TRANSFER

Do You
Remember?

Think back for a moment to one of your high school English, science, or history classes. Select a particular subject, one that you did not go on to study in college. Imagine the teacher, the room, the textbook. If you can do all this, you are using your information-processing strategies for search and retrieval very well. Now remember what you actually studied in class. If it was a science class, what were some of the formulas you learned? How about chemical reactions? Oxidation reduction? If you are like most of us, you may remember *that* you learned these things, but you will not be quite sure exactly *what* you learned. Were those hours wasted? What could have made the learning more memorable and useful? These are essentially questions about the transfer of learning from one situation to another.

### Positive and Negative Transfer

Positive Transfer

Whenever something learned previously influences current learning, **transfer** has occurred. If students learn a mathematical principle in first period and use it to solve a physics problem in fifth period, then *positive transfer* has taken place. Even more rewarding for the teachers involved is the positive transfer that takes place when a math principle is learned in October and applied to a physics problem in March. However, the effect of past learning on present learning is not always so positive. Two examples of *negative transfer* were given in the last chapter: proactive interference (old learning interferes with mastering new information), and retroactive interference (new learning wipes out old information). Two other forms of negative

Negative
Transfer

transfer are functional fixedness and response set, both of which involve responding to a new situation by trying to apply inappropriate old strategies.

As a teacher you will want to encourage positive transfer and discourage negative. Another distinction made between different types of transfer may help you in doing so. This is the distinction between specific and nonspecific, or general, transfer.

## Specific and General Transfer

Specific and
General Transfer

*Specific transfer* occurs when a rule, fact, or skill learned in one situation is applied in another very similar situation. Examples of specific transfer include applying rules of punctuation to write a job application letter and using knowledge of the alphabet to find a word in the dictionary. *General transfer* involves dealing with new problems based on principles and attitudes learned in other, often dissimilar situations. Examples of general transfer are trying analogous thinking to solve the rope-tying or X-ray problems described earlier, and choosing teaching as a career after years of developing a positive attitude toward teachers or schools.

Studies of transfer undertaken in the early twentieth century have probably had more impact on education than any other research conducted by psychologists (Travers, 1977). What were these studies, and why were they so important? What do they have to do with specific and general transfer?

Mental
Discipline

In the early 1900s it was assumed that learning certain subjects, such as Latin and mathematics, provided a kind of mental discipline and taught students how to think. By studying these specific subjects, the theory went, students learned powers of thinking and reasoning that could be applied to all subjects. Given these general beliefs, Thorndike and his colleages conducted research to determine if studying Latin, Greek, and mathematics actually did lead to increased intellectual achievement in other subject areas (Brolyer, Thorndike and Woodyard, 1927). They found there was no general transfer to achievement in other areas. Learning Latin, for example, seemed to transfer primarily to learning more Latin. In other words, transfer was specific and not general.

When the findings of Thorndike's research were publicized, the notion of mental discipline began to fade and many changes in curricula and graduation requirements were made. Thanks to educational psychology (at least indirectly), you did not have to study Greek and Latin throughout your school years.

Thorndike's
Theory of
Transfer

Thorndike's own theory of transfer states that learning one particular skill is likely to improve the learning of another skill only to the extent that the two skills overlap or have common elements. The more similar two particular skills are, the more likely it is that learning one of them will transfer to learning the other. The stress is on specific transfer, at least as far as skills are concerned. Learning to drive one automatic shift car prepares you quite well for driving another identical model, fairly well for driving another car with automatic transmission, less well for driving a standard shift, and not at all well for driving a motorcycle. But some specific transfer does take place in each case, since each type of vehicle has elements in common.

Importance
of Both General
and Specific

Although Thorndike chose to stress specific transfer, both specific and general transfer are important in the classroom. In the basic skills areas, students need to learn a great deal of information that they will apply directly every day. But beyond these basic skills, it is difficult to predict the specific knowledge students will need in the future. As a child growing up in Texas in the 1950s and 1960s, it would have been very hard for the first author to learn many of the specific skills needed to deal with fuel shortages and high costs of energy. With gasoline selling for 27 cents per gallon, the politics of oil supply and demand and concerns for ecology and conservation were not a part of the high school curriculum. But learning to use a slide rule was taught. Now calculators have made this skill obsolete. Undoubtedly changes as extreme and unpredictable as these await the students you will teach. For this reason, the general transfer of principles, attitudes, and problem-solving strategies will be just as important to these students as the specific transfer of basic skills.

## Teaching for Positive Transfer

Many of the principles you have already encountered in this and in the previous chapter will help you teach for positive transfer. Here we will consider three issues: What should be learned to enhance transfer? How should the material be presented? How should it be practiced and performed?

**What Should Be Learned?**    When you realized how much you had forgotten from high school, you may have asked yourself, "What *is* worth learning? What *should* the content of instruction be?" Right now we are concerned about what content is most likely to transfer positively to other situations.

Basic Skills    The first answer is an obvious one. The learning of basic skills such as reading, writing, computing, and speaking will definitely transfer to other situations, because these skills are necessary for later work in and out of school. All later learning depends on positive transfer of the basics to new situations. Certainly in the early grades this content is critical. Reading and writing, in fact, continue to be important throughout the students' educational careers and beyond. Study skills are also useful in a wide range of situations and should be included in every curriculum.

Using Gagné's Heirarchy    The second answer to questions about subjects that promote positive transfer involves Gagné's hierarchy of intellectual skills. As we noted in the first section of this chapter, the learning of more advanced and complex knowledge appears to be based on having a good store of well-organized

*One way to insure positive transfer is to teach skills that will be valuable in the future.*

(Ken Karp)

prior knowledge. Thus, teaching for transfer includes carefully laying the groundwork in teaching concepts and rules that will be needed later.

A third aspect of deciding what to teach for maximum transfer involves making guesses about what students will need to know and do in the future. Students are likely to use the information they learn if it is necessary for success in further education, adult life, and careers. Besides the basic skills we mentioned earlier, teachers might decide to focus on survival skills, such as writing job applications, reading government forms, calculating insurance needs, figuring income tax, locating and evaluating needed services, mathematics for household finances, borrowing money for college, job interview skills, computer literacy, and study skills for college. Many concepts and principles can be learned and practiced within the context of these survival skills.

Finally, teachers can emphasize procedural knowledge (knowing how to do something) as well as declarative knowledge (facts and principles). Experts in a given field know many facts, but they also have a vast fund of procedural knowledge about how to accomplish tasks in their field. Students can be helped to develop problem-solving skills that include procedural knowledge and metacognitive strategies for monitoring progress (Travers, 1982).

**How Should Material Be Presented?**   The first answer, and perhaps the most important, is *thoroughly*. The more completely information is understood, the more likely it is that positive transfer will be encouraged and negative transfer avoided (Ellis, 1965; Travers, 1982). This thorough understanding means incorporating the new information meaningfully into existing schemata — that is, encoding the information so that it can be stored in long-term memory and later retrieved. All suggestions given in the previous chapter for making learning and remembering meaningful should help you teach for transfer. In addition, it appears that principles are more likely to be transferred if students not only understand them, but can describe the principles verbally (Travers, 1982).

Second, students will be more likely to transfer information to new situations if they have been actively involved in the learning process. Of course, active involvement does not mean one particular method, such as discovery learning. Involvement can be in the form of discussion, independent library research, group experiments, or mental activity during lectures. The important theme is student engagement with the material. Involvement should lead to greater understanding and thus to an increase in positive transfer.

**How Should New Learning Be Practiced?**   To enhance positive transfer, newly mastered concepts, principles, and generalizations should be used in a wide variety of situations. Some of these applications should involve complex unstructured problems. Since many of the problems faced in later life, both in school and out, do not come to the students complete with instructions, students must practice using what they have learned to solve problems that are not clearly defined.

Positive transfer is also more likely to occur if students practice new skills under conditions similar to those they will have to work under later. You will be expected to perform as a student teacher under conditions very similar to those in a real assignment. As a teacher, you may decide that students should take open book, oral, essay, or group tests, depending on the conditions of performance that will be expected of them later. One way to match practice conditions with likely future performance conditions is to use simulations. Such approaches have been very successful in training pilots, physicians, and drivers (Bower and Hilgard, 1981).

**Overlearning**

Another way to ensure greater transfer is to encourage **overlearning.** This simply means asking students to practice a task past the point of attaining the desired criterion. Many of the basic facts students learn in elementary school, such as the multiplication tables, are traditionally overlearned. They are practiced long after students fully understand them. This overlearning helps students retrieve the information quickly and accurately when it is needed. Overlearning is one reason why most people can easily repeat important telephone numbers and simple addition facts. The Guidelines here should be of help in teaching for transfer.

# *Guidelines*

## *Encouraging Positive Transfer*

**1. Make sure all students have adequate opportunity to master the basics.**

**EXAMPLES**
- Focus on reading, mathematics, and language in elementary school.
- Consider individualized instruction for students with particular difficulties.

**2. Help students in later grades apply and improve reading and writing skills.**

**EXAMPLES**
- Prepare students for reading assignments by studying needed vocabulary, reviewing the organization of the material, setting purposes for reading.

**3. Relate content being learned to the future needs of students.**

**EXAMPLES**
- Choose problems from real experiences.
- Introduce lessons by showing how the information will be helpful later.

**4. Make sure students thoroughly understand the new information.**

**EXAMPLES**
- Get the student actively involved in the learning through discussions, experiments, brainstorming, and so on.
- Require students to explain principles in their own words.

**5. Provide practice for new learning in a wide variety of situations.**

**EXAMPLES**
- Use problems, games, worksheets, and peer tutoring to practice language and mathematical skills.
- Occasionally present ambiguous, ill-defined problems that students can solve using recently learned principles.

**6. Rehearse information until overlearning occurs.**

**EXAMPLES**
- Drill facts students need to recall quickly and accurately.
- Have short and frequent, rather than long and infrequent, repetition and review.

## SUMMARY

1. Much of cognitive theory involves answering questions about how different kinds of information are learned by different people.

2. Gagné has suggested five basic categories of learning outcomes: (1) intellectual skills (discriminations, concepts, rules, and higher-order rules); (2) verbal information; (3) attitudes; (4) motor skills; and (5) cognitive strategies.

3. Concepts are categories used to group similar events, ideas, or objects. We probably learn concepts from prototypes of the category, then refine our knowledge by adding an understanding of relevant and irrelevant features.

4. Lessons about concepts include four basic components: concept name, definition, attributes, and examples. Actual teaching of the concept may follow a rule-example or an example-rule format.

5. Bruner's work has focused on learning through discovery following his belief that students learn best when they themselves discover the structure of the subject being studied. Bruner suggests classroom learning be inductive.

6. Ausubel suggests that learning be deductive, based in part on his belief that people need to develop internal hierarchies, headed by general concepts or subsumers, to master details and have a system for subsuming more specific concepts.

7. Expository teaching makes use of advance organizers to introduce basic concepts and subordinate content arranged in terms of similarities and differences.

8. Students often find it difficult to solve problems because of functional fixedness or rigidity. They should be encouraged to use systematic approaches, apply analogies, and become actively involved in an attempt to find solutions.

9. Studies of experts indicate that experts organize their knowledge around general principles that describe the right solutions for whole classes of problems.

10. A critical element in solving problems in school subjects is representing the problem in an accurate way. This can lead to a sudden insight into the solution.

11. The transfer of learning from one situation to another may be either positive (the use of a math formula in physics class) or negative (the problem of functional fixedness). It may also be specific (the use of language skills in writing letters) or general (the use of problem-solving strategies to solve new problems).

## KEY TERMS

| | | |
|---|---|---|
| attitudes | rule-eg method | functional fixedness |
| motor skills | eg-rule method | response set |
| verbal information | structure | insight |
| intellectual skills | coding system | generate-test method |
| cognitive strategies | intuitive thinking | analogical thinking |
| concept | discovery learning | declarative and procedural |
| defining attributes | expository teaching | knowledge |
| prototype | subsumer | transfer |
| positive and negative | advance organizer | overlearning |
| instances | problem solving | |

# Teachers' Forum

## "Do It Again?"

Overlearning a task is often recommended because it decreases the effect of interference and allows the students to recall the information or perform the task "automatically" when they need to do so. In order to overlearn, students must rehearse and repeat the learning task many times. Yet pure drill and rote repetition often become boring and ineffective because student attention is lost. What are some methods you use to provide interest and variety in necessary repetition of material?

**Making Repetition Interesting**

For all subject areas requiring immediate recall, drill can take many varied, exciting forms. Flashcards, perhaps the most commonly used form of drill, can be used in countless game-type settings in which teams of students oppose one another. For those who learn best through auditory techniques, teacher-made tapes are valuable tools. Variations on well-known games are also very effective in reinforcing information. "Beat the Clock," "Bingo," "Tic-Tac-Toe," "Concentration," and "Jeopardy" are but a few popular games providing structure for drill activities. Timed tests and peer-tutoring sessions have also proved to be effective techniques. Another area that deserves exploration is professionally prepared duplicating books which cleverly combine drill activities with riddles, codes, shade-ins, and dot-to-dot exercises.

Jacqueline M. Walsh, Sixth-Grade Teacher
*Agnes E. Little Elementary School, Pawtucket, Rhode Island*

**Projects**

Not only do drill and rote repetition become boring and ineffective, but the retention is usually short-lived. . . . I strive for understanding through a variety of experiences. I am a project-oriented teacher. The children in my class learn by doing. Repetition, yes, but in a different setting, through a new experience, using a new game, getting involved in a new project. They must experience to learn. We've been hearing it for years: "Experience is the best teacher." I believe it!

Joan M. Bloom, First-Grade Teacher
*Henry Barnard Lab School for Rhode Island College, Providence, Rhode Island*

**Letting Students Ask the Questions**

One method I use to provide interest and variety in the necessary repetition of material is to motivate students to make mini-quizzes and then provide the opportunity for them to play teacher while giving the quiz to the rest of the class. I also allow students to create games with various subject matter and then play them with the rest of the class.

Sharon Klotz, Sixth-Grade Language Arts Teacher
*Kiel Middle School, Kiel, Wisconsin*

# Reading Difficulties

Imagine that two of your students are way behind the others in reading ability. You initially thought it would help if you gave them very interesting material at a much lower reading level. However, the other students caught on quickly and began to make fun of the "easy readers." At that point, both students with reading problems refused to have anything to do with the books you gave them. One student is a tough member of one of the most popular groups in school. The other is a shy student with few friends.

**Class Discussions**

A discussion with the entire class on rates of cognitive skill development might prevent cruel remarks about individual progress. The purpose is not to discover present aptitude, but to lay the foundation for future achievement. Tutorial work with each other in *all* subject areas may help students realize various rates of development, as well as develop empathy. The emphasis should be on returning to and successfully completing the foundation work necessary for future success in reading.

Barbara L. Luedtke, High School Physical Education Teacher
*Appleton High School-East, Appleton, Wisconsin*

**Individualized Approach**

As a reading teacher, I would recognize the fact that I am not individualizing the program properly. I would assign each of the students in the class a totally different book. We have a reading laboratory in my school which effectively eliminates this problem. My classes meet there twice each week in small groups from two to six students. They are grouped according to ability and specific skills. The students become so involved in their own tasks that they haven't time to "check up" on each other. Unless the students are incompatible, I would allow them to work together. Occasionally for various reasons we have students working alone successfully.

Shirley Wilson Roby, Sixth-Grade Reading Teacher
*Lakeland Middle School, Shrub Oak, New York*

**Mastery Learning**

One solution to this problem may be mastery learning. The classroom can be divided into learning labs, with students working at their own rates. If the problem has already become serious in terms of interpersonal rivalries, I would try several approaches. I would speak to the individuals who have been harassing the slow readers and explain the situation. I might also give a value lesson ... that would put everyone at the disadvantage the two slow readers experience consistently. Finally, I might adjust learning activities to correct the problem in my classroom, or I might seek outside help from special or resource teachers. ...

Wayne A. Ginty, High School Social Studies Teacher
*Lockport Senior High School, Lockport, New York*

# SUGGESTIONS FOR FURTHER READING AND STUDY

ANDERSON, J. R. Acquisition of cognitive skill. *Psychological Review*, 1982, *89*, 369–406. A fairly technical but clearly written summary of the development of a cognitive skill from a declarative stage (facts about the skill domain are interpreted) to a procedural stage (the domain knowledge is directly embodied on procedures for performing the skill).

ANDERSON, J. R. *Cognitive psychology and its implications*. San Francisco: W. H. Freeman, 1980. A very well written text with excellent explanations and many examples. The concepts are complex but this book helps clarify them.

ANDERSON, R., SPIRO, R. and MONTAGUE (EDS.). *Schooling and the acquisition of knowledge.*, Hillsdale, N.J.: Lawrence Erlbaum, 1977. This is a collection of chapters on cognitive learning. Not light reading, but focus is on classrooms.

BIGGE, M. L. *Learning theories for teachers* (4th ed.). New York: Harper and Row, 1982. This latest edition of a classic text discusses both behavioral and cognitive views of learning, with an emphasis on the latter.

BRANSFORD, J. D. *Human cognition: Learning, understanding, and remembering*. Belmont, California: Wadsworth, 1979. A very readable but thorough introduction to the field of cognitive psychology.

BROWN, A. Metacognitive development and reading. In R. Spiro, B. Bruce, and W. Brewer (Eds.), *Theoretical issues in reading comprehension*. Hillsdale N.J.: Lawrence Erlbaum, 1980. Ann Brown is one of the leading authorities on the role of metacognition in learning. This chapter is an excellent explanation of the relationship between metacognitive abilities and important learning tasks in school.

CAVANAUGH, J. C. and PERLMUTTER, M. Metamemory: A critical examination. *Child Development*, 1982, *53*, 11–28. This is a fairly technical review of the concepts, theory, and research related to metamemory. It is both a criticism of previous work and a suggestion for needed revisions in conceptualization and research methods.

CRAIK, F. I. and LOCKHART, R. S. Levels of processing: A framework for memory research. *Journal of Verbal Learning and Verbal Behavior*, 1972, *11*, 671–684. This article presents Craik's and Lockhart's criticisms of the "stages" of memory theories (short-term, long-term, memory) and proposes an alternative view suggesting that how well something is remembered is determined by how deeply the information is processed.

HALL, J. F. *An Invitation to learning and memory*. Boston: Allyn and Bacon, 1982. This text covers both behavioral and cognitive views, but clearly emphasizes the cognitive perspective.

HART, L. A. *Human brain and human learning*. New York: Longman, 1983. In this book, Hart proposes a new approach to teaching and learning based on research on the human brain—an interesting contrast to more traditional views.

HIGBEE, K. L. Your memory: *How it works and how to improve it*. Englewood Cliffs, N.J.: Prentice-Hall, 1977. A very interesting and useful guide—not just for teaching but for anyone who wants to "remember better."

KLATZKY, R. L. *Human memory: Structures and processes* (2nd ed.). San Francisco: W. H. Freeman, 1980. A classic text that presents the information processing approach clearly and completely.

LEVIN, J. The Mnemonic 80s: Keywords in the classroom. *Educational Psychologist*, 1981, *16*, 65–82. This article summarizes the applications of the keyword method for the classroom teaching.

NEISSER, W. Cognitive and reality: *Principles and implications of cognitive psychology*. San Francisco: W. H. Freeman, 1976. A short but thorough discussion of perception, attention, schemata, and memory by a major figure in cognitive psychology.

NORMAN, D. A. *Learning and Memory*. San Francisco: W. H. Freeman, 1982. A concise and intriguing statement from one of the most important researchers in the field of cognitive psychology.

PRESSLEY, M. Elaboration and memory development. *Child Development*, 1982, *53*, 296–309. A review of research on how children use elaboration, spontaneously or with instruction, to improve memory. Educational applications such as the keyword method are discussed as well.

PRESSLEY, M., LEVIN, J. and DELANEY, H. D. The Mnemonic keyword method. *Review of Research in Education*, 1982, *52*, 61–91. A thoughtful review of research on the keyword method by educational psychologists who have been instrumental in developing the approach.

REED, S. K. *Cognition: Theory and applications*. Monterey, California: Brooks/Cole pub. company, 1982. A current and readable basic text with sections on information processing, representing and organization of knowledge, and complex cognitive skills.

RUMELHART, D. E. and ORTONY, A. The representation of knowledge in memory. In R. Anderson, R. Spiro, and W. Montague (Eds.), *Schooling and the acquisition of knowledge*, Hillsdale, N.J.: Lawrence Erlbaum, 1977. A carefully written explanation of the role of schemata in learning and remembering.

# SUGGESTIONS FOR FURTHER READING AND STUDY

ANDERSON, T. H. Study strategies and adjunct aids. In R. J. Spiro, B. C. Bruce, and W. F. Brewer (Eds.), *Theoretical issues in reading comprehension.* Hillsdale, N.J.: Lawrence Erlbaum, 1981. This chapter summarizes the research on study strategies in reading.

BRANSFORD, J. D., STEIN, B. S., SHELTON, T. S., and OVINGS, R. A. Cognition and adaptation: The importance of learning to learn. In J. Harvey (ed.), *Cognition, social behavior, and the environment.* Hillsdale, N.J.: Lawrence Erlbaum, 1982. This is a very interesting chapter about the skills used when people learn new information and use it later in new situations.

BRANSFORD, J. D. STEIN, B. S., VYE, N. J., FRANKS, J. J., AUBLE, P. M., MEZYNSKI, K. J., and PERFETTO, G. A. Differences in approaches to learning: An overview. *Journal of Experimental Psychology: General,* in press. This article summarizes ideas about differences between successful and unsuccessful learners.

BROWN, A. L., CAMPIONE, J. C. and DAY, J. D. Learning to learn: On training students to learn from text. *Educational Researcher,* 1981, *9,* 14–21. A very helpful review of research on different learning strategies for reading and studying prose.

CHAMPAGNE, A. B., KLOPFER, L. E., and ANDERSON, J. H. Factors influencing the learning of classical mechanics. *American Journal of Physics,* 1980, *48,* 1074–1079. This article describes how intuitive ideas about the ways objects move can interfere with learning scientific principles of motion.

EGGEN, P. D., KAVCHAK, D. P. and HARDER, R. J. *Strategies for teachers: Information processing models in the classroom.* Englewood Cliffs, N.J.: Prentice-Hall, 1979. This very practical book describes five different models for teaching, including approaches based on the work of Bruner and Ausubel.

FARNHAM-DIGGORY, S. *Cognitive processes in education: A psychological preparation for teaching and curriculum development.* New York: Harper and Row, 1972. This book covers a broad range of topics from cognitive development to creativity. It is one of the few that tries to bridge the gap between cognitive psychology and education.

FENKER, R. *Stop studying — start learning: Or how to jump start your brain.* Fort Worth, Texas: Tangram, 1981. A highly readable and humourous guide for becoming an "expert" student.

KIRBY, J. R. and BIGGS, J. B. (Eds.) *Cognition, development and instruction.* New York: Academic Press, 1980. Chapters by leading educational psychologists of individual differences, metamemory, cognitive development, and instruction.

KLEIN, G. A. and WEITZENFELD, J. Improvement of skills for solving ill-defined problems. *Educational Psychologist,* 1978, *13,* 31–41. This article discusses many approaches to solving well-defined problems and then describe the skills needed to solve ill-defined problems.

LARKIN, J., MCDERMOTT, J., SIMON, D. P. and SIMON, H. A. Expert and novice performance in solving physics problems. *Science,* 1980, *208,* 1335–1342. Intriguing ideas about the factors that influence expert performance, especially the role of representing and organizing knowledge.

LUITEN, J., WILLIAM, J. A. and ACKERSON, G. A meta-analysis of the effects of advanced organizers on learning and retention. *American Educational Research Journal,* 1980, *17,* 211–218. This article summarizes many studies on the effectiveness of advanced organizers.

MAYER, R. E. *Thinking, problem solving, cognition.* San Francisco: W. H. Freeman, 1983. This new book by the authors of *Thinking and problem solving* is an interesting text with many visual aids. There are sections on historical perspectives, basic thinking tasks, information processing, and implications of the cognitive approach for learning and teaching.

POLYA, G. *How to solve it: A new aspect of mathematical method* (2nd ed.). Princeton, N.J.: Princeton University Press, 1957. A classic little book on problem solving that has had a large impact.

PRESSELY, M. and LEVIN, J. R. (Eds.). *Cognitive Strategy research: Educational Applications.* New York: Springer, 1983. A sophisticated collection describing research on cognition strategies that has direct implications for teaching.

RESNICK, L. B. Instructional psychology. In M. Rosenzeveig and L. M. Porter (Eds.), *Annual Review of Psychology.* Palo Alto: Annual Reviews, 1981. This chapter discusses the implications of findings in cognitive psychology for teaching reading, mathematics, science, and problem solving.

STERNBERG, R. and DAVIDSON, J. The mind of the puzzler. *Psychology Today,* 1982, *16,* 37–144. In this fascinating article the authors describe differences between good and bad problem solvers.

TRAVERS, R. M. W. *Essentials of learning: The new cognitive learning for students of education* (5th ed.). New York: Macmillan, 1982. A classic reference on learning theory for teachers.

TUMA, D. T. and REIF, F. *Problem solving and education: Issues in teaching and research.* Hillsdale, N.J.: Lawrence Erlbaum, 1980. In this text several experts on problem solving discuss research and applications.

# 8

# Motivating Students

Motivation is at the heart of many of the most important concerns of teachers. "Why don't the students pay attention?" "Kids today don't seem to care about school." "The trouble is these students have no motivation!" If you have spent much time in schools, you have heard these laments before. Most educators have made similar comments at one time or another. Is lack of motivation really at the heart of school failure? We will examine this question and several others here.

We begin with a discussion of the meaning of the term motivation and a consideration of three general views: behavioral, cognitive, and humanistic. These approaches provide varying frameworks for considering motivation; more specific theories have been offered to explain just why people are moved to behave as they do. In the next section we will examine some of the most influential theories by addressing three questions: (1) What factors should be considered before the learning activity? (2) What can the teacher do during the lesson to encourage motivation? (3) How can the outcome of the learning experience foster continuing motivation? In answering these questions, we will discuss the importance of student attitudes, needs, curiosity, and interests; the role of different goal structures and team learning; and the motivational effects of experiencing competence and reinforcement. Each of these theories will help teachers better understand what motivates their students, but more information is needed. The next section focuses on a factor that can unintentionally influence motivation—teacher expectations. From this we will turn to anxiety, a problem that should concern teachers even though it is often overlooked.

By the time you have completed this chapter, you should have a relatively good idea of the role of motivation in the classroom, both theoretical and practical. More specifically, you should be able to do the following:

- Define the concept of motivation from the behavioral, cognitive, and humanistic points of view and describe a representative theory from each perspective.
- List Maslow's seven levels of needs and give a classroom example of each.
- Discuss possible motivational effects that success and failure may have on different students.
- Describe several potential effects of teacher expectations on two different students: one the teacher believes will fail and one the teacher believes will do well.
- Present at least two strategies for teaching a required basic subject to a student who does not care about learning it and to a student who is very anxious.

We being with the most basic question: What is motivation? As you will soon see, the term is often used incorrectly.

## WHAT IS MOTIVATION?

Definition of Motivation

**Motivation** is usually defined as something that energizes and directs behavior. Obviously, this is a very general definition, one that could be applied to many different factors affecting behavior. We all know how it feels to be moving energetically toward a goal. Psychologists have tended to be more specific in developing concepts of motivation, generally centering on three questions. First, what is it that originally causes a person to initiate some action? Second, what causes a person to move toward a particular goal? And third, what causes a person to persist in attempts to reach that goal? Psychologists have suggested many different answers based on such factors as instincts, drives, needs, incentives, and social pressure. As with many other important concepts in psychology, the major explanations of motivation fall into two categories: cognitive and behavioral (Weiner, 1972). There is also a widely influential humanistic view.

**Three Views of Motivation**

No matter what explanations are given for the causes of motivation, psychologists agree that we should not talk about unmotivated students. All behavior is motivated, even that of students staring out the window and avoiding schoolwork. What teachers usually mean when they say that students lack motivation is that students are not motivated to do what the teacher has in mind. A second area of agreement involves the importance of motivation. Classroom teachers (Lufler, 1978) and researchers (Walberg and Uguroglu, 1980) identify the need to motivate students toward appropriate goals as one of the critical tasks of teaching.

*Many activities compete for students' attention today. Will they ever be as enthusiastic about their work as they are about their music? How could these interests be used to motivate students?*

(Ken Karp)

# Behavioral Views of Motivation

**Initiation, Direction, Persistence**

As we saw in Chapter 5, behavioral psychologists have developed concepts such as contiguity, reinforcement, punishment, and modeling to explain why people behave as they do. Within this view, behavior is initiated by internal or external stimuli, such as hunger pangs or the sight of food on television. Previous learning or habits then determine what direction the behavior will take. The hungry person may, for example, open the refrigerator that in the past has provided food. Behavior persists until the sustaining stimulus (hunger pangs or a bowl of ice cream) disappears. In other words, motivation can be explained by environmental events that stimulate actions or by physical conditions such as hunger (Weiner, 1972). Motivation caused by external events or outside rewards that have nothing to do with the learning situation itself generally is called **extrinsic motivation.**

**Extrinsic Motivation**

Grades, points, and other rewards for learning are attempts to create extrinsic motivation.

Within the strict behavioral framework, to motivate students is really to apply the principles described in Chapter 5 to increase, decrease, or develop behaviors. Because these principles have been studied extensively in classrooms, they provide important sources of help for teachers. We will devote the next chapter to behavioral methods for motivating students and managing classrooms. Since we will be concentrating on behavioral views of motivation there, we will give little attention to the strict behavioral approach now.

**Recent Changes in Behavioral Views**

But to imply that behavioral approaches to motivation focus only on reinforcement and punishment would be an inaccurate representation of current trends in the area. The recent work of Bandura and the social learning theorists has extended the traditional behavioral view of motivation to include such cognitive factors as expectancies (What will I get out of doing this?), intentions (I want to finish this so I can do something else), anticipations (This will take too long, so I won't do it), and self-evaluations (I am not very good at that, so I will avoid it). In fact, some psychologists classify Bandura's theory as a cognitive approach (Bower and Hilgard, 1981). We discuss it under behavioral theories because it provides a bridge to cognitive approaches.

**Two Sources of Motivation**

**Social-Learning Theory.** Bandura (1977) suggests two basic sources of motivation. The first is our thoughts about possible future outcomes of behavior: Will I pass or fail? Will I be liked or laughed at? These thoughts are based on past experiences and the consequences of past actions. From these, the person tries to imagine future consequences. A second source of motivation is the active setting of goals. According to Bandura, the goals we set become our standards for evaluating performance. We tend to persist in our efforts until they meet the standards we have set. As we work toward the goals, we imagine all the positive things that will occur when we reach the goals and all the negative things that will occur if we do not. Upon reaching the goal, we may be satisfied for a short time, but we often begin again by setting new goals and raising our level of aspiration.

**Importance of Goals**

The types of goals we set will influence the amount of motivation we have to reach them. Goals that are specific, moderately difficult, and likely to be reached in the near future tend to enhance motivation and persistence.

*(Hugh Rogers/Monkmeyer Press Photo Service)*

*Students will be more persistent in working independently if they are moving toward goals that are clear, specific, moderately difficult, and attainable.*

Specific goals provide clear standards for judging performance. Moderate difficulty provides the best opportunity for actually reaching a reasonably challenging goal. Finally, good intentions for distant goals are often overshadowed by more immediate concerns. But goals that can be reached fairly soon are less likely to be abandoned or pushed aside in the day-to-day business of coping.

Some people seem to be more effective than others at setting goals, evaluating their own performance, and reinforcing themselves for accomplishment. But teachers can help students develop skills in these areas. When students adopt the learning goals of the class as their own objectives, they become more self-motivated to achieve in school. According to the social-learning theorists, students probably will value the goals set by the teacher if these goals are clear, specific, reasonable, moderately challenging, and attainable within a relatively short period of time. With its emphasis on the active setting of goals, the social-learning approach to motivation has moved in a much more cognitive direction.

## Cognitive Views of Motivation

Importance of Perceptions

One of the central assumptions in cognitive views of motivation is that people do not respond automatically to external events or to physical conditions such as hunger; they respond to their perceptions of these events. You may have had the experience of being so interested or involved in a project that you missed a meal. You did not even realize you were hungry until you noticed the time. In contrast to the behavioral view, the cognitive view emphasizes **intrinsic** (internal) sources of motivation, such as the satisfaction of learning or of accomplishment.

Intrinsic Motivation

Some cognitive theories assume that humans have a basic need to understand their environment and to be competent, active, and effective in coping with the world (R. W. White, 1959). This is similar to Piaget's idea of equilibration, the need to assimilate new information and make it fit cognitive schemes — in other words, the need to understand. People are seen as active and curious, searching for information to solve personally relevant problems, ignoring even hunger or enduring discomfort to focus on self-selected goals. People work hard because they enjoy the work and because they want to understand.

Motivation in the cognitive framework is based on choices, decisions, plans, interests, goals, and calculations of likely success or failure. The effects of this last factor, expectations of success or failure, play an important part in a current cognitive conceptualization of motivation, attribution theory.

Quest for Understanding

**Attribution Theory.**    **Attribution theory** can be seen as the most cognitive of all the influential theories of motivation. According to its developer, Bernard Weiner, "the central assumption of attribution theory, which sets it apart from pleasure-pain theories of motivation, is that the search for understanding is the (or *a*) basic 'spring of action'" (Weiner, 1979, p. 3). This assumption is again reminiscent of Piaget's ideas about equilibration and making sense of the world.

In the classroom, Weiner notes, the quest for understanding often leads to questions about success and failure. Students may ask themselves: "Why did I flunk my midterm?" "What's wrong with my essay?" Weiner believes that students, and all people for that matter, attempt to explain why things happened as they did, to make attributions about causes. Students may thus attempt to explain their grades by listing factors such as ability, effort, mood, luck, help, interest, or clarity of instructions.

Three Attributions

Weiner has grouped the various causes students are likely to give for success or failure under three general headings. The first head contrasts internal causes (factors within a person) with external causes. Examples of internal causes are ability, effort, and mood. External causes include the difficulty of the task, the teacher's attitude toward you, luck, or help from others. The second heading contrasts stable and unstable causes. Ability is a stable cause, mood is unstable. The third head contrasts controllable and uncontrollable causes. For example, you can control the amount of help you get in studying, but you cannot control your luck or mood on the day of the test.

Most causes for success or failure given by students can be categorized on each of these three dimensions. For example, ability is an internal, stable, and uncontrollable cause; luck is external, unstable and uncontrollable. Weiner (1979) believes each dimension has important implications for motivation.

Internal/External Causes

The internal-external dimension, for example, seems to be closely related to feelings of confidence, self-esteem, pride, guilt, or shame (Weiner, 1980). If success or failure is attributed to internal factors, success will lead to pride and failure to shame. If the causes are seen as external, gratitude might follow success and anger could follow failure.

Stable/Unstable Causes

The stability dimension seems to be closely related to expectations about the future. If, for example, students attribute their success (or failure) to stable factors such as ability or the difficulty of the test, they are likely to expect to succeed (or fail) on similar tasks in the future. But if they attribute the outcome to unstable factors such as mood or luck, they are likely to expect changes in the future when confronted with similar tasks.

**Controllable/ Uncontrollable Causes**

The control dimension is probably related to feelings of confidence and future expectations, although more research is needed to confirm this. If success is attributed to controllable factors, the student can take greater pride in it and expect to achieve it again in the future. If success is thought to be caused by uncontrollable factors, the student is more likely to be merely grateful and to hope that the luck will continue.

**Apathy and Depression**

**Attributions and Student Motivation.** In the classroom, the greatest problems of motivation are likely to arise when students attribute failures to internal, stable, and uncontrollable characteristics such as ability. They may seem apathetic, resigned to failure, depressed, helpless, or "unmotivated" (Weiner, Russell and Lerman, 1978). Apathy is a logical reaction to failure if students believe the causes are their own doing (internal), are unlikely to change (stable), and are beyond their control anyway. Students who view their failures this way are less likely to seek help (Ames and Lau, 1982). Such students need encouragement to see how the situation might change. They also need to experience realistic success. One promising approach is to emphasize the connection between past efforts and past successes. Telling students that "trying harder" will lead to future achievement is not particularly effective. They need real evidence that effort will pay off (Schunk, 1982).

*If students believe that their hard work can lead to success, then motivation will be greater. If they believe they lack ability or that other factors beyond their control cause them to fail, a sense of helplessness may develop.*

At the heart of attribution theory is the notion of individual perception. If students believe they lack the ability to deal with higher mathematics, they are likely to act on this belief even if their actual abilities are well above average. These students are likely to have little motivation for mathematics simply because they expect to do poorly in it. Fanelli (1977) suggests that teachers approach students with these words: "You *might* be able to do it if you try." This keeps the options for realistic success open, both in the teacher's mind and in the students', without setting the stage for great disappointment if initial efforts meet with failure.

## Humanistic Approaches to Motivation

Third-Force Psychology

Humanistic interpretations of motivation emphasize personal freedom, choice, self-determination, and striving for personal growth. With these emphases, the humanistic psychologists tend to be in harmony with many of the cognitive approaches. Perhaps most important is the fact that both views stress intrinsic motivation.

Definition of Needs

In addition, many humanistic theories describe the role of needs. According to Kolesnik (1978, p. 149), a **need** can be defined as "any type of deficiency in the human organism or the absence of anything the person requires, or thinks he requires, for his overall well being." Human beings are seen as seldom if ever having their needs met completely and perfectly. Improvement is always possible. People are thus motivated by the needs, or the tensions created by the needs, to move toward goals they believe will help satisfy the needs. Let us see how one very influential humanistic theory of motivation deals with this central concept.

**Maslow's Hierarchy.** Abraham Maslow has had a great impact on psychology in general and on the psychology of motivation in particular. Maslow (1970) has suggested that there is a hierarchy of human needs. Lower-level needs for survival and safety are the most important and maintain control over behavior when they are not being met. But if people are physically comfortable and secure, they will be stimulated to fill slightly higher-level needs — namely, social needs for belonging and self-esteem within their own group. When these needs are more or less satisfied, people turn to the higher-level needs for intellectual achievement, aesthetic appreciation, and finally

Self-Actualization

self-actualization. **Self-actualization** is Maslow's term for self-fulfillment and the realization of personal potential. Figure 8–1 offers a visual representation of Maslow's hierarchy.

Maslow (1968) has called the four lower needs — survival, safety, belonging, and self-esteem — **deficiency needs.** When these needs are not met, motivation increases to find ways of satisfying them: The hungrier a person is, the harder that person will search for food. When deficiency needs are satisfied, the motivation for focusing on them decreases. Maslow has labeled the three higher-level needs — intellectual achievement, aesthetic appreciation, and self-actualization — **being needs.** When these needs are met, a person's motivation to reach them does not cease; rather motivation increases to seek further fulfillment. For example, the more a person is successful in efforts to know and understand, the more that person will strive for increased knowledge and understanding. Unlike the deficiency needs, these being needs can never be completely filled. The motivation to achieve them is endlessly renewed.

## Figure 8–1    Maslow's Hierarchy of Needs

| | |
|---|---|
| Highest level | *Self-actualization:* Self-fulfillment and the realization of all that a person is capable of being. |
| | *Aesthetic appreciation:* The search for order, structure, and beauty. |
| | *Intellectual achievement:* The need to understand and explore. |
| | *Self-esteem:* The desire to gain approval and recognition. |
| | *Belonging:* The need to be accepted and loved. |
| | *Safety:* The need to feel physically and psychologically secure and free from danger. |
| Lowest level | *Survival:* The very basic need for food, water, air, and shelter. |

Data based on Hierarchy of Needs in "A Theory of Human Motivation" in **Motivation and Personality,** 2nd edition, by Abraham H. Maslow. Copyright © 1970 by Abraham M. Maslow. By permission of Harper & Row, Publishers Inc.

Criticisms    Maslow's theory has been criticized for the very obvious reason that people do not always appear to behave as the theory would predict. Most of us move back and forth, motivated by many different needs at different times. Some people deny themselves safety or friendship to focus on the higher-level needs of knowledge and understanding. But Maslow's theory does have a number of important implications for teachers.

Implications    Students' desires to fill lower-level needs may at times contradict your own desire to have them achieve higher-level goals. Students who come to school hungry, sick, or hurt are unlikely to be motivated to seek knowledge and understanding. If the classroom is a fearful, unpredictable place and students seldom know where they stand, they are likely to be more concerned with security and less with learning. Belonging to a social group and maintaining self-esteem within that group also are important to students. If doing what the teacher says conflicts with group rules, students may choose to ignore the teacher's wishes or even defy the teacher.

Maslow's theory also offers certain implications for achieving higher-level needs. A student's success in mastering a body of knowledge or creating a beautiful object may well lead to increased motivation and the setting of even higher goals (Sears, 1940; Atkinson and Raynor, 1974; and Moulton, 1965).

# MOTIVATION AND TEACHING

A Model
of Motivation
in Teaching

One way to organize the vast amount of information on motivation is to consider the factors that influence motivation at different times in the learning process itself (Wlodkowski, 1981). As students begin a lesson or class, they bring with them particular attitudes and needs. Both influence motivation to participate. During the lesson, the immediate stimulation of the activities and the students' affect or feelings about the experience itself have powerful effects on motivation. If the students are left with a sense of competence from their own accomplishments or their efforts are reinforced in other ways at the end of the lesson, they will be more motivated to pursue similar tasks in the future. Figure 8–2 represents these six factors acting together to influence the learner's motivation.

## Figure 8–2 Factors Influencing Motivation at Different Times in the Learning Cycle

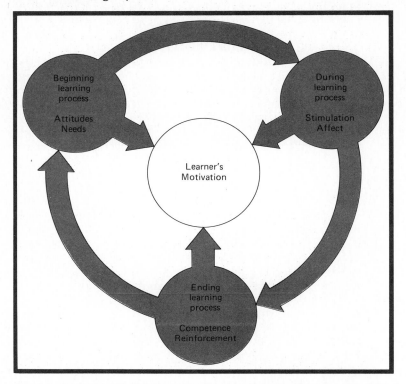

*From R. J. Wlodkowski, 1982. **Motivating and Teaching: A practical guide.** Washington, D.C.: National Education Assoc. Press. Copyright 1978 by R. J. Wlodkowski. Used with permission.*

## Before Learning: Attitudes and Needs

Before beginning an activity, Wlodkowski (1981) suggests that teachers ask two questions related to motivation: (1) What can I do to guarantee a positive attitude toward the upcoming activity? (2) How can I best meet my students' needs through this activity?

*Creating Positive Attitudes*

To answer the first question, you must know what factors influence attitudes toward the subject. We discussed the formation of positive and negative attitudes about school when we considered the applications of classical conditioning in Chapter 5. Applying these principles would mean making the conditions surrounding the subject as positive as possible. In addition to associating pleasant experiences with learning, teachers can also confront negative attitudes directly. In math classes, teachers might ask how many students believe the material is too hard. What is the basis for those impressions? What would make the material easier? As indicated in Figure 8–2, attitudes are greatly influenced by prior experiences with similar situations, so the development of positive attitudes is an ongoing challenge to teachers.

A great deal has been written about needs and motivation. For teaching, the most fully developed and relevant work involves the need to achieve.

**Achievement Motivation.** David McClelland and John Atkinson were among the first to concentrate on the study of **achievement motivation** (McClelland, Atkinson, Clark and Lowell, 1953). People who strive for excellence in a field for the sake of achieving and not for some reward are considered to be high in the need for achievement. This need has been labeled *n-Ach* for convenience. To evaluate an individual's need to achieve, McClelland used the **Thematic Apperception Test,** often called the **TAT** (Murray, 1938), although other methods are now available.

Assessing
Achievement
Motivation

In the TAT, people are shown ambiguous pictures and asked to tell or write stories about them. The stories are scored by identifying the themes or needs implied. A major assumption behind such a test is that people project their own fantasies, thoughts, and needs into the characters and situations in their stories. For this reason, tests such as the TAT are called **projective tests.** Here is an example of a story that was scored high on n-Ach:

High n-Ach

The boy is trying to reconcile the philosophies of Descartes and Thomas Aquinas — at the tender age of 18. He has read several books on philosophy and feels the weight of the world on his shoulders.

Looking at the same picture, another individual wrote a story that received a low n-Ach score:

Low n-Ach

Ed is thinking of leaving home for a while in the hope that this might shock his parents into getting along.

Origins
of Achievement
Motivation

The stories are taken from Atkinson and Birch, (1970) and Atkinson and Raynor (1974). The origins of high achievement motivation are assumed to be in the family and cultural group of the child. If achievement, initiative, and competitiveness are encouraged and reinforced in the home, a child is more likely to develop a high need for achievement (Kolesnik, 1978). Children who see that their actions can have an impact on their environment and who are taught how to judge a good performance are more likely to grow up with the desire to excel (Morris, 1982).

Even though the need to achieve is assumed to be a relatively stable characteristic, it is not the only factor that influences behavior; the environment can play a role as well. For example, competitive situations encourage greater striving for achievement. In addition, people are selective. Students with a high need to achieve may work hard in areas that are important to them and their plans for the future, but be content to slide by in subjects that seem irrelevant.

Need to Avoid
Failure

Atkinson (1964) added a new consideration to the theory of achievement when he noted that there is also a need to avoid failure. He believes both the need for achievement and the need to avoid failure are present in all people. If a person's need to achieve in a particular situation is greater than the need to avoid failure, the overall tendency, or **resultant motivation,** will be to take the risk and try to achieve. An extended example should help clarify Atkinson's views.

An Example

A coach wants the school team to try a new routine at the gymnastic meet coming up in two months. The routine involves three very difficult new movements. If the movements are executed well, the team is certain to win the meet. If the team tries and fails, it is sure to lose. Rachel is the best member of the team and could probably master the movements with ease.

But she insists on perfecting the old routine instead of learning a new one. She is immobilized by the thought that she might embarrass herself in front of that many people. For Rachel, the fear of failure is greater than the need for achievement in this particular situation. Another member of the team, Lee, is eager to try the new routine. While she is not as good a gymnast as Rachel, she is less fearful of being embarrassed and is willing to work at mastering the new movements. She is generally the last to leave every practice session and seems to look forward to new challenges. For Lee, the need for achievement overcomes any fear of failure.

If students' motivation to achieve is greater than their motivation to avoid failure, their desire to pursue a problem is often enhanced when they experience a moderate amount of failure. They are determined to achieve, so they try again. (If Lee, for example, were to fall off the balance beam, she would be likely to try even harder to master that particualar movement.) On the other hand, success gained too easily can actually decrease motivation for high-achievement-oriented students. (Remember Lee's desire to try the new movements, not just to rely on the old ones.)

The opposite effects are likely with students who are motivated by the need to avoid failure. They tend to be discouraged by failure but encouraged by success. Rachel, for example, might quit the team if she were embarrassed publicly by mistakes. If the old routine won the meet, however, she probably would experience unqualified pleasure. Another type of reaction is possible for people who are very fearful of failure: They may set unrealistically high goals that are almost guaranteed to produce failure.

*Simple games or group learning experiences in the classroom will give the teacher some sense of various students' needs to achieve and of their needs to avoid failure. Such knowledge will enable the teacher to help the students set and achieve realistic goals.*

(David S. Strickler/Monkmeyer Press Photo Service)

Research findings have indicated a number of other specific differences between people high in achievement motivation and those who are more motivated by the need to avoid failure. People high in achievement motivation tend to select moderately challenging problems, while those low in achievement motivation are more likely to select either very easy or unreasonably difficult problems (Atkinson and Litwin, 1960). Highs also tend to work longer before giving up on difficult problems (French and Thomas, 1958; Weiner and Kukla, 1970). In choosing work partners, highs tend to choose people who are good at the task at hand, while lows tend to choose people who are friendly (French, 1956).

Those high in need for achievement perform best in competitive situations, learn fast, assume responsibility readily, are self-confident and energetic, but also are more tense (Morris, 1982). Finally, in groups of students with comparable IQ scores, those with high achievement motivation make better grades in school (Atkinson and Raynor, 1974).

Teaching
Strategies

As a teacher, it may help in planning activities to have some sense of which of your students need to achieve and which need to avoid failure. According to the theory, students who are highly motivated to achieve are likely to respond better to more challenging assignments, stricter grading, corrective feedback, new or unusual problems, and the chance to try again. Students who are more concerned about avoiding failure are likely to respond better to less challenging assignments, ample reinforcement for success, small steps in learning, more lenient grading, and avoidance of public recognition of mistakes.

**Level of Aspiration.** The compromise between the high goals we would like to reach and our fear of failing if we aim too high determines our **level of aspiration.** This is the goal we believe we can attain and are willing to work toward (Kolesnik, 1978). A high level of aspiration involves challenging and difficult goals. When people are successful, they tend to raise their levels of aspiration.

Results
of Failure

The results of failure are less predictable. A great deal depends on the individual's attributions for the causes of the failure. Failure on one part of the task may not cause people to lower their expectations for ultimate success. They may simply try another path (Farnham-Diggory, 1972). A student who hopes to go to medical school may not change plans with the first low grades in chemistry, but decide instead to go to summer school. However, when alternatives run out and all grades are too low, the student has to find another goal, perhaps a career in some other aspect of health care. When neither alternative paths to the goal nor an acceptable substitute is available, the individual is likely to become demoralized, and motivation suffers (Farnham-Diggory, 1972).

Failure may have positive as well as negative effects. Some experience with failure can be valuable, since students who are used to constant success can be devastated by setbacks. Learning to persist in the face of failure is a very important ability (Clifford, 1979; W. Foster, 1981). We will consider this issue more thoroughly in the chapter on grading.

Encouraging
Appropriate
Aspirations

At times all students may need help finding alternative paths to reach their goals or new and more realistic goals. In addition, some students may need support in aspiring to higher levels in the face of sexual or ethnic stereotypes about what they "should" want or what they "should not" be able to do well.

**Meeting Students' Needs.** Maslow's theory can suggest ways to plan activities that increase motivation. To make students feel safer and more secure with difficult material, you might organize extra tutoring assistance (Wlodkowski, 1981). Needs for belonging and self-esteem might be met in part by allowing students to work in teams. We will discuss this possibility more fully later in the chapter. If the teacher has taken students' attitudes and needs into account in planning the lesson, motivation to participate is more likely. The next challenge is to keep motivation high during the lesson itself.

## During the Learning Process: Interests and Emotional Climate

What can teachers do to stimulate student interest during the lesson? What can be done to maintain a positive emotional climate (Wlodkowski, 1981)?

**Student Interests and Motivation.** One seemingly logical way to motivate students during a lesson is to relate learning experiences to the interests of the students. This is not always an easy or even a desirable strategy; there are times when students must master basic skills that hold no intrinsic interest for them. But students' interests can be part of many teaching strategies. Sylvia Ashton-Warner (1963), for example, describes a system for teaching reading by using the students' own stories about topics of interest to them. If a teacher knows what students are interested in, much of the classroom work can be related to those concerns.

Discovering Student Interests

There are a number of ways to determine students' interests (Rust, 1977). The most direct route is to ask the students themselves, either with a questionnaire or by talking to them. Students may also be asked to rank a number of activities from the most to the least preferred. In classrooms where there is some free time, observations may help. How do students spend free time? Their activities are keys to their interests. Teachers may also watch for attentiveness during classroom lessons. This is one of the methods for assessing audience interest in television programs. In teaching, you may become aware of certain times when everyone is suddenly focused on you or busily working at some assigned tasks. Noting the tasks or topics at these points is one way to find out what parts of current classroom practice hold the most interest for your students.

Incorporating Interests in Teaching

Once you have an understanding of your students' interests, you can apply this knowledge in your teaching. Three examples should show some of the many ways student interests can encourage classroom motivation.

One teacher used the adolescent interest in music to make the science laboratory a more pleasant place to work.

A music teacher encouraged an interest in Bach by helping students see how the Beatles used a similar style.

A history teacher discovered that some students were interested in historical novels. "What was the truth about Anne Boleyn?" one student asked. A brief argument ensued, with the other historical-novel fans giving their opinions. The library assignment that followed was geared to help students see how historical novels rely on (and bend) history. The students were also given a chance to learn about historical documents and to debate the questions about Anne Boleyn. If any of these students developed a permanent interest in historical inquiry, it might be traced in part to their early romantic interest in the life of Anne Boleyn.

In this last example, the teacher is also modeling an inquiring approach, a willingness to follow the threads of student interest.

**Stimulating Curiosity.**    Providing opportunities for students to become curious is one important route to enhancing motivation. Vidler (1977) notes that if the environment is unchanging, boredom will result. What is there in the classroom for students to become curious about? One teacher we know has an "interesting table." The table itself is ordinary, but students have been asked to bring in strange items from home, items that may be beautiful, difficult to identify, suitable for a number of uses, and so on. Many questions are undoubtedly raised by the interesting things the students provide.

*Arousing Curiosity*    Teachers also can encourage motivation by beginning a lesson or unit with a display designed to arouse curiosity. Such curiosity-provoking experiences should be matched to the cognitive abilities of the students. For younger students, the chance to manipulate and explore may be the most effective way to stimulate curiosity. For older students, well-constructed questions or abstract, logical puzzles can have the same effect.

With older students and adults, the presentation of problems involving paradoxes and contradictions may be the best way to stimulate curiosity (Vidler, 1977). Other possbilities are role plays and simulations (Stewart, 1980). An example can be found in a NASA simulation experiment that asks students the most important items to take on a space trip. This exercise might be a good opener for a unit about the moon or about space travel.

*Paradox*    A realistic paradox can be used to stimulate curiosity in any subject area. Think, for example, of the growing global concern about world energy sources. With diminishing energy supplies, some developed countries are having to shut down manufacturing plants or limit production. Meanwhile, developing countries that are the major source of oil demand high prices in order to reach a standard of living similar to that in the developed countries.

*Curiosity of this type is easily encouraged; in fact, it is almost impossible to stifle. So deeply rooted is the motivation to learn in young children that it has sometimes been called instinctive.*

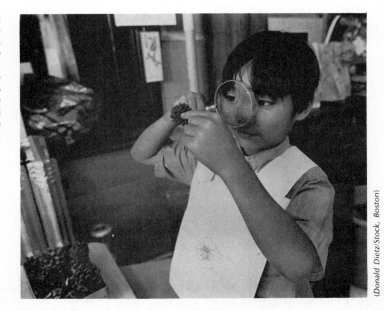

(Donald Dietz/Stock, Boston)

What should the United Nations recommend? What should United States policy be? What should people in any given country do about it? This situation, presented to students in a social studies class, could stimulate thinking and prepare students to gain more knowledge about the subject.

**Ambiguous Assignments**

Another approach to stimulating curiosity is found in what Peter Snyder (1975), a teacher for thirteen years, calls "ambiguous assignments." Students are given a long list of different possibilities and instructed to proceed as they see fit. Examples are found in Figure 8–3. Snyder notes that "life is an ambiguous assignment and people need to develop the skills to deal with it" (Snyder, 1975, p. 47). Whether or not you agree with this assumption, you may find occasional open-ended assignments useful in encouraging curiosity and creativity.

**Figure 8–3**    **Stimulating Curiosity through Ambiguous Assignments**

INSTRUCTIONS:
Choose one of the following assignments and carry it out as you see fit.
1. Present a brief activity to represent the most important moment in the last 10 years.
2. Find a new use for something.
3. Select the best character in the book you are reading and develop a project on that character.
4. Collect a series of pictures and use them to illustrate, without words, a mathematical or arithmetical principle.
5. Find evidence that change exists.
6. Complete a project on nature.
7. Demonstrate the relationship between mathematics and language.
8. Write something (poem, essay, story) that reflects what you heard on a sound-effects record (teacher to provide the record).
9. Describe the relationship between power and growth.
10. Create something that relates to the Civil War.
11. Complete a mathematical project.
12. Define words in a nonverbal way, such as:
    Draw a picture that represents force.
    Bring in an object that represents gentle.
    Make a sound that is permissive.

From P. Snyder. The ambiguous assignment. **Media and Methods,** 1975, **12,** 47.

If you let your mind play with your own subject area, you can probably come up with many ideas about engaging your students' natural desire to respond to interesting or appropriately challenging situations. Although the stimulation of curiosity is a valuable first step in enhancing motivation, other methods may prove more helpful in maintaining it.

**Maintaining a Positive Emotional Climate.**    In the classroom, students function as part of a large group. Johnson and Johnson (1975, 1978) have given considerable attention to this factor in their work on motivation. They have found that motivation can be greatly influenced by the ways in which we relate to the other people who are also involved in the accomplishment of a goal. Johnson and Johnson have labeled this interpersonal factor the **goal structure** of the task. There are three such structures: cooperative, competitive, and individualistic as shown in Figure 8–4.

**Figure 8–4**  **Different Goal Structures**

| Goal Structure | Type of Interaction |
|---|---|
| Cooperative | Students perceive they can reach their goal if and only if the other students also reach the goal. |
| Competitive | Students perceive they can reach their goal if and only if the other students do not reach the goal. |
| Individualistic | Students perceive their own attempt to reach a goal is unrelated to other students' attempts to reach goals. |

*Adapted from D. Johnson and R. Johnson. **Learning together and alone: Cooperation, competition, and individualization.** Englewood Cliffs, N.J.: Prentice-Hall, 1975, pp. 7 and 32.*

Advocates
of Cooperation

Johnson and Johnson stress the appropriateness of a cooperative goal structure for most common school learning situations. Many psychologists would disagree with this emphasis on the grounds that individual differences in abilities require more individualistic approaches to learning concepts, principles, and so on. Johnson and Johnson base their belief that cooperative goal structures are superior for these learning tasks on a number of research studies. For example, when the task involves complex learning and problem-solving skills, several psychologists have found that cooperation leads to higher achievement than competition. (Edwards and De Vries, 1974; Davis, Laughlin, and Komorita, 1976). In addition, cooperative learning seems to result in improved ability to see the world from another person's point of view (Bridgeman, 1977).

**Using Cooperative Techniques.**   In the cooperative goal structure, each person's individual efforts contribute to the benefit of the individual and the group. All the people in the group are working toward a single outcome, and materials can be shared. The interpersonal interaction with peers that students seem to enjoy so much becomes a part of the learning process. The need for belonging described by Maslow is more likely to be met. Cooperation generally works best when there is a chance for high interaction, mutual sharing and helping, and coordination of effort.

Examples
of Cooperative
Learning

Among the many specific activities that can be approached cooperatively are those found in the following examples:

Students can work together in conducting local surveys to see if people are using less electricity than they did a year ago.

All the students in a class may gain a better understanding of the difference between an acre and a hectare if they work together to mark out and measure the two different areas.

Class decisions can be made about problems such as whether underdeveloped countries should be given nuclear power plants.

Cooperative learning is not limited to specific and elaborate activities like these. Many of the most ordinary assignments can be enhanced by cooperation. If ten new definitions need to be learned in a science class, why not let students divide them up and teach one another? (Be certain, however, that everyone in the group can accomplish the task.) Sometimes a cooperative effort ends with one or two students doing the work of the entire group. Work groups should be monitored to make sure that each person is contributing and that no hostilities are developing. The fact that problems sometimes do occur may in itself be useful. Learning to negotiate, to share responsibility, and to deal with interpersonal hostilities can be valuable throughout life.

In practice, the effects of learning in a group probably vary, depending on what actually happens in the group and who is in it. Even if the group as a whole is successful, there is no guarantee that every student has benefited equally. If only a few people take responsibility for the work, these people will learn, but the nonparticipating members probably will not. Students who ask questions, get answers, and attempt explanations are more likely to learn than students whose questions go unasked or unanswered. For very shy and introverted students, individual learning may be a better approach (Webb, 1980, 1982).

Robert Slavin and his associates have developed a system for overcoming the disadvantages of the cooperative goal structure while maintaining its advantages. The system is called **Student Teams–Achievement Divisions** or **STAD** (Slavin, 1978). Each team has about five members, and there is a mix of different abilities, ethnic backgrounds, and sexes. Students work in these teams to prepare for twice-weekly quizzes. Individual team member's scores on these quizzes are totaled to determine the winning team for each week. Thus everyone, not just the most able or motivated, must work hard. This avoids the problem of having unequal contributions to a group project.

To make sure that each team member can contribute equally to the group total, the students are given points by comparing their performance to the performance of the other students in their achievement division. These divisions are established based on tests of ability, with six students in each division. The top six students are assigned to division 1, the next six to division 2, and so on. Students are never actually grouped for teaching based on these divisions or even told that the divisions exist. But when the students take tests, they earn points for their team depending on how well they performed in relation to others in their own achievement division. The person scoring at the top of his or her division earns 8 points, the second earns 6, and so on. So improvement pays off for all students. Those with less ability can still earn the maximum points for their team by scoring at the top of their division. To prevent students from being stuck in one division, the top person in each is moved up to a tougher division at regular intervals. When division 1 gets too big, it is split into 1A and 1B.

There are many parallels to sports leagues in the STAD approach, so the system usually appeals to students. Research indicates that students are more involved in their work, learn more, have better attitudes towards other races, and feel more liked by classmates when the STAD approach is used. Similar results have been obtained with a technique called the **jigsaw classroom**, as indicated in Box 8–1. In this approach, the main goal is improved interracial relations.

Most of the research on different goal structures has focused on competition and cooperation. Much less research has studied the individualistic goal

## BOX 8–1 THE JIGSAW CLASSROOM

Elliot Aronson and colleagues (1978) watched the sudden desegregation of the public schools in Austin, Texas, in the 1970s. At times there was violence in the high schools. While many emergency strategies might have proved useful for the immediate situation, Aronson et al. decided to try to develop a plan for changing the basic process of schooling so that *"Children could learn to like and trust each other not as an extracurricular activity but in the course of learning their reading, writing, and arithmetic"* (Aronson et al., 1978, p. 23). These researchers turned to the elementary school in the hope of reaching students before deep-seated distrust of different racial groups had developed.

Aronson and colleagues felt the competitive class environment was a major factor in undermining trust and liking among students. The researchers' answer to this dilemma was the jigsaw classroom. The major characteristic of the jigsaw classroom is cooperative learning. Students come to treat each other as needed resources, sources of important information for learning. Reinforcement for competition is replaced by reinforcement for cooperation. Aronson and colleagues describe the following true example of the jigsaw technique in a fifth-grade class:

Students in the class were divided into working groups of six. Boys and girls, Anglo and minority students, were mixed in the group. Each of the six students in the work groups was given a different paragraph describing the life of Joseph Pulitzer. Students were told that everyone would be tested over all the material. Each student had part of the information, but no one had it all. The students had to teach each other. They had to learn to listen to one another.

For Carlos, a student in one of the groups, this approach was very difficult at first. His first language was Spanish, and he could barely be understood in English. Without meaning to, the teacher had avoided giving Carlos any practice in speaking because he embarrassed himself and the teacher when he tried to answer questions in class. At first the members of Carlos's team were frustrated by the boy's inability to make himself understood. But after a reminder from the teacher that the test would cover Carlos's material too, the students became more skillful at "interviewing" Carlos about his part of the story. As he answered, Carlos gained the practice in speaking he had sorely needed but had avoided for years. The other students came to know Carlos better and discovered that he was not "dumb" at all.

Research on the use of these cooperative learning techniques indicated that participation in a jigsaw classroom led to greater liking of self, classmates, and school in general than participation in a traditional competitive class. Achievement for Anglo students was the same in both types of classrooms. But achievement for black and Chicano students was greater in the jigsaw classrooms. These results were found even though the teachers used the cooperative learning technique for as little as three or four hours per week (Aronson et al., 1978).

*When students work together it is important to make sure that each person is contributing. Spot checks on individual efforts may be necessary.*

structure. This goal structure involves a person working alone, not competing or cooperating with anyone else. An example is a class where students work independently and are evaluated based on their own achievements, regardless of how others do in the class.

## At the End of the Learning Experience: Competence and Reinforcement

What factors influence motivation at the end of the learning experience? If you look at Figure 8–2, you see the terms *competence* and *reinforcement*. Wlodkowski (1981) suggests the following two questions to guide planning so that lesson outcome fosters motivation: How does this activity increase student feelings of competence? What is the reinforcement this activity provides for students?

Developing
a Sense
of Competence

To increase feelings of competence, you might help students see the connections between their actions the outcome of the lesson. What did they do to overcome problems they encountered? If they made mistakes and did not correct them, how might they monitor their work more effectively next time? In raising these questions, the teacher is attempting to nurture a sense of competence and responsibility. Several psychologists have suggested that this sense of personal causation is the key to motivation, and they have designed a special program to teach it.

**Origins and Pawns: A Special Program to Enhance Competence.**    In 1976, Richard de Charms published a book called *Enhancing motivation: Change in the classroom,* describing the results of a four-year effort to enhance motivation in several elementary and junior high classrooms. The program was based on earlier studies of classroom motivation and the characterization of students as "origins" and "pawns." We will look first at the results of his earlier studies and then at the program itself.

Origins and Pawns

According to de Charms (1968), **origins** are people who are in control of their own achievement, due to skills they have developed at goal setting, their ability to plan strategies to reach these goals, and their willingness to take responsibility for their own actions. **Pawns** are people who are at the mercy of the environment and feel helpless in the face of outside forces. Some situations seem to encourage pawnlike behavior, while others seem to encourage people to be achievement-oriented origins. De Charms believes that schools should create environments where students will have many chances to act as origins, although not all students may be able to do so immediately.

As a result of these earlier studies, de Charms became involved in a special program to enhance motivation in the schools. The elementary and junior high teachers in the program were asked to introduce their students to a number of the concepts we have been discussing in this chapter: (1) self-concept, (2) achievement motivation, (3) realistic goal setting, and (4) the origin-pawn distinction. Games, exercises, creative writing, journals, art-work, and other techniques were used to promote student understanding. Figure 8–5 shows one of the methods for teaching the origin-pawn concept to sixth and seventh graders.

Framework for Self-motivation

Reflected in this exercise and in the others used in the program is the framework for self-motivation. Students were asked to set reasonable goals, make concrete plans to reach those goals, devise ways of evaluating their progress, and assume personal responsibility. These steps are in many ways reminiscent of the social-learning theorists' ideas about motivation described earlier, as well as the research on metacognitive skills discussed in the chapters on cognitive learning. In addition, by helping students to see themselves as origins, de Charms is encouraging them to view their successes and failures as the outgrowth of internal, controllable causes. All these factors contribute to a sense of personal competence.

Based on the results of the special motivation program, de Charms concluded that "motivation training for personal causation enhances both motivation and academic achievement when embedded in subject-matter material" (de Charms, 1976, p. 210). He also noted that the origin concept, with its emphasis on personal responsibility, was a much better source of motivation for both teacher and student than externally imposed tests of accountability.

**Figure 8–5   Training Students To Be Origins**

---

*Purpose and approach:* In order to teach students to be origins, a set of words that described origin behavior was developed along with a gimmick (the use of the letter *p*) to hold student attention.

Definition
of origin: An origin is someone who

    **(a)** takes *personal responsibility,*

    **(b)** *Prepares* his work carefully,

    **(c)** *Plans* his life to help him reach his goals,

    **(d)** *Practices* his skills,

    **(e)** *Persists* in his work,

    **(f)** has *patience,* for he knows that some goals take time in reaching,

    **(g)** *Performs,* for he knows he has to do things in order to reach his goals,

    **(h)** checks his *progress,* i.e., uses feedback,

    **(i)** moves toward *perfecting* his skills, paying special attention to improvement.

Activity:    After students were introduced to these ideas, they were asked to set a goal and construct a checklist to keep track of the number of times they acted in accordance with their goal.

---

Adapted from Richard de Charms. **Enhancing motivation. Change in the classroom.** © 1976 by Irvington Publishers, Inc., New York. Reprinted by permission.

---

Extrinsic
Reinforcement

**Reinforcement for Learning.**   Not every lesson successfully completed will enhance a sense of competence. Some activities involve necessary drill, repetition, and practice. Students may feel "competent enough" and not have much interest in completing these lessons. In this case, the teacher may decide to provide extrinsic reinforcement for successful completion of the work. In addition, some students—those with less ability, a low need for achievement, inadequate preparation, a history of failing in a particular subject, or a poor academic self-concept—may need extra incentives at first in tackling a difficult task. In these situations, the teacher may plan the lesson to include systematic reinforcement. The next chapter describes many

Cautions

approaches for applying the principles of reinforcement (and punishment) to enhance motivation, as well as a discussion about when not to use these principles. These cautions are included because the inappropriate use of reinforcers can undermine students' natural interest in a subject (Deci, 1975).

The Guidelines here give some general principles for applying theories of motivation. In addition, Figure 8–6 lists questions and theories that can guide lesson planning and enhance motivation before, during, and at the end of the learning activity, along with examples of how the questions might be answered. Many of these suggestions are taken from a collection of articles written by elementary and secondary school teachers called "Motivating Today's Students" (Gray, Schulman, Dunn, Workman, Spielberg, Farah and Jones, 1981).

To this point we have considered the deliberate process of planning lessons. In the next sections we examine subtle and often unplanned factors that might affect student motivation.

# Guidelines

*Applying the Theories of Motivation*

**1. Make sure that students have a sufficient chance to fulfill their needs for affiliation and belonging.**

EXAMPLES
- Provide some time for peer interaction, possibly as a reinforcement for positive academic and social behaviors.
- Consider forming cooperative work groups for some tasks.

**2. Make the classroom a pleasant and safe place.**

EXAMPLES
- Choose assignments to ensure that each student experiences success more often than failure.
- Do not permit ridicule or public criticisms of a student by other students.

**3. Recognize the possibility that students come to school with different patterns of needs based on past experiences.**

EXAMPLES
- Students who are overly concerned with achievement may need help in relaxing.
- Students who have a great need to avoid failure may need ways of demonstrating their learning privately.

**4. Help students take appropriate responsibility for their successes and failures.**

EXAMPLES
- Model self-criticism.
- Invite guest speakers who are willing to speak about their own successes and failures.

**5. Encourage students to see the connections between their own efforts and accomplishments.**

EXAMPLES
- Discuss reasons for particular successes as well as failures.
- Avoid making quick judgments about the reasons for students' success or failure.

**6. Help students set reasonable short-term goals.**

EXAMPLES
- Encourage students who set low goals to raise them a little at a time.
- When students set unrealistically high goals, suggest alternatives.

**7. Fit the difficulty of the assignment to the students.**

EXAMPLES
- For students who are high in achievement motivation, you may occasionally want to give problems so challenging the students will fail on their first attempt.
- For students who fear failure, less difficult problems may be appropriate.

**Figure 8–6  Encouraging Motivation Before, During, and After a Learning Experience**

*QUESTION:* What can I do to guarantee positive student attitudes for this activity?

THEORY: Pavlov and classical conditioning.

STRATEGIES: In general, make the conditions surrounding the activity positive and confront negative attitudes directly.

SPECIFIC IDEAS: Puzzles and games that demonstrate the concepts you are teaching; discussions of students' misconceptions about the material; try new desk arrangements; music; posters to make the learning environment more pleasant.

*QUESTION:* How do I best meet the needs of my students through this activity?

THEORY: Maslow's hierarchy of needs; McClelland and Atkinson's achievement theory.

STRATEGIES: In general, make the learning environment safe and make achievement attainable for all the students.

SPECIFIC IDEAS: Be fair and consistent yourself so students can trust you; use students' names; allow students to work in teams on anxiety-provoking projects such as oral reports; provide tutors for students who are having trouble; reveal yourself to your students; set reasonable goals.

*QUESTION:* What about this activity will keep my students interested while they do it?

THEORY: Piaget's equilibration.

STRATEGIES: In general, be flexible and change when student interest wanes; plan for active student involvement.

SPECIFIC IDEAS: Ask intriguing questions and pose puzzling problems; use simulation games; have field trips on the subject; try independent study for some students or interdisciplinary projects such as "The American Way of Death."

*QUESTION:* How can I make the emotional climate positive for this activity?

THEORY: Cooperative learning.

STRATEGIES: In general, take student concerns into account and minimize unhealthy competition.

SPECIFIC IDEAS: Make requirements, instructions, and grading standards clear; experiment with learning teams; enjoy the activity yourself; recognize the humor in situations.

*QUESTION:* How does this activity affirm students' sense of competence?

THEORY: White's competence theory and de Charms' personal causation.

STRATEGIES: In general, let students know where they stand academically and help them take responsibility for completing work.

SPECIFIC IDEAS: Have students keep track of the assignments they complete in a notebook; break long projects up into shorter steps; have students discuss what was especially hard about the assignment and how they conquered it.

*QUESTION:* What reinforcement does this activity provide?

THEORY: Reinforcement theory.

STRATEGIES: In general, make sure that positive consequences follow work well done.

SPECIFIC IDEAS: Send home color-coded weekly report cards for younger students (green is doing fine, yellow means caution, needs improvement, red indicates problems); at the end of a unit on fractions have a Fraction Festival with fraction games and refreshment divided using fractions; allow free time for those who finish early.

# TEACHER EXPECTATIONS

Pygmalion in
the Classroom

Over 15 years ago, a study by Rosenthal and Jacobson (1968) captured the attention of the national media in a way that few studies by psychologists have since. Articles in newspapers across the country reported the seemingly remarkable effects of "Pygmalion in the classroom," a phrase taken from the title of the book written about the experiment. The study also caused great controversy within the professional community. Debate about the meaning of the results continues, and so does research (Braun, 1976; Brophy, 1982; Mendels and Flanders, 1973; Snow, 1969; Wilkins and Glock, 1973).

What did Rosenthal and Jacobson do that caused such a stir? Briefly, they picked several students at random in a number of elementary school classrooms, then told the teachers that these students probably would make significant intellectual gains during the year. According to Rosenthal and Jacobson, the students did indeed make larger gains than normal that year.

Self-Fulfilling
Prophecy

The researchers presented data suggesting the existence of a self-fulfilling prophecy in the classroom. **Self-fulfilling prophecy** in this case meant that the expectations and predictions of the teachers about how well students would do in the future in some way brought about the very behaviors the teachers expected.

Criticisms

The original study was heavily criticized for the experimental and statistical methods used (Elashoff and Snow, 1971; Snow, 1969), and several researchers such as Claiborn (1969) and Wilkins and Glock (1973) tried but were unable to replicate the findings. However, other researchers have found results supporting the idea that teachers' expectations can influence student performance (Cornbleth, David and Button, 1974; Good, 1970; Pippert, 1969).

Brophy and Good (1970) suggest that teacher expectations may affect students in the following manner. Teachers begin by forming expectations about how well different students will do in the class. The teachers then treat the students differently, based upon their expectations. If they expect a student to do well, the student may be given more encouragement or more time to answer a question. Because the students are being treated differently, they respond differently, often in ways that complement the teachers' expectations. Students given more time and more encouragement answer correctly more often. If these different treatments are repeated daily for months, the students given more time and encouragement will do better academically and score better on achievement tests.

A Model
of the Process

Braun (1976) has developed a general model to describe where teacher expectations come from, how they are communicated to students, and how they are perpetuated by changes in student behavior. Figure 8–7 shows the basic factors in the model. All the elements are based on actual research findings, so there is evidence that these factors may indeed be very influential.

## Sources of Expectations

As you can see in Figure 8–7, Braun lists ten possible sources of teacher expectations. Intelligence test scores are an obvious source, especially if teachers do not interpret the scores appropriately (see Chapter 4 for a discussion of this issue). Sex also influences teachers. Most teachers tend to expect boys to present more behavior problems than girls. Oddly enough, names also might be influential.

**293**

**Figure 8–7   Teacher Expectations and Changes in Student Behavior: Braun's Model**

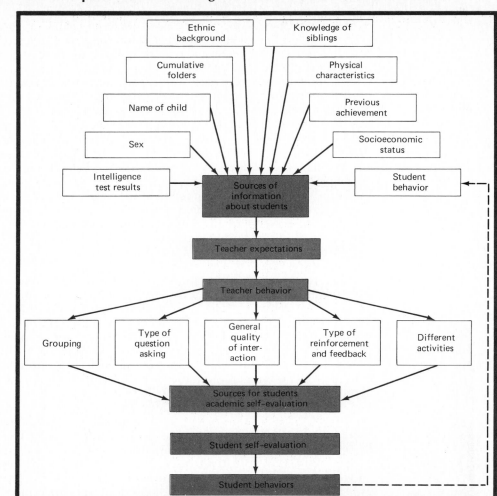

Adapted from C. Braun. Teacher expectations: Socialpsychological dynamics. *Review of Educational Research,* 1976, *46,* 185–213. Copyright © 1976 American Educational Research Association, Washington, D.C.

The notes from previous teachers and the medical or psychological reports found in cumulative folders (permanent record files) are another obvious source of expectations. Knowledge of ethnic background also seems to have an influence, as does knowledge of older brothers and sisters. The influence of students' physical characteristics is shown in several studies, indicating that teachers hold higher expectations for attractive students. Previous achievement, socioeconomic class, and the actual behaviors of the student also offer important sources of information.

How
Expectations
Affect Students

Given these and other sources of information, teachers form expectations about students' probable classroom behavior and academic achievement. These expectations may be accurate predictors. The problems come when teachers use the information to form expectations that turn out to be inaccurate, or when accurate predictions are followed by decisions to use inappropriate teaching methods.

If you remember the discussion of self-concept in Chapter 3, you should be able to make a connection between teacher communication of low expectations and the student's self-esteem. Many students use the teacher's behavior as a mirror in which to view a reflection of themselves. If the reflection they see seems to say "You probably won't be able to do this," their self-esteem is likely to suffer. Of course, students differ. Some are more sensitive than others to the teacher's opinions. The teacher's evaluation may be very significant to one student and disregarded as unimportant by another. In general, the self-esteem of students who are younger, dependent on the teacher, conforming, and who like the teacher may be more influenced by the teacher's views (Brophy, 1982).

*Teachers can communicate expectations by the way they respond to students' requests for help.*
*Who gets a second explanation and who is told, "I discussed that already.*
*Why weren't you listening?"*

(Ken Karp)

## Teacher Behavior and Student Reactions

In Figure 8–7, you also will find five areas in which teachers might behave differently toward students. The first and last of these involve instructional strategies, such as grouping and different activities. The other three involve teacher-student interaction, such as question asking, general quality of interaction, and reinforcement. We begin with a discussion of the instructional strategies.

**Grouping Students**

Different grouping processes may well have a marked effect on students. It appears that even very young students assigned to low reading groups are aware of their grouping and tend to prefer friends from higher-ability groups. Teachers also seem to prefer students in the higher reading groups (McGinley and McGinley, 1970). Rist (1970) described a teacher in a kindergarten class who assigned students to three separate work tables after just a few days, based on guesses about intellectual ability. The lowest-ability table was the one farthest from the teacher's desk. Students at that table had difficulty hearing the teacher and received less attention from her. Certainly these students had reason to believe the teacher expected less of them and in turn to expect less of themselves.

**Assigning Different Activities**

Once teachers assign students to ability groups, they usually assign different learning activities. To the extent that teachers choose activities that challenge students and increase achievement, these differences are probably necessary. Activities become inappropriate when students are ready for more challenging work but are not given the opportunity because teachers believe they cannot handle it. It may be appropriate to teach at a slower pace and to cover less material with certain students, but the pace and quantity should increase when the students are ready for more. Setting higher standards leads to greater achievement for all students (Doyle, Hancock and Kifer, 1971; Pidgeon, 1970).

Another problem occurs when teachers make accurate predictions about student abilities, but select the wrong teaching methods. For example, a teacher may correctly decide that one group of students will have great difficulty with a particular lesson and another will learn the new material easily. In both cases, the teacher might decide to spend little time with these students, since one group "can't benefit from help" and the other "doesn't need help." Both groups are thus robbed of the chance to do their best (Brophy, 1982).

Whatever the group and activity assignments, the amount and quality of student-teacher interaction is likely to have a crucial effect on students. This factor may seem less obvious, but it is a central part of students' experiences in the classroom. Researchers have looked specifically at the three middle factors in Braun's model—question asking, quality of interaction, and reinforcement—in an attempt to explain what effect variations might have on students.

**Questions Asked**

Students who are expected to achieve tend to be asked more questions, given more chances and a longer time to respond, interrupted less often, and asked harder questions than students who are expected to do poorly (Allington, 1980; Cornbleth, Davis and Button, 1974; Rosenthal, 1973; Willis, 1970). If you think about this from the teacher's perspective, it is understandable. Calling on high-expectation students is a much easier and more rewarding way to have a class discussion. Very often these are the students who have the best answers. Getting extra practice in class participation means that these students become skilled at discussion and thus make having a class discussion more fun.

According to Rosenthal (1973), teachers tend to encourage responses from students if they hold high expectations for the students. This means giving these students more time to answer, giving clues and prompts, and generally communicating their belief that the students can answer the question. When teachers have high expectations for students, they tend to be more encouraging in general, smiling at these students more often and showing greater warmth nonverbally through such responses as leaning toward these students and nodding their heads as the students speak (Woolfolk and Brooks, 1983). If expectations for students are low, the students may be asked easier questions and given less time. They are also much less likely to be prompted.

It appears that feedback and reinforcement also differ according to teacher expectations. Brophy and Good (1974) found that teachers demand better performance from high-achieving students, are less likely to accept a poor answer from them, and praise them more for good answers. If low-achieving students give inadequate answers, teachers are more likely to accept or even reinforce the poor performance or to criticize the students for wrong answers. Even more disturbing is the finding that low-achieving students receive less praise than high-achieving students for similar correct answers. On tests when an answer is "almost right," the teacher is more likely to give the benefit of the doubt (and thus the better grade) to high-achieving students (Finn, 1972).

This inconsistent feedback can be very confusing for low-ability students. Imagine how hard it would be to learn when your wrong answers were sometimes praised, sometimes ignored, and sometimes criticized while your right answers received little recognition (Good, 1982).

Behaviors from all five categories taken together can communicate to students just how they are viewed by a very significant person, their teacher. Especially for young students, the teacher's view can help shape self-esteem. Returning to Weiner's ideas about attribution discussed earlier, if youngsters see the inevitable mistakes that accompany learning as a consequence of their own lack of ability, they are likely to lower their level of aspiration. Decreased motivation follows lowered expectations. The student and the teacher set lower standards, persistence is discouraged, and poorer performance results. Students start saying "I don't know" or just not saying anything rather than risking failure again. Teachers accept this poor performance and attribute it to lack of ability. The lower expectation for the student is confirmed and, as the dotted line in Figure 8–7 shows, the cycle continues.

Even when student performance does not fit expectations, the teacher may rationalize and assume, for example, that the low-ability student must have cheated or the high-ability student must have been upset that day. It may take many disconfirmations to change the teacher's beliefs about a particular student's abilities. Thus expectations often remain in the face of contradictory evidence (Brophy, 1982; Darley and Fazio, 1980).

Research has indicated that this cycle can be broken. Not all teachers form inappropriate expectations or act on their expectations in unconstructive

## *Guidelines*

### *Avoiding the Negative Effects of Teacher Expectations*

**1. Use information from tests, cumulative folders, and other teachers carefully.**

EXAMPLES
- Some teachers avoid reading cumulative folders for several weeks at the beginning of the year.
- Be critical and objective about the reports you hear from other teachers, especially "horror stories" told in the teachers' lounge.

**2. Be flexible in your use of grouping strategies.**

EXAMPLES
- Review the work of students in different groups often and experiment with new groupings.
- Use different groupings for different subjects.

**3. Make sure all the students are challenged.**

EXAMPLES
- Avoid saying, "This is easy, I know you can do it."
- Give a wide range of problems and encourage all students to try a few of the harder ones for extra credit.

**4. Be especially careful about how you respond to low-achieving students during class discussions.**

EXAMPLES
- Give them prompts, clues, and time to answer.
- Give ample praise for good answers.

**5. Use materials that show a wide range of ethnic groups.**

EXAMPLES
- Check readers and library books. Is there ethnic diversity?
- Ask your librarian to find multi-ethnic stories, filmstrips, etc.

ways (Babad, Inbar and Rosenthal, 1982). The Guidelines given here may help you avoid some of these problems.

Next we examine one other factor that may have subtle effects on motivation and is often overlooked: anxiety.

## ANXIETY IN THE CLASSROOM

Students who worry that they will not be able to complete a task satisfactorily often end up with a feeling of **anxiety**, or "an experience of general uneasiness, a sense of foreboding, a feeling of tension" in situations where the cause of these feelings is not apparent (Hansen, 1977, p. 91). These feelings may be more or less intense, but they do seem to have significant effects on behavior. In fact, one researcher found that academic failure led to dropping out of school for more than 20 percent of the students who were extremely anxious, while only 6 percent of the students who were seldom anxious dropped out for this reason (Spielberger, 1966).

- If a few materials are available, ask students to research and create their own, based on community or family resources.

**6. Be fair in disciplinary procedures.**

EXAMPLES
- Make sure equal offenses merit equal punishment.
- Set clear rules so that students have a fair warning.

**7. Communicate to all students that you believe they can learn — and mean it.**

EXAMPLES
- Return papers that do not meet standards with specific suggestions for improvements.
- If students do not have the answers immediately, wait, probe, and then help them think through an answer.

**8. Involve all students in learning tasks and in privileges.**

EXAMPLES
- Use some system for calling on or contacting students to make sure you give each student practice in reading, speaking, answering questions, etc.
- Make privileges dependent on appropriate class behaviors for all students.

**9. Monitor your nonverbal behavior.**

EXAMPLES
- Do you lean away or stand farther away from some students?
- Do you avoid touching some students?
- Does your voice tone vary with different students?

## Individual Differences in Anxiety

Trait or State

Psychologists disagree about whether anxiety should be considered a general trait all people possess in different amounts or simply a response to particular situations (Spielberger, 1966). It is likely that both types of anxiety exist. A person who has a general tendency to become anxious is more likely to respond to many types of situations with sweaty palms, a rapid heartbeat, and that feeling of foreboding described by Hansen. This is called **trait anxiety.** Individuals with this trait generally experience anxiety in a wider range of situations and may feel the anxiety more intensely than others. The second type is **state anxiety.** This occurs in specific threatening situations when the normal reaction is to feel anxious. Thus a person who is not usually anxious may become so under certain circumstances (Shuell, 1981a).

Effects of Anxiety

Researchers have found a number of relationships between anxiety and academic performance. People who are highly anxious tend to score lower on tests of intellectual aptitude than people who are less anxious (Sarason, Davidson, Lightall, Waite and Ruebush, 1960). Although we do not know for

**Time Pressures**

certain, it appears that high anxiety is the cause of the poor performance instead of the poor performance being the cause of the anxiety. Anxiety appears to improve performance on simple tasks or on skills that have been practiced at length, but interfere with the accomplishment of more complex tasks or skills that are not thoroughly practiced (Ball, 1977).

In the classroom the conditions surrounding a test can influence how well a highly anxious individual performs. For example, Hill and Eaton (1977) found that very anxious fifth- and sixth-graders worked as quickly and accurately as their less anxious classmates when there was no time limit imposed for solving arithmetic problems. However, with a time limit the very anxious students not only made three times as many errors as their classmates, they also spent about twice as much time on each problem and cheated twice as often as the less anxious group. Conditions that arouse fears about losing in a competitive situation or not completing work may bring out the worst in highly anxious students. In fact, Williams and Hill (1976) found that very anxious students outperformed all other groups when they did not have to put their names on test papers, thus removing some of the personal cost of failing.

Recently, Sigmund Tobias (1979) has suggested a model to explain how anxiety interferes with learning and test performance. When students are learning new material, attention is very important. You will not learn what you never notice or take in. Highly anxious students evidently divide their attention between the new material and preoccupation with concerns about how nervous they are feeling. So instead of concentrating on a lecture or reading, they keep noticing the tight feelings in their chest, perhaps saying to themselves, "I'm so tense, I'll never understand this stuff!" Thus, from the beginning the anxious student may have missed much of the information to be learned.

But problems do not end here. Even if they are paying attention, anxious students have more trouble learning material that is difficult, that requires them to rely on short- and intermediate-term memory, and that is not very well organized (sounds like some of our lectures). Finally, as we saw in Hill's research, anxious students often know more than they can demonstrate on a test that "really counts." So anxiety interferes at several points in the learning and testing cycle.

## Coping with Anxiety

Teachers should help highly anxious students to set realistic goals, since these individuals often have difficulty making wise choices. They are likely to select either extremely difficult or very easy tasks. In the first case, they will probably fail and this could increase their sense of hopelessness and foreboding about school. In the second case, they probably will succeed but miss the sense of satisfaction that encourages greater effort and eases their fears about schoolwork. A good deal of guidance may be needed when these students choose both short-term and long-term goals.

Since anxiety appears to interfere with attention and the ability to remember (Wittrock, 1978), the most effective instruction for highly anxious students, at least those of average or high ability, appears to be quite structured, allowing the students to repeat parts of the lesson that were missed or forgotten (Seiber, O'Neill and Tobias, 1977). Programmed instruction offers one solution. It is structured, allows students to repeat parts missed, and minimizes the failure that is often dreaded by anxious students. Other possibilities are audio or video tapes that can be rewound to repeat sections that were missed. Oosthoek and Ackers (1973) found that being able to rewind a tape helped anxious students to learn, and they took advantage of this possibility more than nonanxious students using the same materials.

Tests

The greatest anxiety-arousing situation in schools at every level is the test. Students know that test results will influence decisions about future education and employment, so testing tends to arouse anxiety in everyone. As we already have seen, students who are highly anxious do not shine on standardized and timed tests, or any important classroom test. These tests often include complex, unfamiliar, and difficult material, just the type that makes the task harder for anxious students.

If students tend to be anxious, it is likely that their test scores will not be valid measures of their abilities. In these cases you can develop other, more informal methods for evaluation. The Guidelines here give some ideas for dealing with anxiety, both in classroom lessons and in testing.

# Guidelines

## Dealing with Anxiety

**1. Use competition carefully.**

EXAMPLES
- Monitor activities to make sure no students are being put under undue pressure.
- During competitive games, make sure all students involved have a reasonable chance of succeeding.

**2. Avoid situations in which highly anxious students will have to perform in front of large groups.**

EXAMPLES
- Ask for volunteers if performances are needed.
- Give anxious students practice in speaking before smaller groups.

**3. Make sure all instructions are clear.**

EXAMPLES
- Write test instructions on the board or test papers instead of giving them orally.
- Check with students to make sure they understand.

**4. Avoid unnecessary time pressures.**

EXAMPLES
- Give occasional take-home tests.
- Make sure all students can complete classroom tests within the period given.

**5. Remove some of the pressures from major tests and exams.**

EXAMPLES
- Teach test-taking skills; give practice tests; provide study guides.
- Avoid basing most of a report-card grade on one test.

## SUMMARY

1. The study of motivation is essentially a study of the many different factors that lead people to initiate actions directed toward specific goals and then persist in their attempts to reach these goals.

2. Psychologists agree that all goal-directed behavior is motivated, but they disagree about the factors that cause motivation.

3. Behaviorists tend to stress extrinsic motivation caused by external stimuli and reinforcement. Physical conditions such as hunger may also be involved.

4. Social-learning theorists emphasize the motivational roles of a person's thoughts about future consequences and the person's ability to set goals.

5. Cognitive psychologists stress a person's active search for meaning, understanding, and competence. The attribution theory of motivation suggests that the causes people give for their successes and failures have a strong effect on their future performances.

6. Humanists stress intrinsic motivation and emphasize the need for personal growth. Maslow has suggested that people are motivated by a hierarchy of needs moving toward self-actualization.

7. Students' attitudes toward learning can be influenced by the conditions of the learning activity.

8. Teachers also must take into account the needs of the student, especially need for achievement.

9. The achievement theory of motivation focuses on the desire to succeed and the need to avoid failure.

10. Among the many methods a teacher can use to enhance motivation are displays, questions, and activities that stimulate curiosity; simulations; lessons based on the students own interests; and activities that call for cooperative effort.

11. The successful completion of a learning experience should leave the student with feeling of competence. If the lesson is routine, the teacher may have to build reinforcement into the activity so that successful completion leads to positive consequences for the students.

12. Several studies have pointed to the important role teacher expectations may play in motivating students. Teachers tend to treat students differently depending on their own views of how well the students are likely to do.

13. Anxiety may be a personality trait or something caused by particular situations.

14. In the classroom, anxiety may improve performance on simple tasks but interfere with performance on more difficult assignments and tests.

## KEY TERMS

motivation

extrinsic motivation

intrinsic motivation

attribution theory

need

self-actualization

deficiency needs

being needs

achievement motivation

Thematic Apperception Test (TAT)

projective tests

resultant motivation

level of aspiration

goal structure

Student Teams-Achievement Divisions (STAD)

jigsaw classroom

origin/pawns

self-fulfilling prophecy

anxiety

trait/state anxiety

# Teachers' Forum

## Cumulative Records

When teachers read students' cumulative records, they learn certain facts and form opinions even before they meet the students in the classroom. Preconceptions (and perhaps misconceptions) may lead to expectations, which in turn influence how the teachers behave toward the students. What is the role of cumulative records? How can you use the information they contain without forming premature expectations of performance and behavior?

**Read Selectively**

Cumulative records contain essential health information and clinically diagnosed conditions of which a teacher must be aware. At the beginning of each year, I examine the records for this information alone. Additionally, the records contain each previous teacher's assessment of a child's performance and behavior. I purposely ignore these observations, as a child's developmental processes and environmental circumstances may cause dramatic differences in performance and behavior from one year to the next. Since children do react differently to each teacher's personality and method of teaching, I use caution at the end of the year in preparing the cumulative record for the next teacher. Each child needs a fresh start each year.

Arleen Wyatt, Third-Grade Teacher,
*Happy Valley Elementary School, Rossville, Georgia*

**Form Your Own Opinions First**

I feel the cumulative record is definitely an asset to the classroom teacher. However, I seldom refer to the records until I have given myself a couple of weeks with the children in order to form my own opinions.

Once I have made a generalization about a child, I refer to the records. If my feelings are confirmed, I carry on. If I have formed a different opinion from previous teachers, I usually approach them to find out how and why we were discrepant in our thinking.

Joan M. Bloom, First-Grade Teacher
*Henry Barnard Lab School for Rhode Island College, Providence, Rhode Island*

**Different Information for Different Problems**

Cumulative records should be used as a reference tool. I like to check achievement test scores and IQ scores prior to beginning instruction with the students so I know if the materials I am using are at the child's instructional level. I also like to check the health records to see if there are any physical problems of which I should be aware. After the first quarter grading period, I like to check last year's grades to see how the child compares at the present time. I generally use the remainder of the information after I myself see a problem. . . .

Sharon Klotz, Sixth-Grade Teacher
*Kiel Middle School, Kiel, Wisconsin*

## A Discouraged Student

You have a student who has a history of failing grades. He has become very discouraged and is on the verge of quitting altogether. How can you motivate this student to keep trying and prevent his joining the ranks of the dropouts?

**The Importance of Success**

The student has probably not experienced success recently, which would contribute to low self-image and a discouraged attitude. A one-on-one discussion to emphasize the student's successes and contributions may be helpful to improve self-image or give him or her a "vision" of what he or she could be. That personalized attention, along with rewarding good classroom work, behavior, and effort with praise, stickers, and prestige duties could motivate the learner. The key is to discover what motivates that student and use it as a positive reinforcement.

Barbara L. Luedtke, Secondary Physical Education Teacher
*Appleton High School — East, Appleton, Wisconsin*

**Help the Student Get Started**

Several factors produce academic failure: a home situation in which students are physically or emotionally abused; an attempt to control their parents or to gain attention; an inadequate self-image; a career they perceive does not require academic skills.

Generally, I have been most successful working with each student to: (1) discuss steps to get work done; (2) set achievable work goals; (3) provide materials that are not brought to class; (4) let the student know I have a sincere interest in him as a person, as well as a student. Interviews with people working in his career area can often convince the student that basic skills are important for success in getting a job. Ultimately, unless the student decides to do the work because he will benefit, little can be done to get him to be academically successful.

Ruth Roberts, Seventh-Grade Earth Science/Biology Teacher
*Greece Athena Junior High School, Rochester, New York*

## A Bad Case of Test Anxiety

One of your students has a very severe case of test anxiety. Although he performs very well in class and hands in excellent homework, he seems to panic everytime you give a test. On test days, he enters class with a strained look on his face. While taking the test, he spends most of his time chewing on his fingernails. His test papers are always a blotted mess, with answers changed left and right. His test scores are not disastrous, but you're sure he could do better if he weren't so worried. What would you do to help this student get over his test anxiety?

**A Variety of Approaches**

First talk with the parents to see if excessive pressure to do well is coming from home. Do not put great emphasis on [such statements as] "We're going to have a test on Friday" or "Let's see how much you know about this chapter." Do not weigh test scores too heavily in determining report-card grades. Talk with the student and help him see that his daily work is important in the same way a test grade is. Give practice tests two or three days before the actual test is scheduled using the same test whenever possible. Record the score only if the student is satisfied with the grade.

Give the student a second opportunity on the actual test day to retake the test if he chooses and let him keep the higher of the two scores. Change the format of the test; a test does not always have to resemble what the student is conditioned to thinking of as a test; multiple choice items can be changed to crossword puzzles.

Carol Gibbs, Sixth-Grade Teacher
*Happy Valley School, Rossville, Georgia*

**A Stress on the Reasons for Testing**

A student with test anxiety can be helped by increasing his or her understanding of tests and testing situations. A private talk together to explain that the learning that comes about as a result of the human tendency to find out what was not known at test time could be very important in this case. Practice testing under lower pressure as a study technique would probably be helpful to this student. Even taking, as formally as possible, the little quiz items in the paper or magazines could add a calming practice effect, especially if another person can be asked to evaluate the responses. Techniques in test taking are discussed in many books and these readings could form a basis for self-study to increase the student's understanding of testing and to lessen anxiety. Reproducing one or two of these articles to have on hand for anxious students could be a very humane and helpful teaching technique.

Larry A. Irwin, Middle-School Principal
*Brentwood Middle School, Greeley, Colorado*

# 9

# Managing Classroom Behavior

Many books have been written about how to deal with disruptive students, how to discipline, and how to manage classrooms. In this chapter and the next, we present several approaches. Of them, behavioral learning principles have proved particularly helpful, in part because these principles have been tested and found effective in laboratories and schools all over the world.

We look first at methods that focus on positive behaviors; then we turn to strategies for helping students develop new skills and abilities. Since there are times when teachers must deal directly with undesirable behaviors, we also present methods for coping with these problems. After examining strategies for managing large groups, we turn to two special programs that have proved effective in situations where other systems have failed: token reinforcement programs and contingency contracts. Next we discuss several ways of involving students in their own learning through self-management. Finally, we explore a number of ethical issues involved in the application of behavioral techniques.

By the time you have finished this chapter, you should be able to do the following:

- Describe how teachers use and misuse attention to reinforce changes in student behavior.
- List items that may be most reinforcing in the classes you will be teaching.
- Plan strategies for applying cueing, modeling, and shaping to help students master new skills and abilities.
- Suggest effective techniques for stopping problem behavior.
- Give examples of how the entire class can be made responsible for student behavior.
- Describe two special programs for classroom management.
- Suggest ways in which students can become responsible for their own behavior.
- List cautions that must be considered in the use of any behavioral management technique.

We begin with methods for increasing positive behavior.

## FOCUSING ON POSITIVE BEHAVIORS

Reinforcement

To increase a behavior is to reinforce it, whether the behavior is spelling words correctly or hitting baseballs. As we noted in Chapter 5, actions followed by reinforcers probably will be repeated in similar situations in the future. The classroom teacher can capitalize on this principle simply by reinforcing positive behaviors.

This seems like an easy enough technique to apply—but in truth it takes substantial effort. Misbehavior is easy to recognize. Positive behavior, on the other hand, is often overlooked. We all tend to be good critics, able to point out what is wrong more readily than what is right. Praising seems to be less natural than criticizing.

## Reinforcing with Teacher Attention

Using Teacher Attention to Improve Behavior

A study by Madsen illustrates the importance of teacher attention as a reinforcer for most students. In this classic study (Madsen, Becker and Thomas, 1968), two problem students in a second-grade class were the subjects. These two spent about half their time in school hitting, fighting, destroying school property, running around the room, and disturbing other pupils. Several approaches were tested systematically to see if improvements followed. Setting explicit class rules and repeatedly reminding the students of the rules did nothing to stop the problems. Ignoring inappropriate behavior and emphasizing the rules also had little effect. If anything, the disruptive behavior increased.

Praising Good Behavior and Ignoring Bad

Next the teacher began to give praise and attention to the students when they were working or playing constructively. The teacher said things such as, "I like the way you are working so quietly!" The teacher also continued to make the rules explicit and to ignore any infractions. This combination of rules, ignoring problem behavior, and praising positive behavior seemed to work. For the first time, there was a significant decrease in the disruptive behavior.

Then the teacher returned to the original classroom procedures used before the study began. The rate of disruption returned to the earlier level, making it clear that the combination of rules, praise, and ignoring was the effective ingredient. When the teacher resumed these procedures, the two students immediately became less disruptive. This gave even more evidence of a definite cause-and-effect relationship. The treatment led to changes. The changes disappeared when the treatment was removed, but reappeared when the treatment was once again applied.

McAllister, Stachowiak, Baer, and Conderman (1969) have found similar results for high school students using a combination of praising the entire class for appropriate behavior and expressing disapproval to individual students who talked out of turn. Based on the results in your classes, praise might be combined with ignoring inappropriate behaviors or with individual reprimands.

These simple procedures have led to improvements in academic subjects such as spelling and mathematics at both the elementary and secondary levels (Zimmerman and Zimmerman, 1962; Kirby and Shields, 1972), paying greater attention to the teacher in elementary classes (Broden, Bruce, Mitchell, Carter and Hall, 1970), and the completion of more assignments in secondary classes (Marlowe, Madsen, Bowen, Reardon and Logue, 1978).

The Prevalence of Criticism

But even though it makes good sense (and is probably good management) to pay attention to positive behaviors, this appears to be difficult in many classrooms. In a study of seventh-graders, Thomas and associates found that the teachers' average rate of verbal disapproval was almost three times the average rate of verbal approval (Thomas, Presland, Grant and Glynn, 1978). At every grade level White (1975) recorded more overall disapproval than approval among the teachers she studied.

*Teacher attention, whether approving or disapproving, is one of the strongest reinforcers of student behavior. Which behavior here merits teacher attention? Which is best ignored?*

For a teacher with a class of 20 to 35 students, it probably is difficult to learn to praise frequently. The problem behaviors are obvious to everyone, and the student working quietly is not trying to attract attention. Because we worry that ignoring misbehavior might "encourage" others to break the rules, we are afraid to overlook even minor infractions. So, the teacher's time is consumed by disapproving. But if we consider the possible effects of teacher praise, it may be well worth the additional effort needed to use it.

**Effective Praise**

There are several cautions, however. Simply "handing out compliments" will not improve behavior. To be effective, praise must (1) be contingent on the behavior to be reinforced, (2) specify clearly the behaviors being reinforced, and (3) be believable (O'Leary and O'Leary, 1977). In other words, the praise should be sincere recognition of a well-defined behavior, so students understand what they did to warrant the recognition.

Unfortunately, teachers who have not received special training often violate these conditions (Brophy, 1981). Research indicates that teachers seldom specify clearly the behaviors they are praising. In one study, this specification occurred only 5 percent of the time (Anderson, Evertson and Brophy, 1979). Of course students may understand the connection without a clear statement from the teacher, but often they understand less than the teacher assumes. At times, teachers fail to make praise contingent on appropriate behavior and may even praise wrong answers. Finally, teachers make praise seem insincere by saying positive words with facial expressions or voice tones that do not fit.

**Other Functions of Praise**

Teachers often use praise for purposes other than reinforcement. Brophy (1981) gives several examples of applications of praise that provide little reinforcement. In dealing with students who often fail, teachers may use

310

praise to counterbalance criticism when improvement occurs. It may carry the not-so-hidden message, "I was right. I knew you weren't trying. You deserved my earlier criticism."

When they grow tired of nagging but still need to make a point, teachers may praise the behavior of a "good" student ("I like the way Ken is . . ."). If done publicly, this can be embarrassing for most students since they easily detect the manipulation and lack of sincerity.

Sometimes praise simply indicates that students have completed the assigned work and can move on. This is the "fine, fine" type of praise and is not particularly reinforcing. As students grow older, most interactions in class are focused on academics. Except for occasionally unexpected good answers, praise in the upper grades is reserved for the cooperative but slow student who seems to need encouragement. Brophy calls this "praise as a consolation prize."

**Problems with Praise**

Some psychologists object to the use of praise in teaching. They suggest that the emphasis should be on learning for its own sake, not learning to win the approval of teachers or other authorities. At the end of the chapter we will discuss these and other criticisms of various approaches based on external reinforcement.

## Alternatives to Problem Behaviors

**Reinforcing Alternatives**

Any negative behavior (hitting, forgetting homework, and so on) can be viewed as an absence of positive behavior (cooperative play or turning in homework on time). In other words, if students are playing cooperatively, they cannot be hitting one another at the same time. One aspect of dealing with any problem behavior should be reinforcing more desirable behaviors when they do occur. If you simply try to stop negative behaviors without providing alternatives, students are likely to find their own replacements. The new situation may be as bad or worse than the original.

The following examples offer suggestions for accentuating the positive in your own classroom:

If students are hitting each other, you might begin to look for chances to reinforce them for playing quietly together. This will give them an alternative way of gaining teacher attention and of interacting in a group.

Cheating is a common problem in many classrooms. Instead of repeatedly punishing offenders, you might look for ways to reward independent work or to give some credit for answers that, while not correct, show a good attempt.

If you are dealing with cases of lying, you might want to find ways of praising truthful statements while letting the students know you will deal with voluntary admissions of wrongdoing in a fair and moderate way.

**Positive Practice**

**Positive practice** is a strategy for helping students replace one behavior with another. This approach is especially appropriate for dealing with academic errors. When students make a mistake, they must correct it as soon as possible and practice the correct response. Foxx and Jones (1978) and Ollendick, Matson, Esveldt-Dawson, and Shapiro (1980) used this procedure, combined with positive reinforcement, to improve spelling. Students were rewarded for the words they spelled correctly and had to practice their misspelled words in a variety of ways (writing correctly in sentences, spelling phonetically, writing a full dictionary definition, and so on). The combination of positive reinforcement and practice led to 100 percent accuracy in spelling and was preferred by the students to more traditional systems for studying misspelled words. The same principle could be applied when students break classroom rules. Instead of being punished, the student might be required to practice the correct alternative action.

Another approach for increasing desirable behavior involves negative reinforcement. The basic principle is to give students an alternative. If you stop doing $x$ and start doing $y$, you can get out of this unpleasant situation. Negative reinforcement helped the first author's daughter get dressed for school by herself. She was told: "Elizabeth, as soon as you put on your clothes, you can come out of the bathroom and join us for breakfast. If you hurry, we will have lots of time to talk and maybe a few minutes to play. But don't come out until you are finished." This system was met at first with protests and a few tears, but soon Elizabeth quickly put on her clothes so she could leave the relatively boring bathroom and join the family for breakfast. Before we tried it, Elizabeth would spend up to an hour getting dressed.

Notice that a negative behavior (dawdling) was dealt with by focusing on a positive behavior (getting dressed quickly). The reinforcement for dressing quickly was positive — namely, the appearance of breakfast and the company of her parents. But negative reinforcement, the disappearance of an unpleasant situation (being stuck alone in a boring bathroom), also played a role.

In second grade, Elizabeth's teacher used negative reinforcement to help the class learn math facts. As soon as a student answered every problem correctly two weeks in a row on Friday's timed test of addition and subtraction, he or she did not have to take the test any more. Successful students got to watch their classmates endure the weekly unpleasantness of "Take out your pencil . . . ." A system like this one is appropriate when all the students have the ability to master the material, but may need some incentive to do so.

We will discuss negative reinforcement more thoroughly when we describe methods for dealing with undesirable behaviors. Negative reinforcement, which is often mistakenly equated with punishment, actually offers an excellent alternative to punishment. For now, it is enough to remember that both positive and negative reinforcement can be useful in increasing desirable behavior, the first by focusing directly on postiive behavior and the second by offering an alternative that leads to a postive outcome.

## Selecting the Best Reinforcers

There are many reinforcers other than teacher attention already available in most classes. In fact, teachers often grant privileges and tangible rewards, such as the.chance to talk to other students or feed the class animals, in a rather haphazard way. By making the same privileges and rewards directly contingent upon learning and positive behavior, the teacher may greatly increase both learning and desired behavior.

Whatever your source of reinforcers, a very helpful guide to choosing the most effective ones is found in the **Premack principle,** named for David Premack (1965). According to the Premack principle, a high-frequency behavior (a preferred activity) can be an especially effective reinforcer for a

*What would students do with free time in school? Many would play one of the hundreds of electronic games now available. Students can earn time to play these games when school work is completed.*

(Ken Karp)

low-frequency behavior (a less preferred activity). This is sometimes referred to as "Grandma's rule": First do what I want you to do, then you may do what you want to do.

**Getting Ideas from Students**

If no work demands were placed on students, what would they do? The answer to this question can suggest many possible reinforcers. For most students, talking, moving around the room, sitting near a friend, being exempt from assignments or tests, reading magazines, or playing games are preferred activities. The best way to determine appropriate reinforcers for your students may be to watch what they do in their free time. If you find yourself saying to a student, "Stop doing that and pay attention!" or "Please put that away until the end of class!" you have probably found a perfect reinforcerer for the student. Another good method is to ask the class for ideas. Questionnaires like the one in Figure 9–1 can elicit suggestions. Remember that what works for one student may not be right for another: Serralde De Scholz and McDougall (1978), for example, found that average and fast learners tended to value approval, praise, and being correct much more than slow learners. For students with learning problems, tangible rewards, activities, and privileges may be most effective.

313

**Figure 9–1   Getting Student Ideas about Reinforcement**

NAME _____ Grade _____ Date _____

Please answer all the questions as completely as you can.

**1.** The school subjects I like best are:
**2.** Three things I like most to do in school are:
**3.** If I had 30 minutes free time at school each day to do what I really like, it would be:
**4.** My two favorite candies are:
**5.** At recess I like most to (three things):
**6.** If I had $1 to spend on anything, I would buy:
**7.** Three jobs I would enjoy in the class are:
**8.** The two people I most like to work with in school are:
**9.** At home I really enjoy (three things):

Source: Adapted from G. Blackman and A. Silberman, **Modification of child and adolescent behavior,** 2d ed., pp. 281–83. © 1975 by Wadsworth Publishing Co, Inc. Reprinted by permission of publisher.

In applying the Premack principle, it is important to remember that the low-frequency behavior must happen first. Consider the Premack principle and note what is wrong with the following conversation:

STUDENTS:   Oh, no! Do we have to diagram sentences again today? The other classes got to discuss the film we saw in the auditorium this morning.

TEACHER:   But the other classes finished the lesson on sentences yesterday. We're almost finished too. If we don't finish the lesson, I'm afraid you'll forget the rules we reviewed yesterday.

STUDENTS:   Why don't we finish the sentences at the end of the period and talk about the film now?

TEACHER:   Okay, if you promise to complete the sentences later.

The teacher in this example had a perfect opportunity to use the Premack principle. Discussing the film could have served as a reinforcer for completing the lesson on sentences. As it is now, the class could easily spend the entire period discussing the film. Then, just as the discussion becomes fascinating, the teacher must play the role of police officer and insist that the class return to the sentences.

We do not mean to suggest that a teacher should follow a lesson plan as if it were carved in stone. But in this situation the teacher seemed to have a good reason for continuing with the lesson. Instead of letting the students discuss the film first, she might have said: "I promise you that if we all concentrate, we can finish the sentences in twenty minutes. You will understand the lesson and we will be through with it. Then we can spend the rest of the period discussing the film. That way, if the discussion becomes interesting I won't have to stop it in the middle to finish the sentence lesson." In this case, both teacher and students would have achieved their goals.

# *Guidelines*

## *Focusing on Positive Behavior*

**1. Whenever possible, focus attention on the students who are following the rules and ignore those who are behaving inappropriately.**

EXAMPLES
- If a few students are not paying attention at the beginning of a lesson, praise those who are "ready to listen."
- Use misbehavior as a personal cue to find some positive behavior to reinforce.

**2. Make sure that all students, even those who often cause problems, receive some praise, privileges, or other rewards when they do something well.**

EXAMPLES
- Review your class list occasionally to make sure all students are receiving some reinforcement.
- Remain alert to possibilities of praising those students who tend to create problems.

**3. Establish a variety of reinforcers.**

EXAMPLES
- Use the Premack principle to decide on effective reinforcers.
- Let students suggest their own reinforcers or choose from a "menu" of reinforcers with "weekly specials."

No matter what reinforcers are best in your classroom, you will benefit from stressing the positive. The Guidelines offered here should help summarize the many methods of reinforcing positive behavior. But what if the behavior you want to encourage never occurs? A teacher cannot provide a positive consequence for an action that never takes place. In the following section we describe several systems for developing new behaviors.

## DEVELOPING NEW BEHAVIORS

In this section we will discuss three approaches to helping students learn new behaviors: cueing, modeling, and shaping. Both cueing and modeling have been introduced before. Shaping is based on two principles that also should be familiar to you by now: reinforcement and extinction. In instituting new behaviors, cueing and modeling are usually considered first, since shaping is a much more time-consuming strategy.

### Cueing and Prompting

As we explained in Chapter 5, a **cue** is a stimulus that provides information about what behavior is appropriate and will be reinforced in a particular situation. Cues are useful in helping students demonstrate behaviors they are physically capable of performing but seldom or never perform on their own. Every student in the room, for example, may be able to get his or her materials ready and begin working immediately after the class bell rings, but few will do so automatically. The bell could serve as a cue, but many students have learned to ignore the bell—possibly because they have not been reinforced for paying attention to it.

The problem in this situation is to teach the students to respond in a positive way (by working) to an antecedent stimulus in their environment (the bell). One approach would be to provide a prompt—an additional cue—just after the first cue has occurred. Wesley Becker and his associates offer two principles for using this approach (Becker, Engelmann and Thomas 1975). First, make sure the environmental stimulus that you want to become a cue occurs right before the new prompt you are using, so students will learn to respond to the cue and not just rely on the prompt. Second, fade the prompt as soon as possible so students do not become dependent upon it.

Based on these two principles, the strategy for teaching students to get ready for work after hearing the bell might be this:

*FIRST DAY*
The teacher begins by saying, "We have been wasting quite a bit of time settling down to work after the bell rings. I have a new system to help us get going more quickly. When the bell rings, I am going to turn on this buzzer. As soon as every person has his or her work started, I will turn off the buzzer." Then the teacher implements the procedure, upon hearing the class bell.

*FIRST WEEK*
The teacher continues the process and praises the students who begin working as soon as the bell rings.

*SECOND WEEK*
At this point the teacher begins to wait longer before turning the buzzer on, but she continues to reinforce students for beginning work promptly. By the end of the week, she does not use the buzzer at all, but continues to praise the students who respond appropriately to the bell.

Notice that this strategy followed the two principles stated earlier: first the cue (the bell), then the prompt (the buzzer), and then the gradual fading of the prompt. In addition, this strategy also used negative reinforcement. Negative reinforcement offers an escape from an unpleasant situation. As soon as the students started working, the teacher removed the unpleasant stimulus of the buzzer.

Often the problem is that students are not able to perform a particular action. In this case, the strategy of modeling might be considered.

## Modeling

As we noted in Chapter 5, modeling (or vicarious conditioning) can be an effective and efficient means of teaching new behavior. Few studies have tested this type of modeling in classroom situations, but indications are that interest and work in this area will increase in coming years. The studies that have been conducted offer encouraging results. Zimmerman and Pike (1972),

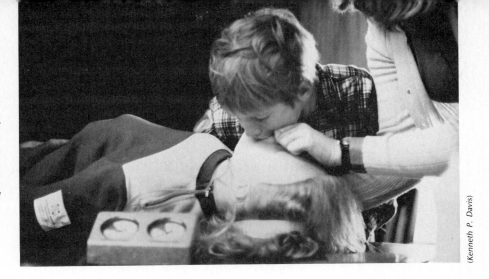

*It would be difficult to master a skill such as cardio-pulminary resuscitation without first observing a demonstration of the skill and then having the chance to practice, as this student is doing with a specially designed mannequin.*

for example, found that modeling plus praise was much more effective than praise alone in helping second-grade students learn to ask questions in a small group. Swanson and Henderson (1977) also used modeling to help preschool children learn to ask questions. They found the most effective teaching strategy to be viewing a videotape model of children asking questions, combined with the chance to practice these skills later with appropriate feedback.

Modeling has long been used to teach dance, sports, crafts, and skills in home economics, chemistry, shop, and other subjects. We also teach students a number of new behaviors unintentionally by our own actions. The following are examples of some deliberate attempts to apply modeling in teaching:

> A student asks a question and the teacher says, "That question requires some critical thinking. Let me be sure I understand the problem before I try to think through the answer. . . ." The teacher then goes on to model good critical thinking and problem-solving strategies by "thinking out loud."

> A teacher is concerned that many of the girls in her high school class have very stereotyped ideas about careers for women. She invites several women from the community who have nontraditional jobs to speak to the class during Career Study Week.

In some situations, a good cue or even a good model will not help students learn to behave in new ways. Shaping may be appropriate in these cases.

## Shaping

What happens when students continually fail to gain reinforcement because they simply cannot meet the criteria? Consider these examples:

> A fourth-grade student looks at the results of the latest mathematics test. "No credit on almost half of the problems again because I made one dumb mistake in each problem. I hate math!"

A tenth-grade student tries each day to find some excuse for not participating in the softball game in gym class. The student cannot catch a ball and now refuses to try.

In both situations the students are receiving no reinforcement for their work because the end product of their efforts is not good enough. A safe prediction is that the students will soon learn to hate the class, the subject, and perhaps the teacher and school in general.

**Shaping through
Successive
Approximations**

One way to prevent this problem and help the students learn the needed behaviors is the strategy of **shaping,** also called **successive approximations.** Shaping involves reinforcing progress instead of waiting for perfection. In order to use shaping, the teacher must break down the final complex behavior the student is expected to master into a number of small steps. Krumboltz and Krumboltz (1972) describe four different methods for establishing the small steps:

**Different
Methods
of Shaping**

1.  *Reinforce individual aspects of a task.* A complex skill can be broken down into all its subskills, and the student can be reinforced for mastering each subskill. A research paper, for example, could be broken down into outlining skills, using the index and table of contents, summarizing information from several sources, drawing conclusions, writing footnotes, and so on.

2.  *Reinforce increased accuracy.* Sometimes a student can perform the desired behavior, but the results are not very accurate. The teacher in this case might want to emphasize improvements in accuracy. A language teacher, for example, might first reinforce a vague approximation of the correct pronunciation of *Monsieur,* then continue to raise standards gradually until pronunciation is near native.

3.  *Reinforce increasingly longer intervals of the desired behavior.* Students often can perform in a desirable fashion, but only for a few minutes at a time. They can be encouraged to extend this period of time with a gradually increasing criterion for reinforcement. For example, a student who frequently talks to others during class may be reinforced for remaining quiet for five minutes, then eight minutes, then twelve, and so on.

4.  *Reinforce increasingly longer intervals of participation.* Students are sometimes reluctant to participate because they have been embarrassed in the past. In this case, a teacher could begin by reinforcing even the smallest contributions of a student who seldom participates in class. This should probably be done in a matter-of-fact way, since extravagant praise may be embarrassing to a shy student.

Many behaviors can be improved through shaping, especially skills that involve persistence, endurance, increased accuracy, greater speed, or extensive practice to master. Because shaping is a time-consuming process, however, it should not be used if success can be attained through cueing or modeling. The Guidelines presented here for all three procedures—cueing, modeling, and shaping—help clarify these distinctions.

To this point, we have presented strategies with a positive focus. For the most part, these approaches involve various methods for delivering positive reinforcement. In the next section, we discuss systems that focus on undesirable behavior. We have deliberately begun with the more positive strategies because we believe that these approaches should be considered first, before more negative methods are tried.

# *Guidelines*

## *Developing New Behaviors*

1. **If students are already capable of performing a behavior but seldom or never do, you may want to provide a cue to remind them of the appropriate behavior.**

EXAMPLES
- Use signs as prompts to remind students to put materials away if the mess itself is not a cue for neatness.
- Provide verbal cues in your instructions before students tackle something they are likely to do wrong.

2. **If students have never encountered a desired behavior, you may want to provide a model of this behavior.**

EXAMPLES
- Use films showing the desired behavior being reinforced.
- Provide feedback and reinforcement when students practice the behavior they have seen modeled.

3. **If the final behavior is far beyond the current abilities of the students, you may want to try successive approximations, or shaping.**

EXAMPLES
- Begin by giving partial credit to a student having difficulty with a particular task; then gradually change the criterion.
- Give a student who is afraid of speaking in class a chance to answer questions calling for simple one- or two-word replies and gradually change the criterion.

## COPING WITH UNDESIRABLE BEHAVIOR

No matter how successful you are at accentuating the positive, there are times when you must cope with undesirable behavior, either because other methods do not seem sufficient or because the behavior itself is dangerous or calls for direct action. For this purpose, negative reinforcement, satiation, and punishment all offer possible solutions.

### Negative Reinforcement

Negative
Reinforcement
in the
Classroom

Remember the basic principle of negative reinforcement presented in Chapter 5: if an action stops something unpleasant, then the action is likely to occur again in similar situations. An example is found in the seat-belt buzzer mechanism in a car. Fastening the seat belt stops the buzzer in the car. After fastening the seat belt for several weeks, you may continue to do so, for a while at least, even if your buzzer breaks down. Negative reinforcement operates in a number of other everyday situations. Parents, for example, learn to rock their babies in certain ways when the rocking stops the baby's crying. (A crying baby is definitely an unpleasant situation.)

Negative reinforcement may also be used to enhance learning. To do this, you must place students in mildly unpleasant situations so they can "escape" when their behavior improves. Consider these examples:

A teacher says to a third-grade class, "When the art supplies are put back in the cabinet and each of you is sitting quietly, we will go outside. Until then, we will miss our recess."

A high school teacher says to a student who seldom finishes in-class assignments, "As soon as you complete the assignment, you may join the class in the auditorium. But until you finish, you must work in the study hall."

Negative
Reinforcement
vs. Punishment

You may wonder why these examples are not considered punishment. Surely, staying in during recess or not accompanying the class to a special program is punishing. But the focus in each case is on *increasing* specific behaviors by removing something aversive as soon as the desired behaviors occur. When behavior is increasing, the process is reinforcement. Since the consequence involves removing or "subtracting" a stimulus, the reinforcement is *negative*. In addition, there is the issue of control. These are unpleasant situations, but in each case the students retain control. As soon as they perform the appropriate behavior, the unpleasant situation ends.

In contrast, punishment occurs after the fact, and the student cannot so easily terminate it. The third-grade teacher could have used punishment by saying, "Since you are so noisy and haven't put away your art supplies, we will miss 15 minutes of recess!" The high school teacher also could have used punishment by saying, "Because you haven't completed your assignment again, I want you to go to the study hall and work instead of attending the special program." In these situations, the students would have had no options. Control of the unpleasant condition would have remained in the hands of the teacher. Only by defying or outwitting the teacher could the students have had an impact.

An equally important difference between negative reinforcement and punishment is found in the potential effect each is likely to have. The ultimate effect of negative reinforcement, when used successfully, is to increase some positive behavior. The effect of punishment is to suppress behavior. Negative reinforcement contains a means for ending a certain behavior by increasing an alternative. At best, punishment simply will help you stop or suppress an undesirable behavior.

Rules
for Applying
Negative
Reinforcement

Krumboltz and Krumboltz (1972) offer several rules for negative reinforcement. First, describe the desired change in a positive way. Second, don't bluff. Make sure you can enforce your unpleasant situation. Third, follow through despite complaints. And fourth, insist on action, not promises. If the unpleasant situation terminates when students promise to be better next time, you have reinforced making promises, but not making changes.

## Satiation

Another way to stop problem behavior is to insist that students continue the behavior until they are tired of doing it. This procedure should be applied with care. Continuing some behaviors may be very dangerous. For example, a command to smoke every cigarette in a pack would be highly undesirable.

A Classroom
Example
of Satiation

An example of a more appropriate use of **satiation** is related by Krumboltz and Krumboltz (1972). In the middle of a ninth-grade algebra class, the teacher suddenly noticed that four students were making all sorts of unusual motions. When the teacher asked them what they were doing, they initially said it was nothing. When encouraged, they finally admitted they were bouncing imaginary balls. The teacher pretended to greet this idea with enthusiasm and suggested the whole class do it. At first, there was a great deal of laughing and joking. After a minute this stopped, and one student even quit. The teacher, however, insisted that all the students continue. After five minutes and a number of exhausted sighs, the teacher allowed the students to stop. No one bounced an imaginary ball in that class again.

Teachers also may allow students to continue some action until they stop by themselves, if the behavior is not interfering with the rest of the class. This can be done by simply ignoring the behavior. Remember that responding to an ignorable behavior may actually reinforce it.

In using satiation, a teacher must take care not to give in before the students do. It is also important that the repeated behavior is the one you are trying to end. If the algebra teacher above had insisted that the students write, "I will not bounce imaginary balls in class" 500 times, the students would have become satiated on writing rather than on bouncing balls.

## Punishment

The Need for a
Two-Pronged
Attack

As we have already noted, **punishment** is at best a means of suppressing behavior, either by the presentation of something negative or by the removal of something positive. It does not, in and of itself, lead to any positive behavior. Thus, whenever you consider the use of punishment, you should make it part of a two-pronged attack. The first prong is to carry out the punishment and suppress the undesirable behavior. The second prong of the attack is to give students an alternative, something to do instead, generally with some form of reinforcement.

Punishment is a very popular method for influencing behavior in schools. However, the approach has not eliminated problems. This lack of impact may be due in part to the fact that we know very little about what constitutes effective punishment. Many methods may stop misbehavior for a few minutes, but punishment should have a more lasting effect. Three strategies—reprimands, response cost, and social isolation—have proved successful in some situations (O'Leary and O'Leary, 1976a).

The Benefits of
Private Criticism

**Reprimands.**   A study by O'Leary and his associates examined the effects of soft, private **reprimands** versus loud, public reprimands on decreasing disruptive behavior (O'Leary, Kaufman, Kass and Drabman, 1970). Reprimanding a problem student quietly so that only the student can hear the statement seems to be much more effective. When the teacher in the study spoke to the offenders loud enough for the entire class to hear, the disruptions increased or continued at a constant level. Perhaps the students enjoyed the public recognition ("You really got the teacher going today, didn't you?"). Perhaps public condemnation encourages a student to save face by having the last word. At any rate, the additional initial effort required to use soft reprimands seems to be a good investment in making lasting improvements.

The Loss of a
Reinforcer

**Response Cost.**   The concept of **response cost** is familiar to anyone who has ever paid a fine. For certain infractions of the rules, people must lose some reinforcer (money, time, privileges, pleasures). In a class, the concept of response cost may be applied in the following way. Five problem talkers in a sixth-grade classroom begin each day with 15 marks beside their names on the blackboard. Each time one of the students talks without permission, she or he erases one mark from the board. For each mark remaining at the end of the day, the student gets two minutes of free time. As the students improve, they begin the day with fewer marks. But each mark is now worth more minutes of free time, so the potential reward is still 30 minutes. Later, the number of minutes of available free time is decreased as well.

**Social Isolation.**    One of the most controversial behavioral methods for decreasing undesirable behavior is the strategy of **social isolation,** often called **time out from reinforcement.** The process involves removing a highly disruptive student for 5 to 10 minutes. The student is placed in an empty, uninteresting room alone. The idea behind this procedure is that the classroom is a reinforcing place, and removal from the classroom will act as a mild punishment. We have referred to this procedure as social isolation, rather than time out, because it is not always certain whether leaving a classroom is really leaving reinforcement. Everyone can remember classes that were not all that reinforcing. It seems likely that the factor acting to decrease behavior is the punishment of brief isolation from other people (Drabman and Spitalnik, 1973; O'Leary and O'Leary, 1976a).

Social isolation is used most often with problem students in special classes.

*Social isolation, sometimes called "time out from reinforcement," can be an effective punishment if administered cautiously. However, the teacher in this picture may be removing the "isolating" effect unless he is just beginning or just ending the isolation period.*

Many schools, in fact, do not have the facilities for implementing the procedure in all classes. A trip to the principal's office or a chair in the corner of the room does not have the same effect as sitting alone in an empty room. To use the procedure, teachers also must be able to ensure that a sometimes reluctant student stays in the time-out room. With older students, this becomes increasingly difficult. For very resistant problems, however, social isolation can be quite effective. Simply removing a student from the room temporarily (never for more than 15 minutes) may be a kinder way to cope with misbehavior than harsh words and hard punishment.

**Problems with
Social Isolation**

Great care should be exercised with social isolation. Consultation with a school psychologist or specially trained teacher is recommended before attempting this procedure unless it is a regular part of school policy. Social isolation is easily abused. It also may be improperly applied. Some schools believe they are using social isolation when a student is sent to a detention room. But other people are usually in the room, and there is little isolation. Also the average stay in a detention room is longer than 15 minutes.

Foxx and Shapiro (1978) offer an alternative to social isolation called nonexclusionary time out. In this procedure, all students who are following the class rules are allowed to wear a ribbon or badge or some other object that is easily removed. If a student misbehaves, the teacher removes the ribbon and the student is not allowed to participate in class for 3 minutes. When the time is up, if the student is behaving appropriately, the ribbon is returned and the student may again participate. The ribbon serves as a cue to the teacher and to the other class members, telling them when to ignore and when to reinforce each student.

**Negative
Associations**

**Some Cautions.** Any procedure that involves unpleasant events should be handled with caution. Punishment can have several negative side effects. Most of us have strong emotional reactions to being punished. The people or situations involved in the punishment tend to become associated with these negative feelings, possibly through a process similar to classical conditioning. We all tend to avoid people and situations associated with pain or unpleasantness in the past. Students may learn to fear or hate teachers, subjects, and events that have been punishing, especially if the students have experienced little balancing reinforcement in those situations.

Attempting to escape or avoid unpleasant situations is also a predictable human response. If the consequences of failing are too severe, students may learn to cheat. If the consequences of attending school are too unpleasant, students may cut class or drop out altogether.

**A Model
for Aggression**

Finally, the reaction of an adult to the misbehavior of a student teaches the student an important lesson. The adult's response is a model of how to deal with problems. If you listen to the conversation or watch the play of young students, you often see problems solved through aggression. Some part of that aggression may be learned from the disciplinary procedures of the adults working with the students.

Although negative control has potentially harmful side effects, some behaviors must be stopped. If a student has no desire to change and seldom evidences any positive behaviors that could be reinforced, punishment may be necessary to stop or at least slow down the problem behavior so that other responses may occur and be reinforced. In addition, actions that are genuinely dangerous to the student, to others, or to school property at times must be punished.

It is obvious that effective punishment requires hard work and careful management. The teacher who chooses to use punishment may profit from the Guidelines presented here, adapted from the work of Becker, Engelmann, and Thomas (1975).

# *Guidelines*

## *Punishment*

**1. Try to structure the situation so you can use negative reinforcement rather than punishment to change behavior.**

EXAMPLES
- Allow the student to escape an unpleasant situation by performing the desired behavior.
- Insist on student action, not promises.

**2. Make the punishment immediate and unavoidable.**

EXAMPLES
- If possible, avoid delayed detention as a punishment.
- Don't argue or negotiate with students once you have decided punishment is necessary.

**3. Give one warning only.**

EXAMPLES
- Establish some sort of cue to warn students that punishment will follow a continued behavior.
- Let the students know that a single warning will be given.

**4. Remain calm and matter-of-fact.**

EXAMPLES
- Avoid vindictive or sarcastic words that the students might model.
- Put the stress on the need to end the problem behavior rather than on dislike of the student.

**5. Be consistent in your application of punishment.**

EXAMPLES
- Keep the focus on the undesirable behavior rather than on the misbehaving students, and punish all cases of this behavior.
- Avoid inadvertently reinforcing the behavior you are trying to eliminate.
- Let students know in advance the consequences of breaking the rules.

**6. Be sure punishment for misbehavior is balanced by praise for an incompatible behavior.**

EXAMPLES
- If a student is punished for being disruptive, praise him when he is working quietly.

**7. Examine the effects of punishment — is the behavior decreasing?**

EXAMPLES
- What you perceive as a punisher may be experienced by the student as a reinforcer.
- Use effective punishment, such as private reprimands and response cost, not public harangues and ridicule.

# SPECIAL PROGRAMS FOR CLASSROOM MANAGEMENT

In some situations, you may want to consider using a much more formal system of reinforcers. Three possibilities are group consequences, token programs, and contingency contracts.

## Group Responsibility

Playing the<br>Good Behavior<br>Game

Reinforcement for the class can be based on the cumulative behaviors of every member of the class, usually by adding each student's points to a class total. The Good Behavior game is an example of this approach. A class is divided into two teams. Specific rules for good behavior are established. Each time a student breaks one of the rules, that student's team is given a mark. The team with the fewest marks at the end of the period receives a special reward or privilege (longer recess, first to lunch, and so on). If both teams earn fewer than a preestablished number of marks, both teams receive the reward. Harris and Sherman (1973) found that a criterion of as few as four marks worked effectively in maintaining good behavior. Most studies indicate that while the game produces only small improvements in academic achievement, it can produce definite improvements in the behaviors listed in the good behavior rules.

A variation of this game was effective in improving the behavior of an extremely disruptive group while they were in the library. The librarian worked with the students to set rules, divided the class into teams, and gave points to one or both teams several times during the period, if everyone on the team was following the rules. The winning team members, or both teams if each received the necessary number of points, collected their reward in the regular classroom once each week (Fishbein and Wasik, 1981). Other researchers have found that the Good Behavior game is more effective than teacher attention in controlling disruptive behavior in fourth- and fifth-grade classes. In addition, the teachers preferred the game over the techniques of praising good behavior and ignoring undesirable behavior (Warner, Miller and Cohen, 1977).

Earning Rewards<br>for Group<br>Performance

A second approach involves basing reinforcement on the behavior of the group as a whole. Wilson and Hopkins (1973) conducted a study using group responsibility to lower noise levels. Radio music served as the reinforcer for students in a home economics class whenever the noise was below a predetermined level. When the noise exceeded the level, the radio was turned off. Given the success of this simple method, such a procedure might be considered in any class where music or similar reinforcers do not interfere with the task at hand. Another example is a method developed by Switzer, Deal, and Bailey (1977) to eliminate stealing in three second-grade classrooms. Each day the teachers said, "If I don't notice anything missing this morning, you will have 10 minutes of free time after you have had your snack." Whenever anything was taken, the teacher left the room for a few minutes. If the articles were returned, the free time was still given.

**Cautions.**   In many ways, programs using group consequences have been just as successful as those based on individual consequences. However, caution is needed in applying group approaches. Some systems require individual students to earn points for the whole group. In such situations there is likely to be pressure on these students from the rest of the class. If the students are genuinely unable to perform the required behavior, then failure

325

is probable. The consequences of failure may be great, especially for students who have difficulties making friends.

Even with procedures involving all students, peer pressure may be heavy on students who are not contributing sufficiently to the class point total or who are responsible for the loss of points. This peer pressure is not always easy for the teacher to monitor. Recently we saw an entire class break into cheers when the teacher announced that one boy was transferring to another school. The chant, "No more points! No more points!" filled the room. The points referred to a system of giving one point to the whole class each time anyone broke a rule. Every point meant 5 minutes of recess lost. The boy who was transferring had been responsible for many losses. He was not very popular to begin with and the point system, though quite effective in maintaining order, had led to greater rejection for him.

Peer pressure in the form of support and encouragement, however, can be a positive influence. Teachers might show students how to give support and constructive feedback to classmates. If a few students seem to enjoy sabotaging the system, those students may need separate arrangements.

Group responsibility is just one of many special programs. In the next section, we will look at two slightly more complex approaches.

## Token Reinforcement Programs

Often it is difficult to recognize and reinforce all the students who deserve it. A **token reinforcement system** can help solve this problem by allowing all students to earn tokens for both academic work and positive classroom behavior. The tokens may be points, checks, holes punched in a card, chips, play money, or anything else that is easily identified as the student's property. Periodically the students exchange the tokens they have earned for some desired reward.

According to O'Leary and Drabman (1971), token programs have successfully reduced disruptive behaviors, increased studying, and led to greater academic achievement in a variety of classrooms. For example, token programs have been used with elementary students to increase attention levels (Ferritor, Buckholdt, Hamblin and Smith, 1972); to help students follow class rules (Harris and Sherman, 1973); and to maintain attention to assignments (Bushell, Wrobel and Michaelis, 1968). Progress has also been made with elementary school students in improving skills in arithmetic, spelling, reading, and social studies (Hawkins, Sluyter and Smith, 1972; Kirby, Holborn and Bushby, 1981); in strengthening writing skills (Brigham, Grabard and Stans, 1972); and even in encouraging creativity in the writing of short stories (Mahoney and Hopkins, 1973). In the secondary grades, token programs have been used successfully to help students complete assignments (Rickard, Melvin, Creel and Creel, 1973); to lower noise levels (Wilson and Hopkins, 1973); and to decrease disruptive behaviors (Main and Munro, 1977).

A good example of the application of a token program can be found in Project Success Environment, conducted in a very difficult inner-city school system (Rollins, McCandless, Thompson and Brassell, 1974). Sixteen teachers were trained in a summer workshop to use praise-and-ignore techniques and token reinforcement. The following year they implemented these procedures

*For the most part, the best reinforcers are obvious, since students do little to hide their likes and dislikes. To provide greater variety of reinforcement, however, the teacher should be on the lookout for subtler indications of interest, such as extra time spent on an experiment.*

(Julie O'Neill/Stock, Boston)

in their first-, second-, third-, sixth-, and eighth-grade classrooms. The performance of the students in all these classrooms was compared with the performance of similar students in 14 comparison classrooms.

**Procedures**    Throughout the year, all the project teachers used the praise-and-ignore techniques for reinforcing appropriate behaviors. In addition, students were given tokens for positive behaviors—in this case, checks on reward cards. During the first three weeks, the reinforcement was given mainly for following conduct rules. After the third week, reinforcement was shifted to academic achievement. Checks were at first given fairly continuously and predictably; later they were dispensed more intermittently and unpredictably. During the third and fourth months, the rewards that could be purchased with the tokens were changed from candy and toys to activities and school supplies. By the fourth month, students could earn time in an activity room supervised by paraprofessionals. Toys, games, and comic books were provided in the elementary school activity rooms. Games, magazines, radios, and records were available in the middle school activity room. Over the course of the year, the number of checks needed to earn the rewards increased.

**Results**    With such an elaborate project, one would hope that the results were substantial. They were. The 16 project classes and the 14 comparison classes were observed during the entire year, and a number of major differences were noted. First, the project teachers reinforced students about twice as often and punished students much less than the teachers in the comparison classes. Second, the students in the project classes exhibited dramatically less disruptive behavior. Third, the project students also spent a much greater amount of time working on their assignments. Perhaps the most exciting

327

# *Guidelines*

## *Token Reinforcement Programs*

**1. Establish a clear set of rules stating the behaviors that will earn tokens.**

EXAMPLES
- Number of problems completed correctly.
- Description of positive social behaviors.

**2. You may want to have different goals for different groups of students.**

EXAMPLES
- Focus on cooperative behaviors for students who are disruptive.
- For "good" students, give tokens for enrichment work, peer tutoring, completion of special project, and so on.

**3. Select tokens that will work well in your particular class.**

EXAMPLES
- Colored chips for younger students.
- Points for older students.

**4. Offer a variety of rewards at different "prices."**

EXAMPLES
- Rewards that can be purchased for a few tokens so that all students will be motivated to try.
- Rewards that make more extensive efforts seem worthwhile.

**5. Gradually increase the requirements for each token.**

EXAMPLES
- Begin with one token for each correct answer, then for every three correct answers, and so on.
- Offer tokens initially for 5 minutes of attention to assignments, eventually for a whole day of appropriate work.

**6. Gradually change from tangible rewards to privileges and time focused on enjoyable learning experiences.**

EXAMPLES
- With young students, start with candy or toys and end with assisting the teacher and free reading time.
- With older students, start with such things as magazines and move toward monitoring privileges and free time to spend on independent projects.

result of the program, however, was the fourth finding. The project students improved greatly in both academic aptitude and achievement. Their gains on the California Test of Mental Maturity and the California Reading Achievement Test were twice as large as the gains made by the comparison students.

Additional Benefits
Although a token program is time-consuming, the benefits may make it all worthwhile. In addition to improving target behaviors, it may offer a number of fringe benefits. Within a well-organized program, few students are likely to be overlooked. The special privileges and jobs that are often given just to the best students—assisting the teacher, serving as a leader, working on

independent projects — can be made a part of the reward system available to all students. Each student involved in a token-reinforcement program also has visual evidence of the progress being made, in the form of tokens that can be counted daily. Finally, students can learn a number of valuable lessons in a token program. They can learn that they have some control over their lives, that their behaviors have certain relatively dependable consequences. They also can learn some lessons about the realities of our economic system — namely, that in order to have access to rewards, one must earn them.

Variations

Several variations are possible in designing a token program. In some programs students have been trained to be managers, dispensing tokens and freeing the teacher to focus on other activities. Winett, Krasner, and Krasner (1971), for example, developed a system that used a rotating student monitor to reinforce class members for reading independently while the teacher worked with other students. Another variation is to allow students to earn tokens in the classroom and exchange them for rewards at home. These plans are very successful when parents are willing to cooperate. Usually a note or report form is sent home daily or twice a week. The note indicates the number of points earned in the preceding time period. The points may be exchanged for minutes of television viewing, access to special toys, private time with parents, or saved for larger rewards such as trips.

Whatever the variation, a number of basic steps should be taken in setting up a token reinforcement program. The Guidelines given on the preceding page list the essential ones.

## Contingency Contract Programs

Negotiating
a Contract

In a **contingency contract** program, the teacher draws up an individual contract with each student describing exactly what the student must do to earn a particular privilege or reward. In some programs, students participate in deciding on the behaviors to be reinforced and the rewards that can be gained. The process of negotiating can be an educational experience in itself, as students learn to set reasonable goals and abide by the terms of a contract.

A sample contract is given in Figure 9–2. Note that it lists positive behaviors in very specific terms and describes just how these behaviors are to be recorded. The reinforcement is also stated in very specific terms and in this case offers a reward not only to the shy student involved, but also to a friend. The shy student's friendship thus becomes more desirable for others in the class.

The few pages devoted to token reinforcement and contingency contracts here can offer only an introduction to these programs. Suggested readings at the end of the chapter provide greater detail. If you want to set up a large-scale reward program in your classroom, you probably should seek professional advice. Often the school psychologist, counselor, or principal can help. In addition, you should consider the cautions about using reward systems discussed at the end of this chapter. Applied inappropriately, methods that provide external rewards can undermine the students' intrinsic motivation to learn (Deci, 1975; Lepper and Green, 1978).

The goal of most teaching is to help students become independent learners. In the next section we look at some management techniques students can use in or out of school.

**Figure 9–2** **A Sample Contract for Changing Classroom Behaviors of a Shy Student**

A contract between _____(student)_____ and _____(teacher)_____.

If_____(student's name)_____ fills the following requirements _____(teacher's name)_____ will provide the reward listed below.

REQUIREMENTS  **1.** Ask or answer at least three questions during class discussion each day. The questions asked or answered should be recorded in your notebook and reported to me at the end of the day.

**2.** Talk with two different students each day during activity time about any topic. The conversations should be reported to me at the end of the day.

REWARD  For each day the requirements are met, 15 minutes of free time alone or with any friend either in the activity center, the library, or the playground.

*Source: Adapted from R. Martin and D. Lauridsen. **Developing student discipline and motivation: A series for teacher in-service training.** Champaign, Ill.: Research Press, 1974, p. 58.*

# SELF-MANAGEMENT

If one goal of education is to produce people capable of educating themselves, students must learn to regulate and manage their own lives, set their own goals, and provide their own reinforcement. In adult life, rewards are sometimes vague and goals often take a long time to reach. For example, we began writing this text several years before the final reinforcement of seeing the completed book. Along the way we had to set small objectives and reinforce ourselves for the completion of each chapter. Life is filled with tasks that call for this sort of **self-management.** Yet psychologists are only now beginning to understand the process (Coates and Thoresen, 1979).

## Approaches to Self-Management

Students may be involved in any or all of the steps in implementing a behavior change program. They may help set goals, observe their own work, keep records of it, and evaluate their own performance. Finally, they can select and deliver reinforcement.

Self-imposed Standards

Several studies have shown that, in general, students work as hard under self-imposed standards as they do under standards imposed by adults (Felixbrod, 1974). But no matter who sets the goals, higher standards tend to lead to higher performance (McLaughlin and Gnagey, 1981).

Unfortunately, student-set goals have a tendency to become lower and lower. Teachers can help students maintain high standards by monitoring the goals set and reinforcing high standards (O'Leary and O'Leary, 1976a). In one study, a teacher working with first-grade students helped students raise the number of mathematics problems they set for themselves each day by praising them whenever they increased their objective by 10 percent. The students maintained their new higher work standards, and the improvements even generalized to other subjects (Price and O'Leary, 1974).

Self-Recording and Self-Evaluation

Students may also participate in the recording and evaluation phases of a reinforcement program. Some examples of behaviors that are appropriate for self-recording are time spent studying, the number of assignments completed, time spent practicing a skill, number of books read, and number of times out of seat without permission. Using a self-monitoring system, a student keeps a chart or diary recording the frequency or duration of each behavior. Because cheating on records is a potential problem, especially when students are rewarded for improvements, intermittent checking by the teacher and bonus points for accurate recording may be helpful (Hundert and Bucker, 1978). Self-evaluation is somewhat more difficult because it involves

---

### BOX 9–1 SELF-MANAGEMENT IN COLLEGE

Both research and the experiences of most educators indicate that classroom teachers feel great time pressures (Pettigrew and Wolf, 1982). Being unable to find the time to accomplish all that is required may be one reason people leave the profession (Chapman and Hutcheson, 1982). These demands on time become painfully evident to students when they begin their student teaching semester. That time period, with assignments from college courses and new responsibilities in the classroom, is one of the most hectic of the college career. One semester recently, the first author and a colleague decided to test some self-management techniques with their students during this busy time.

Four sections of student teachers participated in the project. One of the classes was randomly chosen to serve as a control group. Students in the remaining three sections read a popular book on how to manage time and avoid procrastinating (Lakein, 1973), attended a lecture on the major points of the book, with special emphasis on the techniques of written planning and self-monitoring, and saw a film on the topic. Then the students were invited to participate in a self-management project. Those who volunteered set goals for each day, completed written plans outlining when and where they would accomplish these goals, and kept a log noting how they spent their time each day. From this log they could identify the activities, people, and places that were wasting their time. In addition, they could recognize their most and least productive periods during the day.

Several assignments were due the last week of the semester, but could be handed in at any point. When the students had finished the class and were fully involved in student teaching, they received a questionnaire about the course and their teaching experiences. We recorded when all assignments and questionnaires were handed in and checked to see if the self-management training had affected performance in any way. Results of the analyses indicated significant differences among the groups in promptness in returning assignments and questionnaires. For example, in the group that did not receive training, 59 percent returned the questionnaire. In the group that read the book, saw the film, and attended the lecture, 65 percent returned the questionnaire. But in the group that did all the preceding plus written planning and self-monitoring, 77 percent returned the questionnaire, a very high rate of response.

The students who participated were enthusiastic about the project. Many intended to continue setting goals and making written plans each night in order to make the most of their time.

making a judgment about quality. Very few studies have been conducted in this area, but it appears that students can learn to evaluate their behavior with reasonable accuracy (Santogrossi, O'Leary, Romanczyk and Kaufman, 1973).

**Self-Reinforcement**

Self-recording or self-evaluation alone does not ensure a change in the desired direction. The behaviors the students record must have reliable consequences. The final step in many self-management programs is student involvement in reinforcement. Rewarding yourself for a job well done leads to higher levels of performance than simply setting goals or keeping track of progress (Bandura, 1978). Given this, you may want to think of some creative way to reinforce yourself when you finish this chapter.

We have been focusing on the external aspects of self-management — goals, recording, evaluation, and rewards. But as we all know from experience, merely stating an objective and recording efforts will not guarantee success. Along the way we must concentrate, ignore distractions, and work to accomplish goals. Some of us are better at this than others, and some students are more capable than their classmates in this area. In the previous chapter, we discussed the skills related to self-motivation. For many students in your classroom, these skills will not come naturally; they must be taught.

*Jennie's teacher is encouraging her to take responsibility for her own reading progress by keeping a record of the number of pages read each week. The next step is to make sure reinforcement follows improvement.*

## Examples of Self-Management

A Creative Writing Program

Ballard and Glynn (1975) describe one program in which a third-grade teacher used self-management to encourage the development of creative writing abilities. At 1:00 each afternoon, the 37 students in the class were given a creative writing period. They were encouraged to write about anything that interested them and to use as many action words and describing words as possible. After a while, the teacher asked the students to record on special sheets the number of sentences, action words, and describing words in their stories each day. The students did this, but no increase in sentences, action words, or describing words followed. Then the teacher allowed the students to earn free activity time based on some aspect of their writing. This time was self-monitored, with periodic checkups by the teacher. At this point, radical improvements were seen in all aspects of student writing. Not only did the number of sentences, action words, and describing words increase, but the overall quality improved, as judged by independent raters at a university.

Self-Management in Sports

A second example of self-management is found in a study by McKenzie and Rushall (1974). The coaches of a competitive swim team with members from ages 9 to 16 were having difficulty persuading swimmers to maintain high work rates. Then the coaches drew up four charts indicating the training program to be followed by each member, and posted these near the pool. The swimmers were given the responsibility of recording number of laps and completion of each training unit. Because the recording was public, swimmers could see their own progress and that of others, give and receive congratulations, and keep accurate track of the work units completed. This seemed to offer a good deal of reinforcement. Work output increased by 27 percent when the charts were introduced. The coaches liked the system because swimmers could begin to work immediately without waiting for instructions. The coaches could then devote their time to training individuals.

Self-Management for Impulsive Students

The third example involves teaching students to give themselves silent instructions about the task at hand. At first the teacher may have students say the instructions out loud, to make sure they understand the system. Later the instructions may be whispered, and finally simply "thought." This approach has helped impulsive students slow down and consider each alternative more carefully. Poor readers have been taught a set of self-instructions to guide reading. They learn to ask themselves questions about the content as they go along, outline each passage in their heads, relate the ideas in the reading to other information, and so on (Meichenbaum, 1977).

One important aspect of the self-instructional approach is to give students something concrete to do that focuses their attention. But the instructions must involve a task that fits the goals of the particular situation. Asking questions as you read not only helps maintain attention, but also helps you better understand what you are reading. Some other system, like imagining painful punishment every time your mind wanders, might keep you focused on the book, but it probably would not improve comprehension.

The Guidelines given here may prove helpful if you decide to apply self-management techniques in your classroom. Keep in mind the need for adequate reinforcement; self-recording and self-evaluation alone do not seem to work. Before concluding this chapter on methods of changing behavior, we will look at some of the ethical issues related to the use of behavioral strategies.

333

## PROBLEMS AND ISSUES

The preceding sections have provided an overview of several strategies for changing classroom behavior. These strategies are tools that may be used responsibly or irresponsibly.

### Ethical Issues

The ethical questions related to the use of the strategies described in this chapter are similar to those raised by any process that seeks to influence people. Here we will present two major concerns. First, which of the many goals that could be chosen are most acceptable in a school setting? Second, which of the many strategies that could be used seem most appropriate for students in public schools?

**Selecting Goals.** In selecting goals, the question that seems to arise most often is whether to focus on classroom conduct or academic achievement.

According to the *Preliminary Report of the Commission on Behavior Modification of the American Psychological Association,* "there appears to be a wide consensus that simply improving classroom conduct does not necessarily result in academic change" (1976, p. 6).

Cautions about Inappropriate Goals

This leads us to one of the most obvious potential abuses of behavior modification. The strategies described in this chapter could be applied exclusively to teach students to sit still, raise their hands before speaking, and remain silent at all other times (Winett and Winkler, 1972). This certainly would be an unethical use of the techniques. It is true that a teacher may need to establish some organization and order, but stopping with improvements in conduct will not ensure academic learning.

On the other hand, in some situations, reinforcing academic skills may lead to improvements in conduct (Ayllon and Roberts, 1974). Emphasis should be placed, whenever possible, on academic behaviors. Academic improvements generalize to other situations more successfully than changes in classroom conduct, which often are exhibited in the classroom where they are learned but nowhere else (O'Leary and O'Leary, 1976b). Of course, academic and social behaviors may be improved simultaneously.

**Selecting Strategies.**  In any learning situation, a teacher may choose to change a student's behavior through positive or negative means. If a student is writing a love note in class, for example, the teacher can choose to approach the problem by punishing love note writing or by reinforcing behaviors incompatible with love note writing. As we have already noted, punishment may involve a number of undesirable side effects. In light of these possible side effects, it makes sense to begin with positive reinforcement strategies whenever possible and turn to punishment only when these fail.

Use the Least Restrictive Procedures First

A set of guidelines originally prepared to select programs for retarded students offers a logical progression of strategies that may be applied in any classroom setting. These guidelines recommend that the first procedures should be those that are "the least intrusive and restrictive, the most benign, practical, and economical (in the long run) in implementation, but yet optimally effective" (*Preliminary Report of the Commission on Behavior Modification of the American Psychological Association,* 1976). When simpler, less restrictive procedures fail, the more complicated procedures should be tried. Applying these guidelines to the strategies presented in this chapter, we have created the general hierarchy found in Figure 9–3.

**Figure 9–3    Choosing Strategies for Classroom Management**

| | |
|---|---|
| *First try:* | Praising positive behaviors and ignoring undesirable behaviors. |
| *If that doesn't work, try:* | Praise-and-ignore techniques with vicarious reinforcement, prompting and cueing, soft reprimands, modeling, or shaping. |
| *If that doesn't work, try:* | Praise-and-ignore techniques with negative reinforcement, satiation, response cost, or social isolation. |

A second consideration in the selection of a strategy is the impact of the strategy on the individual student. For some students, even a soft reprimand might be overkill. Simply reinforcing the appropriate behavior of a nearby student might work better. If a student has a history of being severely punished at home for bad reports from school, a home-based reward program might be very harmful to that student. Reports of unsatisfactory progress at school could lead to increased abuse at home. The responsibility of fitting the strategy to the special needs of each student calls for some expenditure of time to gather information. This will be especially true of the more elaborate programs.

Before introducing a program such as token reinforcement, a teacher must examine all the possible consequences for all the students. To gather information about the students and the possible results of such a program, teachers ideally should seek outside consultation.

## Criticisms of Behavioral Methods

We believe that, properly used, the strategies in this chapter can help students learn academically and grow in self-sufficiency. However, there are definite limitations and cautions involved. Effective tools do not automatically produce excellent work. The indiscriminate use of even the best tools can produce major problems.

Critics of behavioral methods point to two basic problems that may arise with the application of these methods in classrooms. First, they believe these methods may lead to a decreased interest in learning. Second, they believe the programs may have had a bad effect on the students who are not involved.

**Decreased Interest in Learning.**   Some psychologists stand firmly behind the belief that "token programs lead to token learning." They fear that rewarding students for all learning will cause the students to lose interest in learning for its own sake (Deci, 1975; Lepper and Green, 1978; Lepper, Green and Nisbett, 1973). Recent studies have suggested that using reward programs with students who are already interested in the subject matter, in fact, may cause students to be less interested in the subject when the reward program ends. But for students who are not initially interested in the subject, being in a reward program not only increases achievement, it also appears to increase interest in the subject itself.

The lesson here is straightforward. Fit rewards to the individual. If a student is already being reinforced in a subject (by interest in the subject, parental or teacher approval, or some other factor), there is no need to add reinforcers. If, however, the student does not find a subject reinforcing, then reward programs may help kindle an interest (O'Leary and O'Leary, 1976b). In most situations, reward programs can be gradually phased out and learning maintained by teacher attention and student success. If the reward system cannot be removed successfully, perhaps the material is not appropriate for the student. If you use reward systems for individuals rather than for the entire class, you must consider the impact on other students.

**Impact on Other Students.**   Using a reward program or giving one student increased attention may have a detrimental effect on the other students in the

"GETTING AN 'A' OR A STAR IS ALLRIGHT, BUT I'D LIKE SOME SORT OF PROFIT-SHARING PLAN AROUND HERE."

(Sidney Harris)

classroom. Is it possible that other students will learn to be "bad" in order to be included in the reward program? Most of the evidence on this question suggests that reward programs do not have any adverse effects on students who are not participating in the program *if* the teacher believes in the program and explains the reasons for using it to the nonparticipating students (Christy, 1975).

Whatever was maintaining the "good" behavior of the nonparticipating students (teacher approval, interest in the subject) will probably continue maintaining good behavior. If the conduct of some students does seem to deteriorate when their peers are involved in special programs, many of the same procedures discussed in this chapter should help them return to previous levels of appropriate behavior.

## SUMMARY

1. Many studies have demonstrated the powerful effects of teacher attention. Simply by recognizing some student action, a teacher may encourage the behavior to be repeated.

2. Teachers can apply this principle by paying attention to and praising positive behaviors and whenever possible ignoring undesirable behaviors.

3. Students need guidance in what to do as well as what *not* to do. Negative reinforcement and positive practice may help students adopt alternatives for inappropriate or incorrect responses.

4. The choice of additional forms of reinforcement can be based in part on the Premack principle: Popular activities can serve as reinforcers for less popular activities.

5. If students are already able to act in certain ways but seldom do, a teacher may want to use cues to encourage the behavior.

6.  If students do not know how to perform the behavior, a model may help.

7.  The most time-consuming process for developing a new behavior is shaping. This involves breaking down the behavior to be learned into small steps, then reinforcing gradual step-by-step progress toward the final goal.

8.  Using negative reinforcement, a teacher can put students in a mildly unpleasant situation and allow them to leave the situation only when their behavior improves.

9.  With satiation, a teacher can insist that students continue the problem behaviors until they have no more desire to carry them out.

10. When all else fails, some form of punishment such as a private reprimand, the loss of privileges (response cost), or isolation may be necessary.

11. Because students are influenced by their peers, it sometimes is productive to enlist the help of the whole class. Possibilities include rewarding the class for points achieved by every individual or making rewards contingent on the behavior of the class as a whole.

12. Two special programs based on behavioral learning principles have been especially effective in dealing with more difficult problems in classroom management: token reinforcement and contingency contracts.

13. Many of the methods described in this chapter can be applied by students to manage their own behavior. Students can participate in setting goals, keeping track of progress, evaluating accomplishments, and selecting and giving reinforcement. In addition, students can learn to "talk themselves into working" by using specific instructions to focus their attention on the task at hand.

14. Whenever possible, teachers should focus on academic improvement, not just following class rules, use positive reinforcement before trying negative reinforcement, satiation, or punishment, and to seek professional help before implementing a large-scale program.

15. Critics of behavioral methods suggest that reinforcing a student for accomplishments may undermine the student's natural interest in learning or cause classmates to be jealous.

## KEY TERMS

| | |
|---|---|
| positive practice | response cost |
| Premack principle | time out from reinforcement |
| cue | social isolation |
| shaping (successive approximation) | token reinforcement |
| satiation | contingency contract |
| punishment | self-management |
| reprimand | |

## SUGGESTIONS FOR FURTHER READING AND STUDY

BECKER, W. *Parents are teachers: A child management program.* Champaign, Ill.: Research, 1971. A classic with many good ideas for both parents and teachers.

BUCKLEY, N. K. and WALKER, H. M. *Modifying classroom behavior: A manual of procedures for classroom teachers* (Rev. ed.). Champaign, Ill.: Research Press, 1978. Here you will find a basic guide for teachers who wish to use behavioral methods of classroom management. The revised edition describes ways of involving parents in school-based programs.

DRABMAN, R. S. and TUCKER, R. D. Why classroom token economies fail. *Journal of School Psychol-*

ogy, 1974, *12*, 178–188. This article surveys the common problems encountered when token economies are used in classrooms, lists traps to avoid, and offers a number of points to consider before setting up such a program.

HERMAN, T. M. *Creating learning environments: The behavioral approach to education.* Boston: Allyn & Bacon, 1977. This textbook on behavioral approaches to teaching includes discussions of setting goals and using reinforcement and punishment, as well as a number of other behavioral topics such as programmed instruction.

HOWELL, R. G. JR. and HOWELL, P. L. *Discipline in the classroom: Solving the teaching puzzle.* Reston, Va.: Reston Publishing Co., 1979. In addition to discussing behavioral principles in a very practical way, this book has chapters on teacher anxiety, the school environment, group dynamics, curriculum, and communication.

KRUMBOLTZ, J. D. and KRUMBOLTZ, H. D. *Changing children's behavior.* Englewood Cliffs, N.J.: Prentice-Hall, 1972. This very readable and practical book presents 13 principles for teaching students along with a number of examples and case studies.

MEICHENBAUM, D. *Cognitive behavior modification: An integrative approach.* New York: Plenum, 1977. Meichenbaum's text describes his work with impulsive children and the basic principles of cognitive behavior modification.

O'LEARY, S. G. and K. D. Behavior modification in the schools, in H. Leitenberg (Ed.) *Handbook of behavior modification and behavior therapy.* Englewood Cliffs, N.J.: Prentice-Hall, 1976. In this article, you will find a very thorough, clearly written, and interesting description of how behavioral learning principles have been applied to school problems.

O'LEARY, K. D. and O'LEARY, S. G. (Eds.). *Classroom management: The successful use of behavior modification.* (2nd ed.). New York: Pergamon, 1977. A classic collection of articles on behavioral methods for classroom management by experts in the field.

WOLFGANG, C. H. and GLICKMAN, C. D. *Solving discipline problems: Strategies for classroom teachers.* This book discusses behavioral approaches to management as well as many alternatives. It is a thorough and readable introduction.

H&H Enterprises publishes a series of booklets called *How to be a better behavior manager.* The series editors are N. Azrin, V. Besalel, R. V. Hall, and M. C. Hall. The address for the series is: Box 1070-BT, Lawrence, Kansas, 66044. Some of the booklets are:

*How to use positive practice*
*How to plan for generalization*
*How to maintain behavior*
*How to teach through modeling and imitation*
*How to use planned ignoring*
*How to select reinforcers*
*How to use reprimands*
*How to use shaping*
*How to use overcorrecting*

# Teachers' Forum

## Does Positive Reinforcement Work?

Once there was a teacher who attended a workshop on behavior management and decided to implement what he learned. His plan was to ignore undesirable behavior and praise desirable behavior. He focused on a student who frequently took 5 to 10 minutes to sharpen her pencil. He ignored the pencil-sharpening behavior when it occurred and praised her for not being at the pencil sharpener several times during the day. However, the behavior persisted, and he returned to his previous management method which, although ineffective, at least made him feel better. He concluded the behavior management principles he had learned did not work. Would you agree? What advice would you give this teacher?

*Clear Positive Goals*

Behavior management should attempt to make the child responsible for his or her own behavior in a positive manner. I think the teacher's trouble was focusing on the negative behavior — time at the pencil sharpener. Instead, I would talk with the child about spending time on task. We would negotiate an individual contract that would reward extended periods of time on task (and not at the pencil sharpener). Then praise for working would be in order, while time at the pencil sharpener would gradually diminish. The behavior management principle would remain the same, but the goal would be more clearly defined for both child and teacher.

Arleen Wyatt, Third-Grade Teacher
*Happy Valley Elementary School, Rossville, Georgia*

*Carefully Chosen Reinforcers*

No, I do not agree that behavior management principles do not work. On the contrary, I believe they always work! My advice: First, start with concrete rewards: stars, stickers, stamps, etc. Next, draw up a chart. Set goals. For instance: Establish with the student that the sharpener may be used once in the morning, once in the afternoon. Draw up a student-teacher contract to establish goals. If child complies at the end of the morning, reward with a star; same for afternoon. When drawing up a contract, include a reward: For example, 5 stars equals 10 minutes "free time" or an extra trip to the library.

Patricia Frank, Fourth- and Fifth-Grade Teacher
*Cambridge School, South Brunswick, New Jersey*

## A Consistently Late Student

One of your students is almost always late to class. She generally has a pass, and she always has a good excuse. Usually it has something to do with one of the numerous extracurricular groups with which she is involved. Although you do hate having her miss the beginning of class each day, the biggest problem is in her entrances. She invariably manages to disrupt the rest of the class by making a production number of her entrance or by stopping to talk briefly to one of the other students. What steps would you take to put an end to these entrances? What, if anything, would you do to discourage her lateness?

**A Search for Answers**

I'd begin by asking myself: Is Linda's tardiness a personal message that my class isn't really important? If so, is she right? Do Linda's entrances threaten my own position center-stage? If so, am *I* right? If my answers demonstated that the problem was entirely external, I would talk with Linda, impressing on her the influence she has as a school leader and asking her help in promoting promptness and [an appropriate] attitude once the bell rings. How could she refuse? Then I'd get busy and plan in detail the most exciting, educational, and relevant first ten minutes of class possible for the next six weeks.

Rachel D. Morton, Seventh-Grade Language Arts Teacher
*Star Middle School, Star, North Carolina*

**Removal, Reduction, and Modification**

There are three methods to resolve a disruptive behavior: (1) removal; (2) reduction; (3) modification. To remove the disruption, inform the students that the door will be closed after establishing a reasonable passing time. Anyone not in class should report to the guidance or administration office. For the reduction [and modification] of disruption, (a) allow the student two tardinesses biweekly; additional incidents will result in after-school retention; (b) enlist the cooperation of the extracurricular advisor to encourage the student's punctuality; (c) explain to the student how you feel about the effect of her entrances upon the students. The conflict should be immediately and mutually resolved.

Ruth P. Roberts, Seventh-Grade Science Teacher
*Athena Junior High School, Rochester, New York*

**A Series of Conferences**

I would first question her need to disrupt the class upon entrance. The obvious reason for such behavior is that it is an attention-getting device. My steps for dealing with the entrance problem would be as follows: first, I would ignore her behavior and speak with her privately about the matter. In the conference, I would encourage her to believe that she is somebody and that it isn't necessary to try to prove anything. I would also remind her that such grand entrances will not longer be acceptable; second, if the conference proved to no avail, I would suggest that she, her parents, and I discuss the situation (I am assuming her parents care about her school activites); third, if the results of the parental conference were unsatisfactory, I would give notice that the matter would have to be referred to the assistant principal; fourth, if Steps 1, 2, and 3 failed to remedy the situation, I would recommend that serious disciplinary action be taken toward the girl. (Step 4 would be a last ditch effort and probably serve to complicate the matter. I could only hope that Step 1 alleviated the problem.)

James C. Fulgham, High-School Latin Teacher
*Brainerd High School, Chattanooga, Tennessee*

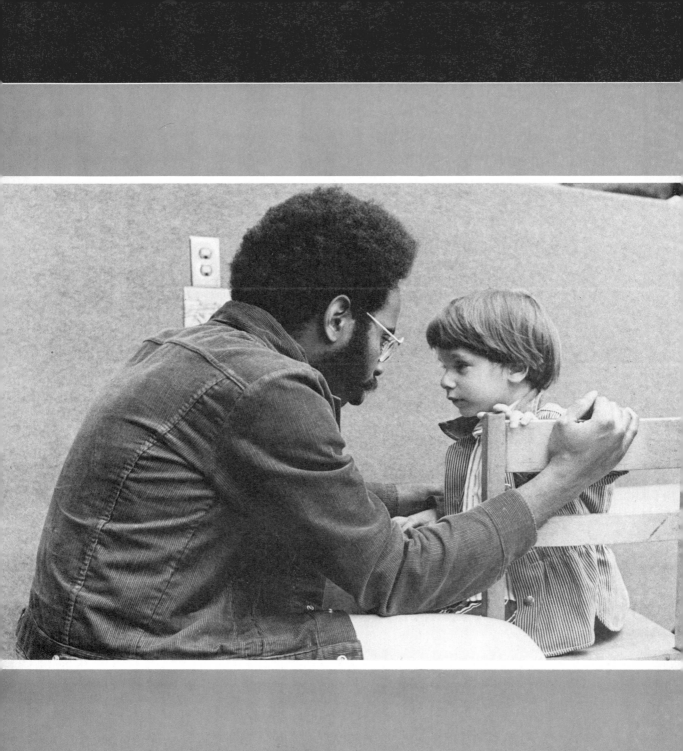

# 10

# Classroom Discipline and Communication

**OVERVIEW**     Although we have been talking about discipline and management throughout this book, we are now ready to examine several key aspects of these issues in depth. Few topics in educational psychology are as important to teachers. We all know that teachers must cope with a wide range of discipline problems. Students involved in disrupting class cannot be involved in learning. Often the disruption prevents anyone in the room from learning. In fact, good classroom management is one of the most influential factors in encouraging academic learning (Good, 1979).

One very important role for the teacher in achieving a well-managed class is that of leader. Different situations require different types of leadership, but this matching is the responsibility of the teacher. There are two main tasks for a leader: The first is to establish a good working atmosphere, and the second is to maintain that positive environment when problems arise.

Several steps help to establish good discipline in a classroom. The first is planning. This includes deciding on rules and procedures, as well as determining consequences for following or breaking the rules. Long before the students arrive, the teacher should try to foresee what organization will be needed and determine how to respond to the inevitable problems. The next step is teaching students how to follow the rules. This job must begin the first day of class. In fact, results of research we will examine in this chapter indicate that the first few weeks of school are critical in establishing patterns of effective discipline and good communication between teacher and students.

Having set up a successful management system, the teacher must maintain it. One of the best ways is to prevent problems from occurring at all. Some teachers are very successful at prevention. A second step is to respond appropriately and constructively when problems do arise (as they always do!). For instance, what will you do when students challenge you openly in class, when one student asks your advice on a difficult personal problem, when you catch a student cheating, or when another "disappears" psychologically and refuses to participate? We will examine the ways that teachers can communicate effectively with their students in these and many other situations.

By the time you have finished this chapter, you should be able to do the following:

- Describe an appropriate class situation for using democratic, teacher-centered, or laissez-faire leadership.
- Create a list of rules and procedures for the class you will be teaching.
- Develop a plan for organizing your first week of teaching.
- Explain Kounin's suggestions for preventing management problems.
- Describe how you might respond to a student who seldom completes work.
- Suggest two different approaches to dealing with a conflict between teacher and student or between two students.

# LEADERSHIP IN THE CLASSROOM

Bany and Johnson divide the teacher's job into three major activity patterns, as shown in Figure 10–1. Even though leadership is essential to successful teaching, teaching involves more than leadership. Some of the teacher's time and effort is directed toward instruction, some toward evaluation. But it is the teacher as a group leader who creates an efficient organizational structure and good working environment so that instruction and evaluation can take place. A group that is totally disorganized, unclear about its goals, or constantly fighting will not be a good learning group. The leadership pattern includes establishing (facilitating) a positive learning environment and maintaining that environment so that instruction and evaluation can take place.

On the first day of class, the teacher faces a room filled with individuals. Perhaps a few small cliques, friendships, or rivalries already exist. But there is no sense of group unity, no set of rules for conduct in the group, no feeling of belonging. If teachers are successful leaders, they will help students develop a system of relationships that encourages cooperation.

*Creating Standards and Rules*

Standards and rules must be established that maintain order, ensure justice, and protect individual rights, but do not contradict school policy. What happens when one student hurts another? How do students get to go to the drinking fountain, pencil sharpener, nurse's office? What do students who finish assignments early do with their extra time? How can individuals gain recognition and reinforcement in the group? Students need procedural knowledge such as this so they can solve the daily problems involved in being members of the class and behaving appropriately.

*Maintaining a Positive Atmosphere*

No matter how skillful the teacher is in uniting students and establishing a positive atmosphere, the task is never complete. Regular maintenance is necessary. Conflicts arise. The needs of individual members change. A new

**Figure 10–1   Three Activity Patterns of the Teacher**

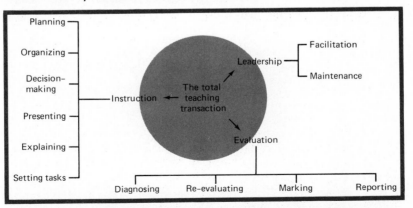

*Reprinted with permission of Macmillan Publishing Co., Inc., from **Educational social psychology** by M. A. Bany and Lois V. Johnson. Copyright © 1975, Macmillan Publishing Co., Inc.*

kind of learning task requires a new organizational structure. Sometimes outside pressures such as holidays, upcoming tests or athletic contests, or family troubles cause stress in the classroom. Another task for the teacher is to restore a positive environment by helping students cope with conflict, change, and stress.

## Styles of Leadership

If you remember the teachers you have had and their styles of leading, you can probably recall three strategies for organizing a class and making decisions.

**Teacher-directed Leadership**

One strategy could be called **teacher-directed leadership.** The teacher set the objectives, planned assignments, chose materials, evaluated work, and set class rules pretty much without help from the class. Teacher-directed leadership need not mean negative or arbitrary control. As you will see in Chapter 12, several studies have found that teachers who are effective in helping students learn basic skills are warm and caring, but also make most of the instructional decisions themselves.

**Democratic and Laissez-Faire Leadership**

Much has been written encouraging teachers to be the second type of leader, called **democratic** or **participatory.** You probably remember such teachers. They involved students in class planning and decision making. You may have had other instructors who led by not leading at all, by being completely permissive. This is called **laissez-faire leadership,** the third style. Which of these three styles is most effective? Does effectiveness depend on the students or the situation?

**Giving Students Choices**

Recent investigations into the effects of giving students choices, conducted in real classrooms, found surprising results (Rosenshine, 1977). In three separate studies of elementary school students from low and middle socioeconomic backgrounds, giving students free or limited choice of activities, work groups, and seating selection, and making students responsible for class planning, were consistently associated with low achievement and little time spent engaged in academic activities (Soar, 1973; Stallings and Kaskowitz, 1975; Solomon and Kendall, 1976). In addition, the classes

*This teacher exerts his leadership in a relaxed, unauthoritarian manner. The goals of classroom leadership are always the same, a positive psychological climate and efficiency of learning. There are as many different ways to achieve these goals, however, as there are different teachers.*

Elizabeth Hamlin/Stock, Boston.

studied by Solomon and Kendall were loud, disorderly, and boisterous; students made little gain in creativity, self-esteem, inquiry, and writing ability when they chose their own activities and were responsible for class planning.

One explanation for this distressing relationship between student choice and lower achievement is that students with many choices are more susceptible to distraction (Rosenshine, 1977). You may have had a similar experience. An instructor tells you to choose a term project, to do anything you want. To decide on a project, you spend some time in the library. While browsing through the references you notice an intriguing article on job opportunities in your field or you spot a book a friend has said is great. Two hours later, you remember that you must decide on a project. You finally get a few ideas, only to discover that the library does not have the books you would need to do the project. Since you must turn in a description of your intended project the next day, you pick one of the remaining possibilities. But there is no time to make sure all the references are available.

In another class, you are given the choice of three projects along with lists of possible references for each (available in the library). You quickly choose your topic and go straight to the right books. It is still possible to be distracted, but there are simply fewer opportunities.

Before we decide that open-ended term projects are bad, we should consider the objectives of each instructor. If the first instructor intended that students decide for themselves what they wanted to learn and then work independently to learn it, an open-ended assignment would be appropriate. Dealing with the distraction is part of the learning experience. Tests of academic content (such as those used in the research reviewed by Rosenshine) would not measure progress toward the teacher's objective of making choices and learning independently. Other outcome measures would be needed.

You should be cautious in interpreting results showing that student choice is related to *little* learning. As Rosenshine warns, "These results do *not* mean that all attempts at informality in the classes studied were disastrous, but rather that *extremes* (our emphasis) of student autonomy and self-direction were usually associated with less task orientation and student engagement, and consequently, less student gain on all measures" (Rosenshine, 1977, p. 12). The following example shows some of the difficulties with unguided choice.

Ms. Wilson listened to her student teacher as she enthusiastically explained her plan to give the second-graders an opportunity to choose what they wanted to do. Ms. Wilson decided to let Ms. Morse give it a try. In different areas of the room, she put out various science materials for the children—magnets, magnifying glasses, weights and measures. She showed all the materials to the children, then told them to choose an area where they would like to go. It turned out to be a very unproductive afternoon. Some areas had too many children, some none; some children wandered from group to group, never getting involved in anything. Many materials were misused; others were used with no particular purpose in mind.

In evaluating the lesson, Ms. Wilson and Ms. Morse discussed the need for specific objectives and clear directions. The children needed more guidance about what could be done with the different materials. Ms. Morse wanted to try the lesson again, this time giving the second-graders a choice, but a clear, directed choice. After making many changes, Ms. Morse tried again. In each area, there were specific directions. The children had a definite purpose as

## *Guidelines*
### *Allowing Students to Make Choices*

**1. The younger the child, the more clear-cut and structured choices should be.**

EXAMPLES
- Elementary school students may be given a choice of several books on a particular topic.
- High school students may be given a choice of topics and books (from a specified list).

**2. Totally unlimited and unguided choice is probably not an effective teaching strategy for most students. Always monitor choices.**

EXAMPLES
- "When you choose your topic, meet with me for a planning session. Topics are due ..."
- Use progress checks to make sure students are not getting lost or distracted.

**3. The level of choice you give students should fit your objectives. If the point is to learn material as efficiently as possible, giving a choice of topic will probably not be a helpful strategy.**

EXAMPLES
- Give more choices when independent learning is an objective.
- Make tests fit the objectives.

---

they experimented with the science materials. The number of children in each area was limited, but the children were provided with time to go to at least two different areas. This time the lesson was a success; the children enjoyed an opportunity to choose, and they learned something from the activity. They requested more afternoons like this one.

The lesson in these findings is not to abandon student choice, but to use choice appropriately. The Guidelines given here should help. In selecting a style of classroom leadership, you will also have to consider a number of other issues.

### Factors in Classroom Leadership

What sort of a leader will you be? Your answer will depend on the subject and grade you teach, the policies of the school, the abilities and expectations of the students, and your own personality. Figure 10–2 presents some of the advantages and limitations of various leadership styles.

Flexibility in Leadership

We do not mean to give the message that you must choose one leadership style and stick with it forever. As with any teaching plan, you will change when the situation warrants change. You may be quite directive in one class, but you may experiment with more democratic methods in another. You might assign one project that is completely open-ended. With some students, you may direct work step-by-step; with others, you may give choices. At the beginning of the year you could be quite directive, and move to more student

**Figure 10–2  Advantages and Limitations of Different Leadership Styles**

| Style | Advantages | Limitations | Potentially Effective in These Situations |
|---|---|---|---|
| Teacher-directed leadership ("Today we will be learning . . .") | 1. Associated with greater achievement gain and engaged time in elementary classrooms. <br> 2. Prevents wasted time and students floundering to make decisions. <br> 3. Allows the teacher to select appropriate activities for individuals. <br> 4. Anxious students perform better with more structure and direction. | 1. Does not give students practice in making choices, becoming self-sufficient. <br> 2. Unless the teacher is also fair, warm, and friendly, can lead to rebellion. <br> 3. Might encourage apathy and dependence on teacher. | 1. Basic skill learning in elementary grades. <br> 2. Large classes, in general, where total democratic or laissez-faire leadership would immobilize class. <br> 3. Begin with teacher direction when this is what students are used to, even if planning to move to other methods. <br> 4. Teaching students who are anxious or fearful. |
| Democratic or student participation leadership ("Let's decide together what we should do about . . .") | 1. Morale will probably be high. <br> 2. Students will learn to be more self-sufficient, depending less on the teacher. <br> 3. Students may be more motivated and committed to class activities, since they were able to help plan them. <br> 4. Helps students practice the life skills of negotiation and making decisions in groups. | 1. Students are not as knowledgeable as the teacher. Their ideas may not be the best approaches to learning the material. <br> 2. Hours may be spent reaching group decisions instead of learning. <br> 3. Achievement, for some children at least, will be lower. | 1. Teaching smaller classes. <br> 2. Teaching subjects where objectives are general and can be reached in a variety of ways. <br> 3. Teaching high-ability students who are not anxious. <br> 4. Possibly more appropriate with older children. |

| Style | Advantages | Limitations | Potentially Effective in These Situations |
|---|---|---|---|

**Figure 10–2** (continued)

| Style | Advantages | Limitations | Potentially Effective in These Situations |
|---|---|---|---|
| Laissez-faire leadership ("It is up to you to use this time to learn what you want.") | 1. Allows some students to excel and discover new reservoirs of creativity.<br>2. Forces students to assume total responsibility for learning. If they are successful in class they may continue to assume responsibility for learning outside the classroom.<br>3. Provides an arena in which to learn about students: Who emerges as a leader? How do individuals handle uncertainty and conflict? | 1. Achievement may be very low.<br>2. Students, parents, and school administrators may be dissatisfied.<br>3. Some students will be totally overwhelmed and lost. | 1. With a few very creative or able students.<br>2. In classes where individual creativity is a primary focus.<br>3. In very small classes.<br>4. As a class experiment to study group processes, communication, leadership, decision making, or anarchy. |

participation later on. If you teach elementary students, you might combine strong teacher direction for basic skills teaching in the morning with more student direction in the afternoon for projects and creative experiences.

No matter what style you choose, you cannot abdicate your role as leader. One way or another, you are responsible for creating and maintaining an organizational structure and learning environment that promotes student growth. This process begins even before there are students in the room to lead. It starts with planning months before the first day of class.

## PLANNING GOOD MANAGEMENT

In making plans for your class, much of what you already have learned in this book should prove helpful. Here we will review some ideas from previous chapters.

## A Look Back at What You Already Know

Problems are prevented when individual variations, like those discussed in Chapters 2, 3, and 4, are taken into account in instructional planning. Sometimes students become involved in disruption because the work assigned is not at their level. A student who reads at the fourth-grade level, but who is told to read silently 10 pages of a text written at the eighth-grade level, will be restless, distractible, discouraged, and a prime candidate for trouble. The student who is bored by lessons well below her ability level may also be interested in finding more exciting activities to fill her time. Over the summer, before you start teaching, you might find out about the range of achievement levels in your class so you can plan to have appropriate materials. If you want to avoid forming expectations about the abilities of particular students before you see their work in your own class, you might ask for a list of scores without names.

In one sense, teachers are preventing discipline problems whenever they make an effort to motivate students. A student involved in mastering course objectives is usually not simultaneously involved in a clash with the teacher or other students. All plans for motivating students are steps toward preventing problems.

In Chapters 5 and 9 you learned that teachers often perpetuate inappropriate behavior by reinforcing it with attention. You can prevent some classroom problems by making rules clear and specific and establishing consequences, for breaking rules. The first week of class is too late to make these plans. As you will see in a minute, effective teachers have these rules and consequences worked out before the students arrive.

Assuming you know to reinforce appropriate behavior, take individual variations into account in planning, and motivate students to value and learn the material, what else can you do? Researchers have recently examined this question and found some answers that seem to work for teachers.

## Some Research Results

Over the past several years, educational psychologists at the Research and Development Center for Teacher Education, the University of Texas at Austin, have studied classroom management. The general approach is to observe and videotape in a large number of classrooms, with intensive observations the first week of school and less frequent visits later in the year. The most and least effective teachers are identified based on the behavior of their classes later in the year.

Next the researchers look at the videotapes of the first weeks of class to see how the effective teachers "got started." Other comparisons are made between the teachers who ultimately have well-behaved, achieving classes and those who have classes with many problems. Based on these comparisons, management principles are developed. These principles are taught to a new group of teachers to see if applying the principles in fact leads to good classroom management. The results have been quite positive. Teachers who apply the principles have fewer problems; their students spend more time working and less time disrupting; and achievement is higher.

The findings of these studies are the basis for two books on classroom management, one for elementary school teachers (Evertson, Emmer, Clements, Sanford, Worsham and Williams, 1984) and another for secondary school teachers (Emmer, Evertson, Clements, Sanford and Worsham, 1984). Many of the ideas in the following pages are taken from these manuals.

## Planning Rules and Procedures

**The Need
for Organization**

At the elementary school level, teachers must lead 20 to 30 students of varying abilities through many different activities each day. Materials must be distributed, collected, and stored. Students often have to move from one area of the room to another or even into other rooms. Often the teacher must work with a small group while the rest of the class is expected to complete assignments on their own. Without efficient rules and procedures, a great deal of time is wasted answering the same question over and over. "My pencil broke. How can I do my math?" "I'm finished with my workbook. What should I do now?" "Steven hit me!"

At the secondary school level, teachers must deal with over 100 students each day, using many materials and perhaps changing rooms. In addition, these teachers face older students who are more likely to challenge their authority. The effective managers studied by Emmer, Evertson and their colleagues at the University of Texas had planned rules and procedures to cope with these situations.

**Procedures**

**Procedures** describe how to accomplish activities in the classroom. At the elementary level, teachers must develop procedures describing the use of desks, storage space, learning centers, shared materials, the teacher's desk, the drinking fountain, sink, pencil sharpener, and bathroom; how and when to go outside the room to the library, office, nurse, gym, playground, lunchroom; how to get permission to speak in class; signals that mean "stop

*Students must be taught the rules and procedures for day-to-day life in the classroom. Simple activities like sharpening a pencil can be the source of problems.*

Ken Karp

what you are doing and look at me"; how to make, collect, record, and return assignments, distribute and collect materials, move around the room, make up work, behave in small groups; what to do during free time, fire drills, public address system announcements; how to assign student monitors, and many others (Evertson et al., 1984).

At the secondary level the procedures are different, but many of the questions remain. How will materials and assignments be distributed and collected? Under what conditions can students leave the room? How do students respond to the bells at the beginning and end of the period? What about late or incomplete work? How will grades be determined? In addition, certain classes need special procedures related to equipment, safety, and supplies (Emmer et al., 1984). Figure 10–3 gives a few examples of specific procedures for elementary and secondary classes.

**Figure 10–3   Examples of Procedures for Elementary And Secondary Classrooms**

---

ELEMENTARY

1.   *Standards for student upkeep of desks and storage areas.*     Some teachers set aside a particular period of time each week for students to clean out their desks; others suggest this be done every day.
2.   *Rules concerning table manners, behavior, noise level in the lunchroom.* Some schools have special awards or contest for behavior in the lunchroom. If your students are too noisy or misbehave a lot, you may wish to establish a reward system for good behavior, or include lunchroom behavior as part of your in-class reward system.
3.   *Methods for informing students about assignments. When and how will you give instructions for assignments?*     Many teachers write the daily assignments on the chalkboard, listed by the reading groups. Other teachers use individual assignment sheets, placed in a folder or notebook for each student. This requires much more time for the teacher, but can be rewarding for the students, when they are allowed to check off or color in a square as assignments are finished.

SECONDARY

1.   *When the tardy bell rings, what are students supposed to do?*     When the bell rings, most effective managers expect talking to stop. A good idea is to have a regular beginning class routine for the first 4 or 5 minutes of class. Students should begin the activity as soon as the bell rings.
2.   *Procedure for dismissing the class.*     Most effective teachers require all students to be in their seats and quiet before they may be dismissed. Because students do not want to be late for their next class, they will generally settle down quickly if you enforce this requirement.

ELEMENTARY OR SECONDARY

1.   *Passing out and collecting materials and supplies.*     To avoid traffic jams, plan distribution stations carefully. Use more than one station. When possible, save time by placing some or all necessary materials or supplies on students' desks or work tables before class starts. Assign student helpers to: (1) help pass out supplies and materials; (2) monitor supply stations or check out/in special equipment; and (3) monitor cleanup of work areas or equipment.

---

*Source: Adapted from Evertson, et al. 1984 and Emmer et al. 1984.*

**Rules** specify expected and forbidden actions in the class. Unlike procedures, rules are often written down and posted. In establishing rules, you should consider what type of atmosphere you want to create. What student behaviors do you need in order to teach effectively? What limits do the students need to guide their behavior (Canter and Canter, 1976)? It is better to have a few general rules that cover many specifics rather than to list all the dos and don'ts. But if specific actions are forbidden, such as chewing gum or smoking in the restrooms, then a rule should make this clear.

5 Rules for Elementary Classes

**Elementary School.** As examples of general rules for elementary school teachers, Evertson and colleagues (1984) suggest five items: (1) *Be polite and helpful*. This applies to behavior toward adults and other students. (2) *Take care of your school*. This might include picking up litter, caring for school property, returning library books, not marking on walls, desks, busses, and so on. (3) *Behave in the cafeteria*. Here students need guidance and examples to make clear what "behaving" means, including how to act in line, type of talking permitted, what to do with food, trays, trash, sharing of food, and so on. (4) *Do not hit, shove, or hurt others*. Again, students need clear explanations of what the teacher means by "hurting." (5) *Keep the bathroom clean*.

Whatever the rules, students need to be taught the behaviors that are included and excluded in each rule. Examples, practice, and discussions will be required before learning is complete. The examples in Box 10–1 show how two teachers explained rules to their students.

If you teach elementary school students, you may discover that you have different rules for different activities. Since this can be confusing until the students learn the rules, you might consider making signs that list the rules for each activity. Then you can post the sign before the activity as a reminder to the class and yourself about the expected behavior. Of course, these rules must be explained and discussed before the signs can have their full effect (Canter and Canter, 1976). Figure 10–4 gives an example of one teacher's signs.

5 Rules for Secondary Classes

**Secondary School.** Rules for secondary students might include these five suggested by Emmer and colleagues: (1) *Bring all needed materials to class*. The teacher must specify type of pen, pencil, paper, notebook, texts, and so on.

**Figure 10–4  Rules for Different Work Areas in an Elementary Class**

---

*Quiet Work*
1. No talking
2. Follow directions
3. Complete assignments

*Rug Time*
1. Sit on rug
2. Keep hands·to self
3. Raise hands

*Transition Periods*
1. Follow directions
2. Walk
3. Clean up

*Free Choice*
1. Choose an activity
2. Follow directions
3. Share supplies

*P.E.*
1. Follow directions
2. Take turns
3. Use equipment appropriately

---

*Source: Adapted from Canter and Canter, Rules for different work area in elementary class in* **Assertive discipline: A take-charge approach for today's educator.** *Los Angeles: Canter & Associates, 1976.*

# BOX 10–1 TEACHING THE RULES ON THE FIRST DAY OF CLASS

## A PRIMARY-GRADE TEACHER

The teacher greets the children as they enter, helps them put on their name tags, and has them tape laminated name strips to a desk. When most of the children are in, she calls roll, checking her pronunciation of names, instructing them in how to answer, and smiling at each one as they respond.

She discusses the rules that are posted: (1) Speak softly; (2) walk in the room; (3) finish your work. She has the children give examples of soft and loud, as well as reasons why each rule is important. She also discusses the stop and go signs beside the door and explains how to turn them around when going to the restroom.

She discusses with the children how to come up and sit on the rug and then has them come up. They listen to a story record, then sing familiar songs and learn one new one.

They discuss some things they did during the summer that they enjoyed.

The teacher holds up a sheet of white paper and explains that they are going to find pictures of things starting with *M*. She demonstrates how to fold it into four sections and how to write a capital and a small *M* in a corner of each section. She shows them a stack of magazines she has at hand and goes through one, having them tell her names of things pictured that begin with *M*. She says they will cut one *M* picture to glue into each section, and when they finish they can use the other sheet of paper she gives them to draw a summer activity they enjoy. She tells them to be sure to put their names on the backs of both papers, telling them that they can copy from their name strips if they need to. She then has the children repeat the instructions back to her.

## A SECONDARY ENGLISH TEACHER

He begins introductions by asking students to write his name, the course title, and room number on the first line of their papers. The information is written on the front board. The teacher tells a little about himself and his name. He talks about the importance of the course (eighth-grade English). He gives reassuring answers to questions about the high school placement tests they will take later in the year.

Next the teacher explains that today they will discuss rules and procedures for the class so that students will know just what he expects from them. He also tells them that they will be expected to take notes (with his help) and that they will finish the task tomorrow and will have to have the papers signed by parents and turn them in, then keep them in their class notebooks. He stresses the importance of neatness on this paper. In the following discussion of basic rules and procedures for the class, the teacher states each requirement in a short sentence, repeating each several times and allowing time for students to copy from an overhead transparency. He walks around the room checking on student work.

Eight minutes before this shortened period is to end, the teacher tells students to put the rules away and to get out another paper. Using a poster display he has prepared, he shows students how to head their paper and gives them a short assignment to be handed in today in class. This task is to copy several sentences that are written on the board and circle all the nouns. The teacher demonstrates by circling a noun in the first sentence. Students work on this activity while the teacher monitors.

When the bell is about to ring, the teacher has students pass up their papers and prepare to leave. They leave when dismissed by the teacher.

*Adapted from Evertson, et al. 1984 and Emmer et al. 1984.*

(2) *Be in your seat and ready to work when the bell rings.* Many teachers have a standard beginning activity for the class, such as a warmup exercise on the board or a requirement that students have paper with a proper heading ready when the bell rings. (3) *Obtain permission before speaking or leaving your seat.* There may be exceptions to this rule, such as being able to sharpen pencils or come to the teacher's desk when the teacher is not presenting a lesson. (4) *Respect and be polite to all people.* This covers fighting, verbal abuse, and general troublemaking. (5) *Respect other people's property.* Here property includes the school's, the teacher's, and that belonging to other students. Again, rules must be explained and taught. Box 10–1 presents an example of a secondary school teacher explaining the rules to his class.

Clear
and Logical
Consequences

**Consequences.** As soon as you decide on your rules and procedures, you must consider what you will do when a student breaks a rule or does not follow a procedure. It is too late to make this decision after the rule has been broken. For many infractions, a logical consequence is to have the student go back and do it right. Students who run in the hall may have to return and walk properly. Incomplete papers can be redone. Materials left out should be replaced.

You will have to determine positive and negative consequences for student actions. The previous chapter discussed the role of consequences in class management. Our main point here is that these decisions must be made early so students can be informed about the consequences of following or breaking the rules in your class.

If you have thought through the rules and procedures you will need to teach effectively, and determined consequences for following and breaking rules, you are on your way to having a well-managed class. Now you must continue to encourage good discipline by getting off to a good start.

*This teacher has posted the consequences for interrupting during a meeting. One interruption receives a warning. Students who interrupt again must sit under the loft, and the third violation leads to extra work.*

Stan Wakefield

## The First Weeks of Class

What do effective teachers really do during those first critical days and weeks? A recent study by Emmer, Evertson, and Anderson (1980) gives us some idea. These researchers sent trained observers into the classrooms of 29 third-grade teachers on the first day of class. The observers made extensive narrative records of the processes in each room. Observers also assessed the task involvement of the students every 15 minutes. Each classroom was observed 8 to 10 times during the first three weeks of the school year, and then about once every three weeks from November until the end of school.

**Effective Managers for Elementary Students.**  Using the later observations, Emmer and colleagues were able to identify two subgroups of teachers: those who were very effective managers over this year, and those who were not effective. Comparing the first-week activities of the two groups, it was clear that they used very different activities and behaviors for management at the beginning of the year. In the effective teachers' classrooms, the following characteristics were noted:

A Good Start

1. Rules and procedures were integrated into workable systems, and students were taught these systems directly.
2. The very first day was well organized: name tags were ready; interesting activities that could be done individually were immediately provided.
3. Teachers stayed with their students.
4. When all students were present, the teachers began to teach the class the most needed rules and procedures, explaining clearly, giving examples and reasons.
5. During the first weeks, effective managers spent quite a bit of time teaching the rules. Some used guided practice to teach procedures; others used rewards to shape behavior. Most taught students to respond to some signal like a bell.
6. The teachers worked with the group as a whole at first on enjoyable academic activities. They did not rush to get students into groups or to get them started in readers. This whole-class work gave the teachers a better opportunity to continue monitoring all students' learning of the rule and procedures.
7. Misbehavior was stopped quickly in a firm but not harsh manner.

A Bad Start

In contrast, in the ineffective teachers' classrooms the following characteristics were noted:

1. Rules and procedures were not workable or were vague. Students wandered aimlessly, not knowing exactly how to deal with essentials like sharpening pencils and going to the restroom.
2. Procedures were not taught, practiced, or consistently enforced.
3. Teachers often left the room. Many became absorbed in paperwork or in helping one student.
4. Students had to ask each other what they should be doing or simply talked because they had nothing productive to do.
5. The teachers became less effective leaders, and students had to fill the leadership void.
6. Consequences of both positive and negative behaviors were not clear to students, nor were the consequences consistently presented.

Even though effective managers lost some instructional time during the first few weeks of the year by focusing on rules and procedures, they gained

Ken Karp

*Good discipline begins the first day of class. Students should have something interesting to do right away, and the teacher should avoid becoming engrossed with one or two people.*

time over the entire year. Their classes were seldom interrupted by student misbehavior or general confusion and disorganization. The first few weeks are an important investment in positive management for the whole year.

**Other Ideas for Getting Started**

Dreikurs and colleagues have some other recommendations for getting started effectively (Dreikurs, Grunwald and Pepper, 1971). In an elementary school classroom, the teacher should have a variety of activities planned so that each student will form a good impression of the new class and not become bored by one or two long lessons the first day. The teacher should be familiar with the students' names, be able to pronounce them correctly, and have some positive information about each student that can be mentioned in a private greeting. During the first morning, the teacher should make sure students can recognize and pronounce his or her name. A simple set of rules and a daily routine should be made clear in a relaxed and cheerful discussion.

Praise and positive expectations should be directed toward the group as a whole, to begin to build group spirit. Statements such as "I think this is going to be a good class," "We are going to learn a lot together," said with genuine conviction, are better than statements that emphasize differences between students, such as "Jason has already learned how to put his materials away quickly before lunch."

**Getting Started in Secondary School**

**Effective Managers for Secondary Students.**    What about getting started in the secondary school? It appears that many of the differences between effective and ineffective elementary school teachers still hold at the secondary level. Again, effective managers focus on establishing rules, procedures, and expectations on the first day of class. These standards for academic work and class behavior are clearly communicated to students and consistently enforced during the first weeks of class. Student behavior is closely monitored, and infractions of the rules are dealt with quickly. In classes with lower-ability

**358**

students, work cycles are shorter. Better teachers do not require these students to spend long, unbroken periods of time on one type of activity. Instead, they move students smoothly through several different tasks in each period. In general, effective teachers keep careful track of each student's progress so students cannot avoid work without facing consequences (Emmer and Evertson, 1982).

With all this close monitoring and consistent enforcement of the rules, you may wonder if effective secondary teachers must be grim and humorless. Not necessarily. The effective managers in one study also smiled and joked more with their students (Moskowitz and Hayman, 1976). As any experienced teacher can tell you, there is much more to smile about when the class is cooperative and well behaved.

We have been talking to this point about getting started on the right foot. But, as we said at the beginning of this chapter, constant maintenance is required.

# MAINTAINING EFFECTIVE DISCIPLINE

Preventing
Problems

Jacob Kounin (1970) studied classroom management by observing effective and ineffective teachers in action. He located a group of teachers whose classes were relatively free of problems and a group of teachers whose classes were continually plagued by chaos and disruption. By observing what teachers actually did, Kounin discovered that the two groups of teachers were not very different in the way they handled discipline once problems arose. The difference was that successful managers were much better at *preventing* problems.

## Preventing Problems

In his observations of effective teachers, Kounin noted that these individuals were skilled at leading a group and keeping activities moving. They made sure students had something productive to do at all times. There were few times when students simply had to wait or watch others work. Activities were well organized and moved at a good pace. Even though these effective teachers were experts at group management, they were aware of individual students, so no one could "hide" in the group.

Kounin concluded that effective classroom managers were especially skilled in four areas: "withitness," overlapping activities, group focus, and movement management (Doyle, 1977). More recent research continues to confirm the importance of these factors (Emmer and Evertson, 1981).

**Withitness.** **Withitness** is the ability to communicate to students that you are aware of what is happening in the classroom, that you "don't miss anything." With-it teachers seem to have "eyes in the back of their heads." They avoid becoming absorbed or interacting with a few students, since this encourages the rest of the class to wander.

Timing and
Target Errors

These teachers stop minor disruptions effectively before they become major. They also know who instigated the problem, and they make sure the right people are dealt with. In other words, they do not make what Kounin called *timing errors* (waiting too long before intervening) or *target errors* (blaming the wrong student, letting the real perpetrators escape the responsibility for their behavior).

If two problems occur at the same time, effective managers deal with the most serious one first. For example, a teacher who tells two students to stop whispering but ignores even a brief shoving match at the pencil sharpener communicates to students a lack of awareness. Students begin to believe they can "get away with almost anything," if they are clever (Charles, 1981).

Being withit does not mean publicly correcting every minor infraction of the rules. This kind of public attention may actually reinforce the misbehavior, as we saw in an earlier chapter. Teachers who frequently correct students do not necessarily have the most well-behaved classes (Irving and Martin, 1982). The key is to know what is happening so you can prevent problems. Emmer and colleagues (1984) suggest four simple ways to stop misbehavior quickly:

4 Ways to Stop
Misbehavior

1. Make eye contact or move closer to the offender. Other nonverbal signals such as pointing to work might be helpful. Make sure the student actually stops the inappropriate behavior and gets back to work. If you do not, students will learn to ignore your signals.

2. If students are not performing a class procedure correctly, remind the students of the procedure and have them do it correctly.

3. In a calm, unhostile way, ask the student to state the correct rule or procedure, then follow it.

4. Tell the student in a clear, assertive, and unhostile way to stop. (We will discuss more about assertive messages to students in a later section.)

Although it is undeniably important to be firm and consistent in handling problems, Kounin found that dealing with the right offender at the right time was even more critical for good class management (Charles, 1981).

Handling
a Group

**Overlapping and Group Focus.** **Overlapping** is the ability to keep track of and supervise several activities at the same time. Success in this area also requires constant monitoring of the class. In many ways, a teacher must continually manage what Dunkin and Biddle (1974) have called a "three-ring circus." For example, a teacher might have to check the work of an individual and at the same time keep a small group working by saying, "Right, go on" (Charles, 1981).

**Group focus** is the ability to keep as many students as possible involved in appropriate class activities, avoiding a focus on one or two students. This means that all students should have something to do during a lesson. If someone is working a problem at the board, the other students should work the same problem at their desks. The teacher might ask everyone to write the answer to a question, then call on individuals to respond while the rest of the class compares their answers. Choral responses might be required while the teacher moves around the room to make sure everyone is participating (Charles, 1981). The goal is for each individual to be involved and accountable for knowing the information being presented.

Smooth
Transitions

**Movement Management.** **Movement management** is the ability to keep the lessons and the group moving by making smooth transitions, maintaining an appropriate pace, and using variety when changes are necessary. The effective teacher avoids abrupt transitions, such as announcing a new activity before gaining the students' attention or starting a new activity, then going back to the old activity (Charles, 1981). In all these situations one-third of the class will be doing the new activity, many will be on the old lesson, several will be asking other students what to do, some will be taking the opportunity to have a little fun, and most will be confused.

Avoiding Slowdowns

Another type of error involves problems with what Kounin called *slowdowns*, or taking too much time to start new activities. Sometimes teachers give too many directions. ("Everyone take out a piece of paper . . . Now get a pencil . . . Print your name in the upper left hand corner . . . Let's see the names . . . Now put the date in the upper left corner . . . Today is . . . ). By the time the teacher finishes, the students have lost interest in the project and gone on to entertain themselves. Another problem arises when teachers have students work one at a time while the rest of the class is expected to wait and watch. Charles (1981) gives this example:

> During a science lesson the teacher began, "Row one may get up and get their beakers. Row two may get theirs. Now row three. Now, row one may line up to put salt in their beakers. Row two may follow them," and so forth. When each row had gotten the salt, the teacher had them go row by row to get some water. This left the rest of the class sitting at their desks with no direction. At best they were doing nothing. Probably they were dreaming up something with which to entertain themselves.
>
> . . . After every child had the necessary elements . . . the teacher proceeded. "Okay, Roy, now pour the vinegar into the water while we watch. Now Susie, it's your turn. Patti, you're next." The teacher had the students do the activity singly when it would have made sense to have the class do it together (pp. 52–54).

A teacher who successfully demonstrated withitness, overlapping activities, group focus, and movement management would have a class filled with actively engaged students who could not escape the teacher's all-seeing eye. This need not be a grim classroom; more likely it would be a busy class with students who experience success in learning instead of turning to misbehavior to gain attention and achieve status. One of the best ways of coping with discipline problems is preventing them by keeping the entire group focused on learning productively.

Kounin's work relied on observation of teachers to determine effective management strategies. He identified relationships between teacher actions and student involvement in learning. He did not ask teachers to try different strategies and then measure the impact of those strategies on students. A large study conducted recently in first-grade classrooms did use a more experimental approach by having teachers actually test different management techniques.

## Techniques for Primary Grades

Testing Management Strategies

In order to identify principles of classroom organization and management that are related to student learning, Anderson and colleagues (Anderson, Evertson and Brophy, 1979) gave one group of teachers an instructional model to follow when teaching reading. The model consisted of principles that previous research indicated were probably important in managing classrooms and preventing discipline problems. The teachers were observed using the principles, and student learning was measured. Another group of teachers, who had not been given the instructional model to test, was also observed and their students' achievement was measured.

Based on the results of this study, 12 of the original principles were identified as being related to reading achievement. The 10 principles most relevant to class management are listed below:

Management
Principles

1. Transitions should be quick and orderly. Before change and movement begin, students should know where they are expected to go and what they will be doing next. Shouting orders while children attempt to move and listen at the same time is ineffective.

2. Materials for the reading group should be arranged before the children are called. Instruction should begin immediately as soon as all children arrive.

3. Arrange small groups of childen for working so that they face the wall and the teacher has her back to the wall and faces the room. In this position, she can work with the small group while monitoring the rest of the class. In addition, the students in the group are less distracted by action in the room.

4. Give a *brief* overview of the content at the beginning of the lesson.

5. Make sure students understand directions or explanations by asking them to summarize or by questioning them about the explanation.

6. Call on children in order around the circle instead of randomly.

7. Avoid calling on volunteers.

8. Gently discourage students from calling out answers.

9. Make sure that each student has a chance to respond, practice, and receive feedback.

10. Meet reading groups for as long as possible, depending on the attention spans of the children (about 25 to 35 minutes for an average-ability first-grade group).

Anderson and colleagues reached two conclusions about management that support several principles of cognitive learning discussed in Chapter 6. First, young students may not process information in the same way that we do. The classroom is filled with stimuli competing for students attention. It is not always obvious to students what is important. Teachers must clearly direct the students' attention and help them focus on the appropriate material. Second, young students learn by doing and being actively involved. Management strategies that keep all students participating will encourage learning.

## Special Problems with Secondary Students

Emmer and colleagues (1984) list four special problems that can threaten any management system. The effective secondary school teachers they studied had several good ways to handle these problems.

Incomplete
Work

The first problem is the student who seldom completes work. If the student is able to do the work, the teacher must keep accurate records so everyone will be sure what the student is actually doing. The teacher may need to contact the parents, principal, counselor, or other teachers for help. But the most important factor is to enforce the established consequences for incomplete work. Do not pass the student because you know he or she is "bright enough" to pass. Canter and Canter (1976) suggest teachers make it clear to these students that the choice is theirs: They can do the work and pass or not do the work and face the consequences.

The second problem involves students who continually break the same rules. They constantly forget materials or speak without raising their hand, for example. Emmer and colleagues make these suggestions. Seat the students away from others who might be influenced by them. Try to catch the students before they break the rules, but if rules are broken, be consistent in applying established consequences. Do not accept promises to do better next time. Teach the students how to monitor their own behavior. Some of the self-management techniques described in the previous chapter should be helpful. Finally, remain friendly with the students. Try to catch them in a good moment so you can talk to them about something other than their rule-breaking.

The defiant, hostile student can pose real problems for many teachers. If there is an outbreak, you should try to get out of the situation as soon as possible; everyone loses in a public power struggle. One possibility is to give the student a chance to save face and cool down by saying, "It's your choice to cooperate or not. You can take a minute to think about it." If the student complies, you may talk later about controlling the outbursts in class. If the student refuses, you can tell him or her to wait in the hall until you get the class started on work and can step outside for a private talk. If the student refuses to leave, send another class member for the assistant principal. Again, follow through. If the student complies before help arrives, do not let him or her off the hook. If the problem is frequent, you might have a conference with the counselor, parents, or other teachers. If the problem is an unreconcilable clash of personalities, the student should be transferred to another teacher.

The final type of problem is violence or destruction of property. The first step is to send for help and get the names of participants and witnesses. Then get rid of any crowd that may have gathered; an audience will only make things worse. Do not step in to break up a fight without help. Make sure the school office is aware of the incident. Usually the school has a policy for dealing with these situations.

The studies described thus far by Kounin, Anderson, Emmer, and others have looked to classroom interactions for ideas about building a positive learning environment. Another source of help for teachers in managing classrooms is theory and research on **group dynamics** from social psychology. As we noted earlier in the chapter, the teacher is the leader of the classroom group, responsible for establishing and maintaining a good working atmosphere. Group cohesiveness and shared norms characterize a positive atmosphere (Weber, 1977).

## Group Cohesiveness and Norms

In order to work well together, group members must be unified and **cohesive**—that is, they must have a positive group spirit. Such students identify with the group and are glad to be members. You have probably experienced this group spirit and identification as a member of a team, club, or performing ensemble. Johnson and Bany (1970) offer a number of suggestions for building group unity, three of which are found in the Guidelines given here.

A good working atmosphere also means that members of the group share common **norms.** These norms are standards for how work will be done, how good is good enough, how people will treat each other, how rule-breakers

# Guidelines
## Developing Group Cohesiveness

**1. Being a member of the group should be desirable and attractive to students. Students must be able to be proud or at least satisfied to be in the group. (You can see the problem some classes, labeled by students "dummy" English or math, would have in making members glad to be a part of the class.)**

EXAMPLES
- Model pride in being a part of the group.
- Point out things the group does well.

**2. Goals should be clear to students and valued by most members of the group.**

EXAMPLES
- When possible, involve students in setting goals.
- Give an overview of the day's goals at the beginning of class.

**3. Communication among members should be encouraged as much as possible without detracting from instruction.**

EXAMPLES
- Use group projects, teams, task forces, and small and large discussion groups to encourage communication while still working on the course material.
- Allow time at the end of the period to talk if the work gets done first.

*Adapted from L. V. Johnson and M. A. Bany, **Classroom management: Theory and skill training.** New York: Macmillan, 1970.*

will be dealt with. Teachers begin to establish unity and norms on the first day of class.

### The Lessons of Experience

Teacher-Tested Ideas

We have described approaches to maintaining a positive climate in the classroom by emphasizing problem prevention, group cohesiveness, and shared group norms. Sometimes teachers learn a few helpful strategies from experience. Figure 10–5 is a checklist of teacher-tested suggestions for managing classrooms and preventing problems.

# THE NEED FOR COMMUNICATION

We believe communication between teacher and students is essential when problems arise. Communication is more than "teacher talk — student listen." It is more than simply the words exchanged between individuals. We communicate in many ways.

## Figure 10–5 Teacher-Tested Ideas for Preventing Classroom Problems

1. Do not talk to the chalkboard, talk to the class. Do not turn your back to the class for long periods of time.
2. Begin class on time.
3. Do not use lowered grades or extra work as punishment for inappropriate class behavior.
4. If a rule is broken, warn students once, then follow through with the previously established consequence for breaking the rule.
5. Intervene immediately in serious matters threatening the safety of students (for example, fights).
6. Do not use sarcasm.
7. Be polite to students and reinforce student politeness.
8. Be firm and consistent in dealing with deliberate misconduct. Do not let yourself be talked out of a position you have taken, but do not take a position you cannot hold in the first place. In other words, do not make threats you cannot carry out, then back down.
9. Communicate to the class in a confident manner that you expect their cooperation.
10. Remain calm and pleasant; do not overlook serious disruptions.
11. Use punishment only as a last resort when positive procedures or problem solving have not improved the situation.
12. Move around the room and know what is happening in each area. Do not become engrossed with a few students.

Source: Adapted from R. L. Schain and M. Polner, **Using effective discipline for better class control.** Englewood Cliffs, N.J.: Prentice-Hall, 1964.

## Communication and Metacommunication

Messages
to Students

TEACHER: Carl, Where is your homework?

CARL: I left it in my Dad's car this morning.

TEACHER: Again? You will have to bring me a note tomorrow from your father saying that you actually did the homework. I won't grade it without the note.

MESSAGE RECEIVED BY CARL You are lying. I can't trust you. I need proof you did the work.

TEACHER: Sit every other desk. Put all your things under your desk. Jane and Laurel, you are sitting too close together. One of you move up here!

MESSAGE RECEIVED BY JANE AND LAUREL I expect you two to cheat on this test.

A new student comes to Ms. Lincoln's kindergarten. The child is messy and unwashed. Ms. Lincoln puts her hand lightly on the girl's shoulder and says, "I know you will like it here." Her muscles tense and she leans away from the child.

MESSAGE RECEIVED BY
  THE STUDENT   I don't like you. I think you are bad.

**Message Sent and Message Received**

In all interactions, there is a message sent and a message received. Sometimes teachers believe they are sending one message, but their voice tones, body positions, choice of words, or gestures communicate a different message. The underlying or hidden message is the **metacommunication.** Students may hear the metacommunication, at some level, and respond to it without ever stopping to say to themselves "The Teacher said . . . but I know she means . . ." For example, a student may respond with hostility if he or she feels insulted by the teacher (or by another student), but the student may not be able to say exactly where the feeling of being insulted came from. Perhaps it was in the voice tone, not the words, of the teacher. In such cases, the teacher may feel attacked for no reason. "What did I say? All I said was . . . ." The first principle of communication is that people respond to what they think was said or meant, to what they heard, not necessarily to the message sent or intended.

**Paraphrasing**

There are many exercises you can try in your college courses, or in your classroom when you become a teacher, to practice sending and receiving messages accurately. Students in our classes have told us of one instructor at the college who encourages accurate communication using the paraphrase rule. In class discussion, before any participant, including the teacher, is allowed to respond to any other participant, he or she must summarize what the previous speaker said. If the summary is wrong, indicating the speaker was misunderstood, the speaker must explain again. The respondent then tries again to paraphrase, until the speaker agrees that the listener has heard the correct message.

There are a few advantages to using the paraphrase rule:

1.  Students listen more carefully to each other, since they must paraphrase correctly before speaking themselves.
2.  Students learn to be clearer in their communications by hearing how other people interpret their messages.
3.  Sometimes two people only think they disagree (or agree) on a subject. Often one person disagrees with something the other person never meant to say.

Paraphrasing is more than a classroom exercise. It can be the first step in communicating with your students. Before a teacher can do anything to deal appropriately with a student problem, he or she must know what the real problem is. A student who says, "That was the dumbest book. Why did we have to read it?" may really be saying, "The book was too difficult for me. I couldn't read it and I feel dumb." A teacher who responds to the Why question with a justification for the choice of reading material has missed the point. The student may feel even worse. Now he is not only dumb, he has also missed out on an experience the teacher believes is important. He will never catch up! The crucial first step in responding to a classroom problem is determining what sort of response is needed.

# Diagnosis: Who Owns the Problem?

Whose Problem
Is It?   Thomas Gordon (1974) has described a system for determining what kind of response is needed in a problem situation. Gordon's system begins with this question: Who owns the problem? If it is really the student's problem, a response called active listening (or empathetic listening) is recommended. As you will see later, active or empathetic listening is closely related to the process of paraphrasing. If the teacher owns the problem, then other approaches are called for.

Deciding who owns the problem is critical. If the student owns the problem, the teacher becomes a counselor and supporter, helping the student find his or her own solution. Since it is not the teacher's problem, the teacher cannot assume responsibility for it. If the teacher owns the problem, the teacher must find a solution through problem solving with the student.

It is often difficult to stand back from classroom problems and take an objective look. As a teacher, you may find many student behaviors unacceptable, unpleasant, or troubling. According to Gordon, the key to good teacher-student relationships is determining why you are troubled by the behavior and whose problem it is. Here are three troubling situations:

1. A student writes obscene words and draws explicit illustrations in an encyclopedia.
2. A student tells you that his mother and father had a bad fight and he hates his father.
3. A student quietly reads a newspaper in the back of the room.

Teacher's
Problem   Why are these behaviors troubling? If you are bothered and feel unaccepting of the student's behavior because it has a concrete tangible effect on you as a teacher and you are blocked from reaching your goals by the student's action, then *you* own the problem. It is your responsibility to confront the student and seek a solution. A teacher-owned problem appears to be present in the first situation described above, the young pornographer.

Student's
Problem   If you feel annoyed or unaccepting of the student's behavior because you wish he or she would feel or act differently, or because you are embarrassed for the child, then it is probably the student's problem. The test question is this: Does this student's action concretely and tangibly affect me or prevent me from fulfilling my role as a teacher? The student who hated his father in the second situation above did not prevent the teacher from teaching, even though the teacher may have wished that the student felt differently about his father. The problem is really the student's, and he must find his own solution.

Situation 3 is more difficult to diagnose. We have lengthy debates in our class about whose problem it is when a student reads a newspaper in class. One argument is that the teacher is not interfered with in any way, so it is the student's problem. Another argument is that teachers might find the paper reading distracting during a lecture, so it is their problem and they must find a solution. In a gray area such as this, it probably depends on the teacher and how he or she actually experiences the student behavior.

Having decided who owns the problem, it is time to act.

## Counseling — The Student's Problem

Consider the following dialogue:

STUDENT: This book is really dumb! Why did we have to read it?

TEACHER: You are upset that you had to read the book. It seemed like a worthless assignment to you. [Teacher paraphrases the student's statement, trying to hear the emotions as well as the words.]

STUDENT: Yeah! Well it wasn't really worthless. I mean I don't know if it was. I couldn't read it.

TEACHER: You had difficulty with the book. You weren't able to read it, and that bothers you.

STUDENT: Sure, I felt really dumb. I know I can write a good report, but I need a different book for reading.

TEACHER: Would you like to choose one?

STUDENT: Great! I have two ideas . . .

**Empathetic Listening**

Here the teacher used what Charles Kelley (1974) calls **empathetic listening** to allow the student to find a solution. By trying to hear the student and avoiding jumping in too quickly with advice, solutions, criticisms, reprimands, or interrogations, the teacher kept the communication lines open. Here are a few *unhelpful* responses the teacher might have made:

**Unhelpful Responses**

I choose the book because it is the best example of . . . in our library. You will need to have read it for your English II class next year. [Teacher justifies choice, so student cannot admit that this important assignment is too difficult.]

Did you really read it? I bet you didn't do the work and now you want out of the assignment. [Teacher accuses, and student hears, "She doesn't trust me!" and must defend himself or accept the teacher's view of him.]

*With both students speaking at once, does either know what the other is saying? Can the other students follow either argument? It might be interesting to find out by introducing the paraphrase rule.*

Sybil Shelton/Monkmeyer Press Photo Service

Your job is to read the book, not ask me why. I know what's best. [Teacher pulls rank, and student hears "You are too dumb or immature to decide what is good for you!" Student can rebel or passively accept the teacher's judgment.]

Empathetic listening can be a helpful response when students bring problems to you. To make such a response, you reflect to the student what you hear him or her saying. This reflection is more than a parroting of the student's words; it is a statement that captures the emotions, intent, and meaning behind the words. Sokolove, Sadker, and Sadker (1977, p. 249) summarize the components of empathetic listening as follows:

Making
an Empathetic
Response

1. Blocking out external stimuli.
2. Attending carefully to both the verbal and nonverbal messages of the speaker.
3. Differentiating between the intellectual and emotional content of the message.
4. Making inferences regarding the feelings experienced by the speaker.

When students realize they have been heard, and not evaluated negatively for what they have said and felt, they are free to trust the teacher and talk more. Sometimes the true problem surfaces only later in the conversation. In their study of effective and ineffective elementary school teachers, Emmer and colleagues found that teachers who had well-managed classrooms with few discipline problems were good listeners and used their listening skills to identify the concerns of their students correctly (Emmer, Evertson and Anderson, 1980).

## Confrontation and Assertive Discipline

Now let us assume a student is doing something that actively interferes with teaching. The instructor decides the student must stop. The problem is the teacher's. Confrontation, not counseling, is required.

"I" Messages

**"I" Messages.**   Gordon (1974) recommends sending an **"I" message** if the teacher must intervene and change the student's behavior. Basically this means telling students, in a straightforward, assertive, and nonjudgmental way, what they are doing, how it affects you as a teacher, and how you feel about it. The students are then free to change voluntarily, and often do. Here are some "I" messages:

When you leave your locker open, I sometimes bump into it and hurt myself.

When you all call out answers, I cannot concentrate on each answer and I feel frustrated.

These are student actions that bother the teacher, so the problem is the teacher's and not the student's.

**Assertive Discipline.**   Lee and Marlene Canter (1976) suggest other approaches for dealing with the teacher's problem. They call their method **assertive discipline.** It involves teacher behavior that is neither wishywashy and passive nor hostile and aggressive. Teachers are assertive when they make their expectations clear and follow through with established consequences. Students then have a clear choice: They can follow the rules or accept the consequences. Many teachers are ineffective with students because they are either passive or hostile.

The passive or nonassertive response style involves five key mistakes. (1) Instead of telling the student directly what to do, the teacher tells, or often *asks*, the student to accomplish an intermediate goal. For example, instead of telling the student to stop shoving, the teacher might ask the student to *try* to stop or *think about* stopping. (2) The teacher says something about the behavior without telling the child what to do. The teacher might say, "Why are you doing that? Don't you know the rules?" or "Sam, you are disturbing the class." (3) The teacher might clearly state what should happen, but never follow through with the established consequences, giving the students "one more chance" every time. (4) A related problem is using threats but seldom following through, often because the threat is too severe. (5) Finally, teachers may ignore behavior that should receive a response or wait too long before responding.

A hostile response style involves different mistakes. (1) Teachers may make "you" statements condemning the student without stating clearly what the student should be doing. For example, they may say, "You should be ashamed of the way you're behaving!" "You never listen!" "You are acting like a baby!" (2) They threaten the students angrily, but often don't follow through, as in "You'll be very sorry you did that when I get through with you!" (3) The consequences they impose are too severe. For example, one teacher observed by Canter and Canter (1976) told a student in PE class that he would have to sit on the bench for three weeks. A few days later the team in the class was short one member and the teacher let the student play, never returning him to the bench to complete the three week "sentence." (4) At times teachers get so fed up with students that they respond with physical force. Often a teacher who has been passive may explode when students persist in misbehaving.

*Miss Applegate may have gone too far in being assertive with this class.*

© 1979 Leo Cullum. Reprinted with permission.

"GOOD MORNING, CHILDREN. MY NAME IS MISS APPLEGATE. ONE FALSE MOVE AND I'LL KILL YOU."

In contrast to passive and hostile styles, an assertive response communicates to the students that you care too much about them and the process of learning to allow inappropriate behavior to persist. Assertive teachers clearly state what they expect. To be most effective, the teachers often look into a student's eyes when speaking, address the student by name, perhaps touching the student's shoulder while talking. The teachers' voice tone is calm, firm, and confident. They are not sidetracked by accusations such as: "You just don't understand!" or "You don't like me!". Assertive teachers do not get into a debate about the fairness of the rules. They expect changes, not promises or apologies. Box 10–2 gives examples of passive, hostile, and assertive responses to several common situations.

---

## BOX 10–2 PASSIVE, HOSTILE, AND ASSERTIVE TEACHER RESPONSES

*A 3rd grade teacher had a number of children who frequently would push and shove in order to be first in line. This would result in constant fighting and yelling before the class went outside. Before lunch the problem occurs again.*

### Non-Assertive Response

The teacher walks up to the children and states, "I don't know what's wrong with you children. You're pushing and shoving again. You children need to learn how to line up like good boys and girls. Now I want you all to try to do so."

### Hostile Response

The teacher walks up to the children who were pushing and grabs them and roughly yanks them to the back of the line. Once they are at the end of the line she angrily states, "You push and shove others, I'll push and shove you!"

### Assertive Response

The teacher firmly tells the children, "Stop pushing and shoving." To back up her words, she makes all the children who were pushing and shoving go to the back of the line.

*An 8th grade science teacher had a problem with students frequently cheating on tests, During an exam he observed several students openly looking at each others' papers.*

### Non-Assertive Response

The teacher states, "Don't forget, I have told you if I catch anyone cheating they will be sorry. So I hope any of you who may be thinking of cheating won't do it."

### Hostile Response

He storms up to the students and rips up their papers angrily stating, 'I hate cheaters. You should be ashamed of yourselves."

### Assertive Response

He calls the students to his desk and firmly states, "There is no cheating in this class! I saw you looking at each other's papers, so you all get an 'F' on the test."

Source: Adapted from Canter and Canter (1976) Passive, Hostile and assertive teacher responses in **Assertive discipline: A take-charge approach for today's educator.** Los Angeles: Canter & Associates, 1976.

**Conflict and Negotiations.** If "I" messages or other assertive responses fail and the student persists, teacher and student are in a conflict situation. When two individuals are in conflict, their actions are incompatible. Johnson (1972) states that an interpersonal conflict exists "whenever an action by one person prevents, obstructs, or interferes with the actions of another person" (p. 203). In a conflict, each participant believes he or she cannot win unless the other person loses.

Several pitfalls are present when two people are in conflict. One common pitfall is that the two individuals become less able to perceive each other's behavior accurately. Research has shown that the angrier you get with other people, the more you see them as the villains and yourself as an innocent victim. Their mistakes are vividly clear to you, but your own actions seem perfectly justified. Since you feel the other people are in the wrong and they feel just as strongly that it is all your fault, very little mutual trust is possible. A cooperative solution to the problem is almost impossible. In fact, by the time the discussion has gone on a few minutes, the original problem is lost in a sea of charges, countercharges, and self-defense (Johnson, 1972).

Imposing
a Solution
or Giving In

There are three methods of resolving a conflict between teacher and student. One is for the teacher to impose a solution. This may be necessary during an emergency, such as when a defiant student refuses to go to the hall to discuss a public outbreak. The second method is for the teacher to give in to student demands. It is possible that you might be convinced by a particularly compelling student argument, but generally it is a bad idea to be talked out of a position.

A Better
Solution

There are problems when either the teacher or the student gives in completely. In each case, someone is the loser and has no impact on the final decision. Gordon recommends a third approach, which he calls the *no-lose method*. Using this strategy, the needs of both the teacher and the students are taken into account in the solution. No one person is expected to give in completely, and all participants retain respect for themselves and each other.

Steps

The no-lose method is a six-step problem-solving strategy:

1.  *Define the problem:* What exactly are the behaviors involved? What does each person want? (Use active listening to help students pinpoint the real problem.)
2.  *Generate many possible solutions:* Brainstorm, but allow *no* evaluation of any ideas yet.
3.  *Evaluate each solution:* Any participant may veto any idea. If no solutions are found to be acceptable, brainstorm again.
4.  *Make a decision:* Choose one solution through consensus, no voting allowed. In the end everyone must be satisfied with the solution.
5.  *Determine how to implement the solution:* What will be needed? Who will be responsible for each task? What is the timetable?
6.  *Assess the success of the solution:* After trying the solution for a while, ask: "Are we satisfied with our decision? How well is it working? Should we make some changes?

We have described the suggestions of Charles Kelley, Lee and Marlene Canter, and Thomas Gordon for counseling and confronting students because these approaches give teachers specific strategies to try in difficult situations. We have used these methods ourselves and found them helpful. By focusing on listening and problem solving, we have found it easier to see the student's side of an issue and remain positive toward students as individuals, even when their behavior is a problem.

## SUMMARY

1. It is the responsibility of the teacher as leader to establish and maintain an atmosphere in the classroom that encourages learning.

2. There are three basic types of leadership: teacher-centered, democratic, and laissez-faire.

3. The most effective teachers set rules and establish procedures for handling predictable problems. Consequences should be established for following and breaking the rules, so the teacher and the students know what will happen in either case.

4. During the first days of class teachers must spend the necessary time to teach rules and procedures, then monitor students to make sure they are following these guidelines.

5. Quick and consistent responses to infractions of the rules characterize effective teachers. The first days should be organized so that enjoyable activities are available for everyone and students spend little time with nothing to do.

6. To create a positive environment, teachers must actively prevent problems by taking individual differences into account, maintaining student motivation, and reinforcing positive behavior.

7. Successful problem preventers are skilled in four areas described by Kounin: withitness, overlapping, group focus, and movement management.

8. Studies by Evertson, Emmer, and colleagues have identified the specific management strategies of successful elementary and secondary teachers.

9. Communication between teacher and student is essential when problems arise. All interactions between people, even silence or neglect, communicate some meaning.

10. Techniques such as empathetic listening, assertive discipline, conflict resolution, and problem solving can be aids for teachers in maintaining beneficial communication with students.

## KEY TERMS

teacher-directed leadership

democratic/participatory leadership

laissez-faire leadership

procedures

rules

withitness

overlapping

group focus

movement management

group dynamics

cohesive group

norms

metacommunication

empathetic listening

"I" message

assertive discipline

## SUGGESTIONS FOR FURTHER READING AND STUDY

CHARLES, C. M. *Building classroom discipline: From models to practice.* New York: Longman, 1981. Describes seven models of discipline including Kounin and Canter, then presents twenty strategies based on insights from these models.

EMMER, E. T. and EVERTSON, C. M. Synthesis of research on classroom management. *Educational Leadership*, 1981, *38*, 342–345. In just a few pages these two experts on classroom management summarize the results of the best research in the area.

GORDON, T. *T.E.T.: Teacher effectiveness training.* New York: Peter H. Wyden, 1974. Gordon's very popular book gives many examples of his now-famous active listening and I messages, along with other problem-solving techniques for dealing with classroom problems.

DREIKURS, R., GRUNWALD, B. B., and PEPPER F. C. *Maintaining sanity in the classroom: Illustrated teaching techniques.* New York: Harper and Row, 1971. This very useful book for teachers gives both a theoretical framework and many techniques for dealing with the whole range of classroom problems.

# Teachers' Forum

## Management Tips for New Teachers

Classroom management is always of concern to a beginning teacher. One reason for this concern is that teacher effectiveness is related to student behavior. Obviously little teaching and learning can take place if much time is taken up handling disruptions and uncooperative behavior. Based on your experiences, what ideas and practices would you recommend to a new teacher?

**Sensitivity and Consistency**

Establish an open, loving, caring environment so that your charges can receive lots of positive strokes.... Know your students and their backgrounds. Be alert to the signs they send—I'm tired, I'm hurt, I'm hungry —and be ready to act, before they "act out."... Be sure your expectations and rules are clearly understood, and be consistent with their applications. Be aware that our tolerance levels vary from day to day—if we permit inappropriate behavior today, we will see it again tomorrow.... Busy, involved students have little time or interest in misbehavior. Be ready to change your pace, plans, or activities if necessary.... Keep your voice well modulated. Learn to give silent messages to offenders. Be ready to relieve tensions with a smile or a laugh.

Joan H. Lowe, Fifth-Grade Teacher
*Russell Elementary School, Hazelwood, Missouri*

**Enthusiasm and Organization**

There's no substitute for well-organized, enthusiastic teaching. If your students are interested and you are well-prepared, behavior is easier to manage.... Start with these assumptions: You like to teach; your students want to learn; you have something important to give them. Establish, from the beginning, the division of roles: You are the teacher, fully in charge; they are the students, there to learn. A folksy, chummy, pal-like demeanor diminishes your authority.... Whatever your game plan for discipline, whether it be names posted, seating changed, extra assignments, ejection, or after-school detainment, administer it consistently—consistency in your expectations and in what you will not tolerate. Do it with firmness, no shouting. Do it fairly, without sarcasm or shaming. And, from the beginning, try hard to create a climate of optimism and cheerfulness, expecting the very best effort from everyone. Your classroom is a good place to be. Learning something is the most satisfying thing in the world. Hindsight has taught me that the best teachers do these things. I wish I could have taught this way more often.

Harriet Chipley, Elementary Art Teacher
*Lookout Mountain Elementary School, Lookout Mountain, Tennessee*

## Finding Time to Listen

Empathetic listening is an excellent way to gain a student's trust and cooperation, but it requires uninterrupted time, free from distractions. In a busy school day with a classroom of students, how do you find time to have a personal conversation with one student?

| | If a student asks for a little one-on-one time, I usually arrange an after-school or lunch period get-together in which I can be available for a chat. But, more than likely, the need for personal and special attention arises out of an in-class problem or disturbance for which some private conversation to get at the roots of the situation is due. In that case, I plan a way for the student to help me with some task in the art room, usually during a free period, so that we can talk privately. This works well in a depart-mentalized system such as ours. For the self-contained classroom, such privacy might be more difficult to achieve. What if that classroom teacher set up a regular early-morning or after-school helper system? The designated student would take his or her honored turn and be an important assistant. There'd be lots of time for teacher and pupil to get to know each other better. |
|---|---|

**Making Yourself Available**

Harriet Chipley, Elementary Art Teacher
*Lookout Mountain Elementary School, Lookout Mountain, Tennessee*

## Balancing Paperwork and the Needs of the Class

Imagine yourself in the following situation. There is a great deal of paper work you must take care of at the beginning of each period: attendance sheets, daily memos from the administration, the collection of special assignments, and miscellaneous forms. While you attend to this, students leave their seats, drop books, and sharpen pencils endlessly. It usually takes 5 to 10 minutes to calm them down before class can start. What, if anything, would you do to change this situation? What would you tackle first?

**A Survey of the Options**

The first priority is for the teacher to gain immediate control of the class. Teacher attention must first be directed to the students rather than the paperwork. I feel that he/she has several alternatives that include the following: (1) Assign attendance sheets, memos, etc. to individual students. (2) Set up a routine where students come into the room and immediately begin some assigned activity. This may have to be timed at first. As soon as students are busy, the teacher is free to handle paperwork. (3) Jointly compose a set of class rules. If these rules are followed, the previously wasted time could be used for special activities at the end of the period.

Darline Reynolds, Junior-High-School Teacher
*Spirit Lake Junior High, Spirit Lake, Iowa*

**Setting Meaningful Tasks**

In business education subjects, the problem can be solved as follows: The traditional typewriting warm-up for the first 10 minutes of the period can be modified to serve as an accuracy practice drill. A timer is set when the class bell rings and a short typing assignment is placed on the blackboard. Students who complete the assignment perfectly (optional 1 error for slow classes) get a plus. . . . Large numbers of pluses will increase the quarterly grades. . . . These techniques have helped decrease lateness to my classes, have allowed me the time I need to complete the necessary clerical work at the beginning of the period, and act to increase the students' knowledge and skills. I believe that these techniques may be adapted to any subject. A small task with a time limit is an excellent tool for the beginning of any class period.

Estelle Sickles, Business Education Teacher, Grades 9–12
*Hempstead High School, Hempstead, New York*

# 11

# Designing Instruction: Objectives, Formats, and Settings

On Sunday nights every week, thousands of teachers across the country sit making out lesson plans. Often they begin by outlining activities for the week: lecture on Monday, show a film on Tuesday, and so on. Although this seems like a reasonable way to proceed, an important step is missing. The teacher has not yet asked this question: What is the purpose of these activities? More specifically, the teacher has not yet decided what the students are supposed to learn. If the teacher is unclear about the purpose of the activities, the students probably will be even more confused. They are likely to greet any new material with the common refrain, "Will this be on the test?"

Because teachers so frequently begin in the middle by selecting activities rather than at the beginning by determining purposes, we devote a large part of this chapter to the subject of objectives. We look first at some basic definitions of instructional objectives, their function in the classroom, several different kinds of objectives, and a number of criticisms of objectives. Next, we consider how to select objectives, for a lesson or a whole course, based on task analysis and taxonomies of learning outcomes.

Once a teacher has a clear set of purposes in mind, the next step is to decide how to structure the lesson. We discuss several teaching strategies based on the size of the group and the role of the teacher. These strategies include recitation, lecturing, group discussion, seatwork, and individualized instruction. In the final section we consider how to match the physical environment of the classroom to the objectives and activities of the lesson. By the time you have finished this chapter, you should be able to do the following:

- Give several reasons for using instructional objectives.
- Write objectives, applying Mager's or Gronlund's approach.
- Use task analysis to develop a sequence of objectives.
- Create objectives for cognitive, affective, or psychomotor learning.
- Tell how you would go about planning objectives for an entire course.
- Describe situations in which you would choose each of the following formats for teaching: recitation, lecture, group discussion, seatwork, and individualized instruction.
- Draw floor plans to fit the physical environment of your classroom to your learning goals and teaching methods.

Now, let's start at the beginning by considering what the students should learn.

## OBJECTIVES FOR LEARNING

A Definition
of Instructional
Objectives

The seven items listed above in the overview are examples of instructional objectives. Although there are many different approaches to writing objectives, each assumes that the first step in teaching is to decide what changes will take place in the learner, what will be the outcome of teaching. This leads us to a general definition of an **instructional objective:** a clear and unambiguous description of your educational intentions for your students.

Behavioral and Cognitive Objectives

Objectives vary from the extremely general to the extremely specific. They also vary according to the teacher's philosophical approach. Objectives written by people holding behavioral views of learning tend to focus on observable and measurable changes in the learner. Behavioral objectives generally start with such terms as "list, define, add," or "calculate," and continue with a specific description of what the learner is expected to do. Those favoring the cognitive view of learning generally state objectives more in terms of internal changes. Their objectives are more likely to begin with words such as "understand, recognize, create," or "apply." Both groups, however, agree that objectives are more than simple summaries of course content, outlines of topics to be covered, or lists of activities. Objectives are descriptions of changes in the learners.

## The Value of Objectives

Some advocates of instructional objectives have been extremely enthusiastic. At times their zeal has done a disservice to their cause, but many of the advantages they claim for objectives are worth examining.

**Student Achievement.** The effects of providing students with instructional objectives are not clear-cut. Some studies have found that giving a list of objectives to students at the beginning of a unit increases student learning; other studies indicate no significant impact at all (Duchastel and Merrill, 1973; Duell, 1974). If giving students objectives does not increase learning in every situation, then *under what conditions* do objectives increase learning?

Objectives with Unorganized Material

Tobias and Duchastel (1974) examined this question by comparing studies of the use of objectives with highly organized material such as programmed instruction versus loosely organized material such as lectures and films. From this comparison, it appears that instructional objectives are most helpful when the activities are less organized and structured. Since few teaching activities are as organized as programmed instruction, this finding supports a broad use of instructional objectives.

Focusing Attention

Duell (1974) makes a similar point. She believes that objectives will help students learn if the objectives bring information to their attention that might otherwise have been overlooked. If the importance of some information is not clear from the learning materials and activities themselves, instructional objectives will probably help focus student attention and thus increase achievement (Duchastel, 1979).

Avoiding "Word Magic"

**Improved Communication.** In day-to-day classroom interaction, a good number of a teacher's verbal and nonverbal messages may be ambiguous. For example, a teacher may know that one goal of teaching is to foster good citizenship. Almost everyone would agree that good citizenship is important. This kind of vague purpose is a good example what Dyer (1967) has called "word magic."

Goals stated in word magic sound great. But no one really knows what they mean. What will the students be doing when they are good citizens? How does a teacher communicate the idea of good citizenship to students?

379

**380**

**Designing
Instruction:
Objectives,
Formats, and
Settings**

One day the teacher may consider that questioning authority is a sign of good citizenship. Another day the same action may be considered bad citizenship (especially if it is the teacher's authority being questioned). Specifying learning objectives can help teachers clarify for themselves the changes they believe are important for their students. This will not only make the changes easier to reach, but will also improve communication between teacher and student.

Avoiding
Haphazard
Planning

**Planning and Testing.**     Each day teachers must plan to do something; they must select or create activities and put those activities into some meaningful order. But an infinite number of possible activities exists. Which ones are best? Some criteria must be used to make these decisions. A reasonable approach is to select activities that will help students learn something worth knowing—or, in other words, help them master an important objective. If intended changes in student behavior are not made the central concern in planning, other concerns can take their place. Planning may become haphazard. It may begin to revolve around whatever happens to be available that week in the audiovisual center.

Criteria
for Evaluation

In almost every class, teachers must evaluate performance. Distinctions are made between good and poor work. All evaluation, in fact, implies learning objectives. Even if a teacher never specifies objectives, students will become aware of them when the tests or assignments are graded and it is too late to profit from the information. If, for example, the top grades go to students who are best at memorizing facts, all the students will realize that the objective was to memorize facts. If, on the other hand, the objectives are supplied in advance, both students and teacher will face evaluation knowing what the criteria are. Students' understanding of the objectives will make studying easier and more efficient. For the teacher, an early statement of objectives will make preparing tests simpler.

*If teachers begin
planning by
deciding what
students should
learn, lessons and
tests will be better
coordinated. But
this is a
time-consuming
process and often
means "homework"
for teachers.*

Frank Siteman/Stock, Boston

**A General Statement about Objectives.**    Because part of the development of instructional objectives took place in industry and the military, the techniques often sound somewhat mechanistic. The following argument states our own position.

Humanizing
Teaching

There is nothing less humane and caring than playing the guess-what-you-should-be-learning game with students. Using instructional objectives properly can be a way of humanizing the educational process. If a teacher first considers what students should be able to do after completing a unit, the teacher is likely to identify the outcomes that are important and enduring. If the teacher considers which objectives are most attainable, the teacher will probably have to consider the strengths and weaknesses of each student, and thus tailor the teaching to the individuals in the class. If the teacher offers learning objectives to the students, the students will have a chance to take more responsibility for their own learning. If using learning objectives increases student achievement, then the power of knowledge, competence, and success is passed on to the student.

## Kinds of Objectives

One of the factors that distinguishes the approaches to writing objectives is the level of specificity required.

**From the General to the Specific.**    In our discussion thus far, you have seen the words "goal," "purpose," "outcome," and "objective." As you may have guessed, there are several levels of goals for education. At a very general, abstract level are the grand goals society might have for graduates of public schools. For example, education should promote intellectual development and effective citizenship. At the other end of the continuum are specific subobjectives describing single behaviors. Bill Neuman, for example, should hold a pencil properly, and Mary Delgado should spell the word "vote" correctly.

At the most general level, goals are so vague that they become meaningless as potential guidelines for instruction. One teacher's definition of how to promote intellectual development might be very different from another teacher's definition. On the other hand, listing every new behavior for every student in the class would require a computer and many bottles of aspirin.

Behavioral and
Cognitive Views

Most psychologists and educators would agree that we need something between grand generalities and specific item-by-item instructions for each student. But here the agreement ends. As we have seen, cognitivists tend to favor terms such as "understand" and "appreciate." Behaviorists tend to prefer "list" and "identify." Cognitive objectives thus tend to be more general and less clearly measurable than behavioral objectives. They also tend to be less restricting. Consider the examples given in Figure 11–1.

Operationalizing

In a sense, the ideas listed in the more general objectives in Figure 11–1 have been **operationalized** in the more specific objectives. The unobservable changes found in the first set of objectives have, in the second set, been defined in terms that can be measured. How can you tell if a student can reason, understand, or appreciate? One way is to give the student a specific task that will provide evidence for the change. Here, we will look at one well-developed method of writing more specific objectives.

## Figure 11–1  General and Specific Objectives

| General Objectives | More Specific Objectives |
|---|---|
| The student can reason in solving simple arithmetic problems. | The student can solve simple arithmetic problems written in a new form: $3 + 4 = ?$ and $3 + 4 = \mathbf{x}$. |
| The student understands the concept of meter in poetry. | The student can correctly identify the meter of any poem. |
| The student appreciates teamwork. | The student passes the ball when appropriate. |

Writing
Behavioral
Objectives

Three Parts

**Mager's Behavioral Objectives.**    Robert Mager has developed a very influential system for writing instructional objectives. Mager's idea is that objectives ought to describe ''what the student will be doing when demonstrating his achievement and how you will know he is doing it'' (Mager, 1962, p. 53). Mager's objectives are generally regarded as behavioral.

According to Mager, a good objective has three parts. First, it must have a verb phrase describing the intended student behavior. (Here the idea of operationalizing is very important.) Second, it must list the conditions under which the behavior will occur (this is essentially a definition of the testing situation). Third, it must give the criteria for acceptable performance on the test. Figure 11–2 shows how the system works.

Using Mager's format, we could write a number of objectives for this chapter. We will develop one here as an example: writing instructional objectives. First we would have to specify the behavior involved. This part of the objective might be to *write* instructional objectives appropriate for students in your subject area. Then we would have to look at conditions of performance—for example, in class and without the aid of any course materials. Finally, we would have to give certain performance criteria. The number and the type of objectives could be given here: three valid objectives, each containing all three components described by Mager. If we reorganize a bit for clarity, the final objective could be written as in the extract on the next page.

## Figure 11–2  Mager's Three-part System

| Part | Question to Ask | Example |
|---|---|---|
| Student behavior | Do what? | Mark statements with an F for fact or an O for opinion. |
| Conditions of performance | Under what conditions? | Given an article from a newspaper. |
| Performance criteria | How well? | 75% of the statements correctly marked. |

*From Mager, R. F. **Preparing instructional objectives.** © 1962 by Fearon, Palo Alto, CA. Reprinted by permission.*

In class, without the aid of any course material, you will write three instructional objectives appropriate for students in your subject area. Each objective must contain all three components described by Mager.

Mager's system, with its emphasis on final behavior, requires a great deal of specificity. Mager contends that such an effort is worthwhile. He believes that often students can teach themselves if they are given well-stated objectives. Norman Gronlund offers a different approach.

Stating
Cognitive
Objectives

**Gronlund's Objectives.** Gronlund (1978) believes that an objective should be stated first in general terms ("understand," "appreciate," and so on). Then the teacher should clarify the meaning of the objective by listing a few sample behaviors providing evidence that the student has reached it. Gronlund's system is often used for writing cognitive objectives. An example is found in Figure 11–3.

Gronlund's point is that the goal in the example given in Figure 11–3 really is to understand. The teacher does not want the student to stop with defining, identifying, or distinguishing. Instead, the teacher looks at performance on these sample tasks to decide if the student really understands. In fact, the teacher could have chosen three different tasks to test understanding.

Objectives
as Samples
of Ability

Gronlund's emphasis on behavioral objectives as samples of student ability is important. A teacher could never list all the behaviors that might be involved in truly understanding some subject area. But stating an initial general objective makes it clear that understanding is the purpose.

Gronlund's approach is more inclusive than Mager's. It also saves time. According to one critic of Mager's approach, 10,000 different objectives would be needed to specify all the student outcomes possible from reading one particular educational psychology text (MacDonald-Ross, 1974). Surely a sample of only 50 to 100 of the possible 10,000 objectives would be realistic in any one course.

The methods presented here are not mutually exclusive. For example, a teacher might decide to use Gronlund's method of stating general aims and Mager's guidelines for specifying the sample objectives. The most recent research on instructional objectives tends to favor approaches similar to Gronlund's. It seems reasonable to state fewer objectives in more general terms, while still clarifying these statements with samples of specific behaviors (Dressel, 1977).

**Figure 11–3    Gronlund's Combined System of Writing Objectives**

| Part | Example |
|------|---------|
| General objective | Understands the terms used in plane geometry. |
| Subobjective A | Defines the terms in his or her own words. |
| Subobjective B | Identifies the meaning of the terms when used in context. |
| Subobjective C | Distinguishes between those terms that are similar in meaning. |

Adapted from N. E. Gronlund. *Stating behavioral objectives for classroom instruction* (2nd ed.). Toronto: Macmillan, 1978, pp. 4–5.

Both Mager's and Gronlund's systems assume that a teacher will know in advance all the final behaviors the students must master. Does this mean that a teacher must anticipate every outcome of learning? Is there no room for spontaneity in the classroom?

**Eisner's Expressive Objectives.**   Several years ago, Eisner (1969) began to stress the importance of what he called **expressive objectives.** An expressive objective clearly defines an activity for the student. However, exactly what each student might learn from the activity is not specified, since it is not always possible to determine the outcomes of every activity.

We believe expressive objectives can be valuable supplements to objectives focused on outcomes. Teaching would be terribly dull if every activity had an ironclad set of anticipated outcomes. In practice, the two types of objectives may work well together. For example, one expressive objective might be to have students interview local residents about some controversial issue. Although such an experience might lead to a variety of outcomes for students, the teacher need not try to guess them all in advance. However, the teacher might define some specific instructional objectives, such as learning interviewing techniques or methods of drawing conclusions from data, to prepare the students for the activity. After the interviewing process, the teacher might once again define some specific objectives based on unanticipated outcomes of the experience. For example, if many students got lost while interviewing, a specific objective on map reading might be in order.

Little work has been done in the area of expressive objectives since Eisner presented his ideas. The danger in relying too heavily on them is that a teacher can fall into the old trap of specifying activities without thinking about what students should learn from them.

As we said at the beginning of the section, not all educators believe writing objectives is valuable. Many of the criticisms are worth considering.

## Criticisms

We will consider three common criticisms of objectives and then offer a set of Guidelines to help teachers avoid problems.

**The Time Factor.**   A number of critics have stated that specifying an objective for every learning outcome requires more time than most teachers have. Those in favor of objectives have often labeled this idea an admission of laziness. But MacDonald-Ross's (1974) finding that 10,000 objectives would be needed to define all the outcomes of a typical education psychology text lends support to the notion that time may be a factor worth considering. Two possible solutions are to acknowledge that not all outcomes will be specified and to get help from outside sources.

Sources
for Objectives

Many publications provide lists of potential objectives. One source is the Instructional Objectives Exchange, which has collected and rated objectives in many areas. Originally a nonprofit organization, this is now a private company.˙

**The Trivialization Factor.**   According to some critics, instructional objectives are likely to be unimportant because trivial, short-term goals are easier to specify. Of course, it is always easier to teach and evaluate low-level abilities.

David S. Stricker/Monkmeyer Press Photo Service

*The objection has been raised that the distribution of course objectives amounts to spoonfeeding the students. Why are instructional objectives more susceptible to this criticism than other forms of instruction? Does the charge hold up?*

This is true whether objectives are stated or not: There are teachers who have not heard of objectives but nevertheless have been teaching trivia for years. Using objectives will not force a teacher to teach low-level abilities, but it might make the possibility more likely. In addition, if objectives are too precise and teachers try to stick to the objectives every year, the curriculum tends to stagnate. The teacher may ignore new developments if they are not in the objectives.

Many critics feel that the use of instructional objectives has a potential effect of spoon-feeding students. If only low-level abilities are specified as outcomes, and tests are merely a collection of instructional objectives turned into questions, spoon-feeding is indeed likely. The students' abilities to question and explore might well be limited. But this does not have to be the case.

Consider this objective, prepared for a relatively high-level secondary course in history:

Objectives for High-Level Abilities

In class, without access to notes, given three presidential elections between 1900 and 1944, write a 200-word essay describing how domestic policy might have changed if the defeated presidential candidate had been elected.

On the test, the teacher selects the elections of 1900, 1912, and 1940. Since these particular years were not specified in the objective, students must know a number of facts. What presidents were chosen in each election year between 1900 and 1944? Who ran against them? What was the domestic policy advocated by each candidate? What key events occurred during each president's term in office? Besides understanding these facts and concepts, the students would have to be able to make inferences, give evidence to support hypotheses, and think divergently (come up with many possible right answers). This is hardly spoon-feeding!

385

**386**

Designing
Instruction:
Objectives,
Formats, and
Settings

**The Difficulty of Writing Objectives for Some Subjects.** It may be relatively easy to write objectives tor math classes, but what about objectives in art classes? Several advocates of objectives insist that teachers in all fields, even in the humanities and arts, make judgments about student work. Therefore, they claim, the criteria for making judgments can be applied to determine learning objectives (Popham, 1969). The argument is that if you can judge a good painting when you see one, you can write objectives that will specify how you decide if the painting is good. This position makes some sense. But, as MacDonald-Ross (1974) points out, just because you know a good painting when you see one does not mean you can write objectives describing how all good paintings would be evaluated.

The problem of writing objectives in some subjects is real. It might again be worthwhile to supplement the objectives you write with those available from such sources as the Instructional Objectives Exchange. And in spite of these very real problems, we believe objectives should play an important role in teaching. The Guidelines given here may be of use whether you decide to make thorough use of objectives or just prepare them for certain assignments.

# Guidelines

## Instructional Objectives

**1. Avoid word magic or phrases that sound noble and important but say very little.**

EXAMPLES
- Keep the focus on specific changes that will take place in the students in your class.
- Ask students to explain the meaning of the objectives.

**2. Decide upon activities after setting objectives.**

EXAMPLES
- If the goal is the memorization of vocabulary, give the students memory aids and practice exercises.
- If the goal is the ability to develop well thought out positions, consider position papers, debates, team projects, or mock trials.

**3. Make sure your tests are related to your objectives.**

EXAMPLES
- Write objectives and rough drafts for tests at the same time.
- Weight the tests according to the importance of the various objectives and the time spent on each.

**4. Do not exclude objectives that seem to be of value even though the outcome cannot be specified.**

EXAMPLES
- Expressive objectives such as making gifts to take to a nursing home during the holidays.
- Evaluate students by degree of participation rather than test grade.

# TASK ANALYSIS

When teachers sit down to decide what students should learn, they confront an overwhelming number of possibilities. Several solutions have been proposed to this dilemma. Here we will look at one of the most influential methods of determining learning objectives, task analysis.

## The Basic Method

*Origin of Task Analysis*

The procedure involved in **task analysis** was originally developed by R. B. Miller (1962) during World War II to help the armed services train personnel. Miller's system begins with a definition of the final performance requirement, what the trainee or student must be able to do at the end of the program or unit. Then the objectives that will lead to the final goal are identified and specified. The procedure is the obvious one of breaking skills and processes down into subskills and subprocesses.

*Task Analysis in the Classroom*

In the classroom, the teacher begins by asking: "What will the students have to do before they can reach the final goal I have in mind?" The answer to this question may help identify several underlying skills. For the sake of argument, let's say five skills are identified. The teacher next asks: "What must the students be able to do to succeed at each of these five skills?" The answer this time should produce a number of subskills for each of the basic skills. This movement backward to list the skills underlying the task at hand should give a full picture of all the abilities a student must have to accomplish the objective successfully. If a student has trouble with the final task, the problem could be with the subskills.

## An Example of Task Analysis

Consider an example. Assume students must write a position paper based on library research. What skills and subskills are required to complete such an assignment? Figure 11–4 offers the beginning of a task analysis for this assignment.

*Different Reasons for Failure*

If the teacher assigned the position paper without analyzing the task and skills required, what could happen? Some of the students might not know how to use the card catalog. They might search through one or two encyclopedias, then write a summary of the issues as described in the encyclopedia. The teacher wanted a synthesis of several sources, but these students wrote book reports. They would receive very low grades on the assignment. Another group of students might know how to use the card catalog, tables of contents, and indexes, but have difficulty reaching conclusions. They might hand in lengthy papers listing a number of summaries about different ideas. These students would also get low grades, but for different reasons. A final group of students might be able to draw conclusions, but their written presentations might be so confusing and grammatically incorrect that the teacher could not understand what they were trying to say. Each of the groups failed, but for different reasons.

A task analysis gives a picture of the logical sequence of steps leading toward an ability. Knowing this sequence, the teacher can make sure students have the necessary skills before they are given an assignment. In addition,

**Figure 11–4   Task Analysis for a Library Assignment: A Simplified Analysis**

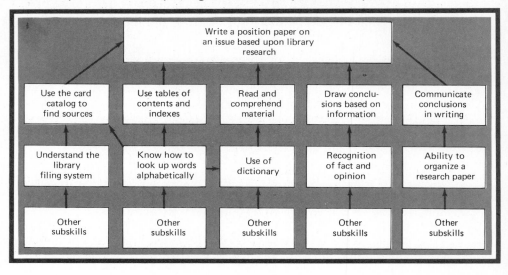

when students have difficulty, the teacher can pinpoint problem areas. If a task analysis had been done on the assignment we just described, the teacher could have written several different objectives for the students. Some students would have to work on mastering the supporting objectives before they could tackle the final assignment. Other students could go right to the library and begin work.

**Using Student Errors**

The process can also work in reverse. Student errors can highlight the subskills required to complete a task successfully. If you have not done a task analysis before giving an assignment, you can use the information from student errors in analyzing the task before presenting it to next year's class. Each year of experience can lead to better teaching.

*Not every student is as competent as this girl in using the card catalog. If this task is a necessary part of an assignment, many students will have trouble unless they are first taught how to use the materials.*

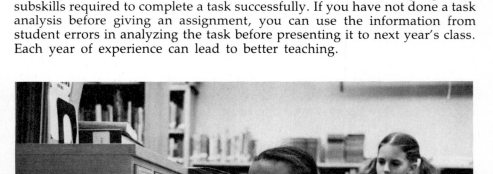

Ken Karp

# TAXONOMIES

Three Domains
of Objectives

Several years ago, as interest in defining educational objectives was increasing, a group of experts in educational evaluation led by Benjamin Bloom studied the idea of defining objectives systematically. After years of work they developed a **taxonomy,** or classification system, of educational objectives. Objectives were divided into three **domains: cognitive, affective,** and **psychomotor.** A handbook describing the objectives in each area was eventually published. In real life, of course, behaviors from these three different domains occur simultaneously. While students are writing (psychomotor), they are also remembering or reasoning (cognitive), and they are likely to have some emotional response to the task as well (affective). One reason for considering these areas separately is to accentuate the affective and psychomotor areas because schools often focus on cognitive changes alone.

## The Cognitive Domain

Six basic objectives are listed in Bloom's taxonomy in the cognitive domain (Bloom, Engelhart, Frost, Hill and Krathwohl, 1956):

1.   *Knowledge:* Remembering something previously encountered without necessarily understanding, using, or changing it.
2.   *Comprehension:* Understanding the material being communicated without necessarily relating it to anything else.
3.   *Application:* Using a general concept to solve some problem in a particular situation.
4.   *Analysis:* Breaking something down into its parts.
5.   *Synthesis:* Creating something new by putting parts of different ideas together to make a whole.
6.   *Evaluation:* Judging the value of material or methods as they might be applied in a particular situation.

Limitations
of a Hierarchy

It may be helpful to consider these objectives as a hierarchy, each skill building on those below, but this may not be an accurate picture. It is very difficult to divide intellectual abilities into separate skills that build on each other. For example, Pring (1971) suggests that you cannot separate comprehension of terms or symbols from a working knowledge of how to apply them. In certain fields, such as mathematics, the levels in the hierarchy do not seem to fit the structure of knowledge in the subject very well. But Bloom's taxonomy does encourage educators to think systematically about objectives and broadens our view about possible outcomes (Furst, 1981).

Consider how the taxonomy of cognitive outcomes might suggest objectives for a course. Figure 11–2 gave one example of a specific objective at the *analysis* level in a social studies class, distinguishing between fact and opinion in news stories. At the *synthesis* level, an objective for the class could be this:

Objectives
at the Higher
Levels

Given a list of three facts, write a two-paragraph news story taking a position on an issue and documenting the position with the facts.

At the level of *evaluation,* the objective might be:

Given two articles that present contradictory views of a recent event, decide which article gives the fairer presentation and justify your choice.

**Evaluation and Cognitive Objectives.**  The progression from one level to another can also be helpful in planning evaluation, since different types of test items are appropriate for objectives at the various levels. Gronlund (1982) suggests that knowledge objectives can best be measured by **objective tests,** particularly in situations where good multiple-choice questions can be constructed. Such tests will also work with the comprehension, application, and analysis levels of the taxonomy.

Objective tests will not be adequate for measuring synthesis- and evaluation-level objectives. For these levels, the **essay test** is more appropriate. Like the objective test, the essay test will also work at the middle levels of the taxonomy, but it will not work well in measuring knowledge objectives. Thus the teacher has a choice of methods for measuring middle-level objectives. When it comes to the lowest and highest levels, however, the teacher must take care to see that the evaluation methods fit the objectives.

## The Affective Domain

The objectives in the taxonomy of the affective domain run from least committed to most committed (Krathwohl, Bloom and Masia, 1956). At the lowest level, a student would simply pay attention to a certain idea. At the highest level, the student would adopt an idea or a value and act consistently with that idea. The five basic objectives in the affective domain are given below:

1.  *Receiving:* Being aware of or attending to something in the environment; this is the I'll-listen-to-the-concert-but-I-won't-promise-to-like-it level.

2.  *Responding:* Showing some new behavior as a result of experience; at this level a person might applaud after the concert or hum some of the music the next day.

3.  *Valuing:* Showing some definite involvement or commitment; at this point a person might choose to go to a concert instead of a film.

4.  *Organization:* Integrating a new value into one's general set of values, giving it some ranking among one's general priorities; this is the level at which a person would begin to make long-range commitments to concert attendance.

5.  *Characterization by Value:* Acting consistently with the new value; at this highest level, a person would be firmly committed to a love of music and show it openly and consistently.

Like the basic objectives in the cognitive domain, these five objectives are very general. To write specific learning objectives, you must state what students will actually be doing when they are receiving, responding, valuing, and so on. For example, an objective for a nutrition class at the valuing level might be this:

After completing the unit on consumer action, at least 50 percent of the class will support the junk food boycott project by giving up candy for a month.

This objective raises some interesting questions about evaluation. How can you determine whether students act on their values? Should grades depend on supporting a junk food boycott?

**Evaluating Affective Objectives.**  There are at least two ways in which assessing affective objectives may be helpful. Often it is desirable to evaluate

390

these objectives for diagnostic purposes, to see what values students bring to class. Final evaluation may also help teachers gauge their success in bringing about a desired change in attitudes or values.

Suppose, for example, that an important goal in a science class is commitment to ethics in conducting and reporting research. If the teacher learns at the beginning of the course that students approve of falsifying scientific results to further one's position, the teacher will have a ready-made affective goal to pursue throughout the course. If the teacher learns that students still feel this way at the end of a course, the teacher may wish to approach that topic a little differently the next time.

It is difficult to measure the attainment of affective objectives. How can a teacher be sure, for example, that students have given up candy in support of a junk food boycott? The best method may be to ask them to report anonymously on their candy consumption. If grades were attached to individual signed replies, the process might counteract the desire to reach another affective goal, honesty. In most cases, we would suggest that affective measures not be graded.

Techniques for measuring affective objectives are far from precise. Students may tend to express the views they think the teacher desires, even on an anonymous questionnaire. But the influence of affective goals often extends well beyond the classroom, in values such as an appreciation for reading or a positive attitude toward science that may continue throughout life. As a teacher, you cannot help teaching values. It may be wise to measure the lasting results of your teaching.

## The Psychomotor Domain

Until recently, this area has been overlooked for the most part by teachers not directly involved in physical education. A taxonomy of the objectives in the psychomotor domain was not developed until the early 1970s (Harrow, 1972). It is arranged from the lowest level of observable movements to the highest. The six basic objectives in the taxonomy are given below:

1. *Reflex movements:* Actions that occur involuntarily in response to some stimulus (stretching, blinking, posture adjustments).

2. *Basic fundamental:* Inherent movement patterns that are formed from a combination of reflex movements (walking, running, jumping, pushing, pulling, manipulating).

3. *Perceptual abilities:* Translation of stimuli received through the senses into appropriate movements (following verbal instructions, dodging a moving ball, maintaining balance, jumping rope).

4. *Physical abilities:* Basic movements and abilities that are essential to the development of more highly skilled movements (distance running, weight lifting, toe touching, basic ballet exercises).

5. *Skilled movements:* More complex movements requiring a certain degree of efficiency (movements involved in sports, dance, and the fine arts).

6. *Nondiscursive communication:* Ability to communicate through body movement (gestures, facial expressions, choreographed dance movements).

Objectives in the psychomotor domain should be of interest not only to teachers of physical education, but to a wide range of educators, including those in fine arts, vocational-technical education, and special education.

Many other subjects, such as chemistry, physics, and biology, also require specialized movements and well-developed hand-eye coordination. Using lab equipment or art materials means learning new physical skills. Here are two examples of psychomotor objectives:

Psychomotor
Objectives

Four minutes after completing a one-mile run in 8 minutes or under, your heart rate will be below 120.

Without referring to notes or diagrams, assemble the appropriate laboratory apparatus to distill _____.

**Methods of Evaluating Psychomotor Objectives.**   Learning in the psychomotor area really means developing a particular performance ability. How do you assess a student's performance? The obvious answer is to ask the student to demonstrate the skill and observe the student's proficiency. In some cases, the performance of the skill results in a product, so assessment of the product can be substituted for observation of the actual performance. An art student learning to use the potter's wheel, for example, should be able to produce a pot that is symmetrical, stands by itself, and meets a number of other criteria.

Assessing
Performance

In writing a psychomotor objective, you have specified the performance outcome to be measured. This is the first step in evaluation. Such objectives usually include action verbs such as "run," "operate," or "build." Performance standards for the task should also be specified. These include clear descriptions of the elements of the task, the proper sequence for performance, and guidelines for judging correct movements.

The next step is to draw up a clear description of the testing situation. This should include the purpose of the test, the equipment or materials to be used, and the testing procedure, including required performance, time limits, and

*The most logical way to evaluate psychomotor objectives is to observe while the student performs the required movements. This student is working on a project that combines cognitive objectives (reading and measuring) with skilled movements (coordinating stirring, rolling dough) and probably affective objectives too, since the results should be fun to eat!*

Ken Karp

**Figure 11–5    Checklist for Evaluating the Use of an Oral Thermometer**

_____ 1.   Removes thermometer from container by grasping nonbulb end.
_____ 2.   Wipes thermometer downward from nonbulb end with fresh wiper.
_____ 3.   Shakes down thermometer to less than 96° while holding nonbulb end.
_____ 4.   Places bulb end of thermometer under patient's tongue.
_____ 5.   Tells patient to close lips but to avoid biting down on thermometer.
_____ 6.   Leaves thermometer in patient's mouth for 3 minutes.
_____ 7.   Removes thermometer from patient's mouth by grasping nonbulb end.
_____ 8.   Reads temperature to the nearest two-tenths of a degree.
_____ 9.   Records temperature reading on patient's chart.
_____ 10.  Cleans thermometer and replaces in container.

Adapted from N. E. Gronlund. **Constructing achievement tests** (2nd ed.). Englewood Cliffs, N.J.: Prentice-Hall, 1977, p. 98. Adapted with permission of publisher.

**Using a Checklist**

method of scoring. These instructions should be in written form to ensure that all students tested will be completing the same task (Gronlund, 1982).

When students are actually performing, you need a checklist or rating scale so you can focus on the important aspects of the skill being evaluated. A checklist usually gives the measurable dimensions of performance, along with a series of blank spaces for judgments. An example is found in Figure 11–5. A rating scale generally follows the same plan but has a numerical scale to rate each aspect of performance, rather than blanks for "yes" or "no" judgments.

Once you have learned to write and evaluate objectives in all three domains, your job is not over. You will be teaching more than single skills and lessons. You must plan an integrated program of study and then evaluate progress in that program.

## The Big Picture: Course Objectives

In planning objectives for an entire unit, many teachers develop a **behavior-content matrix.** The first step is to decide the general objectives for the course, stated in broad terms. Each general objective is then broken down into two components. The first is student behavior — that is, knowledge of facts, knowledge of concepts, ability to generalize, and so on. The second component is course content — that is, the subjects to be covered in the course. If one of the general objectives in an English class is to enhance appreciation of American literature, student behaviors might include knowledge (of authors, historical periods, book titles), ability to compare (different styles, different themes), and ability to criticize. The course content component would include the different novels, poems, short stories, and so on that you wished to cover.

**Using a Behavior-Content Matrix**

In drawing up the matrix or chart, the teacher would list student behaviors across the top, usually from simplest to most complex, and content areas down the side. At each square where a particular behavior intersects with a particular content area, the teacher can write instructional objectives. In this way, the teacher makes sure all important behaviors and topics are considered as possible objectives. Priorities can be set, with several objectives for some squares and none for others, depending on the outcomes the teacher is

**Figure 11–6    A Behavior-Content Matrix for a Unit on Decimals**

| Content | Behaviors | | | | |
|---|---|---|---|---|---|
| | Knowledge | Comprehension | Application | Analysis | **Total** |
| Multiplication | | 1 | 1 | 1 | **3** |
| Addition and Subtraction | | | 1 | 1 | **2** |
| Division | | 1 | 1 | 1 | **3** |
| Renaming | 2 | 2 | | 1 | **5** |
| Definitions | 2 | | | 1 | **3** |
| **Total** | **4** | **4** | **3** | **5** | **16** |

From Hills, **Measurement and evaluation in the classroom.** Columbus, Ohio: Merrill, 1976, p. 8.

seeking. At test time, the teacher can emphasize key areas by asking more questions from the most important squares.

If you develop a behavior-content matrix for a course, you may avoid many of the potential problems with instructional objectives. You are less likely to present trivial objectives or "spoon-feed" students. A behavior-content matrix also makes it possible to see all the objectives of a course at once and to organize them in the most logical sequence.

Figure 11–6 gives an example of a plan for a unit on decimals. Examples of other plans for many different subject areas at both the elementary and secondary levels can be found in a handbook prepared by Bloom, Hastings, and Madaus (1971).

Let us assume you have developed the objectives for your class and have a general idea of the goals for the entire year. What next? You still need to decide what to do on Monday. The following section describes a variety of methods for turning objectives into action in the classroom.

# BASIC FORMATS FOR TEACHING

We begin with the strategy many people associate most directly with teaching: reciting and answering questions.

## Recitation and Questioning

Structure, Solicit, React

The **recitation** approach to teaching has been with us for many years. A teacher poses questions, and students answer them. The teacher's questions generally follow some sort of plan to develop a framework for the subject matter involved. The students' answers are often followed by reactions from the teacher, such as statements of praise, correction, or requests for further information. The pattern from the teacher's point of view is one of structure

**395**
**Designing
Instruction:
Objectives,
Formats, and
Settings**

(setting a framework), solicitation (asking questions), and reaction (praising, correcting, and expanding) (Clark, Gage, Marx, Peterson, Staybrook and Winne, 1979). These steps are repeated over and over again.

Let us consider the heart of recitation, the soliciting or questioning phase, by looking first at the different kinds of questions that might be asked, and then at ways of fitting the questions to the students.

**Kinds of Questions.**    Much has been written to describe the kinds of questions teachers could ask. Some educators have estimated that high school teachers ask an average of 395 questions per day (Gall, 1970). What are these questions like? Bloom's taxonomy of objectives in the cognitive domain is often used to categorize questions as being at the knowledge, comprehension, application, analysis, synthesis, or evaluation levels. Figure 11–7 offers examples of different questions at the different levels.

*Convergent
and Divergent
Questions*

Questions may also be **convergent** (asking for only one right answer) or **divergent** (asking for many possible right answers). Questions about concrete facts are convergent: Who ruled England in 1540? Who wrote *Peter Pan*? Questions dealing with opinions or hypotheses are divergent: Why did the United States go to war in 1898? What do you think of nuclear power plants?

Quite a bit of space in education textbooks has been devoted to urging teachers to ask both high-level (analysis, synthesis, and evaluation) and divergent questions. Is this really an effective approach? Recent research has provided several surprises.

*The Value
of Factual
Questions*

**Fitting the Questions to the Students.**    Stallings and Kaskowitz (1975) and Soar (1973) have found that the frequency of knowledge questions, comprehension-level questions, convergent questions, and single-answer questions is positively related to student learning. In these studies, high-level questions were negatively related to student learning. But three facts should be kept in mind in interpreting these results. The students were in primary grades; they were from low socioeconomic backgrounds; and their achievement was measured with test questions at the knowledge and comprehension levels.

**Figure 11–7   Classroom Questions**

| Category Name | Type of Thinking Expected | Samples |
|---|---|---|
| Knowledge (remembering) | Student simply recalls or recognizes information as it was learned. | "Define. . . ." "What is the capital of . . . ?" "Who was the first . . . ?" "What did the text say about . . . ?" |
| Comprehension (understanding) | Student demonstrates understanding of the material; questions require mental reorganization or interpretation, not just recall. | "Explain in your own words. . . ." "Compare. . . ." "What is the main idea of . . . ?" "Describe what you saw. . . ." |
| Application (solving) | Student uses information to solve a problem. A single correct answer is expected. | "Which principle is demonstrated in . . . ?" "Given the length and width, calculate. . . ." "Apply the rules of . . . to solve the following. . . ." |
| Analysis (analyzing) | Students must think critically; identify reasons, motives; make an inference based upon several bits of information; take apart a conclusion to see if it is supported by evidence. | "What factors influenced the writings of . . . ?" "Why was Washington, D.C. chosen . . . ?" "Which of the following are facts and which are opinions?" "Based upon your experiment, what is the chemical . . . ?" |
| Synthesis (creating) | Student performs original thinking, creates an original plan, proposal, design, story, and so on. No single correct answer. | "What's a good name for this . . . ?" "How could we raise money for . . . ?" "What would the United States be like if the South had won . . . ?" |
| Evaluation (judging) | Student judges the merit of an idea, offers an opinion, uses standards to evaluate a product or idea. | "Which U.S. Senator is the most effective?" "Should students be given choices in . . . ?" "Which painting do you prefer?" "Why would you favor . . . ?" |

Adapted from M. Sadker and D. Sadker, Questioning skills. In J. Cooper (ed.), **Classroom teaching skills: A handbook.** Lexington, Mass.: D.C. Heath, 1977, pp. 156–174.

Other investigators have reached different conclusions. For example, Redfield and Rousseau (1981) examined 14 studies and concluded that more higher-order questions can lead to achievement gains when teachers are trained to use this approach appropriately.

Questions for High and Low Ability Students

It appears that both types of questions can be effective. However, different patterns seem to be better for different students. The best pattern for lower-ability students is simple questions allowing a high percentage of correct answers, encouragement, help when the student does not have the correct answer, and praise. For high-ability students, the successful pattern is harder questions with fewer correct answers from the students and a rapid pace with little encouragement or discussion after student answers, except to correct or criticize wrong answers. A mix of higher- and lower-level questions seems helpful for this group (Medley, 1977; Ward and Tikunoff, 1976). This pattern may sound somewhat harsh. You must weigh your own goals for student learning against your goals for student self-esteem. Some students respond well to constructive criticism; others are troubled by criticism, especially in public.

## Lecturing and Explaining

Some studies have found that teachers lecture during one-sixth to one-fourth of all classroom time. Teachers in the high grades lecture more than teachers in the low grades (Dunkin and Biddle, 1974). You will probably learn about how to lecture in your methods classes. Many different approaches are available; the system you choose depends on your objectives and the subject you are teaching. You will want to keep in mind, for example, the age of your students. The younger your students, the briefer and simpler your explanations should be. You may also want to follow a basic three-part format: tell the students what you are going to say (and why), say it, and then tell them what you said.

Advantages of Lecturing

In considering the lecture method, you will have to make decisions about when to use it. Lecturing is appropriate for communicating a large amount of material to many students in a short period of time. The teacher can integrate information from many sources and give students a more complete understanding of a subject in less time than it would take for the students to integrate all the information themselves. Lecturing is a good method for introducing a new topic, giving background information, and motivating students to learn more on their own. Lecturing also helps students learn to listen accurately and critically. Finally, lecturing gives a teacher a chance to see which students appear confused and make on-the-spot changes to help them understand (Gilstrap and Martin, 1975). Lectures are therefore most appropriate for cognitive and affective objectives at the lower levels of the taxonomies described earlier.

Disadvantages of Lecturing

With all these advantages, lecturing may sound like the ideal method. But consider these four disadvantages. First, you may find that some students have trouble listening for more than a few minutes at a time and simply tune you out. Second, lecturing puts the students in a passive position and may prevent them from asking questions. Third, students learn and comprehend at different paces, while the lecture proceeds at the lecturer's own pace. Finally, the material covered in a lecture may often be communicated just as

**398**
**Designing
Instruction:
Objectives,
Formats, and
Settings**

well in a text assignment or a handout (Gilstrap and Martin, 1975). If your objectives include having students analyze a problem, synthesize (create) original products such as solutions, arguments, essays, poems, short stories, paintings, and so on, or evaluate work, then you must go beyond lecturing to methods that require more direct student involvement.

### Group Discussion

Group discussion is in some ways similar to the recitation strategy described earlier. A teacher may pose questions, listen to student answers, react, and probe for more information. But in a true group discussion the teacher tries to assume a less dominant role. Students ask and answer each other's questions and respond to each other's answers. The teacher becomes the moderator, trying to involve as many of the students as possible in the discussion, keeping the discussion on the topic (one of the hardest tasks), and helping students summarize and draw conclusions.

Advantages
of Discussion

Again, choices about when to use group discussion can best be made with an understanding of the advantages and disadvantages of the method in

## *Guidelines*
### Leading Class Discussion

**1. Invite the participation of shy children.**

EXAMPLES
- "What's your opinion, Joel?"
- "We need to hear from some other students. What do you think, Kevin?"
  *Note*: Do not wait until there is a deadly silence to ask these shy students to reply. Most people hate to break a silence, even more confident and verbal people. Also, be sure the question directed to such students is one that invites an easy response.

**2. Direct student comments and questions back to another student.**

EXAMPLES
- "That's an unusual idea, Steve. Kim, what do you think of Steve's idea?"
- "That's an important question, John. Ed, do you have any thoughts about how you'd answer that?"

**3. Make sure you understand what a student has said. If you are unsure, other students may be unsure as well.**

EXAMPLES
- Ask a second student to summarize what the first student said; then the first student can try again to explain if the summary is incorrect.
- "Karen, I think you're saying. . . . Is that right or have I misunderstood?"

**4. Probe for more information.**

EXAMPLES
- "That's a strong statement. Do you have any evidence to back it up?"
- "Tell us how you reached that conclusion. What steps did you go through?"

**399**

Designing
Instruction:
Objectives,
Formats, and
Settings

relation to your objectives. On the positive side, the students are directly involved and have the chance to participate. Group discussion helps students learn to express ideas clearly, to justify opinions, and to tolerate different views. Group discussion also gives students a chance to ask for clarification and get more information. Finally, students can assume responsibility by sharing the leadership of the group with the teacher (Gilstrap and Martin, 1975). Thus group discussions are appropriate for such objectives as evaluation of ideas, development of tolerant attitudes, and synthesis of personal viewpoints.

**Disadvantages of Discussion**

Of course, there are disadvantages. First, class discussions are quite unpredictable and may easily digress into an exchange of ignorance. Second, some members of the group may have great difficulty in participating and may become anxious if forced to speak. Third, a good deal of preparation may be needed to assure that participants have a common background of knowledge on which to base the discussion. Finally, large groups are often unwieldy. In many cases, a few students will dominate the discussion while the others daydream. The Guidelines included here may help you keep your group discussions on track.

**5. Bring the discussion back to the subject.**

**EXAMPLES**
- "Let's see, we were discussing . . . and Sarah made one suggestion. Has anyone a different idea?"
- "Let me try to summarize what has happened thus far before we continue."

**6. Give time for thought before asking for responses. Some students find it easier to speak if they write down a few ideas first.**

**EXAMPLES**
- "How would your life be different if television had never been invented? Jot down your ideas on paper and we will share reactions in a minute." After a few minutes, "Jean, will you tell us what you wrote?"

**7. Encourage children to look at and talk to one another. You set the stage early in the discussion by the way you answer student questions. If you give your opinion, you may find the discussion turning into a press interview where you are the expert and students are the reporters.**

**8. When a student finishes speaking, look around the room to judge reactions.**

**EXAMPLES**
- If other students look puzzled, ask them to describe why they are confused.
- If students are nodding assent, ask them to give an example of what was just said or further evidence to back up the argument.

Adapted from R. Dreikurs, B. B. Grunwald, and F. C. Pepper. *Maintaining sanity in the classroom: Illustrated teaching techniques.* New York: Harper and Row, 1971, pp. 100–120.

## Seatwork

Very little is known about how to use **seatwork** effectively. We have seen that students spend a great deal of their school day working alone at their seats. This type of solitary study can lead to learning. If properly designed and supervised, independent work can help students master a range of objectives, from simple drill and practice of knowledge to doing thoughtful evaluations of complex ideas.

To benefit from independent work, students must stay involved and do the work. As we will discuss more thoroughly in the next chapter, effective teachers supervise students, keeping them actively involved in the materials so that the time spent on seatwork is not wasted. For example, research indicates that being available to students doing seatwork is more effective than offering help to students before they ask for it (Rosenshine, 1977).

**Effective Seatwork**

But what kinds of tasks and materials keep students involved? One clue is found in a study by Kounin and Doyle (1975). When the teachers in this study arranged materials beforehand for their preschool students, the students were more attentive to the task. When the students had to stop to find needed materials, they often became distracted. Perhaps structure is especially important when students work on their own. The objectives of the task should be clear, and all the materials that might be needed should be provided.

Now we turn to one of the most widely discussed methods, individualized instruction. We will give this particular method somewhat more coverage than the others because of the great amount of planning it often involves.

## Individualized Instruction

**Characteristics of Individualized Instruction**

Individualized instruction does not necessarily mean independent work. **Individualized instruction** involves students working with learning plans that have been designed to meet their own needs, interests, and abilities.

*Individualized instruction does not have to mean individuals working alone. Students working in groups on activities designed to meet their needs are taking part in individualized instruction.*

**Modifying Lessons to Fit Individual Needs.**   To tailor a learning activity to individual students, a teacher might vary one or more of the following: (1) the pace of learning, (2) the instructional objectives, (3) the activity or the materials, (4) the reading level, or (5) the methods of expressing learning.

*Varying Pace*

Perhaps the simplest form of individualized instruction is to let students work at their own pace on the same assignment. To allow students to move at their own pace through a fixed body of material, the material must be broken down into a sequence of objectives and learning activities or assignments. After mastering one objective, a student can move on to the next.

*Objectives*

A second variable in individualized instruction is found in choice of learning objectives. If you establish a set of objectives, then pretest the class on the objectives, you may find that many students are already able to do much of the work. Instead of insisting that each student move through the same sequence of objectives, you can tailor the objectives to the needs, interests, and abilities of different students or different groups of students. A low-ability student might need to work on objectives related to concete skills. The steps in the task and the objectives would have to be small and specific. A gifted student might work toward objectives that call for high-level thinking and abstraction. For this student, the steps need not be small. Clearly, you need a variety of objectives across many ability levels to accommodate a heterogeneous group of students.

*Activities*

Another variable in individualized instruction is the learning activity itself. Even if students are moving toward the same objectives, they might use different means to achieve those objectives. One student might rely on the textbook, while another might read library books or newspaper stories. A third student could use audiovisual resources. Students with reading problems, students who have impaired vision, or students who have difficulty remembering what they read might listen to tapes or play simulation games together. Gifted students might do independent library research.

*Reading Level*

A fourth variable is reading level. All your students may be capable of working toward the same objective, but some may require material at a lower reading level than the rest. Most of the students in a high school class may be able to write a two-page paper comparing the Great Depression and the present economic situation, but some of them may need background reading material at the junior high level or even lower. It is not always possible to find such a wide range of reading materials. Information sources other than the printed word may have to be included.

*Expressing Learning*

A last variable that can be tailored to fit the needs of individual students is the way in which students are required to express or demonstrate learning. Students who have difficulty with written expression might be given oral tests or asked to tape record their answers to written tests. Gifted students might demonstrate learning by completing major papers or projects. For other students, frequent tests might be better. Some learning can also be expressed nonverbally, by drawing pictures, graphing relationships, making a model, or assembling a collage.

*Contracts*

**Special Programs for Individualized Instruction.**   Individual contracts offer an obvious means of varying instruction to meet individual needs. In Chapter 9 we described the use of contingency contracts and gave an example of a contract for an elementary school student. There are many different types of contracts. A teacher must decide who will determine the topic, objectives, materials, evaluation procedure, and time limits. Quite often a successful program combines both teacher and student decisions.

Contracts may be successful with students of any age, but young students need smaller objectives, shorter time limits, greater structure, and fewer choices. If you want your students to become more able to work independently, but still want to give them clear guidelines, contracts can be helpful.

Learning
Centers

A **learning center** can be set up in one corner of a classroom, in a hall or closet, or at a table. In some schools, entire rooms are set aside for learning centers in such subjects as mathematics or writing. The main purpose of a learning center is to engage students in activities that often involve manipulating materials. Many educators who advocate learning centers have been influenced by Piaget and his findings concerning the importance of concrete experiences for cognitive development. The objectives for the learning center program may be enrichment, skill building, or exploration (Blackburn and Powell, 1976).

In an enrichment center, students can follow up on a topic that has been covered in class. After a common lesson, they can use the center to pursue the topic at their own ability level and in keeping with their own interests and needs. Assume that science class has spent several days learning about photosynthesis. For the remainder of the unit, each student may be asked to complete three activities listed in the activity card file at a learning center. To make sure a student does not choose three similar activities, the cards could be color-coded (Blackburn and Powell, 1976).

Learning
Packages

**Learning packages** generally offer more structure than learning centers, but choices are still available to the students. Objectives are specified, but students may be given alternative ways of reaching them. In addition, students are given a chance to progress at their own pace. Among the items that may be included in a learning package are these: (1) a rationale explaining the reasons for completing the package; (2) objectives; (3) a variety of activities; and (4) a self-test.

When an entire class is organized around learning packages, students are usually required to complete several packages before taking a major test. The self-test in each package gives students an opportunity to evaluate their own strengths and weaknesses before facing a test that will be graded. Perhaps the most difficult part of preparing learning packages is writing at the students' level. The packages must be clear, well organized, and easy to follow, since students working alone or in groups must use the package as a guide.

Whatever method is chosen to individualize instruction, a teacher must know the subject well in order to break it down into small units and to arrange the units into a meaningful sequence. Most of the methods also rely heavily on clear objectives. Since students are often working on their own, without the teacher's direct control, they must know what they are expected to learn before they can make good choices about how to learn. Objectives describe these expectations.

Today, no discussion of teaching methods would be complete without an examination computer-assisted instruction. This is such an important area that we have devoted an entire section to it in the appendix immediately following this chapter.

# SETTINGS FOR ACHIEVING OBJECTIVES

In recent years, psychologists have become interested in the role of the physical environment in classroom learning. Instead of taking the room arrangement for granted, many teachers are discovering how to match the setting to objectives and activities. To understand the impact of the physical environment on learning in classrooms, you should be familiar with two basic ways of organizing space.

**Arranging Space by Territory**

Indignant cries of "This is *my* desk!" quickly become familiar to many elementary school teachers. In most traditional classrooms, a student's desk is inviolable territory. The spatial principle underlying this type of classroom arrangement is territoriality. The space is divided into individual territories that belong to their owners, at least until the teacher changes everyone's seat. This type of organization is particularly suitable for lessons addressed to the whole class at once.

**Arranging Space by Function**

A second way of arranging space is by function. In this arrangement, space is divided into interest areas or work centers that contain curriculum materials for specific topics, directions for activities, and work surfaces. Everyone has access to all areas. This type of arrangement is best for situations where small groups of students work simultaneously on a variety of activities.

These two ways of organizing space are not mutually exclusive; many teachers use a design that combines the two. Individual pupil desks are placed in the center, with interest areas in the back or around the periphery of the room. This allows flexibility for both large and small group activities.

Whichever way you choose to organize your classroom space, the environment must be suitable to the curriculum topic, your learning objectives, the type of lesson, the students, and you. If you read the box on messy teachers, you'll find another reason to think about the physical environment of your classroom.

## Interest-Area Arrangements

**Research on Space**

Recent research on this topic has shown that the design of interest areas can influence the way the areas are used by students. For example, working with a classroom teacher, Carol Weinstein (1977) was able to make changes in interest areas that helped the teacher meet her objectives of having more girls involved in the science center and having all students experiment more with a variety of manipulative materials. In a second study, changes in a library corner led to more involvement in activities related to literature throughout the class (Morrow and Weinstein, 1983).

Teachers are often puzzled by how to design interest areas that match their objectives for the students. Here are several suggestions.

**Decide What Activities You Want the Classroom to Accommodate.**  For example, if you are in a self-contained elementary classroom, you might wish to set up interest areas for reading, arts and crafts, science, and math. If you are teaching one particular subject on the junior or senior high level, you may wish to divide your room into several areas, perhaps for audiovisual activities, small group instruction, quiet study, and projects. List these

## BOX 11–1 MESSY TEACHERS

A schoolteacher who maintains a messy classroom is usually assumed to be disorganized.

This is no surprise.

But two Rutgers University researchers have learned that observers of that classroom may also conclude that the teacher is less stimulating, less dependable, lazy, unresponsive to student needs, unable to inspire good student behavior, lacking in creativity, and probably doesn't enjoy the job!

Dr. Carol Weinstein and Dr. Anita Woolfolk made these discoveries during their study of "The Classroom Setting as a Source of Expectations about Teachers and Pupils," recently published in the *Journal of Environmental Psychology*.

"Any person going through public school from kindergarten through 12th grade spends 14,000 hours in a classroom," Weinstein states. "But the schoolroom atmosphere is just so familiar that most of us aren't even aware of what is being communicated. We wanted to find out."

For their project on classroom design, slides depicting actual elementary schoolrooms were shown to three groups of subjects, who were asked to evaluate both the teacher who supposedly set up that learning environment and the students using it. No people were visible in any slide.

Two basic classroom arrangements were shown: the "traditional," with desks in rows, and the "open" classroom, with its interest-area plan. Rooms of both types varied in degree of orderliness. In "neat" rooms, work surfaces were clear, materials and books tidily arranged on shelves, and bulletin boards organized. The "messy" rooms were cluttered with clothing and papers; books and materials were strewn about; items hung askew on the bulletin boards.

The results clearly showed that teachers and pupils in neat rooms were judged much more favorably than their counterparts in the disorderly rooms, and pupils associated with neat rooms were assumed to be happier and better behaved.

When Weinstein showed the slides to fifth-graders, the youngsters' preference for neat over messy rooms was unanimous. "Not one child wanted to learn in a disorderly room, regardless of design," she reports. "They really notice and care. Neatness is obviously something they value."

And what about open versus traditional classrooms?

In both popular and professional literature, open classrooms are associated with a student-centered orientation, creativity, and flexibility, Weinstein and Woolfolk point out, while traditional row seating is linked to an emphasis on rigid authority, conformity, and regimentation.

The adult subjects in this experiment clearly corroborated these assumptions. However, they viewed the teachers as being equally organized and students as being equally well behaved in both types of rooms — as long as the rooms were neat!

For the fifth-graders in the study, spatial arrangement had no impact on their ratings. This may be due to the positive educational experiences these particular children have had in traditional classrooms, Weinstein believes.

"What we've learned so far," Weinstein asserts, "is that the physical setting must be considered. It is not more important than curriculum or interpersonal relations, but increased understanding of how people consciously or unconsciously use the environment as a source of information can help all who care about improving the quality of education in our schools."

*Source: Adapted from a Rutgers News Service release, Rutgers–The State University, New Brunswick, New Jersey, February 5, 1982.*

**405**

Designing
Instruction:
Objectives,
Formats, and
Settings

activities in a column, and next to each note whether any pose special spatial requirements. For example, art and science should be near the sink; science should also be near the windows if you wish to grow plants; a quiet study area should not be in front of the door; small group instruction should be near the board.

**Draw Several Floor Plans, Then Choose the Best.**   Use graph paper if possible, and draw to scale. As you work, keep in mind the following principles:

Principles
of Class Design

1.   *What are the fixed features?* What are the "givens" of the room that you must deal with — the locations of doors, windows, sockets. You probably do not want to have your audiovisual center in a corner without a plug!

2.   *Have easy access to materials.* Materials should have a clearly labeled place of their own, and these places must be easy to reach if you want students to use them. Shelves toward the center of the room seem to be more likely to attract attention than those placed in the corners. There should be enough shelves so that materials do not have to be placed in piles on top of each other.

3.   *Students need clean, convenient surfaces on which to use equipment.* The closer this surface is to the materials, the better.

4.   *Work areas should be private and quiet.* Tables or work areas should not be placed in the middle of traffic lanes, and a person should not have to pass through one area to get to another. Noisy activities should be placed as far as possible from quiet ones, and you can increase the feeling of quiet and privacy by placing partitions such as bookcases or pegboards between areas or within large areas.

5.   *There should be ease of supervision in each area.* If you plan to put up partitions, make sure they are low enough for you to see over them comfortably. If your classroom is too much like a maze, you will have difficulty surveying the goings-on in a quiet, efficient way.

6.   *Avoid dead spaces and racetracks.* Check to see that you have not placed all the interest areas around the outside of the room, leaving a large dead space in the middle. You also want to avoid placing a few items of furniture right in the middle of this large space, creating a racetrack around the furniture. Both encourage rowdiness, perhaps because they resemble playgrounds and so communicate to the pupils that it is okay to run here.

7.   *Provide choices.* Different people have different spatial needs. Some people prefer closed, small spaces in which to work; others may find such places too confining.

8.   *Provide flexibility.* At times you may wish to have students work alone, in small groups, or with many others. If you cannot arrange to have spaces for all these possibilities at one time, try to ensure that your design is flexible enough so that it can be changed to meet the requirements of new activities.

Testing Your
Plan

**Try the New Arrangement; Evaluate and Make Changes.**   Only by monitoring the use of the environment can difficulties be identified and solved. Even then, the suggestions we have presented cannot guarantee that students will select materials and work purposefully with them. Rather, the common goal of these suggestions is to remove as much physical friction from the classroom system as possible so that students can easily select and use materials. Incidentally, do not neglect to enlist the aid of your students. They have to live in the room too, and designing a classroom can be a very educational, challenging experience!

# Personal Territories

Effects of
Seating Position

Can the physical setting influence teaching and learning in classrooms organized by territories? Almost all the **environment-behavior research** in these classrooms has examined the relationship between seating position and variables such as personality, attitudes toward school, grades, and class participation. Let us look briefly at a few of the most intriguing studies.

Firsthand experience in traditional classrooms tells us that the most interested students sit at the front, and those who yearn for an early escape station themselves as close to the door as possible. Does research support this observation? In an extensive research project examining elementary and secondary classes, Adams and Biddle (1970) found that verbal interaction was concentrated in the center front of the classroom and in a line directly up the center of the room. The data were so dramatic that Adams and Biddle coined the term **action zone** to refer to this area of the room.

The questions that followed were these: "Do students who are interested in a course and who wish to participate select seats in the front, or do teachers assign front seats to students who tend to participate?" "Does a front-seat position somehow cause students to become more interested and involved in class?" The questions remain unresolved, but front-seat location does seem to increase participation from those students who are predisposed to speak in class, whereas a seat in the back will make it more difficult to participate and easier to sit back and daydream (Woolfolk and Brooks, 1983). In addition, even though most rooms have an "action zone" where participation is greatest, this area is not always front and center. In some classes it may be on one side or near a particular learning center (Good, 1983).

Alternatives
to Row Seating

Many teachers vary the seating in their classrooms so the same students are not always consigned to the back of the room. Another reason to change seating is to make the arrangement more appropriate for particular objectives and activities. Since too much rearranging can be a waste of time and an invitation to chaos, Musgrave (1975) distinguishes between home base formations, semipermanent arrangements that are suitable for a wide number of teaching-learning situations, and special formations, which give needed variety and are best suited to a particular lesson.

Home-Base
Formations

Figure 11–8 shows several home-base formations other than rows and columns. Horizontal rows share many of the advantages of row and column arrangements. Both are useful for independent seatwork, presentations, and recitations; they encourage students to focus on the teacher; and they simplify housekeeping. Horizontal rows permit a small amount of interaction among neighbors, so students can more easily work in pairs. This formation is also best for demonstrations, since students are closer to the teacher. However, it is a poor arrangement if a teacher wishes to encourage student interaction.

Clusters of four or circle arrangements are best for student interaction. Circles are especially useful for discussions, while still allowing independent seatwork. Clusters permit students to talk, help one another, share materials, and work on group tasks. Both arrangements, however, are poor for whole-group presentations and may make class control more difficult.

Special
Formations

Figure 11–9 shows several special formations. The debate arrangement and interest stations are probably familiar. The stack formation, where students sit close together near the focus of attention, should only be used for short periods of time, since it can lead to discipline problems. On the other

**407**

Designing
Instruction:
Objectives,
Formats, and
Settings

hand, it can create a feeling of group cohesion and is helpful when the teacher wants students to watch a demonstration, brainstorm on a class problem, or see a small visual aid.

Although the physical environment can hinder or aid the realization of a teacher's goals in ways that are real and important, it is not all-powerful. Arranging desks in a circle will not guarantee increased participation in a discussion. A cozy reading area will not solve reading problems. Nevertheless, it is essential that teachers consider the classroom space at the same time that they focus on the objectives and teaching methods. All play an important role in the establishment of an optimal learning environment.

**Figure 11–8    Some Home Base Formations**

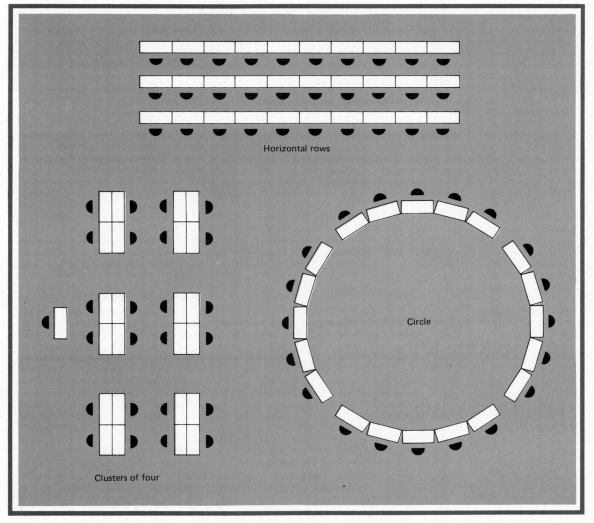

*Adapted from G. R. Musgrave,* **Individualized instruction: Teaching strategies focusing on the learner.** *Boston: Allyn and Bacon, 1975, pp. 49, 52, 54.*

**Figure 11–9  Some Special Formations**

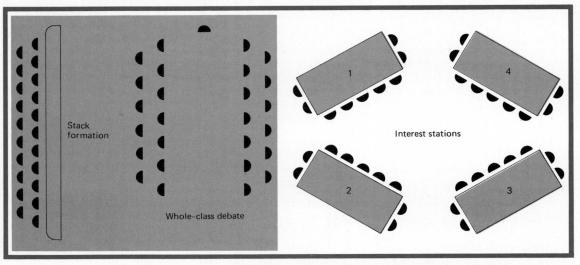

*Stack formation*

*Whole-class debate*

*Interest stations*

Adapted from G. R. Musgrave, **Individualized instruction: Teaching strategies focusing on the learner.** Boston: Allyn and Bacon, 1975, pp. 48, 63, 65.

## SUMMARY

1. Instructional objectives are statements of intended changes in the students.

2. They offer three major benefits to teachers and students. (1) Knowing the purpose of a learning experience helps students master the material. (2) The use of objectives can improve teacher-student communications. (3) Objectives can be invaluable in planning effective activities and in writing fair and balanced tests.

3. Three different approaches to writing objectives are Mager's very specific behavioral objectives, Gronlund's combination of general and specific objectives, and Eisner's expressive objectives.

4. Major criticisms of instructional objectives include the fact that they are time-consuming to write, the fact that trivial objectives are easier to create, the difficulty of writing objectives for some subjects, and the restrictions they place on student's abilities to explore knowledge on their own.

5. Using the task analysis system, a teacher identifies all the subskills needed to master a particular skill and then writes specific objectives for each subskill.

6. Benjamin Bloom and others have developed taxonomies listing basic objectives and a number of subobjectives for the cognitive, affective, and psychomotor domains.

7. One well-developed method for planning an entire unit is a behavior-content matrix, a grid combining student behaviors with specific items of course content.

8. There are a number of formats for teaching: recitation and questioning, lecturing, group discussion, seat work, and individualized instruction.

9. To individualize instruction the teacher can vary the pace, objectives, activities, reading level, or method for expressing learning.

10. There are two basic kinds of spatial organization, territorial (the traditional classroom arrangement) and functional (dividing space into interest or work areas).

11. Four steps to follow in organizing a classroom include: (1) decide what activities you want your classroom to accommodate; (2) draw a number of floor plans; (3) choose the plan you like best; and (4) try it out, evaluate it, and redesign it if necessary.

**KEY TERMS**

| | |
|---|---|
| instructional objectives | behavior-content matrix |
| operationalize | recitation |
| expressive objectives | convergent/divergent thinking |
| task analysis | seatwork |
| taxonomy | individualized instruction |
| domains: cognitive, affective, | learning center |
| psychomotor | learning package |
| objective test | environment-behavior research |
| essay test | action zone |

## SUGGESTIONS FOR FURTHER READING AND STUDY

COOPER, J. M., HANSEN, J. MARTORELLA, P. H., MORINE-DERSHIMER, G., SADKER, D., SADKER, K., SHOSTAK, R., SOKOLOVE, S., TENBRINK, T., and WEBER, W. A. *Classroom teaching skills: A handbook.* Lexington Mass.: D.C. Heath & Co., 1977. Each chapter in this book was written by an expert in the field. Topics include setting objectives, individualizing instruction, questioning skills, and making effective presentations.

DRESSEL, P. L. The nature and role of objectives in instruction. *Educational Technology,* 1977, *17,* 7–15. This article surveys current thinking about a balanced and sensible approach to using instructional objectives.

EMMER, E. T. and MILLETT, G. B. *Improving teaching through experimentation: A laboratory approach.* Englewood Cliffs, NJ: Prentice-Hall, 1970. A brief but very practical book about how to determine readiness, communication objectives to students, motivate, and evaluate. There are case studies and guidelines for evaluating your own teaching.

FURST, E. J. Bloom's taxonomy of educational objectives for the cognitive domain: Philosophical and educational issues. *Review of Educational Research,* 1981, *51,* 441–454. A thoughtful critique of Bloom's taxonomy.

GILSTRAP, R. L. and MARTIN, W. R. *Current strategies for teachers: A resource for personalizing instruction.* Pacific Palisades, CA: Goodyear, 1975. Among the many different strategies discussed here are lecturing, group discussion, drill, independent study, group projects, discovery, learning centers, and learning packages.

GRONLUND, N. E. *Stating behavioral objectives for classroom instruction* (2nd ed.). Toronto: Macmillan, 1978. This is a very practical book telling how to be sensible about using instructional objectives but still reap the benefits of this strategy.

GRONLUND, N. E. *Constructing achievement tests* (3rd ed.). Englewood Cliffs, NJ: Prentice-Hall, 1982. Gronlund describes how to plan evaluation for cognitive, affective, and psychomotor objectives.

KAPFER, M. B. (Ed.). *Behavioral objectives: The position of the pendulum.* Englewood Cliffs, NJ: Prentice-Hall, 1978. This book has chapters by many experts on the use of behavioral objectives in instruction.

MAGER, R. *Preparing instructional objectives.* Palo Alto, CA: Fearon, 1962. Perhaps the most influential work on how to write behavioral objectives. Mager's book is written with style and humor in branching-program format.

REDFIELD, D. L. and ROUSSEAU, E. W. A meta-analysis of experimental research on teacher-questioning behavior. *Review of Educational Research,* 1981, *51,* 181–193. These researchers compare the results of many studies on teacher questions and student learning.

WEINSTEIN, C. The physical environment of the school and student behavior. *Review of Educational Research,* 1979, **49,** 577–610. This article offers a very thorough review of recent research on the physical aspects of schools and classrooms, particularly as those features affect student behavior.

SOMMER, R. *Tight spaces: Hard architecture and how to humanize it.* Englewood Cliffs, NJ: Prentice-Hall, 1974. A classic book about how to make the physical environment more appropriate for human activities.

# Teachers' Forum

## Where Do Objectives Come From?

Sources of instructional objectives can range from those found in teachers' manuals and curriculum guides to those written by individual teachers and tailored to fit each class. How do you proceed in establishing instructional goals for the subject matter you teach? How do you present these goals to the students?

**Objectives for Gifted Students**

There are few materials for instruction of the gifted and talented compared to regular instructional programs, so GT teachers write much of the curriculum, sharing developed units with other GT teachers throughout the system. Teachers choose unit topics that may be presented at an introductory level in the regular classroom, then expand them in the GT class; or the topics may not be part of the regular classroom program at all. . . . [C]urriculum for the gifted and talented . . . should provide a differentiated program, taking the student where he/she is and moving him/her into areas of skill development that would not be possible in the regular classroom setting. In addition, the curriculum should establish objectives dealing with the highest levels of affective and cognitive skills (e.g., analysis, synthesis, evaluation). It should be open-ended and allow the *student* to choose an investigation, to develop goals and method of execution, to determine what constitutes a finished product, to evaluate the product, and to present/demonstrate the product to others in the class. . . .

Richard D. Courtright, Gifted and Talented Teacher
*Ephesus Road Elementary School, Chapel Hill, North Carolina*

## The Individual Contract Program: Pitfalls

This year you have decided to individualize your teaching by using contracts. About two-thirds of the students enjoy this method and are thriving under it. But you find that the other students are lost when they have to work independently. They wander about the room and work only when you supervise them directly. You simply don't have time to work with all these students individually each day.

**Independence or Supervision?**

First I would want to determine if these children understand fully what the contracts are and how they are expected to proceed. If this is not the problem, but they require a more structured environment, I would group this third of the class and continue their instruction with direct teacher supervision. I would use those parts of the contracts they could handle independently. . . . Another possible approach would be to pair with another teacher for part of the day—giving independence to those who can handle it and supervision to those who cannot.

Charlotte Ross, Second-Grade Teacher
*Conert Avenue School, Elmont, New York*

**Gradual Transition**

No one method works for all children. I have found that some children require more structure than others for successful learning. I place these children in a small group and give them more direct supervision. I gradually introduce more and more independent assignments to them as the children appear to be able to handle the independence. Eventually, most are able to work more independently, and the few remaining are easier to work with on an individual basis.

Arleen Wyatt, Third-Grade Teacher
*Happy Valley Elementary School, Rossville, Georgia*

## The Discussion Method: Pitfalls

Your student teacher is a strong advocate of the discussion method and relies almost solely on this teaching strategy. You have noticed, however, that a number of the students never participate and seem to be totally turned off by this teacher. Others participate occasionally, but have recently begun to get more and more bored. At this point, the class seems to revolve around a small group of students who admire the student teacher.

**Consider the Alternatives**  I would speak directly with the student teacher. . . . I would present the student teacher with as many learning techniques as possible and suggest that he/she find more appropriate means to reach the objectives. The student teacher should evaluate for him/herself the value of using the discussion mode alone. This should be accomplished early so as not to lose the class's interest or cause discipline problems.

Wayne A. Ginty, Tenth-Grade Social Studies Teacher
*Lockport Senior High School, Lockport, New York*

**A Repertoire of Strategies**  If the goals for students are total participation, critical thinking practice, and interest and enjoyment in learning, then student teachers must develop a repertoire of teaching strategies. Questioning techniques, variety of media, programs for individual needs and interests, and ways to integrate specific concepts into an overall scheme for the learner would have to supplement the discussion method to compensate for individual differences. The student teacher should participate in an interaction analysis with audio-video equipment to make a personal evaluation. The evaluation may point out that sole use of the discussion method has turned into an "ad lib" situation, and maximum teacher-student interaction has not been achieved. The feedback can serve as a basis for future needs and planning.

Barbara L. Luedtke, Secondary Physical Education Teacher
*Appleton High School — East, Appleton, Wisconsin*

**Using a Planning Web**  When working with a student teacher in developing a curriculum, I use a planning web to identify the content and list the many ways each section can be taught. With this information, the student teacher selects a different strategy for each section. This enables the person to experiment with several methods, select the one with which he/she feels most comfortable, and practice a variety of teaching strategies. . . . To monitor the number of students who participate during each class period, I audit the student teacher by video or audio-taping the lessons. The student teacher's assignment is to listen and/or watch the presentation and to time teacher versus student participation. Additionally, I will observe lessons during which I mark on a seating chart the number of responses each student makes during a class period. The student teacher and I [then] discuss strategies by which additional student participation can be achieved. . . .

Ruth Roberts, Seventh-Grade Earth Sciences/Biology Teacher
*Greece Athena Junior High School, Rochester, New York*

# Appendix:

# Computer-Based Education

**OVERVIEW**
As you glance at this page, a revolution is taking place around you. Signs of it can be seen everywhere—on TV, in magazines, in offices, in private homes, and in schools. The computer age has arrived, and in the opinion of some, will be significant enough to be labeled that way by historians (Johnson, 1981). That computer usage is rapidly increasing in our society is probably not shocking news. But you may be asking this: "What implications will the computer age have for me as a prospective teacher?" Although computers have been used for many different functions over the past three decades, it is only recently that they have had a significant impact in schools. This appendix is intended to acquaint you with past and current developments, including the origin of computers, their features and operation, and their specific applications to education and teaching. Special emphasis will be placed on **microcomputers,** the major force behind today's computer revolution. These small, relatively inexpensive systems make it possible for homes and schools to enter the computer age on a large scale.

When you complete this appendix, you should be able to:

- Describe major events in the origin of computer-based education.
- Distinguish among the types of computer applications and systems used in education.
- Describe the considerations involved in selecting hardware and software for computer-based education.
- Evaluate computer-based lessons in terms of strengths and limitations for teaching.

Before beginning our journey into the world of computers, we present a glossary of important terms in Figure 11A–1 (the same terms are also defined in the Glossary in the back of the book). One of the least appreciated by-products of the computer revolution is the proliferation of new terminology to describe things both familiar and strange. For a much more thorough review of computer terms, an excellent resource is an article by Douglas and Edwards in the October 1979 issue of *Educational Technology.*

**Figure 11A–1  Common Computer Terms**

BASIC. An acronym for Beginners All-purpose Symbolic Instructional Code, the most popular programming language for microcomputers.

Byte. The basic unit of information in a computer. The symbol K refers to 1024 bytes, and is used to specify the size of a computer's memory (32K = 32 × 1024 bytes).

CAI. An acronym for computer-assisted instruction—use of computers directly for teaching.

CBE. An acronym for computer-based education—general applications of computers in support of classroom teaching and management.

Chip (Microchip). A tiny piece of silicon smaller than a fingernail on which circuit elements are etched for carrying out computer operations.

CMI. An acronym for computer-managed instruction—use of computer for support functions such as testing, recordkeeping, scheduling, and prescribing.

Hardware. The physical equipment that goes into a computer, consisting of mechanical, magnetic, electrical, and electronic devices.

Monitor. A video display unit, which uses a cathode ray tube (CRT) to generate characters. It resembles a regular TV set, but has a higher degree of resolution (greater clarity).

Peripherals. Accessory devices, such as printers and modems, which transfer information when connected to a computer.

Software. The programs and accompanying documentation for use with computers.

Stand-alone. A computer unit that functions independently of other units. Microcomputers belong to this category.

Timesharing. A system in which separate computer terminals are dependent on a central computer for operation.

## THE ORIGIN OF COMPUTER-BASED EDUCATION

The First Computer

Changes with the Microchip

It was only a relatively short time ago that the first general-purpose computing machine made its appearance. Its name was ENIAC, and it was built at the University of Pennsylvania in 1946 at the cost of approximately $500,000 (1946 dollars!). It weighed 30 tons and required 1,500 square feet of floor space. Inside, it contained 18,500 special vacuum tubes which required 130,000 watts of power.

Technology improved steadily over the years. Vacuum tubes were replaced by transistors, which reduced the bulk of computers by a factor of 10 (Thompson, 1979). But even with this significant shedding of poundage, computers remained pretty much in the heavyweight division. In 1971, however, an event of major importance sent these transistor-laden creatures the way of the dinosaur almost overnight. The event was the development of the **microchip,** a one-quarter-square-inch piece of material on which thousands of electronic circuits (replacements for tubes and transistors) could be implanted. By 1980, the number of vacuum tube equivalents that could be etched on a microchip ranged from 60,000 to 70,000. By 1981, the number had increased to 750,000 tube equivalents. Using microchips, transmissions of impulses (switchings) can take place in several nanoseconds, one-thousand-millionths of a second (Shane, 1982). Awe-inspiring figures, no doubt, but what does it all mean? The answer is cost efficiency, high power, and seemingly limitless possibilities for miniaturization. The descendant of ENIAC is a device that sells for a very small fraction of ENIAC's cost and has the bulk and weight of a typewriter.

What does all this have to do with computer-based education? Our brief delay in getting to that subject actually mirrors real life, except that the wait for CBE was anything but brief. The reason is simple. The pioneers of the computer age were engineers, mathematicians, and physicists. Neither their inventions nor their interests were geared toward education. But in the rapidly expanding computer industry, there was a need to train new personnel quickly and efficiently. What better way to do this than by using the computers themselves to do the training? In the late 1950s, members of the computer industry became some of the first users of CBE, applying it to instruction and training in their own field (Suppes and Macken, 1978).

Programmed
Instruction

Interest in **programmed instruction** provided impetus for the involvement of educators soon thereafter (Burns and Bozeman, 1982). If you have read the section on programmed instruction presented in Chapter 5 and have had any previous exposure to CBE, you can appreciate how natural computers might have seemed as a means of presenting programmed lessons. Throughout the 1960s, many projects were intitiated by corporations and universities to develop and evaluate such applications. Among the most successful of these efforts was the Stanford Program directed by Patrick Suppes, which after only two years of operation provided daily computerized instruction in reading or mathematics to approximately 400 disadvantaged students (Burns and Bozeman, 1982; Suppes, Jerman and Brian, 1968). But this was only the beginning. By the late 1960s, numerous CBE systems were emerging all over

PLATO

the country. The PLATO system, which we will briefly review below, was one of the most successful of these efforts.

But only a very small proportion of children received any exposure to CBE. Even today, the percentage is relatively limited. For instance, was CBE available at your elementary school or high school? The answer for most readers is probably "No." But with the emergence of microcomputers—in a few years that response may be quite rare. The computer age, though a little slow in getting started in education, is exploding onto the scene with great force.

# ORIENTATION AND SYSTEMS OF CBE

## Instruction versus Management

CAI

Thus far in our discussion, we have referred to educational applications using only the general label CBE (computer-based education). But the term *education,* being so all-encompassing, gives little impression of the types of applications. Therefore, we will introduce two new labels: CAI, computer-assisted instruction, and CMI, computer-managed instruction. In computer-

CMI

assisted instruction, the computer, not a person or textbook, presents the lesson. The systems referred to earlier (such as PLATO) exemplify this orientation. Computer-managed instruction is using the computer to help manage or supervise instruction. Typical functions include recordkeeping, testing, scheduling, prescribing, and time and resource management.

## Together versus Alone

How is CBE made available in classrooms? Although fairly detailed classifications have been made of the different possibilities (Bork, 1978), for simplicity we will restrict our analysis to two basic categories: timesharing versus stand-alone.

In a **timesharing system,** students sit at separate terminals connected to a main computer through direct wiring, phone lines, or microwaves. The main computer may be in the same room as the terminals, in another room in the school, or at a location many miles away. The terminal will typically contain a keyboard to receive student responses and a television-type (cathode ray tube or CRT) screen to display information from the computer. The terminal does not function as a computer, but only as a device for transmitting information. The PLATO system provides an excellent example of timesharing. Operated by the Computer-Based Education Research Laboratory at the University of Illinois and Control Data Corporation, it has over 1000 terminals connected to its main computer in Urbana, Illinois (Alderman, Appel and Murphy, 1978; Brenner and Agee, 1979). Communication between the computer and the user terminal takes place by microwaves for nearby locations and over telephone lines for remote locations. Lessons appear on a special plasma panel that can produce animation as well as complex graphics. Teachers write their own lessons using a special language called TUTOR. Users have access to any PLATO lesson stored in a cental library and can communicate directly with any other user on the system.

The second major type of computer system is the **stand-alone unit.** Here each "terminal" is actually a computer, capable of storing and processing information. The most obvious example of a stand-alone unit is the microcomputer (Apple, Pet, Commodore, Radio Shack brands) now advertised and sold everywhere. A student positioned at one of these receives the lesson independently of all other students and of any other computer. But an individual microcomputer can also be made part of a timesharing system by connecting it to a central computer. PLATO terminals are now being developed to function in both stand-alone and timesharing capacities (Brenner and Agee, 1979).

In thinking about these classifications, it is natural to wonder which provides the better basis for CBE. The answer is that each can be advantageous, depending on the circumstances. Timesharing offers the advantage of a coordinated system permitting centralized storage of records and access to an existing library of programs. A disadvantage, however, is that when the main computer is not operating for some reason (this is called **downtime**), CBE becomes unavailable to all students for that period (regardless of the teacher's lesson plans). Another consideration is that a timesharing operation may be expensive as a result of requiring special terminals and access to a large computer. A single PLATO terminal, for example, costs between $2000 and $4000. Stand-alone units will eliminate the downtime problem and may reduce expenses, but sacrifice the advantages of timesharing. In the next few years you can expect many new developments that combine the advantages of timesharing and stand-alone units.

*Timesharing* (margin note)

*Stand-alone* (margin note)

## MICROCOMPUTERS IN THE CLASSROOM

### Hardware

*Components of a Microcomputer* (margin note)

Microcomputers, like people, come in many different shapes and sizes, but all share certain common features. All microcomputers possess capabilities for receiving, processing, and transmitting information. A typical microcomputer, as shown in Figure 11A–2, looks something like a typewriter that

**416**

**Figure 11A–2   Microcomputer and Peripherals**

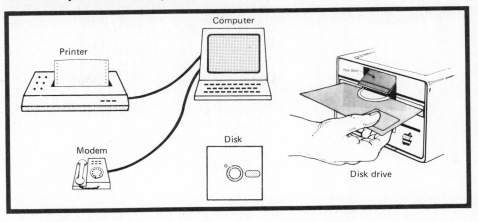

grew a television set where its head should be. The typewriter part or keyboard provides the primary means through which the user transmits information *to* the computer. What looks like a TV screen is actually called a monitor. Its function is to display information from the computer. Its advantage over a regular TV is that it is constructed for that function and thus provides a clearer picture (greater resolution). The heart of the computer, which is not visible in the diagram, is its central processing unit (CPU), made up of the microchips we talked about earlier. The CPU carries out the logical decisions and calculations, in association with the computer's memory.

What we have been describing is called **hardware**—the physical equipment that goes into a computer system. Hardware not directly associated with the main computing functions is called **peripherals.** Two peripherals already introduced are the keyboard and monitor. Here are some others:

**Peripherals**

1. **Disk drive:** If your only peripherals were a keyboard and a monitor, you could send and receive information, but would have no way of storing it outside the computer's memory. Any CAI program you wanted to use would have to be manually entered into the computer's memory each time. A disk drive is a device for storing information on, and reading it from, a plastic **disk** similar to a 45 rpm record. The disk drive can access any location on the disk instantaneously. It is reliable and efficient, and probably an almost essential peripheral for CBE functions.

2. *Tape recorder.* Another device for storing information is a conventional cassette tape recorder. It is much less expensive than the disk drive, but using it is time-consuming and also risky should tapes become severed or tangled. Disk drives are much preferred.

3. **Printer.** Displays on a monitor are only temporary; once a new one appears, what was previously on the screen can no longer be viewed. Printers, much like typewriters, print information on paper, providing what is called a *hard copy.* Hard copies are especially valuable in doing programming, as the entire program can be examined at one's convenience. The monitor screen, having limited space, permits examination of only a small segment at a time. Other obvious advantages of hard copies are for printing records of student performance, generating homework exercises for students to take home, writing letters and memos, and so on.

4.  *Game paddles.* Many computer games and some CAI lessons call for a rapid, coordinated type of response that cannot be achieved through pressing keys. Game paddles, a relatively inexpensive peripheral, make such responding possible through manipulation of push buttons and circular dials.

5.  **Modem.** The modem, which is essentially a telephone coupler, permits connection to a main computer or other microcomputers over regular phone lines. You "call up" the other computer, place the phone in the modem, and your microcomputer becomes a "terminal" capable of communicating with that computer. As a result, you can share information with others, play a game of chess with someone thousands of miles away, or access data sources such as the stock market, news wire services, and the Library of Congress.

For the most part, the essential (or most useful) peripherals are the keyboard, monitor, and disk drive. In many brands of microcomputers, these peripherals are standard; in others, only the keyboard is standard since the monitor and drive must be purchased separately. What is the cost of this basic setup? A realistic price is from about $800 to $3000, with the actual amount depending on size, capabilities, and manufacturer. By adding peripherals (perhaps a modem or extra disk drive), you can build a more powerful and flexible system. Another factor in price is the size of the computer's memory, expressed in number of **kilobytes** or **K** (roughly, the capacity to store 1000 characters). For simple home or educational applications, as little as 4K may suffice. Many commercial programs, however, will require between 16K and 48K. Most good educational programs require 48K or more.

*The Computer's K*

## Software

CBE does not rest on hardware alone; something called software is also required. **Software** refers to the programs that tell the computer what to do. When not being used by the computer, software resides in a storage medium such as a disk or tape cassette. The important point is that a school can own the most elaborate computer system, with every peripheral imaginable, but the value of any CAI it provides will ultimately depend on the quality of the software used ("garbage in, garbage out," as some programmers say). How is educational software acquired? Let us see.

*Computer Languages*

**Using Computer Languages.** The most direct way to obtain educational software is to do the programming yourself. Microcomputers are designed to make programming as simple as possible. The standard microcomputer programming language is BASIC, which stands for Beginners All-purpose Symbolic Instruction Code. BASIC involves the use of simple Engish words and common mathematical expressions, making it one of the easiest languages to learn. Other languages that are becoming increasingly popular for microcomputers are PASCAL, an alternative to BASIC designed to minimize errors and simplify revisions (Bork and Franklin, 1979) and Logo, a special language designed for young children (Papert, 1980).

For some people, programming is tremendously enjoyable. For others, just the idea of learning something as "difficult" and "technical" as computer programming is tremendously threatening. Such resistance is unfortunate. Today, with the new programming languages, the excellent self-tutorial manuals, and the computer literacy courses appearing in many college curriculums, just about everyone can learn the fundamentals of programming.

As an illustration of how logical and straightforward programming is, we have listed the statements of an instructional program written in BASIC in Figure 11A–3. The program randomly generates different multiplication problems involving numbers between 1 and 100, evaluates the student's

**Figure 11A–3** **CAI Program on Multiplication Written in BASIC**

| Statements | What They Mean |
|---|---|
| 10 HOME | Clears the screen. |
| 20 X = INT(RND(1)*100) + 1 | The RND command will randomly generate a number between 0 and 99. The INT converts it to whole number. We add 1 so that X will be a whole number between *1* and *100*. Let's pretend the number 12 is generated. |
| 30 Y = INT(RND(1)*100) + 1 | The same as for statement 20, except now we need a second number, Y, to be multiplied. Let's pretend the number 40 is generated. |
| 40 PRINT X; "*"; Y; " = ?" | This will print the problem on the screen for the student to see. It will look like this: 12 * 40 = ? |
| 50 PRINT | Skips a line to make a more readable display. |
| 60 A = X*Y | Assigns the correct answer to location (variable label) A. |
| 70 INPUT "ENTER ANSWER"; Z | Asks for response from student. Will assign that response to location Z. The screen now looks like this: 12 * 40 = ? |
| | ENTER ANSWER |
| 80 IF (Z = A) THEN 120 | Student's answer, Z, is compared to the actual answer, A. If it matches, we skip to #120. If not a match, continue to #90. |
| 90 PRINT "INCORRECT" | Indicates that the answer was incorrect. |
| 100 PRINT X; "*"; Y; " ="; A | Prints the problem and the correct answer on the screen. Example: 12 * 40 = 480 |
| 110 GOTO 130 | Skips to #130 (remember #120 is only for correct answers). |
| 120 PRINT "CORRECT" | Indicates that the answer was correct. |
| 130 INPUT "DO YOU WANT ANOTHER? (Y/N)"; Y$ | Asks if another problem is desired. Assigns answer Y or N to location Y$. |
| 140 IF Y$ = "Y" THEN 10 | If Y was selected in #130, we go back to statement 10 and start again. If Y wasn't selected, we continue to the next statement. |
| 150 END | End the program. |

*Notes*
1. *The computer follows the statements in numerical order. The particular numbers used (10 or 20) do not matter as long as the sequence is correct.*
2. *Different computer brands use slightly different versions of BASIC (sort of like a dialect). This program is written in the Applesoft version. The symbol * is used to represent multiplication in this version, as conventional signs, × or ·, are unavailable.*

answers, and provides appropriate feedback. Adjacent to each program statement in the figure is an explanation (translation) of what is being done at that particular point. If you are saying to yourself, "Well, I'll skip that one — programming is not for me," there is a very good chance you are one of the people we were just talking about. Give it a try; we are counting on your discovering it is not so complicated after all. The *advantages* of authoring your own software are (1) programs can be tailored to *your* specific instructional objectives, and (2) it can be very enjoyable, if you like programming. The *disadvantages* are that such programs (1) take a great deal of time, and (2) will generally not approach the quality of professional programs.

**Using Authoring Systems.** To help instructors who have little computer background, special authoring languages have been developed. Unlike conventional programming languages, authoring languages contain built-in logic and a much more limited series of commands (Schuyler, 1979). The instructor simply learns the meaning of the commands and when to use them. The programming that makes them operate is automatically incorporated in the lesson. *Advantages:* (1) The program can be tailored to specific instructional objectives; and (2) familiarity with conventional programming languages is not necessary. *Disadvantages:* (1) Such programs tend to be relatively restricted in what they can do because only certain routines may be available; and (2) the amount of time it takes to study the commands and the accompanying documents may approach that required for learning conventional languages. (For a more detailed analysis of the pros and cons of authoring languages, see Merrill, 1981.)

**Purchasing Commerical Software.** Before the days of microcomputers, publishing companies had little incentive to produce educational software. After all, only a small number of schools and practically no individual households owned computers. The microcomputer revolution has changed that situation. Educational programs now exist and are continually being developed in just about all subjects at all different levels. Not only is commercial software easily attainable, it is relatively inexpensive. A high-quality CAI program in spelling or algebraic rules, for example, might be purchased for as little as $30, with a reasonable upper limit of about $200–$250. Some advantages of commercial software are: (1) numerous selections, (2) immediate availability, and (3) professional quality. Some disadvantages are: (1) the exact lessons needed may not be available; (2) those that are available may not teach or interpret the content in the way desired; and (3) costs, though relatively inexpensive, may be monumental for teachers working from a limited supply budget or from personal funds.

**Hiring a Professional Programmer.** Contracting with a professional programmer to create customized educational software is another option. The advantages are that programmers (1) can tailor the lesson to your exact needs, and (2) normally provide professional quality work. The disadvantages are that (1) the level of skill of those who claim to be professionals varies widely, making such arrangements somewhat risky; (2) professional time can be *very* costly unless the programmers are paid employees of the school district; and (3) programmers may misinterpret instructions or have their own ideas, resulting in a program that works differently from what was expected.

**Obtaining Free Software.**   Most educators do not know about the variety of means through which free software can be obtained (Price, 1982). Computer journals and books frequently contain program listings and accompanying descriptions. All one needs to do is buy the journal or book and copy the programs. Another source is clubs and individuals interested in sharing their libraries or working out trades. The advantages of free software are obvious. But what is available (1) may not fit your needs, (2) may be low in quality, and (3) in some cases be illegal—piracy is becoming a serious problem.

The success of any CBE system depends on both the hardware and software that is acquired.

## COMPUTERS VERSUS CONVENTIONAL TEACHING METHODS

What, if anything, can computers do for education that conventional teaching methods cannot? What types of tasks are they best equipped to perform? Robert Taylor (1980), in his book, *The Computer in the School: Tutor, Tool, Tutee,* envisioned three roles for the computer in education. The first is to function as a *tutor* for students by presenting material, evaluating responses, and deciding, on the basis of the evaluation, what to present next. The second is to function as a *tool* by helping students and teachers perform calculations, analyze data, keep records, or write papers. The third is to function as a *tutee* by having student and teacher tell *it* what to do through programming, using BASIC, Logo, PASCAL, or some other language. The tutor role is what traditionally thought of as CAI, whereas the latter two roles (tool and tutee) are newer conceptions. Given the prominence and longer tradition of the tutor role, let us examine some of its attributes, starting first with those that appear advantageous for teaching.

### Advantages

**Self-Pacing.**   It is an established fact in education that students learn at different rates. CAI is particularly well suited to accommodate those differences. The fast worker (or high achiever) can move through the CAI lesson rapidly and progress to the next, without having to wait for classmates to catch up. Students experiencing difficulty, however, can move at a slower pace, reviewing troublesome sections and requesting additional practice until mastery is achieved. In contrast, lecture-recitation methods are group-paced—all students receive the instruction at the same time and at the same rate.

**Drill and Practice.**   Though it is easy for teachers to agree with the idea that "practice makes perfect," providing the right amount for each individual is almost an impossible task. In this regard, the computer, because it possesses nearly limitless patience and endurance, has an important advantage. Having nowhere to go after class, it is content to sit there and present drill as long as the student likes. A spelling program, for example may store hundreds of words on a disk to be presented in different amounts and different orders to individuals, based on need. Another example is the program on multiplication illustrated in Figure 11A–3. By using a random number generator, the program creates new examples, as many as desired, upon request. Drill-and-practice programs are available in virtually all subjects and are probably the easiest CAI programs for teachers to write themselves.

Individualizing Instruction

**Personalized Feedback and Instruction.**    Like programmed instruction, CAI is expressly designed to foster active student responding. Once a response is given, immediate feedback can be presented, indicating whether it was correct or incorrect. But, unlike programmed instruction, CAI permits information about that response, along with other pertinent information (the students' name, pretest score, and so on), to be stored and used to generate personalized messages and prescriptions. For example, we could easily embellish our math program (Figure 11A–3 again) so that if a student misses more than 5 out of the first 10 examples, he or she is directed to a particular section of the textbook and told to complete a certain number of exercises. We could further arrange the program so that, based on analyses of pretest score and success on early examples, the *difficulty level* and/or *number* of new examples is appropriately increased or decreased (Ross and Rakow, 1981; Tennyson and Rothen, 1977). Numerous options for personalized instruction, some learner-controlled and others program-controlled (Park and Tennyson, 1980), are possible.

Lessons for the TV Generation

**Multisensory Presentations.**    Picture the following scene: A second-grader is receiving a CAI lesson on sentence construction. A list of words is displayed on the monitor, from which he is to choose appropriate articles, nouns, and verbs to construct a proper English sentence. He types his entry: "The boy chases the ball." Suddenly the screen flashes in all different colors, a buzzer sounds, and his sentence appears in large letters in the middle of the screen accompanied by the message: "Good work, Billy, that is a proper sentence." The screen goes blank, and a few seconds later a little ball appears and starts rolling across the screen followed by a boy chasing it (while clicking sounds reproduce the cadence of the boy's steps). The sentence has come alive! Computers have the ability to utilize a variety of presentation modes, including text, illustrations, movement, and sound. This adds diversity to a lesson, which can reduce boredom while providing alternatives for students who may have difficulty learning from a particular mode, such as reading text or interpreting pictures.

Life-like Learning

**Simulations.**    Certain skills are extremely difficult or prohibitively expensive to teach under realistic conditions. The vocational education instructor, for instance, might find his principal somewhat reluctant to approve a request to purchase a gasoline engine for each of his 20 students. Similarly, the physics teacher may detect an uneasiness among parents when she asks their permission to teach the principles of flight by giving the students rides in a glider she built. Actual experience may be the best teacher, but if that is not feasible, an excellent alternative can be working with a simulation or model. The computer's capabilities for graphics, animation, and user interaction makes simulation a natural and highly valuable CAI component (Dellow and Ross, 1983). Excellent programs have been developed that simulate such processes as the operation of gasoline engines, flying an airplane, collective bargaining in business, and the functioning of the heart.

*Working at a computer terminal need not be solitary. Students can try to solve problems together. The interaction is part of the learning.*

Ken Karp

The complexity that can be structured into a microcomputer simulation is illustrated by a program entitled "Three Mile Island" (MUSE Company). It takes several hours to learn the rules and procedures, but it is an exciting experience when mastered. The program includes different multicolored and animated displays of a nuclear reactor. When a valve malfunctions and the water heats up, the blue water running in the tubes changes to red. Alarms go off and trouble, meaning "meltdown," is definitely on the way unless you beat the clock and make the correct decisions. Giving students real nuclear reactors to work with is simply not feasible for many reasons. Having them read about them in a textbook is certainly important, but may not be very involving or provide much feel for actual decision-making processes. Simulations provide a valuable means of filling these gaps.

**Learning as Child's Play**

**Games.** "It is 1847 and you have just spent $200 of your $900 life savings to attempt the trip from Independence, Missouri, to Oregon City over the Oregon Trail. On the way you may encounter many potential hazards, such as Indian attacks, rustlers, illness, and inclement weather. Be careful and good luck." With these ominous warnings and the tune "Home on the Range" playing in the background, our sixth-grade pioneers venture forth to test their skill on a program entitled "Oregon Trail" (Minnesota Educational Computing Consortium). Although not simulations in the sense of mirroring actual occurrences, computer games such as "Oregon Trail" can provide students with an appreciation and background for different educational topics. While on the "trail," the students learn about the different problems pioneers experienced, the geographical layout of the territory (a map repositions the wagon after each day of travel), historical facts, and how to manage finances through purchase of different provisions.

**Motivation**

The motivational value of games can easily be exploited in virtually any CAI lesson by making learning into a contest. To return once again to our multiplication program in Figure 11A–3, we could add a few more statements to keep a record of the student's performance and to announce, at the end of each problem, how he or she is doing relative to some standard. With a few more touches, we could have the computer solve the same problems at, say, an 80 percent accuracy level and "compete" directly against the student. Friendly, low-pressure competition seems to be a good motivator for learning at all educational levels, and CAI is well equipped to establish those conditions.

**Developing Problem-Solving Skills.**    In a slightly different category than the games just described are games that place primary emphasis on problem-solving skills and divergent thinking. Many of these games neither teach meaningful information nor simulate anything real. Instead, they establish the players as main characters in a fantasy adventure. The object may be to free a princess who has been kidnapped by an evil wizard, defeat a sinister magician who is terrorizing a kingdom, find a treasure hidden in a haunted house, or free oneself from captivity on a mysterious island. Success at these endeavors depends on how skillfully the computer is employed to obtain information and to translate strategies into actions. The important player qualities appear to be flexible (divergent) thinking and a high tolerance for frustration, since obvious or conventional solutions will almost certainly fail. If played an hour or two each day, an individual game can take weeks or even months to complete.

One of the many popular adventure games is "Wizard and the Princess" (On-Line Systems). You begin your adventure in the peaceful village of Serenia, possessing only some basic supplies and the goal of getting from that point to an unknown location somewhere north to rescue a princess who has been kidnapped by an evil wizard. Through trial and error, you learn how to communicate with the computer to take desired actions ("go north," "examine rock," and so on). As you advance, the scenery, which is produced in high-resolution graphics, changes from village to desert to forest to ocean and eventually (provided you endure), to the wizard's castle.

Creativity    Do such games actually foster creative thinking? As noted in Chapter 4, creativity is hard to define and to identify in students. What can be said for now is that these computer games seem to emphasize the very skills traditionally associated with creativity (that is, original, fluent, and flexible responding). When played in groups, they can also resemble creative thinking exercises, such as brainstorming, in which players provide mutual encouragement for devising numerous and diverse possible solutions. The creativity question will no doubt be receiving a great deal of attention by educational researchers as adventure games become more widely used in school settings.

**Reinforcement.**    One idea emphasized throughout this text is the importance of reinforcement for sustaining positive behaviors. Attention and praise are often sufficient for that purpose, but when schoolwork is especially difficult and demanding, offering additional incentives may prove desirable. But this is when many teachers experience a problem. Identifying appropriate rewards can be difficult, particularly in the higher grades (Wasicsko and Ross, in press.)

A clue to how computers might be of assistance can be found these days just about everywhere—amusement parks, supermarkets, airports, shopping malls. People of all ages have become infatuated with computer games and will sacrifice food, sleep, and a good part of their weekly spending money for the experience ("Games That Play People," 1982). What is important to us, as educators, is the fact that nearly all children and adolescents find it extremely reinforcing to interact with computers in game situations. Making such games available as a reward for doing work can thus serve as a powerful incentive.

Popular videogames like Pac-Man can be obtained easily and fairly cheaply for use with microcomputers. Should something more intellectually stimulating be desired, the examples we discussed earlier "Prisoner" or "Oregon Trail" or a game like computer chess should serve the purpose. One drawback of most computer games, however, is the noise factor: designating a separate room for games (preferably in another building) is strongly recommended.

**Management.**    Last but not least in our analysis are functions relating to CMI. Microcomputers are proving highly useful in helping with the management of classrooms and schools. Common uses are maintaining records and inventories of instructional resources, tracking students' achievement through computerized "grade books," generating individualized instructional prescriptions, scheduling learning activities, keeping instructional files and financial records, administering and scoring tests, supporting clerical tasks through word-processing capabilities, and even controlling environmental conditions in buildings (Eisele, 1981.)

One example of microcomputer software school administrators might find especially useful is VisiCalc (Visicorp Personal Software). Through this program, the computer can display a ledger sheet containing every budget element and calculate instantly the effects of specific changes. Change, for example, the percentage increase in teacher salaries or equipment purchases, and the new bottom line figure for that year's expenses is immediately displayed. Considerable time in the budget-making process can be saved as a result.

## Limitations

Having just considered so many positive attributes of computers for teaching, you may be wondering what the limitations might be. First, although computers can provide feedback and encouragement for students, such communications hardly have the same meaning as those provided by human beings. All of us have been in situations in which desire for approval from meaningful others provoked our best performances and the greatest pride when we finished. Recognition from a teacher, a parent, or classmates can be an extremely powerful force in children's lives. In contrast, we can easily enjoy a positive message from the computer ("good response," "nice going, Fred"), but recognize that it is delivered without conviction or feeling. As we turn the computer off, we know it will immediately forget us and our brilliant performance of just a few minutes ago. One's teacher and classmates, however, will remember for quite some time.

Second, although computers can do wonderful things with graphics displays and sounds, many students find them awkward to use for reading text. A textbook contains a complete set of material in a relatively small, manageable package. Each page can contain a substantial amount of print — and you can hold the book at any distance from your eyes to make the page easiest to read. In contrast, the computer's monitor presents a relatively small display. Paging through different sections and reading the text presented is much more difficult than in a book. In short, computers make very costly and inefficient "page turners." Lessons that require extensive text explanation might be best presented exclusively or in part through printed manuals.

**Limited
Flexibility**

Third, even with the most elaborate programming, CAI lacks the flexibility and timeliness that teachers can provide in interactions with students. Based on how a student is achieving or feeling at a particular time, a perceptive teacher can choose from many alternatives (discontinue the lesson, vary teaching methods, provide reinforcement, switch to another subject) to select an appropriate course of action. CAI has many adaptive capabilities, but they are much more limited by comparison.

**Need for
Practice**

Fourth, there are many skills requiring practice in realistic contexts. CAI can do an excellent job, for example, in teaching a child the rules of baseball, but is a poor substitute for a coach and playing field to develop skills in throwing, fielding, and batting. The same condition would apply to numerous other activities, such as learning to play a piano, give a speech, use a dictionary, or drive a car. Computer simulations would hardly provide sufficient preparation.

**Need for Good
Software**

Fifth, CAI refers only to a system of teaching. As such, its effectiveness depends on the quality of the lessons (software) it makes available. In an earlier section we discussed different means of acquiring software. Although many options exist, the software obtained may not teach the subject in the manner desired. In such cases, using CAI just because it is available would be a poor decision for all concerned.

**Need for
Hardware**

Sixth, although unavailability of software is a serious problem, the real crisis today is a shortage of hardware (Grady, 1982). In the face of recent school closings, budget cuts, and taxpayer rebellions, few school systems have the funds to purchase sufficient hardware to support CAI or CMI. How serious is the hardware shortage? One estimate, from *Time Magazine,* is that the present ratio between students and computers is 400:1 ("Here Come the Microkids," 1982). Using different figures, another estimate is that the computer time now available to the average student is only a little more than 6 minutes per week (Grady, 1982). For many school systems, CBE is still mostly a promise for the future rather than a present reality.

In light of these considerations, CBE is most sensibly regarded as resource for helping teachers, not as a means for replacing them. It is interesting that teachers who voice the latter concern are most frequently the ones who have had little or no experience with CBE. The strengths and limitations of computers in educational roles are *complementary* to those of human teachers. Research has shown that teachers who work with computers for the first time generally characterize their experiences and computers quite favorably. If you use computers in your teaching, the Guidelines here should help you select the appropriate systems.

# *Guidelines*

## *Selecting Microcomputer Hardware and Software*

**1. Compare different computer brands based on how well they fit your needs.**

EXAMPLES
- Make sure that memory capacity is neither too small nor excessive.
- Compare prices of different brands and of the same models sold by different vendors.
- Be certain that appropriate software is easily accessible for the model purchased.
- Be certain that appropriate peripherals (such as a disk drive) can be acquired if they are not standard features of the model.
- Make sure servicing is readily available.
- Ask different vendors to demonstrate their products at your school.
- Observe CBE systems at other schools and determine the teachers' level of satisfaction with the brands selected.

**2. Learn the fundamentals of programming.**

EXAMPLES
- Work through a self-tutorial manual.
- Take a computer literacy or programming course.
- Write and try out simple CAI programs in your teaching area.
- Become familiar with one or more authoring languages.

**3. Keep apprised of the software available in your teaching area.**

EXAMPLES
- Check the catalogs sold in bookstores.
- Examine advertisements in computer magazines.
- Communicate with other teachers who are using CBE.

**4. Exercise caution in purchasing software.**

EXAMPLES
- If possible, obtain a preview copy from the company.
- Read the software reviews published in computer magazines.
- Solicit recommendations from other teachers.

**5. Carefully plan working arrangements with professional programmers.**

EXAMPLES
- Ensure that the programmer is reliable and competent.
- Clearly define the type of program you want. Provide a flowchart or outline detailing the design.
- Keep apprised of the status of the project at all stages of its development.

**6. Take advantage of free software that is available.**

EXAMPLES
- Check computer magazines.
- Join a local computer club.
- Arrange trades with others who collect software.

# WHAT THE RESEARCH SHOWS

In a review published in 1980, Kulik, Kulik, and Cohen analyzed findings from 59 independent studies of computer-based college teaching. They concluded that in comparison with conventional (lecture) instruction, CAI made small but significant contributions to course achievement; produced slightly more favorable attitudes toward instruction and toward the subject matter; and substantially reduced the amount of time needed for instruction. Burns and Bozeman (1981) reviewed 40 studies that focused specifically on uses of CAI in mathematics instruction. The evidence indicated that CAI, used for either drill-and-practice or tutorials, produced higher achievement than conventional methods at both the elementary and the high school levels. In a third review, Orlansky and String (1981) examined results from 30 studies comparing computer-based instruction (both CAI and CMI) to conventional instruction in military settings. Those findings showed slight advantages in achievement under CAI, considerable savings in course completion times under both CAI and CMI, and an "overwhelming preference" by students for CAI and CMI.

How do instructors feel about CBE? Does familiarity in their case breed contempt or contentment? This question has received less attention than the other issues reviewed, but where evaluations have been made, contentment generally seems to be the rule (Alderman et al., 1978; Hansen, Ross and Bowman, 1978; Ragosta, Holland and Jameson, 1982). But not in all cases. Orlansky and String (1981), for example, found greater incidence of unfavorable attitudes among military instructors in eight out of nine comparisons.

In interpreting the findings, it is important to keep in mind that many variables, all of which cannot be experimentally controlled, influence learning in real settings. Making valid comparisons between teaching methods thus becomes very difficult. Also, many of the findings reviewed come from projects in which establishing CAI was the main concern. The CAI programs examined thus tend to be ones that were carefully thought out and applied to subjects directly amenable to that type of teaching. Another factor to consider is the Hawthorne effect, discussed in the appendix to Chapter 1. That CAI is "new and exciting" and traditional instruction is "old and routine" might work to its advantage when it is introduced in schools. These considerations suggest the need for caution before concluding from the results that CBE is, in general, more effective than traditional methods. The important point is that the evidence unquestionably supports the value of using CBE in a variety of educational and training settings.

## SUMMARY

1. Starting with the invention of ENIAC, the first general purpose computer, in 1946, advancements in computer technology took place rapidly.

2. Interest in computer-based education (CBE) was spurred by the programmed instruction movement in the late 1950s and early 1960s.

3. The major forms of CBE are computer-assisted instruction (CAI), using computers to present or teach lessons; and computer-managed instruction (CMI), using computers for functions such as recordkeeping, prescribing, and keeping inventories.

4. Both CAI and CMI can be made available through timesharing systems, in which separate computer terminals transmit information via a central computer, and through stand-alone systems, in which the computers operate as self-sufficient units.

5. Advantages of timesharing are centralized storage of records and access to an existing library of programs. A stand-alone system, however, eliminates computer downtime problems and tends to be less costly to establish.

6. Microcomputers are inexpensive, portable, easily accessible, and extremely well equipped for CBE applications.

7. Essential microcomputer hardware or physical equipment consists of the computing unit (CPU) itself and peripherals such as a keyboard and monitor for transmitting information. Other common peripherals are disk drives, tape recorders, printers, game paddles, and modems.

8. Software refers to the actual programs used to provide directions to the computer. Software can be acquired in a variety of ways by: (1) having teachers write their own programs; (2) purchasing commercial software; (3) contracting with a professional programmer; (4) taking advantage of the available free programs.

9. Computers have the potential to facilitate the learning and teaching process in a number of ways: self-pacing of instruction; drill-and-practice; personalized feedback and instruction; multisensory presentations; simulations; games for teaching information, developing problem-solving skills, and providing reinforcement; and management functions.

10. The limitations are that computers are less capable than human beings at providing meaningful support and encouragement; they are less flexible and creative in making instructional decisions; and computer presentations are not well-adapted for lessons involving extensive amounts of text.

11. The evidence, overall, is generally supportive of CAI, indicating small to moderate achievement gains, considerable savings in course completion time, and more favorable student attitudes toward instruction.

## KEY TERMS

| | | |
|---|---|---|
| microcomputer | hardware | disk drive |
| BASIC | monitor | disk |
| CAI | peripherials | printer |
| CBE | software | modem |
| CMI | stand-alone unit | downtime |
| byte | timesharing | kilobytes (K) |
| chip (microchip) | programmed instruction | |

## SUGGESTIONS FOR FURTHER READING AND STUDY

AVNER, A., MOORE, C., and SMITH, S. Active external control: A basis for superiority of CBI. *Journal of Computer-Based Instruction*, 1980, 6, 115–118. This article relates the advantages of computer-based instruction to the students' active processing of information.

PAPERT, S. *Mindstorms.* New York: Basic Books, 1980. A classic in the field of artificial intelligence and computers.

TAYLOR, R. P. (Ed.). *The computer in the school: tutor, tool, tutee.* New York: Teachers College Press, 1980. This book describes the roles that the computer will assume in classrooms.

AHL, D. H. BASIC computer games, microcomputer edition. Morristown, NJ: Creative Computing Press, 1978. An excellent source of programs for teachers.

# 12

# Using Effective Teaching Strategies

**OVERVIEW**  Teachers make many decisions affecting the lives of students. These decisions range from how to position the desks to how long to spend teaching reading or reviewing homework each day. Even when students are working independently or in small unsupervised groups, they are influenced by decisions the teacher has made about such things as materials, grouping, and timing. Research on teaching is beginning to identify some of the elements of effective instruction.

In this chapter, we examine what is known about the role of the teacher in student learning. Are there particular characteristics that distinguish effective from ineffective teachers? We will spend some time examining this important question and then shift our focus to the organization of instruction and different patterns of teaching. Here the main question will be one that guides much of the teacher's planning: "How can I keep the students actively involved in the learning activities?" As you will see, results of research offer many answers to this question.

Next we turn our attention to the teaching of basic skills. Research in recent years has identified a cluster of principles to guide the teaching of reading, mathematics, and other subjects that focus on mastery of basic information and procedures. Then we explore effective teaching beyond the basics by discussing the problems of matching teaching strategies to the demands of the subject matter and the aptitudes of the students.

By the time you have finished this chapter, you are likely to have many new ideas about methods and approaches to try in the classroom. More specifically, you should be able to do the following:

- Describe a number of characteristics that effective teachers seem to share.
- List certain things that effective teachers generally seem to do.
- List at least two specific strategies for keeping elementary and secondary students actively involved in a lesson, giving reasons for each.
- Give an example of a lesson based on the principles of direct instruction.
- Plan a unit in your subject for a low-ability class.
- Choose one lesson in your own area and explain how you would go about presenting it to the students you will be teaching.

Let us begin with the person who must make these many decisions about teaching strategy, you the teacher. How can you make yourself most effective in the classroom?

## THE SEARCH FOR THE KEYS TO SUCCESS

The search for the secret of successful teaching is not a new one. In the 1950s the Committee on Criteria of Teaching Effectiveness of the American Educational Research Association stated that "after 40 years of research on teacher effectiveness, during which a vast number of studies have been carried out, one can point to few outcomes ... that a teacher education faculty can employ in planning or improving teacher-education programs'' (American Educational Research Association, 1953, p. 657). More recently, several widely publicized studies have concluded that teachers have very little impact on student learning. These reports, the Coleman Report (Coleman et al., 1966) and Jencks' study of the relationship between family and school (Jencks et al., 1972), among others, have led many people to the conclusion that factors such as social class and student ability are the main influences on student learning. The studies seem to demonstrate that teachers have little effect on students.

## Do Teachers Make a Difference?

Criticisms
of Coleman and
Jencks

A closer look at the Coleman and Jencks reports reveals many problems in the design of the research (T. Good, 1982; Program on Teaching Effectiveness, 1976). The studies looked mainly for **correlations** between such things as the verbal ability or social class of the teachers and general intellectual skills of the students. Schoolwide averages were generally used. The studies did *not* try to relate what actually happened in individual classrooms to the achievement of the students in those classrooms. They did *not* examine the effects of individual teachers within each school. Furthermore, since the research was purely correlational, we have no basis for inferring a causal relationship. (See Chapter 1 for a discussion of why correlational research will not allow a determination of cause.) The fact that there appears to be no relationship between the average social class of the teachers in a school and the general intellectual skills of the students really does not answer this basic question: Do individual teachers make a difference in the day-to-day learning of their students?

Teachers
Do Make
a Difference

In the past two decades, several classroom studies have demonstrated that teachers do, in fact, make a difference in student learning. Some researchers have studied such characteristics as the teacher's knowledge of subject matter or attitude toward the students. Other researchers have observed the actual performance of teachers, how they used group size or praise in instruction, for example. These teacher characteristics and performances have been examined to determine their impact on such outcomes as student attitudes toward school and achievement. One study by Stallings and Kaskowitz (1975) found that instructional methods had at least as great an impact on student learning as the entering abilities of the students.

The Role
of Student
Behavior

The relationships between teaching strategies and student learning are complicated. The actions of a teacher cannot magically result in student learning; the link is student behavior. The teacher does something, such as explain a concept or make an assignment. The teacher's performance affects what the student does in class and how the student processes the informa-tion. This in turn affects student learning. Students learn only through their own thinking or acting in particular situations. But what the teacher does influences what the students will do and therefore, to a large extent, what the students will learn. So in this chapter, we will focus on teacher performance and the resulting student behaviors.

## Methods for Studying Effective Teaching

If you wanted to identify the keys to successful teaching, how would you go about it? You might ask students, principals, college professors of education, or experienced teachers to list the characteristics of good teachers. You might make observations in classrooms, rate different teachers on certain traits, and then see which traits were associated with teachers whose students achieved the most or were the most motivated to learn. You could identify teachers whose students, year after year, learned more than students working with other teachers; then you could watch the more successful teachers and note what they do. You might also train teachers to apply several different strategies to teach the same lesson, and then determine which strategy led to the greatest student learning.

All these approaches and more have been applied studying effective teaching. We will be most interested in the research that has been done in classrooms and that has used student learning or other important changes in student behavior as the criterion for effectiveness. Expert opinions from outside the classroom can be informative, but they can also be wrong. But it is helpful to know something about the opinions of one group of experts within the classroom—the students themselves.

## Student Ratings

At some point during your college career, you have probably completed a questionnaire to evaluate one of your professors. What do the results of such questionnaires tell about the effectiveness of teachers? Do students actually learn more from highly rated teachers?

A study by Rodin and Rodin published in 1972 caused a great deal of controversy by concluding that student liking for college instructors was negatively correlated with learning in the course. In other words, the more the students liked an instructor, on the average, the less they learned in his or her class! This study was criticized by many researchers, and contradictory findings have since been reported.

One later study looked at student learning in two different colleges and two different courses (Frey, Leonard and Beatty, 1975). These investigators used the same questionnaire in both colleges to measure student opinions. Through a statistical technique called **factor analysis,** the researchers were able to group the 21 items on the questionnaire into seven factors: (1) clarity of presentation, (2) workload, (3) personal attention, (4) class discussion, (5) organization and planning, (6) grading, and (7) students' perception of their own accomplishment.

Factors Related to Learning

When the results of the questionnaires were compared with the final examination scores of the students, three of the factors were indeed positively correlated with student learning. Students seemed to learn more with instructors they rated high in clarity of presentation (factor 1) and general organization and planning (factor 5). Students who perceived themselves as having learned (factor 7) also tended to learn more.

Again we must caution you that this research demonstrated a correlation between certain factors and student learning, not a causal effect. We do not know, for example, if clarity caused learning or if students who learned more could see the clarity of presentation more readily. There may even have been some other factor, such as an excellent textbook, causing the instructor to be clearer and the students to learn more. But we do know that, in this study at least, teacher clarity and student learning were related positively.

The results in this last study are a bit more comforting than Rodin and Rodin's findings. But the question remains: Is overall student satisfaction with a class related to learning? Consider these hypothetical teachers:

Bill Heath's classes were known for their lively and interesting discussions. Students enjoyed participating and felt at ease. Bill was a favorite professor with many of his students because he took personal and genuine interest in them, in their concerns and ideas. Although the classes (and Bill himself) were often disorganized, the workload and grading standards were always more than fair. Students sometimes kidded Bill about being an absent-minded professor, but attendance in his classes was excellent.

Ann Lopez was quite a different kind of professor. Her classes were thoroughly organized and her presentations almost always very clear. She seemed to be able to make even difficult concepts understandable with her careful explanations. Former students described Ann (or Dr. Lopez, as almost everyone called her) as being businesslike, serious, and somewhat distant. Students often complained that the workload in Ann's class was too heavy and her grading too demanding. Although few students felt close to Ann, most respected her expertise.

Which teacher would you expect to be the most effective? We could predict that Ann Lopez would be rated highly by her students on clarity and organization. These factors were correlated with student learning in the study by Frey, Leonard, and Beatty. Bill Heath might be better liked and even receive a higher overall rating from his students. Attendance in his classes is probably better. Still, students in Ann Lopez's classes might learn more. What are your own goals as a teacher? Is it possible to achieve student satisfaction and promote student learning at the same time?

**Liking and
Learning**

Cromack (1973) gives a clue to the liking-learning mystery. In his study, 17 public school teachers presented a 20-minute minilesson to different groups

*Is it enough that this teacher has the attention of his students, or should he also have their affection? Can students be objective enough to evaluate the effectiveness of a teacher they do not particularly like? Should student ratings be a factor in teacher accountability?*

of students. Cromack determined how much the students learned and how satisfied they were with the lesson. Only 2 of the 17 teachers were effective on both counts. The correlation between teachers' rankings on "helping students learn" and "student satisfaction" was only 0.04. In other words, there was no significant relationship between the two variables (Good, Biddle and Brophy, 1975).

While there may be a relationship between certain student judgments about teachers and learning, it appears that a teacher's overall rating is not necessarily related to student learning. In fact, Peck and Veldman (1973) found that the teachers who were rated by their students as the least pleasant and interesting were the most successful in promoting student learning over three consecutive years. Factors other than the teacher's effectiveness often influence student ratings. For example, college students tend to give higher ratings to instructors who have more lenient grading standards, especially in required courses (DuCette and Kenney, 1982).

Many Goals
for Teaching

Of course, academic learning is not the only important criterion for assessing teacher effectiveness. As a teacher, you may want your students to enjoy school, be absent less often, develop positive self-concepts, and feel a certain confidence in dealing with the material you present. You may also want them to take more courses in your subject or later work in the area. In Chapter 3 we described the results of research indicating that affective objectives such as these are very important to experienced teachers (Prawat et al., 1981). Information from student questionnaires can be of great help in reaching these goals. Results may also provide ideas about changes in course content. But keep in mind the possibility that the most popular teachers in the eyes of the students are not always the teachers who help students learn the most (Abrami, Perry and Leventhal, 1982).

## Characteristics of Effective Teachers

Another approach to the study of teacher effectiveness is to look at specific characteristics of teachers and the effect each may have on learning. We will examine three such characteristics: knowledge, clarity, and warmth.

Knowledge
of the Subject

**Knowledge and Education.**  Do teachers who know more about their subject areas have a more positive impact on their students? The relationship between teacher knowledge of the subject and student learning is not clearly defined and appears to be an indirect one. Teachers who know more about their subject do not necessarily have students who learn more. But teachers who know more may tend to be clearer in their presentations or to use more effective teaching strategies (McDonald, 1976c). Knowledge is probably necessary but not sufficient for effective teaching.

Knowledge
of Teaching
Methods

There is some evidence pointing toward a relationship between a teacher's knowledge of teaching *methods* and student learning (McDonald, 1976b). One study by Cantrell, Stenner, and Katzenmeyer (1977) found that teachers who scored high on a test of behavioral principles of classroom management (the information found in Chapters 5 and 9) and who had positive attitudes toward students were more successful than teachers with less knowledge of these methods. Another study of 31 Head Start teachers found that teachers with more formal education, teacher experience, and hours of training were more successful in helping students achieve educational and social objectives.

The students with the more experienced and educated teachers learned significantly more (Seefeldt, 1973).

**Organization and Clarity.**    When students discuss a class, phrases such as "very clear," "confusing," or "hard to follow" are often heard. As we saw in the study by Frey, Leonard, and Beatty (1975), student ratings of clarity of presentation and general organization are related to learning in college courses. The same appears to be true in elementary and secondary classes. In fact, when Barak Rosenshine and Norma Furst (1973) reviewed about 50 studies of teaching, they concluded that clarity was the most promising teacher behavior for future research. Let's look at some of the evidence.

David Ryans has found that teachers at both the elementary and secondary levels who are systematic and consistent in their teaching tend to maintain better morale in their classrooms than disorganized teachers (Ryans, 1960). Teacher clarity affects student learning as well as morale. For example, ninth-grade algebra teachers who were rated as clearer by students and classroom observers had students who improved more in their comprehension of algebraic concepts (McConnell, 1977). Similar results have been found in other subjects (Kennedy, Cruickshank, Bush and Meyers, 1978) and at other grade levels (Good and Grouws, 1977). Turning once again to the college level, students who were taught by a teacher who was rated as clear learned significantly more than students taught the same material in a lesson rated as unclear (Hines, Cruickshank and Kennedy, 1982; Land and Smith, 1979).

How to be
Vague

Hiller believes there may be an important connection between clarity, knowledge of the subject, and student learning (Hiller, 1971). He studied over 30 twelfth-grade social studies teachers during two minilessons. Teachers with more knowledge of the subject tended to be less vague in their explanations to the class. The less vague the teacher, the more the students learned. Vagueness was assessed by counting the number of times 233 words and phrases such as "somewhere," "not many," "not sure," "anyway," and "sometimes" occurred.

Hiller suggests that lack of knowledge may cause teachers to be vague or to be anxious and nervous, which in turn causes them to be vague. Either way, students get lost (Dunkin and Biddle, 1974). Perhaps the effect of a teacher's lack of knowledge depends on how the teacher copes with the situation. An advanced understanding of chemistry probably will be less important in teaching fourth-grade science than eleventh-grade chemistry. But if lack of knowledge causes the teacher to feel anxious or to choose a poor teaching method to hide the ignorance, the teacher's lack of knowledge can interfere with student learning at every grade level.

Student Grade
Level

You may have noticed that most studies of teacher clarity involve students at the later elementary, secondary, and college levels. In the very early grades there is less extended verbal teaching and more small group, drill and practice, and seatwork. Being clear probably becomes increasingly significant as teaching includes more explanation and lecture (Rosenshine, 1979).

Preparing
for Clarity

Recent research offers guidelines for being clearer in the classroom (Evertson et al., in press; Hines et al., 1982). While you are planning the lesson, try to anticipate the problems your students will have with the material. Sources of information include the teacher's manual for texts and experienced teachers. In addition, you might do the written parts of the lesson yourself to identify possible problems. Have definitions ready for new

Ken Karp

terms and prepare examples for concepts. Organize the lesson in a logical sequence and build in checkpoints to see if the students are following the explanations. Checkpoints might include oral or written questions or problems.

**Clarity during Lessons**

During the lesson, emphasize the important aspects of the material. You can do this from the very beginning by making the purpose of the activity clear. Summarize parts of the lesson as you go along. Watch your pace. After more difficult sections, stop to give students a chance to think. Probe to make sure they understand. Don't overlook anyone in this checking; some students are experts at hiding in a group or following the lead of the better pupils to guess right answers. Ask students to summarize your main points (you may be surprised at their responses).

In general, stick with your plan and do not digress or interrupt the flow with extraneous comments. Signal transitions from one major topic to another with phrases such as, "the next . . . ," "now we will leave . . . and turn to . . . ," "the second step is. . . ." You might help students follow the lesson by putting an outline or list of key points on the board or overhead projector. Continually monitor the group to see if everyone is following the lesson. Look for confident nods or puzzled blank stares. You should be able to tell if most students are keeping up with the material.

Throughout the lesson, choose words that are familiar to the students. Define new terms and relate them to what students already know. Be precise. avoid vague words and ambiguous phrases such as "some," (something, someone, sometime, somehow), "not very" (not very much, not very well, not very hard, not very often) "most," "not all," "sort of," "more or less." Use specific names instead of "it," "them," "thing," and so on. Avoid pet phrases such as "you know?" and "OK?"

After the lesson get feedback to see if students understood the material. You might have the students do a few problems in class while you circulate among them to make sure they have grasped the information. This way you have a chance to correct misunderstandings immediately. If homework is assigned, check this quickly so you can note any problems that require additional explanation. Finally, you might tape record a lesson to check yourself for clarity. This can be an eye-opening experience.

**Warmth and Enthusiasm.**    Teachers vary in level of knowledge and clarity in presenting material. They also vary in the enthusiasm they communicate for the subject and their students. According to Rosenshine and Furst (1973), ratings of teachers' enthusiasm have been related to student growth in several studies. Warmth and understanding of teachers, as measured by rating scales, have also been related to judgments of effective teaching (Ryans, 1960). Again, these are correlational studies. The results do not tell us that teacher enthusiasm *causes* student learning, only that the two variables tend to occur together. When teachers have been trained to be more enthusiastic, their students have been more attentive and involved, but not necessarily better on tests of content (Gillett and Gall, 1982).

But just knowing that warmth and enthusiasm are good qualities for teachers will not tell you how to act in the classroom. Warmth and enthusiasm are **high-inference characteristics,** difficult to define objectively. Just how do warm, enthusiastic teachers communicate? Are there particular behaviors or skills that can be defined more specifically? Mary Collins (1978) "operationalized" enthusiasm to include rapid, varied and excited vocal delivery, lively eyes, demonstrative gestures, expressive face, use of descriptive words, an easygoing acceptance of students' ideas and questions, and a generally high energy level. Reading this list made us think of the teacher as an entertainer or performer, a role we described in the first chapter (Box 1–1). We were intrigued when we encountered a book on the subject, described in Box 12–1.

**Other Factors.**    While teacher knowledge, clarity, organization, and enthusiasm appear to be important factors, identifying them did not end the search for the keys to success in the classroom. Several basic problems remained. Most of the studies that identified these characteristics simply reported correlations between teacher and student behaviors. No causal relationships were established. Maybe it is easier to be enthusiastic when students are involved and learning. Perhaps student learning causes teacher enthusiasm instead of the reverse.

Another reason why it has been difficult to identify particular behaviors related to student learning is that teachers are not consistent in their actions or stable over time. In fact, in some studies teachers completely reverse themselves (Campbell 1972). Other studies also have found little or no relationship between teacher behavior on one occasion and another (Shavelson and Dempsey, 1975).

What does this mean? Are teachers effective one day and ineffective the next? We all have our bad days, but surely there is some consistency in a teacher's effect on students. The problem is not with the teacher but with the

## BOX 12–1 TEACHING AS PERFORMING

*Dr. Morris Burns, a professor at Colorado State University, has taught courses in theater arts and directed plays for 16 years. Summarized here are some of his ideas about the similarities between teaching and acting, taken from the book* Teaching as Performing, *by William Timpson and David Tobin (1982).*

**1.** "Reading" an Audience or Class.

In the theater, a production is not a production until it is played to an audience. Similarly, the final test for any lesson or lecture must be its effect on the students. During performances, directors will attend to any signs that they are losing their audiences: is there much shifting in the seats or coughing that spreads like wildfire? If teachers can learn to decode similar warning signals in their classrooms, they will then be able to vary their tempo or movements or activities in an effort to recapture the attention of their students . . . .

**2.** Becoming the Needed Character.

With respect to acting, this ability is an obvious one. For the teacher it may be less obvious, yet it is equally vital . . . . Burns has . . . found himself approaching a totally new course with a certain amount of fear, even though he feels confident about his material. In that kind of situation he must tell himself that he is confident, and he must act in a confident manner. "I've gone over the material. I know it. I'm convinced of its validity." When he finally enters the classroom, Burns radiates assuredness. This is acting—and his students are the benefactors.

**3.** Adding Appropriate Movement, Gestures, and Expressions.

Actors will spend weeks poring over the physical enactments of their characters. What does a particular character look like? How does the character move? . . . For actors, the study of movement fulfills the physical requirements of the script and also reveals much about the psychological attitude of their characters. For teachers, these lessons are equally relevant. Appropriate and energetic movements will add to the material and convey a certain excitement to students. Directors and actors work hard to provide physical variety as well as eliminate unnecessary or excessive movements. The actor wants to be sure that all movements are meaningful; so should the teacher. Economy of movement is central to presentational clarity and power. Study, attention to detail, direction, and rehearsal are essential to successful movement.

Be especially attentive to the use of your eyes. As a listener or viewer, eye contact with the speaker or performer adds an important personal dimension. With practice—and the mirror is an excellent tool—moods and emphases, rewards and concerns can also be conveyed.

**4.** Making Effective Use of Vocal Range and Potential.

One of the primary tools shared by actors and teachers is of course the voice. Given that words dominate so much of what occurs on stage or in the classroom and that actors receive extensive training in voice, it certainly seems that educators are remiss in not providing similar training for teachers. Vocal range, strength, and flexibility can add valuable variety, emphasis, and even drama to any lesson. Silence as well can prove valuable.

Adapted from Timpson & Tobin, **Teaching as performing: A guide to energizing your public presentation,** Englewood Cliffs, NJ: Prentice-Hall, 1982.

# Guidelines

*Effective Teaching*

**1. Organize your lessons carefully.**

**EXAMPLES**
- Begin lessons with a brief outline written on the board or develop an outline as the lesson progresses.
- Provide objectives to help focus student attention on the purpose of the lesson.

**2. Strive for clarity in your explanations.**

**EXAMPLES**
- Use concrete examples that relate to the students' own lives.
- Give explanations at several levels so all students will understand, not just the brightest.

**3. Communicate an enthusiasm for your subject and the day's lesson.**

**EXAMPLES**
- Tell students why the lesson is important.
- Be sure to make eye contact with the students.

**4. Keep all students involved.**

**EXAMPLES**
- Make sure students who finish early have something productive to do.
- Reinforce students for independent work and for sticking with a task.

**5. Balance goals for student learning with goals directed toward encouraging students to like your subject and school in general.**

**EXAMPLES**
- Use student questionnaires to make adjustments in your teaching.
- Combine a focus on academic skills with special student interests whenever possible.

**6. Constantly broaden your knowledge in your area.**

**EXAMPLES**
- Read journals which report new research and present others' ideas.
- Go to workshops and conventions; take a course at a nearby college.

idea that a particular way of teaching is always appropriate for every student, grade, or subject. Good teachers change their style to fit the situation. "Teacher behavior is moderated, *as it should be,* by the kinds of students and the variety of settings that teachers work in" (Berliner, 1976, p. 9).

The key to effectiveness may be found not in single teacher behaviors, but in teaching patterns. Before we look at the strategies, however, note that the research on specific behaviors can still offer a number of very useful suggestions. The Guidelines here should help you put some of these ideas to work.

# THE ROLE OF STUDENT BEHAVIOR

In research on effective teaching, the emphasis has recently shifted from studying teacher behaviors to examining different variables involved in effective instruction (Rosenshine, 1977; Waxman and Walberg, 1982). One factor identified in study after study has been the behavior of the students themselves.

The Link: Student Behavior
The most important link between teacher performance and student learning is student behavior. As you saw in the chapters on cognitive learning, the way the student processes information is a central factor in determining what is learned and remembered. The most important student behavior may be active time spent on specific learning tasks (Denham and Lieberman, 1980). This time is often called **academic engaged time.** We will look first at the role this factor plays in learning, and second at the way academic engaged time may be increased.

## Academic Engaged Time

It seems almost ridiculously simplistic to state that students will learn only the material they have a chance to learn. If a class does not reach the last three chapters in a textbook, you cannot expect the students to learn the information in those chapters. Nevertheless, in their studies of effective teaching, a number of researchers have overlooked the importance of giving the students a chance to learn—that is, of academic engaged time. In a few studies standardized tests have been used to measure learning in classes where over half the material on the tests was never covered in class.

Opportunity to Learn
There are two important aspects of academic engaged time: the opportunity to learn, and the students' use of this opportunity. Almost every study examining the first aspect, opportunity to learn, has found a significant relationship between content covered and student learning (Armento, 1977; Good and Beckerman, 1978). In fact, the correlations between content covered and student learning are usually larger than the correlations between specific teacher behaviors and student learning (Rosenshine, 1979).

Attention to Learning
But even if students have an opportunity to learn, they may still choose to let the opportunity go by. The cognitive perspective on learning highlights the importance of the students' cognitive processes during instruction. So the second aspect of academic engaged time, the students' *use* of the opportunity, is just as important as the first. Bloom (1976) reviewed 15 studies of student attention and found a very high correlation between student attention and learning. Even higher correlations have been reported in studies that measured only attention to academic subjects (Rosenshine, 1979).

From research findings such as these we can derive one important principle of effective teaching. Teachers who keep their students actively involved in academic tasks, no matter what method is used, are more likely to be effective in helping students learn. This notion may not be particularly revolutionary, but it does place the emphasis where it belongs—not on the method, but on the impact of the method on the students. This is an emphasis shared by most teachers. One of the their major concerns in planning lessons is selecting activities that will encourage active student participation and involvement (Clark and Yinger, 1979; Shavelson and Stern, 1981).

This leads us to an important question: What can teachers do to keep students "academically engaged?"

## Encouraging Involvement

We have already discussed many factors that can keep students engaged. In the chapter on motivation we noted several approaches, including building positive attitudes and curiosity, relating lessons to student interests, encouraging cooperative learning, and planning for reinforcement and feelings of competence. In other chapters we discussed the application of behavioral principles and Kounin's ideas for group management. In this chapter we have mentioned teacher clarity and enthusiasm, two factors directly related to student engagement. What else can teachers do?

Supervision    **Lesson Format.**    The format of the lesson affects student involvement. In general as teacher supervision increases, student academic engaged time also increases (Emmer and Evertson, 1981). For example, Good and Beckerman (1978) found that student time-on-task was greater in small and large groups led by the teacher than in individual seatwork or whole-class activities without teacher leadership. Rosenshine (1979) reports that supervised students are off-task only about 5 percent of the time. But unsupervised students working alone and pacing themselves are off-task about 15 percent of the time and in transition from one activity to another about 10 percent of the time. This does not mean that teachers should eliminate independent work for students; it simply means that this type of activity usually requires careful monitoring.

Task Cues    When the task provides continuous cues for the student about what to do next, involvement will be greater (Kounin and Gump, 1974). For example, students making a collage will usually continue to work until all the background is covered. Activities with clear steps are likely to be more involving, since one step leads to the next. When students have all the materials they need to complete the task, they tend to stay involved (Kounin and Doyle, 1975).

*When students have all the materials they need and the task encourages involvement, less teacher supervision is necessary.*

In a group lesson attention is greater if every student is expected to respond, verbally or nonverbally, to each question (McKenzie and Henry, 1979). When the task requires a response, the signals to participate are continuous, since students may stay involved in order to respond. If individuals answer, students can ignore the lesson until they are asked a question. Students will also continue working to find an answer if they are curious or simply personally interested in the question. Here again, the task keeps them involved and they resist distractions.

**Completing Assignments**

**Involvement without Supervision.** Of course, teachers cannot supervise every student all the time or rely on curiosity. Systems must keep students working and completing assignments on their own. In Chapter 10 we discussed the research of Carolyn Evertson, Ed Emmer, and colleagues in both elementary and secondary schools (Emmer et al., 1980; Emmer and Evertson, 1984). They found that effective teachers at both levels had well-planned systems for encouraging students to be responsible for completing work. We will look at each of these more carefully, drawing suggestions from Evertson et al. (1984) and Emmer et al. (1984).

*1. Work requirements.* Effective teachers make clear to students the routine work requirements of headings, paper size, pen or pencil use, neatness, and so on. At the beginning of the year, pay special attention to teaching, practicing, and correcting these routines. Decide what you will do about late or incomplete work and absences. If a pattern of incomplete work begins to develop, deal with it early, by contacting parents if necessary. Make due dates reasonable and stick to them unless the student has a very good reason for lateness.

**Making Assignments**

*2. Communicating assignments.* With younger students, write assignments on the board, in the same place each day. Demonstrate how to do the assignment, do the first question together, or provide a sample worksheet to make sure students know what to do. With older students, assignments may be dictated, posted, or given in a syllabus. But remind students of upcoming assignments. Even college students forget requirements listed on the syllabus and never mentioned again. If an assignment is complicated or has several parts, give students a sheet describing what to do, resources, due dates, and so on. Older students should be told your criteria for grading assignments.

**Monitoring Work**

*3. Monitoring work in progress.* When you make an assignment in class, make sure each student gets started correctly. If you check only those who raise their hands for help, you will miss students who *think* they know what to do and are wrong, students who are too shy to ask for help, and students who do not plan to do the work at all. Check progress periodically. In discussions and recitations, make sure everyone has a chance to respond so you can check each student, not just the volunteers.

**Checking Work**

*4. Turning in and checking work.* In the elementary grades, you might have students put completed work in designated boxes or in a certain place on the desk. Tests and homework assignments can be passed in a standard direction. (Sound familiar? "Pass your papers to the front."). Older students can take some responsibility for checking one anothers' papers, but graders should sign their names and you must make spot checks for accuracy.

*5. Academic feedback.* We will discuss procedures for establishing grading systems in Chapter 15; here we want to emphasize the importance of immediate feedback. In the elementary grades, students should get papers back the following day. A teacher described by Evertson et al. (1984) had students come to her desk one at a time each day to discuss their work. Completed work was quickly graded and the grade recorded as the student watched. This way the students saw immediate results of their efforts. Good work can be displayed in class and graded papers sent home to parents each week. Students of all ages can keep records of grades, projects completed, and so on. A special problem for older students is completing long-term assignments and projects. You might break up these assignments into several phases, giving feedback at each point. For example, students may be required to turn in a topic, then a list of books, then an outline, then a rough draft, and finally a finished paper.

Student Records

In studying factors that increase academic engaged time, researchers have identified several effective teaching patterns. They have also discovered that different patterns are appropriate for different learning outcomes and different students.

# EFFECTIVE TEACHING FOR DIFFERENT SUBJECTS

A great deal of progress has been made lately in understanding how to teach basics such as reading and mathematics. We will look at some of the research, but a strong caution is called for at this point. In describing effective instruction, we will be speaking about one very specific kind of effectiveness. In most of the studies we will describe, effectiveness is defined as an improvement in student performance on classroom or standardized achievement tests.

Cautions
in Interpreting
Research

This limitation leads us to some other cautions in evaluating the studies. First, the studies do not really tell us about other objectives such as helping students to mature emotionally and socially. Second, the studies generally center on the American classroom as it is at present. Other forms of education may be equally or more effective. Finally, the results are generally for a group of students. We cannot say if methods that are successful on the average will be successful with particular individuals. The research presented here should give you some guidelines for experimenting in your own class. But your judgment of the impact of each strategy on your students will be the criterion for using or abandoning any of the approaches.

## Basic Skills: Direct Instruction

Several psychologists have identified one teaching approach that is related to improved student learning. Barak Rosenshine (1979) calls this approach **direct instruction**. Tom Good uses the term **active teaching** to refer to similar basic characteristics. The goal of direct instruction is mastery of basic skills, reading and mathematics, as measured by the tests commonly given in schools. Let us look at a typical situation.

An Example
of Direct
Instruction

Lee Cohen teaches third grade in a moderate-sized suburban school. She allocates 60 minutes a day, in two 30-minute sessions, to reading instruction. Most of the time her students stay focused on the reading task because she constantly monitors the room, even when she is working with small groups or individuals. Students who are not working are brought back to the task by some communication from the teacher. Often the message is a glance or a private reminder. The tone is firm but gentle. Both teacher and students are aware of the objectives for most of the activities. Lee has chosen the materials purposefully and arranged the activities in a logical sequence. Transitions from one activity to the next are smooth and orderly. The central figure in the classroom is definitely the teacher, but a pleasant atmosphere prevails. There is a sense of seriousness about the academic work and mutual respect among students and teacher.

Themes
of Direct
Instruction

The five basic themes that characterize direct instruction are all found in the classroom described above. First, there is definite organization. The objectives are clear. The activities are intentionally chosen, divided into small teachable steps, and related to the objectives. Second, there is an emphasis on involvement. The students are productively engaged in important academic tasks each day. Third, there is a clear sense of direction. The teacher is a strong leader who sets instructional goals, chooses materials, and paces the lessons. Fourth, each student is taught until she or he masters the materials. Finally, the atmosphere is busy but pleasant.

Rosenshine (1978b) has expanded on these basic characteristics and added a number of specific details for teachers who wish to make use of the principles of direct instruction in the elementary grades. His ideas are found in Figure 12–1.

**Figure 12–1    Suggestions for Using Direct Instruction in the Primary Grades**

1. Approximately two-thirds of classroom time should be spent on reading, arithmetic, and language arts; approximately one-third should be spent on story reading, social studies, science, art, music, and/or independent projects.
2. Students should receive most of their instruction in small groups of five to eight members who can all handle the same material successfully at the same pace.
3. Students should be seated in a semicircle facing the corner with their backs to the room. When working with individual groups, teachers should sit with their backs to the corner so they can watch the rest of the room.
4. New skills should be presented in small steps, first through modeling, then by having students recite with the teachers, and finally by having students recite alone.
5. Pace should be quick and students should have many chances to respond in each lesson.
6. Most responses should be choral, giving all students a great deal of practice. Students should not be singled out when they make mistakes; instead, the whole group should repeat a response until everyone is correct.
7. About one-third of the time, individual students should be asked to respond so the teacher can make sure all students have mastered the task.
8. Student responses should be corrected first through modeling the right response, then by leading the group in the correct response, and finally by testing the group response. The modeling-leading-testing pattern should be repeated as necessary. Prompts may also be used.
9. Reinforcement should be given in the form of praise and tokens (exchangeable for rewards and privileges).
10. The progress of each student should be monitored through frequent tests and daily work sheets.

*Adapted from B. Rosenshine. **Instructional principles in direct instruction.** Paper presented at the annual meeting of the American Educational Research Association, Toronto, April, 1978, pp. 2–9.*

**Basic Skills at All Ages**

Direct instruction appears to be one successful system for teaching basic skills. This approach is related to achievement in junior high mathematics computation and application (Good, 1982) and to reading improvement in remedial reading classes in secondary schools (Stallings, 1980). Are the principles of direct instruction appropriate for reaching other learning outcomes? On this question there is disagreement, as you will see.

## Beyond the Basics

**Open Methods**

In a chapter called "Direct Instruction Reconsidered," Penelope Peterson (1979) compared more traditional teacher-centered instruction, similar to direct instruction, with more open, informal methods. She concluded that teacher-centered instruction leads to better performance on achievement tests, while the open, informal methods are associated with better performance on tests of creativity, abstract thinking, and problem solving. In addition, the open methods are better in improving attitudes toward school, and stimulating curiosity, cooperation among students, and lower absence rates (Stallings and Kaskowitz, 1975).

**Effective Teaching in Different Subjects**

When the goals of teaching involve problem solving and mastering processes rather than creating products, and when the students are average or above in their knowledge of the subject many approaches besides direct instruction can be effective. If this is true, results of research on effective teaching in different subjects should show these distinctions. Figure 12–2 lists some of the effective and ineffective patterns identified by McDonald (1976a). What patterns do you detect?

*When the teacher wants to encourage independent learning, creativity, and problem solving, then more indirect instructional methods may be the best.*

Ken Karp

**Figure 12–2    Effective Teaching in Different Grades and Subjects**

| Grade and Subject | Effective | Less Effective |
|---|---|---|
| Second-grade reading and mathematics | Independent, carefully monitored seatwork<br>Small group teaching<br>Direct individual instruction<br>Rapid student access to teacher for instruction or correction | Teaching the class as a whole |
| Second-grade reading only | A variety of materials | Attempting to achieve many different goals within a single instructional period |
| Second-grade mathematics only | Covering a large amount of material with a wide range of content and skills | Using a variety of materials<br>Having students come to the board to work problems for the whole class |
| Fifth-grade reading | Class discussions<br>Giving explanations<br>Questions and answers<br>Independent work<br>In-depth analysis of a few materials<br>Continuous reading of more complex material | Using a variety of materials<br>Letting students' attention wander |
| Fifth-grade mathematics | Small group teaching and/or teaching the class as a whole<br>Covering a large amount of material with a wide range of content and skills | Using a variety of materials<br>Individualized instruction<br>Independent work |

Adapted with permission from F. McDonald, *Beginning teacher evaluation study, Phase II 1973–74* (Executive Summary Rep.), Princeton, N.J.: Educational Testing Service, 1976, pp. 23–38.

**Less Direct for Older Students**

Effective methods for teaching both math and English with younger students and for teaching math with the fifth-graders fit the principles of direct instruction. But successful approaches for teaching English with the older students involve discussion, questioning, independent work, in-depth analysis, and complex material—very different from the drill-and-practice, teacher-led learning of direct instruction. The learning goals in the upper grades in English are more likely to involve abstract thinking, creativity, and problem solving. These goals probably require methods other than direct instruction. This is in keeping with Tom Good's conclusion that teaching should become less direct as students mature or when the goals involve affective and process outcomes (Good, 1982).

Thus far we have seen that different methods are appropriate for different learning goals. Now we consider the needs of different students.

# EFFECTIVE TEACHING WITH DIFFERENT STUDENTS

In Chapter 4 we explored several ways that students differ: socioeconomic status, culture, intelligence, creativity, cognitive style. In Chapter 8 we discussed the need for achievement, locus of control, and anxiety. Can one method of teaching be equally effective with everyone? Even without turning to research for an answer to this question, you might say "No," and you would be right. As we discussed variations among students in previous chapters, we often gave ideas about appropriate teaching methods. In this section we examine what recent research on teaching effectiveness tells us about dealing with differences.

## Strategies with Younger and Older Students

**Teaching Younger Students**

Some educators believe that the task of teaching students in the preschool years through third grade is so different from teaching older students that the two groups of teachers should complete separate and vastly different training programs (Brophy, 1976). In the early grades, effective instruction seems to involve (1) little verbal discussion, (2) highly structured teacher presentation of new material, (3) immediate chances to practice new skills, (4) drill and more drill, (5) speedy individual feedback, and (6) a large amount of carefully chosen and well-supervised individual learning exercises (Brophy and Evertson, 1976; Brophy, 1976).

Students in the early grades are mastering basic skills. They must learn these skills thoroughly so that peformance becomes almost automatic. Students in the higher grades are using the basic skills to learn facts and concepts in various content areas. Only in the grades above third and fourth are class discussion, independent learning, and lectures likely to be helpful. One explanation for the need to use different approaches at different levels is that many students below fourth grade are preoperational in their thinking (Brophy, 1976). In order to benefit from ideas presented in a purely verbal format, a student must be able to think and process information at least at a concrete operational level. (A more complete discussion of the development of thinking is given in Chapter 2.)

*McDonald found that methods of teaching mathematics should probably vary according to the age level of the students. While individualized instruction can be particularly beneficial in the early grades, the teacher here uses a group-oriented approach, more appropriate for her older class.*

*Elizabeth Hamlin/Stock, Boston.*

Evidence for these principles was found in the large study of many classrooms conducted by Fred McDonald (1976a) and described earlier. McDonald found that young students do not benefit from teaching that relies heavily on words, discussion, or verbal interaction. Older students in reading classes seem to need opportunities to talk, to ask and answer questions, to discuss, and to probe the subject matter. The need for drill in the early grades and discusion in the later grades is probably related, as noted above, to the developmental level of the students.

William Tikunoff, David Berliner, and R. C. Rist (1975) tried an entirely new approach to classroom research. They decided to study second- and fifth-grade classrooms in the way an anthropologist might study another culture—that is, by sending a sensitive observer into the class to record all the important events occurring each day. Instead of counting particular teacher and student behaviors or rating teachers, the observers prepared narrative descriptions of the classes.

**Studying
Effective
Teachers**

Observations were made of 40 teachers: 10 effective and 10 less effective reading teachers and 10 effective and 10 less effective mathematics teachers. From the 40 narratives, the researchers were able to identify 21 different dimensions that discriminated between effective and less effective teachers at both grade levels and in both subjects. Some of the dimensions described teacher behaviors and attitudes; others focused on the students or the class. These characteristics are presented in Figure 12–3.

**Figure 12–3**    **Effective Teaching in Second- and Fifth-Grade Reading and Math Classes**

| Type of Characteristic | Effective | Less Effective |
|---|---|---|
| Teacher behavior | Listens to students<br>Is consistent in messages to class<br>Monitors student learning<br>Changes pace of lesson to fit student needs<br>Promotes student self-sufficiency<br>Makes spontaneous use of unexpected events in lessons<br>Uses structuring in preparing lessons | Belittles students<br>Fills time with busy work<br>Makes illogical statements<br>Treats class as a whole for control purposes<br>Speaks abruptly |
| Teacher characteristics | Accepting<br>Optimistic<br>Knowledgeable about subject matter | Seeks recognition of self from students |
| Student behavior | Cooperative<br>Engaged | Defiant |
| Class characteristic | Convivial<br>Other adults involved in class | |

Adapted from W. J. Tikunoff, D. C. Berliner, and R. C. Rist. **An ethnographic study of forty classrooms of the beginning teacher evaluation study known sample** (Tech. Rep. 75-10-5). San Francisco, Calif.: Far West Laboratory for Educational Research and Development, October 1975, pp. 550–551.

The characteristics in Figure 12–3 give a general picture of effective teaching at the second- and fifth-grade levels. It is possible that these qualities may be part of effective teaching in all elementary grades, or even at higher levels. Further research is needed, however, before we can say for sure that each of the variables consistently discriminates between good and poor teaching.

We should note that the findings of Tikunoff, Berliner, and Rist (1975) also indicate additional characteristics that seem to be uniquely associated with effective teachers of *particular* grades. For example, effective teachers of young students, in addition to evidencing the behaviors listed in Figure 12–3, were also aware of the developmental levels of their students and the need to individualize instruction. The management styles of effective and less effective second-grade teachers also varied. Effective teachers praised students, called them by name, moved around the room, encouraged students, waited for answers, and were warm and polite. Less effective second-grade teachers harassed, ignored, rushed, shamed, and distrusted students, while moralizing and being sarcastic. However, these factors did *not* seem to be significant in fifth-grade classrooms. Perhaps a nurturing atmosphere is more conducive to learning for very young students.

You may be thinking that the positive and negative characterisitcs listed here are simply common sense. Who would doubt that a warm, flexible teacher is more effective than a sarcastic, harassing one? But remember that all the characteristics just named *did not* discriminate between effective and less effective fifth-grade teachers, only second-grade teachers. When effective and less effective fifth-grade teachers were compared, only three characteristics were added to the list in Figure 12–3. Less effective fifth-grade teachers tended to exclude classroom offenders from activities, allowed themselves to be manipulated by students, and used nonverbal cues such as snapping fingers to control students behavior. It thus appears that slightly different management styles may be appropriate for older and younger students. The teacher who is effective with older students must be firmly in control of the class, or too much instructional time will be spent dealing with behavior problems. A warm, nurturing atmosphere seems to be less important in encouraging learning for older students.

## Students with Different Aptitudes

Although most teachers do not teach a wide range of ages in one class, they are usually expected to work with students of varying aptitudes. The question of how to adapt teaching to the needs of the individual student has been studied and debated for years. Countless answers have been suggested, and many solutions attempted. Honors courses, vocational courses, experiences in the performing arts, cooperative work-study programs, independent study, and many other options are available to older students. These choices are attempts to adapt to individual interests and aptitudes. Another approach has been compensatory, remedial, or "lower track" classes for students whose achievement is below average.

Whatever the merits or limitations of these solutions, they still leave classroom teachers with the problem of how to reach the individuals in their classes. Even if the students in a class are fairly similar in ability (a rare occurrence), they will differ in so many other ways that no one method will be equally successful with all of them. This fact has been demonstrated repeatedly by psychologists doing research on aptitude-treatment-interactions.

**Aptitude-Treatment-Interactions.**    The term **aptitude-treatment-interaction** or **ATI** refers to the fact that individual differences related to learning (aptitudes) interact with particular teaching methods (treatments) so that what works well with one person may not work well with another whose aptitudes differ (Cronbach and Snow, 1977). You encountered a few examples of ATIs in Chapter 8 when we discussed methods that work well for nonanxious students but are much less effective with highly anxious students.

ATI Research

Recent studies by Penelope Peterson and colleagues at the University of Wisconsin provide examples of ATI research (Peterson, Janicki and Swing, 1980). In one of these studies, two experienced social studies teachers taught each of their three ninth-grade classes with an inquiry, lecture-recitation, or public issues approach. The students in each class varied in verbal ability, anxiety level, attitude toward social studies, and personality factors such as need to achieve by conforming or by working independently. Results indicated that student differences did interact with teaching method. Figure 12–4 presents the relationship between verbal ability and method. As you can see, students with high verbal ability performed better on a test when they had the lecture-recitation lesson, and students with lower verbal ability performed best on the test when they had participated in the public issues approach.

Higher-Order
Interactions

The interaction shown in Figure 12–4 is only one of the results of Peterson's study. Several other **higher-order interactions** were identified.

**Figure 12–4**    **An Aptitude-Treatment Interaction in the Teaching of Social Studies**

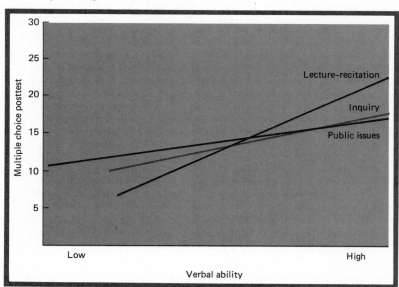

Adapted from Peterson, Janicki, and Swing, Aptitude-treatment interaction effects of three social studies teaching approaches. *Review of Educational Research*, 1980, *17*, p. 354.
Copyright © 1980, AERA, Washington, D.C.

Higher-order interactions involve more than two variables. These interactions become increasingly complex and difficult to interpret. For example, Peterson found a three-way interaction involving student anxiety, student ability, and type of instruction. The anxiety level of high-ability students did not affect how well they responded to each teaching method. But anxiety was a factor for low-ability students. In the low-ability group, high-anxiety students did poorly with the public issues approach but responded well to the inquiry method. Low-anxiety students had the opposite reaction, performing better with public issues than inquiry.

Even with promising results such as those found by Peterson and colleagues, it has been difficult to draw clear implication for teaching from the ATI studies. Tom Good and Deborah Stipek (1983) describe the problem this way:

**Problems with
Applications**

Perhaps the most fundamental, even insurmountable, reason for educators' inability to derive principles from most ATI research is that even when aptitudes and skills are precisely specified and the instructional program is taught by a good teacher, there is simply no single effective educational treatment. Cronbach claims that ATI research is characterized by inconsistent results and higher-order interactions. Apparently, techniques that work in one setting with one group of students do not necessarily work in another setting with another group or students, even for the same teacher. (pp. 9–10)

While it is difficult at this time to derive teaching principles from the ATI research, there is at least one important implication of the findings: When students are having difficulty learning with one teaching approach, it makes sense to try something else. If you can form some hypotheses about the students' particular needs and the nature of the mismatch between their aptitudes and the current teaching approach, you might be able to find a better alternative.

*A New Theory in Educational Psychology: Anti-bodies-treatment-interactions!*

| Flexibility Is the Key | Teaching effects are more complex than we might think, and flexibility is the key. Be prepared to adapt your methods for different students, subjects, and objectives. A second contribution of the ATI research is in the area of ability. While findings are not entirely consistent, there are several implications for teaching students of varying abilities. |
|---|---|

**Ability Differences among Students.** In Chapter 4 we discussed the concept of intelligence and some of the controversies surrounding it. When we use the term "ability" in this chapter, we do not mean a theoretical notion of potential, but instead readiness to profit from instruction (Cronbach and Snow, 1977; Good and Stipek, 1983). In the classroom, this usually translates into prior achievement or having the necessary background knowledge to learn new material. Of course, other factors influence how easily an individual will learn new material, including motivation, academic self-concept, and level of cognitive development.

| Teaching Students with Limited Knowledge | If we look at ATI studies involving prior knowledge, we can identify some consistent findings. When students are quite knowledgeable about a particular subject, achievement is generally comparable with different teaching methods. But when students have little prior knowledge, the method makes a difference. The less the students know, the more they need instructional support, probably in the form of improved materials, help in focusing and sustaining attention, and systematic feedback (Tobias, 1981, 1982). |
|---|---|

For example, effective materials might be organized around clear instructional objectives and include visual support such as graphs, diagrams, models, illustrations, and other aids. The help in focusing attention could include many of the special techniques we have described for increasing academic engaged time. One goal of this extra instructional support is to reduce the information processing demands made on the students (Corno, 1980; Snow, 1977). The materials and the teaching methods help the students organize the information, direct their attention to the critical features, and relieve some of the burden on their memories.

These principles should serve as general guidelines for you in teaching students who have limited knowledge in your subject. But these students often have other problems as well. They may lack interest or motivation. Often they have failed repeatedly in school, and their attitudes are not positive. Some may be disruptive in class, unable to work independently for more than a short time. Frequently teachers are given a whole class of these "low achievers." Even though this may be a smaller class than average, discipline problems are usually greater than average (Evertson, 1982). Carol Evertson provides the slice of life from a low-achieving junior high mathematics class found in Box 12–2, "Please Sit Down and Get to Work!"

The situation she describes would strain even the most patient teacher. What can teachers do with difficult classes such as this one? Based on their study of effective and ineffective secondary school teachers, Ed Emmer and Carol Evertson identified some successful practices for working with low-ability classes.

**Lesson Formats for Low-Ability Classes.** In most secondary school subjects, teachers follow a lesson format that involves an opening, the teacher making a presentation to develop the content of the lesson, the students working on problems or questions based on the teacher's presentation, and finally a closing. With a low-ability class, this standard format can invite

*(The teacher has just put the assignment on the board.)*

Marie says, "I don't have a book." The teacher says, "Look on those shelves," pointing. Marie says, "Those ain't ours." The teacher says, "Some of them are." Marie gets herself a book. Chico raises his hand and says, "I need help." About five students start the assignment right away. (There are 12 students present.) The others are talking, have their hands raised, or are going to the teacher's desk. The teacher says, "Come on up, Randy," when she calls on him. When he gets there, Larry is already there. The teacher says, "Larry, leave him alone." Larry stands and visits by the teacher's desk. Chico puts his hand up again. The teacher says, "Chico, what do you need?" He says, "Help." The teacher says, "Okay, wait a second." Larry sits down by the teacher's desk and looks on as she tells him something. Chico calls out, "Miss _____, are you going to help me?" She says, "Yes, Chico, but come up here." He says, "Aw, Miss, it's too far." The teacher ignores him, and he goes to the teacher's desk. (At this point, five students, virtually half the class, are at the teacher's desk.) The teacher helps Larry briefly and he sits down. Larry talks to Benny. The teacher says, "Benny, I don't want to talk to you again." Benny says, "I have a question." She says, "Then, come up here." He doesn't go up. The teacher is trying to work with Chico now. Chico teases the teacher. The teacher says, "Come on around here." Chico says something about his shoes. He does go around to the other side of the desk, but he continues to tease. She grabs his arm and shakes it, saying, "Settle down, Chico."

*Taken from Evertson et al, 1984.*

problems because the students are expected to pay attention to one activity for long blocks of time.

**Length of Lessons**

Teachers who are successful with low-ability classes tend to have more than one cycle of content development and student seatwork in each period (Ebmeier and Ziomek, 1982). The teacher may make a short presentation, have the students work briefly, then continue the lesson with another segment of content development, then more student practice on the skill being developed, and perhaps another teacher presentation followed by student seatwork (Evertson, 1982). This pattern keeps the students attentive by giving small doses of information and work. The teacher can make sure every student understands each step. The different activities are short enough to be within the limits of the students' attention spans.

**Making Students Responsible**

To make students more responsible for their own work, Emmer and colleagues (1984) suggest short daily assignments. Students should keep a record of grades on every assignment and average grades each week so they can see the results of their work (or lack of work). Class participation should be a part of the grading system, with daily or weekly grades awarded for appropriate contributions. In addition, students can be taught some of the learning strategies more successful students tend to apply automatically (see Chapter 7). It is especially important to give low-achieving students techniques for monitoring their own learning and problem-solving processes so they can tell when they are using the strategies correctly (Brown, Campione and Day, 1981).

**Encouraging Atmosphere**

With all this structure and emphasis on work, the atmosphere of the class should remain as friendly and supportive as possible. Students who have failed repeatedly are more likely to need the kind of genuine encouragement and nurturance that is effective with younger students (Stallings, 1981). Other ideas for working with low-ability students that have proved successful in research on effective teaching are listed in Figure 12–5.

**Figure 12–5**    **Approaches That Help and Hinder Low Achievers in Learning Basic Skills**

| Factors That Help | Factors That Will Not Help |
| --- | --- |
| Instruction broken down into steps, short activities sequenced by the teacher. | Long, unbroken periods of seatwork or independent work, with student choice of activities. |
| Plenty of practice (repetition) with frequent correction and praise; clear and immediate feedback about right and wrong answers. | Little practice, or independent practice without prompt feedback. |
| A lot of supervision and help, in whole-class or group settings. | Individualized, self-paced instruction; independent work; situations calling for pupil self-control or self-direction. |
| Protecting students from interruptions. | Teacher or other students' interrupting while students work. |
| Materials or questions at a level of difficulty at which students have a high rate of success. | Challenging materials or questions, or work in which students are not likely to know most of the answers. |
| Many opportunities and much encouragement to answer teacher questions. | Few opportunities or little encouragement to answer questions frequently. |
| Mostly narrow teacher questions with a "right" answer. | Mostly open-ended questions. |
|  | Nonacademic conversation. |
| Calling on nonvolunteers or using patterned turns to select students to answer questions. | Selecting only volunteers when calling on students to answer questions. |
| "Staying with" a student until he or she answers a question. | Quickly letting someone else answer; leaving a student with little or no feedback. |
| Short and frequent, rather than long and occasional, paper and pencil activities. | Games, artwork, interest centers. |
| *Specific* praise for good performance. | Vague or general praise or praise when it is not especially deserved. |
| Covering material thoroughly. | Covering a lot of material quickly. |

**Source:** *Adapted from Emmer et al., 1984, and Ebmeier and Ziomek, 1982.*

*Carmine L. Galasso*

*Students who lack knowledge in a subject need extra support in learning. This support could include teacher guidance and supervision, well oranized materials, and carefully sequenced objectives.*

**Teaching High Achievers.** The research on aptitude-treatment interactions indicates that a wider range of methods and approaches can be effective with high achievers. During lecture-discussion sessions, these students tend to learn more if the teacher asks both factual questions and questions that require higher-level thinking, keeps the pace of class rapid and the tasks challenging, sets high standards, and points out errors clearly (Brophy and Evertson, 1976). The more nurturant style of teaching seems less important in encouraging learning for high achievers, although this would not hold for every individual. (In the next chapter we will present more detailed information about teaching very able students.)

**Ability Grouping.** We have described teaching strategies for high- and low-ability classes. Many secondary schools group students in classes by ability. What are the effects of this system? A recent review of 52 different studies of ability grouping concluded that: (1) Ability grouping has little positive *or* negative effect on the achievement or self-concept of average and below-average secondary students. (2) Generally, beneficial effects on achievement are found when high-ability students were grouped together in special classes or honors programs. (3) All students' attitudes toward the subject are slightly more favorable in grouped classes (Kulik and Kulik, 1982).

*Research on Ability Grouping*

## INTEGRATING IDEAS ABOUT EFFECTIVE TEACHING

Teaching is complicated. Some of the methods that are supposed to work for every situation simply do not. As a teacher, you will have to make judgments based on your students and the subjects you teach. You will probably have to teach one way to one group of students and another way to others. Young students, students with lower abilities, and highly anxious students may need more structure and direction. Older students and students of higher ability may need more freedom as well as higher performance standards. Before we leave the topic of effective teaching strategies, we will make an attempt to integrate the many different ideas that have been presented.

*Cautions*

The findings of several recent studies describing effective teaching can be combined only to a certain extent. Since almost all the research thus far is correlational, we cannot say for sure what works. To make matters worse, we have already seen that different techniques are more successful with different kinds of students. And even if several studies agree that one particular approach is associated with learning gains, we must remember that the measure of gain is usually based on a class average. In each class some students may do very poorly when taught by the method that seems most effective for the majority of students. With these cautions in mind, let's imagine two elementary teachers who practice many of the strategies discussed in this chapter. We will also examine a secondary classroom that seems to work.

## A Second-Grade Class That Works

Effective
Teaching in the
Primary Grades

In this class, students generally work on individually tailored assignments at their seats while the teacher works with small groups. For reading, a variety of materials keep the students interested. In mathematics, a single workbook is used to move students step-by-step through the basic mathematics skills. This work is supplemented by lots of concrete experiences with counting, weighing, mixing, cutting, and other activities designed to build number concepts.

The teacher seldom instructs the class as a whole, although small groups are used more for reading than for mathematics. Work is assigned according to the achievement level of each student, and all students spend quite a bit of time on drill and repetition. Students also receive rapid feedback about right and wrong answers.

The teacher monitors student progress by constantly moving around the room, watching for students who need help. The class is managed positively whenever possible, through praise, support, and encouragement. Although the lessons are carefully planned, the teacher takes advantage of unusual events that happen to arise. When students rush to the window to watch the first snowfall of the season, the teacher uses this opportunity to teach new "snow vocabulary." In order to make smooth transitions from one activity to another, the teacher avoids ending abruptly. New activities are introduced with a few sentences about why the task is important, what the objective of the lesson is, or what the class will be doing for the next few minutes. The teacher likes the students and strongly believes all of them can learn.

## A Fifth-Grade Class That Works

Effective
Teaching in the
Middle Grades

If you spent much time in this class, you would hear the teacher asking questions, listening carefully to answers, explaining, probing, correcting, and asking more questions. Many of the discussions focus on short stories or articles the whole class has read. Even though the teacher does not use individualized instruction, each student's work is monitored and most of the students are involved most of the time. In math class, the teacher works with the whole class or sometimes with small groups, but does not send any students off to work on their own. The students usually complete the math workbook by the end of the year.

Although the atmosphere of the class is businesslike, the teacher is willing to capitalize on the unexpected. The discovery of some graffitti on the back wall led to a class project to create a mural in an appropriate place, as well as to some interesting discussions about self-expression and the limits of individual freedom. The students understand the reason for most of the assignments. When the teacher gives a minilecture or explains a concept, the presentation is generally very clear. The teacher likes and accepts the students and believes they all can learn.

## A Secondary Class That Works

Less is known about effective teaching patterns in the secondary grades. The 21 characteristics of effective teaching in Figure 12–3 may well be as important for secondary teaching as for elementary. We do know that more lecturing, explaining, and discussing occur in the secondary classroom. Based on the research from college classrooms and some studies using student ratings as criteria for effective teaching, we can create a hypothetical class. But you should keep in mind the probability that there are many patterns of effectiveness for different ages and subjects at the secondary level.

Effective Teaching in the Upper Grades

An effective secondary class might have a teacher who is both well organized and enthusiastic. Lectures would be clear but not too long. While speaking, the teacher might move around the room, making eye contact with as many of the students as possible. Materials would be at the appropriate level of difficulty for each student. This may require quite a range of materials, since the range of abilities is often very great in secondary classes. To the extent possible, the teacher would tailor the lessons to fit the needs of individual students. Some students might be given one assignment. Others might be given a number of choices. Still others might be told to design their own projects.

## Teacher Effectiveness: Conclusions

If you teach your fourth-grade students mathematics in a large group, will they automatically learn? Not if your explanations are confused and vague. Not if you lose control of the class. Not if you hate talking to the whole class, become very anxious, and make no sense as a result. Could a dynamic, knowledgeable, well-organized, enthusiastic teacher have good results using a less effective grouping strategy to teach mathematics? It is very possible. Could a biology teacher produce students who did well on achievement tests at the end of the year, but hated the subject so much they vowed never to dissect another animal as long as they lived? Again, it is possible.

A teacher must make a number of decisions about the organization of classroom instruction. There are no guarantees that the methods you choose will work. In making choices, you must consider the effects the methods are likely to have when used with your subject and your students. You should also consider your own strengths. Finally, you must consider the overall goals you wish to achieve.

Serious Teaching and Enjoyment in School

We have seen that factors such as teacher control of the class, drill, factual questions, clarity, and task orientation are all associated with student learning, at least in certain classes and with certain students. Keep in mind that by student learning we mean the kind of cognitive learning measured on most classroom and standardized tests. As Rosenshine (1979) has said, this may seem like a grim picture of teaching. Actually, the effective classrooms we have described are pleasant and convivial places. Still, some studies have found that more open, flexible, and less structured methods may lead to lower absence rates, more cooperation among students, and higher scores on nonverbal problem-solving tests of reasoning (Stallings and Kaskowitz, 1975). Perhaps the best teacher makes use of the research findings on teacher effectiveness but also includes activities that foster emotional and social growth, and some lessons that are just fun. After all, we want students to learn to read, but we also want them to stay in school.

Rosenshine describes some small "free schools" that combine both approaches:

Mornings in these schools are spent in structured programs in reading, writing, and mathematics. The teachers make the assignments but the children complete them anywhere in the room in a relaxed and informal manner. These assignments are from the same sequential, structured workbooks and readers that are used in traditional schools. Although each child works at his own task and at his own pace, no more than two activities, such as reading and writing, occur at the same time.

# Guidelines

## Organizing Instruction

**1. Vary the amount of structure to fit the needs of the students.**

EXAMPLES
- Give clear directions and very specific objectives when working with young, more anxious, or more dependent students.
- Make occasional use of the open-ended ambiguous assignments described in Chapter 8 when working with older, less anxious students.

**2. Allow many opportunities for students to learn basic skills thoroughly in the early grades.**

EXAMPLES
- Turn drill and practice into games.
- Provide brief worksheets that can be traded for rewards or privileges when completed.

**3. Allow students in junior and senior high school ample opportunity to explore a limited amount of material in depth.**

EXAMPLES
- Hold discussions or debates after students finish reading a short article or handout.
- Have thought-provoking questions ready for discussion.

**4. Use unexpected events as vehicles for teaching.**

EXAMPLES
- Teach new words and concepts related to electricity and sound transmission when students are excited by an electrical storm.
- Discuss seeing events from several different perspectives after a disappointing loss in sports.

**5. Use positive management strategies when possible.**

EXAMPLES
- Do not belittle students; give private reprimands and focus on the behavior, not the person.
- Avoid punishing the whole class for offenses of a few.

Although the atmosphere is relaxed, informal, and respectful, the setting is large group, teacher-centered, and structured. Afternoons are given to projects, exploration, messing around, trips, and discussion. Fridays are for hobbies and crafts. Thus, the school teaches didactic goals, such as reading and math, in a didactic way; and spends the remaining time on more open activities. (Rosenshine, 1977, pp. 23–24)

The Guidelines given here should be of help in making some of the instructional decisions you will face as a teacher.

---

**6. Match grouping to the age of the students and the subject taught.**

EXAMPLES
- Avoid teaching basic skills to the class as a whole in early grades; try direct instruction.
- Try larger groups or whole-class instruction for mathematics in upper elementary grades.

**7. Make sure the objectives for various materials are clear.**

EXAMPLES
- In the elementary grades, provide certain basic materials such as workbooks that present information in meaningful sequence.
- When teaching with supplemental materials in any grade, make sure the purpose of the materials and the instructions are clear to the students.

**8. Balance cognitive and affective objectives.**

EXAMPLES
- In the early grades, include a pleasant, ungraded, activity each day, preferably in the afternoon.
- In the later grades, allow students free time when work is completed to participate in a variety of self-selected projects.
- Have a surprise Friday celebration for work well done.

**9. Structure learning tasks so the student stays involved with the task.**

EXAMPLES
- Ask many students or the class as a whole to respond to each question.
- State clear steps leading to task completion; have all materials readily available.
- Plan systems to encourage students to be responsible for completing their work.
- As much as possible, supervise students while they are working.

**10. Be flexible; if one approach does not work with some students, try another.**

EXAMPLES
- If teacher praise does not seem motivating to a student, try a self-management approach or provide more challenging work.
- If a student does not understand a concept, use more concrete examples or let a peer explain it to him.

1. For years researchers have tried to unravel the mystery of effective teaching. The search for characteristics and personality traits indicated that teacher knowledge, clarity, and enthusiasm play a role in effective instruction.

2. But in trying to pin down teacher behaviors that were successful in every situation, psychologists found that what was important in one situation might be irrelevant in another.

3. In terms of student behaviors and effectiveness, recent research indicates that the longer students are actively engaged in learning tasks, the more they will learn.

4. Factors that encourage engagement are teacher supervision, certain characteristics of the task itself, and an effective system for making, monitoring, and checking assignments.

5. The results of many large-scale studies point to a cluster of principles that are effective in teaching basic skills. This approach has been labeled direct instruction. Other less teacher-directed, more informal methods appear to be appropriate for learning to think abstractly and to solve problems creatively.

6. Effective teaching methods must fit not only the subject, but also the student.

7. Younger students learn better in supportive and nurturing environments. As students grow older, teaching methods can be less directive. Low-ability students continue to need the structure offered by the principles of direct instruction as well as an emotionally supportive learning environment.

8. The findings of recent research on effective teaching raise an important issue for teachers. If certain methods promote academic learning but leave students with a dislike for the subject matter, a teacher must make careful decisions about overall goals.

## KEY TERMS

correlation

factor analysis

academic engaged time

direct instruction

active teaching

aptitude-treatment interaction (ATI)

higher-order interaction

high inference characteristics

# SUGGESTIONS FOR FURTHER READING AND STUDY

BERLINER, D. C. Developing conceptions of classroom environments: Some light on the T in studies of ATI. *Educational Psychologist*, 1983, *18* 1–13. This article describes eleven different basic activities structures that occur in classrooms.

BROPHY, J. Successful teaching strategies for the inner-city child. *Phi Delta Kappan*, 1982, *63*, 527–530. Research-based suggestions for helping these students to be successful in school.

CRONBACH, L. J. and SNOW, R. L. *Aptitudes and instructional methods.* New York: Irvington, 1977. A classic in the field of aptitude-treatment interactions.

DENHAM, D. and LIEBERMAN, A. (Eds). *Time to learn.* Washington, D.C.: National Institute of Education, 1980. A series of articles on academic engaged time and learning.

*The Elementary School Journal*, 1983, Volume 83, Number 4. This is a special issue on "Research on Teaching." There are articles by Jere Brophy on classroom organization, Barak Rosenshine on teaching functions, Rhona Weinstein on how children perceive teachers and instructional methods and Steward Purkey on effective schools.

EMMER, E. T. and EVERTSON, C. M. Synthesis of research on classroom management. *Educa-*

*tional Leadership*, 1981, *38*, 342–345. In a few pages, these researchers summarize the implications of recent research on effective teaching.

EPSTEIN, J. (Ed.). *Masters: Portraits of great teachers.* New York: Basic Books 1981. A series of essays about gifted teachers written by one of their equally able students.

GAGE, N. L. *The Scientific basis of the art of teaching.* New York: Teachers College Press, 1978. A concise discussion on what we really have learned from research about teachers, how this knowledge might be applied, and how research might be improved.

GALLOWAY, C. Teaching and nonverbal behavior. In A. Wolfgang (Eds.), *Nonverbal behavior: Applications and culture implications.* New York: Academic Press, 1979. A very interesting discussion about how teachers can influence students through facial expressions, gesture, voice tone, and other behavior outside words.

GOOD, T. Teacher effectiveness in the elementary school: What we know about it now. *Journal of Teacher Education,* 1979, *30,* 52–64. A thoughtful integration of the research on effective elementary school teaching.

LORTIE, D. *Schoolteacher: A sociological study.* Chicago: The University of Chicago Press, 1975. This is a classic study of teaching as an occupation. The emphasis is on teachers' views, beliefs, and feelings about their lives in the classroom.

MCDONALD, F. *Teachers do make a difference.* Princeton, N.J.: Educational Testing Service, 1976. McDonald's booklet offers a review of important recent research on effective teaching. The conclusion is that teachers do make a difference but the process is complicated.

PETERSON, P. and WALBERG, H. (Eds.) *Research on teaching: Concepts, findings and implications.* Berkeley, CA: McCutchan, 1979. This book has chapters by many of the top researchers on such topics as direct instruction, teacher thinking and decision making, and teaching effectiveness.

PETERSON, P. L. JANICKI, T. C. and SEVING, S. R. Aptitude-treatment interaction effects of three social studies teaching approaches. *American Educational Research Journal,* 1980, *17,* 339–360. This article reports the results of two carefully conducted studies that examine relationships among different teaching approaches (lecture-recitation, inquiry, and public issues discussion) and different student attributes (ability and anxiety level).

RUPLEY, W. H. and CHEVRETTE, P. Research in effective classroom instruction: Important findings for preservice and inservice teacher educators. *Action in Teacher Education: The Journal of the Association of Teacher Educators,* 1982, *4,* 73–79.

STALLINGS, J. Allocated academic learning time revisited, or beyond time on task. *Educational Researcher,* 1980, *9,* 11–16. This article reviews previous research and suggests ways that teachers can be trained to increase student learning.

TIMPSON, W. M. and TOBIN, D. N. *Teaching as performing: A guide to energizing your public presentation.* Englewood Cliffs, N.J.: Prentice-Hall, 1982. Advice about being a better teacher by taking your "cues" from performers.

# Teachers' Forum

## Reviving Interest in Learning Centers

A conscientious and energetic teacher spent her first two years of teaching constructing excellent learning centers. They had clear objectives, were well-organized and attractive, allowed the students to work independently in groups or individually, and provided different levels of work and varied resource materials. Previous students had been enthusiastic about the centers, but this year center time is greeted by a collective moan. The students dawdle and seem to drudge through the work. What is the teacher to do?

**Creating Interest**

It appears that this group of children is not oriented to center work. I would withdraw all centers for a brief period of time. Then I would bring one particularly interesting center back into the classroom. I would carefully and ceremoniously select a small group of students, make them feel quite special to have been selected, and allow them to spend some time with me working on the center. During this time they would be excused from some other work. As we worked together daily, they would begin to see how exciting center work can be. Others would soon be anxious to join in our fun. Gradually, other centers could be introduced without overwhelming the students or stifling their newly acquired enthusiasm.

Arleen Wyatt, Third-Grade Teacher
*Happy Valley Elementary School, Rossville, Georgia*

**Providing a Balance**

Too much of anything, learning centers included, can lead to boredom; a variety of experiences creates interest and maintains enthusiasm. Learning centers, unless they provide intermittent student/teacher–student/student interaction and have general relevance (and practicality) to ongoing classroom activity, would seem to create an imbalanced educational program.

Jacqueline G. Dyer, Second- to Eighth-Grade Teacher
*Classical Junior Academy, St. Louis, Missouri*

**Readiness and Interest**

One of the first things I would want to determine is if these children had been exposed previously to learning centers. If so, what had been their experience? If not, were they able to work independently and achieve success? Do they need to be introduced to the concept gradually? I would want to tap their interest and create a learning center around that. Can the students become involved and contribute ideas?

Perhaps even before this, I would want to have an open discussion and find out just what is causing the class moan.

Charlotte Ross, Second-Grade Teacher
*Covert Avenue School, Elmont, New York*

## Feedback from Student Evaluations

Once teachers settle into their assignments, they often have little professional interaction with other teachers and even less knowledgeable and helpful criticism. In the search for feedback, teachers may decide to use student evaluations. Would you advise them to do so? What are some pitfalls they might encounter?

**Triangular Feedback**

Feedback from students can be helpful if the criteria are clear. Legitimate areas of concern should be emphasized to avoid popularity contests. Students would be capable of determining fairness, availability, motivation, control, preparedness, and other factors governing the teaching setting; but student ability to give professional-level feedback is questionable. Perhaps a triangular form of evaluation would serve best: one-third student feedback, one-third administrative/professional feedback, and one-third self-evaluation.

Barbara L. Luedtke, Secondary Physical Education Teacher
*Appleton High School — East, Appleton, Wisconsin*

## A Disaster

You have just finished grading the first library research papers of the year, and the results are disastrous. The idea seemed simple enough. You gave each student a different current topic, told them to look the topic up in different periodicals, and then write a two-page summary of the information they found, listing sources. From the results, you can see that some students used nothing but encyclopedias, others gave just their own views, and some copied their entire papers from the sources.

**Accept the Blame**

(1) Accept much of the blame. It appears to me that the students weren't adequately prepared for the assignment in the first place. (2) Be patient.

James C. Fulgham, Secondary Latin Teacher
*Brainerd High School, Chattanooga, Tennessee*

**Act as a Model**

Usually in such cases I do a report (research paper) with my fourth-grade students. I bring in periodicals so that the students *see* the references. I have students tell what they have read and I encourage them to record these words and not the words of the author. At all levels I would make every effort to give individual topics that were of interest to them. For the students who used only one reference, I would consider requiring them to hand in notes from various sources on different days.

Louis G. Harrold, Fourth-Grade Teacher
*Greenwood School, Warwick, Rhode Island*

# Teaching Exceptional Students

**OVERVIEW**      Teachers today must be able to work with a wide range of students. In the past, students with identifiable learning problems, students we now call exceptional, were often segregated in special education classes. Today, many spend at least part of the day with regular teachers. In addition, students in the classrooms of the 1980s often come from different cultural backgrounds.

In the category of exceptional students are both the handicapped and the gifted. Handicapped students are the mentally retarded, physically handicapped, emotionally disturbed, learning disabled, and behavior problem students. Recent changes in federal legislation require that many handicapped students formerly taught in special classes must now be taught in the regular classroom. One consequence of these legal rulings is that you probably will have at least one exceptional student in your class, whatever grade you teach. We will discuss the new laws, their effects on classrooms, and how to cope with them.

This chapter is organized around the kinds of problems and abilities students might have. As we discuss each problem area, we will describe how a teacher might recognize a student displaying the problem, seek help from school and community resources, and plan instruction based on the individuals' strengths and weaknesses.

By the time you complete this chapter, you should be able to do the following:

- Discuss the potential problems in categorizing and labeling students.
- Discuss the steps involved in diagnostic-prescriptive teaching.
- List indicators of hearing, vision, language, and behavior problems, as well as indicators of specific learning disabilities and mental retardation.
- Adapt your teaching methods to meet the needs of exceptional students.
- Discuss the implications of Public Law 94-142 for your teaching.
- Describe how you might recognize and teach a gifted student in your class.
- Explain the options for multicultural and bilingual teaching.

When we hear the words "exceptional student," most of us immediately think of labels such as "retarded," "emotionally disturbed," or "dyslexic." In the following section we examine these labels and the process of categorizing people.

## WHAT DOES IT MEAN TO BE EXCEPTIONAL?

Limited Options      One problem facing exceptional students until recently was a lack of options. If a child could not be taught in the regular classroom, using standard methods, the school had the right to refuse to educate the person at all. A student who was mildly cerebral palsied or partially sighted might need only extra materials, equipment, or tutoring to succeed in a normal classroom. Yet the school could deny its facilities to the student, forcing him or her to attend a separate program designed for individuals with much more serious handicaps. This situation has changed dramatically in the past decade.

The practice of separating students with learning problems and physical handicaps from "normal" students relied on the process of labeling. Today there is great controversy over the issue of labeling.

## What's in a Name: Caution in the Use of Labels

Labels Are
Judgments

No child is born "mildly retarded" or "learning disabled" in the same way that a child is born female or with the blood type O negative. The decision that an individual is retarded is a judgment based on the way the individual performs certain tasks. As Jane Mercer has stated: "Persons have no names and belong to no class until we put them in one. Whom we call mentally retarded, and where we draw the line between the mentally retarded and the normal, depend upon our interest and the purpose of our classification" (Mercer, 1973, p. 1).

The Disease
Model

**Labels and Decisions.** For many years, the purpose of using labels to put students in groups was to determine if they were eligible for special services in the school or community. The focus of special education was diagnosis and classification, deciding what was "wrong" with students so they could receive the appropriate "treatment." The model for this procedure is like the disease model used by physicians: The assumption is that each disease has a particular treatment, which usually is effective.

Unfortunately, few specific "treatments" automatically follow from a diagnosis such as mental retardation. Many different teaching strategies and materials are appropriate for students labeled retarded. Similarly, a student who has been categorized as partially sighted may benefit from the same techniques used to teach students whose sight is perfect but who have great difficulty remembering what they see. Critics of labeling claim the categories

*This 1914 photograph depicts the traditional approach to dealing with exceptional children, with students labeled "handicapped" separated from "normal" students. Not only has this segregation lessened considerably in recent years, but the labeling itself has become controversial.*

Louis Hine/New York Public Library

have no educational relevance, since the label does not tell the teacher which methods or materials to use with individual students.

Labels Affect
Perception
**Labels as Stigmas.** Many educators believe children labeled as different from peers are permanently stigmatized. Teachers, friends, and the students themselves set expectations for achievement based on the label and not the individual. When everyone assumes students will fail, they often respond with failure. Several research studies have demonstrated the powerful effects of labels (for example, Foster, Ysseldyke and Reese, 1975; Gottlieb, 1974). In these studies, the same information (test scores, videotape interview, and so on) about a student was presented to two different groups of teachers. One group was told that the student was normal. The other group was told the student had a particular problem (for example, that he or she is retarded, emotionally disturbed, "dull," or learning disabled). The teachers who believed the student had some kind of problem usually saw the student's behavior as disturbed. In other words, believing something was wrong with a student led teachers to *see* more wrong.

Other Sources
of Stigma
Labels are not the sole source of stigma for exceptional students. There is some evidence that the behavior of "special" students is one cause of difficulties in their interpersonal relationships; that is, students who are very slow learners, who disrupt class, or who repeatedly fail are liked less by their classmates regardless of the presence or absence of a formal label (Gottlieb, 1974). However, the presence of a label may add to these difficulties, especially for older students.

Benefits
of Labels
Some educators argue that, for younger students at least, being labeled as special helps protect the child. For example, if classmates know a student is retarded, they will adjust their standards and be more accepting of his or her limitations. Being classified also means that parents and teachers have some guidelines in seeking information from research on particular problems. Labels sometimes open doors to special programs or financial assistance. Labels probably both stigmatize and help students (Gottlieb, 1974). But until we are able to make diagnoses with great accuracy, we should be very cautious about describing a complex human being with one word.

## Beyond the Labels: Teaching Students

When a teacher or parent is confronted with students having obvious difficulties in learning and/or interacting, students who cannot cope with their world as easily as others the same age, something must be done. Avoiding special attention and help in order to avoid placing a label on such students is not a satisfactory answer to the problem. The best way to prevent the students, their peers, and their teachers from forming negative attitudes about the situation is to help these students learn and change their behavior.

To be effective, teachers need to know which instructional strategies to use. In previous years, the diagnosis of an exceptional student was often considered complete when the correct category was determined so the student could be placed in the appropriate special class. Today, diagnosis is not considered complete until a "prescription" is written describing the teaching techniques that have been tried and found effective for the student.

**Diagnostic-Prescriptive Teaching: Evaluation without Labels.**    The steps in the **diagnostic-prescriptive cycle** are these: (1) determine current functioning; (2) identify teaching strategies that might help the student learn; (3) test these techniques with the student; (4) write a plan for teaching the student based on the results of the trial teaching; and (5) evaluate progress frequently. With this approach, there is less emphasis on testing outside the classroom or school by specialists such as neurologists or psychologists. Instead, specially trained teachers play a major role in diagnosis and planning. Let us follow three students through the diagnostic-prescriptive cycle.

**Sandy, Bill, and Jean: Three Examples of Diagnosis without Labels.** Sandy is an 8-year-old girl in a suburban school. Although her teachers have given her hours of extra attention, Sandy is falling farther and farther behind in all subjects. She requires much longer to learn and must move very slowly, practicing new skills more than other children. Sandy also has difficulty in her relationships with other children. She sometimes explodes angrily.

An individual intelligence test is given, and Sandy receives a score of 60. She is low in all abilities measured on an achievement test. Because she needs special help in all subject areas, Sandy is assigned to a self-contained class for children who need more individual attention than the regular teachers can give. Sandy still joins her old class for art (one of Sandy's strengths) and recess. The regular teacher works with the special teacher to plan a behavior management program focused on Sandy's relationships with classmates and on her tantrums.

Bill is a handsome 13-year-old boy. He is quite bright but avoids writing whenever possible. His grades are beginning to suffer because his school-work requires more and more writing. Testing reveals that Bill has great difficulty translating the information he hears into its written equivalent. He becomes confused and cannot seem to write what he has in mind. His sentences become disorganized and are left unfinished. Bill is assigned to the resource room for one hour each day to work on written expression. The

resource teacher's aide also gives Bill some tests from his regular classes orally so he can begin to salvage his sinking grades. In addition, the resource teacher helps Bill's regular teachers adapt his assignments to avoid his writing problem until he can make some progress in overcoming it.

Jean is a 17-year-old girl who has a congenital orthopedic problem. She has had major surgery on three occasions and countless minor operations and physical therapy treatments. Although a very bright student, Jean has had to miss quite a bit of school, and her grades have suffered. Testing revealed no learning problems other than a mild hearing impairment. A hearing aid has practically eliminated this source of difficulty. It was decided that tutors and home teachers would be provided when Jean was out of school. The only extra help Jean needed during the time she attended school was assistance with her wheelchair, books, and materials. A few changes were made in the high school itself when Jean entered. Ramps were installed, and Jean's classes were moved to the first floor. Students were assigned to move Jean from one class to another and carry her books. Two of these helpers became her close friends. The three girls plan to go to the same college and be roommates.

You can see that some of the prescriptions for Sandy, Bill, and Jean involve building on strong areas to compensate for weaknesses. Other approaches involve trying to correct the weaknesses directly. Which is best?

*The teacher who suspects that a student's learning difficulty may stem from a physical, emotional, or mental disorder should consult a specialist or a specially trained teacher. Simply naming the problem is the smallest part of the diagnosis, which should extend to a detailed prescription of teaching methods that hold promise for the student.*

Norman Hurst/Stock, Boston

Flexibility
Is the Key

**Teaching to Strengths or Weaknesses.** There is disagreement among professionals as to whether teachers should remediate and correct learning "weaknesses" or build on learning "strengths" so the student can use strengths to compensate for the problem. Say a student has great difficulty reading. As a consequence, he has fallen far behind in all his classes because all subjects require some reading, even subjects he understands well, like mathematics and science. If you were the student's teacher, would you direct your attention toward teaching him to read, or toward using methods that do not rely on reading to teach the subject matter he is missing? Since the answer to this question varies for each individual student, it is probably best to try both approaches. Do not let students fall behind in all other subjects by insisting that they learn only from the printed word. In addition, do not give up on teaching them to read! Flexibility is crucial for regular teachers working with handicapped students.

## STUDENTS WITH LEARNING PROBLEMS

In this section we take an in-depth look at the major problems. Remember, however, that many students have more than one handicapping condition.

### Physical and Health Problems

A Range
of Problems

Many students have health problems that do not interfere with their progress in school. Some students must have special **orthopedic devices,** such as braces, shoes, crutches, or wheelchairs, to participate in a normal school program. Accidents, disease, or birth defects can lead to conditions that require these devices. If the school has the necessary architectural features, such as ramps, elevators, and accessible restroom facilities, and if teachers make allowance for the physical limitations of students, very little needs to be done to alter the usual educational program for them. We will look at two problems, epilepsy and cerebral palsy, in more detail, since these conditions are so often misunderstood.

**Epilepsy.** We often have more misinformation than information about **epilepsy.** The exact causes are unknown, but the seizures that accompany some forms result from uncontrolled, spontaneous firings of neurons in the brain. Not all seizures are the result of epilepsy; temporary conditions such as high fevers or infections can also trigger seizures (Wilson, 1973).

Petit Mal
Epilepsy

There are two types of epilepsy you might encounter in the classroom. The first, *petit mal epilepsy,* is characterized by a temporary loss of contact with the outside world. The student may stare, not respond to questions, drop what is being held, and miss what has been happening for a few moments. *Grand mal epilepsy* is characterized by uncontrolled jerking movements that ordinarily last 2 to 5 minutes. When the student regains consciousness, he or she may be very weary, confused, and need to sleep (Hallahan and Kauffman, 1982).

Grand Mal
Epilepsy

The major problem for students with petit mal seizures is that they miss the continuity of the class interaction. If seizures are frequent, they will find the lessons confusing. As a teacher, you should simply question these students to be sure they are understanding and following the lesson. Be prepared to repeat yourself periodically. Since petit mal seizures are not dramatic, the condition may go undetected. If a child in your class appears to daydream frequently, does not seem to know what is going on at times, or cannot remember what has just happened when you ask, you should consult the school psychologist or nurse.

Teacher's
Reaction

A grand mal seizure requires a reaction from the teacher. The old idea of putting a stick or pencil in a student's mouth to protect the tongue during a grand mal seizure should be *forgotten.* Anything hard might injure the child. The major danger to students having a seizure is that they will hurt themselves by striking a hard surface during the violent jerking that accompanies the seizure. But do not try to restrain the child's movements. Simply lower the child gently to the floor, away from furniture or walls. Move hard objects away. Some experts advise turning the student's head to the side and gently placing a soft material like a handkerchief between the back teeth. Check with the student's parents to find out how the seizure is usually dealt with. If one seizure follows another and the student does not regain consciousness in between, get medical help right away (Hallahan and Kauffman, 1982).

As a teacher, your reaction to a seizure is very important. The other students in the class will be upset if you are upset. If you seem fearful or disgusted, they will learn to respond in similar ways. The class should be prepared for the possibility of seizures occurring during school. Mistaken ideas, such as that the condition is contagious, should be clarified. When the student having the seizure regains consciousness, he or she should not be greeted by a classroom of staring children.

**Cerebral Palsy.** Damage to the brain and central nervous system before, during, or in the early years after birth can cause a child to have difficulty moving and coordinating his or her body. The problem may be very mild, so the child simply appears to be a bit clumsy, or so severe that voluntary movement is practically impossible. The most common form of **cerebral palsy** is characterized by **spasticity** (involuntary contraction of muscles).

The damage to the brain may be such that only movement is affected. Children with this form of cerebral palsy may simply wear a brace or be in a wheelchair and need no special educational program. But many children with cerebral palsy have secondary handicaps such as sensory deficits or speech problems (Bigge and Sirvis, 1982). In the classroom, these secondary handicaps are the greatest concern. The teacher may use strategies for many different learning problems in working with children who have cerebral palsy. Box 13–1 tells the story of one such child.

---

### BOX 13–1 TOMMY

*The following excerpts were taken from an article entitled, "For Tommy at 13, No New Freedoms," by Barbara Meyer. (New York Times, Jan. 24, 1982, p. 26.)*

Twelve . . . going on 13 . . . becoming a teenager. We can all probably recall the inner excitement and ambivalent feelings that we experienced at the prospect: Physical changes, anticipation of new freedoms, going to high school, more-difficult studies, sports, dating, driving.

Tommy is 12, almost 13. He is about to become a teenager. Period. Tommy has cerebral palsy, severe enough to keep him in a wheelchair. He is unable to speak and he wears a hearing aid.

The changes will take place. That cute little fellow with the ready smile is already showing signs of becoming a pimply-faced, misshapen adolescent with flailing, uncontrollable movements.

And he's becoming so moody! Still sounds like any other adolescent, doesn't he?

The only difference is that Tommy will still be in a wheelchair, unable to speak or hear well, and still flailing his arms when he completes his rite of passage.

Tommy will have no new freedoms. His boundaries were set at birth. He is now in a special school, and will be going on to another special school. He will never be part of the adolescent steps in crowded halls, the good-natured pushing and yelling, cutting classes, flirting, the highs and lows of friendships and romances.

He will never know the exhilaration of victory or pain of defeat in an athletic event. He can never look forward to that star-spangled day of slipping a new driver's licence into his wallet. . . .

The President declared 1981, and part of 1982, as the Year of the Disabled Person. There are mandated access ramps to public buildings, parking spaces identified for the handicapped, telephone booths scaled down for wheelchairs, nondiscrimination laws for hiring the disabled.

Fine, just fine.

But what about Tommy? You can't mandate kids to play with him after school. You can't give other people the patience and sincerity to spend time trying to understand what he tries to communicate to them.

You can't insist that people stop talking down to him as though he were a 2-year-old.

He has a great sense of humor. Can't they see that?

He's lonely. Can't they feel that?

He's frustrated. He's starting to realize just how disabled he is. Don't they know that? . . .

**Adjustment and Self-Concept.**   Although many students with health problems seem to need only medication or special equipment in order to learn in the regular classroom, they may also need extra emotional support and counseling. A student wearing a brace may be no different from others when it comes to translating French or solving long-division problems, but that student's life outside the classroom may be quite different.

Peer Relationships

It is especially important for students with serious health problems to receive genuine praise and recognition for their successes. Because physical handicaps often interfere with the normal play and physical activity of children, the development of peer relationships may be affected. Teachers should be sensitive to the social successes of all their students, but handicapped students sometimes need extra support in their attempts to become a part of the classroom group.

## Impaired Vision or Hearing

Students with severe hearing or vision losses, especially younger students who have not yet learned how to function in regular classrooms, spend most of their school time in special classes. Students with mild impairments or with more severe problems who have had special training are frequently placed in regular classrooms for most or all of their instruction.

Oral v. Manual Approaches

**Hearing Impairment.**   In the past, educators have debated whether oral or manual approaches are better for children with hearing impairments. Oral approaches involve **speech reading** as well as training students to use whatever limited hearing they might have. Manual approaches include **sign language** and **finger spelling.** Research indicates that children who learn some manual method of communicating perform better in academic subjects and are more socially mature than students who are exposed only to oral methods.

Today the trend is to combine both approaches (Hallahan and Kauffman, 1982). There is a new appreciation for signing, both as a means of communication and as a very expressive language. The first author encountered an example of this wider acceptance at a production of "A Christmas Carol." The entire play was interpreted in signs for the audience by two women standing in front of the stage. Many people in the audience, including the author's daughter, were fascinated by the interpretation and enjoyed this addition to the play.

Causes of Hearing Impairment

Hearing losses may be caused by genetic factors, maternal infections such as rubella during pregnancy, complications during birth, or early childhood diseases such as mumps or measles. Many children today are protected from hearing loss by vaccinations against such infections.

Signs of hearing problems are turning one ear toward the speaker, favoring one ear in conversation, or misunderstanding conversation when the speaker's face cannot be seen. Other indications are not following directions, frequently asking people to repeat what they have said, mispronouncing new words or names, or being reluctant to participate in class discussion (Charles and Malian, 1980). The Guidelines given here should help you in teaching students with impaired hearing.

# *Guidelines*

*Teaching the Hearing-Impaired Student*

**1. Make sure the student is seated where he or she can see your lip movements clearly.**

EXAMPLES
- Lighting should be sufficient to see clearly, but students should not be facing windows or a bright light.
- Do not stand with your back to the windows or a bright light; this casts your face in shadow and makes lip reading difficult.

**2. Speak naturally, in complete grammatical sentences.**

EXAMPLES
- Do not overemphasize lip movements or speak more slowly than usual.
- Do not speak too loudly, especially if the student is wearing a hearing aid.

**3. Avoid visual distractions that would draw attention away from the lips.**

EXAMPLES
- Excessive makeup or jewelry can be distracting.
- Overuse of hand gestures can draw attention inappropriately.

**4. Make it easy for the student to see your face.**

EXAMPLES
- Use an overhead projector to allow you to speak and write while still maintaining eye contact with students.
- Try not to move around the room while speaking.

Adjusting to Glasses

**Visual Impairment.** Mild vision problems can be overcome with corrective lenses. Difficulties sometimes arise when a student forgets or refuses to wear glasses. One solution in these situations is a token reinforcement program. For example, the teacher makes the following contract with the student: "At ten random times during the day I will stop by your desk. If you are wearing your glasses at that moment, you get a check on this card taped to the top of your desk. As soon as you have five checks (or whatever number is appropriate), you may choose a reward from this list."

Only about .1 percent of the students in this country have visual impairments so serious that special education services are needed. Most of this group needing special services is classified as having **low vision.** This means they can see objects close to them but have difficulty seeing at a distance. These children may need only large-print readers to remain in the regular classroom. A small group of students, about 1 in every 2500, is **educationally blind.** These students must have Braille materials, recordings, or readers (Kirk and Gallagher, 1983).

**5. Encourage the hearing-impaired student to face the speaker during class discussions.**

EXAMPLES
- Allow the student to move around the room to get the best possible view of the speaker.
- Use small group discussion.

**6. Make sure directions, assignments, and class materials are understood.**

EXAMPLES
- Write assignments or directions on the board or use mimeographed handouts.
- If this is not possible, a hearing student may be asked to take notes for the hearing-impaired student.
- Ask the hearing-impaired student to repeat or explain class material. Do *not* simply ask, "Do you understand?"

**7. Learn how a hearing aid operates.**

EXAMPLES
- Ask the child or special teacher to demonstrate it to the class.
- Encourage the child to assume responsibility for the care of the hearing aid.

**8. Keep in close contact with other professional personnel involved in the child's education.**

EXAMPLES
- Exchange visits with the special class teacher.
- Check with the child's therapist regularly to note changes and differing needs.

Special Materials

Special materials and equipment that help visually handicapped students to function in regular classrooms include large-print typewriters, variable-speed tape recorders (allowing teachers to make time-compressed tape recordings, which speed up the rate of speech without changing the voice pitch), special calculators, the abacus, three-dimensional maps, charts, and models, and special measuring devices. For students with visual problems, the quality of the print is often more important than the size, so watch out for trouble with handouts and ditto sheets. You can buy ditto masters that print in black, red, or green. These may be easier to read than the standard purple we all know and love. The Instructional Materials Reference Center of the American Printing House for the Blind (1839 Frankfort Avenue, Louisville, KY 40206) has catalogs of instructional materials for visually impaired students.

Signs of Vision Problems

Students who have difficulty seeing often hold books very close to or far away from their eyes. They may squint, rub their eyes frequently, or complain that their eyes burn or itch. The eyes may actually be swollen, red, or encrusted. Students with vision problems may misread material on the blackboard or describe their vision as being blurred (DeMott, 1982). They may be very sensitive to light or may hold their heads at an odd angle (Charles and Malian, 1980). Any sign of impairment should be reported to a qualified school official.

## Communication Disorders

Language is a complex, learned behavior. Language disorders may arise from many sources, since so many different aspects of the individual are involved in learning language. A child with a hearing impairment will not learn to speak normally. A child who hears inadequate language at home will learn inadequate langage. Children who are not listened to or whose perception of the world is distorted by emotional problems will reflect these problems in their language development. Since speaking involves movements, any impairment of the other motor functions involved with speech can cause language disorders. Because language development requires thinking, any problems of cognitive functioning can affect the growth of language.

**Speech Impairments.** Students who cannot produce sounds effectively for speaking because of disturbances in articulation, voicing, or because they stutter are considered to have a **speech impairment.** About 5 percent of the population of school-age children has some form of speech impairment. Articulation problems and stuttering are the two most common problems.

**Articulation disorders** include substituting one sound for another ("I tought I taw a puddy tat"), distorting a sound (*shoup* for *soup*), adding a sound (*ideer* for *idea*), or omitting sounds (*po-y* for *pony*) (Cartwright, Cartwright and Ward, 1981). Keep in mind that most children are 6 to 8 years old before they can successfully pronounce all English sounds in normal conversation. The sounds of the consonants *l, r, y, s,* and *z* and the consonant blends *sh,* ch, *zh,* and *th* are the last to be mastered.

**Voicing problems** include speaking with an inappropriate pitch, quality, loudness, or flexibility (Wiig, 1982). A student with any of these problems should be referred to a speech therapist. Recognizing the problem is the first step. Be alert for students whose pronunciation, loudness, voice quality, speech fluency, and rate are very different from those of their peers. Listen to students who seldom speak. Are they simply shy, or do they have difficulties with language?

**Stuttering** generally appears between the ages of 3 and 4. In about 50 percent of the cases, stuttering disappears during early adolescence (Wiig, 1982). The Guidelines presented here give some ideas for dealing with this problem in the classroom.

**Oral Language Disorders.** There are four types of language disorders: (1) the absence of verbal language, due possibly to deafness at birth, brain damage, or severe emotional problems; (2) qualitatively different language, such as merely echoing what is said, caused by hearing loss, learning disabilities, mental retardation, or emotional problems; (3) delayed verbal communication, possibly caused by hearing loss, brain damage, emotional problems, poor teaching or parenting, or inadequate language models; and

# Guidelines

*Helping the Student Who Stutters*

**1. Allow the student time to speak.**

EXAMPLES
- Do not call on the student suddenly, with no warning.
- Let the student know a little before his or her turn is coming up.

**2. Listen to the content of what is said, not to the trouble the student has in saying it.**

EXAMPLES
- Don't correct the speech or finish the sentence for the student.
- Monitor your nonverbal communication. Does your facial expression show impatience?

**3. Give the student classroom responsibility.**

EXAMPLES
- Appoint such a student to a position that will gain respect from classmates.
- Let the student demonstrate skills that require little speaking.

**4. Some days will be easier for this student than others: watch for this.**

EXAMPLES
- Give special opportunites to recite on good days.
- Encourage extra interaction with other classmates on good days.

**5. Try to establish a regular routine.**

EXAMPLES
- The student should follow the same rules as any other student, but pressure should not be put on speaking.
- Develop a schedule so the student knows what's coming next most of the time.

**6. Do not allow the student to use stuttering to avoid a class assignment.**

EXAMPLES
- If a task is oral and the student feels he or she cannot do it, assign the work in written form.
- Encourage some verbal interaction in good days.

**7. Do not allow peers to make fun of the stutterer.**

EXAMPLES
- Model patience and interest when the child talks.
- Read a story written from an exceptional student's viewpoint and discuss with the class.
- Talk with students privately and explain the effects of their ridicule on the stutterer.

(4) interrupted language, often due to hearing loss or injury later in childhood (Hallahan and Kauffman, 1982). As we noted in Chapter 2, language *differences* are not necessarily language *disorders*. Students with language disorders are those who are markedly deficient compared to other students of

their own age and cultural group. Students who seldom speak, who use few words or very short sentences, or who rely on gestures to communicate should be referred to a qualified school official for observation or testing.

## Behavior Disorders

Definition of Behavior Disorders

Students with behavior disorders can be among the most difficult to teach in a regular class. Luckily there are strategies, based on behavior modification, that are very effective in helping these students. Behavior becomes a problem when it deviates so much from appropriate behaviors for the child's age group that it significantly interferes with (1) the child's own growth and development and/or (2) the lives of others. Clearly, deviation implies a difference from some standard, and standards of behavior differ from one situation, age, culture, or time period to another. What passes for team spirit in the football bleachers would be seen as disturbed behavior in a religious service. Let us look here at some of the most common problems.

Delinquency

**Conduct Problems.** When conduct problems come to the attention of the courts, they are called **juvenile delinquency.** Three forms of delinquency have been identified (Ross, 1974). Impulsive delinquents have learned the rules of conduct of their culture but occasionally, or perhaps only once or twice, break a law when there is little chance of being caught. Many adolescents, if they are truthful, will remember one prank or theft that went undetected. If the consequences of breaking the law are positive enough, the behavior might be repeated.

The second type of delinquent is called unsocialized, because he or she failed to develop the internal controls that prevent most people from breaking laws. Researchers looking for causes of this type of delinquency have suggested overstrict or inconsistent parental discipline, lack of family cohesiveness, parental rejection and hostility, and criminal role models in the family as possible causes. The final type of delinquency is called social, because it usually arises in gangs. These groups have their own standards and norms that reward members for illegal or antisocial behavior. Gangs are not confined to the lower socioeconomic classes, but may develop wherever students are left on their own and turn to each other for support, affection, praise, or clear rules of conduct.

Not all children whose conduct is a problem could be called delinquents. Some students exhibit behaviors such as "attention seeking, boisterousness, rudeness, hyperactivity, and physical and verbal aggression" (Graubard, 1973, p. 249). Although these behaviors are not illegal, they are extremely troubling to teachers. The management strategies described in Chapters 9 and 10 are useful in dealing with them.

Definition of Hyperactivity

**Hyperactivity.** You probably have heard and may even have used the term **hyperactivity.** The notion is a modern one; there were no "hyperactive" children 30 or 40 years ago. Today, if anything, the term is applied too often and too widely. Hyperactivity is not one particular condition; it is "a set of behaviors—such as excessive restlessness and short attention span—that are quantitatively and qualitatively different from those of children of the same sex, mental age, and SES" (O'Leary, 1980, p. 195).

Hyperactive children are not only more physically active and inattentive than other children, they have difficulty responding appropriately, working steadily toward goals (even their own goals), and may not be able to control their behavior on command, even for a brief period of time. The problem behaviors are generally evident in all situations and with every teacher. It is hard to know how many children could be classified as hyperactive. The most common estimate is 5 percent of the elementary school population (O'Leary, 1980).

Causes

There is great disagreement about the cause or causes of hyperactivity. The list includes subtle damage to the brain, often called minimal brain damage or MBD, slower than normal neurological development, chemical imbalances in the body, genetic factors, allergies to foods, lead poisoning, maternal drinking or smoking during pregnancy, and simply inappropriate learning (Reid and Hresko, 1981). There is some evidence for each of these possibilities. Certain treatments work better with some individuals than with others, so the underlying problem may not be the same for each child.

Role of Drugs

As a teacher or parent, you are more concerned with cures than causes. Unfortunately, there are no completely effective approaches. Many children, about 700,000, receive stimulant medication, usually Dexedrine or Ritalin. We know little about the long-term effects of drug therapy. However, the short-term effects include possible improvements in social behaviors such as cooperation, attention, and compliance. Research suggests that about 70 percent of hyperactive children are more manageable when on medication, but there are negative side effects (increased heart rate and blood pressure, interference with growth rate, insomnia, weight loss, nausea) for many (O'Leary, 1980; Walden and Thompson, 1981). In addition, there is no evidence of improvement in academic learning or peer relationships, two areas where hyperactive children have great problems. Since students may appear to improve dramatically in their behavior, parents and teachers, relieved to see change, may assume the problem has been cured. It hasn't. The students still need special help in learning.

Methods

The methods that have proved most successful in helping hyperactive students learn new skills are based on the behavioral principles described in Chapters 5 and 9—for example, token reinforcement programs, contingency contracts, and self-management procedures. Even if students in your class are on medication, it is critical that they also learn the academic and social skills they will need to survive. This will not happen by itself, even if behavior improves with medication.

Behavioral Strategies

**Emotional Disturbance.** Certainly attention seeking, rudeness, or aggression may be seen as symptoms of emotional disturbance. Chapters 5 and 9 described several strategies that are useful in helping emotionally disturbed students. For example, a child who is overly fearful of a particular situation, like gym class, may be helped to overcome the fear through gradual desensitization. Because the difficulty with emotionally disturbed students is often that their behavior is inappropriate, behavior modification strategies have frequently proved helpful.

Lately many people have become concerned about the seeming increase in suicide among adolescents. Box 13–2, "A Psychiatrist Looks at Adolescent Suicide," discusses this issue. In recent years, a new category of exceptional

## BOX 13–2 A PSYCHIATRIST LOOKS AT ADOLESCENT SUICIDE

*The following is taken from James Toolan's article, "Depression and suicide in children: An overview," which appeared in the* American Journal of Psychotherapy, *1981, 35, 311–312.*

Suicide is one of the most common causes of death in older adolescents and college-age students — unfortunately in some of the most capable and brilliant. If anything, the suicidal level appears to be increasing rather than decreasing, particularly in the young, and the present statistics on suicidal attempts are absolutely meaningless. Even completed suicides are suspect, because so many are disguised as accidents . . . .

The other statistic to be kept in mind is the number of accidents reported. Accidents occur much more frequently than suicidal attempts, and probably many or even most accidents are semi-intentional. I question whether there are many genuine accidents in life. I am extremely skeptical about one-car automobile accidents. When you work with depressed people you can sometimes have an uncanny notion of who is going to attempt or commit suicide in the disguised fashion of an accident.

Another attitude concerning suicide that we must always question is the one expressed by the comment, "Oh well, it was just a gesture — an attempt to gain attention." The "Friday night special" in the emergency room presents the typical young female who is upset because her boyfriend or husband has gone off with another woman. Band-Aids are put on her wrists or her stomach washed out, and she is sent home and told not to come back. But why would anyone make a suicidal gesture unless he or she were desperate? Her boyfriend did run out on her — she has a right to be depressed — but does she have to use this method of calling attention to her plight? People who resort to this extreme are in my opinion really desperate. They urgently need help and should be seen as soon as possible after the attempt. As an example, a patient was admitted at midnight who definitely attempted to kill herself. The nurse notes at 5 A.M., "unhappy because she did not succeed," the psychiatrist comes in at 10 A.M., the patient has her makeup on and is looking fine, saying, "I want to go home — it was all a mistake. I just lost count of the pills." Denial, by that time, has altered the clinical picture. We have to be very skeptical about such a sudden change of mood following a suicidal attempt, and I think a period of observation is needed in order to truly evaluate such patients. Suicidal patients are often very difficult because they so frequently deny the seriousness of their attempts. All of us who work with youngsters should keep this in mind.

students has been identified. The category is controversial, partly because professionals cannot agree on who belongs in it.

## Specific Learning Disabilities: What's Wrong When Nothing Is Wrong?

How do you explain a student who is not mentally retarded, emotionally disturbed, educationally deprived, or culturally different; who has normal vision, hearing, and language capabilities, and who still cannot learn to read, write, or compute? One explanation is that the student has a **specific learning disability**. The federal government gives this definition:

Definition    "Specific learning disability" means a disorder in one or more of the basic psychological processes involved in understanding or using language, spoken or written, which may manifest itself in an imperfect ability to listen, think, speak, read, write, spell, or to do mathematical calculations. The term includes such conditions as perceptual handicaps, brain injury, minimal brain dysfunction, dyslexia, and developmental aphasia. (*Federal Register*, August 23, 1977)

The definition goes on to say that the disorders of listening, thinking, and so on are *not* due primarily to other conditions, such as mental retardation, emotional disturbance, or educational disadvantages.

**Students with Learning Disabilities.** As with any of the groups of problems described thus far, students with learning disabilities are not all alike. Figure 13–1 is a partial list of characteristics displayed by students

**Figure 13–1    Characteristics of Learning-Disabled Students**

1. Test performance indicators
   a. Poor geometric figure drawing.
   b. Poor performance on group tests.
2. Impairments of perception and concept formation
   a. Impaired discrimination of size.
   b. Impaired discrimination of right-left and up-down.
3. Disorders of speech and comprehension
   a. Impaired discrimination of auditory stimuli.
   b. Slow language development.
4. Disorders of motor function
   a. Frequent delayed motor milestones.
   b. General clumsiness or awkwardness.
5. Academic achievement and adjustments
   a. Reading and spelling disabilities.
   b. Poor printing, writing, or drawing ability.
6. Disorders of thinking process
   a. Poor ability for abstract reasoning.
   b. Difficulties in concept formation.
7. Emotional characteristics
   a. Reckless and uninhibited.
   b. Poor emotional and impulse control.
   c. Low tolerance for frustration.
8. Characteristics of social behavior
   a. Social competence below average for age and measured intelligence.
   b. Behavior often inappropriate for situation and consequences apparently not foreseen.
9. Variation of personality
   a. Overly gullible and easily led by peers and older youngsters.
   b. Frequent rage reactions and tantrums when crossed.
   c. Excessive variation in mood and responsiveness from day to day and even hour to hour.
10. Disorders of attention and concentration
   a. Short attention span for age.
   b. Impaired ability to make decisions, particularly from many choices.

*Source: Adapted from Bryan and Bryan 1975, pp. 40–42. Copyright 1975 and 1978, Alfred Publishing Co., Inc. Bryan, T. H. and Bryan, J. H.* **Understanding learning disabilities.** *Port Washington, N.Y.: Alfred Publishing Co., 1975, by permission of Mayfield Publishing Co.*

diagnosed as learning disabled, but many students with other handicaps and many normal students might have some of the same characteristics. To complicate the situation even more, not all students with learning disabilities will have these problems, and few will have all the characteristics listed here.

There is no agreement about the causes of learning disabilities. Explanations include lack of dominance of one side of the brain, mild or slight physical damage to the brain, chemical imbalances in the body due to allergies to foods and additives, poor early nutrition, genetic factors, immaturity of the central nervous system, underdeveloped perceptual motor skills, poor teaching, lack of motivation, and inadequate structure in the educational program (Mercer, 1982). You can see that some explanations look inside the student for causes, whereas others look outside the student.

Early Diagnosis
Early diagnosis is important so that learning disabled students do not become terribly frustrated and discouraged. The students themselves do not understand why they have such trouble learning. They may develop bad learning habits trying to compensate, or they may try to avoid some subjects. To prevent these fears and bad habits from developing, students should be referred to the appropriate professionals in the school.

Perceptual Training
Controversy also exists about how best to help these students. Many programs have been developed to "train" the underlying learning processes, such as Marianne Frostig's techniques for improving visual perception (Frostig and Horne, 1964). In general, attempts to train perceptual processes directly have not been very successful in improving academic performance (Reid and Hresko, 1981). A more promising approach seems to be to

Study Skills
emphasize study skills and methods for processing information in a given subject like reading or math. Many of the principles of cognitive learning can be applied to help all students improve attention, memory, and problem-solving abilities. No set of teaching techniques will work for every learning-disabled child. You should work with the special education teachers in your school to design appropriate instruction for individual students. The Guidelines given here may also be of help.

## Mental Retardation

Before the 1970s, **mental retardation** was often defined simply as a score below a particular cutoff point on an intelligence test. Since one school district might use a cutoff of, say, 75 while another might use a cutoff of 67, a student could be labeled mentally retarded in one district but not in another. Using an IQ score alone is *never* an appropriate way to classify a student as retarded. Almost every definition of mental retardation includes the idea that mentally retarded individuals cannot adapt adequately to their environment.

AAMD Definition
**Definition and Prevalence.**   In 1973, the American Association on Mental Deficiency (AAMD) gave the following definition: "Mental retardation refers to significantly subaverage general intellectual functioning existing concurrently with deficits in adaptive behavior, and manifest during the developmental period" (Grossman, 1973, p. 11). This definition gives three important factors in identifying mental retardation:

Three Key Factors
1.    Intellectual functioning must be significantly below average. (This is usually defined as a score lower than two standard deviations below the mean on an individual intelligence test—for example, a score below 70 on the WISC-R.)

# *Guidelines*

## *Learning-Disabled Students*

**1. Allow students to use their learning strengths to master course content.**

EXAMPLES
- If a student cannot read, find other ways to present the facts and ideas.
- If a student cannot write but speaks well, let him or her use a tape recorder for some assignments.

**2. Work on the learning problem directly.**

EXAMPLES
- If the student cannot read, teach reading—don't make the student do a social studies assignment from a textbook.
- If the student has difficulties in remembering, teach memory strategies and systems for making written records.

**3. Break assignments into very small steps.**

EXAMPLES
- Identify the steps that give the student the most trouble and concentrate on them.
- Use task analysis to put material into a meaningful sequence (see Chapter 11).

**4. Make sure students are being reinforced for their successes.**

EXAMPLES
- Experiment with token reinforcement programs.
- Allow students to serve as tutors for subjects they know well.

**5. Students should be exposed to special teaching approaches effective with learning-disabled students.**

EXAMPLES
- Learn some of the teaching methods and incorporate them into your classroom. They may be useful with slow learners as well.
- Encourage the student to obtain special tutoring, if possible.

**6. Do not use the LD label as an excuse for the student not learning.**

EXAMPLES
- Keep appropriate expectations for performance, learning-disabled students are usually of average or above-average intelligence.
- Remember that learning-disabled is the most general of the exceptional student categories. It does not describe a specific condition.

2. Adaptive behavior must also be so deficient that the individuals do not meet the standards of personal independence and social responsibility expected of people their age in their own cultural group.

3. Finally, these deficiencies of intellectual functioning and adaptive behavior must have appeared before age 18. Problems occurring after that point are assumed to be due to other factors, such as brain damage or emotional disturbance.

Of the three factors, "The test of social adequacy is the most basic indicator of retarded mental development. If a person is socially and economically self-sufficient, low test scores are relatively meaningless" (Smith and Neisworth, 1975, p. 307). This caution is especially important when interpreting the scores of students from different cultures. Students who have limited verbal ability but are perfectly capable in social situations and have adequate adaptive behavior are *not* retarded.

Prevalance
Only about 1 to 2 percent of the population fits this definition of retarded in both intellectual functioning and adaptive behavior (Hallahan and Kauffman,

**Figure 13–2  Developmental Characteristics of Mentally Retarded Individuals**

| Degrees of Mental Retardation | Preschool Age 0–5: Maturation and Development | School Age 6–20: Training and Education | Adult 21 and over: Social and Vocational Adequacy |
|---|---|---|---|
| Mild | Can develop social and communication skills; minimal retardation in sensorimotor areas; often not distinguished from normal until later age. | Can learn academic skills up to approximately sixth-grade level by late teens. Can be guided toward social conformity. "Educable." | Can usually achieve social and vocational skills adequate to minimum self-support but may need guidance and assistance when under unusual social or economic stress. |
| Moderate | Can talk or learn to communicate; poor social awareness; fair motor development; profits from training in self-help; can be managed with moderate supervision. | Can profit from training in social and occupational skills; unlikely to progress beyond second-grade level in academic subjects; may learn to travel alone in familiar places. | May achieve self-maintenance in unskilled or semi-skilled work under sheltered conditions; needs supervision and guidance when under mild social and economic stress. |
| Severe | Poor motor development; speech is minimal; generally unable to profit from training in self-help; little or no communication skills. | Can talk or learn to communicate; can be trained in elemental health habits; profits from systematic habit training. | May contribute partially to self-maintenance under complete supervision; can develop self-protection skills to a minimal useful level in controlled environment. |
| Profound | Gross retardation; minimal capacity for functioning in sensorimotor areas; needs nursing care. | Some motor development present; may respond to minimal or limited training in self-help. | Some motor and speech development; may achieve very limited self-care; needs nursing care. |

*Source:* S. A. Kirk and J. J. Gallagher. **Educating exceptional children** (3rd ed.). Boston: Houghton Mifflin, 1979, p. 142. Reprinted by permission of Houghton Mifflin Co.

1982). Of this group, most—about 75 percent—are mildly retarded. Only 20 percent of all retarded individuals are moderately retarded, and only 5 percent are severely or profoundly affected. Figure 13–2 describes typical behaviors for mildly, moderately, severely, and profoundly retarded people at different ages.

**Causes.**    We know of organic (physical) causes of retardation for only about 10 to 25 percent of the individuals involved. One is **Down's syndrome**, sometimes called mongolism, a condition caused by having a small extra chromosome. Children with Down's syndrome range in intelligence from very severely retarded to almost normal.

Down's
Syndrome

Older mothers are much more likely to have children with Down's syndrome. If a woman is under 30, the chances are only 1 in 3000 that she will have such a child. But the chances for a woman between 40 and 44 are 1 in 70. There is no known cure, but the condition can be detected early in pregnancy through the process of amniocentesis, withdrawing a small amount of fluid from the uterus that can be examined for several chromosomal problems, including Down's syndrome.

Other Causes

Other known causes of mental retardation include maternal infections such as rubella during pregnancy, blood type incompatibility between the mother and the unborn baby, premature birth, and an inherited disease called phenylketonuria, or PKU (Kirk and Gallagher, 1983). At this point in our knowledge it is reasonable to assume that some biological weakness interacts with a combination of environmental factors to produce mental retardation.

**Teaching Retarded Students.**    As a regular teacher, you will have very little contact with severely or moderately retarded children, but you may encounter mildly retarded children. In the early grades these students may simply learn more slowly than their peers. By the third or fourth grade, they will probably have fallen far behind their classmates.

Mildly Retarded

Learning goals for mildly retarded students between the ages of 9 and 13 include basic reading, writing, arithmetic, learning about the local environment, social behavior, and personal interests. At the junior and senior high school level, the emphasis is on vocational and domestic skills; literacy for living (using the telephone book, reading signs, labels, and newspaper ads, completing a job application, making change); and job-related behaviors like being courteous and punctual, health care, and citizenship (Robinson and Robinson, 1976).

Effects of Being
in Regular
Classes

The impact of regular class placement for retarded students is not certain. Simply placing a retarded student in a regular class does not guarantee that he or she will be accepted (Goodman, Gottlieb and Harrison, 1972). In fact, there is evidence that retarded students are more accepted when they spend *less* time in the regular class (Kirk and Gallagher, 1983). Without extra support from teachers, retarded students can be as isolated from nonretarded peers in a regular class as they are in a special class. Many children must be taught how to make and keep friends, and retarded children often need this kind of guidance most of all. In terms of academic achievement, it appears that favorable results in regular classrooms are most likely with younger students whose handicaps are mild to moderate (Kirk and Gallagher, 1983).

The Guidelines here list suggestions for teaching students with below-average general intelligence.

# Guidelines

## Teaching Retarded Students

1. Determine readiness: however little a child may know, he or she is ready to learn the next step.
2. Objectives should be simply stated and presented in the smallest terms.
3. Specific learning objectives should be based on an analysis of the child's learning strengths and weaknesses.
4. Present material in small, logical steps. Practice extensively before going to the next step.
5. Skills and concepts should be practical — focused on the needs and demands of adult living.
6. Do not skip steps. Students with average intelligence can form conceptual bridges from one step to the next. Retarded children need every step and bridge made explicit. Make connections for the students. Do not expect them to "see" the connections.
7. You may have to present the same idea in many different ways.
8. Step back to a simpler level if you see the student is not following.
9. Be especially careful to motivate the student and maintain attention.
10. Find materials that do not insult the student. A junior-high age boy may need the low vocabulary of "See Spot Run" but will be insulted by the age of the characters and the content of the story.
11. Focus on a few target behaviors or skills so you and the student have a chance of experiencing success. Everyone needs positive reinforcement.
12. Retarded students must overlearn, repeat, and practice more than children of average intelligence. They must be taught how to study. They must review frequently and practice their newly acquired skills in many surroundings.

# MAINSTREAMING

We have been discussing the many special problems of exceptional students in detail because you may well encounter such students in your classroom, no matter what grade or subject you teach. Recent legislation has played an important role in bringing these students into the mainstream.

## Public Law 94–142

Impact of PL 94–142

On November 29, 1975, the Education for All Handicapped Children Act was signed by President Gerald R. Ford. The major purpose of the law is to ensure that all handicapped children have available to them a free public education appropriate to their needs. PL 94-142 has three major points of interest to teachers: the concept of "least restrictive placement"; the individualized education program (IEP); and the protection of the rights of handicapped students and their parents.

**Least Restrictive Placement.** The law requires the states to develop procedures for educating each child in the **least restrictive placement**. This means a setting that is as normal and as much in the mainstream of education of possible. Some handicapped students might spend most of the day in a special class and also attend one or two regular classes in physical education and art. Mainstreaming *does not* mean that students with severe physical, emotional, or cognitive problems must be placed in regular schools that cannot meet their needs. But students who can benefit from involvement with their nonhandicapped peers should be educated with them, even if doing so calls for special aids, services, training, or consultation for the regular teaching staff.

It is probably clear to you now that each student is unique and may need a different program to make progress. The drafters of PL 94-142 recognized this problem.

**The IEP (Individualized Education Program).** The **IEP** is written by a team including the student's teacher or teachers, a qualified school official, the parent(s) or guardian(s), and the student (when possible). The program must be updated each year and must state in writing:

1. The student's present level of achievement.
2. Goals for the year and short-term measurable instructional objectives leading to the year-end goals.
3. A list of specific services that will be provided to the student and when those services will be initiated.
4. A description of how fully the student will participate in the regular school program.
5. A schedule telling how the student's progress toward the objectives will be evaluated, when the program will be revised, and approximately how long the services described in the plan will be needed.

**The Rights of Students and Parents.** Several stipulations in PL 94-142 protect the rights of parents and students. Schools must have procedures maintaining the confidentiality of school records. Testing practices must not discriminate against students from different cultural backgrounds. Parents have the right to see all records relating to the testing, placement, and teaching of their child. If they wish, parents may obtain an independent evaluation of their child. At the meeting where the IEP is developed, parents may bring an advocate or representative. Students whose parents are unknown or unavailable must be assigned a surrogate parent to participate in the planning. Parents must receive written notice (in their native language) before any evaluation or change in placement is made.

Parents have the right to challenge the program developed for their child and are protected by due process legal procedures. Clearly, all these safeguards could complicate the process of planning for exceptional students. But the rights of handicapped students and their parents were not protected well enough by earlier procedures.

The future of PL 94-142 is not certain; the legislation may be changed or even repealed. Still, the economic realities of the educational system probably will require regular teachers to handle more instead of fewer handicapped students because the money for expensive specialists and programs will not be available in most schools.

## Making the Programs Work

Designs for Teaching

Lloyd Dunn (1973a) has suggested 11 designs for teaching exceptional students. The designs are presented in Figure 13-3. At the top of the inverted pyramid are the plans that integrate the student most completely into the regular school program. As you move down the pyramid, the plans remove the student more and more from the regular program.

**Figure 13–3    Designs for Teaching Exceptional Students**

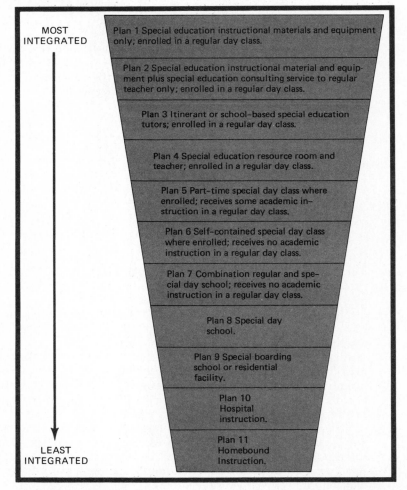

MOST INTEGRATED

Plan 1 Special education instructional materials and equipment only; enrolled in a regular day class.

Plan 2 Special education instructional material and equipment plus special education consulting service to regular teacher only; enrolled in a regular day class.

Plan 3 Itinerant or school–based special education tutors; enrolled in a regular day class.

Plan 4 Special education resource room and teacher; enrolled in a regular day class.

Plan 5 Part-time special day class where enrolled; receives some academic instruction in a regular day class.

Plan 6 Self-contained special day class where enrolled; receives no academic instruction in a regular day class.

Plan 7 Combination regular and special day school; receives no academic instruction in a regular day class.

Plan 8 Special day school.

Plan 9 Special boarding school or residential facility.

Plan 10 Hospital instruction.

Plan 11 Homebound Instruction.

LEAST INTEGRATED

*Adapted from L. M. Dunn, An overview. In L. M. Dunn (Ed.),* **Exceptional children in the schools: Special education in transition,** *2nd ed. Copyright © 1973 by Holt, Rinehart and Winston, Inc. Reprinted by permission of Holt, Rinehart and Winston, CBS College Publishing.*

*Often students with learning or behavior problems are assigned to music or art classes as part of the mainstreaming process. If you plan to teach these subjects, you should learn all you can about exceptional students.*

Ken Karp

Ideally, each student is assigned to the most integrated program he or she can handle. Then students are moved up to a more integrated program as soon as possible. For example, students with severe reading problems might first be assigned to plan 4 or 5. They would spend a large portion of the day in a resource room or special education classroom learning to read, and also attend regular classes where reading was not as important. As progress is made in reading, they would spend less time in the special class and more time in regular classes. At some point, they might stop going to the special class but meet with a reading tutor a few times a week (plan 3). Finally, they would attend only regular classes, but their teachers might be given special materials to use in teaching them, as well as consultation in how to help them continue to improve while in the regular classes (plans 1 or 2).

Mainstreaming Is not Enough

**Problems with Least Restrictive Placement.**    Although all educators favor improving educational programs for handicapped students, some have criticized the move toward mainstreaming. Teachers in regular classes have not been prepared to teach students with special learning problems. It is not clear that a student with special problems will learn more just by being placed in a class with nonhandicapped peers.

Whatever the placement, the teachers working with the students must have the materials, methods, knowledge, skills, and support from the school to create a learning environment appropriate for the needs of that student. Administrators must not use mainstreaming as a way to cut costs by moving handicapped students into less expensive regular classrooms. Regular teachers will need additional training and support services to provide high-quality educational programs for exceptional students.

There are many possibilities for providing extra help for regular teachers working with handicapped students, including resource rooms, helping teachers, and special materials or equipment.

**Resource Rooms and Helping Teachers.**   A **resource room** is a classroom with special materials and equipment and a specially trained teacher. The resource room can be used in many ways. Students may come to the resource room on a regular basis for from 30 minutes to several hours each day. During this time, they receive instruction individually or in small groups. Students are helped to overcome learning problems by developing skills they lack or by learning how to compensate for weaknesses. The rest of the day the students are in regular classes. The resource teacher works every day with several groups of students from all grades in the school.

The resource room might also be used as a crisis center. Individual students could spend an hour, a day, or a week in the resource room during a crisis period, when the regular teacher is unable to give the student the attention and guidance he or she needs. Many resource teachers are trained in crisis intervention and counseling. They can help both the regular teacher and the student recover from a difficult situation.

Besides working with students directly, a resource teacher might also work with them indirectly by giving the regular teacher ideas, materials, or actual demonstrations of teaching techniques. Ideally, all the teaching techniques that are found to be effective with a particular student in the resource room will be taught to the regular teachers so that they can take over most of the responsibility for the student's instruction. In other words, the resource teachers function as a diagnostic-prescriptive teachers, since they can test various materials and methods with the students.

**Special Materials and Equipment.**   It is sometimes possible to provide special materials and equipment so that a handicapped student will not have to leave the class for instruction. Having special large-print books and recordings will allow many partially sighted or blind students to remain in class. Some students have excellent vision but cannot read or interpret information they receive visually. These students may need tutors who will

read to them and record class material for listening at home. Students who can read but are far behind their classmates in reading level are often helped by high-interest, low-vocabulary books. These stories are written to interest older students, but the vocabulary is very simple.

For some students with coordination problems, special writing equipment is available. Large-print typewriters may be helpful to students with vision problems. Learning to type has been demonstrated in one study to help high school students who were at least two years behind in reading improve their achievement (Fuhr, 1972).

There is another group of individuals with special educational needs who are often overlooked by the schools: these are the gifted and talented.

## STUDENTS WITH SPECIAL ABILITIES: THE GIFTED

In the past, providing an enriched education for extremely bright or talented students was seen as almost undemocratic, elitist, or un-American. Why use extra resources for students who already had so much ability when handicapped students needed the resources so desperately? But there is a growing recognition that gifted students are being poorly served by most public schools. It is a tragedy whenever students are prevented from fulfilling their potential, whether they are retarded or gifted.

# Who Are the Gifted?

Types
of Giftedness

As usual, there is no agreement on what constitutes a **gifted student.** In fact, individuals can have many different types of gifts. Renzulli (1982) suggests that we distinguish between the academically gifted and "creative/productive giftedness." The first type learns lessons very easily and quickly and generally scores well on tests of intelligence. However, these indicators do not predict success in later life. The second group tends to excel in situations that require the application of information to solve problems in new and effective ways. These characteristics are more likely to be associated with success in later life.

Based on these ideas, Renzulli has developed a definition of giftedness that includes three factors. The first is above-average general ability. The second is high levels of task commitment or motivation to achieve in certain areas. Finally, he suggests that a high level of creativity is important. When these three factors come together, the individual is in a position to make valuable, significant contributions. In this text we include very bright, creative, or talented students in the gifted category.

Truly gifted children are not the students who simply learn quickly and with little effort. The work produced by gifted students is original, creative, outstanding, extremely advanced for their age, and potentially of lasting importance.

What do we know about these remarkable individuals—people former United States Commissioner of Education Sidney P. Marland, Jr., has called "our most neglected students"?

Terman's Work

A classic study investigating the characteristics of the gifted was started by Terman and associates (1925, 1947, 1959). This huge project is following the lives of 1528 gifted boys and girls and will continue until the year 2010. The subjects all have IQ scores in the top 1 percent of the population (140 on the Standard-Binet individual test of intelligence). They were identified on the basis of teacher recommendations and IQ tests, so they probably fall into Renzulli's (1982) academically gifted category.

Terman and colleagues found that these gifted children were larger, stronger, and healthier than the norm. They often walked sooner and were more athletic. However, nongifted siblings of gifted children are also larger and healthier than the general population. It appears that physical health and achievement may go along with being gifted, but being gifted does not always go along with being physically able (Laycock and Caylor, 1964).

Adjustment

Another surprising finding was that Terman's subjects were more emotionally stable than their peers and became better-adjusted adults than the average. They had lower rates of delinquency, emotional problems, divorces, drug problems, and so on. Of course, the teachers in Terman's study who made the nominations may have selected students who were better adjusted initially. It would be incorrect to say that every gifted person is superior in adjustment and emotional health. Many problems confront a gifted child. "To have the intelligence of an adult and the emotions of a child combined in a childish body is to encounter certain difficulties" (Hollingworth, 1942, p. 282). Some of these difficulties are boredom; frustration in moving slowly in classes; concern with right, wrong, evil, meaning, and other abstract issues when most peers are concerned with baseball or passing math class; and isolation from peers who share these concerns.

From the descriptions thus far it may seem to you that identifying a gifted child would be simple. This is not always the case. Many parents provide early educational experiences for their children. A preschool or primary student coming to your class may read above grade level, play an instrument quite well, or whiz through every assignment. How do you separate the gifted from hard-working or parentally pressured students?

## Recognizing Gifted Students

Since there are many talents and abilities, there are many ways to recognize gifted students.

**Individual Intelligence Tests.**  To identify academically gifted students, the best single predictor is still the individual IQ test. Many schools have a cutoff of the top 3 percent for the child's ethnic or cultural group (an IQ of about 130 for white, native-born Americans). An individual intelligence test is costly, time-consuming, and far from perfect. Many eminent individuals, including Copernicus, Rembrandt, Bach, Lincoln, LaVoisier, and Locke, would not have made this cutoff (Cox, 1926).

**Teacher Observation.**  Teachers are successful about 10 to 50 percent of the time in picking out the gifted children in their classes (Fox, 1981). Seven questions emerged from a study by Walton (1961) as the best to ask teachers in identifying gifted children: (1) Who learns easily and rapidly? (2) Who uses a lot of common sense and practical knowledge? (3) Who retains easily what he has heard? (4) Who knows about many things of which other children are unaware? (5) Who uses a large number of words easily and accurately? (6) Who recognizes relations, comprehends meanings? (7) Who is alert, keenly observant, responds quickly?

**Other Sources of Information.**  Group achievement and intelligence tests tend to underestimate the IQs of very bright children. Still, these tests are often administered routinely and may give some useful information, if the results are interpreted with caution. When schools rely on a cutoff of 130 on a group test like the Otis Quick-Scoring Mental Ability Test, they are likely to miss 50 to 75 percent of the students who would score 130 or above on the individual tests of IQ. A cutoff score of 115 will identify around 90 percent of these students (Fox, 1981).

Group tests might be appropriate for screening, but not for making placement decisions. Several studies at the University of Connecticut have found that students scoring in the top 20 percent but below the top 5 percent on traditional measures of academic ability performed just as well in a special program for the gifted as students in the same program who scored in the top 5 percent (Reis, 1981).

**Artistic Talent**  Especially for recognizing artistic talent, experts in the field can be called in to judge the merits of a child's creation. Science projects, exhibitions, performances, auditions, and interviews are all possibilities. Creativity tests may provide additional information. Not all children with very high IQs also score high on creativity tests, and vice versa. However, scores on creativity and IQ tests are positively related, and tests of creativity may identify some children not picked up by other measures, particularly minority students who may be at a disadvantage on the other types of tests.

Assuming you have identified students who need special educational programs, what should those programs be?

## Teaching the Gifted

There are at least two issues in making educational plans for gifted students. One is the question of how should students be grouped and paced. The other is determining what teaching methods are effective.

Resistance
to Acceleration

**Grouping and Pacing.** There continues to be popular resistance to plans that allow gifted students to begin school early or to accelerate. Most careful studies indicate that truly gifted students who begin primary, elementary, junior high, high school, college, or even graduate school early do as well as and usually better than nongifted students who are progressing at the normal pace. Social and emotional adjustment do not appear to be affected negatively. Gifted students tend to prefer the company of older playmates and may be miserably bored if kept with children of their own age. Skipping grades may not be the best solution for a particular gifted student, but it does not deserve the bad name it has received (Daurio, 1979).

Flexibility

Increasingly, more flexible programs are being instituted for gifted students. Before- or after-school programs, summer institutes, courses at nearby colleges; classes with local artists, musicians, or dancers; independent research projects; selected classes in high school for younger students; honor classes; or special interest clubs are all possible arrangements for giving gifted students appropriate learning experiences. There is some evidence that grouping gifted students together, at least for part of the school day, is beneficial to them (Martinson, 1961). But simply grouping students together will not automatically lead to excellence. The teaching methods, materials, and curricula must be appropriate.

*"Classrooms" for gifted students can be in museums, libraries, or anywhere else that allows independent, high-level learning.*

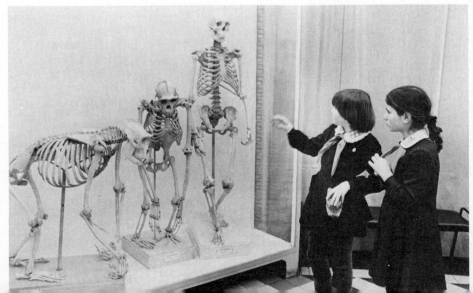

Neil Goldstein

# *Guidelines*

## *Teaching Gifted Students*

**1. Allow time for independent work, quiet, privacy, and solitude.**

EXAMPLES
- Allow students to pursue independent projects in the library.
- Some class time can be devoted to independent work.

**2. Use computers and advanced learning materials to allow students to master material independently.**

EXAMPLES
- Have a variety of advanced texts available to take home.
- If computers are available, encourage students to design teaching programs for computer-assisted instruction.

**3. Use delayed, intrinsic, and social reinforcement rather than immediate and concrete rewards.**

EXAMPLES
- Avoid emphasis on grades.
- Have students share creations with the class.
- Have students analyze and criticize their own work.

**4. Involve students in planning their own curriculum.**

EXAMPLES
- Help students set their own learning goals.
- Have problem-solving sessions to identify assignments.

**5. Focus on problem solving, divergent thinking, and long-term projects rather than frequent tests on factual information.**

EXAMPLES
- Avoid frequent testing and grading.
- Focus on a few large projects instead of many small assignments.

**Teaching Strategies.**   Teaching methods for gifted students should encourage abstract thinking, the development of formal operational thought, creativity, and independence, not simply learning greater quantities of facts. A number of these ideas are included in the Guidelines we have given here. In working with gifted and talented students, teachers must be imaginative, flexible, and unthreatened by the capabilities of their students.

Another group of students with special problems and special abilities often have not received an appropriate education in America's schools—those students whose culture and language differs from that of the majority.

## MULTICULTURAL AND BILINGUAL EDUCATION

Alternatives to the Melting Pot     Since the beginning of the twentieth century, American institutions have tended to promote a blending of the diverse subcultures of the nation into a single unit. As new immigrants arrived they were expected to be assimilated—that is, to enter the melting pot and become like those who had arrived earlier. The concept of **multicultural education** rejects both assimilation and the existence of separate cultures. According to this concept, American society should undergo a gradual transformation to a society that values diversity, or **cultural pluralism.**

## Making Multicultural Education Work

How can an educational program be designed to meet the needs of members of various ethnic minority groups? The student must feel secure in order to learn. A comfortable and nonthreatening learning environment can be created by accepting the student's individuality and beginning with routines that are not in conflict with the student's culture. Where English is not the student's first language, some specific issues arise. In schools where there are large minority-language (say, Spanish-speaking) populations, the classroom can be made more like home by using the child's home language for instruction in the early years.

Self-Esteem

An attitude of self-esteem and pride is an important accomplishment of the school years. Sometimes the self-image and occupational aspirations of minority children have actually declined in the early years in public school (Diggs, 1974). By presenting the accomplishments of particular members of that ethnic group or by bringing the patterns of culture into the classroom (foods, dress, music), teachers can help students maintain a sense of pride in their cultural group. Students from other cultures will also benefit from learning more about the diversity of American society.

Tiedt and Tiedt (1979) provide a book full of suggestions for multicultural teaching. Here are just a few:

Methods

Ask students to draw a picture of themselves or bring in a photograph. On a page with this picture, have each student list all their different group memberships. Display the pages around the room or bind them into a book (see Figure 13–4).

**Figure 13–4    A Student's Picture of Herself, with a List of Her Membership
in Different Groups**

Sue Wong is . . .

a girl
a daughter
a member of the Wong family
a Californian
a San Franciscan
a member of this class
a twelve-year-old
a Chinese-American
a U.S. citizen

From P. L. Tiedt and I. M. Tiedt. **Multicultural education: A handbook
of activities, information and resources.** © 1979 by Allyn and Bacon, p. 144. Reprinted by permission.

Study one cultural group in depth, such as Native Americans, Puerto Ricans, Chicanos, Afro-Americans, or Vietnamese Americans.

Create a learning center based on a paticular culture. Use maps, postcards, books, encyclopedias, recordings of the native language, pictures, posters, flags. Have students draw maps. Calculate distances, convert money, illustrate stories about holidays, or write for more information to the appropriate public or private agencies within the particular country.

Introduce lessons based on a multicultural calendar. Tiedt and Tiedt provide a calendar for each school month.

### Bilingual Education

All citizens should learn the official language of their country. But when and how should instruction in English begin? Is it better to teach the child to read first in the native language, or to begin reading instruction in English? Do children need some oral lessons in English before reading instruction can be effective? Should other subjects such as mathematics and social studies be taught in the primary (home) language until the child is fluent in English?

*One outcome of multicultural education should be an increased appreciation of the contributions of many cultures to our daily experiences.*

Irene Springer

| Methods | Two approaches to bilingual education suggest diverging answers to these questions (Engle, 1975). The **native language approach** is based on the idea that while it is essential that the child learn the majority language, students have a right to keep their own native language. Teachers should work with the language the children exhibit, gradually building knowledge of the majority language as appropriate. The **direct method** emphasizes development of the majority language as the primary goal and does not try to use the child's native language as a medium of instruction. Research evidence can be shown to support either approach, but final answers are not yet possible. |
|---|---|

Research on Bilingual Education

Engle (1975) has made some generalizations about research findings in the area of bilingual education. Oral training in the second language is important in the early grades and should precede direct instruction in reading. In other words, students should be taught to speak the second language before they learn to read in it. Often programs in bilingual education will not show student gains for several years. No matter what program of instruction is used, bilingual students will initially make slower progress than their single-language counterparts. They pay a price for the later potential gain of fluency in two languages. However, over the years, bilingual progress does not need to retard development of the primary language.

## SUMMARY

1. Education for exceptional students has changed greatly. In the past, the focus of testing was on diagnosis and labeling, then separate placement.

2. One important recent change is the development of diagnostic-prescriptive teaching: students are tested, their learning strengths and weaknesses are identified, and then effective teaching methods and materials are found for each individual.

3. The key to helping students with special learning abilities and difficulties is to focus on the behavior of the student, especially learning strengths and weaknesses.

4. Recent legislation has required an appropriate education for *all* handicapped students.

5. Part of this education is participation with nonhandicapped students whenever possible (mainstreaming) and an individual education plan (IEP) for each student.

6. Regular classroom teachers will need support and training. Resource rooms and helping teacher teams are two possible sources of support and consultation.

7. Students with special abilities, talents, and creativity often receive an inappropriate education in the public schools.

8. A wide range of approaches can be used to identify potentially productive students, such as auditions, science fairs, contests, individual intelligence tests, and parent nominations.

9. Many programs are appropriate for these students, including acceleration, special summer schools, Saturday clubs, individual projects, honors classes, and early college.

10. Today we are turning away from the melting pot or assimilation idea and turning toward valuing a broad diversity of cultural patterns.

11. This pluralist approach can work in the multicultural classroom through creating a nonthreatening environment and bringing examples of the culture into the classroom to encourage pride.

12. There are two approaches to teaching bilingual students, the native language and the direct method.

**KEY TERMS**

| | |
|---|---|
| diagnostic-prescriptive teaching | juvenile delinquency |
| orthopedic devices | hyperactive |
| epilepsy | specific learning disability |
| cerebral palsy | mental retardation |
| spasticity | Down's syndrome |
| speech reading | least restrictive placement |
| sign language | individualized educational program (IEP) |
| finger spelling | resource room |
| low vision | gifted students |
| educationally blind | muticultural education |
| speech impairment | cultural pluralism |
| articulation disorder | native language approach |
| voicing problems | direct method |
| stuttering | |

## SUGGESTIONS FOR FURTHER READING AND STUDY

CHARLES, C. M. and MALIAN, I. M. *The special student: Practical help for the classroom teacher.* St. Louis: C. V. Mosby, 1980. This is an excellent overview of the legal requirements and teaching methods for working with exceptional students in the regular classroom.

THE COUNCIL FOR EXCEPTIONAL CHILDREN (1920 Association Drive, Reston, Va 22091) publishes several journals for teachers including: *Journal for the Education of the Gifted, Teaching Exceptional Children, Exceptional Children* (this journal reports results of research).

GLOVER, J. and GARY, A. *Mainstreaming exceptional children: How to make it work.* Pacific Grove, Calif.: Boxwood Press, 1976. A short book with many ideas about assessment, placement, individualized instruction, and evaluation for mainstreamed students.

HALLAHAN, D. P. and KAUFFMAN, J. M. *Exceptional children: Introduction to special education* (2nd ed.). Englewood Cliffs, NJ: Prentice-Hall, 1982. One of the best introductions to the field, this book has chapters about mental retardation, learning disabilities, speech and language disorders, hearing and visual impairment, physical handicaps, giftedness, and current trends in special education.

HARING, N. (Ed.). *Exceptional children and youth.* Columbus, Ohio: Charles E. Merrill, 1982. A good basic text with chapters contributed by experts in the field.

KIRK, S. A. and GALLAGHER, J. J. *Educating exceptional children,* (4th ed.). Boston: Houghton Mifflin, 1983. A classic in the field of special education, organized like the Hallahan and Kauffman text, by categories of exceptionality.

O'LEARY, K. D. Pills or skills for hyperactive children? *Journal of Applied Behavior Analysis,* 1980, *13,* 191–204. A very thorough review of the research on different methods for helping hyperactive children.

REID, D. K. and HRESKO, W. P. *A cognitive approach to learning disabilities.* New York: McGraw-Hill, 1981. The new cognitive orientation to learning brings insights to the problems of learning disabled students.

*Teaching Gifted Children* and *Learning Disabilities Guide,* each published nine times a year by Croft-NEI, 24 Rope Ferry Road, Waterford, CT, 06386.

WOODWARD, D. M. *Mainstreaming the learning disabled adolescent: A manual of strategies and materials.* Rockville, MD: Aspen Systems Corp., 1981. It is difficult to find a book on this topic. Woodward's text is a very practical resource for teachers.

WOOLFOLK, A. E. The schools and individual excellence. *Journal for the Education of the Gifted,* 1982, *7,* No. 1, 39–49. This article describes several factors in schooling that contribute to the psychological development of highly productive and talented individuals.

# Teachers' Forum

## Class Acceptance of the Handicapped

You have in your class this year two mainstreamed students: a girl with cerebral palsy and a boy with a severe speech impairment. Although both are above average intellectually, their handicaps cause them to seem "dumb." The other students in the class avoid these two and are beginning to call them names, such as "weirdo" and "retard." How can you help these mainstreamed students to become accepted members of the class?

**Prepare the Class**

Accepting handicapped children is considerably easier if the teacher accepts them and is not uncomfortable about the impairment. . . . The class has to be prepared to receive and accept children who are different. There are many books dealing with stories of handicapped children, which if read and discussed can help these children who are more fortunate gain an understanding of others. . . . Another useful technique is role-playing. A teacher I know had her class spend an entire day using just one hand. After this experience, most were able to understand and gain some identification with a handicapped child who has just one good hand.

Charlotte Ross, Second-Grade Teacher
*Covert Avenue School, Elmont, New York*

**Satisfy Normal Curiosity**

My experience has been that the children in the classroom are curious about the nature of the problems of the mainstreamed students. If this curiosity is not satisfied through acceptable explanations, ignorance and fear can lead to inappropriate behavior such as name calling. While the mainstreamed children are out of the classroom, have an honest discussion with the other students. Answer their questions about the nature of each mainstreamed child's problems, such as how it happened, if it's contagious, and how it feels. With knowledge comes understanding, and the other students [will] always treat the mainstreamed children remarkably well.

Arleen Wyatt, Third-Grade Teacher
*Happy Valley Elementary School Rossville, Georgia*

**Plan for Involvement**

. . . [S]ome prior "in-service" should be held for the regular students to acquaint them with the handicapping conditions of their mainstreamed peers. In addition, every opportunity should be provided for the mainstreamed students to achieve visible successes within the regular class. Class discussions using appropriate kit material of individual differences without pointing out specific students is a useful technique, as are (1) teacher modeling, (2) cooperative group activity where all students are given tasks within their capabilities, (3) peer tutoring groups, and (4) materials that help the mainstreamed students display the strengths of their particular learning style.

Jacqueline G. Dyer, Second- to Eighth-Grade Teacher
*Classical Junior Academy, St. Louis, Missouri*

## The Case of the Mislabeled Student

For most of the day you have a student in your class who has been tested and designated as ED (emotionally disturbed). However, you have noticed that his behavior seems to be no worse than that of a few other students and definitely within the class norm. Also, you notice that his Individualized Educational Program (IEP) is written only for academic areas, with no attention to his problem behaviors. What would you do in a case like this?

**Reevaluate and Reconsider**

After researching the school records to make sure there was no available information on any behaviors that led to the student being labeled as ED, I'd do a week's observation of classroom behavior, recording all behaviors — positive and negative — at ten-minute intervals. I'd then present my concerns regarding the inappropriate identification and the incomplete IEP to the building-level special services committee, and refer the student for a reevaluation. I'd suggest having the school psychologist observe the student to confirm the findings, and conduct any testing deemed appropriate by the committee. After confirmation that the ED label is not appropriate, I'd have a teacher-student-parent conference to inform the parents of the change and develop an appropriate plan for academic goals, counseling, and a follow-up reevaluation. Regardless of the outcome, if the student is not behaving in an identifiably ED manner, in the classroom he should be treated as if there were no label.

Richard D. Courtright, Gifted and Talented Teacher
*Ephesus Road Elementary School, Chapel Hill, North Carolina*

## Ethnic Slurs

One of the students in your class, a member of an ethnic minority, gets into a heated discussion with a member of another ethnic minority. The subject has nothing to do with ethnic background, and you are rather pleased that the discussion seems to be arousing so much enthusiasm. Suddenly, however, one of the students makes a particularly vicious reference to the other student's ethnic membership. The entire class sits hushed, waiting for your decision.

**Directing Group Discussions**

I would remind the class that such remarks have little meaning in an otherwise valuable discussion, that such remarks not only weaken or destroy a discussion, but that they can be made of any ethnic group. I would immediately direct the discussion back to what they had previously enjoyed, pointing out some of the excellent, perhaps thought-provoking, statements they had made. I would compliment them on their good ideas. In the future I might take a more active role in their discussions, not to lead or guide, but to assist in direction. This "name-calling" often takes place when the discussion has lost its zest and is winding down. This is a good time for the teacher to redirect the discussion or to introduce a new topic.

Shirley Wilson Roby, Sixth-Grade Reading Teacher
*Lakeland Schools, Shrub Oak, New York*

## Mainstreaming Problems

What have been some of the problems you have encountered in teaching exceptional students in the regular classroom? How did you go about solving the problems?

The art curriculum is an excellent vehicle for handling the exceptional child. The clear intention is to stimulate individual and personal responses to a given task. In an environment that stresses different and creative solutions, all children are encouraged to find their own answers, regardless of their developmental level. Indeed, many exceptional students whose academic disabilities are severe sometimes have great creative ability.

I think now of one particular student whose ability in every area is very limited. He cannot understand much about the aesthetic concepts taught, but the art room has been a happy experience for him. He seems to take pleasure in whatever he does there. In an atmosphere of praise and encouragement, his peers give him helpful hints and we all salute his efforts.

Harriet Chipley, Elementary Art Teacher
*Lookout Mountain Elementary, Lookout MT., Tennessee*

## Skipping Two Grades?

Imagine that you have an especially bright student in your class, who is way beyond the others in ability to think about concepts. She also seems much more mature than the other students and she doesn't seem to have many friends in the class. Her parents would like to have her advanced two grade levels. The school administration has asked you to express your opinion about such a move. What would you advise? What reasons would you give both to the administration and to the student's parents?

I would advise advancing the student two grade levels. Since she seems more mature than the other students and it appears that she has few friends in her class, my challenging her academically would have little bearing on her socialization, which I deem important in her overall development. I would advance that rationale to the administration and her parents using appropriate statistics on the talented and gifted.

Margie C. Gallagher, Sixth-Grade Teacher
*Perrysburg Middle School, Perrysburg, Ohio*

Although she seems mature in her present grade level, moving her up two grades might eventually erode that maturity. It seems to be too much of a "jump" for any youngster. The academic work may be a challenge, but socially she may not be ready for students two years older. I would suggest she be advanced one grade level. This could be done with the provision that she receive enrichment activities as well as the classroom lessons. The teacher should try to encourage her to participate and make friends with the children in class. Evaluation of her social and academic progress should be made at periodic intervals, and parents, teachers, and child could discuss their perceptions, feelings, and progress to date.

Marilyn Dozoretz, Sixth-Grade and Prekindergarten Teacher
*Build Academy Public School, Buffalo, New York*

# 14

# Measuring Achievement and Aptitude

Would it surprise you to learn that published tests such as the college entrance exams and IQ tests are creations of the twentieth century? In the nineteenth and early twentieth centuries, college entrance was generally based on grades, essays, and interviews. Adults were chosen for jobs mainly by interview and intuition. From your own experience, you know that testing has come a long way since then.

What would you like to know about testing? How should you prepare yourself or your students for tests? How should you make up tests? How should you interpret test scores? In this chapter, we look mainly at the last question, leaving the others for Chapter 15. We do this because the best way to ensure that the tests you give are appropriate is to begin with an understanding of how test scores are determined and what they really mean.

First we consider testing in general, including the various methods of interpreting test scores. Then we look at the different kinds of standardized tests used in schools. By the time you have completed this chapter, you should be able to do the following:

- Calculate mean, median, mode, and standard deviation.
- Discuss the relationships among percentile ranks, standard deviations, $z$ scores, $T$ scores, and stanine scores.
- Explain how to improve reliability and validity in testing.
- Interpret the results of achievement, aptitude, and diagnostic tests in a realistic manner.
- Take a position on the truth-in-testing issue and defend your position.
- Describe how to prepare students (and yourself) to take standardized tests.

We begin with a look at the meaning of two terms that are essential in any discussion of testing: measurement and evaluation.

## MEASUREMENT AND EVALUATION

Evaluation    All teaching involves **evaluation.** At the heart of evaluation is judgment— making decisions based on values. In the process of evaluation, we compare information to criteria and then make judgments. Teachers must make literally hundreds of decisions that involve judgments. "Should we use a different text this year?" "Is the film appropriate for my students?" "Will Sarah do better if she repeats the first grade?" "Should Terry get a B− or a C+ on the project?"

Measurement    **Measurement** is the process of applying a set of rules to describe events or characteristics with numbers. Measurement tells how much, how often, or how well by providing scores, ranks, or ratings. Measurement makes it possible for a teacher to turn observations into numbers. Instead of saying "Sarah doesn't seem to understand addition," a teacher might say "Sarah answered only 2 of the 15 problems correctly on her addition worksheet."

Measurement also allows a teacher to compare one student's performance on one particular task with a standard or with the performances of the other students.

Not all the evaluative decisions made by teachers involve measurement. Some decisions are based on information that is difficult to measure accurately: student preferences, information from parents, previous experiences, even intuition. But measurement does play a large role in many classroom decisions, and properly done, it can be a source of unbiased data for making evaluations. The decisions based on measurement are not always valid. Skillful measurement requires an understanding of many concepts. Let us start with testing, a common form of measurement in the classroom.

# UNDERSTANDING TESTING

The answers students give on any type of test have no meaning by themselves; we must make some kind of comparison to interpret test results. Two basic types of comparison are possible. A test score can be compared to the scores obtained by other people who have taken the same test. You may have taken a college entrance exam. The score you received on that test told you (and the admissions offices of colleges) how your performance compared to performances of many other people who had previously taken the same test or one very like it. The second type of comparison is to a fixed standard. Most tests required for a driver's license are based on this kind of comparison. If you have a driver's license, the decision to issue your license probably was made by comparing your score with a fixed score that the motor vehicle agency felt indicated sufficient knowledge about driving.

Two Kinds
of Comparisons

The two kinds of comparisons made in testing thus involve comparisons with other people (norm-referenced testing) and comparisons with fixed standards (criterion-referenced testing).

## Norm-Referenced Tests

Raw Score

In **norm-referenced** testing, the other people who have taken the test provide the norms for determining the meaning of a given individual's score. You can think of a norm as being the typical level of performance for a particular group. By comparing the individual's raw score (the actual number correct) to the norms, we can determine if the score is above, below, or around the average for that group.

Norm Groups

There are at least three types of norm groups (comparison groups) in education. One frequently used norm group is the class or school itself. When a teacher compares the score of one student in a tenth-grade American history class with the scores of all the other students in the class, the class itself is the norm group. If the teacher happens to have three American history classes, all of about the same ability, then the norm group for evaluating individual performance might be all three classes.

Districtwide

Norm groups may also be drawn from wider areas. Sometimes, for example, school districts develop achievement tests to see how well the students in the district are doing. When students take this test, their scores may be compared to the scores of all the other students at their grade level throughout the district. A student whose score on the achievement test was in the top 25 percent at a particularly good school might be in the top 15 percent for the entire district. Some tests have national norm groups. When students take a test such as the college entrance exam, their scores are compared with the scores of other students all over the country.

Norm-referenced tests are constructed with certain objectives in mind, but the test items themselves tend to be samples of many different abilities rather than clusters of items assessing a limited number of specific objectives. One assumption with norm-referenced testing is that "each item provides a separate and independent indication of some aspect of achievement in the domain of learning encompassed by the test" (Ebel, 1978, p. 3). A student's score on a norm-referenced test tends to reflect the student's general level of functioning in a domain of knowledge or subject area, rather than mastery of specific skills and information.

Norm-referenced tests are especially useful in measuring overall achievement when students have come to understand complex material by different routes. They also provide a reasonable approach when all the students in a group being tested have mastered the basics, but some have gone on to higher levels of sophistication and competence. Norm-referenced tests give a way to measure this wide range of achievement. Finally, norm-referenced tests are appropriate when only the top few candidates can be admitted to a program.

Hopkins and Antes (1979) list several limitations of norm-referenced measurements. Results of a norm-referenced test do not tell you if students have mastered the prerequisite knowledge and skills for moving on to more advanced material. Knowing that a student is in the top 3 percent of the class on a test of algebraic concepts will not tell you if he or she is ready to move on to trigonometry. *Everyone* in the class might have failed to reach the criterion indicating sufficient mastery of algebraic concepts.

Norm-referenced tests are also less appropriate than criterion-referenced tests for measuring affective and psychomotor objectives. To measure psychomotor learning, a clear description of standards is necessary to judge individuals. Even the best gymnast in any school performs certain exercises better than others and needs specific guidance about how to improve. In the affective area, attitudes and values are personal; comparisons among individuals are not really appropriate. For example, what is an "average"

*These students, and others like them all over the country, are taking the College Board examination. This is one example of a norm-referenced test. Each person's score will be compared to the scores of others who have taken the test.*

performance on a measure of political values or opinions? Finally, norm-referenced tests tend to encourage competition and comparison of scores. Some students compete to be the best. Others, who see that being the best seems impossible, may compete to be the worst! Either goal has its casualties.

## Criterion-Referenced Tests

When test scores are compared to a given criterion or standard of performance, the term **criterion-referenced** is applied to describe the test. In deciding who should be allowed to drive a car, it is important to determine just what standard of performance is appropriate for selecting safe drivers. It does not matter how your test results compare to the results of others. If your performance on the test was in the top 10 percent but you consistently ran through red lights, you would not be a good candidate for receiving a license even though your score was high.

Importance of
Objectives

Criterion-referenced tests measure the mastery of very specific objectives. The results of a criterion-referenced test should tell the teacher exactly what the students can do and what they cannot do, at least under certain conditions. Norm-referenced tests are based on objectives as well, and the individual items on the two types of tests could be very similar. But criterion-referenced tests should assess several specific objectives thoroughly, to get a good idea of the student's particular skills. Norm-referenced tests are more likely to sample many abilities. However, the major difference between the two types of tests is in the comparison that gives meaning to the raw scores. With norm-referenced tests, the comparison is to the performance of others. With criterion-referenced tests, the comparison is to a preset standard.

Setting
Standards

Criterion-referenced measurement is especially appropriate for lower-level knowledge and comprehension objectives when students must be able to do something that can be fairly directly measured (Hopkins and Stanley, 1981). For example, a criterion-referenced test would be useful in measuring the ability to add three-digit numbers. A test could be designed with 20 different problems. The standard for mastery could be set at 17 out of 20 correct. (The standard is often somewhat arbitrary, but may be based on such things as the teacher's experience with other classes, the difficulty of the problems, or professional judgment.) If two students make scores of 7 and 11 it does not matter that one student did better than the other, since neither met the standard of 17. Both need more help. In describing either student to parents, the teacher might say that the student has not yet fully mastered addition of three-digit numbers.

Advantages
of Criterion-
Referenced
Tests

There are many instances when comparison to a preset standard is more important than comparison to the performance of others. The teaching of basic skills provides many examples. It is not very comforting to know, as a parent, that your child is better than most of the students in class in reading if all the students are unable to read material suited for their grade level. Sometimes standards for meeting the criterion must be set at 100 percent correct. You probably would not like to have your appendix removed by a surgeon who left instruments inside the body only 10 percent of the time.

Limitations

Criterion-referenced tests are not appropriate for every situation. To develop a criterion-referenced test, we must be able to establish specific objectives for the subject to be taught and tested. Not every subject can be broken down into a set of specific objectives that exhausts all possible learning outcomes. And as we noted in Chapter 11, often the true objective is understanding, appreciating, or analyzing. Moreover, standards are important in criterion-referenced testing, yet they often tend to be arbitrary. When deciding if a student has mastered the addition of three-digit numbers comes down to the difference between 16 or 17 problems being right, it seems hard to justify one particular standard over another. Finally, at times it is valuable to know how the students in your class compare to other students at their grade level both locally and nationally. Remember, too, that admission to college is based in part on a test given to students all over the country. You will want your students who plan to go to college to have the good chance on such a test.

### Comparing the Two

Figure 14–1 offers a comparison of norm-referenced and criterion-referenced tests. It may be of some help when you decide what kinds of tests to give your own students. There is much more, however, to be considered before you make final decisions.

**Figure 14–1    Deciding on the Type of Test to Use**

---

Norm-referenced tests may work best when you are
- Measuring general ability in certain areas such as English, algebra, general science, or American history
- Assessing the range of abilities in a large group
- Selecting top candidates when only a few openings are available

Criterion-referenced tests may work best when you are
- Measuring mastery of basic skills
- Determining if students have prerequisites to start a new unit
- Assessing affective and psychomotor objectives
- Grouping students for instruction

---

## TEST SCORES: WHAT DO THEY MEAN?

On the average, more than 1 million standardized tests are given each school day in classes throughout this country (Lyman, 1978). Most of these are norm-referenced standardized tests. For this reason, we will explore test scores for standardized norm-referenced tests in detail. When we refer to standardized tests in the remainder of this chapter, we mean norm-referenced tests, unless otherwise noted.

### Basic Concepts

Standardized
Tests

**Standardized tests** are the official-looking pamphlets and piles of forms purchased by school systems and administered to students. More specifically, a standardized test is "a task or set of tasks given under standard conditions and designed to assess some aspect of a person's knowledge, skill, or personality. . . . A test yields one or more objectively obtained quantitative scores, so that, as nearly as possible, each person is assessed in the same way" (Green, 1981, p. 1001). The tests are meant to be given under carefully controlled conditions, so that students all over the country undergo the same experience when they take the tests. Standard methods of developing items, administering the test, scoring it, and reporting the scores are all implied in the term, standardized test.

The test has also been through a standardization process that involves trying out all the items and the instructions to make sure they work, and then rewriting and retesting when necessary. The final version of the test is administered to a **norming sample,** a large sample of subjects as similar as possible to the students who will be taking the test in school systems throughout the country. This norming sample serves as a comparison group for all students who later take the test.

The test publishers provide one or more ways of interpreting each student's raw score (number correct) by comparisons with the norming sample. Many of the comparisons are based on measurements of the central tendency and standard deviation of a frequency distribution. We will examine these terms before we describe methods for comparing scores with norming samples.

**Frequency Distributions.** A **frequency distribution** is simply a listing of the number of people who obtain each score on a test or other measuring device. Figure 14–2 shows a frequency distribution of the scores of 19 students on a

**Figure 14–2** **A Frequency Distribution for Scores of 19 Students on a Test of Spelling**

| Raw Scores on Spelling Test | | Frequency Distribution of Raw Scores | |
|---|---|---|---|
| Student | Score | Score | Number of Students Receiving the Score |
| 1. Peter | 55 | 40 | 1 |
| 2. Elizabeth | 100 | 45 | 1 |
| 3. Carol | 85 | 50 | 2 |
| 4. Robert | 95 | 55 | 1 |
| 5. Lorraine | 40 | 60 | 2 |
| 6. Ed | 85 | 65 | 1 |
| 7. Marion | 75 | 70 | 1 |
| 8. Ray | 60 | 75 | 3 |
| 9. Mary | 50 | 80 | 1 |
| 10. Ellen | 85 | 85 | 3 |
| 11. Charles | 75 | 90 | 1 |
| 12. Tanya | 80 | 95 | 1 |
| 13. Alec | 60 | 100 | 1 |
| 14. Treena | 50 | | 19 |
| 15. Denise | 65 | | |
| 16. Jonas | 75 | | |
| 17. Rachel | 70 | | |
| 18. Anna | 45 | | |
| 19. Ramon | 90 | | |
| | 1340 | | |

**Figure 14–3    Histogram of a Frequency Distribution**

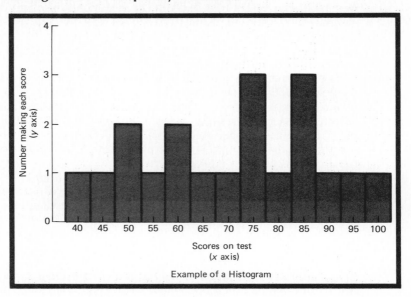

Example of a Histogram

spelling test. The information is often expressed as a simple graph where one axis (the *x* or horizontal axis) indicates the possible scores and the other axis (the *y* or vertical axis) indicates the number of subjects who attained each score. A graph, in this case a **histogram,** or bar graph, of the spelling test scores is represented in Figure 14–3.

**Mean, Median, Mode**

**Measurements of Central Tendency and Standard Deviation.**    You have probably had a great deal of experience with means. A **mean** is simply the arithmetic average of a group of scores. To calculate the mean, you add the scores and divide the total by the number of scores in the distribution. For example, the total of the scores in Figure 14–2 is 1340, so the mean is 1340/19, or 70.53. The mean offers one way of measuring **central tendency,** of finding a score that is typical or representative of the whole distribution.

Two other measures of central tendency are the median and the mode. The **median** is the middle score in the distribution, the point where half the scores are larger and half are smaller. In Figure 14–2 the median of the 19 scores is 70. Nine scores in the distribution are greater than 70, and nine are less. The **mode** is the score that occurs most often. The distribution in Figure 14–2 actually has two modes, 75 and 85, which makes it a **bimodal distribution.**

While the measure of central tendency gives a score that is representative of the group of scores, it does not tell you anything about how the scores are distributed. Two groups of scores may both have a mean of 50 but be very different. One group might contain the scores 50, 45, 55, 55, 45, 50, 50; the other group might contain the scores 100, 0, 50, 90, 10, 50, 50. In both cases the mean, median, and mode are all 50, but the distributions are quite different.

**Standard Deviation**

The **standard deviation** is an index of how much scores spread out around the mean. The larger the standard deviation, the more spread out the scores in the distribution. The smaller the standard deviation, the more the scores tend to "crowd together" around the mean. For example, in the distribution 50, 45, 50, 55, 55, 45, 50, the standard deviation will be much smaller than in the distribution 100, 0, 50, 90, 10, 50, 50. Another way of saying this is that distributions with very small standard deviations have less **variability** in the scores.

The standard deviation is relatively easy to calculate if you remember your high school math. It does take time, however. The process is similar to taking an average, but square roots are used, generally along with a square root table. To calculate the standard deviation, you follow these steps:

Steps
to Calculate
the Standard
Deviation

1. Calculate the mean (written as $\bar{X}$) of the scores.
2. Subtract the mean from each of the scores. This is written as $(X - \bar{X})$.
3. Square each difference (multiply each difference by itself). This is written $(X - \bar{X})^2$.
4. Add all the squared differences. This is written $\Sigma (X - \bar{X})^2$.
5. Divide this total by the number of scores. This is written

$$\frac{\Sigma(X - \bar{X})^2}{N}$$

6. Find the square root. This is written

$$\sqrt{\frac{\Sigma(X - \bar{X})^2}{N}}$$

which is the formula for calculating the standard deviation.

Figure 14–4 shows how to apply the steps to calculate the standard deviation of a set of test scores. The *Student Guide* that accompanies this text provides a more complete explanation of the standard deviation and a short-cut method for estimating it with classroom test data.

Using the SD
to Interpret
Results

Knowing the mean and the standard deviation of a group of scores gives you a better picture of the meaning of an individual score. For example, suppose you received a score of 78 on a test. You would be very pleased with the score if the mean of the test were 70 and the standard deviation were 4. In this case, your score would be 2 standard deviations above the mean, a score well above average, as you can see in Figure 14–5.

Consider the difference if the mean of the test had remained at 70 but the standard deviation had been 20. In the second case, your score of 78 would be less than 1 standard deviation from the mean. You would be much closer to the middle of the group, with an above-average but not a high score. Knowing the standard deviation tells you much more than simply knowing the range of scores. One or two students may do very well or very poorly no matter how the majority scored on the tests.

Standard deviations are very useful in understanding test results. They are especially helpful if the results of the tests form a **normal distribution,** like those in the two example tests in Figure 14–5. You may have met the normal distribution before. It is the famous bell-shaped curve.

**The Normal Distribution.** This is the most famous frequency distribution, in part because it describes many naturally occurring physical and social

## Figure 14–4  Calculating the Standard Deviation

The following steps illustrate how to calculate the standard deviation of these 16 scores: 16, 14, 30, 25, 12, 18, 22, 12, 26, 28, 25, 20, 24, 12, 16, 11.

| Step 1 | Step 2 | Step 3 |
|---|---|---|
| Find the Mean of the Scores | Subtract the Mean (We will use 19 to avoid Decimals) from Each Score | Square Each Resulting Difference |
| $\dfrac{\text{Total of scores}}{\text{Number of scores}} = \dfrac{311}{16} = 19.44$ | $16 - 19 = -3$<br>$14 - 19 = -5$<br>$30 - 19 = 11$<br>$25 - 19 = 6$<br>$12 - 19 = -7$<br>$18 - 19 = -1$<br>$22 - 19 = 3$<br>$12 - 19 = -7$<br>$26 - 19 = 7$<br>$28 - 19 = 9$<br>$25 - 19 = 6$<br>$20 - 19 = 1$<br>$24 - 19 = 5$<br>$12 - 19 = -7$<br>$16 - 19 = -3$<br>$11 - 19 = -8$ | $(-3)^2 = 9$<br>$(-5)^2 = 25$<br>$(11)^2 = 121$<br>$(6)^2 = 36$<br>$(-7)^2 = 49$<br>$(-1)^2 = 1$<br>$(3)^2 = 9$<br>$(-7)^2 = 49$<br>$(7)^2 = 49$<br>$(9)^2 = 81$<br>$(6)^2 = 36$<br>$(1)^2 = 1$<br>$(5)^2 = 25$<br>$(-7)^2 = 49$<br>$(3)^2 = 9$<br>$(-8)^2 = 64$ |

| Step 4 | Step 5 | Step 6 |
|---|---|---|
| Then Add these Squared Differences: | Divide the Total by the Number of Original Scores | Find the Square Root |
| 9<br>25<br>121<br>36<br>49<br>1<br>9<br>49<br>49<br>81<br>36<br>1<br>25<br>49<br>9<br>64<br>___<br>613 | $\dfrac{613}{16} = 38.31$ | $\sqrt{38.31} = 6.19$<br>= standard deviation |

**Figure 14–5   Two Tests with the Same Mean and Different Standard Deviation**

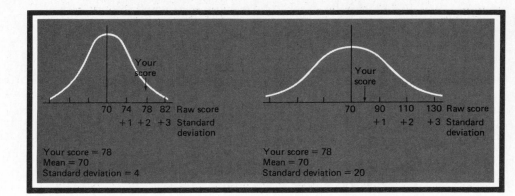

phenomena. Many scores fall in the middle, giving the bell its puffed appearance. Fewer and fewer scores are included as you look out toward the end points, or *tails,* of the distribution.

Mean, Median, and Mode the Same

The normal distribution has been throughly analyzed by statisticians. The mean of a normal distribution is also its midpoint. Half the scores are above the mean, and half are below it. In a normal distribution, the mean, median, and mode are all the same point.

Another convenient property of the normal distribution is that the percentage of scores falling within each area of the curve is known, as you can see in Figure 14–6. A person scoring within 1 standard deviation of the mean obviously has a lot of company. Many scores pile up here. In fact, 68 percent of all scores are located in the area plus and minus 1 standard deviation from the mean. About 16 percent of the scores are higher than 1 standard deviation

**Figure 14–6   The Normal Distribution**

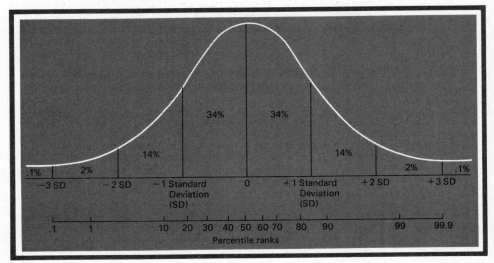

515

above the mean. Of this higher group, only 2.5 percent are better than 2 standard deviations above the mean. Similarly, only about 16 percent of the scores are less than 1 standard deviation below the mean, and of that group only about 2.5 percent are worse than 2 standard deviations below. At 2 standard deviations from the mean in either direction, the scorer has left the pack behind.

The SAT college entrance exam offers one example of a normal distribution. The mean of the SAT is 500 and the standard deviation is 100. If you know people who made scores of 700, you know they did very well. Only about 2.5 percent of the people who took the test did any better because only 2.5 percent of the scores are better than 2 standard deviations above the mean in a normal distribution.

## Types of Scores

Now we have enough background information for a discussion of the different kinds of scores you may encounter in reports of results from standardized tests. We begin with two types of scores that require very little calculation to understand: percentile rank scores and grade-equivalent scores. Then we look briefly at slightly more complicated standard scores.

**Percentile Rank Scores.**   The concept of ranking is the basis for one very useful kind of score reported on standardized tests: a **percentile rank score.** In percentile ranking, each student's raw score is compared with the raw scores obtained by the students in the norming sample. The percentile rank shows the percentage of students in the norming sample who scored at or below a particular raw score. If a student's score is the same or better than three-quarters of the students in the norming sample, the student would score at the 75th percentile, or have a percentile rank of 75. You can see that this does *not* mean that the student had a raw score of 75 questions answered correctly or even that the student answered 75 percent of the questions correctly. Rather, the 75 refers to the percentage of people in the norming sample whose scores were equal to or below this student's on the test. Another way to describe a percentile rank of 75 is to say that only 25 percent of the people in the norming sample had higher scores on the test. A percentile rank of 50 means that a student has scored as well or better than 50 percent of the norming sample and achieved an average score.

Figure 14–7 illustrates one problem in interpreting percentile scores. Differences in percentile ranks do not mean the same thing in terms of raw score points in the middle of the scale as they do at the fringes. The graph shows Joan's and Alice's percentile scores on the Fictitious Test of Excellence in Language and Arithmetic. Both students are about average in arithmetic skills. One equaled or surpassed 50 percent of the norming sample; the other, 60 percent. But in the middle of the distribution, this difference in percentile ranks means a raw score difference of only a few points. Their raw scores actually were 75 and 77. In the language test, the difference in percentile ranks seems to be about the same as the difference in arithmetic, since one ranked at the 90th percentile and the other at the 99th. But the difference in their raw scores on the language test is much greater. It takes a greater difference in raw score points to make a difference in percentile rank at the extreme ends of the scale. On the language test, the difference in raw scores is about 10 points.

**Figure 14–7    Percentile Ranking Scores at Different Points on the Normal Distribution Curve**

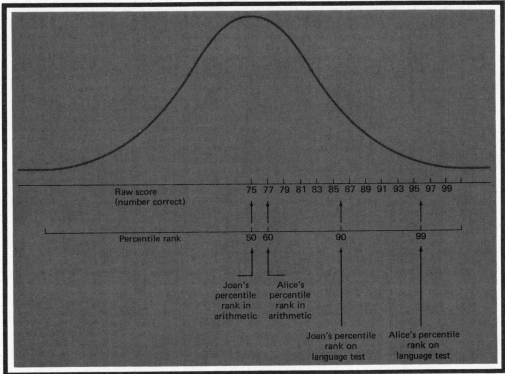

Determining Grade-Equivalents

**Grade-Equivalent Scores.    Grade-equivalent scores** are generally obtained from different norming samples for each grade level. The average of the scores of all the tenth-graders in the norming sample defines the tenth-grade equivalent score. Suppose the raw score average of the tenth-grade norming sample was 38. Any student who attains a raw score of 38 on that test will be assigned a grade-equivalent score of tenth grade. Grade-equivalent scores are generally listed in numbers, such as 8.3, 4.5, 7.6, 11.5, and so on. The whole number gives the grade and the decimals stands for tenths of a year, but they are usually interpreted as months.

Suppose a student with the grade-equivalent score of 10 is a seventh-grader. Should this student be promoted immediately? No! Different forms of the test are often used at different grade levels, so the seventh-grader may not have experienced test items that would be given to tenth-graders. It may be that the seventh-grader has succeeded with almost all the items appropriate for seventh grade. This would place the student well above the average seventh-grader, who would have a grade equivalent score of 7.0. However, only a few of the items on the test may really be appropriate for ninth- or tenth-graders. In other words, the high score may represent superior mastery of material at the seventh-grade level, rather than a capacity for doing advanced work. Even if an average tenth-grader would do about as well as our seventh-grader on this particular test, the tenth-grader certainly knows much more than this test covered.

Because grade-equivalent scores are misleading and so often misinterpreted, especially by parents, most educators and psychologists strongly believe they should not be used at all. To avoid this confusion, other forms of reporting should be used.

*z* Scores **Standard Scores.** As you may remember, one problem with percentile ranks is the difficulty in making comparisons among ranks. A discrepancy of a certain number of raw-score points has a different meaning at different places on the scale. With standard scores, on the other hand, a difference of 10 points is the same everywhere on the scale.

**Standard scores** derive their name from the fact that they are based on the standard deviation. A very common standard score is called the **z score**. A z score tells how many standard deviations above or below the average a raw score is. In the example described earlier in which you were fortunate to get a 78 on a test where the mean was 70 and the standard deviation was 4, your z score would be +2, or 2 standard deviations above the mean. If a person were to score 64 on this test, the score would be 1.5 standard deviation units below the mean, and the z score would be −1.5. A z score of 0 would be no standard deviations above the mean—in other words, right on the mean.

To calculate the z score for a given raw score, just subtract the mean from the raw score and divide the difference by the standard deviation. The formula is:

$$z = \frac{X - \bar{X}}{SD}$$

*T* Scores Since it is often inconvenient to use negative numbers, other standard scores have been devised to eliminate these difficulties. The **T score** has mean of 50 and uses a standard deviation of 10. If you multiply the z score by 10 (which eliminates the decimal) and add 50 (which gets rid of the negative number), you get the equivalent *T* score as the answer. The person whose z score was −1.5 would have a *T* score of 35.

$$-1.5 \times 10 = -15$$
$$-15 + 50 = 35$$

The scoring of the College Entrance Examination Board test is based on a similar procedure. The mean of the scores is set at 500, and a standard deviation of 100 is used. But small differences in raw scores on the College Board tests can give large differences in standard scores, so be careful not to attach much importance to small differences between these scores. Figure 14–8 compares the three types of standard scores we have considered, showing how each would fall on a normal distribution curve.

Stanine Scores Before we leave this section on types of scores, we should mention one other widely used method. **Stanine scores** combine some of the properties of percentile ranks with some of the properties of standard scores. Stanine scores are always whole numbers between 1 and 9 (the name "stanine" is from the words "standard nine"). The mean is 5, and the standard deviation is 2. Each unit from 2 to 8 is equal to half a standard deviation. Stanine scores also provide a method of considering a student's rank, because each of the nine scores includes a range of percentile scores in the normal distribution.

## Figure 14–8 Three Types of Standard Scores on a Normal Distribution Curve

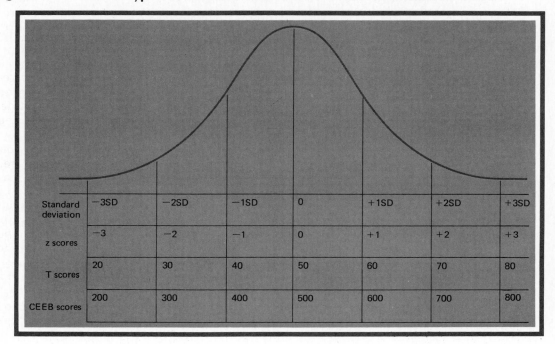

| Standard deviation | −3SD | −2SD | −1SD | 0 | +1SD | +2SD | +3SD |
|---|---|---|---|---|---|---|---|
| z scores | −3 | −2 | −1 | 0 | +1 | +2 | +3 |
| T scores | 20 | 30 | 40 | 50 | 60 | 70 | 80 |
| CEEB scores | 200 | 300 | 400 | 500 | 600 | 700 | 800 |

## Figure 14–9 Stanines

| Stanines | 1 | 2 | 3 | 4 | 5 | 6 | 7 | 8 | 9 |
|---|---|---|---|---|---|---|---|---|---|
| Percentage of all scores in each stanine | 4% | 7% | 12% | 17% | 20% | 17% | 12% | 7% | 4% |
| Cumulative percentages | 4% | 11% | 23% | 40% | 60% | 77% | 89% | 96% | 100% |

These scores have all the advantages of other standard scores but are less precise. Each stanine score represents a wide range of raw scores. This has advantages, since it encourages teachers and parents to view a student's score in more general terms instead of making fine distinctions of a few points. Figure 14–9 shows the percentage of the raw scores in each stanine.

### Interpreting Test Scores

One of the most common problems with the use of tests is misinterpretation of scores. Often this takes the form of believing that the numbers are exact estimates of a student's ability. No test provides a perfect picture of a person's abilities; a test is only one small sample of behavior. You probably have had the experience of feeling that you really understood a subject only to have the test ask several questions you were not expecting or felt were simply unfair. Was the test an accurate measure of your ability? Two factors are important in developing good tests: validity and reliability. Both must be considered in interpreting test scores.

Definition
of Validity
**Validity.**   The most important single characteristic of any test is **validity** (Lyman, 1978). Validity has to do with interpretations based on test results. A test has validity if it measures what it is supposed to measure or predicts what it is supposed to predict. To be a valid test of intelligence, the questions must measure intelligence and not reading speed or lucky guessing. Tests of mathematics achievement ought to measure what students have learned in mathematics and not level of anxiety about math. But a test cannot be judged as valid or invalid except in relation to a specific purpose. For example, a particular test might be a valid instrument for predicting success in college but not a valid measure of creativity or even a good predictor of success on the job. Another test might be a good measure of the tendency to give socially acceptable answers but not of attitudes.

Content Validity
There are several aspects to validity. The most important for teachers are content validity, predictive or criterion validity, and construct validity.

Tests have **content validity** if they measure the skills and abilities covered in a course or unit. This implies that all important topics will be tested and no extraneous topics will be included. Again, think back to your experience. Have you ever been given a test where almost all the questions dealt with only a few concepts from the lecture or a few pages in the textbook? Perhaps worse is taking a test with questions that were never even covered in lecture or text. Another problem that decreases content validity is a test made up of items that students can complete successfully without ever reading the book or attending class. Content validity means that the test measures the important outcomes of the educational experience. One way to improve content validity is to use the behavior content matrix described in Chapter 11 for planning the test.

Predictive
Validity
Establishing content validity is basically a matter of logic, good judgment, and careful planning. **Predictive** or **criterion validity** involves an additional consideration. The test must make fairly accurate predictions. To have predictive validity, a test used to select students for a special training program must discriminate between students who will do well in the program and those who will not.

Construct
Validity
**Construct validity** is more difficult to establish. A test has construct validity if it measures the attribute or "construct" it is intended to measure. Examples of constructs include intelligence, creativity, musical aptitude, scholastic aptitude, and achievement motivation. Construct validity has to do with the meaning of the test score and how it should be interpreted. Several psychologists have suggested that this is the heart of validity. They believe that content and predictive validity are not separate types of validity, but instead are types of evidence to establish if the test actually measures the construct it is intended to measure (Cronbach, 1970; Messick, 1981).

For teachers, consideration of construct validity is especially important when a test is unfamiliar. How would you determine if a test you were examining actually measured what the title of the test implied? Just because a standardized instrument is labeled a test of intelligence, for example, does not mean it is a good test of this attribute for your students. Check the manual to see how results of this test correlate with other established measures of intelligence for students like your own.

A number of factors may interfere with the validity of tests given in classroom situations. Standardized tests must be chosen so that the items on the test actually measure content covered in the classes. This match is absent more often than we might assume. Students must also have the necessary skills to use the test. If students score low on a science test not because they lack of knowledge about science but because they have difficulty reading the questions, do not understand the directions, or do not have enough time to finish, the test is not a valid measure of science achievement.

Sometimes speed of responding is intentionally measured on a test. This type of test is called, not surprisingly, a **speed test**. But if understanding of subject is being measured, a **power test** is more appropriate. On tests of this type, ample time is given for completing the test.

In order to be valid, tests must also be reliable, even though reliability alone will not guarantee validity.

**Reliability.** If you took a standardized test on Monday, then took the same test again one week later and received about the same score each time, you would have reason to believe the test was **reliable**. If 100 people took the test one day and then repeated it again the following week and the ranking of the individual scores was about the same for both tests, you would be even more certain the test was reliable. (Of course, this assumes that no one looks up answers or studies before the second test.) A reliable test gives a consistent and stable "reading" of a person's ability from one occasion to the next, assuming the person's ability remains the same. A reliable thermometer works in a similar manner, giving you a reading of 100° C each time you measure the temperature of boiling water.

Reliability does not always refer to similar performance on two separate administrations of the same test. The term also can be used to refer to the internal consistency or precision of a test. This type of reliability is calculated by comparing a person's performance on half of the questions on the test with that student's performance on the other half. If the student did quite well on all the odd-numbered items and not at all well on the even-numbered items, we might assume that the items were not very consistent in measuring the abilities they were trying to measure (Cronbach, 1970).

You can see why a test must be reliable to have any type of validity. A test that is unstable and inconsistent cannot be trusted to measure achievement in a course or predict future performance. If an instrument gives different readings on different occasions even though the situation remains unchanged, the instrument must not be measuring the same construct every time.

**True Score.** To understand how to improve reliability on a test, you should be familiar with the somewhat complex definition of the term **true score**. All tests are imperfect estimators of the qualities they are trying to measure. There is error involved in every testing situation. Sometimes the errors are in your favor, and you may score higher than your ability might warrant. This occurs when you happen to review a key section just before the test or are unusually well rested and alert the day of an unscheduled "pop" quiz. Sometimes the errors go against you. You are getting sick the day of the examination, have just gotten bad news from home, or focused on the wrong material in your review. If a student could be tested over and over again without becoming tired or memorizing the answers, the average of the test scores would bring you close to a true score. A student's true score can thus be conceptualized as the mean of all the scores the students would receive if the test had been repeated many times.

The Range for the True Score

But in reality students take a test only once. The score each student receives is made up of a true score plus some amount of error. How likely is it that the score obtained in the one testing is identical to the true score? The answer to the question depends on how reliable the test is. The more reliable the test, the less error in the score the student actually obtains. On standardized tests, test developers take this into consideration and make estimations of how much the students' scores would probably vary if they were tested repeatedly. This estimation is called the **standard error of measurement**. It represents the standard deviation of the distribution of scores from our hypothetical repeated testings. A reliable test is thus one with a small standard error of measurement.

Improving Reliability

To improve reliability, test makers must reduce the error involved in measurement. The most effective way to do this is to add more items to the test. Generally speaking, longer tests are more reliable than shorter tests.

**Confidence Interval.** Teachers should never base an opinion of a student's ability or achievement on the exact score the student obtains. Many test companies now report scores using a **confidence interval** or "standard error band" that encloses the student's actual score. This allows a teacher to consider the range of scores within which a student's true score might be.

Overlapping Score Bands

Let us assume, for example, that two students in your class take a standardized achievement test in Spanish. The standard error of measurement for this test is 5. (This type of information will be available in the test manual.) One student receives a score of 79; the other a score of 85. At first glance, these scores seem quite different. But when you consider the standard error bands around the scores instead of the scores alone, you see that the bands overlap. The first student's true score might be anywhere between 74 and 84 (that is, the actual score of 79 plus and minus the standard error of 5). The second student's true score might be anywhere between 80 and 90. If these two students took the test again, they might even switch rankings. It is crucial to keep in mind the idea of standard error bands when selecting students for special programs. No child should be rejected simply because his or her obtained score misses the cutoff by one or two points. The student's true score might well be above the cutoff point.

One caution is in order in interpreting the meaning of the true score. An individual's true score on a given test is an estimate of the score the person would attain if we could eliminate all sources of error. The true score is not "true" in the sense that it is a perfect estimate of the individual's general ability in the area being tested. A test can be very reliable, have a small standard error of measurement, and still lack validity. For example, a test of "intelligence" could be developed that yielded very consistent and stable scores, but did not predict school learning at all. The individual's true score on this test would not be a "true" indicator of intelligence.

The Guidelines given here should be of help in increasing the validity and reliability of the standardized tests you give, as well as the tests you prepare yourself. Now let us examine how standardized tests are used in schools.

# *Guidelines*

## *Increasing Validity and Reliability*

**1. Make sure the test actually covers the content of the unit of study.**

EXAMPLES
- Compare test questions to course objectives.
- Use local achievement tests and local norms when possible.
- Check to see if the test is long enough to cover all important topics.
- Are there any difficulties your students experience with the test, such as not enough time, level of reading, and so on? If so, discuss these problems with appropriate school personnel.

**2. Make sure students know how to use all the test materials.**

EXAMPLES
- Several days before the testing, do a few practice questions with a similar format.
- Demonstrate the use of the answer sheets.
- Ask students questions to make sure they understand.
- Check with new students, shy students, slower students, and students who have difficulty reading to make sure they understand the questions.

**3. Follow instructions for administering the text exactly.**

EXAMPLES
- Practice giving the test before you actually use it.
- Follow the time limits exactly.

**4. Make students as comfortable as possible during testing.**

EXAMPLES
- Do not create anxiety by making the test seem like the most important event of the year.
- Help the class relax before beginning the test, perhaps by telling a joke or having everyone take a few deep breaths. Don't be tense yourself!

**5. Remember that no test scores are perfect.**

EXAMPLES
- Interpret scores using bands instead of a single score.
- Ignore small differences between scores.

# STANDARDIZED TESTS

Cummulative Folders

Several kinds of standardized tests are used in schools today. If you have seen cumulative folders, with testing records for individual students over several years, you know how many ways students are tested in schools in this country. There are three broad categories of standardized tests: achievement, diagnostic, and aptitude (including interest). As a teacher, you will probably encounter more achievement and aptitude tests. An excellent source of information on all types of published tests in a series called the *Mental*

*Measurements Yearbooks.* These yearbooks, once edited by Oscar K. Buros and now done by psychologists at the Univeristy of Nebraska, contain reviews of every major test, with information on the strengths and weaknesses of each, age levels, and how to order.

### Achievement Tests: What Has the Student Learned?

The most common standardized tests given to students are **achievement tests**. These are meant to measure how much a student has learned in specific content areas such as reading comprehension, language usage, grammar, spelling, number operations, computation, science, social studies, mathematics, and logical reasoning.

We already have discussed the importance of using standardized tests that actually measure the topics covered in your class. If an achievement test is not appropriate for the students, the results will measure general test-taking skills and general cognitive abilities, not knowledge of the material the teacher wants to test. Let us assume your school district has selected an appropriate test. What happens next?

**Administering an Achievement Test.** One reason standardized tests are called standardized is that they are meant to be given in a standard way to all students. Instructions should be the same for every group. Time limits must be met exactly. Students should be made as comfortable as possible about taking the test, within the limits set by the testing procedures. (In other words, making students comfortable by giving specific help with the actual questions either before or during the test is not allowed.)

"WHAT WITH THE PRIMARY MENTAL ABILITY TEST AND THE DIFFERENTIAL APTITUDE TEST AND THE READING READINESS TEST AND THE BASIC SKILLS TEST AND THE I.Q. TEST AND THE SEQUENTIAL TESTS OF EDUCATIONAL PROGRESS AND THE MENTAL MATURITY TEST, WE HAVEN'T BEEN LEARNING <u>ANYTHING</u> AT SCHOOL."

© 1978 American Scientist Magazine. Sidney Harris.

As a teacher, you will undoubtedly give standardized tests. The results will be meaningless unless you administer them properly, following the procedures exactly as given in the instructions. If you are well prepared, organized, and relaxed, it will help your students relax and perform better on the test.

**Using Information from an Achievement Test.** Information about several questions is available from achievement test data. Test publishers usually provide individual profiles for each student, showing scores on each subtest. Figure 14–10 is an example of an individual profile for a fifth-grade student on the California Achievement Test. Note that the Individual Test Record reports the scores in many different ways. On the top of the form, after the identifying information, date, school, and so on, is a list of the various tests — Reading Vocabulary, Reading Comprehension, and so on. Beside each test is the raw score (RS), grade-equivalent (OGE), standard score (OSS), national percentile (NP), normal curve equivalent (NCE, a score used for research purposes), and local percentile (LP).

Individual
Profiles

## Figure 14–10 An Individual Test Report

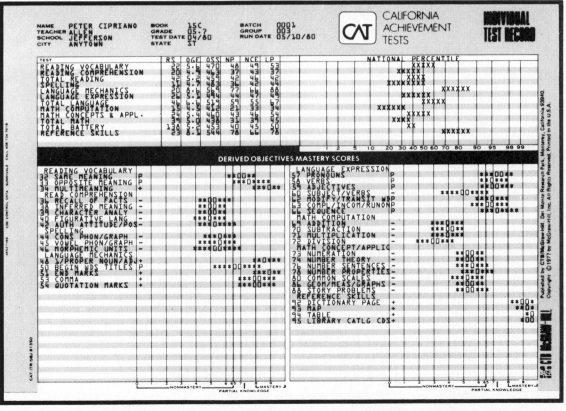

From the California Achievement Tests. Reproduced by permission of CTB/McGraw-Hill, 2500 Garden Road, Monterey, CA 93940. Copyright © 1977 by McGraw-Hill, Inc. All rights reserved. Printed in the USA.

For example, on Reading Vocabulary, Peter scored a grade equivalent of 5.6. His standard score was 470 (where the mean is 500). This is at the 37th percentile nationally and the 53rd percentile in Peter's local area. To the right of these scores we see Peter's test results reported in relation to national norms. Here his percentile ranks are shown with the standard error bands around each to indicate that his true percentile scores could be anywhere within these bands.

The profile in Figure 14–10 tells us a number of things. First, we can see that Peter is apparently strongest in language expression and reference skills. We also can see how Peter's performance compares with both local and national norms. By comparing the two columns under NP (national percentiles) and LP (local percentiles), we see that fifth-graders in Peter's district are achieving at or below the national norms. Peter's score on the total battery, for example, is average for his community but below average nationally.

Criterion-
Referenced
Interpretations

The scores we have just described are all norm-referenced. The bottom portion of the Individual Test Record in Figure 14–10 makes criterion-referenced comparisons, indicating mastery, partial knowledge, or nonmastery for specific skills in reading vocabulary, comprehension, spelling, language mechanics, and so on. This shows how the results from standardized tests can be interpreted in both norm-referenced and criterion-referenced fashion.

Class Profiles

A second type of information might also be provided by the test publishers. Figure 14–11 is a computer-prepared Pupil Item Report for the Metropolitan Mathematics Computation Test, Intermediate, Form F. This

**Figure 14–11   A Test Printout**

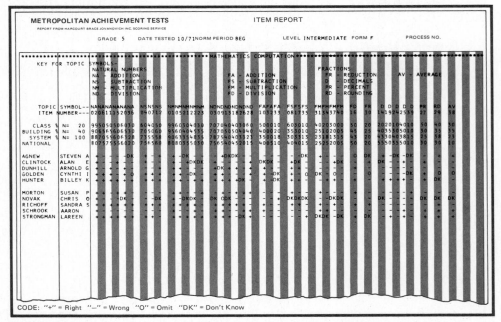

particular printout is for a fifth-grade class. The report tells how each student in the class answered each question and what percentage of the class got each question right. (Since the computer cannot print 100 percent, 99 percent is used when everyone in the class answers correctly.) A second row of numbers tells the percentage of fifth-graders in the building who got each question right. A third row gives the same information for the entire school system, and a fourth gives the percentage correct for fifth-graders nationally.

Quite a bit of information is available from the printout in Figure 14–11. As a whole, the class did well with natural numbers but had some problems with fractions, especially in decimal form. In general, this particular class performed better than the average for the building, school, and nation, except when the questions involved decimals (code D in the printout).

Performance
of Individuals

A look across the page beside each student's name gives some idea of the particular problems each is having in mathematics computation. Steven Agnew needs help in all areas, but he has some grasp of subtracting natural numbers. Billy Hunter seems to do well in most areas. He might review a bit about adding and multiplying fractions and computing averages with fractions. Lareen Strongman needs extra help with adding, subtracting, multiplying, and dividing fractions. Sandra Richoff could work with Billy Hunter, and perhaps others, to study addition and subtraction of fractions. Information from this type of report might be used to individualize instruction and group students with similar needs within the class when mathematics computation is being studied.

From the kind of information found in Figures 14–10 and 14–11, teachers can get a relatively good idea of the strengths and weaknesses of individual students. In fact, the results can be used in a criterion-referenced way to determine each student's progress toward general objectives in the subject, instead of comparing students to one another. For an identification of more general learning problems, however, a number of diagnostic tests have been developed. Since most of these tests are given by specialists such as psychologists, speech therapists, special education teachers, reading specialists, or educational diagnosticians, it is unlikely that you will administer them. There may be times, however, when you will want to use the results of diagnostic tests.

## Diagnostic Tests: Learning Abilities and Problems

Most **diagnostic tests** are given to students individually by a highly trained professional. The goal is usually to identify the specific problems a student is having. Achievement tests, both standardized and teacher-made, identify weaknesses in academic or content areas such as mathematics, computation, or reading; individually administered diagnostic tests identify weaknesses in learning processes. There are diagnostic tests to assess the ability to hear differences between sounds, remember spoken words or sentences, remember a sequence of symbols, separate figures from their background, express relationships, coordinate eye and hand movements, describe objects orally, blend sounds together to form words, recognize details in a picture, coordinate movements, and many other abilities needed to receive, process, and express information. Three diagnostic tests you may encounter are the Illinois Test of Psycholinguistic Abilities (ages 2 to 10), the Woodcock-Johnson

Assessing
Learning
Processes

Psycho-Educational Battery (ages 3 to adult), and the Detroit Tests of Learning Aptitude (ages 3 through adult).

Elementary school teachers are more likely than secondary teachers to receive information from diagnostic tests. There are few such tests for older students. If you become a high school teacher, your students are more likely to be given aptitude tests.

## Aptitude Tests: The Future

Achievement
Aptitude

A distinction is usually made between achievement tests, intended to measure what a student has learned already, and **aptitude tests**, which are meant to predict how well a student will do in learning unfamiliar material in the future. In reality, these are not so much two separate types of tests but instead are extremes on a continuum. Both achievement and aptitude tests measure developed abilities.

Achievement tests may measure abilities developed over a short period of time, such as a week-long unit on map reading, or over a longer period of time, such as a semester. Aptitude tests are meant to measure abilities developed over many years.

It is easier to specify the experiences a student should have had to do well on a test of academic achievement. These experiences are (or should be) closely related to the curriculum. But many different life experiences, inside school and out, might prepare a student to do well on a test of academic aptitude. The greatest difference between the two types of tests is that they are used for different purposes — achievement tests to measure final performance (and perhaps give grades), and aptitude tests to predict how well people will do in particular programs like college or professional school (Anastasi, 1981).

In schools, interest generally focuses on one of two types of aptitude, scholastic and vocational.

Prediction

**Scholastic Aptitude.**    You are likely to have taken a scholastic aptitude test or college entrance examination, probably the SAT or ACT. The purpose of this test was to predict how well you would do in college. Colleges use such scores to help decide on acceptances and rejections. The SAT may have seemed like an achievement test to you, measuring what you had already learned in high school. Although the test is designed to avoid drawing too heavily on specific high school curricula, the questions are very similar to achievement test questions.

In fact, standardized aptitude tests such as the SAT (and the SCAT for younger students) predict future achievement just about as well as standardized achievement tests and previous grades in school do. Since standardized tests are less open to teacher bias than grades are, they may be even fairer predictors of future achievement.

Some psychologists believe grade inflation in high schools has made tests like the SAT even more important. It appears that the validity of the SAT as a predictor of freshman college grades, especially for women, is improving, while the validity of high school records is declining (Bejar and Blew, 1981).

**IQ and Scholastic Aptitude.**    In Chapter 4 we discussed one of the most influential aptitude tests of all, the IQ test. As you saw there, the IQ test as we

**Figure 14–12    The Distribution of IQ Scores**

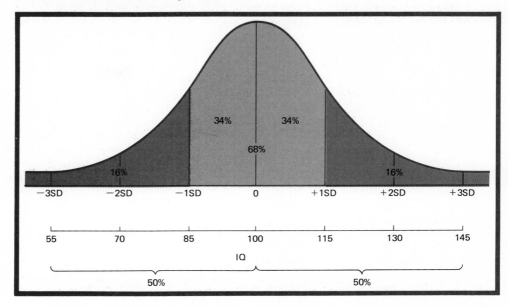

know it could well be called a test of scholastic aptitude. Figure 14–12 shows how IQ scores are distributed based on the results of the major individual tests. Now that you understand the concept of standard deviation, you can better appreciate several statistical characteristics of the tests.

**IQ Is a Standard Score**    For example, the IQ score is really a standard score with a mean of 100 and a standard deviation of 15 (for the Wechsler Scales, the Cognitive Abilities section of the Woodcock-Johnson Psycho-Educational Battery, and the Global Scale of the Kaufman Assessment Battery for Children) or 16 (for the Stanford-Binet and the McCarthy Scales for Children). Thus about 68 percent of the general population would score between +1 and −1 standard deviations from the mean, or between about 85 and 115. Only about 2.5 percent of the general population would have a score higher than 2 standard deviations above the mean—that is, above 130 on the Wechsler Scales.

**Average Range**    A difference of a few points between two student's IQ scores should not be viewed as important. Scores between 90 and 109 are within the average range. In fact, scores between 80 and 119 are considered to range from low average to high average. To see the problems that may arise, consider the following conversation:

PARENT:    We came to speak with you today because we are shocked at our son's IQ score. We can't believe he has only a 99 IQ when his sister scored much higher on the same test. We know they are about the same. In fact, Sammy has better marks than Lauren did in the the fifth grade.

TEACHER:    What was Lauren's score?

PARENT:    Well, she did much better. She scored a 103!

Clearly both students have scored within the average range. The standard error of measurement on the WISC-R varies slightly from one age to the next, but the average standard error is 3.19. Thus the bands around Sammy's and Lauren's IQ scores overlap and would be about 96 to 102 and 100 to 106. The scores are so close that, on a second testing, Sammy might score slightly higher than Lauren.

**Common Mistakes**

Sammy's and Lauren's parents are making other mistakes in the way they are thinking about the results of the IQ tests. Even though individual intelligence tests are better measures of student abilities than group tests, the problems of the testing process in general hold for individual IQ tests as well. An IQ test is a sample of behavior on a given day in a given situation. If a student is tired, sick, upset, fearful, or not really trying to do well, the test score will be affected and the results will not be valid for that student. In addition, IQ tests measure current functioning. Although current achievement predicts future achievement, the prediction is not perfect. Education and experience might change the picture.

**Vocational Aptitude.**   In schools, the school counselor or guidance officer generally is the person most concerned with students' career decisions. It is the responsibility of people in the guidance office to know what aptitude test scores really mean and how to help each student make an appropriate decision. Two kinds of tests, vocational aptitude and vocational interest, may provide useful information for educational planning. But, as with any tests, interpretation must be made with caution.

*Vocational aptitude tests are not, of course, the only important factor in determining career possibilities. Students' ambitions are sometimes inscrutable, showing little apparent relation to natural aptitudes. The career nights sponsored by many high schools provide further guidance in the shaping of those ambitions.*

Less Mahen/Monkmeyer Press Photo Service

**DAT**    If you teach in a junior high or high school, your school may administer vocational aptitude tests to the students. One test designed to measure aptitudes that are relevant to career decisions is the Differential Aptitude Test (DAT). Students in grades 8 through 12 may take the test. Questions cover seven areas: (1) verbal reasoning; (2) numerical ability; (3) abstract reasoning; (4) clerical speed and accuracy; (5) mechanical reasoning; (6) space relations; (7) spelling and language.

The test results on the DAT are converted into percentiles, and a percentile band is reported for each subtest. After the tests have been scored, the guidance counselors in a school should be able to help students relate their DAT profile scores to career planning decisions. In general, people in different occupational groups tend to have different patterns of scores on the DAT.

**Vocational Interest**    In many high schools, tests of **vocational interest** are also given. Two examples are the Kuder Preference Record and the Strong-Campbell Interest Blank. In these inventories students may be asked to indicate which of several activities (such as collecting books, collecting shells, or collecting postcards) they would like most and which they would like least. The pattern of the students' answers is then compared to the answer patterns of adults working in different occupations. It must be remembered, however, that the results on such a test indicate interests, not aptitude or talent.

Occupational interest tests cannot tell you exactly what students will or should be when they grow up. Results of such tests should be interpreted in the light of all the other information available on a student and with some healthy skepticism. As a teacher, you might learn about a student's interests from test results, then use this information to motivate the student. No career option should be permanently closed to an adolescent on the basis of an occupational interest test.

# CURRENT ISSUES IN STANDARDIZED TESTING

**Years of Controversy**    As we said at the beginning of this chapter, before the early twentieth century standardized tests were practically nonexistent. Two factors changed the picture. In 1916 Lewis Terman revised the procedure developed by Binet in France and gave us the Stanford-Binet Intelligence Scale. But the greatest change came when the United States entered World War I in 1917. The army needed a method for evaluating recruits. To solve this problem, psychologists created the Army Alpha and Beta group intelligence tests. By 1919 these had been given to 1.7 million people and had provided valuable information for placing recruits in appropriate training programs.

This success encouraged great interest. Psychologists began to expand testing to civilian populations in high schools, colleges, and industry. Controversy and concern about the widespread use of tests began at that point and has continued ever since (Haney, 1981). In this section we will consider two basic questions: What role should testing play in making decisions about people? Do some students have an unfair advantage in taking tests?

## The Role of Testing

Making
Decisions

In discussing standardized tests, we have emphasized the characteristics of the instruments themselves. But tests are not simply procedures used in research. Many decisions about individuals are made every day based on the results of tests. Should Trevor move on to the next math unit, or does he need more drill on long division? Should Kay be issued a driver's license? How many and which students from the eighth grade would benefit from an accelerated program in science? Who belongs in a special class for the mentally retarded? Who will be admitted to college or professional school? In answering these questions, it is important to distinguish between the quality of the test itself and how the test is used. Even the best instruments can be and have been misused. For example, in earlier years a large number of minority students were inappropriately classified as mentally retarded on the basis of generally valid and reliable individual intelligence scales.

Values

Behind all the statistics and terminology are issues related to values and ethics. Who will be tested? What are the consequences of choosing one test over another for a particular purpose with a given group? What is the effect on students of being tested? How will the test scores of minority students be interpreted? What do we really mean by intelligence, competence, and scholastic aptitude, and do our views agree with those implied by the tests we use to measure these constructs (Messick, 1981)? How will test results be integrated with other information about the individual to make judgments? Answering these questions requires choices based on values, as well as accurate information about what tests can and cannot tell us.

Many people have debated the merits of admission tests; others have been concerned about what might be called "exit" tests.

**Minimum Competence Tests.** We have mentioned in previous chapters that many Americans believe schools should do a better job of teaching the basics. The 1976 Gallup Poll found that 65 percent of the respondents favored a standard, nationwide examination for a high school diploma. This is a surprisingly large number, considering the distrust of tests and dislike for government intervention shared by a large portion of the population (Lerner, 1981). Is the level of competence in reading, writing, and arithmetic too low among today's high school graduates, and will competence testing help?

Rate of Illiteracy

In answer to the first question, Barbara Lerner (1981) notes that the best estimates, taken from the National Assessment of Educational Progress (NEAP, 1976), placed the rate of illiteracy among 17-year-olds at about 20 percent in 1975. Another 40 percent could be classified as semiliterate. These results were based on a test of relatively easy, everyday questions. In 1976, U.S. Department of Labor statistics indicated that only 6.1 percent of all jobs were appropriate for semiliterate individuals. The large number of students who leave high school unable to qualify for any job is a definite problem.

Advantages
of Minimum
Competency
Tests

Will requiring minimum competence tests for promotion and finally for graduation improve the situation? As usual, experts disagree. Lerner believes the close monitoring and clear standards required by minimum competence testing would encourage teachers and students to spend more time teaching and learning the basics. Since academic engaged time is one of the few factors that seems clearly associated with learning, this increased attention should improve achievement. Besides, "no other approach is demonstrably superior to it" (Lerner, 1981, p. 1062).

Disadvantages of Minimum Competency Tests

But many psychologists and teachers believe such tests would be undesirable. Their argument is teachers would have less and less freedom in deciding what and how to teach. The tests would control the curriculum. In working to get everyone to the minimum level, teachers would have to ignore the faster students. New ways of organizing classes would be necessary to prevent holding back everyone while a few students monopolized the teacher's attention. Finally, tests might discriminate against minority students.

Legal Questions

This last factor had a great impact when Florida instituted a functional literacy test for high school graduation. Although the citizens of the state were in favor of the testing, a federal judge ordered the process stopped on the grounds that the tests perpetuated the effects of past discrimination against minority students. Evidence presented during the trial *Debra P.* v. *Turlington* indicated that 20 percent of black seniors and only 2 percent of white seniors were denied diplomas on the basis of the tests. Many of these black students had spent some of their early school careers in segregated schools. The judge felt that denying them diplomas punished these students for having gone to inferior schools and thus violated their right to equal protection under the law (Haney, 1981).

So while many Americans believe tests should be used more often to make decisions about promotion, graduation, and the attainment of minimum skills, other people have grave reservations.

**Truth in Testing.**   Recently, many individuals who are critical of standardized tests for a variety of reasons joined ranks to call for "consumer action" in testing, and the truth-in-testing movement was born. Supporting this movement are various organizations around the country who want the admissions testing process to be more open to public scrutiny. These groups want the public to have complete information about the reliability, validity, costs, and development procedures related to nationwide tests. In addition, they want individual test-takers to receive the correct answers to questions after they complete the test.

New York Law

On January 1, 1980, a truth-in-testing law went into effect in New York covering all major college and professional school admissions tests. Later the Medical College Admissions Test was temporarily exempted, on the ground that there is only a limited number of good questions for this test and they soon would be used up if a new test had to be created every time. Other states are considering legislation similar to New York's.

Effects of Truth in Testing

The advantages of making testing more open are that mistakes, such as the one described in Box 14–1, can be caught. The public may become more sophisticated about testing in general, and publishers may have to be more careful to ensure reliability and validity in their tests. Better assessment procedures, particularly for minority students, may be a consequence (Bersoff, 1981). The disadvantage is that new tests will have to be created continually, adding greatly to the cost of testing for individual students. In addition, it is difficult for researchers to accumulate information and compare results across studies when the tests keep changing.

## BOX 14–1 TOO MANY RIGHT ANSWERS?

Headlines in papers such as the *New York Times* and the *Boston Globe* proclaimed: "Youth Outwits Merit Exam, Raising 240,000 Scores." The youth who caused the question was Daniel Lowen, a student from Florida who had taken the Preliminary Scholastic Aptitude Test (PSAT). After New York passed its truth-in-testing law, the College Board made it a policy to provide the questions and answers to students who took the PSAT. The question that caused the controversy, number 44 on the October 1980 test, showed two pyramids. One had four equal-sized, equilateral faces and a square base. The other had three identical triangular faces and an identical triangular base. The question asked was this: "If the two pyramids were placed together face-to-face with the vertices of the equal-sized equilateral triangles coinciding, how many exposed faces would the resulting solid have?" (Haney, 1981). The correct expected answer was 7, since putting the two pyramids together would cause 2 of the 9 total faces to disappear. Daniel had answered 5 and built a model with his father, a mechanical engineer, to prove that his solution was also correct. The two pyramids can be put together so that four of the exposed faces fall into two planes and become only two faces, not four. The College Board acknowledged that 5 faces was also a correct answer and rescored all the tests, giving credit for that answer too.

When the story reached the public, other solutions to the pyramid problem appeared. Many people argued that the solid rested on its base, so the base could not be an "exposed" face. Depending on whether you consider the base of a solid an exposed face, the answer to the problem could be 5, 6, 7, 8, or 9. The following letter appeared in the *New York Times* in April, 1981:

*TO THE EDITOR:*

The lively public dispute over the correct answer to the question—which at last count had generated at least five different proposed solutions—provides a unique argument in favor of New York State's test disclosure law. Not because the law enables students to catch scoring errors by the test makers—although it does that—but because this example shows what a useful teaching tool provocative, challenging test questions can be.

Imagine turning a bright high school class loose on the latest SAT, with the challenge that they find—and defend—as many answers for each question as possible. Not only would they uncover errors and ambiguities the test makers never dreamed of, but they might stretch their minds in some new and creative directions. . . .

The New York law makes such an exercise possible—and, incidentally, I couldn't imagine a better way of raising those drooping test scores.

Why shouldn't standardized tests be used to teach as well as terrify?

Karl Weber
April 15, 1981

## Advantages in Taking Tests: Fair and Unfair

We have all had plenty of experience with tests that seemed unfair, but often these have been tests in particular classes. In this section we want to consider whether certain groups or individuals have an advantage in taking standardized tests. We will examine three basic issues: Are standardized tests biased against minority students? Can people gain an advantage on admissions tests through coaching? Are there "test-taking skills"?

**Bias in Testing.** As you saw in Chapter 4, the average performance of students from lower SES and minority groups is below that of middle-class students on most standardized measures of mental abilities, although the discrepancies are decreasing for some minority groups (Burton and Jones, 1982). Are tests such as the individual measures of intelligence or college admissions tests biased against minorities? Like many others in educational psychology, this is a complex question.

IQ and School
Abilities

A standard IQ test can be seen as a sample of the student's current abilities to function in a middle-class school culture, a culture that emphasizes verbal skills. In this sense, some students do have less ability than others because they lack familiarity and training in these culturally influenced skills.

Some people argue that the society, not the intelligence test, is unfair, since many students are denied advantages available to others. As Sattler (1974, p. 34) states: "In a sense, *no test can be culture-fair in a culture that is not fair.*" IQ tests measure quite well some of the abilities needed to make it in school. A student who does poorly on an IQ test probably will have more trouble succeeding in school than a student who scores high on the same test. In fact, IQ tests are the most reliable single predictors of school achievement (Sattler, 1982). But this should not be surprising. Remember, Binet and Simon threw out all the test questions that did not predict school achievement when they developed the first IQ test.

Research on test bias shows that most standardized tests predict achievement equally well for all groups of students. The pattern of answers is also similar across different groups. Items that might appear on the surface to be biased against minorities are not necessarily harder for minorities to answer correctly (Jensen, 1980).

Cultural
Differences

Even though standardized aptitude and achievement tests may predict school performance, many people believe there are factors related to the specific content and procedures of such tests that put minority students at a disadvantage. Here are a few factors they suggest:

1.  The language of the test and the tester are often different from those of the students.
2.  The questions asked tend to center on experiences and facts more familiar to the dominant culture.
3.  Answers that support middle-class values often are rewarded with more points.
4.  Being very verbal and talking a lot is rewarded as well. Of course, this is easier if a student feels comfortable in the situation.
5.  Minority children may not be oriented toward achievement and may not appreciate the value of doing well on tests.

Since many of the skills and values listed here are encouraged by families in the dominant culture, it is clear that students from these families have an edge in the testing situation. In the 1970s and 1980s, the question of bias in IQ testing found its way into the courts.

Testing
and Minority
Students

**Testing on Trial.** Throughout the 1970s psychologists frequently found themselves in court to condemn or defend IQ testing. In *Diana* v. *State Board of Education* the issue was the overrepresentation of Mexican-American children in California's public school classes for the mildly mentally retarded. The plaintiff charged that the percentage of Mexican-American children in these classes was higher than the percentage in the school population because IQ tests, given in English, were biased against these children. The court ordered the schools to correct the disproportions and to administer placement tests in a student's native language. The native language requirement for testing later became a part of federal law, PL 94–142, the Education for All Handicapped Children Act.

A few years later, also in California, IQ tests were in the courtroom again, this time in *Larry P.* v. *Wilson Riles*. The case was initiated in 1971 on behalf of minority children placed in classes for the mildly retarded. The issue again was overrepresentation of certain groups of students in these classes and bias in the IQ tests. The case took several years, and an appeal is still in progress.

During the lengthy suit, in 1975, the California State Board of Education declared a moratorium on individual IQ tests for all children being evaluated for placement in classes for the mildly retarded until the issue was decided (Lambert, 1981). In 1979, the court ruled that no intelligence tests could be used to place minority students in special classes for the retarded unless the tests met these standards (Bersoff, 1981):

1.    The scores from the tests had to predict academic achievement and classroom performance fairly well.
2.    Different groups of students (blacks, Mexican-Americans) had to have the same pattern of scores on the tests *and the same mean scores.*

This last requirement meant that standard individual IQ tests could not be a part of the evaluation and placement process for minority students.

In making the decision, the judge assumed that any test yielding different mean scores for different groups of students was automatically biased. This rejects the possibility that some groups of students, for whatever reasons, might be less able in the particular school-related skills measured by the tests.

Ban on IQ
Testing

In the years since the schools in California stopped including IQ tests with the placement procedures, the actual number of students enrolled in classes for the mildly retarded has decreased substantially, but the percentage of minority students remains almost the same, around 50 percent. The IQ testing was only one of many elements in the decision to place a student in a special class. First, the child had to fail in the regular class. Then other test results and teacher recommendations were examined. When IQ tests were given, an average or above-average score kept students who had failed in regular classes out of classes for the retarded and led to placement in other types of special programs more appropriate to their needs (Lambert, 1981). Simply eliminating IQ testing will not help the children who are failing in school. The real question is how to give these students an appropriate education.

**Culture-Fair Tests.**    Concern about cultural biases in testing has led some psychologists to try to develop **culture-fair** or **culture-tree tests.** These efforts have not been very successful. On many of the so-called culture-fair tests, the performance of students from deprived socioeconomic backgrounds and minority groups has been the same or worse than their performance on the standard Wechsler and Binet scales (Costello and Dickie, 1970; Jensen, 1974; Sattler, 1982).

SOMPA

Another attempt to make assessment more appropriate for minority students is the **System for Multicultural Pluralistic Assessment (SOMPA)** designed by Jane Mercer and June Lewis (1977). This process involves several different types of tests, parent interviews, physical and health screening, and an assessment of adaptive behavior. The idea behind SOMPA is to evaluate the student's levels of functioning not only in relation to the standard school skills measured by the WISC-R individual intelligence scale, but also in terms of adaptive behavior in the family and community. The procedure takes the sociocultural level of the student into consideration in estimating learning potential instead of simply comparing the student's performance to standard test norms. A major goal of SOMPA is to distinguish between minority students who are mentally retarded and those who are not retarded, even though their IQ scores on standard tests are low.

SOMPA is an important attempt to make testing more appropriate for the needs of minority children. Like all new approaches, it has problems. The norms for the test are based on a limited sample of children in California. Children in other parts of the country, Texas for example (Oakland, 1979), do not necessarily fit the patterns of the California norms. (The Kaufman Assessment Battery for Children also includes separate norms for the different sociocultural and SES groups, but these are based on a national sample.) Another problem with the SOMPA is that the estimate of learning potential score is not as accurate as standard IQ scores in predicting school achievement.

Students who perform very poorly on standard IQ and achievement tests need special help of some type, no matter what the reason for the low score. While they should not be labeled as retarded, they should not simply continue in the educational program that is leading to failure. SOMPA is very time-consuming, and results do not tell teachers what to do to help students learn more effectively (Sattler, 1982). But the approach does focus attention on the problem of assessment for minority students.

**Research
on Test Bias**

In summarizing her review of test bias, Nancy Cole (1981) says: "First, we have learned there is not large-scale, consistent bias against minority groups in the technical validity sense in the major, widely used and widely studied tests. Second, we have learned that the lack of such bias means neither that the use made of the tests is necessarily socially good nor that improvements in the test cannot be made" (p. 1075). Concern with bias in tests has led publishers to be more careful about the content of test items and the makeup of norm groups. But the real issue involves how tests are used. Teachers and parents must make sure results are used to help students.

**Special Courses**

**Coaching and Test-Taking Skills.** Courses to prepare students for college entrance exams are becoming more popular. In a survey of seven Northeastern states, Alderman and Powers (1980) found that almost one-third of the high schools offered special programs for students taking the SAT. As you probably know from experience, commercial courses are available as well. It is hard to evaluate the effects of these courses.

People who take special courses may be more motivated to do well on the test is the first place. It would not be fair to conduct an experiment on the effects of these courses when students are taking the tests "for real." (How would you like to be in the control group that came for, but didn't get, training before the test that counted for college admission!) So some experiments have studied the effects of training on "practice tests," but results may not be representative of tests taken under normal circumstances (Anastasi, 1981). Given all these limitations, the findings may be far from precise. In general, research has indicated that short high school training programs yield average gains of 10 points in SAT verbal and 15 points in SAT

Practice
math, while longer commercial programs show gains of about 20 (verbal) and 30 points (math). Gains of 20 to 30 points mean that you got about three additional items correct (Messick, 1980; Messick and Jungeblut, 1981).

Two other types of training can make a difference in test scores. One is simple familiarity with the procedures of standardized tests. Students who have a lot of experience with standardized tests do better than those who do not. Some of this advantage may be due to greater self-confidence, less tendency to panic, familiarity with different types of questions (for example, knowing how to read an analogy such as house : garage :: _____ : car), and practice with the various answer sheets (Anastasi, 1981). Even short

# Guidelines

## Taking a Test

**1. Use the night before the test effectively.**

EXAMPLES
- Study the night before the exam, ending with a final look at a summary of the key points, concepts, relationships.
- Get a good night's sleep.

**2. Set the situation so you can concentrate on the test.**

EXAMPLES
- Give yourself plenty of time to eat and get to the exam room.
- Don't sit near a friend. It may make concentration difficult, and you may be tempted to leave early if the friend does to compare notes.

**3. Make sure you know what the test is asking.**

EXAMPLES
- Read the directions carefully. If you are unsure, ask the instructor for clarification.
- Read each question carefully to spot any tricky words, such as "not," "except," "all of the following but one."
- On an essay test, read every question first, so you know the size of the job ahead of you and can make informed selections in case you are given a choice of question to answer.
- On a multiple-choice test, read every alternative, even if you find an early one that seems right.

**4. Use time effectively.**

EXAMPLES
- Begin working right away and move as rapidly as possible while your energy is high.
- Do the easy questions first.
- Don't get stuck on one question. If you are stumped, mark the question so you can return to it easily later, but go on to questions you can answer more quickly.
- If you are unsure about a question, answer it but mark it so you can go back if there is time to reconsider it more carefully.
- On a multiple-choice test, if you definitely will not have time to finish, leave a few minutes to fill in all the remaining questions with the same letter if there is no penalty for guessing.

orientations about how to take tests can help students who lack familiarity and confidence.

**Metacognitive Skills**

A second type of training that appears to be very promising is instruction in general cognitive skills such as problem solving, careful analysis of questions, making sure to consider *all* the alternatives, noticing details and deciding which are relevant for the solution, avoiding impulsive answers, and checking work. These are the kinds of metacognitive and study skills we have discussed before. This type of training is likely to generalize to many intellectual and life tasks (Anastasi, 1981). The Guidelines here give some ideas about how to be a more effective test-taker.

- If you are running out of time on an essay test, do not leave any questions blank. Briefly outline a few key points to show the instructor you "knew the answer and just needed more time."

**5. Know when to guess on multiple-choice or true-false tests.**

EXAMPLES
- Always guess when only right answers are scored.
- Always guess when you can eliminate some of the alternatives.
- Don't guess if the number of wrong answers is subtracted from the number right and you haven't a clue about which alternatives are right or wrong.

**6. Notice patterns in the right response on multiple-choice and true-false tests.**

EXAMPLES
- Are correct answers always longer? shorter? in the middle? more likely one letter, or more often true than false?
- Does the grammar give the right answer away or eliminate any alternatives?

**7. Check your work.**

EXAMPLES
- Even if you can't stand to look at the test another minute, reread each question and make sure you answered the way you intended.
- If you are using a machine-scored answer sheet, check occasionally to be sure the number of the question you are answering corresponds to the number of the answer on the sheet.

**8. On essay tests, answer as directly as possible.**

EXAMPLES
- Avoid flowery introductions. Answer the question in the first sentence and then elaborate.
- Don't save your best ideas till last. Give them early in the answer.
- Unless the instructor requires complete sentences, consider listing points, arguments, and so on by number in your answer. It will help you organize your thoughts and concentrate on the important aspects of the answer.

*Source:* Adapted from W. Pauk. ***How to study in college***, (2d Ed.). Boston: Houghton Mifflin, 1974, pp. 176–185, and R. E. Sarnacki. An examination of test-wiseness in the cognitive test domain. ***Review of Research in Education***, 1979, **49**, 252–279.

## SUMMARY

1. Standardized tests, produced by professional test developers, may be either norm-referenced or criterion-referenced.

2. A norm-referenced test compares the student's performance to the performance of other individuals who took the same or a similar test.

3. A criterion-referenced test compares a student's performance to a fixed criterion, generally with a cutoff point marking passing and failing performance, as on a driver's license exam.

4. A frequency distribution is simply a listing of the number of students who obtained each score on a test. Such a distribution can be graphed, and the central tendency of the scores can be determined by finding the *mean* (arithmetic average), the *median* (middle score), or the *mode* (most frequent score).

5. The standard deviation is an index of how much the scores spread out around the mean. Scores are much more meaningful if listed along with the mean and the standard deviation. In the normal distribution, a bell-shaped curve places 68 percent of the scores within one standard deviation of the mean.

6. A student's score may be reported as a percentile rank (a number indicating the percentage of students who did the same or worse on the test) or as a grade equivalent (showing how closely the student's performance matches that of the average student in a certain grade).

7. Standard scores, which make use of the mean and standard deviation, may also be used. Scores on IQ tests and college entrance examinations are examples of commonly used standard scores.

8. Care must be taken in interpreting test results. Each test is only a sample of a student's performance on a given day. The score is only an estimate of a student's true score.

9. Some tests are more valid than others, in the sense that they measure what they are supposed to measure and the meaning of the scores is clear. Some tests are also more reliable than others—that is, they yield more stable and consistent estimates.

10. Three kinds of standardized tests are used frequently in schools: achievement, diagnostic, and aptitude.

11. There has been a great deal of controversy about large nationwide tests, particularly admissions and minimum competence tests.

12. The most widely used tests are equally valid predictors of school achievement for the various SES and ethnic groups, although the tests can be and have been misused to discriminate against minority students.

13. Teachers must be careful to use the results of tests to improve instruction and not to stereotype students or justify lowered expectations.

14. Performance on standardized tests can be improved if students are given experience with this type of testing and training in study skills and problem solving.

## KEY TERMS

| | | |
|---|---|---|
| evaluation | frequency distribution | bimodal distribution |
| measurement | histogram | standard deviation |
| norm-referenced testing | mean | variability |
| citerion-referenced testing | central tendency | normal distribution |
| standardized tests | median | percentile rank |
| norming sample | mode | grade-equivalent score |

standard score

$z$ score

$T$ score

stanine score

validity (content, predictive, construct)

speed and power tests

reliability

true score

standard error of measurement

confidence interval

achievement test

diagnostic test

vocational interest test

culture-free test

SOMPA

## SUGGESTIONS FOR FURTHER READING AND STUDY

In 1978, the American Educational Association sponsored a debate on norm-referenced versus criterion-referenced testing. The essential arguments were later published in the *Educational Researcher*, 1978, 12, 3–10: Ebel, R. L. The case for norm-referenced testing. Popham, W. J. The case for criterion-referenced testing.

A special issue on testing of the *American Psychologist*, 36, October, 1981. In this special issue of the journal are many short articles on issues such as test bias, coaching, the uses of tests, admissions and minimum competency tests, as well as a "primer" on testing concepts and terms by B. F. Green.

BUROS, O. K. Fifty years in testing: Some reminiscences, criticisms, and suggestions. *Educational Researcher*, 1977, 11, 9–15. This article gives insights about tests past and present from a man whose knowledge of the field was impressive.

FISKE, E. B. Finding fault with the testers. *The New York Times Magazine*, Nov. 18, 1979, 152–162. A very interesting newstory about the criticisms of the Educational Testing Service.

HILLS, J. R. *Measurement and evaluation in the classroom*. Columbus, Ohio, C. E. Merrill, 1976. Available with this book is a workbook of exercises and a set of 11 audio casette tapes, cued to the exercise book.

HOPKINS, K. D. and STANLEY, J. C. *Educational and psychological evaluation* (6th ed.). Englewood Cliffs, NJ: Prentice-Hall, 1981. A basic text on measurement.

LAMBERT, N. M. Psychological evidence in Larry P. V. Wilson files: An evaluation by a witness for the defense. *American Psychologist*, 1981, 36, 937–952. Reading this article, you will see how tests have come under attack in the courts and what some of the counter arguments are.

LYMAN, H. B. Test scores and what they mean (3rd ed.). Englewood Cliffs, NJ: Prentice-Hall, 1978. This is a very readable little text, filled with examples and clear explanations of statistical and measurement concepts.

MILLMAN, J. and PAUK, W. *How to take tests*. New York: McGraw-Hill, 1969. This book has helped many people improve their test-taking skills.

Tests: How good? How fair? *Newsweek*, Feb. 18, 1980, 97. A fairly balanced presentation of the views of both the critics and the supporters of testing.

WILEY, D. E. The vicious and the virtuous: ETS and college admissions. *Contemporary Education Review*, 1982, 1, 85–101. A very thoughtful consideration of admissions tests, their content, strengths, weaknesses, and the role they play in educational decisions.

# Teachers' Forum

## Achievement Tests

Achievement tests have become a way of life in the schools. Administrators and parents, as well as teachers, are interested in the results. However, the tests are an expense to the schools and a source of anxiety to the students (and teachers). What are the advantages and disadvantages of achievement tests? How can the test results be used?

**A Balanced View**

*The advantages are* (1) [Provide] a basis of comparison for evaluating strengths and correcting weaknesses of students, classes, schools and districts. (2) [Provide] support for teacher judgment. (3) [Serve] as a tool for evaluating the worth of texts, instructional materials, and curriculum. *The disadvantages are* (1) Tests do not always test what is taught. (2) Some administrators use tests to evaluate teachers and principals, pitting school against school and teacher against teacher. (3) Some teachers are pressured into teaching the tests, thereby invalidating the results. (4) Some students are not "test takers" and some are "super-guessers," making results unreliable. (5) Test results are too often just filed and forgotten. . . . I use these test results to measure each individual's growth and plan for any significant deviation from the norm.

Joan H. Lowe, Fifth-Grade Teacher
*Russell Elementary School, Hazelwood, Missouri*

## Testing for Minimum Competence

In many states, a recent requirement for high school graduation is that students pass a minimum competence test. They must be able to perform basic skills at a minimum level — for example, eighth grade, before they can receive a diploma. It may be stipulated that students who do not reach this level can graduate if their parents sign a statement acknowledging their level of competence and giving permission for them to graduate anyway. What effect has this legislation had in your school? Has it made a difference in the quality of education for students with low scholastic achievement?

**Positive Effects**

The more demanding requirements for graduation have affected our school greatly. We have developed a learning lab that focuses on skill deficiencies. Our program has also adopted a new track in both social studies and English that includes skills-oriented work. The actual effect . . . has been positive so far. Materials and teaching styles have been adapted to meet the needs of the student. The reading lab has been successful in remediating learning problems.

Wayne A. Ginty, Tenth-Grade Social Studies Teacher
*Lockport Senior High School, Lockport, New York*

**A Step in the Right Direction**

The introduction of a basic competence requirement has distributed the responsibility for the student's learning among the parents, community, student, and educational personnel. The parents and students have now a greater interest in the student's acquisition of skills to pass the tests and receive a certified diploma. Since neither the teachers nor administrators can any longer recommend the low-skilled student for graduation, the parents are more cooperative in providing the support needed to get students academically oriented. . . . The basic competence system that has been introduced to establish a standardized graduation does not remove the mandate that all students who are capable of learning are to be taught. To eliminate the possibility that students will be encouraged to quit school when they reach the proper age, financial penalties in state aid are being recommended by state legislators. To increase the success of students in passing tests, educators are making changes in the content requirements, redefining basic standards at each grade level, and trying alternative teaching strategies.

Ruth Roberts, Seventh-Grade Earth Science/Biology Teacher

*Greece Athena Junior High School, Rochester, New York*

## Coaching?

**You have just been told that all teachers in your school must give standardized achievement tests to their students. The administration has said that the test results will be used to measure only the students, not the teachers. Nevertheless, a general hope has been expressed that the students will do well on the tests.**

**Con**   In view of everything that has come to light recently concerning competency tests, we, as teachers, know that some blame and doubt has been directed toward our performance in the classroom. We also realize that many feel results of standardized tests can be attributed directly to the teacher and that the teacher should be held directly accountable. I would take *no* steps in preparing my students for a test of this nature. I should hope that the tests would indicate how well a student has achieved in certain areas, not how well a teacher has prepared them to take such tests. Preparation for achievement tests would, by its very nature, be counterproductive.

James C. Fulgham, High-School Latin and English Teacher

*Brainerd High School, Chattanooga, Tennessee*

**Be a Good Coach!**   Coaching is an excellent analogy — the coach prepares and psyches up the players, telling them how to perform and what to expect, but the players go on the field and *they* execute what they've learned. Teachers need to coach in order to maximize the results of the *accurate* assessment of student performance. . . . [R]egarding the test, the teacher should tell the students the number, topics, and duration of the subtests, then explain that there are questions they will be unable to answer because of the nature of achievement tests. The teacher should give practice in filling in circles or boxes in booklets or on answer sheets similar to the test (most publishers provide these), and advise students whether it would be beneficial to guess at an answer they don't know (this information is in the testing manual). . . . [T]he teacher can change the room to testing arrangements four or five days ahead of time so students, especially those in open classrooms, will be accustomed to it. Next, he/she should send home a letter suggesting that parents enforce a recommended bedtime during the days of testing. . . . Yes, coach the students. You can't play the game for them, but you can do everything possible to ensure their *best* performance.

Richard D. Courtright, Gifted and Talented Teacher

*Ephesus Road Elementary School, Chapel Hill, North Carolina*

# 15

# Classroom Evaluation and Grading

When they think about elementary or secondary school, many people vividly remember being tested and graded. In this chapter, we will look at both tests and grades, focusing not only on the effects these are likely to have on students, but also on practical means for developing more efficient methods of testing and grading.

We begin with a consideration of the many types of tests teachers prepare each year. Then we turn to grades, looking first at ways teachers can overcome any biases they may bring to the grading process and then at the effects grades are likely to have on students. Because there are so many grading systems, we also spend some time examining the advantages and disadvantages of one system over another. Finally we turn to the very important topic of communication with students and parents. How will you justify the grades you give?

By the time you have finished this chapter, you should be able to do the following:

- Create multiple-choice and essay test items for your subject area.
- Identify possible sources of bias in your own grading policies.
- Make a plan for testing students on a unit of work.
- Discuss the potential positive and negative effects of grades on students.
- Give examples of criterion-referenced and norm-referenced grading systems.
- Assign grades to a hypothetical group of students and defend your decisions in a class debate.
- Role-play a conference with parents who do not understand your grading system or their child's grades.

## CLASSROOM EVALUATION AND TESTING

As a teacher, you may or may not be involved in deciding which grading system will be adopted for your school or class. Many school districts have a standard approach to grading. Still, you will have some choice about how you will use your district's grading system. Will you give tests? How many? What kinds? Will students do projects? How will homework influence grades? Will you grade on improvement? Even if a particular type of grading system is mandatory in your school, you will decide what route you and your students will take to arrive at the end point—the grade itself.

We discussed standardized tests in the previous chapter. But many tests given in classrooms are not provided by outside sources; they are created by the overworked teacher. We begin with a discussion of two basic uses of tests and then examine how to create fair and meaningful tests.

## Two Uses of Tests

Planning instruction necessarily entails determining how to measure achievement. To be sure students have learned anything, you must observe or test their performance in some way. Bloom, Hastings, and Madaus (1971) divide measurement of achievement into two categories: formative and summative.

Planning

**Formative measurement** occurs before or during instruction. It has two basic purposes: to guide the teacher in planning and to help students identify areas requiring concentration. In other words, it is *formative* in the sense that it helps *form* educational plans. Tests or observations of performance closely related to instructional objectives are useful for this purpose. Often students are given a test prior to instruction, a **pretest**. This helps teachers determine what students already know. Sometimes a test is also given to see what areas of weakness remain when instruction is partially completed. This is generally called a **diagnostic test**, but it should not be confused with the standardized diagnostic tests of more general learning abilities. A classroom diagnostic test identifies a student's areas of achievement and weakness. Both pretests and diagnostic tests are examples of formative measurement, and their results do not influence grades.

Grading

**Summative measurement** occurs at the end of a sequence of instruction. Its purpose is to let the teacher and the students know the level of accomplishment attained. Summative measurement provides a *summary* of accomplishment. The final exam is a classic example, although any test or assignment that gives final evidence of achievement is summative.

Purposes

The distinction between formative and summative measurement is really one of purpose or use. The same test can be used for either purpose. If the goal is to obtain information about achievement for planning purposes, the testing is formative. Such a test or assignment does not count toward a grade, but strongly influences instructional planning. If the purpose is to assess final achievement (and help determine a course grade), the measurement is summative.

Although summative testing is the best-known form of classroom assessment, formative tests also have an important role to play. You yourself have probably had the experience of thinking you really understood something until you took the final exam. Then you realized how and why your interpretation was incorrect. If this information had been available before the test, you could have used it to improve your mastery of the topic. Since teachers cannot possibly interview every student on every topic to determine who understands what, formative tests can be very effective. Older students are often able to apply the information from formative tests to "reteach" themselves. Since formative tests do not count toward the final grade, students who tend to be very anxious on "real" tests or who do not perform well on such tests may find this low-pressure practice in test-taking especially helpful.

As we mentioned earlier, it is the use of the results that determines whether a test is formative or summative. Any format is appropriate for creating either type of test. Let us look now at some common formats — objective and essay tests.

# OBJECTIVE TESTING

Multiple-choice questions, matching exercises, true or false statements, and short-answer or fill-in items are all a part of **objective testing**. The word "objective" in this term does not refer to a goal, as in "instructional objectives." Here objective means "not open to many interpretations," or "not subjective." The scoring of these types of items is relatively objective compared to the scoring of essay questions.

**Fit Items to Objectives** Gronlund (1982) suggests that teachers should begin by trying to construct multiple-choice items and switch to other formats only if the subject matter or the type of learning outcome involved makes this desirable. If a number of similar concepts need to be interrelated, a matching item might serve best. If it is difficult to come up with several wrong answers for multiple choice, a true-false question may well solve the problem. Alternatively, the student might be asked to supply a short answer that completes a statement ("fill in the blank"). Sometimes having several different types of items can make the test more interesting for the student. In addition, variety can lower anxiety, since the entire grade does not depend on one type of question that may be difficult for a particular student.

Here we will look closely at the multiple-choice format. As we have noted, this type of objective question will not always be the best solution, but it does offer considerably more than most types of objective questions.

## Using Multiple-Choice Tests

We often assume that multiple-choice items are appropriate only for asking factual questions. But these items can test higher-level objectives as well, through the introduction of novel content. In other words, the item can assess more than recall and recognition if it requires the student to deal with new material by applying the concept or principle being tested.

**Higher-Level Items** In Chapter 11 we discussed Bloom's taxonomy of objectives in the cognitive domain. At the fourth level of the taxonomy is *analysis*. One aspect of analysis is the ability to recognize unstated assumptions. The following multiple-choice item is designed to evaluate this kind of higher-level objective:

An educational psychology professor states, "A $z$ score of $+1$ on a test is equivalent to a percentile rank of approximately 84." Which of the following assumptions is the professor making?

1. The scores on the test range from 0 to 100.
2. The standard deviation of the test scores is equal to 3.4
3. The distribution of scores on the test is normal. (CORRECT ANSWER)
4. The test is valid and reliable.

When objective tests are used, the most difficult part is making up the tests. Essay tests also require skillful construction, but you will find that grading the completed product is generally the major difficulty with essays. Before we turn to essay tests, let us examine some suggestions offered by Gronlund (1982) for constructing and grading multiple-choice tests.

## Constructing and Grading Multiple-Choice Items

Some students jokingly refer to multiple-choice tests as "multiple-guess" tests. Your goal in writing test items is to design them so that they measure student achievement rather than test-taking and guessing skills.

Parts of a
Multiple-Choice
Item

The **stem** of a multiple-choice item is the part that asks the question or poses the problem. The choices that follow are called alternatives. The wrong answers are called **distractors** because their purpose is to distract students who have only a partial understanding of the material. If there were no plausible distractors, students with only a vague understanding would have no difficulty in finding the right answer.

Stating the correct answer so that it is the *only* right answer or so that it is clearly the *best* answer is a challenge. You probably have been on the student side of discussions about whether the correct answer was really correct or whether several of the answers might be correct. The teacher is likely to feel just as bad as the students when half the class selects the same wrong answer and only three people choose the so-called right answer. Often this means the item was poor and should be discarded. Care in designing the alternative answers makes this less likely. The Guidelines presented on the following pages should make the job of writing multiple-choice questions somewhat easier.

# ESSAY TESTING

Some learning objectives are best measured by requiring students to create the answers on their own. An essay question is in order in these cases. The most difficult part of essay testing is judging the quality of the answers, but writing good, clear questions is not particularly easy either. We will look at a number of the factors involved in writing, administering, and grading essay tests, with most of the specific suggestions taken from Gronlund (1982). We will also consider factors that can bias the scoring of essay questions and how to overcome these problems.

## Constructing Essay Tests

Compared to objective tests, essay tests sample a smaller variety and number of learning outcomes, mainly because answering essay questions requires more time than answering short objective questions. Thus, for the sake of efficiency essay tests generally should be limited to the measurement of more complex learning outcomes—that is, outcomes that cannot be measured by short objective questions.

An essay question should present a clear and precise task to the students while letting them know how their essays will be evaluated. Gronlund suggests the following as an example of an essay question that might appear in an educational psychology course to measure an objective at the *synthesis* level (the fifth level) of Bloom's taxonomy in the cognitive domain:

Example of an
Essay Question

For a course that you are teaching or expect to teach, prepare a complete plan for evaluating student achievement. Be sure to include the procedures you would follow, the instruments you would use, and the reasons for your choices.

# Guidelines

## Writing Objective Test Items

**1. The stem should be clear, simple, and present only a single problem. Unessential details should be left out.**

**POOR** ▪ There are several different kinds of standard or derived scores. An IQ score is especially useful because. . . .

**BETTER** ▪ An advantage of an IQ score is. . . .

**2. The problem in the stem should be stated in positive terms. Negative language is confusing. If you must use words such as *not, no,* or *except,* underline them or type them in all capitals.**

**POOR** ▪ Which of the following is not a standard score?

**BETTER** ▪ Which of the following is NOT a standard score?

**3. As much wording as possible should be included in the stem so phrases will not have to be repeated in each alternative.**

**POOR** ▪ A percentile score
a. indicates the percent of items answered correctly.
b. indicates the percent of items right divided by the percent wrong.
c. indicates the percent of people who scored above.
d. indicates the percent of people who scored at or below.

**BETTER** ▪ A percentile score indicates the percent of
a. items answered correctly.
b. items right divided by the percent wrong.
c. people who scored above.
d. people who scored at or below.

**4. Each alternative answer should fit the grammatical form of the stem so no answers are obviously wrong.**

**POOR** ▪ The Stanford-Binet test yields an
a. IQ score.
b. reading level.
c. vocational preference.
d. mechanical aptitude.

**BETTER** ▪ The Stanford-Binet is a test of
a. intelligence.
b. reading level.
c. vocational preference.
d. mechanical aptitude.

**5. Categorical words such as *always, all, only,* or *never,* should be avoided unless they can appear consistently in all the alternatives. Using these categorical words is an easy way to make an alternative wrong, but most smart test takers know they ought to avoid the categorical answers.**

**POOR** ▪ A student's true score on a standardized test is
a. never equal to the obtained score.
b. always very close to the obtained score.

    c. always determined by the standard error of measurement.

    d. usually within a band that extends from plus one to minus one standard errors of measurement on each side of the obtained score.

**BETTER** ▪ Which one of the statements below would most often be correct about a student's true score on a standardized test?

    a. It equals the obtained score.

    b. It will be very close to the obtained score.

    c. It is determined by the standard error of measurement.

    d. It could be above or below the obtained score.

6. **The POOR alternative given in item 5 also has a second problem. The correct answer is much longer and more detailed than the three distractors. This is a clue that *d* is the correct choice.**

7. **You should also avoid including two wrong answers that have the same meaning. If only one answer can be right and two answers are the same, then they both must be wrong. This narrows down the choices considerably.**

**POOR** ▪ The most frequently occurring score in a distribution is called the

    a. mode.

    b. median.

    c. arithmetic average.

    d. mean.

**BETTER** ▪ The most frequently occurring score in a distribution is called the

    a. mode.

    b. median.

    c. standard deviation.

    d. mean.

8. **Using the exact wording found in the textbook is another technique to avoid. Poor students may recognize the answers without knowing what they mean.**

9. **Overuse of "all of the above" and "none of the above" should be avoided. Such choices may be helpful to students who are simply guessing. In addition, using "all of the above" may trick a quick student who sees that the first alternative is correct and does not read on to discover that the others are correct too.**

10. **Obvious patterns also aid students who are guessing. The position of the correct answer should be varied, as should its length. The correct answer should sometimes be the longest, sometimes the shortest, and more often neither the longest nor the shortest.**

11. **In addition to following these suggestions, you may also think ahead about how you will score an objective test. For example, if all the alternatives of multiple-choice items are neatly lined up on the left side of the paper, you can use a blank test as a key. Correct answers can be marked on the key with a felt pen, and the key can be placed next to each student's paper for quick comparison of answers.**

This question requires students to apply information and values derived from course material to produce a complex new product.

Gronlund (1982) offers a number of specific suggestions for constructing and administering essay tests. First, students should be given ample time for answering. If more than one essay is being completed in the same class period, you may want to give suggested time requirements for each. Remember, however, that time pressure increases anxiety and may prevent appropriate testing for some students.

Whatever your approach, do not include a large number of essay questions in an attempt to make up for the fact that an essay test samples limited amounts of material. It would be better to plan on more frequent testing than to include more than two or three essay questions in a single class period. Combining an essay question with a number of objective items is one way to avoid the problem of limited sampling. Finally, do not give students a choice of questions. Each question on the test should be important enough that everyone be required to answer it. If students have a choice of questions, they are actually taking different tests unless everyone happens to choose the same items. Comparisons among students do not make sense when they have been given different tests.

## Evaluating Essays

In 1912 Starch and Elliot began a series of experiments that shocked educators into critical consideration of subjectivity in testing. These researchers wanted to find out the extent to which teachers were influenced in scoring essay tests by personal values, standards, and expectations. For their initial study, they sent the English-language examination papers written by two high school students and duplicated in their original form to 200 high schools. The first-year English teacher in each school was asked to score the paper according to the standards of the school. A percentage scale was to be used, with 75 percent as a passing grade.

The scores on one of the papers ranged from 64 to 98 percent, with a mean of 88.2. The average score for the other paper was 80.2, with a range between 50 and 97. Neatness, spelling, punctuation, and communicative effectiveness were valued to different degrees by different teachers. The following year Starch and Elliot (1913a and b) published similar findings in a study involving history and geometry papers. The most important result of these studies was the discovery that the problem was not confined to any particular subject area. Rather, the individual standards of the grader and the unreliability of scoring procedures were the main difficulties.

**Factors in Essay Scoring.** Certain qualities of an essay itself may influence grades. For example, in a study of grading practices at 16 law schools, Linn, Klein, and Hart (1972) found that neatly written, verbose, jargon-filled essays with few grammatical and construction errors were given the best grades. Recent evidence indicates that other college professors may reward quantity rather than quality in essays, as you can see in Box 15–1.

**Scoring Methods.** Gronlund (1982) offers a number of strategies for grading essays to avoid the undesirable influences described above. If you wrote the essay question with specific objectives in mind, these objectives can act as a guide in establishing criteria for evaluating the students' work. When

## BOX 15–1 "AS I WAS SAYING (AND SAYING AND SAYING) ...'

The October 27, 1981, issue of the *New York Times* featured an article entitled, "Teachers Reward Muddy Prose, Study Finds" (Fiske, 1981). The article described a series of experiments with college and high school English teachers over a six-year period conducted by Rosemary Hake of Chicago State University and Joseph Williams of the University of Chicago. Many English teachers were asked to rate pairs of student essays that were identical in every way but linguistic style. One essay was quite verbose, with flowery language, complex sentences, and passive verbs. The other essay was written in the simple, straightforward language most teachers claim is the goal for students of writing. The teachers consistently rated the verbose essay higher and even perceived different errors in this type of paper.

"The teachers tended to find errors of logic and meaning in the verbose papers and mechanical errors in the others — even though the papers were identical in the errors they contained," Dr. Hake said in an interview. "The operating principle seemed to be that the higher the level of the language, the greater the importance of the errors." (Fiske, 1981, p. C1)

There was one difference between the ratings of high school and college teachers. When the essays were well organized, both groups preferred the wordier versions, but when the essays were poorly organized, only the high school teachers continued to rate wordiness highly. When essays were poorly organized, college teachers seemed to see the flowery language as an attempt to cover up having little substantial to say. The researchers pointed out that this could lead to problems. Students in high school are more likely to receive high grades for "flashy language" than for good arguments and content. When these students get to college, they may receive low grades on their writing. Instead of improving the content, the students may try what worked in high school, more complicated and flowery writing, which does little to raise their grades. Excerpts from the two types of essays follow. How would you rate each?

### DIRECT STYLE
I prefer to live in a large city because there I would be free to do things that cannot be done in a small town. In a small town a person has to live the way his neighbors do. He needs to conform to what they think is the proper way to behave, if he acts or thinks in a way that differs from what they expect, he will be considered suspicious . . . .

### WORDY STYLE
My preference is for life in a large city because there I would have the freedom to do things that can't be done in a small town. In a small town a person's life has to be like his neighbor's. There is a need for his conforming to their beliefs regarding proper behavior, if his actions or thinking is different from their general expectations, he will be the object of suspicion . . . .

possible, a good first step is to construct a model answer; then you can assign points to its various parts. Points might also be given for the organization of the answer, as well as the internal consistency. Grades such as 1 to 5 or A, B, C, D, and F can then be assigned, and the papers sorted into piles. As a final step, the papers in each pile should be skimmed to see if they are relatively comparable in quality. These techniques will help ensure fairness and accuracy in grading.

When grading essay tests with several questions, it makes sense to grade all responses to one question before moving on to the next. This helps prevent the quality of a student's answer to one question from influencing your evaluation of the student's other answers. After you finish reading and scoring the first question, shuffle the papers so that no students end up having all their questions graded first, last, or in the middle (Hills, 1976).

You may achieve greater objectivity if you ask students to put their names on the back of the paper, so that grading is anonymous. A final check on your fairness as a grader is to have another teacher who is equally familiar with your goals and subject matter grade your tests. This can give you valuable insights into areas of bias in your grading practices. But if you decide to do this, be sure that each of you makes comments on separate sheets of paper so you do not influence each other.

Now that we have examined both objective and essay testing, we can compare the two approaches. Figure 15–1 presents a summary of the important characteristics of each.

**Figure 15–1  A Comparison of Objective and Essay Tests**

|  | Objective Tests | Essay Tests |
|---|---|---|
| Types of outcomes measured | Good for measuring outcomes at the knowledge, comprehension, application and analysis levels of Bloom's taxonomy; inadequate for synthesis and evaluation outcomes. | Inefficient for knowledge outcomes; good for comprehension, application, and analysis outcomes; best type for synthesis and evaluation outcomes. |
| Ability to sample content | Possible to sample a large number of items, resulting in broad coverage of the course content. | Possible to sample only a relatively small number of items, resulting in limited coverage. |
| Problems in preparing items | Preparation of good items is difficult and time-consuming. | Preparation of good items is difficult, but easier than objective items. |
| Scoring | Objective, simple, and highly reliable. | Subjective, difficult, and less reliable. |
| Factors distorting student scores | Student achievement scores are apt to be distorted by reading ability and guessing. | Student achievement scores are apt to be distorted by writing ability and bluffing. |
| Probable effect on learning | Encourages students to remember, interpret, and analyze the ideas of others. | Encourages students to organize, integrate, and express their own ideas. |

**Source:** Adapted from N. E. Gronlund. **Constructive achievement tests** (3rd ed.). Englewood Cliffs, N.J.: Prentice-Hall, 1982, p. 73.

# PLANNING A MEASUREMENT PROGRAM

The behavior content matrix presented in Chapter 11 offers one way of making sure the lessons and objectives a teacher presents follow a logical and rational plan. A teacher also must consider the entire unit or year in measuring achievement. Each part of the evaluation program should be designed to suit a specific purpose.

## Planning for Evaluation

At the end of the instructional unit, you will probably want to give a comprehensive test covering all the material that has been studied. Every test requires planning. If you use a behavior content matrix to plan instruction, it also can act as your guide in developing a plan for the unit test. Whatever method you select, you will need to decide how many items students can complete during the testing period and then make sure that the items you write cover all the objectives you have set for the unit. More important objectives should have more items.

Making
a Test Plan
An example of a plan that might be appropriate for a 40-question unit test in government is given in Figure 15–2. From the test plan, you can see that this teacher has decided the most important topic is "major political issues" and the least important is "methods of inquiry." You can also see that the teacher wants to emphasize the ability to understand "generalizations,"

**Figure 15–2  Test Plan for a Unit on Government**

| Content or Topic | Behavior Tested | | | | |
| --- | --- | --- | --- | --- | --- |
| | Concepts | Generalization | Location of Information | Interpretation of Graphs and Symbolic Material | Total Number of Questions |
| Factors affecting politics | 4 | 4 | 1 | 1 | 10 |
| National politics | 2 | 3 | 3 | 2 | 10 |
| Methods of inquiry | 1 | 1 | 2 | 1 | 5 |
| Major political issues | 3 | 6 | 4 | 2 | 15 |
| Total number of questions | 10 | 14 | 10 | 6 | 40 |

while giving considerable attention to "concepts" and the ability to "locate information." "Interpreting graphs" is the least important behavior, but not to be overlooked.

By preparing such a plan, a teacher can avoid a situation where she or he has written 15 great questions (out of 40), only to discover that all 15 ask students to deal with concepts about the same topic. Making a test plan will also improve the validity of tests. You will be able to ask a reasonable number of questions about each key topic, measuring the behaviors you hoped to develop. If you use the plan, you will find that it does not take long, especially if you work from the outside totals columns in toward the specific types of questions.

**Dropping the Lowest Grade**

Students are most comfortable if they know what assignments and tests count toward a grade and when these will occur. Some teachers allow students to drop their lowest grade in order to make them feel more comfortable with the testing procedure. This practice is generally discouraged by measurement experts because then students will be compared on different bases, using different tests. Of course, this assumes some form of norm-referenced grading. In making a general plan, you will have to consider not only this issue, but also the issues of frequency and variety.

**Value of Frequent Tests**

Frequent tests encourage the retention of information and appear to be more effective than simply spending a comparable amount of time reviewing and studying the material (Nungester and Duchastel, 1982). In addition to

*Measurement of student achievement should not rely solely upon tests. Oral reports can be used to supplement written exams, and everyday classroom performance should be considered as well. In each instance, the students should know in advance what will be expected of them and how their performance will be evaluated.*

*David S. Strickler/Monkmeyer Press Photo Service*

**557** formal tests, you may want to use corrected homework as part of formative or summative evaluation. Participation in certain experiences may be credited toward the grade. For example, students may be required to participate in one of several activities, including debates, role-playing, demonstrations, or games. The quality of their participation may or may not be not be graded; the activity itself is the goal. In some subjects teachers keep samples, audio recordings, or portfolios of students' work. When the time comes to assign grades, these work samples give evidence of progress. In Chapter 11 we described methods for assessing affective and psychomotor objectives. These methods might be included in an overall measurement program.

No matter what methods you adopt, you must be fair in applying the methods to individual students.

## Cautions: Being Fair

Voice Quality

You saw earlier that factors such as handwriting and flowery language can influence teachers when they grade essay tests. But the influences do not stop with essays. Oral expression can affect a student's course grades. It appears that such language characteristics as using standard white dialect with appropriate intonation and speaking with a soft, moderately pitched, good-quality voice are associated with receiving better grades from teachers (Frender, Brown and Lambert, 1970; Naremore, 1970; Seligman, Tucker and Lambert, 1972). (See, your mother was right. Be neat and speak softly. You may get a better grade for the same work!)

Teacher's Expectations

In general, it appears that teachers' grading practices can be greatly influenced by expectations about the ability of the students being graded. In several studies, college students have been given tests to score along with fictitious information about the general ability of the students who supposedly did the work. Tests were given a higher score when the subjects believed the test was completed by a student with high ability (Cahen, 1966; Simon, 1969).

Even the student's name can influence grading. In one study elementary school teachers, but not college students, gave higher grades to papers supposedly written by Michael or David than to the same papers written by Elmer and Hubert. For girls, the name Adelle on the paper resulted in more points than the names Karen or Bertha (Hills, 1976).

Teacher's Attributions

The attributions a teacher makes about the causes of student successes or failures can affect the grades the students receive. Teachers are more likely to give higher grades for effort (a controllable factor) than for ability (an uncontrollable factor). Lower grades are more likely when teachers attribute a student's failure to lack of effort instead of lack of ability (Weiner, 1979). It is also possible that grades can be influenced by a **halo effect**—that is, by the tendency to view particular aspects of a student positively based on a generally positive impression of the student. As a teacher, you may find it difficult to avoid being affected by positive and negative halos. A very pleasant student who seems to work hard and causes little trouble may be given the benefit of the doubt (B− instead of C+), while a very difficult student who seems to refuse to try might be a loser at grading time (D instead of C−).

But what about the recipients of these grades? Is it enough that the teacher's evaluation practices are fair?

# EFFECTS OF GRADING ON STUDENTS

It might be worthwhile at this point for you to consider how the many grades you have received over the years have affected you. Since you are a college student, you have probably received your share of high grades. Without them, you might not have reached this educational level. Did you ever receive an F? If you did, how did you feel? What did you do as a result? Grades have many different effects on students.

## Effects of Success and Failure

In Chapter 8 we discussed the possible effects of success and failure on motivation. We saw that motivation to continue work may be greatly influenced by a student's attribution of the causes for past successes or failures. Because student attributions are an individual matter, it is difficult to talk about the overall effects of grades on motivation. It is likely that the effect of any grade is influenced by several individual factors: (1) the student's attribution of the cause for the grade; (2) the grade the student expected to receive; and (3) the grade the student is accustomed to receiving. We have already discussed the issue of attribution and motivation. Now let us examine other aspects of the effects of success and failure, particularly as they relate to grades.

Conformity     **The Effect of High Grades.** For the student who generally achieves high marks, grades tend to be a positive reinforcer. The student is likely to study in the same way and to try to continue the kind of learning that has been rewarded in the past. Some research indicates that if teachers reward conforming answers—answers that agree with or duplicate material from lectures or the textbook—students will try to conform to teacher views in future assignments, even if they did not previously share those views (Bostrum, Vlandis and Rosenbaum, 1961). In addition, there is some evidence that high grades are generally more often achieved by conforming students than by "creative" students (Holland, 1960; Kelley, 1958) and that students who share the teacher's values tend to receive higher grades (Cronbach and Snow, 1977). The long-term effect of grades on the successful student depends partially on the behaviors actually rewarded by the grades.

Rising Aspirations     These findings refer to continually successful students. Such students probably develop a positive view of themselves as academic achievers over time. But suppose a student is not consistently successful. What effect comes with the achievement of unexpected high grades? Such successes may lead to rising levels of aspiration and perhaps to increased effort. For a student who has neither worked hard nor received high grades in the past, a reward for honest initial efforts at a new learning task can be influential, depending on the attributions the student makes about the causes of the new success.

Positive Course Evaluations     But changes do not occur quickly. Over the short term, more liberal grading policies and higher grades appear to improve course evaluations, but not performance on tests or attendance, at least in college (Vasta and Sarmiento, 1979). More lenient standards are related to more positive course evaluations, particularly in required courses (DuCette and Kenney, 1982).

"YOU OUGHT TO BE GLAD THAT I CAN GET SUCH POOR GRADES WITHOUT DEVELOPING AN INFERIORITY COMPLEX.'"

*von Reigew*

**The Effect of Low Grades.**    Some students have received so many Cs and Ds by the time they finish high school that they may begin to feel they have earned a C or D in life as well. Repeated failure can lead to a destructive cycle: failure, lower level of aspiration, reduced efforts to succeed, failure, lower level of aspiration, and so on. Grades assigned to these students are often perceived as punishment. But what is being punished? If a student has been studying a bit, coming to school regularly, and putting in some effort on tests, he or she may begin to feel it is these behaviors that are being punished. If there are no other rewards for these behaviors in the school setting, they are likely to diminish or disappear.

**Negative Effects of Failure**    There is some evidence that high standards, a competitive class atmosphere, and a large percentage of lower grades are associated with increased absenteeism and increased dropout rates (Moos and Moos, 1978; Trickett and Moos, 1974). This seems especially likely with disadvantaged students (Wessman, 1972). While high standards and competition tend to be related to increased academic learning, it is clear that a balance must exist between high standards and a reasonable chance to succeed.

**Positive Effects of Failure**    To this point it sounds as though low grades and failure should be avoided in schools. But the situation is not that simple. (It never is in teaching!) After reviewing many years of research on the effects of failure from several perspectives, Margaret Clifford (1979) concluded that failure can have both positive and negative effects on subsequent performance, depending on the situation and the personality of the students involved.

For example, one study required subjects to complete three sets of problems. On the first set, the experimenters arranged for subjects to experience either 0, 50, or 100 percent success. On the second set, it was arranged for all subjects to fail completely. On the third set of problems, the experimenters merely recorded how well the subjects performed. Those who had succeeded only 50 percent of the time before the failure experience performed the best. It appears that a history of complete failure or 100 percent success may be bad preparation for learning to cope with failure. Some level of failure may be productive for most students, especially if teachers help the students see connections between hard work and improvement. Clifford (1979) summarizes the dangers of easy success:

> Success which comes too easily is not likely to be as highly valued as success which is difficult to achieve. With our educational practices designed to ensure success we may be conditioning students to be intolerant of performance which is less than perfect, to be conservative risk takers in learning situations, to retreat when they encounter failure, and to covet the known rather than venture into the unknown. (p. 50)

The more able your students, the more challenging and important it will be to help them learn to "fail successfully" (Foster, 1981).

**Being Held Back.** So far, we have been talking about the effects of failing a test or perhaps a course. But what about the effect of failing an entire grade — that is, of being "held back?" According to Jackson (1975), there has been extensive research on this question, but much of the research has been so poorly designed that we really do not know much. The one general conclusion Jackson felt was warranted after looking at all the research was that "there is no reliable body of evidence to indicate that grade retention is more beneficial than grade promotion for students with serious academic or adjustment difficulties" (Jackson, 1975, p. 627).

No Clear
Conclusions

This conclusion does not mean that promotion is the better alternative. It simply means that there is no clear answer yet about which policy is better. However, one problem with simply repeating a grade is that, without special help, the same difficulties and lack of understanding may well be encountered again, with similar results — inadequate learning.

## Effects of Feedback

Corrective
Feedback

Several studies of feedback have concluded that it is more helpful to tell students when they are wrong than when they are right, but the most productive approach is to tell them *why* they are wrong (Bloom and Bourdon, 1980). Students often need help in figuring out why their answers are incorrect. Without such feedback, they are likely to make the same mistakes again. Yet this type of feedback is rarely given. In one study, only about 8 percent of the teachers noticed a consistent error in a student's arithmetic computation and informed the student (Bloom and Bourdon, 1980).

Mistaken Rules

Results of research on cognitive learning demonstrate that students are very logical and "intelligent" in making errors — few mistakes are random. The student usually applies some rule or procedure to answer a question or solve a problem in class. The rule may be wrong and may need to be corrected before the student will understand the material. Robert Glaser, in an article entitled "The future of testing: A research agenda for cognitive psychology and psychometrics," said the following:

An important skill in teaching is the ability to synthesize from a student's performance an accurate picture of the misconceptions that lead to error. The task goes deeper than identifying incorrect answers and pointing these out to the student: it should identify the nature of the concept or rule that the student is employing that governs her or his performance in some way (in most cases, the student's behavior is not random or careless, but is driven by some underlying misconception or by incomplete knowledge). (1981, p. 926)

Figure 15–3 shows several examples of mistaken rules that have appeared in the arithmetic computations of students.

Written
Comments

Some research indicates that written comments on completed assignments can lead to improved performance in future work. Page conducted a study in 1958 including 74 classrooms and 2139 students. The results showed that brief written comments placed on objective exams were better than no comments at all in improving subsequent scores on exams. In the past two decades, this study has been repeated at least 17 times with varying results. Very few of the studies have found the overwhelmingly positive results reported by Page. In

**Figure 15–3    Correcting Mistaken Rules**

|  |  |
|---|---|
| 143<br>−  28<br>125 | The student subtracts the smaller digit in each column from the larger digit regardless of which is on top. |
| 143<br>−  28<br>125 | When the student needs to borrow, he adds 10 to the top digit of the current column without subtracting 1 from the next column to the left. |
| 1300<br>−  522<br>878 | When borrowing from a column whose top digit is 0, the student writes 9 but does not continue borrowing from the column to the left of the 0. |
| 140<br>−  21<br>121 | Whenever the top digit in a column is 0, the student writes the bottom digit in the answer; i.e., $0 - N = N$. |
| 140<br>−  21<br>120 | Whenever the top digit in a column is 0, the student writes 0 in the answer, i.e., $0 - N = 0$. |
| 1300<br>−  522<br>788 | When borrowing from a column where the top digit is 0, the student borrows from the next column to the left correctly but writes 10 instead of 9 in this column. |
| 321<br>−  89<br>231 | When borrowing into a column whose top digit is 1, the student gets 10 instead of 11. |
| 662<br>−  357<br>205 | Once the student needs to borrow from a column, he continues to borrow from every column whether he needs to or not. |
| 662<br>−  357<br>115 | The student always subtracts all borrows from leftmost digit in the top number. |

*Source:* "*Diagnostic Models for Procedural Bugs in Basic Mathematical Skills*" *by J. S. Brown & R. R. Burton,* **Cognitive Science,** *1978; 2, 155–192. Copyright 1978 by Ablex Publishing Corp. Reprinted by permission.*

the studies that found comments to be effective, the comments were encouraging and personalized in nature rather than stereotyped (Stewart and White, 1976).

In the end, teachers must decide for themselves whether it is worth the time to write comments on student work. Even though Page (1958) found that comments improved student work, this improvement was evident for only 1 out of every 10 students. Although comments may not always lead to improvement in student performance, our experience indicates that students want some explanation for their grade, especially if it is lower than expected. Without comments, grades sometimes seem arbitrary.

This is especially true for older students. In fact, Steward and White (1976) concluded that the most consistent evidence for the effectiveness of comments was with college students. For younger students, oral feedback may be much more important than written comments. Marble, Winne, and Martin (1978) reached a similar conclusion in a study of written comments in eighth-grade science classes. They suggest that the teacher's time might be better

spent giving students immediate oral feedback. As we noted earlier, oral feedback that helps students pinpoint and correct key misconceptions is especially helpful.

While extensive written comments may be inappropriate for younger students, brief written comments are a different matter. Short, cogent comments can be fun for teacher and students alike. With younger students, the comments may be as simple as these: "Wow," "Bravo," "Super," "A winner." One elementary teacher we know just writes down the first printable word that pops into her head; students never know what will come next. The first author's daughter understood that her paper was particularly good when the second-grade teacher drew a "popcorn man" saying "terrific" in the corner of her test or essay. Having a cartoonlike popcorn man on her paper was more reinforcing than simply receiving a good grade. Such comments also take some of the emphasis off the grade itself.

## Working for a Grade versus Working to Learn

Is there really a difference between working for a grade and working to learn? The answer to this question depends in part on how a grade is determined. If grades are based on tests that require detailed memorization of facts, dates, and definitions, the students' study time will probably be spent learning these details. There will be little opportunity to explore the thought questions that may be found at the end of the chapter. But would students actually explore these questions if their work were not graded?

Cullen and Cullen (1975) gave high school students a one-page library assignment and varied grading conditions in an attempt to find out whether the presence or absence of a grade made a difference. One group was told that completing the paper would mean "extra credit" — that is, it would add points to their grade, but they would not lose points if they did not do the paper. Another group was told that if they did not complete the extra assignment, their course grades would go down. The last group was invited to complete the paper simply for their own interest and enjoyment.

Papers were completed by 64 percent of the group who could lose points, 41 percent of the group who could improve their grades, and only 14 percent of those who had no grade incentive. This study demonstrates that if some assignments count toward the grade and others do not, students are likely to put their efforts where the grades are and let opportunities to complete projects "just for fun" slip through their fingers.

Some research indicates that if students receive external rewards for doing something they enjoy anyway, their motivation may actually diminish. They may be less likely to do the task for its own sake. Salili, Maehr, Sorenson, and Fyans (1976) found that actual performance on a task was not affected by the evaluation conditions, but that future performances often were. The three evaluation conditions in their study were (1) external evaluation (scores reported to the teacher and figured into the final grade; (2) self-evaluation (only the student knew his or her own score); and (3) peer evaluation (scores were indicated publicly but not included in the final grade). While performance on the task was not affected, students in the external evaluation group were less motivated to do tasks similar to the graded task in the future.

Other researchers (Lepper, Greene and Nisbett, 1973; Lepper and Green, 1975) have found that external rewards can decrease both current performance and motivation to continue. (We discussed this issue in Chapter 9.) One recommendation based on these findings would be to give a few *required* but *ungraded* assignments. Even when the work is ungraded, students should receive feedback on the good and the improvable aspects of their work.

As a teacher, you can use grades to motivate the kind of learning you intend students to achieve in your course. If you test only at a very simple but detailed level of knowledge, you may force students to choose between higher aspects of learning and a good grade in your course. If you set objectives more appropriately, including all applicable levels of cognitive,

*The tests and activities that determine grades also determine how students will spend their studying time. The skills and abilities measured on the test should represent worthwhile objectives.*

Ken Karp

affective, and psychomotor functioning, you will allow students to equate studying for learning with studying for a grade. When a grade reflects meaningful learning, working for a grade and working to learn are the same.

The Guidelines given here can act as a summary of the many different effects grades may have on students.

# Guidelines

## Minimizing the Detrimental Effects of Grading

**1. Avoid reserving high grades and high praise for answers that conform to your ideas or those in the textbook.**

EXAMPLES
- Give extra points for correct and creative answers.
- Withhold your opinions until all sides of an issue have been explored.
- Reinforce students for disagreeing in a rational, productive manner.

**2. Make sure each student receives some recognition for the parts of his or her work that are good or correct.**

EXAMPLES
- Give partial credit for partially correct answers.
- Consider token reinforcement, giving tokens for each correct part of work.
- Never lower grades as punishment for inappropriate classroom behavior.

**3. Make sure each student has a reasonable chance to be successful, especially at the beginning of a new task.**

EXAMPLES
- Pretest students to make sure they have prerequisite abilities.
- Individualize instruction based on pretest results.

**4. Balance written and oral feedback.**

EXAMPLES
- Consider giving short, lively written comments with younger students and more extensive written comments with high school students.
- When the grade on a paper is lower than the student might have expected, be sure the reason for the lower grade is clear.
- Tailor comments to the individual student's performance; avoid writing the same phrases over and over.

**5. Make grades as meaningful as possible.**

EXAMPLES
- Tie grades to the mastery of important objectives.
- Give ungraded assignments to encourage exploration.

**6. Base grades on more than just one type of criteria.**

EXAMPLES
- Use essay questions as well as multiple-choice items on a test.
- Grade oral reports and class participation.

Now that we have seen a few of the factors that might bias grading and some of the effects of grades on students, let us examine grading practices themselves. You should be in a good position to evaluate each approach by considering its potential effect on students, how well it fits with the subject matter you will be teaching, and how vulnerable it would be to bias.

In determining a final grade, the teacher must make a major decision. We discussed the issue on which this decision is based in the previous chapter. Should a student's grade reflect the amount of material learned and how well it has been learned, or should the grade reflect the student's status in comparison with the rest of the class? In other words, should grading be criterion-referenced or norm-referenced?

## Criterion-Referenced versus Norm-Referenced Grading

**Criterion Referenced**

In **criterion-referenced grading**, the grade represents a list of accomplishments. If clear objectives have been set for the course, the grade may represent a certain number of objectives met satisfactorily. When a criterion-referenced system is used, criteria for each grade generally are spelled out in advance. It is then up to the student to strive for and reach a level that matches the grade he or she wants to receive. Theoretically, in this system all students can achieve an A if they master the necessary number of specified objectives.

**Norm Referenced**

If grading is **norm-referenced**, the major influence on a grade is the student's standing in comparison with others who also took the course. If a student studies very hard but almost everyone else does too, the student may receive a disappointing grade, perhaps a C, in the course.

Different kinds of information are conveyed by criterion-referenced and norm-referenced testing and grading. Since any number of students can achieve any grade in a criterion-referenced system, there is no need to discriminate among the students. There are enough high grades to go around to those who will work for them. The grade does not imply that the student did better or worse than anyone else. Achievement, not a student's status relative to other members of the class, is reflected in the grade. Motivation to succeed tends to be higher among students when they know they are not obliged to compete for the small number of superior grades available. Actual academic improvement can be greater for these students (Kurtz and Swenson, 1951).

How does this fit in with the traditional purposes of grading? If grades are meant to help sort students out into piles of more and less successful achievers so that they can be grouped for instruction and assessed for college admission and employment, grades should discriminate between those who have performed well and those who have been less successful. In practice, many school systems would look askance at a teacher who turned in a roster filled with As and explained that all the students had attained the objectives. The assumption might be that if all the objectives could be attained by all the students, then more or tougher objectives were needed. Nevertheless, a criterion-referenced system may be acceptable in some schools. Let us consider an example.

**Figure 15–4  Criterion-Referenced Grades at the Secondary Level**

JERICHO JUNIOR HIGH SCHOOL
JERICHO, NEW YORK

EVALUATION

Teacher _____  Student _____

Counselor _____  Dates (from) _____ (to) _____

Analogy as a Thought Process   Grade _____   Subject English

Code: 1 The student has demonstrated that he has met the objective.
2 The student has demonstrated progress toward meeting the objective.
3 The student has demonstrated that at this time he has not met the objective.
4 The student has not demonstrated whether or not he has met the objective.
5 The objective does not apply at this time.

**BASIC INFORMATION:**

_____1. The student can identify comparisons which use *like, as, than,* and *is.*
_____2. The student can identify comparisons which do not use *like, as, than,* or *is. (The teacher threw the student out of class. Student + ball.)*
_____3. *The student can recognize the similarity in two unlike items.*

**UNDERSTANDING:**

_____1. The student can distinguish between the *is* of identity and the *is* of comparison. (I am John. I am a block of wood.)
_____2. The student can distinguish between the literal sense of a poem and the meaning suggested by its comparisons.

**APPLICATION:**

_____1. The student can compose original sentences which make a comparison without using words such as *like, as,* or *than.*
_____2. Given a comparison, the student can extend it into a paragraph.

*Grading and reporting: Current trends in school policies and programs.* Copyright 1972 by National School Public Relations Association. Reprinted by permission.

**A Criterion-Referenced System.**   Criterion-referenced grading has the advantage of relating judgments about a student to the achievement of clearly defined instructional objectives. Some school systems have developed reporting systems where report cards list objectives along with judgments about the student's attainment of each. Reporting is done at the end of each unit of instruction. The junior high report card shown in Figure 15–4 demonstrates the relationship between evaluation and the goals of the unit.

Curving Grades    **A Norm-Referenced System.**   One very popular type of norm-referenced grading is **grading on the curve.** As we noted in the previous chapter, the characteristics of the normal curve, or normal distribution, are well known. For example, we know that two-thirds of the distribution (68 percent) are clustered within 1 standard deviation of the mean. In grading on the curve, the middle of the normal distribution or "average" performance becomes the anchor on which grading is based. In other words, teachers look at the average level of performance, assign what they consider an "average grade" for this performance, and then grade superior performances higher and inferior performances lower.

Using Different Curves

If grading were done strictly on the normal curve, there would be an equal number of As and Fs, a larger number of Bs and Ds, and an even larger number of Cs. The grades would have to form a bell-shaped curve. For example, a teacher might decide to give 10 percent As and Fs, 20 percent Bs and Ds, and 40 percent Cs. This is a very strict interpretation of grading on the curve, and it makes sense only if achievement in the class follows the normal curve.

Grading on the curve can be done with varying levels of precision. The simplest approach is to rank-order the students' raw scores on a test and use this ranked list of scores as the basis for assigning grades. Such a distribution might look like this: 92 91 91 90 83 80 78 76 72 68 65 61 57 54 53 49 48 48 47 46 43 38 36 29. Knowing that two-thirds of the scores in a normal distribution should be in the middle, you might bracket off the middle two-thirds of the scores and plan to give those students Cs (or Bs, if you believed B was an average grade for the class in question). Some people prefer to use the middle one-third of the students rather than two-thirds as the basis for the average grade. Based on these two approaches, grades might be assigned as follows:

### Middle Two-Thirds Assigned Cs

| A | B | C | D | F |
|---|---|---|---|---|
| 92 | 91 91 90 | 83 80 78 76 72 68 65 61 57 54 53 49 48 47 46 43 | 38 36 | 29 29 |

### Middle One-Third Assigned Cs

| A | B | C | D | F |
|---|---|---|---|---|
| 92 | 91 91 90 83 80 78 76 | 72 68 65 61 57 54 53 49 | 48 47 46 43 38 36 | 29 29 |

This approximation to grading on the curve is very rough indeed. In these examples the distance between one letter grade and another is sometimes one point! Given the amount of error in testing, these examples probably do not represent a fair distribution of grades. You can correct some of these problems by introducing common sense into the process. For example, you may believe the following grade assignment is more fair:

Using Common Sense

### Adjusted Grades

| A | B | C | D | F |
|---|---|---|---|---|
| 92 91 91 90 | 83 80 78 76 72 | 68 65 61 57 54 53 | 49 48 47 46 43 38 36 | 29 29 |

In this case, the teacher began with the notion of a normal curve, then added a personal view of fairness and the meaning of the scores to improve the distribution of grades. You may notice that in this case the instructor has used the natural gaps in the range of scores to locate boundaries between grades. Between the A and B categories are 7 points, between the B and C, 4 points, and so on. Of course, if you adopt this system of using natural gaps in the ranking, students will not know the cutoff points for each grade until the end of the unit.

## Preparing Report Cards

No matter what kind of grading system you have, you will undoubtedly give several tests. In addition, you will probably assign homework or projects. Let us assume your unit evaluation plan includes two short tests (mostly multiple-choice questions but one essay), homework, a project, and a unit test. If you had a criterion-referenced system for testing and grading, how would you convert scores on these individual performances to the overall indications of mastery on a report card such as that shown in Figure 15–4? What about using a norm-referenced system? How do you combine results from individual tests and assignments to yield a final distribution of scores for the unit or semester grade?

Reporting Criterion-Referenced Grades

Let us consider criterion-referenced grading first. If you adopt this system, you cannot average or combine test scores or homework grades in a mathematical way. Since tests and assignments measure the mastery of particular objectives, it would be meaningless to average the students' mastery of adding two-digit numbers with their mastery of measuring with a ruler, although both might be objectives in arithmetic. Information from tests and assignments must be used instead to judge whether the student has met each of the objectives. On the report card, the objectives are listed and the student's level of proficiency in each is indicated.

Reporting Norm-Referenced Grades

Norm-referenced grading is a different story. In order to assign grades, the teacher must merge all the scores from tests and projects into a final score. Final grades are assigned based on how each student's final score compares with that of the rest of the students. But the usual procedure of simply adding up all the scores and averaging the total is often not appropriate, and it can be misleading. For example, assume two students took two tests. The tests were equally important and had the same weight in the overall unit. The students' scores were as shown in the tabulation below.

|  | Test 1<br>Class Mean = 30<br>Standard Deviation = 8 | Test 2<br>Class Mean = 50<br>Standard Deviation = 16 | Total<br>Raw Score |
|---|---|---|---|
| Leslie | 38 | 50 | 88 |
| Jason | 30 | 66 | 96 |

*Adapted from Chase (1978, p. 328).*

Total Scores Misleading

If we were to compute an average or rank the students based on their totals, Jason would be ahead of Leslie. But if we look at the class mean and standard deviation for each test, we see a different picture. On one test, Leslie's score was 1 standard deviation above the mean, and on the other her score was at the mean; Jason's record is exactly the same:

|  | Test 1 | Test 2 |
|---|---|---|
| Leslie | +1 SD | Mean |
| Jason | Mean | +1 SD |

If these two tests are really equally important, Jason and Leslie have identical records in relation to the rest of the class on these tests. To compare students' performances on several tests, the scores for each must be converted to a standard scale like a *T* score. More detailed instructions about how to do this are available in Terwilliger (1971). Most teachers do not calculate *T* scores for all their students, but the example shows how you must bring common sense to grading. Gross totals do not always reflect how well one student is doing in relation to others in the class.

## The Point System

One popular system for combining grades from many assignments is a point system. Each test or assignment is given a certain number of total points, depending on its importance. A test worth 40 percent of the grade could be worth 40 points. A paper worth 20 percent could be worth 20 points. Points are then awarded on the test or paper based upon specific criteria. An A+ paper, one that meets all the criteria, could be given the full 20 points; an average paper might be given 10 points. If tests of comparable importance are worth the same number of points, are equally difficult, and cover a similar amount of material, we may expect to avoid some of the problems Jason and Leslie encountered when the means and standard deviations of two supposedly comparable tests varied so greatly.

Let us assume a grade book indicates the scores shown in Figure 15–5.

**Figure 15–5    Points Earned on Five Assignments**

| Student | Test 1 20% 20 points | Test 2 20% 20 points | Unit Test 30% 30 points | Homework 15% 15 points | Project 15% 15 points | Total |
|---|---|---|---|---|---|---|
| Amy | 10 | 12 | 16 | 6 | 7 | _____ |
| Bert | 12 | 10 | 14 | 7 | 6 | _____ |
| Cathy | 20 | 19 | 30 | 15 | 13 | _____ |
| Doug | 18 | 20 | 25 | 15 | 15 | _____ |
| Ed | 6 | 5 | 12 | 4 | 10 | _____ |
| Frieda | 10 | 12 | 18 | 10 | 9 | _____ |
| Grace | 13 | 11 | 22 | 11 | 10 | _____ |
| Herbert | 7 | 9 | 12 | 5 | 6 | _____ |
| Isaac | 14 | 16 | 26 | 12 | 12 | _____ |
| Joan | 20 | 18 | 28 | 10 | 15 | _____ |
| Keith | 19 | 20 | 25 | 11 | 12 | _____ |
| Linda | 14 | 12 | 20 | 13 | 9 | _____ |
| Melody | 15 | 13 | 24 | 8 | 10 | _____ |
| Ned | 8 | 7 | 12 | 8 | 6 | _____ |
| Olivia | 11 | 12 | 16 | 9 | 10 | _____ |
| Peter | 7 | 8 | 11 | 4 | 8 | _____ |

How would you assign grades to students for this unit of work? Here are several possibilities:

1. Find the total number of points for each student and rank the students. Assign grades by looking for natural gaps of several points or imposing a curve (a certain percentage of As, Bs, and so on).

2. Convert each score to a percentage and average the percentages. Rank the students on percentages and proceed as above to look for gaps or impose a curve. Compare the results of this approach with the results of the one above.

3. Rank the students on each assignment. Then calculate each student's average rank for all five assignments. (If two students tie for one rank, they split the difference between that rank and the one below. For example, if two students tie for third place, they each get 3.5 and there is no fourth place.) Use the average rankings to determine overall ranks, then look for gaps or impose a curve on the overall ranks.

You might enjoy having your educational psychology class divide into groups and assign grades to the students in Figure 15–5, based on the three different methods. Even better, have pairs of groups try each method. You can see if your group's grades correspond to those of the other group using the same method. How about comparing the grades assigned by different groups using different methods?

## Percentage Grading

There is another approach to assigning grades to a group of students like those in Figure 15–5. The teacher can decide in advance the percentage of the total number of points that will merit an A, B, C, D, and F. Then any number of students can earn any grade. This procedure is very common; you may have experienced it yourself from the student's end. Let us look at it more closely, because it has some frequently overlooked problems.

Grading symbols such as A, B, C, D, F are probably the most frequent means of reporting at the present time. School systems often establish equivalent percentage categories for each of these symbols. The percentages vary from school district to school district, but two typical ones are as follows:

Two Different
Standards

90–100 = A; 80–89 = B; 70–79 = C; 60–69 = D; below 60 = F
94–100 = A; 85–93 = B; 76–83 = C; 70–75 = D; below 70 = F

As you can see, although both districts have an A to F five-point grading system, the average achievement required for each grade differs between the two.

Assumptions

But can we really say what is the total amount of knowledge available in, for example, eighth-grade science? Are we sure we can accurately measure what percentage of this body of knowledge each student has attained? To use **percentage grading** appropriately, we would have to know exactly what there was to learn and exactly how much each student had learned. These conditions are seldom met, even though teachers use the cutoff points to assign grades as if measurement was so accurate that a one-point difference was meaningful: "In spite of decades of research in educational and psychological measurement, which has produced more defensible methods, the concept [of percentage grading], once established, has proved remarkably resistant to change" (Zimmerman, 1981, p. 178).

## Figure 15–6    Knowledge of Grading Practices

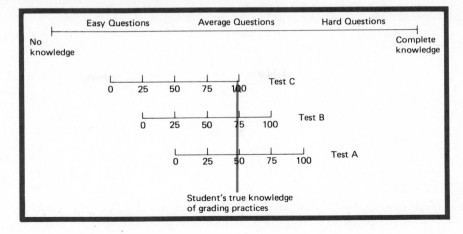

Suppose teachers are required to adhere to such a grading system, using the percentage average from grade books to assign the appropriate letter grade automatically. By giving very easy tests, they could ensure that a large number of students did well and received high grades in the course. By administering more difficult tests, the teacher might well produce more lower and failing grades. Let us assume that teachers want to grade fairly and so attempt to construct and administer tests that truly reflect the content of the course at an appropriate difficulty level. Is precise evaluation of the percentage of knowledge achieved by the student possible by this method?

Look at Figure 15–6. Let us assume we can actually define the domain, *knowledge of grading practices.* We can identify all the skills, information, concepts, facts — all the knowledge that makes up this domain. Next we assume we can order by difficulty all possible questions based on this knowledge. Now we create three valid and reliable tests. On Test A the questions are moderately hard, on test B they are of average difficulty, and on test C they are very easy. A student with a level of knowledge of grading practices as indicated by the arrow in Figure 15–6 would score about 50 percent correct on Test A, 75 percent on Test B, and 100 percent on Test C — depending, of course, on how severely each test is graded.

Any grading system prescribed or suggested by the school can be influenced by particular concerns of the teacher. Do not be fooled by the seeming security of absolute percentages. Your own grading philosophy will continue to operate, even in this system. Because there is more concern today with specifying objectives and criterion-referenced evaluation, especially at the elementary grade levels, several new methods for evaluating student progress against predetermined criteria have evolved. We will look at two: the contract system and mastery learning.

## The Contract System

When applied to the whole class, the **contract system** indicates the type, quantity, and quality of work required for each number or letter grade in the system. Students agree or "contract" to work for a particular grade by meeting the specified requirements. For example, the following standards may be established:

Examples
of Standards

*F:* Not come to class regularly or not turn in the required work.

*D:* Come to class regularly and turn in the required work on time.

*C:* Come to class regularly, turn in the required work on time, and receive a check mark on all assignments indicating they are satisfactory.

*B:* Come to class regularly, turn in the required work on time, and receive a check mark on all assignments except three that achieve a check plus, indicating superior achievement.

*A:* As above, plus a successful oral or written report on one of the books listed for supplementary reading.

Effects
of Contracts

This example contains more subjective judgment than would be ideal. However, contract systems reduce student anxiety about grades and can eliminate subjective judgment to whatever extent the teacher wants by specifying the quantity and quality required for various grades. The contract system can be applied to individual students and function much like an independent study plan.

Problems

Unfortunately, the system can also lead to overemphasis on quantity of work. Teachers may be too vague about the standards that differentiate acceptable from unacceptable work. It is sometimes difficult to tell a student that a particular assignment is completely unsatisfactory ("Is it that bad?"), so many teachers end up accepting almost every piece of work. In addition, if a school system requires a five-point grading system and all students contract for and achieve the highest grade, the teacher will wish administrative approval for the system had been obtained in advance.

The contract system can be modified by including a **revise option.** Then students whose work was not satisfactory or who achieved a check but hoped for a check plus could be allowed to revise their work. A check might be worth 75 points and a check plus 90 points; a check plus earned after revision could be worth 85 points—more than a check but less than a check plus earned the first time around. This system allows students to improve their work but also rewards getting it right the first time. Some quality control is possible, since students earn points not just for quantity, but also for quality. In addition, the teacher might be less reluctant to judge a project unsatisfactory, since students are given a way to improve their work (King, 1979).

## The Mastery Approach

We mentioned earlier that many psychologists are not satisfied with the normal curve model of grading. They believe effective instruction ought to ensure that most students master a majority of the learning objectives. **Mastery learning** is an approach to teaching and grading based on the assumption that, given enough time and the proper instruction, most students can master a majority of the learning objectives (Bloom, 1968; Block, 1971).

Using a Mastery
System

To use the mastery approach, teachers must break a course down into small units of study. Each unit might involve mastering several specific objectives. Students are informed of the objectives and the criteria for meeting each. In order to leave one unit and move on to the next, students usually have to attain a minimum mastery of the objectives. This may be defined as a certain number of questions answered correctly on the unit test. Letter grades for each unit can be based on levels of performance on the unit test. Students who do not reach the minimum level of mastery and students who reach this minimum level but want to improve their performance (thus raising their grade) can recycle through the unit and take another form of the unit test.

Determining Grades Under a mastery system, grades can be determined by the actual number of objectives mastered, the number of units completed, the proficiency level reached on each unit, or some combination of these methods. Students can work at their own pace, finishing the entire course quickly if they are able or taking a long time to reach a few objectives. Of course, if only a few objectives are met by the end of the marking period, the student's grade will reflect this. The Keller plan discussed in Chapter 5 is a version of a mastery approach.

Problems There are problems with this approach. Since all students do not cover the same material, the course must be self-contained. Using a mastery approach to teach Algebra I would not ensure that all students had the prerequisites for Algebra II, since some might never get past solving an equation with one unknown. In addition, teachers must have a variety of materials to allow students to recycle through objectives they failed to meet the first time. Usually just dealing with the same materials all over again will not help. If the entire school uses a mastery system, however, some of these problems are solved.

It is also important to have several tests for each unit. Students quickly figure out that taking the test and failing is better preparation for passing the unit than studying all the material, since an attempt at the test tells them exactly what to study for the next try (Cox and Dunn, 1979). This approach can lead to memorizing and learning a few specifics, but not really understanding the material.

Individual Differences Even though the idea is that most students can master the material if given enough time and appropriate instruction, individual differences persist. Some students will leave a unit with much better understanding than others. Some will work much harder to take advantage of the learning opportunities (Grabe and Latta, 1981). Some will be frustrated instead of encouraged by the chance to recycle ("You mean I have to do it *again*!"). And finally, the word "mastery" may be misleading. Completing a mastery unit successfully usually means that the students are ready to move to the next unit, not that they are "masters" of the information (Cox and Dunn, 1979).

## Grading on Effort and Improvement

Grading on effort and improvement is not really a complete grading system, but rather a theme that can be run through most grading methods.

Penalizing Good Students Should teachers grade students based on how much they learn or on the final level of learning? One problem with using improvement as a standard for grading is that the best students improve the least, since they are already the most competent. Do you want to penalize these students because they knew quite a bit initially and the teaching and testing has limited how much learning they can demonstrate? After all, unless you assign extra work, students can do only so much before they run out of things to do.

Effort Many teachers try to include some judgment of effort in final grades. But effort is difficult to assess. Are you certain your perception of each student's effort is correct? Clement (1978) suggests a system for including a judgment about effort in the final grade called the **dual marking system.** Students are

573

assigned two grades. One (usually a letter) indicates the actual level of achievement. The other, a number, indicates the relationship of the achievement to the student's actual ability and effort. For example, a grade of B could be qualified as follows (Clement, 1978, p. 51):

**Dual Marking System**

$B_1$: Outstanding effort, better achievement than expected, good attitude.
$B_2$: Average effort, satisfactory in terms of ability.
$B_3$: Lower achievement than ability would indicate, poor attitude.

Of course, this system assumes that the teacher can adequately judge true

# Guidelines

## Using Any Grading System

**1. Explain your grading policies to students early in the course and remind them of the policies regularly.**

EXAMPLES
- Give older students a grading handout describing the assignments, tests, grading criteria, and schedule of testing.
- Explain to younger students in a low-pressure manner how their work will be evaluated.

**2. Set reasonable standards.**

EXAMPLES
- Discuss workload and grading standards with more experienced teachers.
- Give a few formative tests to get a sense of your students' range of abilities before you give a graded test.

**3. Base your grades on as much objective evidence as possible.**

EXAMPLES
- Plan in advance how and when you will test.
- Keep a portfolio of student work. This may be useful in student or parent conferences.

**4. Be sure students understand test directions.**

EXAMPLES
- Outline the directions on the board.
- Ask several students to explain the directions.

**5. Ask clear questions focusing on the important material that has been taught.**

EXAMPLES
- Check your questions to see if they have too many "ands," "ors," or "in additions."
- Stay close to your test plan outlining the key objectives in the course.

**6. Watch for cheating during tests.**

EXAMPLES
- Walk around the room.
- Be firm but reasonable when you encounter cheating.

ability and effort. A grade of $D_1$, $D_2$, or $F_2$ could be quite insulting! A grade of $A_3$ or $F_1$ should not be possible. But the system does have the advantage of recognizing hard work and giving feedback about a seeming lack of effort. An $A_2$ might tell very bright students: "You're doing well, but I know you could do better." This could help the students to expect more of themselves and not slip by on high ability. The overall grade—A, B, C—still reflects achievement and is not changed (or biased) by teachers' judgment of effort.

Few teachers are able to create a grading system completely to their own liking; the school system generally has ideas of its own. The Guidelines given here should help you work within whatever system you follow.

---

spot bad questions, gauge the difficulty of the test, and estimate the time needed.

**EXAMPLES**
- Outline the main points of an essay question.
- Use a blank form of an objective test as a key.

**8. Correct, return, and discuss test questions as soon as possible.**

**EXAMPLES**
- Have students who wrote good answers read their responses for the class; make sure it is not the same person each time.
- Discuss why wrong answers, especially popular wrong choices, are incorrect.

**9. As a rule, do not change a grade.**

**EXAMPLES**
- Make sure you can defend the grade in the first place.
- DO change any clerical or calculation errors.

**10. Guard against bias in grading.**

**EXAMPLES**
- Ask students to put their names on the backs of their papers.
- Use an objective point system when grading essays.

**11. Keep pupils informed of their standing in class.**

**EXAMPLES**
- Write the distribution of scores on the board after tests.
- Schedule periodic conferences to go over work from the previous weeks.

**12. Give students benefit of the doubt. All measurement techniques involve error.**

**EXAMPLES**
- Unless there is very good reason not to, give the higher grade in borderline cases.
- If a large number of students miss the same question in the same way, revise the question for the future and consider throwing it out for that testing.

*Source: Adapted from A. M. Drayer, **Problems in middle and high school teaching: A handbook for student teachers and beginning teachers.** Boston: Allyn & Bacon, 1979, pp. 182–187.*

# BEYOND GRADING: COMMUNICATION

No number or letter grade conveys the totality of a student's experience in a class or course. Both students and teachers sometimes become too focused on the end point: the grade. Children and adolescents spend the majority of their waking hours for many months of the year in school, where teachers are the relevant adults. This gives teachers the opportunity and the responsibility to know their students as people.

**Student Conferences**

Every subject area can allow time for teachers to observe students at work and interacting with one another. With a little reorganization, it should also be possible to use some classes as "conference time" when the teacher sees students individually. It is common in elementary schools for teachers to assign marks or make comments concerning each student's nonacademic achievement. Enthusiasm, ability to work with others, conformity to classroom rules, self-confidence, and other aspects of social and motivational behavior may be included in the report. Some secondary schools also report this type of information to parents.

Conferences and careful observation of students in a somewhat structured way can make such judgments more accurate and valuable, subjective though they will continue to be. Observing particular students in a planned way, on some regular schedule, will keep you from being attentive only to the troublemakers and failing to notice the little boy in the back who is squinting at the blackboard and missed the eye screening.

**Parent Conferences**

Conferences with parents are often expected of teachers in elementary school and can be equally important in junior high and high school. At every level, the success of the conference depends on a number of factors. At the simplest level, both parties must be present. By scheduling conferences at a time convenient for the parents and making firm appointments, confirmed in writing or by phone, these problems can be minimized.

**Communication Skills**

The more skilled teachers are in the area of interpersonal communication, the more effective they will be at conducting these conferences. Listening and

*The parent-teacher conference may not seem like a very good idea to the student sitting on the hot seat. Nevertheless, such conferences are a valuable adjunct to the grading system. What shows up only in black and white on a report card may have many shades of gray that can be better dealt with in a full and open discussion.*

Mimi Forsyth/Monkmeyer Press Photo Service

problem-solving skills such as those discussed in Chapter 10 can be particularly important. Especially when dealing with parents or students who are angry or upset, make sure you really hear the *concerns* of the participants, and not just their words.

The conference should not be a time for lecturing parents or students. As the professional, the teacher needs to take a leadership role while remaining sensitive to the needs of the other participants. The atmosphere should be friendly and unrushed. Any observations about the student should be as factual as possible, based on observation or information from assignments. The focus of the conference must be positive if positive results are to be obtained. Begin and end with encouraging and favorable points, even if some problems are raised in between. Information gained from student or parent should be kept confidential.

Privacy Act

A recent ruling, the Buckley Amendment, is likely to have an effect on you as a teacher. Also called the Family Educational Rights and Privacy Act of 1974 and the Educational Amendments Act of 1974, this law states that all educational agencies must make test results and any other information in students' records available to the students and/or their parents. If the records contain information students or parents believe is incorrect, they can challenge such entries and have the information removed if they win the challenge. This means that the information in a student's records must be based on firm, defensible evidence. Tests must be valid and reliable. Your grades must be justified by thorough testing and observation.

We see the effects of the Buckley amendment each year when we write recommendations for students. Students now have the right to see letters of recommendation that were once confidential. Consequently, there is a tendency for many employers or graduate schools to pay less attention to these letters, assuming that the professor has not been candid because the student might see the letter. For this reason, many recommendation forms allow students to waive their right to see the letters.

## SUMMARY

1. Two very important and difficult tasks for teachers are testing students and assigning grades. Many schools have established policies about testing and grading practices, but individual teachers decide how these practices will be carried out.

2. In the classroom, tests may be formative (ungraded, diagnostic) or summative (graded, summarizing the student's learning).

3. Two common formats are objective and essay questions.

4. Objective tests, including multiple-choice, true-false, and matching items, should be written with specific guidelines in mind.

5. Writing and scoring essay questions requires careful planning plus criteria to discourage bias in scoring.

6. Many factors besides quality of work can influence grades: the teacher's beliefs about the student's ability or effort, the student's handwriting or voice quality, the student's general classroom behavior, perhaps even the students' names.

7. The effects of grades on students depend in part on the students' attributions of causes for the success or failure, as well as the students' grading history.

8. High grades tend to encourage continued effort and higher levels of aspiration; low grades tend to discourage effort and lead to lower levels of aspiration.

9. Students need experience in coping with failure, so standards must be high enough to encourage effort and perhaps occasional failure.

10. Grading can be either criterion- or norm-referenced.

11. Criterion-referenced report cards usually indicate how well each of several objectives has been met by the individual student.

12. One popular norm-referenced system is grading on the curve, based on a ranking of the students in the class.

13. Many schools use percentage grading systems, but the degree of difficulty of the tests and the scoring criteria often influence the results.

14. Two alternatives to traditional grading are the contract and mastery approaches.

15. No matter what system you use, you will have to decide whether you want to grade on effort or improvement and whether you want to limit the number of good grades available.

16. Not every communication from the teacher needs to be tied to a grade. Communication with students and parents can be an important step in understanding students and creating effective instruction. In addition, today students and parents have a legal right to see all the information in the students' records.

## KEY TERMS

| | |
|---|---|
| formative measurement | criterion-referenced grading |
| pretest | norm-referenced grading |
| diagnostic test | grading on the curve |
| summative measurement | percentage grading |
| objective testing | contract system |
| stem | revise option |
| distractor | mastery learning |
| halo effect | dual marking system |

## SUGGESTIONS FOR FURTHER READING AND STUDY

BLOCK, J. J. and ANDERSON, L. W. *Mastery learning in classroom instruction.* New York: Macmillan, 1975. This is a volume in the Current Topics in the Classroom Series. Although very short (about 90 pages), it covers such topics as a philosophy of mastery learning, planning and constructing mastery units, preparing students to use the mastery approach, and assigning and reporting grades.

BLOOM, B. S., HASTINGS, J.T., and MADAUS, G. F. (Eds.). *Handbook on formative and summative evaluation of student learning.* New York: McGraw-Hill, 1971. An encyclopedia on the subject of creating classroom tests. There are chapters describing formative and summative classroom evaluation in almost every subject area.

CLIFFORD, M. M. Effects of failure: Alternative explanations and possible implications. *Educational Psychologist,* 1979, 14, 44–52. This article demonstrates that the effects of failure can be positive as well as negative.

GLASER, R. The future of testing: A research agenda for cognitive psychology and psychometrics. *American Psychologist,* 1981, 36, 923–936. Glaser shows the role of cognitive science in designing and interpreting tests.

GRONLUND, N. E. *Constructing achievement tests* (3rd ed.). Englewood Cliffs, NJ: Prentice-Hall, 1982. A complete guide to creating and scoring multiple-choice essay, matching, true-false, and short-answer tests. Very clear — an essential work for teachers who test, and that's everyone!

GRONLUND, N. E. *Preparing criterion-referenced tests for classroom instruction.* New York: Macmillan, 1973. As the author states in the preface: "This book is intended as a practical guide for the preparation and use of criterion-referenced tests in classroom instruction." The book is a very brief and understandable introduction to the principles and uses of criterion-referenced testing. There are chapters on mastery learning, developmental learning, test planning, writing test questions, and applications of criterion-referenced testing in many situations.

# Teachers' Forum

## Problems with CRT

A teacher has decided to use criterion-referenced testing. She likes the idea that students must achieve a certain level of mastery before moving on to new material. It is now only the sixth week of school. The class ranges from two children still studying the first week's assignment all the way to the highest group that is ready for what the teacher had planned to present in the tenth week. Planning for all levels has become impossible, and many children are losing interest. Class discussions seem out of the question because there is no common ground. What should the teacher do now? Can you implement criterion-referenced testing and avoid these pitfalls?

**Try Several Techniques**

Solicit aides, parents, other adults and peers to assist those in need of tutoring. Where possible develop a "jigsaw" procedure where groups are formed containing students with a variety of achievement levels — each member having responsibility for gathering certain kinds of information to share with the "home" groups, thereby fitting the pieces of the "puzzle" together to create the finished product. Examine teaching style, materials, and techniques regularly to determine if adaptations can be made to help the slower-moving students as well as the others. Organization and management of the test results may lessen the classroom problems.

Jacqueline G. Dyer, Second- to Eighth-Grade Teacher
*Classical Junior Academy, St. Louis, Missouri*

**Capitalize on Strengths**

I would use CRT and do so as a basis for forming groups within the classroom. It is possible to keep interest by expanding the learning horizontally instead of vertically. There are many enrichment activities that can be introduced. Does the school have a learning center where the more able student can do research? Can that student help others do experiments, write test questions, or integrate the subject with another discipline?

Charlotte Ross, Second-Grade Teacher
*Covert Avenue School, Elmont, New York*

## Grade-Consciousness

It is probably true that most grading systems diminish the pleasure found in learning for its own sake. Any high school teacher knows that students will put in much more effort when a project or paper is graded instead of merely "required." We teach children to work for the grade, not the knowledge. Is there a need to counteract this grade-consciousness? How do you provide experiences in the joy of learning for your students?

**Explore the Meaning of Grades**

I have always incorporated at least one grade per quarter when everyone gets an A — a personal autobiography is the best to start with. Then listen to the initial proud reactions: "I got an A!" Keep listening: "Hey, stupid got an A, too!" "What is this?" "How can I get an A and Susie get one, too?" Quell the outrage and discuss why they feel *they* deserve an A but no one else does. Then talk about grades and what they mean and don't mean. This helps to let the student understand grades and begin to journey toward self-evaluation.

Bonnie Hettman, High-School English Teacher
*Lima Central Catholic School, Lima, Ohio*

## Parental Pressure

One of your students is under great pressure from his parents to get good grades. As far as you can tell, however, his average grades seem to reflect his true abilities. You have just sent out report cards, and the boy's parents have scheduled a conference with you. They seem to think you may be discriminating against their son in some way or another.

**Plan Ahead**  My first bit of advice is: Don't wait for report card time to communicate with parents! Send home simple weekly progress reports, work samples, tests (good and bad) for parents' signatures, and other information. Keeping parents up to date eliminates virtually all misunderstandings. *Should a problem still exist, then follow this routine:* (1) Greet parents with a positive attitude; acknowledge their concerns and listen; try to get to the root of the problem. (2) Be prepared with data to support the grades (test scores, work samples, standardized test scores, etc.). (3) Emphasize the positive. He does so well in _____. He's so thoughtful, helpful, and cooperative. (4) Have recommendations handy: "Here's how we can work together." Try to help them appreciate the fact that most of us are average people who can accomplish a great deal when we are motivated properly but can be terribly defeated when pressured to do more than our abilities allow.

Joan H. Lowe, Fifth-Grade Teacher
*Russell Elementary School, Hazelwood, Missouri*

**Accept Reality**  I would first check the student's history, including his grades and teachers' comments from previous years, to be certain that the child's work is not slipping. I would have available work samples of his, plus samples of outstanding students for comparison. Test scores, both standardized and class, should be on hand to show his placement in the class. I would discuss with the parents the necessity for us all to accept the student as he is, to give him encouragement and deserved credit when it is due. It might be wise to point out what their son could stand to lose if we all push him too hard: his self-confidence, his leisure time, his happy disposition, and his spirit of cooperation.

Shirley Wilson Roby, Sixth-Grade Reading Teacher
*Lakeland Schools, Shrub Oak, New York*

# Glossary

**Abstract**  A brief summary of the key procedures and results of a research study.

**Academic engaged time**  The active time a student spends on learning tasks. There are two factors that determine this use of time: the amount of opportunity the student has to learn and the student's use of that opportunity.

**Acceleration**  Encouraging students to move more quickly from one cognitive level to another.

**Accommodation**  Piaget's term for the changing or enlarging of established cognitive structures (schemes) in order to understand a novel object or experience.

**Achievement motivation**  Motivation for achievement in a field for its own sake rather than for extrinsic reward.

**Achievement tests**  Tests that measure how much a student has learned in a subject area.

**Action-zone**  The area in a classroom arranged in rows and columns that includes the front row and the center columns. Students seated in this area tend to interact more with the teacher and to be higher achievers.

**Active teaching**  Principles of instruction similar to direct instruction in which the teacher actively directs learning and carefully monitors students to make sure they are doing the work, much of which involves mastering basic skills.

**Adaptation**  According to Piaget the cognitive process through which we deal with the environment by changing the environment (assimilation) or changing ourselves (accommodation).

**Advance organizers**  In Ausubel's approach to teaching, an initial statement about the subject matter, which provides a structure for all additional information thereby making it easier to learn and remember.

**Aggression**  Hostile feelings, physical or verbal behaviors aimed at doing harm to another.

**Altruism**  A desire to help others in need with no expectation of external reward.

**Analogical thinking**  One approach to problem solving in which new or unfamiliar ideas are related to more familiar ones: reasoning by analogy.

**Androgynous**  Having both masculine and feminine psychological characteristics.

**Antecedents**  Events that precede a behavior.

**Anxiety**  A feeling of general uneasiness and tension; a sense of foreboding.

**Aptitude-treatment interaction**  A term that refers to the fact that there is an interaction between an individual student's capabilities and different teaching methods. As a result of this interaction, a particular teaching method may not be equally effective with all students.

**Articulation**  Difficulty in correct pronunciation of appropriate linguistic sounds. Articulation problems may include the substitution of one sound for another or the complete omission of a sound.

**Assertive discipline**  An approach to classroom management developed by Canter and Canter that stresses the rights of teachers to teach and the rights of students to learn.

**Assimilation**  Piaget's term for the process of making sense of experiences and perceptions by fitting them into previously established cognitive structures (schemes).

**Attitudes**  A relatively enduring perception, learned through positive and negative experiences and/or modeling.

**Attribution theory**  A cognitive view of motivation that emphasizes the role of the person's beliefs about the causes for success and failure.

**Autonomy vs. doubt**  This conflict marks Erikson's second stage of development during which young children begin to actively explore their environment.

**Aversive stimulus**  An unpleasant stimulus, one that a subject will work to avoid.

**BASIC**  An acronym for Beginners All-purpose Symbolic Instructional Code, the most popular programming language for microcomputers.

**Behavioral (psychology)**  A theoretical orientation in psychology that emphasizes the study of observable behaviors instead of internal events such as thinking and emotions.

**Behavior-content matrix**  One possible method for organizing teacher goals and objectives. Each general objective is broken down into two components. The first component is student behavior and the second is course content. A matrix or chart is then designed with student behaviors listed across the top and course content down the side. At each point of intersection of these two components the teacher can design specific instructional objectives.

**Being needs**  Maslow's term for the three higher level needs in his hierarchy: intellectual achievement, aesthetic appreciation, and self-actualization.

**Bimodal distribution**  A group of scores that has two modes that is, two different scores that tie for being the most frequently occurring score.

**Bottom-up processing**  Making sense of information by

analyzing the basic elements and combining them to form larger units. For example, in reading this would mean understanding the material by analyzing and recognizing letters and words then building meaning from these basics. The alternative is top-down processing.

**Brain lateralization** The specialization of the two hemispheres of the brain. For most people, the right hemisphere (or half) of the brain appears to be involved with spatial relations, imagery, nonverbal problem solving and simultaneous processing of information. The left side is involved with verbal abilities and sequential processing.

**Brainstorming** One possible strategy for developing creative thought in which ideas are generated but not evaluated until all possible suggestions have been made.

**Branching program** Programmed instruction materials that use a multiple choice format. Each incorrect response directs students onto various remediation frames that clarify the material and send students back to try again.

**Byte** The basic unit of information in a computer. The symbol K refers to 1,024 bytes, and is used to specify the size of a computer's memory (32K = 32 × 1,024 bytes).

**CAI** An acronym for computer-assisted instruction — use of computers directly for teaching.

**Causal relationship** A connection between two or more variables in which cause and effect can be demonstrated, for example, a relationship that allows the researcher to state that A causes B.

**Cause-and-effect relationships** These exist when one variable is shown to have a causative effect on a second variable (or group of variables). This relationship can be demonstrated only in controlled experimental settings.

**CBE** An acronym for computer-based education — general applications of computers in support of classroom teaching and management.

**Central tendency** A score that is typical or representative of a group of scores. The three measures of central tendency are mean, median, and mode.

**Cerebral palsy** Difficulty in movement and coordination resulting from lesions in various parts of the brain which form prior to, during, or soon after birth.

**Chip (microchip)** A tiny piece of silicon smaller than a fingernail on which circuit elements are etched for carrying out computer operations.

**Chromosomes** Long, tiny elements in the body carrying the genes that transmit inherited characteristics from one generation to the next.

**Classical conditioning** A type of learning that occurs when a neutral stimulus is paired with a stimulus that elicits an emotional or physiological response. After repeated pairings of these two stimuli the previously neutral stimulus will elicit a similar response.

**Classroom management** The teacher's responsibility to maintain the classroom as a healthy learning environment, relatively free of behavior problems.

**Classification** An important cognitive ability mastered in Piaget's concrete operational stage which involves the grouping of objects into multiple categories. This

differentiation depends on the ability to focus on one or more characteristics of the objects at once.

**CMI** An acronym for computer-managed instruction — use of computer for support functions such as testing, recordkeeping, scheduling and prescribing.

**Coding system** An organizational framework for putting concepts in a hierarchical relationship so the more specific examples are placed under the broader concepts.

**Cognitive development** The increasing complexity of the mental processes of thinking and problem solving.

**Cognitive (psychology)** A theoretical orientation in psychology that emphasizes the acquisition and use of knowledge to solve problems. Cognitive psychologists study how people learn and remember information, and why some people do these things better than others.

**Cognitive strategies** Cognitive skills for perceiving, analyzing, learning, thinking, and remembering which enable individuals to process the information in the environment. For example, one cognitive strategy for solving new problems is brainstorming.

**Cognitive styles** Stable ways in which people differ in perception, encoding, and information storage.

**Cohesive group** A classroom group that has a sense of unity and shared standards.

**Compensation** A Piagetian term for the knowledge that changes in one dimension can be offset by the changes in another dimension. In order to solve conservation problems one must develop this knowledge.

**Concept** A collection of experiences or ideas that are grouped together based on some common properties.

**Concrete operations** The third stage of Piaget's theory of cognitive development during which children become able to think logically, but only about problems that can be visualized or considered in concrete terms.

**Conditioned response (CR)** In classical conditioning a learned response made to a previously neutral stimulus. This response is acquired through repeated pairings of the neutral stimulus with an unconditioned stimulus.

**Conditioned stimulus (CS)** A previously neutral stimulus that is paired with an unconditioned stimulus and eventually produces a response when presented alone.

**Confederate** An assistant in an experiment who pretends to be a subject as part of the experimental manipulation.

**Confidence interval (or "standard error band")** The student's score plus and minus the standard error of measurement of the test.

**Consequences** Events that follow a behavior.

**Content validity** A test has content validity if it measures the knowledge and skills covered in a class.

**Conservation** The concept that certain properties of an object (weight, length, etc.) remain the same regardless of changes in its other properties (shape, position, etc.).

**Construct validity** A test has construct validity if it is a good measure of the theoretical construct it intends to measure. Examples of theoretical constructs are intelligence and creativity.

**Contiguity learning** A principle of learning stating that whenever two events occur together repeatedly they will become associated. Later, when only one of these events occurs (a stimulus), the other will be remembered too (a response).

**Contingency contract** A behavioral program in which teachers draw up individual contracts with students. The contracts outline specifically what the student must do to be rewarded and what the reward will be.

**Continuous reinforcement** A schedule in which every correct response is reinforced.

**Control group** In an experiment, a group of subjects that receives no special treatment.

**Convergent questions** Questions about concrete facts that have only one correct answer.

**Convergent thinking** A more common type of thinking that results in one conventional solution to a problem.

**Correlation** A statistical method that can determine the direction and strength of a relationship between variables.

**Creativity** An individual's capacity to produce original or novel products or solutions to problems.

**Criterion-referenced grading** In this grading system the criteria for each grade are spelled out in advance and everyone has a chance to earn the highest possible grade.

**Crystallized intelligence** One of Cattell's factors of intelligence—the many abilities that are highly valued and taught by the culture e.g., reading, making change, or balancing a checkbook.

**Cue** A stimulus that gives an individual information about the consequences that will follow different behaviors. Generally speaking, this stimulus sets the occasion for a specific response.

**Cultural pluralism (cultural diversity)** The existence of many different cultures within a group; encouraging different cultures to maintain their distinctive qualities even when they become part of a larger group.

**Culture** The rules for acceptable behaviors, attitudes, and beliefs established by a social group.

**Culture-free test** An attempt to make tests fairer for minority groups by including items that are not biased in favor of or against any cultural group.

**Declarative knowledge** The facts we know; the content of knowledge. See also procedural knowledge.

**Deficiency needs** Maslow's term for the four lowest needs in his hierarchy: survival, safety, belonging, and self-esteem. When these needs are not met one's motivation to satisfy them increases. Once met, however, motivation focusing on them decreases.

**Defining attributes** Features shared by the members of a category which combine to characterize or define that overall category. These features are also referred to as distinctive features. For example, one defining attribute of the category "square" is four equal sides.

**Democratic leadership** One possible strategy for organizing the classroom in which the teacher solicits the opinions and ideas of the class so that decisions are made by consensus. This strategy is also referred to as participatory leadership.

**Dependent variable** In experiments, the variable that may change as a result of changes in the independent variable.

**Developmental crises** The specific struggles an individual encounters at each stage of social development as outlined, for example, in Erikson's theory.

**Development** The orderly changes that occur in an individual over time from conception to death.

**Deviation IQ** A score determined by comparing the individual's performance on an intelligence test with the average performance for that age group. The average is usually set at 100.

**Diagnostic-prescriptive cycle** An approach to the diagnosis of exceptional children which stresses the development of a prescription describing effective teaching techniques for each student. The steps of this cycle are (1) evaluation of current functioning, (2) development of teaching techniques, (3) testing the techniques, (4) writing a plan, (5) frequent evaluation of progress.

**Diagnostic tests** Tests administered to identify specific problems a student is having that interfere with learning.

**Dialect** A variation of a language spoken by a particular group. This variation is usually influenced by geography.

**Direct instruction** An instructional method that emphasizes the mastery of basic skills. This method is characterized by several basic themes: clear organization of content, student involvement, academic engaged time, a strong sense of direction, mastery of materials, and a pleasant, busy atmosphere.

**Direct method** An approach to bilingual education in which the main goal is the development of the majority language and the student's primary language is not used as a medium of instruction.

**Direct observation** A method for collecting information in which a researcher watches the individual or situation while the events of interest are actually happening.

**Discovery learning** Bruner's method for teaching concepts by guiding students through experiences with specific examples of the concepts, then helping the students deduce general rules and relationships. Contrast with expository teaching.

**Discrimination** Distinguishing between and responding differently to two similar stimuli.

**Disk (disc)** A medium, resembling a phonograph record, used for storing information apart from the computer's memory.

**Disk drive** A device for storing information on and retrieving it from disks.

**Distractor** The wrong answers among the alternatives in a multiple choice question. They should be plausible in order to be chosen by students who have only a partial understanding of the subject.

**Distributed practice** Practicing material to be remembered for brief periods of time. There are rest times in between practice times.

**Divergent thinking** A type of thinking used to create several different and unusual solutions to a problem. This type of thought is often equated with creativity.

**Domains** Three areas of classification found in Bloom's

taxonomy for educational objectives. They are cognitive, affective, and psychomotor.

**Down's syndrome (mongolism)** One known organic cause for retardation in which the individual has an extra chromosome.

**Downtime** The time when the computer is out of service for any reason.

**Dual code theory of memory** This theory states that information is stored in memory as visual images and/or verbal representations. Thus, according to this theory, it is easier to remember information that can be represented both visually and verbally since there are two "anchors" in memory.

**Dual marking system** Giving a letter grade for the quality of the work by qualifying this grade with a number indicating effort.

**Education** A formal process through which society transmits its values, beliefs, knowledge and symbolic systems to new members so as to maximize their adaptability.

**Educationally blind** Vision so limited that special teaching materials are necessary.

**Educational psychology** A discipline concerned with understanding and improving the teaching/learning process, using the theories and methods of psychology, as well as its own unique theories and methods.

**Egocentric** Believing that others experience a particular event the same way you do or have the same reactions.

**Eg-rule method** A teaching method in which many examples of a rule are first presented and then a general definition is determined.

**Elaboration** A method for processing information that involves adding meaning, extending, expanding, and forming associations with knowledge already in long-term memory.

**Empathetic listening** One possible approach to student problems in which the teacher listens to the student's communication and then paraphrases what the student has said (including any implicit emotions or meanings).

**Empathy** the ability to feel an emotion as it is experienced by another.

**Environment-behavior research** Studies the effect of physical classroom setting on the behavior of students and teachers.

**Epilepsy** A general name given to a group of nervous diseases marked by spontaneous neuron firings in the brain and resulting convulsions (of varying degrees).

**Equilibration** Searching for a balance between one's cognitive schemes and one's experiences or perceptions of the environment. This balance is achieved through the modification of thought.

**Essay tests** Tests in which students are required to organize cognitive materials and express them in composition or essay form.

**Evaluation** The inspection of all information available concerning the students, teacher, and educational program to ascertain the degree of change in the students and to make valid judgments concerning the educational program being used.

**Experimentation** A method of research in which investigators manipulate one or more variables (independent variables) and measure the effects of this manipulation on another set of variables (dependent variables).

**Expository teaching** Ausubel's approach to instruction which is based on reception rather than discovery.

**Expressive objectives** Eisner's approach to outlining instructional objectives in which teachers clearly define the activities for the students but do not specify exactly what the students might learn from these activities. This approach is based on the belief that it is not always possible to predict the outcome of activities.

**Extinction** The gradual disappearance of a learned response. In operant conditioning this occurs when reinforcement is withheld. In classical conditioning extinction will result when the conditioned stimulus is no longer paired with the unconditioned stimulus.

**Extrinsic motivation** Motivation caused by external events or rewards outside the learning situation itself.

**Faces of intellect** Guilford's theory describing 120 separate intellectual abilities. These abilities involve using different operations (evaluation, convergent production, divergent production, memory, cognition) to act on particular types of content (figural, symbolic, semantic, behavioral) to achieve different types of products (units, classes, relations, transformations, implications).

**Factor analysis** A statistical technique that groups individual items on a questionnaire into several overall categories or factors. This technique allows for the examination of such data in broader terms.

**Feature analysis** A theory of perception stating that we recognize examples of concepts by checking for distinctive features or characteristics that define the concept. For example, we recognize the letter "A" by checking for two lines meeting at approximately a 45 degree angle with a horizontal line going across about half way down.

**Figure-ground** A concept from Gestalt psychology which refers to the way in which individuals organize stimuli to create reality. According to this concept people tend to focus on a basic figure so that it clearly stands out from its background and the stimuli surrounding it become less important.

**Finger spelling** A method for communicating manually that has a specific hand position for each letter.

**Fixed-interval** A reinforcement schedule in which a predetermined fixed-time interval must occur between each reinforced response regardless of the number of responses the subject makes.

**Fixed-ratio schedule** A schedule of reinforcement in which a predetermined, fixed number of responses must occur in between each reinforced response.

**Fluid intelligence** One of the two factors of intelligence outlined by Cattell. It involves basic processes of thinking and problem solving that develop without formal education.

**Foreclosure** One of the alternatives during Erikson's

stage of Identity v. Role Confusion. The individual has made a commitment related to vocation and moral values without seriously considering many choices, usually by adopting the views of parents.

**Formal operations** Piaget's final stage of cognitive development in which students are able to think abstractly and deal with purely verbal or logical problems

**Formative measurement** Occurs before or during instruction for the purpose of guiding or forming educational plans.

**Frames** The small steps or units used in programmed instruction. Most of these steps contain some text and at least one question requiring a response from the students.

**Frequency distribution** A list of the number of people who receive each score on a test.

**Functional fixedness** The inability to use things in a new way. This is one possible barrier to problem solving.

**Generalization** A principle of conditioning stating that once a conditioned response is established, similar stimuli may evoke the same response. The more similar the stimulus, the greater the chance for generalization.

**Generativity vs. self-absorption** This is the alternative presented to individuals in Erikson's seventh stage of development. At this point individuals will develop a sense of generativity by reaching out beyond their own concerns to embrace those of society and future generations. However, people may also become preoccupied with their own well-being and so develop a sense of self-absorption.

**Generate-test method** A method of solving problems by testing solution as they occur to you without systematically limiting the solutions you consider.

**Genes** Carried by the chromosomes, these tiny substances transmit inherited characteristics from one generation to the next.

**Genotype** The genetic makeup of the individual, not necessarily the same as the phenotype or observable characteristics.

**Gestalt** A term that literally means a pattern or configuration and also refers to the belief that people tend to organize their perceptions into patterns in order to make sense of the world around them.

**Goal-directed activity** One of the major cognitive accomplishments of the sensorimotor period in which children begin to direct previously random behavior toward some environmental goal.

**Goal structure** Johnson and Johnson's term for the structure of the interpersonal interactions students become involved in when working towards a goal. They outline three such structures: cooperative, competitive, and individualistic.

**Grade equivalent score** The grade level of the average student whose score equals a given raw score. If your score on a test equals the average score for students who are halfway through the 11th grade, then your grade equivalent score would be 11.5 on that test. This score is so often misinterpreted that it should never be used.

**Grading on the curve** Assigning grades so that they follow a normal curve with an equal number of As and Fs, Bs and Ds, and the largest number of Cs.

**Group dynamics** The study of how groups function and the effects of group membership on individual members.

**Group focus** A teacher's ability to keep as many students as possible involved in class activities.

**Halo effect** The tendency to view particular aspects of a student's performance positively based on a generally positive impression of that student.

**Hardware** The physical equipment that goes into a computer, consisting of mechanical, magnetic, electrical, and electronic devices.

**Hawthorne effect** An influence that can occur in experiments when subjects know they are being studied and change their behavior as a result.

**Heritability ratio** The proportion of the variance among individuals on a particular characteristic that is due to genetic factors, assuming the individuals experienced the same environmental conditions.

**Higher-order interactions** Complex relationships between three or more variables in an experiment that becomes increasingly hard to interpret.

**Histogram** A bar graph showing how many people achieved each score on a test, or, more generally, the frequency of occurrence of each observation.

**Holophrases** Single words used during an early stage of language development to communicate a whole thought or complex idea, for example saying "Juice!" to communicate "My juice is gone and I want more!"

**Hyperactive** An amount of physical activity or movement that is excessive in comparison to other individuals of the same age and culture.

**Hypothesis** A statement about the predicted relationships among the variables being investigated in a study.

**Identity** A Piagetian term for the knowledge that a quantity does not change unless something is added or taken away. In order to solve conservation problems, one must develop this knowledge.

**Identity achievement** One of the alternatives during Erikson's stage of Identity v. Role Confusion. The individual has made a strong commitment after seriously considering many choices related to vocation and moral values.

**Identity diffusion** One of the alternatives during Erikson's stage of Identity v. Role Confusion. The individual remains uncommitted to any choices related to vocation and moral values.

**Identity vs. role diffusion** This alternative marks Erikson's fifth stage of social development. As individuals enter adolescence they must come to grips with the question, Who am I? If adolescents are encouraged to experiment with different roles during this period they may successfully develop an integrated and coherent sense of self. If, however, adolescents are not encouraged or given suggestions in this search for identity they may become trapped in a state of role diffusion.

**I-messages** One of Gordon's strategies for changing student behavior in which teachers describe the problem behavior, the concrete effects that behavior has on them as teachers and how the behavior makes them feel. This approach frees the students to change their behavior voluntarily.

**Independent variable** In experiments, this is the variable changed or treated to determine the effects of these changes on other variables being studied. See also dependent variable.

**Individualized education program (IEP)** A program written for the student by the teacher, parents, a qualified school official, and the student (whenever possible). This program should set forth goals, services, and teaching strategies for that student.

**Individualized instruction** Instruction that has been assigned to meet the needs, interests and abilities of the individual student.

**Industry vs. inferiority** This is the basic alternative in Erikson's fourth stage of development. In this period, children develop a desire to complete productive work on their own.

**Information processing** Theories of learning that assume that individuals have internal mental structures for processes such as perceiving, coding information, and recalling that information.

**Initiative vs. guilt** Erikson's third stage of development is marked by this alternative. In this period children are beginning to test their powers at adult tasks.

**Insight** Sudden realization of the solution to a problem.

**Instructional objectives** A clear and unambiguous description of the goals or changes in the students the teacher wishes to observe as a result of instruction.

**Integrity vs. despair** This is the alternative that marks Erikson's final stage of development. As individuals approach old age they tend to take stock of their lives. Some feel a sense of satisfaction over their accomplishments, others feel intense despair.

**Intellectual skills** Gagne's term for an individual's ability to use symbols.

**Intelligence** The individual's current level of functioning (a product of inherited abilities and experiences) that allows the person to acquire, remember, retrieve, and use knowledge to solve problems and adapt to the world.

**Intelligence quotient (IQ)** A score determined by dividing the individual's mental age by chronological age and multiplying by 100. The formula is IQ = MA/CA × 100.

**Interference** Due to the limited capacity of short term memory storage, older information becomes weaker and will eventually be lost as new information is taken in. When short term memory storage is filled, then any new information will interfere with the retention of older information.

**Intermittent reinforcement** A schedule in which correct responses are reinforced frequently but not every time. This schedule is most effective in maintaining already acquired responses.

**Intimacy vs. isolation** This is the crisis that accompanies Erikson's sixth stage of development. It is based on the ability to successfully develop an intimate relationship with another without fear of losing one's own identity in the process.

**Intrinsic motivation** An internal source of motivation such as curiosity or the desire to learn.

**Intuitive thinking** According to Bruner, the ability to go beyond the information given and to develop hypotheses based on sudden, dramatic perceptions.

**Jigsaw classroom** A classroom design that emphasizes and reinforces cooperation among students as opposed to competition.

**Juvenile delinquency** The violation of laws by individuals under a specific age.

**Keller Plan** A system of individualized instruction that does not require any special materials or computers. This system uses many of the principles of programmed instruction (specific goals, small steps, immediate feedback, and self pacing) and incorporates lectures, proctored testing, and tutoring. This plan is also referred to as The Personalized System of Instruction (PSI).

**Kilobytes (K)** A measure of the computer's memory capacity. Roughly speaking, a kilobyte is the capacity to store 1,000 characters.

**Laissez-faire leadership** One strategy for organizing a class in which the teacher is completely permissive and does not tell students directly what to do.

**Law** A principle that has stood the test of time and repeated investigation.

**Law of effect** Thorndike's law of learning: Any action that produces a satisfying state will be repeated in a similar situation.

**Learning** A relatively permanent change in an individual's capabilities as a result of experience or practice. These internal changes cannot be directly observed, so they must be inferred from changes in the individual's directly observable behaviors.

**Learning center** A specified area of a classroom or school where students can pursue a specific topic at their own ability level. These centers provide materials and activities so that students may pursue individual interests in a subject area. Centers may be used for enrichment, skill building, or exploration.

**Learning package** Self-instructional materials that are written at the students' level and allow them to work at their own pace. Packages specify objectives but present students with alternate ways of reaching objectives.

**Least restrictive placement** Educating a child in the most normal situation that is possible given the child's special problems and needs.

**Level of aspiration** The individual's goals for achievement, often a compromise between the high levels the person wants to achieve and his or her fear of failing in the attempt.

**Levels of processing theory** A theory of memory stating that the depth of processing of information determines how well we will remember that information. Information processed superficially will not be remembered as well as information that is thoroughly processed and connected with knowledge already in memory.

**Linear programs** A set of programmed instruction

materials advocated by Skinner. Linear programs have two important features: (1) students must actively create an answer as opposed to choosing one from a multiple-choice format. (2) frames are designed to keep the amount of errors at a minimum.

**Longitudinal study** A type of research design for studying the same subjects over several years to observe changes that take place across time.

**Long-term memory** Memory for information that exists over long periods of time, perhaps permanently.

**Low vision** Some useful vision within a few feet but limited distance vision.

**Mainstreaming** The movement of students with special learning needs out of special education classes and into regular classes.

**Massed practice** Studying material to be remembered for a single extended period of time.

**Mastery learning** An approach to teaching and grading that is based on the assumption that every student is capable of achieving most of the course objectives if given enough time and the proper instruction.

**Maturation** Genetically preprogrammed changes that occur naturally and spontaneously. These changes proceed regardless of outside influences.

**Mean** The arithmetic average of a group of scores. This is the most commonly used measure of central tendency.

**Meaningful** Associated with knowledge already in long-term memory. Meaningful lessons are well organized, clarify new terms, draw clear connections between related elements and make natural use of knowledge already in long-term memory through examples, analogies, etc.

**Measurement** A process that uses a rule to assign a numerical description to some attribute of a person, object, or event.

**Median** The central score of a distribution; the score which divides the distribution into two equal subgroups. Next to mean, this is the most common measure of central tendency.

**Mental age** A concept used in intelligence testing. Mental age is a derived score based on the assigned age level of the items completed correctly by the test taker.

**Mental retardation** Subaverage, general intellectual functioning accompanied by poor behavioral adaptation both of which have developed before age 18.

**Metacognition** Knowledge about cognitive processes such as thinking, learning, and remembering; awareness of how to monitor and use your own cognitive abilities to solve life problems, for example, knowing when a problem has gotten harder and you need to try a new approach.

**Metacommunication** An underlying or hidden message of a communication. Although this may not be the message the speaker intended to send, it may be the message that is received.

**Metalinguistic** Knowledge about language; knowing the rules and exceptions of language usage.

**Microcomputer** A small computer (about the size of a television or even smaller) that has large capacities because it contains microchips (tiny bits of silicon with thousands of electrical circuits).

**Minimum competency testing** A system that requires students to pass a test of basic information or skills before they can graduate or continue to the next level.

**Mnemonics** The art of memory. The purpose of mnemonics is to connect new information with previously existing knowledge. The strategies of mnemonics are most useful when the information to be learned has very little inherent meaning.

**Mode** The score that occurs most often in a distribution. This is one of three measures of central tendency.

**Modem** A device allowing a computer to use telephone lines to communicate.

**Monitor** A video display unit, which uses a cathode ray tube (CRT) to generate characters. It resembles a regular TV set, but has a higher degree of resolution (greater clarity).

**Moral dilemmas** Hypothetical situations where the "correct" or "moral" course of action is unclear.

**Moratorium** One of the alternatives during Erikson's stage of Identity v. Role Confusion. The individual is in the midst of the identity crisis but probably will soon make a strong commitment to personal vocational and moral values.

**Motivation** Factors that energize and direct behavior toward a goal.

**Motor skills** The knowledge of a sequence of body movements necessary to perform an act and the ability to perform those movements.

**Movement management** A teacher's ability to keep the class moving by using a variety of ideas and changing the pace when necessary.

**Multicultural education** Educational goals and methods that teach students the value of cultural diversity.

**Native language approach** One approach to bilingual education in which teachers work with the language the student naturally exhibits as well as gradually building a knowledge of the majority language.

**Needs** Those things that an individual requires for his overall well-being.

**Negative instances** A stimulus that is *not* an example of a concept.

**Negative reinforcement** The removal of a stimulus after a behavior has occurred that leads to an increase in the behavior. An example would be allowing a child to come out of the corner when he or she is quiet.

**Neobehaviorists** A group of behavioral psychologists who have expanded their view of learning to incorporate changes in certain internal, unobservable states such as expectations, beliefs, thoughts, etc.

**Neutral stimulus** During a classical conditioning experiment, a stimulus that elicits no particular response at first, but later, after conditioning, elicits a response similar to that of the unconditioned stimulus.

**Normal distribution** A bell-shaped distribution. In a normal curve, scores are distributed symmetrically about the mean, and the mean, median, and mode are all the same.

**Norming sample**  A large sample of subjects as similar as possible to the students who will be taking a particular standardized. The scores of this sample serve as a basis of comparison for later scores.

**Norm-referenced grading**  This system reflects a student's standing in comparison with others in the class; few students can earn the highest possible grade in this system.

**Norm-referenced testing**  Tests in which scores are determined by a comparison to the performances of other people who have taken the test.

**Norms**  In referring to groups, the standards for acceptable or "normal" behavior in the group.

**Objective tests**  Tests using multiple choice, fill-in, true-false, or any similar format. Knowledge comprehension, application, and analysis objectives are best measured through the use of objective tests.

**Objective permanence.**  Piaget's term for the understanding that an object exists in the environment apart from one's perception of it and action on it. Children make this cognitive step durng the sensorimotor stage of development.

**Observation**  A method of research in which investigators watch and record behaviors as they occur without any intervention.

**Observational learning (modeling)**  Learning by observing others and notng the consequences of their actions.

**One-way logic**  The ability of preoperational children to think through an operation logically in only one direction. Children at this stage are unable to reverse the direction of the operation.

**Operant conditioning**  A type of learning in which behaviors are strengthened or weakened depending upon their consequences and antecedents.

**Operants**  A Skinnerian term for behaviors that are not simple responses to stimuli but rather are deliberate actions made on the environment. According to Skinner these operants are affected and changed by the consequences that follow them.

**Operationalize**  Defining objectives in specific terms so that they can be more easily observed and measured.

**Operations**  Actions carried out through logical mental thought processes rather than through physical manipulations.

**Organization**  Piaget's term for the systemization of cognitive perceptual information into meaningful patterns called schemes.

**Origins**  De Charm's term for individuals who are in control of their own achievements due to their skills at goal setting and their willingness to take responsibility for their own actions.

**Orthopedic devices**  Devices such as braces, crutches, wheelchairs, etc. used by physically handicapped students.

**Overgeneralization**  In learning language, children may use one word for many similar objects, for example, calling all four-legged animals "dogs."

**Overlapping**  A teacher's ability to supervise and keep track of several activities simultaneously.

**Overlearning**  Practicing a task until it is learned perfectly. At this point practice no longer leads to improvement. The skill is resistant to forgetting and is easily retrieved when needed.

**Overregularization**  In learning language, children may learn a rule and apply it to all situations, even when the result is incorrect, for example, adding "ed" to all words to express past tense ("breaked," "comed," "gived").

**Part learning**  Breaking down a list of items to be learned into smaller segments. This concentration on a limited number of items is a useful strategy since only a few items can enter long term storage at one time.

**Pawns**  DeCharm's term for individuals who feel powerless and think they have no control over their fate.

**Peer rating**  A method for collecting information about students by asking their classmates to make judgments, rankings, ratings, or other evaluations.

**Percentage grading**  Converting performance on class work to a percentage and then assigning grades based on predetermined cutoff such as 93% to 100% is an A.

**Percentile rank**  A comparison of an individual's raw score with the raw scores of the norming sample. This comparison tells the test taker the percent of students in the norming sample whose scores fall at or below his or her own score.

**Perception**  The process of interpreting or giving meaning to the sensations detected by sense organs (vision, hearing, touch, etc.).

**Peripherals**  Accessory devices, such as printers and modems, which transfer information when connected to a computer.

**Personal development**  Changes in an individual's personality over time.

**Phenotype**  The observable characteristics of the individual such as eye color. Not necessarily the same as the genotype or underlying genetic makeup.

**Physical development**  Orderly changes in bodily functions and structure that occur over time.

**Polygenetic inheritance**  Inheritance of a particular characteristic or ability that is affected by many different genes.

**Positive instances**  A stimulus that is an example of concept.

**Positive practice**  A method of correcting students by having them practice the correct response several times immediately after making an error.

**Positive reinforcement**  An object or event that is presented following a behavior and serves to reinforce that behavior. Some examples are food, physical contact, or social praise.

**Prägnanz**  The basic principle of the Gestalt theory of perception stating that we make sense of what we perceive by reorganizing it to be more simple, complete, and regular. In other words, we try to make what we experience fit a category we already know.

**Premack principle**  A principle developed by David Premack stating that engaging in a high-frequency behavior (or preferred activity) may act as reinforcement for the completion of a low-frequency behavior (or less-preferred activity). In the application of this principle the low-frequency behavior should come first.

**Preoperational** The second stage in Piaget's theory of cognitive development. During this stage "childhood logic" is evident. Children are not yet capable of using adult logical operations.

**Presentation punishment** The presentation of a stimulus that has the effect of decreasing or suppressing the behavior that produced it. Examples: spankings, reprimands, running laps.

**Pretest** A formative test given before instruction to determine what the students already know and what they are ready to learn.

**Principle** A relationship between two or more factors that has been established through repeated study and experimentation.

**Printer** A peripheral device which prints characters on paper, producing a "hard copy."

**Problem solving** The creation of a new solution to a novel problem rather than simply applying previously learned rules to the situation.

**Procedural knowledge** The skills and procedures we are able to perform, the use of declarative knowledge.

**Procedures** Systems for dealing with routine and predictable tasks in the classroom such as handing out papers or correcting homework.

**Programmed instruction** A set of instructional materials that students can use to teach themselves about a particular topic. This instructional approach features self-pacing, immediate feedback, and division of materials into small units (frames).

**Projective tests** An indirect method for obtaining a diagnosis of personality organization by interpreting an individual's responses to relatively ambiguous stimuli. These tests are based on the assumption that subjects will project their own needs, attitudes or fears into their responses.

**Propositional networks** Mental structures of interconnected units of knowledge called propositions. A proposition is the smallest unit of information that can be judged true or false.

**Prosocial behavior** Behavior that is beneficial to society (cooperation empathy, altruism, etc.)

**Prototype** The best representative of a particular category.

**Psychology** The study of human behavior, mental processes, development and learning.

**Psychomotor** One of three domains in Bloom's taxonomy for educational objectives. In this domain, teachers outline objectives for student movement and motor skills which are divided into six categories: reflex movements, basic fundamental, perceptual abilities, physical abilities, skilled movements, and nondiscursive communication.

**Psychosocial theory** A theory that describes the relationship between the social relationships and tasks required of an individual in a particular culture, and the psychological development of that individual.

**Punisher** Any event that decreases or suppresses the behavior that produced or preceded it.

**Punishment** Using a punisher to decrease the likelihood that the behavior will occur again. Putting a child in the corner is an example of punishment.

**Random** Without a definite pattern or plan; following no rule.

**Recitation** A specific teaching approach using *structure* (setting a framework), *solicitation* (asking questions within that framework) and *reactions* (praising, correcting, or expanding student responses to those questions).

**Rehearsal** Repeated practice. In the case of memory, the mental rehearsal of information in short term memory is a factor in transferring that information into long term storage.

**Reinforcement** Using a reinforcer to increase the likelihood that the behavior will occur again.

**Reinforcer** Any event that increases the behavior that produced it.

**Reliability** A test is reliable if it is consistent in its measurement on repeated administrations.

**Removal punishment** The removal of a stimulus that has the effect of decreasing or suppressing the behavior that produced it. Examples: fines, loss of privileges.

**Replication** The process of repeating research to assure that different experimenters will get the same results.

**Reprimands** Criticisms for misbehavior. When used as a method for stopping a problem behavior, soft private reprimands are much more effective at decreasing the behavior than are loud and public reprimands.

**Resource room** A separate classroom in which a student can receive extra help in a problem area. A resource room is generally equipped with special materials and a specially trained teacher.

**Response** Any physiological or psychological change or process that results from stimulation.

**Response cost** A behavioral method for decreasing undesirable behavior that involves the loss of a reinforcer as a result of the infraction of rules.

**Response set** A tendency to continue responding in a particular way, even when the situation requires a new response.

**Resultant motivation** The overall tendency of one's motivation, a product of the individual's strongest overriding need. Resultant motivation depends on which need is greater, the need to achieve or the need to avoid failure.

**Reversibility** A Piagetian term for the mental ability to think back through an operation from the end to the beginning. This ability is necessary to the solving of conservation tasks.

**Revise option** This system gives students the option to improve on work already completed in a contract grading system.

**Ripple effect** A process through which student inhibitions are strengthened or weakened by observing the consequences that result when another student performs the inhibited behavior.

**Rule-eg method** A teaching method in which a general

definition or rule is stated first and then particular examples of that rule are considered.

**Rules** Gagne's term for a learned capability to express relationships among two or more concepts. For example, the rule for how to calculate area describes a relationship between length and width.

**Satiation** One method used to stop a problem behavior in which students are required to continue the behavior until they are tired of doing it. In using this approach teachers must take care not to give in before the students do.

**Schema** In cognitive learning, a large, complex unit of knowledge that organizes information. A schema serves as a guide describing what to expect in a given situation, what to look for, how elements should fit together, the usual relationships among elements and so on. A schema is like a model or stereotype.

**Schemes** A Piagetian term for the cognitive framework individuals use to organize experiences and perceptions of their environment. These basic cognitive units become increasingly complex as development occurs. This term refers to both ideas and motor patterns of behavior.

**Seat work** That portion of students' school work that is done independently. Seat work often includes reading, drills, answering questions, completing worksheets, etc.

**Self-actualization** Maslow's term for the realization of personal potential and self-fulfillment.

**Self-concept** How people view themselves physically, emotionally, socially, and academically.

**Self-fulfilling prophecy** A phenomenon in which believing or predicting that something will occur causes it to happen.

**Self-instruction** A method for controlling your own behavior by reminding yourself of the sequence of steps to follow in completing a particular task. This approach has been especially helpful in training impulsive children to be more deliberate.

**Self management** The capability to regulate and manage your own life, set your own goals and provide yourself with reinforcement. Teachers may help students to develop self-management skills through programs that allow them to set their own goals, observe and keep records of their own work and progress, and evaluate their own performance.

**Self-report** A method for collecting information about a person in which the individual being studied responds to questions and provides data directly to the experimenter.

**Semantics** The way meaning is organized in language.

**Sensorimotor** The earliest stage of development in Piaget's theory. This stage occurs during infancy (0–2 yrs.) and is marked by exploration of the environment through motor action and sense perception.

**Sensory register** A brief holding point for sensory information. During this brief period of 1/4 second, we select the information that will be further processed.

**Serial position effect** A phenomenon in which items at the beginning and end of a list are most easily remembered.

**Seriation** A cognitive ability, mastered during the concrete operational stage, involving the arrangement of objects or events in sequential order along some dimension.

**Shaping** A method for developing an appropriate behavior in which the teacher rewards responses that are successively more similar to the ultimate desired response (successive approximations). In order to use this method, teachers must break down the desired complex behavior into a number of smaller steps.

**Short term memory** A phase of memory in which information is held for a relatively short period (approximately 20 seconds) and will disappear unless rehearsed.

**Sign language** A system of hand signals and symbols that communicate words and concepts.

**Skinner box** A small experimental chamber equipped with a food tray and a bar (for rats) or a disc (for pigeons) which is connected to a food hopper.

**Social cognition** The process of understanding the thoughts, viewpoints, emotions, and intentions of other people.

**Social development** Changes in the way an individual relates to other people and to society.

**Social isolation** See time out from reinforcement.

**Social learning theory** A theoretical orientation in psychology that draws on both cognitive and behavioral perspectives to explain how people learn. A major factor in this theory is the role of learning by observing other people.

**Socioeconomic status (SES)** A sociological term used to describe variations in wealth, power, and prestige of individuals in society.

**Software** The programs and accompanying documentation for use with computers.

**SOMPA** System of Multicultural Pluralistic Assessment; an individual test of cognitive, perceptual-motor and adaptive abilities that attempts to take the culture of the individual into account in the assessment process.

**Spasticity** Involuntary contraction of muscles which is characteristic of many forms of cerebral palsy.

**Speech impairment** A classification for students who can't produce efficient speech sounds due to stuttering, difficulties in articulation, or voicing.

**Stand-alone** A computer unit that functions independently of other units. Microcomputers belong to this category.

**Standard error of measurement** An estimation of how much an individual's score would vary if the test were given repeatedly. A reliable test should have a small standard error of measurement.

**Standardized tests** Tests that have been tried out with many students and revised based upon these trials. Standardized tests have standard administration and scoring procedures.

**Stanine scores** Whole-number scores that combine

some of the properties of percentile ranks with some of the properties of standard scores.

**State anxiety** Anxiety arising in response to factors in the situation.

**Stem** That part of a multiple choice item which asks the question or poses the problem.

**Stimulus** Any event in the environment.

**Structure** Bruner's term for the fundamental ideas, relationships, and patterns that make up a subject matter.

**Subsumer** Ausubel's term for the general concept that heads the coding system of a subject area. It is given this name because all other more specific concepts are subsumed under it.

**Student Teams–Achievement Divisions (STAD)** A system developed by Slavin for using cooperation, competition, and rewards to increase student motivation.

**Summative measurement** Occurs at the end of an instructional unit for the purpose of assessing the student's final level of achievement.

**Stuttering** A problem in speaking that involves repeating or prolonging sounds, thus interrupting the normal flow of speech.

**Subjects** The people or animals being studied in a research project.

**Task analysis** A system for breaking down a task into fundamental subskills. The first step is to define the final performance goal and then list the skills necessary to attain that goal. These skills are then broken down into subskills until a full picture is attained of all abilities (in proper sequence) necessary to achieve the ultimate goal.

**Taxonomy** A classification system. Bloom developed a taxonomy for educational objectives that divides those objectives into three domains: cognitive, affective and psychomotor.

**Teacher-directed leadership** One strategy for organizing a class in which the teacher makes the majority of the decisions with little class input.

**Teacher rating** A method for collecting information about students by asking their teachers to make judgments, rankings, ratings, or other evaluations.

**Telegraphic** A stage in learning language when children use only the most important words, as in "Eric want cookie!"

**Test** A series of questions, exercises, or other tasks for measuring ability, skill, knowledge, performance, etc.

**Thematic Apperception Test (TAT)** A projective test developed by Murray in order to measure a person's needs. This test is based upon the assumption that people project their own needs into stories they create about ambiguous pictures.

**Theory** An integration of all known principles, laws, and information pertaining to a specific area of study. This structure allows the investigator to venture explanations for related phenomena and create solutions to unique problems.

**Time decay** The weakening and disappearance of information stored in short term memory caused by the passage of time.

**Time out from reinforcement** A behavioral method that involves the removal of a disruptive student from the classroom. The student is usually sent to an empty, uninteresting room for 5–10 minutes. This procedure is also referred to as *social isolation.*

**Time sharing** A system in which separate computer terminals are dependent on a central computer for operation.

**Token reinforcement** A behavioral program in which students can earn tokens for both good academic work and classroom behavior. When a number of tokens has been accumulated, students may exchange them for toys, food, free-time, privileges, etc.

**Top-down processing** Making sense of information by imposing an organization such as using context or general knowledge to recognize and understand individual elements. In reading this would mean using the sense of the story to recognize unfamiliar words and fill in meaning. The alternative is bottom-up processing.

**Trait anxiety** Anxiety that can be attributed to the individual's tendency to be anxious across many types of situations; a personal characteristic.

**Transfer** A phenomenon in which something that was previously learned facilitates (*positive transfer*) or hinders (*negative transfer*) current learning.

**True score** The mean of all scores an individual would receive if the same test were taken an infinite number of times. This is a theoretical concept never obtained in practice.

**Trust vs. mistrust** This struggle marks Erikson's first stage of development during which infants discover whether they can depend on the world around them.

**T-score** A standard score that converts the average raw score to 50 and uses a standard deviation of 10 so that the inconvenience of negative scores, found when using z-scores, is eliminated.

**Unconditioned response (UCR)** In classical conditioning an emotional or physiological response occurs to a particular stimulus without the benefit of any previous learning. For example, a loud buzzer will cause startle response without any previous conditioning.

**Unconditioned stimulus (UCS)** In classical conditioning, any stimulus that automatically produces an emotional or physiological response without the benefit of any previous learning. For example, in Pavlov's experiments meat produced the physiological response of salivation in the dogs without any previous learning.

**Validity** A test is valid if it measures what it claims to measure.

**Variable** Any characteristic that can change or vary from one person or situation to the next. Age, sex, test scores, attitudes, and number of books read are examples of variables.

**Variable-ratio schedule** A schedule of reinforcement in which a predetermined number of responses, which varies from trial to trial, must occur between each reinforced response.

**Variability** The tendency of scores in a group of scores to be scattered away from the central or average score.

**Variable-interval schedule** A reinforcement schedule in which a predetermined time interval, which varies from trial to trial, must pass between each reinforced response.

**Verbal information** Facts, terms, names, characteristics, etc. The items that make up the content of most lessons presented to the classroom.

**Vocational interest tests** Tests that are used to indicate the vocations a student might be interested in. To determine interests, a student's responses are compared to the responses of adults in various vocations.

**Voicing problems** Speech problems that include inappropriate pitch, quality, loudness, or flexibility.

**Withitness** A teacher's ability to communicate to students that he or she is totally aware of everything that happens in the classroom.

**Z-score** A measurement which indicates how many standard deviations above or below the average a student's raw score is.

# References

ABRAMI, P. C., PERRY, R. P., & LEVENTHAL, L. The relationship between student personality characteristics, teacher ratings, and student achievement. *Journal of Educational Psychology, 1982, 74,* 111–125.

ADAMS, R. S., & BIDDLE, B. J. *Realities of teaching: Explorations with video tape.* New York: Holt, Rinehart and Winston, 1970.

AIKEN, W. M. Story of the eight-year study. New York: Harper, 1942.

AINSWORTH, M. D. S. Infant-mother attachment. *American Psychologist, 1979, 34,* 932–937.

ALDERMAN, D. L., APPEL, L. R., & MURPHY, R. T. PLATO and TICCIT: An evaluation of CAI in the community college. *Educational Technology, 1978, 18,* 40–45.

ALDERMAN, D. L. & POWERS, D. E. The effects of special preparation on SAT-verbal scores. *American Educational Research Journal, 1980, 17,* 239–253.

ALLINGTON, R. Teacher interruption behaviors during primary-grade oral reading. *Journal of Educational Psychology, 1980, 71,* 371–377.

AMERICAN EDUCATIONAL RESEARCH ASSOCIATION, Committee on the Criteria of Teaching Effectiveness. *Journal of Educational Research* (2nd Rep.), 1953, 46, 641–658.

AMES, R. and LAU, S. An attributional analysis of student help-seeking in academic settings. *Journal of Educational Psychology, 1982, 74,* 414–423.

ANASTASI, A. Coaching, test sophistication, and developed abilities. *American Psychologist, 1981, 36,* 1086–1093.

ANDERSON, J. R. *Cognitive psychology and its implications.* San Francisco: W. H. Freeman, 1980.

ANDERSON, L., EVERTSON, C. M., & BROPHY, J. E. An experimental study of effective teaching in first-grade reading groups. *Elementary School Journal, 1979, 79,* 193–222.

ANDERSON, R. C. & MYROW, D. L. Retroactive interference of meaningful discourse. *Journal of Educational Psychology, 1971, 62,* 81–94.

ANDERSON, T. H. Study strategies and adjunct aids. In R. Spiro, B. Bruce, & W. Brewer (Eds.) *Theoretical issues in reading comprehension,* Hillsdale, N.J.: Lawrence Erlbaum, 1980.

ARMBRUSTER, B. B. & ANDERSON, T. H. Research synthesis on study skills. *Educational Leadership, 1981, 39,* 154–156.

ARMBRUSTER, F. E. The more we spend, the less children learn. *The New York Times Magazine,* August 28, 1977.

ARMENTO, B. A. *Teacher verbal cognitive behaviors related to student achievement on a social science concept test.* Unpublished doctoral dissertation. Indiana University, 1977.

ARONSON, E., BLANEY, N., STEPHAN, C., SIKES, J., & SNAPP, M. *The jigsaw classroom.* Beverly Hills, Calif.: Sage Publications, 1978.

ASHER, S. R., ODEN, S. L., & GOTTMAN, J. M., Children's friendships in school settings. In L.

G. Katz (Ed.), *Current topics in early childhood education.* Vol. 1. Norwood, N.J.: Ablex Press, 1977.

ASHTON, P. T. Cross-cultural Piagetian research: An experimental perspective. *Harvard Educational Review,* 1978 (Reprint Series No. 13).

ASHTON-WARNER, S. *Teacher.* New York: Simon & Schuster, 1963.

ATKINSON, J. W. *An introduction to motivation.* Princeton, N.J.: Van Nostrand, 1964.

ATKINSON, J. W. & BIRCH, D. *The dynamics of action.* New York: Wiley, 1970.

ATKINSON, J. W. & LITWIN, G. H. Achievement motive and test anxiety conceived as a motive to approach success and to avoid failure. *Journal of Abnormal and Social Psychology, 1960, 60,* 52–63.

ATKINSON, J. W. & RAYNOR, J. O. *Motivation and achievement.* Washington, D.C.: V. H. Winston, 1974.

ATKINSON, R. C. Mnemotechnics in second-language learning. American Psychologist, 1975, 30, 821–828.

ATKINSON, R. C. & RAUGH, M. R. An application of the mnemonic keyword method to the acquisition of Russian vocabulary. *Journal of Experimental Psychology: Human Learning and Memory, 1975, 104,* 126–133.

ATKINSON, R. C. & SHIFFRIN, R. M. The control of short-term memory. *Scientific American, 1971, 225,* 82–90.

ATKINSON, R. C. & SHIFFRIN, R. M. Human memory: a proposed system and its control processes. In K. W. Spence & J. T. Spence (Eds.), *The psychology of learning and motivation: Advances in research and theory* Vol. 2. New York: Academic Press, 1968.

AUSUBEL, D. P. The facilitation of meaningful verbal meaning in the classroom. *Educational Psychologist, 1977, 12,* 162–178.

AUSUBEL, D. P. *The psychology of meaningful verbal learning.* New York: Grune & Stratton, 1963.

AYLLON, T. & ROBERTS, M. D. Eliminating discipline problems by strengthening academic performance. *Journal of Applied Behavior Analysis, 1974, 7,* 71–76.

BABAD, E. Y. INBAR, J., and ROSENTHAL, R. Pygmalion, Galatea, and the Golem: Investigations of biased and unbiased teachers. *Journal of Educational Psychology, 1982, 74,* 459–474.

BACKMAN, M. Patterns of mental abilities: Ethnic, socioeconomic, and sex differences. *American Educational Research Journal,* Winter 1972, 9, (1), 1–11.

BALDWIN, J. D. & BALDWIN, J. I. *Behavioral principles in everyday life.* Englewood Cliffs, N.J.: Prentice-Hall, 1981.

BALL, S. A postscript: Thoughts toward an integrated approach to motivation. In S. Ball (Ed.). *Motivation in education.* New York: Academic Press, 1977.

BALLARD, K. D. and GLYNN, T. Behavioral self-

management in story writing with elementary school children. *Journal of Applied Behavior Analysis, 1975, 8,* 387–398.

BANDURA, A. *Aggression: A social learning analysis.* Englewood Cliffs, N.J.: Prentice-Hall, 1973.

BANDURA, A. The role of imitation in personality development. *Journal of Nursery Education, 1963, 18.*

BANDURA, A. The self-system in reciprocal determinism. *American Psychologist, 1978, 33,* 344–358.

BANDURA, A. *Social learning theory.* Englewood Cliffs, N.J.: Prentice-Hall, 1977.

BANDURA, A. *Social learning theory.* New York: General Learning Press, 1971.

BANDURA, A., ROSS, D., & ROSS, S. A. Vicarious reinforcement and imitative learning. *Journal of Abnormal and Social Psychology, 1963, 67,* 601–607.

BANY, M. A. & JOHNSON, L. V. *Educational social psychology.* New York: Macmillan, 1975.

BARNES, B. R. & CLAWSON, E. V. Do advance organizers facilitate learning? Recommendations for further research based on an analysis of 32 studies. *Review of Educational Research, 1975, 45,* 638–659.

BARRON, F. & HARRINGTON D. M. Creativity, intelligence, and personality. In M. Rosenzweig & L. W. Porter (Eds.), *Annual Review of Psychology.* Palo Alto, California: Annual Reviews Inc., 1981.

BARTLETT, F. C. *Remembering: A study in experimental and social psychology.* New York: Macmillan Co., 1932.

BAUMAN, R. P. Teaching for cognitive development: Intelligence can be taught. *The Andover Review. A Journal for Secondary Education,* 1978, 83–100.

BAUMRIND, D. The development of instrumental competence through socialization. In A. Pick (Ed.), *Minnesota symposium on child psychology.* Vol. 7. Minneapolis: University of Minnesota Press, 1973.

BECKER, W. C. ENGLEMANN, S., & THOMAS, D. R. *Teaching 1: Classroom management.* Chicago: Science Research Associates, 1975.

BECKER, W. C. & GERSTER, R. A follow-up of follow-through: The later effects of the direct instruction model on children in 5th and 6th grades. *American Educational Research Journal, 1982, 19,* 75–92.

BEE, H. *The developing child* (3rd ed.). New York: Harper and Row, 1981.

BEE, H. L. VANEGEREN, L. F., STREISSGUTH, A. P., NYMAN, B. A. & LECKIE, M. S. Social class differences in maternal teaching strategies and speech patterns. *Developmental Psychology, 1969, 1,* 726–734.

BEJAR, I. I. & BLEW, E. O. Grade inflation and the validity of the Scholastic Aptitude Test. *American Educational Research Journal, 1981, 18,* 143–156.

BELL, R. Q. Parent, child, and reciprocal influences. *American Psychologist, 1979, 34,* 821–826.

BELLEZZA, F. S., Mnemonic devices: Classification, and criteria. *Review of Research in Education,* 1981, 5, 247–275.

BELSKY, J. & STEINBERG, L. D. The effects of day care: A critical review. *Child Development,* 1978, 49, 929–949.

BENBOW, C. P. & STANLEY, J. C. Sex differences in mathematical ability: Fact or artifact? *Science,* 1980, 210, 1262–1264.

BERGER, K. S. *The developing person.* New York: Worth, 1980.

BERGER, S. M. Observer perseverance as related to a model's success. *Journal of Personality and Social Psychology,* 1971, 19, 341–350.

BERKO, J. The child's learning of English morphology. *Word,* 1958, 14, 150–177.

BERLINER, D. C. Impediments to the study of teacher effectiveness. *Journal of Teacher Education,* 1976, 27, 5–13.

BERLINER, D. C., FISHER, C. W., FILBY, N., & MARLIEVE, R. Proposal for Phase III of Beginning Teacher Evaluation Study. San Francisco: Far West Laboratory for Educational Research and Development, 1976.

BERSOFF, D. N. Testing and the law. *American Psychologist,* 1981, 36, 1046–1056.

BIERLY, M. M. Educational psychology: What is it? *Contemporary Psychology,* 1981, 26, 116–118.

BIGGE, J. & SIRVIS B. Physical and multiple handicaps. In N. Haring (Ed.), *Exceptional children and youth.* Columbus, Ohio: Charles E. Merrill, 1982.

BIRNS, B. The emergence and socialization of sex differences in the earliest years. *Merrill-Palmer Quarterly,* 1976, 22, 229–254.

BISPO, E. & WALLACE, F. A career in education: will there be any jobs? In A. B. Calvin (Ed.), *Perspectives on education.* Reading, Mass.: Addison-Wesley, 1978.

BLACKBURN, J. E. & POWELL, W. C. *One at a time all at once: The creative teacher's guide to individualized instruction without anarchy.* Pacific Palisades, Calif.: Goodyear, 1976.

BLACKHAM, G. & SILBERMAN, A. *Modification of child and adolescent behavior* (2nd ed.). Belmont, California: Wadsworth, 1975.

BLOCK, J. H. (Ed.). *Mastery Learning: Theory and Practice.* New York: Holt, Rinehart & Winston, 1971.

BLOCK, J., BLOCK, J. H. & HARRINGTON, D. Some misgivings about the Matching Familiar Figures test as a measure of reflection-impulsivity. *Development Psychology,* 1974, 10, 611–632.

BLOOM, B. S. *Human characteristics and school learning.* New York: McGraw-Hill, 1976.

BLOOM, B. Individual differences in achievement. In L. J. Rubin (Ed.). *Facts and feelings in the classroom.* New York: Viking, 1973.

BLOOM, B. Learning for Mastery, *Evaluation Comment* 1 (2). Los Angeles: Center for the Study of Evaluation of Instructional Programs, University of California, 1968.

BLOOM, B. S. & BRODER, L. J. *Problem solving processes of college students.* Chicago: University of Chicago Press, 1950.

BLOOM, B. S., ENGELHART, M. D., FROST, E. J., HILL, W. H., & KRATHWOHL, D. R. *Taxonomy of educational objectives,* Handbook I: *Cognitive domain. New York: David McKay, 1956.*

BLOOM, B. S., HASTINGS, J. T. and MADAUS, G. F. *Handbook on formative and summative evaluation of student learning.* New York: McGraw-Hill, 1971.

BLOOM, R. & BOURDON, L. Types and frequencies of teachers' written instructional feedback. *Journal of Educational Research,* 1980, 74, 13–15.

BORK, A. Machines for computer-assisted learning. *Educational Technology,* 1978, 18, 17–20.

BORK, A., & FRANKLIN, S. Personal computers in learning. *Educational Technology,* 1979, 19, 7–12.

BOSTROM, R. N., VLANDIS, J. W., & ROSENBAUM, M. E. Grades as reinforcing contingencies and attitude change. *Journal of Educational Psychology,* 1961, 52, 112–115.

BOURNE, L. E., DOMINOWSKI, R. L., & LOFTUS, E. F. *Cognitive processes.* Englewood Cliffs, N.J.: Prentice-Hall, 1979.

BOWER, G. H. & HILGARD, E. R. *Theories of learning* (5th ed.) Englewood Cliffs, N.J.: Prentice-Hall, 1981.

BRANSFORD, J. D. *Human cognition: Learning, understanding, and remembering.* Belmont, Calif.: Wadsworth, 1979.

BRAUN, C. Teacher expectation: Sociopsychological dynamics. *Review of Educational Research,* Spring 1976, 46, (2), 185–212.

BRENNER, L. P. & AGEE, C. C. The symbiosis of PLATO and microcomputers. *Educational Technology,* 1979, 19, 45–52.

BRETZING, B. B. & KULHAVY, R. W. Note taking and depth of processing. *Contemporary Educational Psychology,* 1979, 4, 145–153.

BREWER, W. F. There is no convincing evidence for operant and classical conditioning in humans. In W. B. Weimer & D. S. Palermo, (Eds.), *Cognition and symbolic processes.* Hillsdale, N.J.: Earlbaum, 1974.

BRIDGEMAN, D. *Cooperative, interdependent learning and its enhancement of role-taking in fifth-grade students.* Paper presented at a meeting of the American Psychological Association, San Francisco, 1977.

BRIGHAM, T. A., GRAUBARD, P. S., & STANS, A. Analysis of the effects of sequential reinforcement contingencies on aspects of composition. *Journal of Applied Behavior Analysis,* 1972, 5, 421–429.

BRINDLEY, W. A. Objective Grading of Essay Examinations, *Educational Technology,* 1978, 18, 27–29.

BRODEN, M., BRUCE, C., MITCHELL, M. A., CARTER, V. & HALL, R. V. Effects of teacher attention on·attending behavior of two boys at adjacent desks. *Journal of Applied Behavior Analysis,* 1970, 3, 199–203.

BRODZINSKY, D. M. The relationship between cognitive style and cognitive development: A two-year longitudinal study. *Developmental Psychology,* 1982, 18, 617–626.

BROLYER, C. R., THORNDIKE, E. L., & WOODYARD, E. R. A second study of mental discipline in high school studies. *Journal of Educational Psychology,* 1927, 18, 377–404.

BROMLEY, D. B. Natural language and the development of the self. In C. B. Keasey, (Ed.), *Nebraska Symposium on Motivation,* 1977. Lincoln, Nebraska: Univerity of Nebraska Press, 1978.

BROPHY, J. E. Reflections on research in elementary schools. *Journal of Teacher Education,* 1976, 27, 31–34.

BROPHY, J. E. Research on the self-fulfilling prophecy and teacher expectations. Paper presented at the annual meeting of the American Educational Research Association, New York, March, 1982.

BROPHY, J. E. Teacher praise: A functional analysis. *Review of Educational Research,* 1981, 51, 5–21.

BROPHY, J. E. & EVERTSON, C. *Learning from teaching: A developmental perspective.* Boston: Allyn & Bacon, 1976.

BROPHY J. E. & EVERTSON, C. M. *Process/ product correlation in the teacher effectiveness study: Final report.* Austin: The University of Texas, 1974.

BROPHY, J. E. and GOOD, T. L. Teachers' communication of differential expectations for children's classroom performance: Some behavioral data. *Journal of Educational Psychology,* 1970, 61, 365–374.

BROPHY, J. E., & GOOD, T. L. *Teacher-student relationships: Causes and consequences.* New York: Holt, Rinehart and Winston, 1974.

BROWN, A. Metacognitive development and reading. In R. Spiro, B. Bruce, & W. Brewer (Eds.) *Theoretical issues in reading comprehension,* Hillsdale, N.J.: Lawrence Erlbaum, 1980.

BROWN, A. L., CAMPIONE, J. C. & BARCLAY, C. R. Training self-checking routines for estimating test readiness: Generalization from list learning to prose recall. *Child Development,* 1979, 50, 501–512.

BROWN, A. L., CAMPIONE, J. C. & DAY, J. D. Learning to learn: On training students to learn from tests. *Educational Researcher,* 1981, 9, 14–21.

BROWN, J. S. & BURTON, R. Diagnostic models for procedural bugs in basic mathematical skills. *Cognitive Science,* 1978, 2, 155–192.

BROWN, J. S. & VANLEHN, K. Toward a generative theory of "bugs." In T. Carpenter, J. Moser, & T. Romberg (Eds.), *Addition and subtraction: A developmental perspective.* Hillsdale, N.J.: Erlbaum Press, 1982.

BROWN, R. *A first language: The early stages.* Cambridge, Mass.: Harvard University Press, 1973.

BROWN, R. & HANLON, C. Derivational complexity and order of acquisition in child speech. In J. M. Hays (Ed.), *Cognition and the development of language.* New York: Wiley 1970.

BROWN, R. & McNEILL, D. The "tip-of-the-tongue" phenomenon. *Journal of Verbal Learning and Verbal Behavior.* 1966, 5, 325–337.

BRUNER, J. S. *Beyond the information given: Studies in the psychology of knowing.* New York: Norton, 1973.

BRUNER, J. S. *The process of education.* New York: Vintage Books, 1960.

BRUNER, J. S. *Toward a theory of instruction.* New York: Norton, 1966.

BRYAN, T. H. & BRYAN, J. H. *Understanding learning disabilities.* Port Washington, N.Y.: Alfred Publishing Co., 1975.

BURGESS, W. V. Adolescent development in the secondary school. In A. Calvin (Ed.), *Perspectives on education.* Reading, Mass.: Addison-Wesley, 1977.

BURNS, P. K. & BOZEMAN, W. C. Computer-assisted instruction and mathematics achievement: Is there a relationship? *Educational Technology,* 1981, 21, 32–39.

BURTON, N. W. & JONES, L. V. Recent trends in achievement levels of black and white youth. *Educational Researcher,* 1982, 11, 10–14 +.

BURTON, R. V. The generality of honesty reconsidered. *Psychological Review,* 1963, 70, 481–499.

BUSHELL, D., WROBEL, P. A., & MICHAELIS, M. L. Applying "group" contingencies to the classroom study behavior of preschool children. *Journal of Applied Behavior Analysis,* 1968, 1, 55–61.

BUSS, A. R. & POLEY, W. *Individual differences: Traits and factors.* New York: Gardner Press, 1976.

CAHEN, L. *An experimental manipulation of the halo effect.* Unpublished doctoral dissertation. Stanford University, 1966.

CALLAHAN, R. E. *Education and the cult of efficiency: A study of the social forces that have shaped the administration of the public schools.* Chicago: University of Chicago Press, 1962.

CAMPBELL, J. R. A longitudinal study in the stability of teacher's verbal behavior. *Science Education*, 1972, *56*, 89–96.

CANTER, L. & CANTER, M. *Assertive discipline: A take-charge approach for today's educator.* Los Angeles: Lee Canter and Associates, 1976.

CANTOR, G., DUNLAP, L. L., and RETTIE, C. S., Effects of reception and discovery instruction on kindergartners' performance on probability tasks. *American Educational Research Journal*, 1982, *19*, 453–464.

CANTRELL, R. P., STENNER A. J., & KATZEN-MEYER, W. G. Teacher knowledge, attitudes, and classroom teaching correlates of student achievement. *Journal of Educational Psychology*, 1977, *69*, 180–190.

CARLSON, R. F., KINCAID, J. P., LANCE, S., & HODGSON, T. Spontaneous use of mnemonics and grade point average. *The Journal of Psychology*, 1976, *92*, 117–122.

CARTWRIGHT, G. P., CARTWRIGHT, C. A. & WARD, M. E. *Educating special learners.* Belmont, Calif.: Wadsworth, 1981.

CASE, R. Intellectual development: A systematic reinterpretation. In F. Farley & N. J. Gordon (Eds.), *Psychology and education: The state of the union,* Berkeley, Calif.: McCutchan, 1980.

CASE, R. A. Developmentally-based theory and technology of instruction. *Review of Educational Research*, 1978b, *48*, 439–463.

CASE, R. Piaget and beyond: Toward a developmentally-based theory and technology of instruction. In R. Glaser (Ed.), *Advances in instructional psychology* Vol. 1. Hillsdale, N.J.: Erlbaum, 1978a.

CASTILLO, G. A. *Left-handed teaching: Lessons in effective education.* New York: Praeger, 1974.

CATTELL, R. B. The fluid and crystallized intelligence: A critical experiment. *Journal of Educational Psychology*, 1963, *54*.

CAZDEN, C. B. Some implications of research on language development for preschool education. In R. Hess & R. Bear (Eds.), *Early education: Current theory, research and action.* Chicago: Aldine, 1968.

CHAMPAGNE, A. B., KLOPFER, L. E., & ANDERSON, J. H. Factors influencing the learning of classical mechanics. *American Journal of Physics*, 1980, *48*, 1074–1079.

CHAPMAN, D. W. & HUTCHESON, S. M. Attrition from teaching careers: A discriminant analysis. *American Educational Research Journal*, 1982, *19*, 93–106.

CHARLES, C. M. *Building classroom discipline: From models to practice.* New York: Longman, 1981.

CHARLES, C. M. & MALIAN, I. M. *The special student: Practical help for the classroom teacher.* St. Louis: C. V. Mosby, 1980.

CHASE, C. I. *Measurement for Educational Evaluation* (2nd ed.). Reading, Mass.: Addison-Wesley, 1978.

CHASE, C. I. *Secondary students assess their schools.* Paper presented at the annual meeting of the American Educational Research Association, Los Angeles, 1981.

CHERRY-PEISACH, E. Children's comprehension of teacher and peer speech. *Child Development*, 1965, 467–480.

CHOMSKY, N. *Aspects of a theory of syntax.* Cambridge, Mass.: M.I.T. Press, 1965.

CHOMSKY, N. A review of B. F. Skinner's *Verbal Behavior. Language*, 1959, *35*, 26–58.

CHRISTY, P. R. Does use of tangible rewards with individual children affect peer observers? *Journal of Applied Behavior Analysis*, 1975, *8*, 187–196.

CLAIBORN, W. L. Expectancy effect in the classroom: A failure to replicate. *Journal of Educational Psychology*, 1969, *60*, 377–383.

CLARIZIO, H. F. *Toward positive classroom discipline.* New York: Wiley, 1971.

CLARK, C. M., GAGE, N. L., MARX, R. W., PETERSON, P. L., STAYBROOK, N. G., & WINNE, P. H. A factorial experiment on teacher structuring, soliciting, and reacting. *Journal of Educational Psychology*, 1979, *71*, 534–550.

CLARK, C. M. & YINGER, R. J. Teachers' thinking. In P. Peterson & H. Walberg (Eds.), *Research on teaching: Concepts, findings, and implications.* Berkeley, Calif.: McCutchan, 1979.

CLARK, G. Broadway has a new language. *Time. The Weekly Newsmagazine.* 1980.

CLASEN, D. & SUBKOVIAK, M. College for kids: Enrichment program for Gifted Elementary Children, Paper presented at the annual meeting of the American Educational Research Association, March, 1982.

CLEMENT, S. L. Dual marking system: Simple and effective. *American Secondary Education*, 1978, *8*, 49–52.

CLIFFORD, M. M. Effects of failure: Alternative explanations and possible implications. *Educational Psychologist*, 1979, *14*, 44–52.

COATES, J. F. Population and education: How demographic trends will shape the U.S. *The Futurist*, 1978, *12*, 35–42.

COATES, T. J. & THORESEN, C. E. Behavioral self-control and educational practice or do we really need self-control? In D. C. Berliner (Ed.), *Review of research in education, 7.* Itasca, Ill.: F. E. Peacock, 1979.

COATES, T. J. & THORESEN, C. E. Teacher anxiety: A review with recommendations. *Review of Educational Research*, 1976, 159–184.

COLE, N. S. Bias in testing. *American Psychologist*, 1981, *36*, 1067–1077.

COLEMAN, J. S., CAMPBELL, J., WOOD, A. M., WEINFELD, F. D., & YORK, R. L. *Equality of educational opportunity.* Washington, D.C.: Office of Education, United States Department of Health, Education and Welfare, 1966.

COLEMAN, J. S., HOFFER, T. & KILGORE, S. *High school achievement: Public, catholic, and private schools compared.* New York: Basic Books, 1982.

COLLINS, M. L. Effects of enthusiasm training on preservice elementary teachers. *Journal of Teacher Education*, 1978, *24*, 53–57.

COPI, I. M. *Introduction to logic.* New York: Macmillan, 1961.

CORNBLETH, C., DAVID, O. L. JR., & BUTTON, C. Expectations for pupil achievement and teacher-pupil interaction. *Social Education*, 1974, *38*, 54–58.

CORNO, L. Individual and class level effects of parent-assisted instruction in classroom memory support systems. *Journal of Educational Psychology*, 1980, *72*, 278–292.

COSTELLO, J. & DICKIE, J. Leiter and Stanford-Binet IQ's of preschool disadvantaged children. *Psychological Reports*, 1970, *28*, 755–760.

Council for Exceptional Children for the Bureau of Education for the Handicapped. *The education for all handicapped children act: P.L. 94-142.* Washington, D.C.: United States Office of Education, 1976.

COX, C. C. The early mental traits of three hundred geniuses. In L. M. Terman (Ed.), *Genetic studies of genius, Vol II.* Stanford: Stanford University Press, 1926.

COX, W. F. & DUNN, T. G. Mastery learning: A psychological trap? *Educational Psychologist*, 1979, *14*, 24–29.

CRAIK, F. I. M. Human Memory. *Annual Review of Psychology*, 1979, *30*, 63–102.

CRAIK, F. I. M. & LOCKHART, R. S. Levels of processing: A framework for memory research. *Journal of Verbal Learning and Verbal Behavior*, 1972, *11*, 671–684.

CROMACK, T. Reinforcing and questioning behavior of teachers as a measure of teacher effects. [Final Rep. Project No. 2A 099, Grant No. OEG-1-71-0019 (509)]. Washington, D.C.: Office of Education, United States Department of Health, Education, and Welfare, 1973.

CRONBACH, L. *Essentials of psychological testing* (3rd Ed.). New York: Harper and Row, 1970.

CRONBACH, L. J., & SNOW, R. L. *Aptitudes and instructional methods.* New York: Irvington, 1977.

CROUSE, J. M. Retroactive interference in reading prose materials. *Journal of Educational Psychology*, 1971, *62*, 39–44.

CROWDER, N. A. Automatic tutoring by means of intrinsic programming. In A. A. Lumsdaine and R. Glaser (Eds.), *Teaching machines and programmed learning.* Washington, D.C.: National Education Association Publications, 1960.

CULLEN, FRANCIS T., CULLEN, JOHN B., HAYOW, VANL. & PLOUFFE, JOHN T., The effects of the use of grades as an incentive. *The Journal of Educational Research.* March, 1975.

CURTIS, T. E. Middle school grades. In A. Calvin (Ed.), *Perspectives on education.* Reading, Mass.: Addison-Wesley, 1977.

DALE, L. G. The growth of systematic thinking: Replication and analysis of Piaget's first chemical experiment. *Australian Journal of Psychology*, 1970, *22*, 277–286.

DAMON, W. *The social world of the child,* San Francisco: Jossey-Bass, 1977.

DANSEREAU, D. The development of a learning strategies curriculum. In H. O'Neil (Ed.) *Learning Strategies,* New York: Academic Press, 1978.

DARBY, C. A. JR., KOROTKIN, A. L., and ROMASHKO, T. *The computer in secondary schools: A survey of its instructional and administrative use.* New York: Praeger, 1972.

DARLEY, J. & FAZIO, R. Expectancy confirmation processes arising in the social interaction sequence. *American Psychologist*, 1980, *35*, 867–881.

DAURIO, S. P. Educational enrichment versus acceleration: A review of the literature. In W. George, S. Cohn, and J. Stanley (Eds.). *Educating the gifted: Acceleration and enrichment.* Baltimore: Johns Hopkins Press, 1979.

DAVIS, E. A. The form and function of children's questions. *Child Development*, 1932, *3*, 57–74.

DAVIS, G. A. Research and development in training creative thinking. In J. Levin and V. Allen (Eds.), *Cognitive learning in children: Theories and strategies.* New York: Academic Press, 1976.

DAVIS, J. A. *General social surveys, 1972–1980: Cumulative codebook.* Chicago: National Opinion Research Center, University of Chicago, 1980.

DAVIS, J., LAUGHLIN, P., & KOMORITA, S. The social psychology of small groups: Cooperative and mixed-motive interaction. In M.

Rosenzweig & L. Porter (Eds.). *Annual Review of Psychology*, Palo Alto: Annual Reviews, Inc., 1976, *27*, 501–542.

DEARMAN, N. B., & PLISKO, V. W. *The condition of education, 1981 edition*. Washington, D.C.: The National Center for Educational Statistics, 1981.

DECHARMS, R. *Enhancing motivation: Change in the classroom*. New York: Irvington Publishers, 1976.

DECHARMS, R. *Personal causation*. New York: Academic Press, 1968.

DECI, E. *Intrinsic motivation*, N. Y. Plenum, 1975.

DEIDERICH, P. B. *Short Cut Statistics for Teacher-Made Tests*, Princeton, N.J.: Educational Testing Service, 1973.

DE LISI, R. & STAUDT, J. Individual differences in college students' performance on formal operations tasks. *Journal of Applied Developmental Psychology*, 1980, *1*, 201–208.

DELLOW, D. A., & ROSS, S. M. Implications of personal computers for social science faculty. *Community College Social Science Journal*, in press.

DE MOTT, R. Visually impaired. In N. B. Haring (Ed.), *Education of Exceptional Children: An introduction to special education*. Columbus, Ohio: Charles E. Merrill, 1974.

DE MOTT, R. M. Visual impairments. In N. Haring (Ed.), *Exceptional children and youth*. Columbus, Ohio: Charles E. Merrill, 1982.

DENHAM, C. & LIEBERMAN, A. *Time to learn*. Washington, D.C.: National Institute of Education, 1980.

DETTERMAN, D. K. A job half done: The road to intelligence testing in the year 2000. In R. J. Sternberg & D. K. Detterman (Eds.), *Human intelligence: Perspectives on its theory and measurement*. Norwood, New Jersey: Ablex Publishing, 1979.

DEUTSCH, M. Education and distributive justice: Some reflections on grading systems. *American Psychologist*, 1979, *34*, 391–401.

DIGGS, RUTH W. Education across cultures. *Exceptional Children*, May, 1974, *40*, 578–583.

DOMINICK, J. R. & GREENBERG, B. S. Attitudes toward violence: The interaction of television exposure, family attitudes and social class. In G. Comstock & E. Rubenstein (Eds.), *Television and social behavior* Vol. 3., Washington, D.C.: U.S. Government Printing Office, 1972.

DOUGLAS, C. H., & EDWARDS, J. S. A selected glossary of terms useful in dealing with computers. *Educational Technology*, 1979, *19*, 56–65.

DOYLE, W. The uses of nonverbal behaviors: Toward an ecological model of classrooms. *Merrill-Palmer Quarterly*, 1977, *23*, 179–192.

DOYLE, W., HANCOCK, G., & KIFER, E. Teacher's perceptions: Do they make a difference? Paper presented at a meeting of the American Educational Research Association, New York, 1971.

DRABMAN, R. A. and SPITALNIK, R. Social isolation as a punishment procedure: A controlled study. *Journal of Experimental Child Psychology*, 1973, *16*, 236–249.

DRABMAN, R. S. and TUCKER, R. D. Why classroom token economies fail. *Journal of School Psychology*, 1974, *12*, 178–188.

DRAYER, A. M. *Problems in middle and high school training: A handbook for student teachers and beginning teachers*. Boston: Allyn & Bacon, 1979.

DREIKURS, R., GRUNWALD, B. B. & PEPPER, F. C. *Maintaining sanity in the classroom: Illustrated teaching techniques*. New York: Harper & Row, 1971.

DRESSEL, P. L. The nature and role of objectives in instruction. *Educational Technology*, 1977, *17*, 7–15.

DUCETTE, J. & KENNEY, J. Do grading standards affect student evaluation of teaching? Some new evidence in an old question. *Journal of Educational Psychology*, 1982, *74*, 308–314.

DUCHASTEL, P. Learning objectives and the organization of prose. *Journal of Educational Psychology*, 1979, *71*, 100–106.

DUCHASTEL, P. C. & MERRILL, P. F. The effects of behavior objectives on learning: A review of empirical studies. *Review of Educational Research*, 1973, *43*, 53–70.

DUELL, O. K. Effect of type of objective, level of test questions, and the judged importance of tested materials upon post-test performance. *Journal of Educational Psychology*, 1974, *66*, 225–232.

DUNCKER, K. On solving problems. *Psychological Monographs*, 1945, *58*, (5 Whole No. 270).

DUNKIN, M. J. & BIDDLE, B. J. *The study of teaching*. New York: Holt, Rinehart and Winston, 1974.

DUNN, L. M. An overview. In L. M. Dunn (Ed.), *Exceptional Children in the Schools: Special education in transition*. New York: Holt, Rinehart and Winston, 1973a.

DUNN, L. M. Children with mild general learning disabilities. In L. M. Dunn (Ed.), *Exceptional Children in the Schools: Special education in transition*. New York: Holt, Rinehart and Winston, 1973b.

DURKHEIM, E. *Suicide* (J. A. Spaulding & G. Simpson, trans.). New York: Free Press, 1958.

DYER, H. S. The discovery and development of educational goals. *Proceedings of the 1966 Invitational Conference on Testing Problems*. Princeton, N.J.: Educational Testing Service, 1967.

DYER, J. W., RILEY, J., & YEKOVICH, F. R. An analysis of three study skills: Notetaking, summarizing, and rereading. *Journal of Educational Research*, 1979, *73*, 3–7.

EBEL, R. L. The case for norm-referenced measurements. *Educational Researcher*, 1978, *12*, 3–5.

EBEL, R. L. What are schools for? In H. Clarizio, R. Craig, & W. Mehrens (Eds.), *Contemporary issues in educational psychology*, Fourth Edition. Boston: Allyn and Bacon, 1981.

EBMEIER, H. H. & ZIOMEK. R. L. Increasing engagement rates of low and high achievers. Paper presented at the annual meeting of the American Educational Research Association, New York, March, 1982.

EDUCATIONAL TESTING SERVICE, *Test use and validity: A response to charges in the Nadar /Narin report on ETS*. Princeton, N.J.: Educational Testing Service, February, 1980.

EDWARDS, A. Personal communication. Cook College, Rutgers University, New Brunswick, N.J., 1979.

EDWARDS, J., NORTON, S., TAYLOR, S., WEISS, M., & DUSSELDORP, R. How effective is CAI? A review of the research. *Educational Leadership*, 1975 *33*, 147–153.

EDWARDS, K. J. & DE VRIES D. L. The effects of teams-games-tournament and two instructional variations on classroom process, student attitudes, and student achievement. (Rep. 172), Center for Social Organization of Schools, Johns Hopkins University, 1974.

EGGEN, P. D., KAUCHAK, D. P., & HARDER, R. J. *Strategies for teachers: Information processing in the classroom*. Englewood Cliffs, N.J.: Prentice-Hall, Inc., 1979.

EISELE, J. E. Computers in the schools: Now that we have them . . . ? *Educational Technology*, 1981, *21*, 24–27.

EISEMAN, J. W. What criteria should public school moral education programs meet? *The Review of Education*, 1981, *7*, 213–230.

EISNER, E. W. Instructional and expressive educational objectives: Their formulation and use in curriculum. In W. J. Popham, E.W. Eisner, H. J. Sullivan, & L. I. Tyler, *Instructional objectives*. (Monograph Series on Curriculum Evaluation, No. 3). Chicago: Rand McNally, 1969.

ELASHOFF, J. D. and SNOW, R. E. *Pygmalion reconsidered*. Worthington, Ohio: Charles A. Jones, 1971.

ELKIND, D. Obituary-Jean Piaget (1896–1980). *American Psychologist*, 1981, *36*, 911–913.

ELLIS, H. *The transfer of learning*. New York: Macmillan, 1965.

EMMER, E. T. & EVERTSON, C. M. Synthesis of research on classroom management. *Educational Leadership*, 1981, *38*, 342–345.

EMMER, E. T. & EVERTSON, C. M. Effective classroom management at the beginning of the school year in junior high school classes. *Journal of Educational Psychology*, 1982, *74*, 485–98.

EMMER, E. T., EVERTSON, C. M., & ANDERSON, L. M. Effective classroom management at the beginning of the school year. *Elementary School Journal*, 1980, *80*, 219–231.

EMMER, E. T., EVERTSON, C. M., CLEMENTS, B. S., SANFORD, J. P., & WORSHAM, M. E. *Organizing and managing the junior high school classroom*. Englewood Cliffs, N.J.: Prentice-Hall, 1984.

EMMER, E. T. & MILLETT, G. *Improving teaching through experimentation: A laboratory approach*. Englewood Cliffs, N.J.: Prentice-Hall, 1970.

ENGLE, P. L. Language medium in early school years for minority language groups. *Review of Educational Research*, 1975, *45*, 283–326.

EPSTEIN, R. (Ed.) *Notebooks: B. F. Skinner*. Englewood Cliffs, N.J.: Prentice-Hall, 1980.

EPSTEIN, Y., COHEN, B. & KRESSEL, K. *Children of divorce: Interventions and evaluation*. Unpublished manuscript, Rutgers University, 1980.

ERIKSON, E. *Childhood and society* (2nd ed.). New York: Norton, 1963.

ERIKSON, E. *Dimensions of a new identity*. New York: Norton, 1974.

ERIKSON, E. *Identity, youth, and crisis*. New York: Norton, 1968.

ESTES, W. K. The state of the field: General problems and issues of theory and metatheory. In W. K. Estes (Ed.), *Handbook of learning and cognitive processes* Vol. 1: Concepts and issues. Hillsdale, N.J.: Erlbaum, 1975.

EVANS, E. D. *Transition to teaching*. New York: Holt, Rinehart and Winston, 1976.

EVANS, G. W. & OSWALT, G. L. Acceleration of academic progress through manipulation of peer influence. *Behavior Research and Therapy*, 1968, *6*, 189–195.

EVERTSON, C. M. Differences in instructional activities in high and low achieving junior high classes. *Elementary School Journal*, 1982, *82*, 329–50.

EVERTSON, C. M., EMMER, E. T., CLEMENTS, B. S., SANFORD, J. P., WORSHAM, M. E. & WILLIAMS, E. L. *Organizing and managing the elementary school classroom*. Englewood Cliffs, N.J.: Prentice-Hall, 1984.

FAIRWEATHER, H. Sex differences in brain organization. *The Behavioral and Brain Sciences*, 1980, *3*, 234.

FANELLI, G. C. Locus of control. In S. Ball (Ed.), *Motivation in education*. New York: Academic Press, 1977.

FARNHAM-DIGGORY, S. *Cognitive processes in education: A psychological preparation for teaching and curriculum development.* New York: Harper and Row, 1972.

FAW, H. W., & WALLER, T. G. Mathemagenic behaviors and efficiency in learning from prose. *Review of Educational Research, 1976, 46,* 691–720.

FEIN, G. *Child Development.* Englewood Cliffs, N.J.: Prentice-Hall, 1978.

FELDHUSEN, J. F., SPEEDIE, S. M., & TREFFINGER, D. J. The Purdue Creative Thinking Program: Research and evaluation. *NSPI Journal, 1971, 10,* 5–9.

FELDMAN, R., and PROHASKA, T. The student as Pygmalion: Effects of student expectancy of the teacher. *Journal of Educational Psychology, 1979, 71,* 485–493.

FELIXBROD, J. J. *Effects of prior locus of control over reinforcement on current performance and resistance to extinction.* Unpublished doctoral dissertation, SUNY, Stony Brook, N.Y., 1974.

FENEMA, E. & SHERMAN, J. Sex-related differences in mathematics achievement, spatial visualization and affective factors. *American Educational Research Journal,* Winter 1977, *14*(1), 51–71.

FERRITOR, D. E., BUCKHOLDT, D., HAMBLIN, R. L. & SMITH, L. The noneffects of contingent reinforcement for attending behavior on work accomplished. *Journal of Applied Behavior Analysis, 1972, 5,* 7–17.

FERSTER, C. B. & SKINNER, B. F. *Schedules of reinforcement.* New York: Appleton-Century-Crofts, 1957.

FESHBACH, S. & SINGER, R. D. *Television and aggression.* San Francisco: Jossey Bass, 1971.

FINN, J. Expectations and the educational environment. *Review of Educational Research, 1972, 42,* 387–410.

FISHBEIN, J., & WASIL, B. Effect of the Good Behavior game on disruptive library behavior. *Journal of Applied Behavior Analysis, 1981, 14,* 89–93.

FISKE, E. B. Teachers reward muddy prose, study finds. *New York Times,* October 27, 1981, Cl +.

FLAVELL, J. H. *Cognitive development,* Englewood Cliffs, N.J.: Prentice-Hall, 1977.

FLAVELL, J. H. Metacognitive aspects of problem solving. In L. Resnick (Ed.), *The nature of intelligence,* Hillsdale, N.J.: Lawrence Erlbaum, 1976.

FLAVELL, J. H. Metacognition and cognitive monitoring: A new area of cognitive-developmental inquiry. *American Psychologist, 1979, 34,* 906–911.

FLAVELL, J. H. Cognitive monitoring. In W. Dickson (Ed.), *Children's or communication skills,* New York: Academic Press, 1981.

FLAVELL, J. H., FRIEDRICHS, A. G., & HOYT, J. D. Developmental changes in memorization processes. *Cognitive Psychology, 1970, 1,* 324–340.

FLAVELL, J. H. & WELLMAN, H. M. Metamemory. In R. V. Kail & J. W. Hagen (Eds.), *Perspectives on the development of memory and cognition.* Hillsdale, N.J.: Earlbaum, 1977.

FOSTER, G. G., YSSELDYKE, J. E., & REESE, J. H. I wouldn't have seen it if I hadn't believed it. *Exceptional Children, 1975, 41,* 469–473.

FOSTER, W. Social and emotional development in gifted individuals. Paper presented at the Fourth World Conference on Gifted and Talented, Montreal, 1981.

FOX, L. H. Identification of the academically gifted. *American Psychologist, 1981, 36,* 1103–1111.

FOXX, R. M., & JONES, J. R. A remediation program for increasing the spelling achievement of elementary and junior high school students. *Behavior Modification, 1978, 2,* 211–230.

FOXX, R. M. & SHAPIRO, S. T. The time-out ribbon: A nonexclusionary time-out procedure. *Journal of Applied Behavior Analysis, 1978, 11,* 125–136.

FRECHLING, J. A., EDWARDS, S., & RICHARDSON, W. M. The declining enrollment problem: A study of why parents withdraw their children from public schools. Paper presented at the annual meeting of the American Educational Research Association, Los Angeles, 1981.

FRENCH, E. G. Motivation as a variable in work partner selection. *Journal of Abnormal and Social Psychology, 1956, 53,* 96–99.

FRENCH, E. G. & THOMAS, F. The relation of achievement motivation to problem-solving effectiveness. *Journal of Abnormal and Social Psychology, 1958, 56,* 45–48.

FRENDER, R., BROWN, B., & LAMBERT, W. The role of speech characteristics in scholastic success. *Canadian Journal of Behavioral Science, 1970, 2,* 299–306.

FREY, P. W., LEONARD, D. W., & BEATTY, W. W. Student rating of instruction: Validation research. *American Educational Research Journal, 1975, 12,* 435–443.

FROSTIG, M. & HORNE, D. *The Frostig program for the development of visual perception: Teacher's guide.* Chicago: Follett, 1964.

FUHR, M. L. The typewriter and retarded readers. *Journal of Reading, 1972, 16,* 30–32.

FULLER, F. F. Concerns of teachers: A developmental conceptualization. *American Educational Research Journal, 1969, 6,* 207–226.

FURST, E. J. Bloom's taxonomy of educational objectives for the cognitive domain: Philosophical and educational issues. *Review of Educational Research, 1981, 51,* 441–454.

FURTH, H. and WACHS, H. *Thinking goes to school: Piaget's theory in practice.* New York: Oxford University Press, 1974.

GAGNÉ, R. M. *Essentials of learning for instruction.* Hinsdale, Ill.: Dryden Press, 1974.

GAGNÉ, R. M. Some issues in the psychology of mathematics instruction. Paper presented at the annual meeting of the American Educational Research Association, New York, March, 1982.

GAGNÉ, R. *The conditions of learning* (3rd ed.). New York: Holt, Rinehart and Winston, 1977.

GAGNÉ, R. M. & BRIGGS, L. J. *Principles of instructional design.* New York: Holt, Rinehart and Winston, 1979.

GAGNÉ, R. M. & SMITH, E. A study of the effects of verbalization on problem solving. *Journal of Experimental Psychology, 1962, 63,* 12–18.

GALL, M. D. The use of questions in teaching. *Review of Educational Research, 1970, 40,* 707–721.

GALLUP, G. Eighth annual Gallup Poll of public attitudes toward public schools. *Phi Delta Kappan, 1975; 57,* 227–241.

GALLUP, G. *The Gallup Poll, 1980.* Princeton, N.J.: Opinion Research Corporation, 1980.

Games that play people. *Time Magazine,* January 18, 1982, pp. 50–58.

GARBER, H. & HERBER, R. *The Milwaukee project: Early intervention as a technique to prevent mental retardation.* Storrs: The University of Connecticut, National Leadership Institute, Teacher Education/Early Education, 1973.

GELMAN, R. Preschool thought. *American Psychologist, 1979, 34,* 900–905.

GELMAN, R. & SHATZ, M. Appropriate speech adjustments: The operation of conversational constraints on talk to two-year-olds. In M. Lewis & L. A. Rosenblum (Eds.), *Interaction, conversation, and the development of language.* New York: Wiley, 1977.

GENTNER, D. Evidence for the psychological reality of semantic components: The verbs of possession. In D. Norman & D. Rumelhart (Eds.), *Explorations in cognition,* San Francisco: Freeman, 1975.

GERBER, G. & GROSS, L. Violence profile # 6. Trends in network television drama and viewer conceptions of social reality 1967–73. *Monographs of the Annenberg School of Communications.* Philadelphia: University of Pennsylvania, 1974.

GILLETT, M. & GALL, M. The effects of teacher enthusiasm on the at-task behavior of students in the elementary grades. Paper presented at the annual meeting of the American Educational Research Association, New York, March, 1982.

GILLIGAN, C. In a different voice: Women's conceptions of self and of morality. *Harvard Educational Review, 1977, 47,* 481–517.

GILSTRAP, R. L. & MARTIN, W. R. *Current strategies for teachers: A resource for personalizing education.* Pacific Palisades, Calif.: Goodyear, 1975.

GINSBURG, H. & OPPER, S. *Piaget's theory of intellectual development* (2nd ed.). Englewood Cliffs, N.J.: Prentice-Hall, 1979.

GLASER, R. Educational psychology and education. *American Psychologist, 1973, 28,* 557–566.

GLASER, R. The future of testing: A research agenda for cognitive psychology and psychometrics. *American Psychologist, 1981, 36,* 923–936.

GLEITMAN, H. *Psychology.* New York: W. W. Norton, 1981.

GOLDSTEIN, H., MOSS, J. W. & JORDAN, L. J. *The efficacy of special class training on the development of mentally retarded children.* Urbana: University of Illinois, Institute for Research on Exceptional Children, 1965.

GOOD, T. Classroom research: A decade of progress. Paper presented at the American Educational Research Association, Montreal, April, 1983.

GOOD, T. L. Research on teaching. Paper presented at the national invitational conference on Exploring Issues in Teacher Education: Questions for Future Research, University of Texas at Austin, January, 1979.

GOOD, T. L. Which students do teachers call on? *Elementary School Journal, 1970, 70,* 190–198.

GOOD, T. L. & BECKERMAN, T. M. Time on task: A naturalistic study in sixth-grade classrooms. *Elementary School Journal,* in press.

GOOD, T., BIDDLE, B., & BROPHY, J. *Teachers make a difference.* New York: Holt, Rinehart and Winston, 1975.

GOOD, T. L. & GROUWS, D. Teaching effects: A process-product study in fourth-grade mathematics classrooms. *Journal of Teacher Education, 1977, 28,* 49–54.

GOOD, T. L. & STIPEK, D. J. Individual differences in the classroom: A psychological perspective. In G. Fenstermacher & J. Goodlad, *1983 National Society for the Study of Education Yearbook,* Chicago: University of Chicago Press, 1983.

GOODMAN, H., GOTTLIEB, J., & HARRISON, R. H. Social acceptance of EMR's integrated into a nongraded elementary school. *American Journal of Mental Deficiency, 1972, 76,* 412–417.

GOODNOW, J. Problems in research on culture

and thought. In D. Elkind and J. Flavell (Eds.), *Studies in cognitive development.* New York: Oxford University Press, 1969.

GORDON, N. J. Social cognition, In F. Farley & N. Gordon (Eds.), *Psychology and education: The state of the union.* Berkeley, California: McCutchan, 1981.

GORDON, T. *Teacher effectiveness training.* New York: Peter H. Wyden, 1974.

GORDON, W. J. J. *Synectics: The development of creative capacity.* New York: Harper and Row, 1961.

GOTTLIEB, J. Attitudes toward retarded children. Effects of labeling and academic performance. *American Journal of Mental Deficiency,* 1974, *79,* 268–273.

GRABE, M. & LATTA, R. M. Cumulative achievement in a mastery instructional system: The impact of differences in resultant achievement motivation and persistence. *American Educational Research Journal,* 1981, *18,* 7–14.

GRADY, D. A hard look at the world of educational computing. *Personal Computing,* 1982, *6,* 40–44.

GRAUBARD, D. S. Children with behavioral disabilities. In L. M. Dunn (Ed.), *Exceptional children in the schools:* Special education in transition. New York: Holt, Rinehart and Winston, 1973.

GRAY, J. M., SCHULMAN, M. E., DUNN, H., WORKMAN, B., SPIELBERG, F., FARAH, M. A. & JONES, N. Motivating today's students: A symposium. *Today's Education,* 1981, *70,* 32–44.

GREEN, B. F. A Primer of testing. *American Psychologist,* 1981, *36,* 1001–1012.

GREENO, J. G. A cognitive learning analysis of algebra. Paper presented at the annual meeting of the American Educational Research Association, New York, March, 1982.

GREENO, J. G. Psychology of learning 1960–1980: One participant's observations. *American Psychologist,* 1980, *35,* 713–744.

GRIFFIN, N., CHASSIN, L., & YOUNG, R. D. Measurement of global self-concept versus multiple role-specific self-concepts in adolescents. *Adolescence,* 1981, *16,* 49–56.

GRINDER, R. E. The "new" science of education: Educational psychology is search of a mission. In F. H. Farley & N. J. Gordon (Eds.) *Psychology and education: The state of the union.* Berkeley, Calif.: McCutchan, 1981.

GRONLUND, N. E. *Constructing achievement tests* (2nd ed.) .Englewood Cliffs, N.J.: PrenticeHall, 1977.

GRONLUND, N. *Constructing achievement tests.* (3rd Ed.) Englewood Cliffs, N.J.: PrenticeHall, 1982.

GRONLUND, N. E. *Stating behavioral objectives for classroom instruction* (2nd. ed.). Toronto: Macmillan, 1978.

GROSSMAN, H. (Ed.). *Manual of terminology and classification in mental retardation.* Washington, D.C.: American Association on Mental Deficiency, 1973.

GUERNEY, L. F. *Psychoeducational programming for children coping with parental separation and divorce.* Paper presented at the annual meeting of the American Educational Association, Los Angeles, April, 1981.

GUILFORD, J. P. *The nature of human intelligence.* New York: McGraw-Hill, 1967.

GUTTENTAG, M. & LONGFELLOW, C. Children's social attributions: Development and change. In. C. B. Keasey, (Ed.), *Nebraska Symposium on Motivation, 1977,* Lincoln, Nebraska: University of Nebraska Press, 1978.

HALLAHAN, D. P. & KAUFFMAN, J. M. *Exceptional children: Introduction to special educa-*

tion. Englewood Cliffs, N.J.: Prentice-Hall, 1982.

HALLAM, R. Piaget and the teaching of history. *Educational Research,* 1969, *12,* 3–12.

HANEY, W. Validity, vaudeville, and values: A short history of social concerns over standardized testing. *American Psychologist,* 1981, *36,* 1021–1034.

HANSEN, D. N., ROSS, S. M., & BOWMAN, H. L. Cost effectiveness of Navy computer-managed instruction. In T. A. Ryan (Ed.), *Systems Research in Education.* Columbia, South Carolina: University of South Carolina, December, 1978.

HANSEN, R. A. Anxiety. In S. Ball (Ed.), *Motivation in education.* New York: Academic Press, 1977.

HANSFORD, B. C., HATTIE, J. A. The relationship between self and achievement/performance measures. *Review of Educational Research,* 1982, *52,* 123–142.

HARGADON, F. Tests and college admission. *American Psychologist,* 1981, *36,* 1021–1034.

HARLEY, R. K. Children with visual disabilities. In L. M. Dunn (Ed.), *Exceptional children in the schools: Special education in transition.* New York: Holt, Rinehart and Winston, 1973.

HARRIS, V. W. and SHERMAN, J. A. Use and analysis of the "Good Behavior Game" to reduce disruptive classroom behavior. *Journal of Applied Behavior Analysis,* 1973, *6,* 405–417.

HARROW, A. J. *A taxonomy of the psychomotor domain: A guide for developing behavioral objectives.* New York: David McKay, 1972.

HARTLEY, S. S. Meta-analysis of the effects of individually paced instruction in mathematics. *Dissertation Abstracts International,* 1978, *38* (7-A), 4003.

HARTUP, W. W. Peer interaction and social development. In P. Mussen (Ed.), *Carmichael's manual of child psychology* (3rd Ed.), Vol. 2. New York: Wiley, 1970.

HASSETT, J. But that would be wrong . . . *Psychology Today,* 1981, *15,*(11), 34–50.

HAVIGHURST, R. J. Life-span development and educational psychology In F. W. Farley & N. J. Gordon (Eds.) *Psychology and education: The state of the union.* Berkeley, Calif.: McCutchan, 1981.

HAVIGHURST, R. J. Social backgrounds: Their impact on school children. In T. D. Horn (Ed.), *Reading for the disadvantaged.* New York: Harcourt Brace Jovanovich, 1970.

HAWKINS, R. P., SLUYTER, D. . & SMITH, C. D. Modifications of achievement by a simple technique involving parents and teachers. In M. Harris (Ed.), *Classroom uses of behavior modification.* Columbus, Ohio: Charles E. Merrill, 1972.

HELLER, J. I. & GREENO, J. G. Information processing analyses of mathematical problem solving. In R. Tyler & S. White (Eds.), *Testing, teaching and learning: Report of a conference on research on testing.* Washington, D.C.: DHEW, National Institute of Education, October, 1979.

Here come the microkids. *Time Magazine,* May 3, 1982, pp. 50–56.

HERMAN, T. M. *Creating learning environments: The behavioral approach to education.* Boston: Allyn & Bacon, 1977.

HETHERINGTON, E. M. Divorce: A child's perspective. *American Psychologist,* 1979, *34,* 851–858.

HETHERINGTON, E. M. & PARKE, R. D. *Child psychology: A contemporary viewpoint.* New York: McGraw-Hill, 1979.

HIGBEE, K. L. *Your memory: How it works and*

how to improve it. Englewood Cliffs, N.J.: Prentice-Hall, 1977.

HILGARD, E. R., ATKINSON, R. L., & ATKINSON, R. C. *Introduction to psychology.* (7th ed.). New York: Harcourt Brace Jovanovich, 1979.

HILL, K. T. & EATON, W. O. The interaction of test anxiety and success-failure experiences in determining children's arithmetic performance. *Developmental Psychology,* 1977, *3,* 205–211.

HILL, W. *Learning: A survey of psychological interpretations* (Rev. Ed.). Scranton: Chandler Publishing Company, 1971.

HILL, W. F. *Principles of learning: A handbook of applications.* Palo Alto: Mayfield Publishing, 1981.

HILLER, J. H. Verbal response indicators of conceptual vagueness. *American Educational Research Journal,* 1971, *8,* 151–161.

HILLER, J. H., FISHER, G. A., & KAESS, W. A computer investigation of effective classroom lecturing. *American Educational Research Journal,* 1969, *6,* 661–675.

HILLS, J. R. *Measurement and evaluation in the classroom.* Columbus, Ohio: Charles E. Merrill, 1976.

HINES, C. V., CRUICKSHANK, D. R., & KENNEDY, J. L. *Measures of teacher clarity and their relationships to student achievement and satisfaction.* Paper presented at the annual meeting of the American Educational Research Association, New York, March, 1982.

HOFFMAN, L. W. Changes in family roles, socialization and sex differences. *American Psychologist,* 1977, *32,* (8), 644–657.

HOFFMAN, M. L. Empathy, its development and prosocial implications. In C. B. Keasey, (Ed.), *Nebraska Symposium on Motivation, 1977,* Lincoln, Nebr. University of Nebraska Press, 1978.

HOFFMAN, M. L. Development of moral thought, feeling, and behavior. *American Psychologist,* 1979, *34,* 958–966.

HOFFMAN, M. L. Personality and social development. In M. R. Rosenzweig and L. W. Porter (Eds.). *Annual review of psychology, 28.* Palo Alto: Annual Reviews, Inc., 1977.

HOLLAND, J. L. Prediction of college grades from personality and aptitude variables. *Journal of Educational Psychology,* 1960, *51,* 245–254.

HOLLINGWORTH, L. S. *Children above 180 IQ.* New York: Harcourt Brace Jovanovich, 1942.

HOMME, L., CSANYI, A., GONZALES, M. A., & RECHS, J. R. *How to use contingency contracting in the classroom* (Rev. Ed.). Champaign, Ill: Research Press, 1970.

HOPKINS, C. O. & ANTES, R. L. *Classroom testing: Administration scoring, and score interpretation.* Itasca, Ill.: F. E. Peacock, 1979.

HOPKINS, K. D. & STANLEY, J. C. *Educational and psychological measurement and evaluation.* (6th ed.). Englewood Cliffs, N.J.: Prentice-Hall, 1981.

HORN, J. L. & DONALDSON, G. Cognitive development in adulthood. In O. Brim & Kagan, J. (Eds.), *Constancy, and change in human development,* Cambridge, Massachusetts: Harvard University Press, 1980.

HOUSE, E. R. & LAPAN, S. D. *Survival in the classroom: Negotiating with kids, colleagues, and bosses.* Boston: Allyn & Bacon, 1978.

HUCK, S. & BOUNDS, W. Essay grades: An interaction between graders' handwriting clarity and the neatness of the examination papers. *American Educational Research Journal,* 1972, *9,* 279–283.

HUDGINS, B. B. *Learning and thinking: A*

*primer for teachers.* Itasca, Ill.: F. E. Peacock, 1977.

HULL, F. M. & HULL, M. E. Children with oral communication disabilities. In L. M. Dunn (Ed.). *Exceptional Children in the schools: Special education in transition.* New York: Holt, Rinehart and Winston, 1973.

HUNDERT, J. & BUCHER, B. Pupil's self-scored arithmetic performance: A practical procedure for maintaining accuracy. *Journal of Applied Behavior Analysis,* 1978, *11,* 304.

HUNT, J. Comments on "The modification of intelligence through early experience" by Ramey and Haskins. *Intelligence,* 1981, *5,* 21–27.

HUNT, J. MCV. *Intelligence and experience.* New York: Ronald, 1961.

HUNT, M. How the mind works. *The New York Times Magazine,* January 24, 1982, 30–35+.

HUNTER, I. M. L. Mnemonic systems and devices. *Science News,* 1956, *39,* 75–97.

HYDE, T. S. & JENKINS, J. J. Recall for words as a function of semantic, graphic, and syntactic orienting tasks. *Journal of Verbal Learning and Verbal Behavior,* 1973, *12,* 471–480.

INHELDER, B. & PIAGET, J. *The growth of logical thinking from childhood to adolescence.* New York: Basic Books, 1973.

IRVING, O. & MARTIN, J. Withitness: The confusing variable. *American Educational Research Journal,* 1982, *19,* 313–319.

JACKSON, G. The research evidence on the effects of grade retention. *Review of Educational Research,* 1975, *45,* 613–636.

JACKSON, P. & LAHADERNE, H. Inequalities of teacher-pupil contacts. In M. Silberman (Ed.). *The experience of schooling.* New York: Holt, Rinehart and Winston, 1971.

JAMISON, D., SUPPES, P., & WELLS S. The effectiveness of alternative instructional media: A survey. *Review of Educational Research,* 1974, *44,* 1–61.

JARVIK, L. F. & ERLENMEYER-KIMLING, L. Survey of familial correlations in measured intellectual functions. In J. Zubin & G. A. Jervis (Eds.). *Psychopathology of mental development.* New York: Grune & Stratton, 1967, 447–459.

JENCKS, C., SMITH, M., ACLAND, H., BANE, M., COHEN, D. GINTIS, H., HEYNS, B., & MICHELSON, S. *Inequality: A reassessment of the effect of family and schooling in America.* New York: Basic Books, 1972.

JENSEN, A. R. *Bias in Testing.* New York: Free Press, 1974.

JENSEN, A. R. How biased are culture-loaded tests? *Genetic Psychology Monographs,* 1974, *90,* 185–244.

JENSEN, A. R. How much can we boost IQ and scholastic achievement? *Harvard Educational Review,* 1969, *39,* 1–123.

JENSEN, A. R. Raising the IQ: The Ramey and Haskins study. *Intelligence,* 1981, *5,* 29–40.

JOHNSON, D. & JOHNSON, R. *Learning together and alone: Cooperation, competition, and individualization.* Englewood Cliffs, N.J.: Prentice-Hall, 1975.

JOHNSON, D. & JOHNSON, R. Many teachers wonder . . . will the special needs child ever really belong? *Instructor,* 1978, *87,* 152–154.

JOHNSON, D. W. *Reaching out: Interpersonal effectiveness and self-actualization.* Englewood Cliffs, N.J.: Prentice-Hall, 1972.

JOHNSON, J. W. Education and the new technology: A face of history. *Educational Technology,* 1981, *21,* 15–23.

JOHNSON, L. V. & BANY, M. A. *Classroom management: Theory and skill training.* New York: Macmillan, 1970.

JOHNSON, K. R. & RUSKIN, R. S. *Behavioral instruction: An evaluative review.* Washington, D.C.: American Psychological Association, 1977.

KAGAN, J. Family experience and the child's development. *American Psychologist,* 1979, *34,* 886–891.

KAGAN, J., ROSMAN, B. L., DAY, D., ALBERT, J. & PHILLIPS, W. Information processing in the child: Significance of analytic and reflective attitudes. *Psychological Monographs,* 1964, *78.*

KAMIN, L. J. *The science and politics of IQ.* Potomac, Md.: Erlbaum, 1974.

KAPLAN, E. & KAPLAN, G. The prelinguistic child. In J. Elliot (Ed.), *Human development and cognitive processes.* New York: Holt, Rinehart, and Winston, 1971.

KARPLUS, R. & LAWSON, C. A. *SCIS Teachers Handbook: Science Curriculum Improvement Study.* Berkeley, Calif.: University of California, 1974.

KASH, M. M. & BORICH, G. *Teacher behavior and pupil self-concept.* Reading, Mass.: Addison-Wesley, 1978.

KATZ, L. G. *Developmental stages for preschool teachers.* Urbana, Ill.: ERIC Clearinghouse on Early Childhood Education, 1972.

KAUFMAN, A. & KAUFMAN, N. *The Kaufman Assessment Battery for Children.* Circle Pines, American Guidance Service, 1983.

KAUFMAN, A., BARON, A., & KNAPP, R. Some effects of instructions on human operant behavior. *Psychonomic Monograph Supplement,* 1966, *1,* 243–250.

KAUFMAN, P. The effects of nonverbal behavior on performance and attitudes in a college classroom. *Dissertation Abstracts International,* 1976, *37,* (1-A), 326.

KELLER, F. S. A personal course in psychology. In R. Ulrich, T. Stachnik, & J. Mabry (Eds.). *Control of human behavior* Vol. 1. New York: Scott Foresman, 1966.

KELLEY, C. *Journal of Humanistic Psychology,* 1974, *14.*

KELLEY, E. G. A study of consistent discrepancies between instructor grades and test results. *Journal of Educational Psychology,* 1958, *49,* 328–335.

KENNEDY, J. L., CRUICKSHANK, D. C., BUSH, A. J., & MYERS, B. Additional investigations into the nature of teacher clarity. *Journal of Educational Research,* 1978, *72,* 3–10.

KING, G. *Personal communication.* Austin: University of Texas, June, 1979.

KIRBY, F. D. & SHIELDS, F. Modification of arithmetic response rate and attending behavior in a seventh grade student. *Journal of Applied Behavior Analysis,* 1972, *5,* 79–84.

KIRBY, K. HOLBORN, S. W., & BUSHBY, H. T. Word game bingo: A behavioral treatment package for improving textual responding to signt words. *Journal of Applied Behavior Analysis,* 1981, *14,* 317–326.

KIRK, S. and GALLAGHER, J. J. *Educating exceptional children* (3rd Ed.). Boston: Houghton Mifflin, 1979.

KIRK, S. and GALLAGHER, J. J. *Educating exceptional children* (4th Ed.). Boston: Houghton Mifflin, 1983.

KIRSCHENBAUM, H., SIMON, S., & NAPIER, R. *Wad-ja-get? The grading game in American education.* New York: Hart, 1971.

KLAHR, D. Information processing models of cognitive development: Potential relevance to science instruction. Paper presented at American Educational Research Association Meeting, March, 1978.

KLAUSMEIER, H. J. Instructional design and the teaching of concepts. In J. Levin & V. Allen (Eds.). *Cognitive learning in children: Theories and strategies.* New York: Academic Press, 1976.

KLAUSMEIER, H. & GOODWIN, W. *Learning and human abilities: Educational psychology.* New York: Harper and Row, 1975.

KNAPCZYK, D. R. & LIVINGSTON, G. The effects of prompting question-asking upon on-task behavior and reading comprehension. *Journal of Applied Behavior Analysis,* 1974, *7,* 115–121.

KOHLBERG, L. The cognitive-developmental approach to moral education. *Phi Delta Kappan,* 1975, *56,* 670–677.

KOHLBERG, L. The development of children's orientations toward moral order: Sequence in the development of moral thought. *Vita Humana,* 1963, *6,* 11–33.

KOHLBERG, L. & GILLIGAN, C. The adolescent as a philosopher: The discovery of the self in a postconventional world. *Daedalus,* 1971, *100,* 1051–1086.

KOHLER, W. *The mentality of apes* (E. Winter, trans.). New York: Harcourt, Brace, 1925.

KOLATA, G. B. Math and sex: Are girls born with less ability? *Science,* 1980, *210,* 1234–1235.

KOLESNIK, W. B. *Learning: Educational applications.* Boston: Allyn & Bacon, 1976.

KOLESNIK, W. B. *Motivation: Understanding and influencing human behavior.* Boston: Allyn & Bacon, 1978.

KOUNIN, J. *Discipline and group management in classrooms.* New York: Holt, Rinehart and Winston, 1970.

KOUNIN, J. S. & DOYLE, P. H. Degree of continuity of a lesson's signal system and task involvement of children. *Journal of Educational Psychology,* 1975, *67,* 159–164.

KOUNIN, J. & GUMP, P. V. Signal systems of lesson settings and the task related behavior of preschool children. *Journal of Educational Psychology,* 1974, *66,* 554–562.

KRATHWOHL, D. R., BLOOM, B. S. & MASIA, B. B. *Taxonomy of educational objectives, Handbook II: Affective domain.* New York: David McKay, 1956.

KREUTZER, M. A., LEONARD, C. & FLAVELL, J. H. An interview study of children's knowledge about memory. *Monographs of the Society for the Study of Child Development,* 1975, *40,* (1, whole No. 159).

KRITCHEVSKY, S., & PRESCOTT, E. *Planning environments for young children: Physical space.* Washington, D.C.: National Association for the Education of Young Children, 1969.

KRUMBOLTZ, J. D. & KRUMBOLTZ, H. B. *Changing children's behavior.* Englewood Cliffs, N.J.: Prentice-Hall, 1972.

KULIK, C. & KULIK, J. Effects of ability grouping on secondary school students: A motor-analysis of evaluation findings. *American Educational Research Journal,* 1982, *19,* 415–428.

KULIK, J. A., KULIK, C. C., & COHEN, P. A. Effectiveness of computer-based college teaching, A meta-analysis of findings. *Review of Educational Research,* 1980, *50,* 525–544.

KULIK, J. A., KULIK, C. C. & COHEN, P. A. A meta-analysis of outcome studies of Keller's Personalized System of Instruction. *American Psychologist,* 1979, *34,* 307–318.

KURTZ, J. J., & SWENSON, E. J. Factors related to over-achievement and under-achievement in school. *School Review,* 1951, *59,* 472–480.

LAKEIN, A. *How to get control of your time and your life.* New York: Signet, 1973.

LAMB, M. The father's role in the infant's social world. In J. H. Stevens & M. Mathews *Mother/child/father/child relationships.* Washington,

D.C.: National Association for the Education of Young Children, 1978.

LAMB, M. E. Parental influences and the father's role: A personal perspective. *American Psychologist*, 1979, *34*, 938–943.

LAMBERT, N. M. Psychological evidence in *Lary P. v. Wilson Riles*: An evaluation by a witness for the defense. *American Psychologist*, 1981, *36*, 937–952.

LAND, M. L. and SMITH, L. R. Effects of a teacher clarity variable on student achievement. *Journal of Educational Research*, 1979, 196–197.

LANDSMANN, L. Is teaching hazardous to your health? *Today's Education*, 1978, *67*, 48–49.

LANGER, P. C. What's the score on programmed instruction? *Today's Education*, 1972, *61*, 59.

LARKIN, J, MCDERMOTT, J., SIMON, D. P., & SIMON, H. A. Expert and novice performance in solving physics problems. *Science*, 1981, *208*, 1335–1340.

LARSEN, G. Y. Methodology in developmental psychology: An examination of research on Piagetian theory. *Child Development*, 1977, *48*, 1160–1166.

LAWRENCE, R. S. Teacher biz needs a little show biz. *The New York Times*, January 6, 1980.

LAYCOCK, F. & CAYLOR, J. S. Physiques of gifted children and their less gifted siblings. *Child Development*, 1964, *35*, 63–74.

LEADBEATER, B. J. and DIONNE, J. The adolescent's use of formal operational thinking in solving problems related to identity resolution. *Adolescence*, 1981, *16*, 101–109.

LEPPER, M. R. & GREENE, D. *The hidden costs of rewards: New perspectives on the psychology of human motivation.* Hillsdale, N.J.: Erlbaum, 1978.

LEPPER, M. R. & GREENE, D. Turning play into work: Effects of adult surveillance and extrinsic reward on children's motivation. *Journal of Personality and Social Psychology*, 1975, *31*, 479–486.

LEPPER, M. R., GREENE, D. & NISBETT, R. Undermining children's intrinsic interest with extrinsic reward: A test of the "overjustification" hypothesis. *Journal of Personality and Social Psychology*, 1973, *28*, 129–137.

LERNER, B. The minimum competency testing movement: Social, scientific, and legal implications. *American Psychologist*, 1981, *36*, 1057–1066.

LEVIN, J. R. *The mnemonic '80s: Keywords in the classroom.* Paper #86. Research and Development Center, Madison: University of Wisconsin, 1980.

LEVIN, J. The mnemonic '80's: Keywords in the classroom *Educational Psychologist*, 1981, *16*, 65–82.

LEVIN, J. and ALLEN, V. *Cognitive learning in children: Theories and strategies.* New York: Academic Press, 1976.

LEVIN, J., BERRY, J. K., MILLER, G. E., & BARTELL, N. P. More on how (and how not) to remember the states and their capitals. *Elementary School Journal*, 1982, *82*, 379–388.

LEVIN, J. & PRESSLEY, M. Understanding mnemonic imagery effects: A dozen "obvious" outcomes. *Educational Technology*, in press.

LEVITAN, T. E. & CHANANIE, L. C. Responses of female primary school teachers to sex-typed behaviors in male and female children. *Child Development*, 1972, *43*, 1309–1316.

LICKONA, T. How to encourage moral development. *Learning*, March, 1977.

LIEBERMAN, D. A. *Learning and the control of behavior: Some principles, theories, and applications of classical and operant conditioning.* New York: Holt, Rinehart and Winston, 1974.

LIEBERT, R. M. & SCHWARTZBERG, N. S. Effects of mass media, In M. Rosenzweig & L. Porter (Eds.) *Annual Review of Psychology*, Palo Alto, Calif. Annual Reviews, 1977.

LINDSAY, P. H. & NORMAN, D. A. *Human information processing: An introduction to psychology* (2nd ed.). New York: Academic Press, 1977.

LINDVALL, C. M., TAMBURINO, J. L. & ROBINSON, J. An exploratory investigation of the effect of teaching primary grade children to use specific problem solving strategies in solving simple arithmetic story problems. Paper presented at the annual meeting of the American Educational Research Association, New York, March, 1982.

LINN, R., KLEIN, S., & HART, F. The nature and correlates of law school essay grades. *Educational and Psychological Measurement*, 1972, *32*, 267–279.

LOCKWOOD, A. The effects of values clarification and moral development curricula on school age subjects: A critical review of recent research. *Review of Educational Research*, 1978, *48*, 325–364.

LOEHLIN, J. C., LINDZEY, G., & SPUHLER, J. N. Cross-group comparisons of intellectual abilities. In L. Willerman & R. Turner (Eds.) *Readings about individuals and group differences.* San Francisco: Freeman, 1979.

LOWENBRAUN, S. & SCROGGS, C. Hearing impaired. In N. G. Haring, *Behavior of exceptional children: An introduction to special education.* Columbus, Ohio: Charles E. Merrill, 1974.

LUFLER, H. S. Discipline: A new look at an old problem. *Phi Delta Kappan*, 1978, *59*, 424–446.

LUITEN, J., AMES, W., & ACKERSON, G. A meta-analysis of the effects of advance organizers on learning and retention. *American Educational Research Journal*, 1980, *17*, 211–218.

LYMAN, H. B. *Test scores and what they mean* (3rd ed.). Englewood Cliffs, N.J.: Prentice-Hall, 1978.

MACCOBY, E. E. & JACKLIN, C. N. *The psychology of sex differences.* Stanford: Stanford University Press, 1974.

MACDONALD-ROSS, M. Behavioral objectives: A critical review. *Instructional Science*, 1974, *2*, 1–51.

MCALLISTER, L. W., STACHOWIAK, J. G., BAER, D. M. & CONDERMAN, L. The application of operant conditioning techniques in a secondary school classroom. *Journal of Applied Behavior Analysis*, 1969, *2*, 277–285.

MCCALL, R. B. Nature-nurture and the two realms of development: A proposed integration with respect to mental development. *Child Development*, 1981, *52*, 1–12.

MCCLELLAND, D. C. Testing for competence rather than for intelligence. *American Psychologist*, 1973, *28*, 1–14.

MCCLELLAND, D., ATKINSON, J. W., CLARK, R. W., & LOWELL, E. L. *The achievement motive.* New York: Appleton-Century-Crofts, 1953.

MCCONNELL, J. W. Relationships between selected teacher behaviors and attitudes/achievements of algebra classes. Paper presented at the annual meeting of the American Educational Research Association, New York, April, 1977.

MCCUNE, S. D. & MATTHEWS, M. Building positive futures: Toward a nonsexist education for all children. *Childhood Education.* February, 1976, 178–186.

MCDONALD, F. *Beginning teacher evaluation study. Phase II 1973–74, Executive summary report.* Princeton, N.J.: Educational Testing Service, 1976a.

MCDONALD, F. Designing research for policy-making. Paper presented at the annual meet-

ing of the American Educational Research Association, San Francisco, April, 1976b.

MCDONALD, F. *Teachers do make a difference.* Princeton, N.J.: Educational Testing Service, 1976c.

MCGINLEY, P. & MCGINLEY, H. Reading groups as psychological groups. *Journal of Experimental Education*, 1970, *39*, 36–42.

MCKEACHIE, W. The decline and fall of the laws of learning. *Educational Researcher*, 1974, *3*, 7–11.

MCKENZIE, G. & HENRY, M. Effects of testlike events on on-task behavior, test anxiety, and achievement in a classroom rule-learning task, *Journal of Educational Psychology*, 1979, *71*, 370–374.

MCKENZIE, T. L. & RUSHALL, B. S. Effects of self-recording on attendance and performance in a competitive swimming training environment. *Journal of Applied Behavior Analysis*, 1974, *7*, 199–206.

MCLAUGHLIN, T. F. & GNAGEY, W. J. Self-management and pupil self-control. Paper presented at the annual meeting of the American Educational Research Association, Los Angeles, April, 1981.

MCNEILL, D. Developmental psycholinguistics. In F. Smith & G. Miller (Eds.), *The genesis of language: A psycholinguistic approach.* Cambridge, Mass.: MIT Press, 1966.

MCNEMAR, Q. Lost: Our intelligence? Why? *American Psychologist*, 1964, *19*, 871–882.

MCPARTLAND, J. *The segregated student in desegregated schools: Final report to the Center for the Study of Social Organization of Schools.* Baltimore: Johns Hopkins University, 1968.

MCWILLIAMS, E. Understanding cognition in science and mathematics: Has there been a breakthrough? Symposium at the meeting of the American Educational Research Association, New York, March, 1982.

MADSEN, C. H., BECKER, W. C., & THOMAS, D. R. Rules, praise, and ignoring: Elements of elementary classroom control. *Journal of Applied Behavior Analysis*, 1968, *1*, 139–150.

MADSEN, C. H., BECKER, W. C., THOMAS, D. R., KOSER, L., & PLAGER, E. An analysis of the reinforcing function of "sit down" commands. In R. K. Parker (Ed.), *Readings in educational psychology.* Boston: Allyn & Bacon, 1968.

MAEHR, M. L. Continuing motivation: An analysis of a seldom considered educational outcome. *Review of Educational Research*, 1976, *46*, 443–462.

MAEHR, M. L. *Sociocultural origins of achievement.* Monterey, Calif.: Brooks Cole, 1974.

MAEROFF, G. I. The unfavored gifted few. *New York Times Magazine*, August 21, 1977, 30.

MAGER, R. *Preparing instructional objectives.* Palo Alto, Calif.: Fearon, 1962.

MAHONEY, K. B. & HOPKINS, B. L. The modification of sentence structure and its relationship to subjective judgments of creativity in writing. *Journal of Applied Behavior Analysis*, 1973, *6*, 425–343.

MAHONEY, M. J. & THORESEN, C. E. *Self-control: Power to the person.* Monterey, Calif.: Brooks Cole, 1974.

MAIER, N. R. F. An aspect of human reasoning. *British Journal of Psychology*, 1933, *24*, 144–155.

MAIN, G. C. & MUNRO, B. C. A token reinforcement program in a public junior high school. *Journal of Applied Behavior Analysis*, 1977, *10*, 93–94.

MANASTER, G. *Adolescent development and the life tasks.* Boston: Allyn & Bacon, 1977.

MANSFIELD, R. S., BUSSE, T. V., & KREPELKA, E. J. The effectiveness of creativity training. *Re-*

view of Educational Research, 1978, 48, 517–536.

MARBLE, W. O., WINNE, P. H. & MARTIN, J. F. Science achievement as a function of method and schedule of grading. Journal of Research in Science Teaching, 1978, 15, 433–400.

MARCIA, J. E. Identity formation in adolescence. In J. Adelson, Handbook of Adolescent Psychology, New York: Wiley, 1980.

MARGOLIN, J. B. & MISCH, M. R. Computers in the classroom: An interdisciplinary view of trends and alternatives. New York: Spartan Books, 1970.

MARKMAN, E. M. Realizing that you don't understand: A preliminary investigation. Child Development, 1977, 48, 986–992.

MARLOWE, R. H., MADSEN, C. H., BOWEN, C. E., REARDON, R. C., & LOGUE, P. E. Several classroom behavior problems: Teachers or counselors. Journal of Applied Behavior Analysis, 1978, 11, 53–66.

MARTIN, R. & LAURIDSEN, D. Developing student discipline and motivation: A series for teacher in-service training. Champaign, Ill.: Research Press, 1974.

MARTINSON, R. A. Children with superior cognitive abilities. In L. M. Dunn (Ed.). Exceptional children in the schools: Special education in transition. New York: Holt, Rinehart and Winston, 1973.

MARTINSON, R. A. Educational programs for gifted pupils. Sacramento: California Department of Education, 1961.

MASLOW, A. H. Motivation and personality (2nd ed.). New York: Harper and Row, 1970.

MASLOW, A. H. Toward a psychology of being (2nd ed.). Princeton, N.J.: Van Nostrand, 1968.

MATARAZZO, J. D. Wechsler's measurement and appraisal of adult intelligence. (5th ed.). Fair Lawn, N.J.: Oxford University Press, 1972.

MAYER, R. E. Thinking and problem solving. Glenview, Ill.: Scott Foresman, 1977.

MEDLEY, D. M. The effectiveness of teachers. In P. Peterson & H. Walberg (Eds.), Research on teaching: Concepts, findings, and implications, Berkeley, Calif.: McCutchan, 1979.

MEDLEY, D. M. Teacher competence and teacher effectiveness: A review of process-product research. Washington, D.C.: American Association of Colleges for Teacher Education, 1977.

MEICHENBAUM, D. Cognitive behavior modification: An integrative approach. New York: Plenum, 1977.

MENDELS, G. E. & FLANDERS, J. P. Teacher's expectations and pupil performance. American Educational Research Journal, 1973, 10, 203–212.

MERCER, C. Learning disabilities. In H. Haring (Ed.), Exceptional children and youth. Columbus, Ohio: Charles E. Merrill, 1982.

MERCER, J. Labeling the mentally retarded. Berkeley, Calif.: University of California Press, 1973.

MERCER, J. R. & LEWIS, J. F. System of Multicultural Pluralistic Assessment. New York: The Psychological Corporation, 1977.

MERRILL, P. F. The case against PILOT: The pros and cons of authoring languages for computer applications to instruction. Paper presented at the annual meeting of the American Educational Research Association, Los Angeles, April 13–17, 1981.

MESSER, S. Reflection-Impulsivity: Stability and school failure. Journal of Educational Psychology, 1970, 61, 487–490.

MESSER, S. Reflection-Impulsivity: A review. Psychological Review, 1976, 83, 1026–1052.

MESSICK, S. The effectiveness of coaching for the SAT: Review and reanalysis of research from the fifties to the FTC. Princeton, N.J.: Educational Testing Service, 1980.

MESSICK, S. & JUNGEBLUT, A. Time and method in coaching for the SAT. Psychological Bulletin, 1981, 89, 191–216.

METCALFE, B. Self-concept and attitude toward school. British Journal of Educational Psychology, 1981, 51, 66–76.

MEYER, B. For Tommy at 13, no new freedoms. New York Times, Jan. 24, 1982, p. 26.

MEYERS, P. I. & HAMMILL, D. D. Methods for Learning Disorders (2nd ed.). New York: Wiley, 1976.

MILLER, G. Language and speech. San Francisco: Freeman, 1981.

MILLER, G. A. The keyword method in the learning of verbs. Paper presented at the Annual Meeting of the American Educational Research Association. San Francisco, April, 1979.

MILLER, G. A. The magical number seven, plus or minus two: Some limits on our capacity for processing information. Psychological Review, 1956, 63, 81–97.

MILLER, R. B. Analysis and specification of behavior for training. In R. Glaser (Ed.). Training research and education: Science edition. New York: Wiley, 1962.

MOODY, K. The research on TV: A disturbing picture. New York Times, Spring Survey of Education, April 20, 1980.

MOOS, R. H. & MOOS, B. S. Classroom Social Climate and Student Absences and Grades. Journal of Educational Psychology, 1978, 70, 263–269.

MORRIS, C. G. Psychology: An introduction. (4th ed.). Englewood Cliffs, N.J.: Prentice-Hall, 1982.

MORROW, L. M. & WEINSTEIN, C. S. Increasing children's use of literature through program and physical design changes. Elementary School Journal, 1983, 83, 131–137.

MOSOKOWITZ, B. A. The acquisition of language. Scientific American, 1978, 239, 92–108.

MOSKOWITZ, G. & HAYMAN, M. L. Successful strategies of inner-city teachers: A year-long study. Journal of Educational Research, 1976, 69, 283–289.

MOULTON, R. W. Effects of success and failure on level of aspiration as related to achievement motives. Journal of Personality and Social Psychology, 1965, 1, 399–406.

MUNSON, H. Moral thinking: Can it be taught? Psychology Today, 1979, 13(2), 48 +.

MURRAY, H. A. Explorations in personality. New York: Oxford University Press, 1938.

MUSGRAVE, G. R. Individualized instruction: Teaching strategies focusing on the learner. Boston, Mass.: Allyn & Bacon, 1975.

MUSS, R. E. Social cognition: David Elkind's theory of adolescent egocentrism. Adolescence, 1982, 17, 249–265.

MUSSEN, P., CONGER, J. J. & KAGAN, J. Child development and personality (5th ed.). New York: Harper and Row, 1979.

NAREMORE, R. Teacher differences in attitudes toward children's speech characteristics. Paper presented at the meeting of the American Educational Research Association, 1970.

NARIN, A. & Associates. The reign of ETS: The corporation that makes up minds. Washington, D.C., 1980.

National Assessment of Educational Progress. Functional literacy: Basic reading performance. Denver, Col.: Author, 1976.

National Center for Educational Statistics, A favorable job market seen for teacher graduates in the late 1980's, Washington, D.C.: US Department of Health, Education, and Welfare, May, 1980.

National Education Association, Ranking of the States, 1981. Washington, D.C.: National Education Association, 1981.

National Education Association. Status of the American public school teacher, 1970–71, Research Report 1972-R3, Washington, D.C.: National Education Association, 1972.

National Education Association, Status of the American public school teacher, 1975–76. Washington, D.C.: National Education Association, 1976.

National Education Association, Teacher supply and demand in public schools, 1980–81, Research Memo, Washington, D.C.: National Education Association, 1981.

NEIMARK, E. Intellectual development during adolescence. In F. D. Horowitz (Ed.). Review of child development research (Vol. 4). Chicago: University of Chicago Press, 1975.

NEISSER, U. Cognition and reality: Principles and implications of cognitive psychology. San Francisco: W. H. Freman, 1976.

NELSON, K. Individual differences in language development: Implications for development and language. Developmental Psychology, 1981, 17, 179–187.

NELSON, K. Structure and strategy in learning to talk. Monographs of the Society for Research in Child Development, 1973, 38.

NELSON, L. L. & KAGAN, S. Competition: The star-spangled scramble. Psychology Today, September, 1972, p. 53.

NEWPORT, E. L., GLEITMAN, H., & GLEITMAN, L. R. Mother, I'd rather do it myself: Some effects and non-effects of maternal speech style. In C. Snow & C. Ferguson (Eds.) Talking to children: Language input and acquisition. Cambridge, England: Cambridge University Press, 1977.

NORMAN, D. A. Memory, knowledge and the answering of questions. In R. L. Solso (Ed.), Contemporary issues in cognitive psychology: The Loyola Symposium. Washington, D.C.: V. H. Winston and Sons, 1973.

NUNGESTER, R. J. & DUCHASTEL, P. C. Testing versus review: Effects on retention. Journal of Educational Psychology, 1982, 74, 18–22.

OAKLAND, T. Research on the Adaptive Behavior Inventory for Children and the Estimated Learning Potential. School Psychology Digest, 1979, 8, 63–70.

O'CONNOR, R. D. Modification of social withdrawal through symbolic modeling. Journal of Applied Behavior Analysis, 1969, 2, 15–22.

O'DAY, E. F., KULHAVY, R. W., ANDERSON, W, & MALCZYNSKI, R. J. Programmed instruction: Techniques and trends. New York: Appleton-Century-Crofts, 1971.

OGDEN, J. E., BROPHY, J. E., & EVERTSON, C. M. An experimental investigation of organization and management techniques in first grade reading groups. Paper presented at the annual meeting of the American Educational Research Association, New York, April, 1977.

O'LEARY, K. D. Pills or skills for hyperactive children. Journal of Applied Behavior Analysis, 1980, 13, 191–204.

O'LEARY, K. D. & DRABMAN, R. S. Token reinforcement programs in the classroom: A review. Psychological Bulletin, 1971, 75, 379–398.

O'LEARY, K. D., KAUFMAN, K. F., KASS, R. E., & DRABMAN, R. S. The effects of loud and soft reprimands on the behavior of disruptive students. Exceptional Children, 1970, 37, 145–155.

O'LEARY, K. D. & O'LEARY, S. (Eds.). Classroom management: The successful use of behavior modification (2nd ed.). New York: Pergamon, 1977.

O'LEARY, K. D. & WILSON, G. T. Behavior therapy: Application and outcome. Englewood Cliffs, N.J.: Prentice-Hall, 1975.

O'LEARY, S. G. & O'LEARY, K. D. Behavior modification in the schools. In H. Leitenberg (Ed.). *Handbook of behavior modification and behavior therapy*. Englewood Cliffs, N.J.: Prentice-Hall, 1976a.

O'LEARY, S. G. & O'LEARY, K. D. Behavior modification in schools: concepts, procedures, and ethical issues. Report prepared for the Protection of Human Subjects of Biomedical and Behavior Research. Washington, D.C.: Department of Health, Education, and Welfare, 1976b.

OLLENDICK, T. H., MATSON, J. L., ESVELDT-DAWSON, K. & SHAPIRO, E. S. Increasing spelling achievement: An analysis of treatment procedures utilizing an alternating treatments design. *Journal of Applied Behavior Analysis*, 1980, *13*, 645–654.

O'NEIL, H. F. *Learning strategies*. New York: Academic Press, 1978.

OOSTHOEK, H. & ACKERS, G. The evaluation of an audio-taped course (II). *British Journal of Educational Technology*, 1973, *4*, 55–73.

ORLANSKY, J. & STRING, J. Computer-based instruction for military training. *Defense Management Journal*, 1981, 2nd Quarter, 46–54.

ORNSTEIN, A. C. Teacher salaries: Past, present, and future. *Phi Delta Kappan*, 1980, *61*, 677–679.

ORNSTEIN, A. C. & MILLER,, H. L. *Looking into education: An introduction to American education*. Chicago: Rand McNally, 1980.

OSBORN, A. F. *Applied imagination* (3rd ed.). New York: Scribner's, 1963.

OSBOURNE, R. Children's ideas about electric current. *New Zealand Science Teacher*, 1981, *29*, 12–19.

OTT, E. Bridging the cultural gap. In Cohen, M. D. (Ed.). *Migrant children: Their education*. Washington, D.C.: The Association for Childhood Education International, 1971.

PAGE, E. B. Teacher Comments and Student Performances: A 74 classroom experiment in school motivation. *Journal of Educational Psychology*, 1958, *49*, 173–181.

PAPALIA, D. E. & OLDS, S. W. *Human Development*, New York: McGraw-Hill, 1981.

PAPERT, S. *Mindstorms*. New York: Basic Books, 1980.

PARK, O., & TENNYSON, R. D. Adaptive design strategies for selecting number and presentation order of examples in coordinate concept acquisition. *Journal of Educational Psychology*, 1980, *72*, 362–370.

PARNES, S. J. *Creative behavior guidebook*. New York: Scribner's, 1967.

PATTERSON, C. J., & MISCHEL, W. Effects of temptation-inhibiting and task-facilitating plans on self-control. *Journal of Personality and Social Psychology*, 1976, *33*, 209–217.

PAUK, W. *How to study in college*, (2nd ed.). Boston: Houghton Mifflin, 1974.

PAVIO, A. *Imagery and verbal processes*. New York: Holt, Rinehart, and Winston, 1971.

PAYNE D. A. *The assessment of learning: Cognitive and affective*. Lexington, Mass.: Heath, 1974.

PAYNE, J. The gifted. In N. G. Harding (Ed.). *Education of exceptional children: An introduction to special education*. Columbus, Ohio: Charles E. Merrill, 1974.

PECK, R. F. & VELDMAN, D. J. *Effects of teacher characteristics on cognitive and affective gains of pupils*. Austin, Texas: Research and Development for Teacher Education, University of Texas, 1973.

PEECK, J., VAN DEN BOSCH, A. B., and KREUPELING, W. J. Effect of mobilizng prior knowledge on learning from text, *Journal of Educational Psychology*, 1982, *74*, 771–777.

PENFIELD, W. Consciousness, memory, and man's conditioned reflexes. In K. H. Pribram (Ed.). *On the biology of learning*. New York: Harcourt Brace Jovanovich, 1969.

PETERSON, D. Educable mentally retarded. In N. Haring (Ed.). *Behavior of exceptional children: An introduction to special education*. Columbus, Ohio: Charles E. Merrill, 1974.

PETERSON, P. Direct instruction reconsidered. In P. Peterson & H. Walberg (Eds.), *Research on teaching: Concepts, findings, and implications*. Berkeley, Calif.: McCutchan, 1979.

PETERSON, P., JANICKI, T. C., & SWING, S. R. Aptitude-treatment interaction effects of three social studies teaching approaches. *American Educational Research Journal*, 1980, *17*, 339–360.

PETTEGREW, L. S. & WOLF, G. E. Validating measures of teacher stress. *American Educational Research Journal*, 1982, *19*, 373–396.

PHILIP, H. & KELLY, M. Product and process in cognitive development: some comparative data of the performance of school age children in different cultures. *British Journal of Educational Psychology*, 1974, *44*, 248–265.

PIAGET, J. *The construction of reality in the child* (M. Cook, trans.). New York: Basic Books, 1954.

PIAGET, J. *Origins of intelligence in children*. New York: Norton, 1963.

PIAGET, J. *The science of education and the psychology of the child*. New York: Orion Press, 1970.

PIAGET, J. *Six psychological studies*. New York: Random House, 1967.

PIAGET, J. *Understanding causality* (D. Miles and M. Miles, trans.), New York: Norton, 1974.

PIDGEON, D. A. *Expectation and pupil performance*. London: National Foundation for Educational Research, 1970.

PINES, M. Only isn't lonely (or spoiled or selfish). *Psychology Today*, March, 1981, 15 + .

PIPPERT, R. A. *A study of creativity and faith*. Manitoba Department of Youth and Education 1969, No. 4.

PLATT, W. & BAKER, B. A. The relation of the scientific "hunch" to research. *Journal of Chemical Evaluation*, 1931, *8*, 1969–2002.

PLOMIN, R. & DEFRIES, J. C. Genetics and intelligence: Recent data. *Intelligence*, 1980, *4*, 15–24.

POCZTAR, J. *The theory and practice of programmed instruction: A guide for teachers*. Paris, UNESCO, 1972.

POPHAM, W. J. Objectives and instruction. In W. J. Popham, E. W. Eisner, H. J. Sullivan, & L. I. Tyler, *Instructional objectives* (Monograph Series on Curriculum Evaluation, No. 3). Chicago: Rand McNally, 1969.

PRAWAT, R. S., ANDERSON, A. DIAMOND, B. MCKEAGUE, D. & WHITMER, S. Teacher thinking about the affective domain: An interview study. Paper presented at the annual meeting of the American Educational Research Association, Los Angeles, 1981.

Preliminary Report of the Commission on Behavior Modification. *Case study issues raised by behavior modification in the schools*. Washington, D.C.: American Psychological Association, 1976.

PREMACK, D. Reinforcement theory. In D. Levine (Ed.). *Nebraska symposium on motivation* (Vol. 13). Lincoln, Nebr.: University of Nebraska Press, 1965.

PRESCOTT, G. A. *Metropolitan Achievement Tests: Manual for interpreting*. New York: Harcourt Brace Jovanovich, 1973.

PRESSEY, S. L. A third and fourth contribution toward the coming industrial revolution: in education. *School and Society*, 1932, *36*, 668–672.

PRESSLEY, M. Elaboration and memory development. *Child Development*, 1982, *53*, 296–309.

PRESSLEY, M., LEVIN, J. & DELANEY, H. D. The mnemonic keyword method. *Review of Research in Education*, 1982, *52*, 61–91.

PRICE, G. and O'LEARY, K. D. Teaching children to develop high performance standards. Unpublished manuscript, SUNY, Stony Brook, N.Y., 1974.

PRICE, R. V. Selecting free and inexpensive computer software. *Educational Computer*, 1982, *2*, 24–26.

PRING, R. Bloom's taxonomy: A philosophical critique. *Cambridge Journal of Education*, 1971, *1*, 83–91.

Program on Teaching Effectiveness. A factorially designed experiment on teacher structuring, soliciting, and reacting. (Research and Development Memorandum No. 147). Stanford, Calif.: Stanford Center for Research and Development in Teaching 1976.

PROSHANSKY, H. M. & NEWTON, P. The nature and meaning of Negro self-identify. In M. Deutsch, I. Katz, & A. R. Jensen (Eds.), *Social class, race, and psychological development*. New York: Holt, Rinehart and Winston, 1968.

PURKEY, W. W. *Self-concept and school achievement*. Englewood Cliffs, N.J.: Prentice-Hall, 1970.

PYLE, D. W. *Intelligence*. Boston: Routledge & Kegan Paul, 1979.

RAGOSTA, M. *Computer-assisted instruction and compensatory education: The ETS/LAUSD study*. Princeton, N.J.: Educational Testing Service, Project Report #18, September 1980.

RAGOSTA, M., HOLLAND, P. W. & JAMESON, D. T. *Computer-assisted instruction and compensatory education: The ETS/LAUSD study*. Executive summary to U.S. National Institute of Education, Contract #0400-78-0065. Princeton, New Jersey: Educational Testing Service, June, 1982.

RAMEY, C. T. & HASKINS, R. Early education, intellectual development, and school performance: A reply to Arthur Jensen and J. McVicker Hunt. *Intelligence*, 1981b, *5*, 41–48.

RAMEY, C. T. & HASKINS, R. The modification of intelligence through early experience. *Intelligence*, 1981a, *5*, 5–19.

RAUDSEPP, E. & HAUGH, G. P. *Creative growth games*. New York: Harcourt Brace Jovanovich, 1977.

READ, M. S., HABICHT, J., LECHTIG, A., & KLEIN, R. E. Maternal malnutrition, birth weight, and child development. Paper presented at the International Symposium on Nutrition, Growth, and Development, Valencia, Spain, May, 1973.

REDFIELD, D. L. & ROUSSEAU, E. W. A meta-analysis of experimental research on teacher questioning behavior. *Review of Educational Research*, 1981, *51*, 181–193.

REED, S. K. *Cognition: Theory and applications*, Monterey, Calif.: Brooks/Cole, 1982.

REID, D. K. & HRESKO, W. P. *A cognitive approach to learning disabilities*. New York: McGraw-Hill, 1981.

REIMER, J. PAOLITTO, D. P., & HERSH, R. H. *Promoting moral growth: From Piaget to Kohlberg* (2nd Ed.). New York: Longman, 1983.

REIS, S. M. *An analysis of the productivity of gifted students participating in programs using the revolving door identification model*. University of Connecticut, Bureau of Educational Research, 1981.

RENNER, J. W., STAFFORD, D. G., LAWSON, A. E., MCKINNON, J. W., FRIST, F. E. & KELLOGG, D. H. *Research, teaching, and learning with the Piagetian model*. Norman, Okla.: University of Oklahoma Press, 1976.

RENZULLI, J. Dear Mr. and Mrs. Copernicus: We regret to inform you ... *Gifted Child Quarterly*, 1982, *26*, 11–14.

RESNICK, L. B. Instructional Psychology. In M. Rosenzweig & L. Porter, (Eds.), *Annual review of psychology* Volume 32, Palo Alto, Calif.: Annual Reviews, 1981.

REYNOLDS, W. M. Self-esteem and classroom behavior in elementary school children. *Psychology in the Schools*, 1980, *17*, 273–277.

RICKARD, H. C., MELVIN, K. B., CREEL, J., & CREEL, L. The effects of bonus tokens upon productivity in a remedial classroom for behaviorally disturbed children. *Behavior Theory*, 1973, *4*, 378–385.

RICKARDS, J. P. Notetaking, underlining, inserted questions, and organizers in text: Research conclusions and educational implications. *Educational Technology*, June, 1980, 5–11.

RIST, R. Student social class and teacher expectations: The self-fulfilling prophecy in ghetto education. *Harvard Educational Review*, 1970, *40*, 411–451.

ROBIN, A. L. Behavioral instruction in college classrooms. *Review of Educational Research*, 1976, *46*, 313–355.

ROBINSON, D. W. Beauty, monster or something in between? 25 views of public schooling. *The Review of Education*, 1978, *4*, 263–274.

ROBINSON, F. P. *Effective study*. New York: Harper and Row 1961.

ROBINSON, N. M. & ROBINSON, H. B. *The mentally retarded child* (2nd ed.). New York: McGraw-Hill, 1976.

RODIN, M. & RODIN, B. Student evaluations of teachers. *Science*, 1972, *177*, 1164–1166.

ROEDELL, W. C., SLABY, R. G., & ROBINSON, H. B. *Social development in young children: A report for teachers*. Washington, D.C.: National Institute of Education, U.S. Department of Health, Education, and Welfare, 1976.

ROEMER, R. E. The social conditions for schoolings. In A. B. Calvin (Ed.), *Perspectives on education*. Reading, Mass.: Addison-Wesley, 1978.

ROETHLISBERGER, F. J., and DICKSON, W. J. *Management and the worker*. Cambridge, Mass.: Harvard University Press, 1939.

ROGERS, D. *Adolescents and youth*, 4th ed. Englewood Cliffs, N.J.: Prentice-Hall, 1981.

ROLLINS, H. A., MCCANDLESS, B. R., THOMPSON, M., & BRASSELL, W. R. Project Success Environment: An extended application of contingency management in inner-city schools. *Journal of Educational Psychology*, 1974, *66*, 167–178.

ROSCH, E. H. Cognitive representations of semantic categories. *Journal of Experimental Psychology: General*, 1975, *104*, 192–233.

ROSCH, E. On the internal structure of perceptual and semantic categories. In T. Moore (Ed.), *Cognitive development and the acquisition of language*. New York: Academic Press, 1973.

ROSEN, R. and HALL, E. *Sexuality and modern life*. New York: Random House, 1983.

ROSENSHINE, B. Academic engaged time, content covered, and direct instruction. Paper presented at the annual meeting of the American Educational Research Association, Toronto, April, 1978a.

ROSENSHINE, B. V. Content, time, and direct instruction. In P. Peterson & H. Walberg (Eds.), *Research on teaching: Concepts, findings, and implications*. Berkeley, Calif.: McCutchan, 1979.

ROSENSHINE, B. Instructional principles in direct instruction. Paper presented at the annual meeting of the American Educational Research Association, Toronto, April, 1978b.

ROSENSHINE, B. Primary grades instruction and student achievement. Paper presented at the annual meeting of the American Educational Research Association, New York, April, 1977.

ROSENSHINE, B., and FURST, N. The use of direct observation to study teaching. In R. Travers (Ed.), *Second Handbook of Research on Teaching*. Chicago: Rand McNally, 1973.

ROSENTHAL, R. *Experimenter Effects in Behavioral Research*, enlarged edition. New York: Halsted Press, 1976.

ROSENTHAL, R. The Pygmalion effect lives. *Psychology Today*, 1973, *56–63.

ROSENTHAL, R. & JACOBSON, L. *Pygmalion in the classroom: Teacher expectations and pupils' intellectual development*. New York: Holt, Rinehart and Winston, 1968.

ROSS, A. O. *Psychological disorders of children: A behavioral approach theory, research and therapy*. New York: McGraw-Hill, 1974.

ROSS, S. M., & RAKOW, E. A. Learner control versus program control as adaptive strategies for selection of instructional support on math rules. *Journal of Educational Psychology*, 1981, *73*, 745–753.

RUBIN, Z. *Children's friendships*. Cambridge, Mass.: Harvard University Press, 1980.

RUMELHART, D. E. & ORTONY, A. The representation of knowledge in memory. In R. Anderson, R. Spiro, & W. Montague (Eds.), *Schooling and the acquisition of knowledge*, Hillsdale, N.J.: 1977.

RUST, L. W. Interests. In S. Ball (Ed.), *Motivation in education*. New York: Academic Press, 1977.

RYANS, D. G. *Characteristics of effective teachers, their descriptions, comparisons and appraisal: A research study*. Washington, D.C.: American Council on education, 1960.

SADKER, M. & SADKER, D. Questioning skills. In J. Copper (Ed.), *Classroom teaching skills: A handbook*. Lexington, Mass.: Heath, 1977.

SALILI, F., MAEHR, M. L., SORENSEN, R. L., FYANS, L. J. A further consideration of the effect of evaluation on motivation. *American Educational Research Journal*. Spring 1976, *13* (2), 85–102.

SANTOGROSSI, D. A., O'LEARY, K. D., ROMANCZYK, R. G., & KAUFMAN, K. F. Self-evaluation by adolescents in a psychiatric hospital school token program. *Journal of Applied Behavior Analysis*, 1973, *6*, 277–288.

SARASON, S. B., DAVIDSON, K. S., LIGHTALL, F. F., WAITE, R. R., & RUEBUSH, B. H. *Anxiety in elementary school children*. New York: Wiley, 1960.

SARGENT, E., HUUS, H. & ANDERSEN, O. *How to read a book*. Newark, Delaware: International Reading Association, 1970.

SARNACKI, R. E. An examination of test-wiseness in the cognitive test domain. *Review of Research in Education*, 1979, *49*, 252–279.

SATTLER, J. *Assessment of children's intelligence*. Philadelphia: Saunders, 1974.

SATTLER, J. M. *Assessment of children's intelligence and special abilities* (2nd Ed.). Boston: Allyn & Bacon, 1982.

SCANDURA, J. M., FRASE, L. T., GAGNE, R., STOLUROW, K., STOLUROW, L., & GROEN, G. Current status and future directions of educational psychology as a discipline. *Educational psychologist*, 1978, *13*, 43–56.

SCARR, S. & YEE, D. Heritability and educational policy: Genetic and environmental effects on IQ, aptitude, and achievement. *Educational Psychologist*, 1980, *15*, 1–22.

SCHAB, F. Cheating in high school: Differences between the sexes (revisited). *Adolescence*, 1980, *15*, 959–965.

SCHAFER, A. & GRAY, M. Sex and mathematics. *Science*, 1981, *211*, No. 4479.

SCHAIN, R. L. & POLNER, M. *Using effective discipline for better class control*. Englewood Cliffs, N.J.: Prentice-Hall, 1964.

SCHUNK, D. H. Effects of effort attributional feedback on children's perceived self-efficacy and achievement. *Journal of Educational Psychology*, 1982, *74*, 548–558.

SCHUYLER, J. A. Programming languages for microprocessor courseware. *Educational Technology*, 1979, *19*, 29–35.

SCHWARTZ, B. *Psychology of learning and behavior*. New York: Norton, 1978.

SCHWEINHART, L. J. & WEIKART, D. P. *Young children grow up: The effects of the Perry Preschool Project program on youths through age 15*. Ypsilanti, Mich.: The High Scope press, 1980.

Science Curriculum Improvement Study, *Energy Sources*. Chicago: Rand-McNally, 1971.

SEAGOE, M. V. Educational psychology. In C. W. Harris (Ed.), *Encyclopedia of educational research*. New York: Macmillan, 1960.

SEARS, P. S. Levels of aspiration in academically successful and unsuccessful children. *Journal of Abnormal and Social Psychology*, 1940, *35*, 498–536.

SEEFELDT, C. Who should teach young children? *Journal of Teacher Education*, 1973, *24*, 308–311.

SEIBER, J. E., O'NEIL, H. F., & TOBIAS, S. *Anxiety, learning, and instruction*. Hillsdale, N.J.: Erlbaum, 1977.

SELIGMAN, C., TUCKER, G., & LAMBERT, W. The effects of speech style and other attributes on teachers' attitudes toward pupils. *Language in Society*, 1972, *1*, 131–142.

SELMAN, R. The development of interpersonal reasoning. In A. Pick (Ed.), *Minnesota Symposium on Child Psychology*, 10, Minneapolis, Minn. The University of Minnesota Press, 1976.

SERRALDE DE SCHOLZ, H. C., & MCDOUGALL, R. Comparison of potential reinforcer ratings between slow learners and regular students. *Behavior Therapy*, 1978, *9*, 60–64.

SESNOWITZ, M., BERNHARDT, K. L. & KNAIN, M. Analysis of the impact of commercial test preparation courses on SAT scores. *American Educational Research Journal*, 1982 *19*, 429–442.

SHANE, H. G. The silicon age and education. *Phi Delta Kappan*, 1982, *63*, 303–308.

SHANTZ, C. The development of social cognition. In E. M. Hetherington (Ed.), *Review of Child Development Research 5*, Chicago: University of Chicago Press, 1975.

SHANTZ, D. W. and VOYDANOFF, D. A. Situational effect on retaliatory aggression at three age levels. *Child Development*, 1973, *44*, 149–153.

SHAVELSON, R. J. & BOLUS, R. Self concept: The interplay of theory and methods. *Journal of Educational Psychology*, 1982, *74*, 3–17.

SHAVELSON, R. J., HUBNER, J. J., & STANTON, G. C. Self-concept: Validation of construct interpretations. *Review of Educational Research*, 1976, *46*, 407–442.

SHAVELSON, R. J. & STERN, P. Research on teachers' pedagogical thoughts, judgments, decisions, and behavior. *Review of Educational Research*, 1981, *51*, 455–499.

SHAVELSON, R. S. & DEMPSEY, N. *Generalizability of measures of teacher effectiveness and teaching process* (Beginning Teacher Evaluation Study, Tech. Rep. No. 3). San Francisco: Far West Laboratory for Educational Research and Development, 1975.

SHUELL, T. J. Dimensions of individual differences. In F. H. Farley & N. J. Gordon (Eds.)

*Psychology and education: The state of the union.* Berkeley, Calif.: McCutchan, 1981a.

SHUELL, T. J. Toward a model of learning from instruction. Paper presented at the American Educational Research Association, Los Angeles, April, 1981b.

SHUEY, A. M. *The testing of Negro intelligence* (Rev. Ed.). New York: Science Press, 1966.

SIGEL, I. E. & BRODZINSKY, D. M. Individual differences: A perspective for understanding intellectual development. In H. Hom & P. Robinson (Eds.), *Psychological processes in early education.* New York: Academic Press, 1977.

SILBERMAN, C. Technology is knocking at the schoolhouse door. *Fortune,* 1966, *74,* 120–125 +.

SILBERMAN, H. R., MELARAGNO, R. J., COULSON, J. E., & ESTEVAN, D. Fixed sequence versus branching auto-instructional methods. *Journal of Educational Psychology,* 1961, *52,* 166–172.

SIMON, D. P. & CHASE, W. G. Skill in chess. *American Scientist,* 1973, *61,* 394–403.

SIMON, D. P. & SIMON, H. A. Individual differences in solving physics problems. In R. Seigler (Ed.), *Children's thinking: What develops?* Hillsdale, N.J.: Lawrence Erlbaum, 1978.

SIMON, S. & CLARK, J. *More value clarification.* San Diego: Pennant Press, 1975.

SIMON, S., HOWE, L., & KIRSCHENBAUM, H. *Values clarification: A handbook of practical strategies for teachers and students.* New York: Hart, 1972.

SIMON, W. Expectancy effects in the scoring of vocabulary items: A study of scorer bias. *Journal of Educational Measurement,* 1969, *6,* 159–164.

SINCLAIR, H. From pre-operational to concrete thinking and parallel development of symbolization. In M. Schwebel and J. Raph (Eds.), *Piaget in the classroom.* New York: Basic Books, 1973.

SKINNER, B. F. *Science,* Oct. 24, 1958.

SKINNER, B. F. *Science and human behavior.* New York: Macmillan, 1953.

SKINNER, B. F. The science of learning and the art of teaching. *Harvard Educational Review,* 1954, *24,* 86–97.

SKINNER, B. F. *The technology of teaching.* New York: Appleton-Century-Crofts, 1968.

SLAVIN, R. E. *Cooperative learning.* New York: Longman, 1983.

SLOAN, M. & WALLACE, L. Glossary: Terms associated with exceptional children. Austin, Texas: Educational Service Center, Region XIII, unpublished manuscript, 1972.

SMITH, E. R. & TYLER, R. W. Appraising and recording student progress. *Adventures in American Education Series 3.* New York: Harper, 1942, pp. 251–252.

SMITH, F. *Comprehension and learning: A conceptual framework for teachers.* New York: Holt, Rinehart and Winston, 1975.

SMITH, R. M. & NEISWORTH, J. T. *The exceptional child: A functional approach.* New York: McGraw-Hill, 1975.

SMITH, S. M., GLENBERG, A., & BJORK, R. A. Environmental context and human memory. *Memory and Cognition,* 1978, *6,* 342–353.

SNOW, R. E. Research on aptitude for learning: A progress report. In L. Shulman (Ed.), *Review of research in education,* Itasca, Ill.: Peacock, 1977.

SNOW, R. E. Unfinished Pygmalion. *Contemporary Psychology,* 1969, *14,* 197–199.

SNYDER, P. The ambiguous assignment. *Media and Methods,* 1975, *12,* 46–47.

SOAR, R. S. *Follow-through classroom process measurement and pupil growth 1970–1971: Final report.* Gainesville, Fla.: University of Florida, 1973.

SOKOLOVE, S., SADKER, M., & SADKER, D.

Interpersonal Communications Skills. In J. Cooper (Ed.), *Classroom teaching skills: A handbook.* Lexington, Mass.: Heath, 1977.

SOLOMON, D. & KENDALL, A. J. *Final report. Individual characteristics and children's performances in varied educational settings.* Chicago: Spencer Foundation Project, May, 1976.

SOMMER, R. Classroom Ecology. *Journal of Applied Behavioral Science,* 1967, *3,* 489–503.

SOMMER, R. *Tight spaces: hard architecture and how to humanize it.* Englewood Cliffs, N.J.: Prentice-Hall, Inc., 1974.

SPEARMAN, C. *The abilities of man: Their nature and measurement.* New York: Macmillan, 1927.

SPERLING, G. A model for visual memory tasks. *Human Factors,* 1963, *5,* 19–31.

SPIELBERGER, C. D. (Ed.). *Anxiety and behavior.* New York: Academic Press, 1966.

STALLINGS, J. Allocated academic learning time revisited, or beyond time on task. *Educational Researcher,* 1980, *0,* 11–16.

STALLINGS, J. A. & KASKOWITZ, D. H. A study of follow-through implementation. Paper presented at the annual meeting of the American Educational Research Association, April, 1975.

STANLEY, J. On educating the gifted. *Educational Researcher,* 1980, *9,* 8–12.

STARCH, D. & ELLIOT, E. C. Reliability of grading high school work in English. *School Review,* 1912, *20,* 442–457.

STARCH, D. & ELLIOT, E. C. Reliability of grading work in history. *School Review,* 1913a, *12,* 676–681.

STARCH, D. & ELLIOT, E. C. Reliability of grading work in mathematics. *School Review,* 1913b, *21,* 676–681.

STARR, R. H. Jr. Child abuse. *American Psychologist,* 1979, *34,* 872–878.

STAUB, E. *Positive social behavior and morality: Socialization and development.* (New York: Academic Press, 1979.)

STEFFIN, S. A. Computer simulations: A key to divergent thinking. *Media and Methods,* 1981, October, 12–13.

STEIN, Z. SUSSER, M., SAENGER, G., & MAROLLA, F. Nutrition and mental performance. *Science,* 1972, *173,* 708–712.

STERNBERG, R. J. Factor theories of intelligence are all right almost. *Educational Researcher,* 1980, *9,* 6–13 +.

STERNBERG, R. & DAVIDSON, J. The mind of the puzzler. *Psychology Today,* 1982, *16,* 37–44.

STEWARD, L. G. & WHITE, M. A. Teacher comments, letter grades and student performance. What do we really know? *Journal of Educational Psychology,* 1976, *68(4),* 488–500.

STEWART, J. R. Teachers who stimulate curiosity. *Education,* 1980, *101,* 158–165.

SUCHMAN, J. *Inquiry development program: Developing inquiry.* Chicago: Science Research Associates, 1966.

SUPPES, P., JERMAN, M., & BRIAN, D. *Computer-assisted instruction: The 1965-66 Stanford arithmetic program.* New York: Academic Press, 1968.

SUPPES, P., & MACKEN, E. The historical path from research and development to operational use of CAI. *Educational Technology,* 1978, *18,* 9–12.

SURBER, J. R. & SMITH, P. L. Testing for misunderstanding. *Educational Psychologist,* 1981, *16,* 165–174.

SWANSON, R. A. & HENDERSON, R. W. Effects of televised modeling and active participation on rule-governed question production among native American pre-school children. *Contemporary Educational Psychology,* 1977, *2,* 345–352.

SWITZER, E. B., DEAL, T. E., & BAILEY, J. S.

The reduction of stealing in second graders using a group contingency program. *Journal of Applied Behavior Analysis,* 1977, *10,* 267–272.

TANNER, J. M. *Growth at adolescence,* (2nd ed.). Oxford: Blackwell Scientific Publications, 1962.

TAVIS, C. T. & SADD, S. *The Redbook report on female sexuality.* New York: Delacorte Press, 1977.

TAYLOR, R. P. (Ed.). *The computer in the school: Tutor, tool, tutee.* New York: Teachers College Press, 1980.

TENNYSON, R. D. Concept learning effectiveness using prototype and skill development presentation forms. Paper presented at the annual meeting of the American Educational Research Association, Los Angeles, April, 1981.

TENNYSON, R. D. & PARK, O. The teaching of concepts: A review of instructional design research literature. *Review of Educational Research,* 1980, *50,* 55–70.

TENNYSON, R. D. & ROTHEN, W. Pretask and on-task adaptive design strategies for selecting number of instances in concept acquisition. *Journal of Educational Psychology,* 1977, *69,* 586–592.

TERMAN, L. M., BALDWIN, B. T., & BRONSON, E. Mental and physical traits of a thousand gifted children. In *Genetic studies of genius* Vol. 1. Stanford, Calif.: Stanford University Press, 1925.

TERMAN, L. M. & MERRILL, M. A. *Stanford-Binet Intelligence Scale.* Boston: Houghton-Mifflin, 1960.

TERMAN, L. M. & ODEN, M. H. The gifted child grows up. In *Genetic studies of genius* Vol. 4. Stanford, Calif.: Stanford University Press, 1947.

TERMAN, L. M. ODEN, M. H. The gifted group in mid-life. In *Genetic studies of genius* Vol. 5. Stanford, Calif.: Stanford University Press, 1959.

TERWILLIGER, J. S. *Assigning grades to students.* Glenview, Ill.: Scott, Foresman, 1971.

THOMAS, E. L. & ROBINSON, H. A. *Improving reading in every class: A sourcebook for teachers.* Boston: Allyn and Bacon, 1972.

THOMAS, J. D., PRESLAND, I. E., GRANT, M. D., & GLYNN, T. L. Natural rates of teacher approval and disapproval in grade seven classrooms. *Journal of Applied Behavior Analysis,* 1978, *11,* 91–94.

THOMPSON, T. J. An overview of microprocessor central processing units (CPUs). *Educational Technology,* 1979, *10,* 41–44.

THORNDIKE, E. L. Educational psychology. In *The psychology of learning* Vol. 2. New York: Teachers College, Columbia University, 1913.

THORNDIKE, R. L. & HAGAN, E. *10,000 careers.* New York: Wiley, 1959.

THURSTONE, L. L. Primary mental abilities. *Psychometric Monographs,* 1938, No. 1.

THURSTONE, L. L. Psychological implications of factor analysis. *American Psychologist,* 1948, *3,* 402–408.

TIEDT, P. L. & TIEDT, I. M. *Multicultural education: A handbook of activities, information, and resources.* Boston: Allyn & Bacon, 1979.

TIKUNOFF, W. J., BERLINER, D. C., & RIST, R. C. *An ethnographic study of forty classrooms of the beginning teacher evaluation study known sample* Tech. Rep. No. 75-10-5). San Francisco: Far West Laboratory for Educational Research and Development, 1975.

TIMPSON, W. M. & TOBIN, D. N. *Teaching as performing: A guide to energizing your public presentation.* Englewood Cliffs, N.J.: Prentice-Hall, 1982.

TOBIAS, SHEILA. Sexist equations, *Psychology Today,* 1982, *16,* 14–17.

TOBIAS, S. Anxiety research in educational

psychology. *Journal of Educational Psychology*, 1979, *71*, 573–582.

TOBIAS, S. Adaptation to individual differences. In F. Farley & N. Gordon (Eds.), *Psychology and education: The state of the union*, Berkeley, Calif.: McCutchan, 1981.

TOBIAS, S. When do instructional methods make a difference? *Educational Researcher*, 1982, *11* (4), 4–10.

TOBIAS, S. & DUCHASTEL, P. Behavioral objectives, sequence, and anxiety in CAI. *Instructional Science*, 1974, *3*, 231–242.

TOOLAN, J. M. Depression and suicide in children: An overview. *American Journal of Psychotherapy*, 1981, *35*, 311–322.

TORRANCE, E. P. Predictive validity of the Torrance tests of creative thinking. *Journal of Creative Behavior*, 1972, *6*, 236–262.

TORRANCE, E. P. and HALL, L. K. Assessing the future reaches of creative potential. *Journal of Creative Behavior*, 1980, *14*, 1–19.

TRAVERS, R. M. W. *Essentials of learning*, (4th ed.). New York: Macmillan, 1977.

TRAVERS, R. M. W. *Essentials of learning: The new cognitive learning for students of education*, (5th ed.). New York: Macmillan, 1982.

TREIMAN, D. J. *Occupational prestige in comparative perspective*. New York: Academic Press, 1977.

TRICKETT, E. & MOOS, R. Personal correlates of contrasting environments: Student satisfaction with high school classrooms. *American Journal of Community Psychology*, 1974, *2*, 1–12.

TYLER, L. E. *Individual differences: Abilities and motivational directions*. New York: Appleton-Century-Crofts, 1974.

VAILLANT, G. E. & VAILLANT, C. O. Natural history of male psychological health, X: Work as a predictor of positive mental health. *The American Journal of Psychiatry*, 1981, *138*, 1433–1440.

VALENTINE, C. A. *Culture and poverty: Critique and counter-proposals*. Chicago: University of Chicago Press, 1968.

VAN MONDRANS, A. P., BLACK, H. B., KEYSOR, R. E., OLSEN, J. B., SHELLEY, M. F., and WILLIAMS, D. D. Methods of inquiry in educational psychology. In D. Treffinger, J. Davis, and R. R. Ripple (Eds.), *Handbook on Teaching Educational Psychology*. New York: Academic Press, Inc., 1977.

VASTA, R. & SARMIENTO, R. F. Liberal grading improves evaluations but not performance. *Journal of Educational Psychology*, 1979, *71*, 207–211.

VERNON, P. E. *Intelligence: Heredity and environment*. San Francisco: Freeman, 1979.

VIDLER, D. C. Curiosity. In S. Ball (Ed.), *Motivation in education*. New York: Academic Press, 1977.

VINACKE, W. E. *The psychology of thinking*. New York: McGraw-Hill, 1952.

VITELLO, S. J. & SOSKIN, R. *Mental retardation: Its social and legal context*. Englewood Cliffs, N.J.: Prentice-Hall, in press.

WADSWORTH, B. J. *Piaget for the classroom teacher*. New York: Longman, 1978.

WADSWORTH, B. J. *Piaget's theory of cognitive development: An introduction for students of psychology and education*. (2nd ed.). New York: Longman, 1978.

WALBERG, H. J. & UGUROGLU, M. E. Motivation and educational productivity: Theories, results, and implications. In L. J. Fyans, Jr. (Ed.), *Achievement motivation: Recent trends in theory and research*. New York: Plenum, 1980.

WALDEN, E. L. & THOMPSON, S. A. A review of some alternative approaches to drug management of hyperactive children. *Journal of Learning Disabilities*, 1981, *14*, 213–217.

WALTON, G. *Identification of the intellectually gifted children in the public school kindergarten*. Unpublished doctoral dissertation, University of California, Los Angeles, 1961.

WARD, B. and TIKUNOFF, W. The effective teacher education problem: Application of selected research results and methodology to teaching. *Journal of Teacher Education*, 1976, *27*, 48–52.

WARNER, S. P., MILLER, F. D., & COHEN, M. W. Relative effectiveness of teacher attention and the "Good Behavior Game" in modifying disruptive classroom behavior. *Journal of Applied Behavior Analysis*, 1977, *10*, 737.

WASICKSKO, M. M., & ROSS, S. M. How to create discipline problems. *The Clearing House*, in press.

WAXMAN, H. C. & WALBERG, H. J. The relation of teaching and learning: A review of reviews of process-product research. *Contemporary Educational Review*, 1982, *1*, 103–120.

WEBB, N. M. Group composition, group interaction, and achievement in cooperative small group. *Journal of Educational Psychology*, 1982, *74*, 475–484.

WEBB, N. M. A process-outcome analysis of learners in group and individual settings. *Educational Psychology*, 1980, *15*, 69–83.

WEBER, K. Letter to the Editor. *New York Times*, April 21, 1981.

WEBER, W. Classroom management. In James Cooper (Ed.), *Classroom teaching skills: A handbook*. Lexington, Mass.: Heath, 1977.

WECHSLER, D. *The measurement and appraisal of adult intelligence* (4th ed.). Baltimore: Williams & Wilkins, 1958.

WEINBERG, R. A. Early education and intervention: Establishing an American tradition. *American Psychologist*, 1979, *34*, 912–916.

WEINER, B. The role of affect in rational (attributional) approaches to human motivation. *Educational Researcher*, 1980, *9*, 4–11.

WEINER, B. *Theories of motivation: From mechanism to cognition*. Chicago: Rand McNally, 1972.

WEINER, B. A theory of motivation for some classroom experiences. *Journal of Educational Psychology*, 1979, *71*, 3–25.

WEINER, B. & KUKLA, A. An attributional analysis of achievement motivation. *Journal of Personality and Social Psychology*, 1970, *15*, 1–20.

WEINER, B., RUSSELL, D., & LERMAN, D. Affective consequences of causal ascriptions. In J. H. Harvey, W. J. Ickes, & R. F. Kidd (Eds.), *New directions in attribution research* Vol. 2. Hillsdale, N.J.: Erlbaum, 1978.

WEINSTEIN, C. S. Modifying student behavior in an open classroom through changes in the physical design. *American Educational Research Journal*, 1977, *14*, 249–262.

WESSELLS, M. G. *Cognitive psychology*. New York: Harper and Row, 1982.

WESSMAN, A. Scholastic and psychological effects of a compensatory education program for disadvantaged high school students: Project A B C. *American Educational Research Journal*, 1972, *9*, 361–372.

WEST, C. K., FISH, J. A., & STEVENS, R. J. General self-concept, self-concept of academic ability and school achievement: Implication for causes of self-concept. *Australian Journal of Education* 1980, *24*.

WEST, C. K. & FOSTER, S. F. *The psychology of human learning and instruction in education*. Belmont, Calif.: Wadsworth, 1976.

WHITE, B. L. *The first three years of life*. Englewood Cliffs, N.J.: Prentice-Hall, 1978.

WHITE, B. L., KABAN, B. T., ATTANUCCI, J., & SHAPIRO, B. B. Experience and environment: Major influences on the *development of the young child*. Englewood Cliffs, N.J.: Prentice-Hall, 1978.

WHITE, M. A. Natural rates of teacher approval and disapproval in the classroom. *Journal of Applied Behavior Analysis*, 1975, *8*, 367–372.

WHITE, R. W. Motivation reconsidered: The concept of competence. *Psychological Review*, 1959, *66*, 297–333.

WIIG, E. H. Communication disorders. In H. Haring (Ed.), *Exceptional children and youth*. Columbus, Ohio: Charles E. Merrill, 1982.

WILKINS, W. E. & GLOCK, M. D. *Teacher expectations and student achievement: A replication and extension*. Ithaca, N.Y.: Cornell University Press, 1973.

WILLERMAN, L. *The psychology of individual and group differences*. San Francisco: W. H. Freeman, 1979.

WILLIAMS, J. P. & HILL, K. T. *Performance on achievement test problems as a function of optimizing test presentation instructions and test anxiety*. Unpublished manuscript, University of Illinois.

WILLIS, B. J. The influence of teacher expectations on teachers' classroom interaction with selected children. *Dissertation Abstracts International*, 1970, *30*. University Microfilm No. 70-07647.)

WILSON, C. W. & HOPKINS, B. L. The effects of contingent music on the intensity of noise in junior high home economic classes. *Journal of Applied Behavior Analysis*, 1973, *6*, 269–275.

WILSON, M. I. Children with crippling and health disabilities. In L. M. Dunn (Ed.). *Exceptional children in the schools: Special education in transition*. New York: Holt, Rinehart and Winston, 1973.

WINETT, R. A., KRASNER, L., & KRASNER, M. Child-monitored token reading program. *Psychology in the Schools*, 1971, *8*, 259–262.

WINETT, R. A., & WINKLER, R. C. Current behavior modification in the classroom: Be still, be quiet, be docile. *Journal of Applied Behavior Analysis*, 1972, *5*, 499–504.

WISCONSIN RESEARCH AND DEVELOPMENT CENTER, Images are a key to learning. *Wisconsin Research and Development Center News*, Spring 1979, pp. 1–2.

WISEMAN, S. & NEISSER, U. Perceptual organization as a determinant of visual recognition memory. *Journal of Psychology*, 1974, *87*, 675–681.

WITKIN, H. A., MOORE, C. A., GOODENOUGH, D. R., & COX, R. W. Field dependent and field independent cognitive styles and their educational implications. *Review of Educational Research*, 1977, *47*, 1–64.

WITTROCK, M. C. *Educational implications of recent research on learning and memory*. Paper presented at the annual meeting of the American Educational Research Association, New York, March, 1982.

WITTROCK, M. C. The cognitive movement in instruction. *Educational Psychologist*, 1978, *13*, 15–30.

WLODKOWSKI, R. J. Making sense out of motivation: A systematic model to consolidate motivational constructs across theories. *Educational Psychologist*, 1981, *16*, 101–110.

WLODKOWSKI, R. J. *Motivation and teaching: A practical guide*. Washington D.C.: National Education Association Press, 1978.

WOMEN ON WORDS AND IMAGES, *Dick and Jane as victims: Sex stereotyping in children's readers* (Expanded 1975 Ed.). Princeton, N.J.: P.O. Box 2163.

WONDERLY, D. M. & KUPFERMID, J. H. Promoting postconventional morality: The adequacy of Kohlberg's aim. *Adolescence*, 1980, *15*, 609–631.

WOOLFOLK, A. E. & BROOKS, D. Nonverbal communication in teaching. In E. Gordon (Ed.), *Review of research in education* Vol. 10, Washington, D.C.: American Educational Research Association, 1983.

WOOLFOLK, A. E., and WOOLFOLK, R. L. A contingency management technique for increasing student attention in a small group. *Journal of School Psychology*, 1974, *12*, 204–212.

WRIGHTMAN, L. S., SIGELMAN, C. K., & SANFORD, F. H. *Psychology, A scientific study of human behavior*. Monterey, Calif.: Brooks/Cole, 1979.

YOUNG, T. Teacher stress: One school district's approach. *Action in Teacher Education*, 1980, *2*, 37–40.

YOUNISS, J. *Parents and peers in social development*. Chicago: University of Chicago Press, 1980.

ZIMMERMAN, B. J. & PIKE, E. O. Effects of modeling and reinforcement on the acquisition and generalization of question-asking behavior. *Child Development*, 1972, *43*, 892–907.

ZIMMERMAN, D. W. On the perennial argument about grading "on the curve" in college courses. *Educational Psychologist*, 1981, *16*, 175–178.

ZIMMERMAN, E. H. & ZIMMERMAN, J. The alternation of behavior in a special classroom situation. *Journal of the Experimental Analysis of Behavior*, 1962, *5*, 59–60.

# Author Index

# Subject Index